The Official Report of the Lambeth Conference 1998

The Lambeth Call to Prayer

We, the Bishops of the Anglican Communion, in the Lambeth Conference together in 1998, fortified by our common sharing in prayer, Bible study and worship and the Retreat led by Jean Vanier, recommit ourselves to prayer, following the example of Christ, as the foundation of all our ministry and dedicate ourselves to lead our people to deepen and strengthen their life of prayer.

We call upon all the members of the Anglican Communion to increase our fellowship by using the Anglican Cycle of Prayer in their personal intercession and public liturgy.

> *'You also join in helping us by your prayers, so that many will give thanks on our behalf for the blessing granted to us through the prayers of many.'*
>
> —2 COR 1:11

The Official Report of the Lambeth Conference 1998

Transformation and Renewal

July 18–August 9, 1998

Lambeth Palace; Canterbury, England

Published for the Anglican Communion by

MOREHOUSE PUBLISHING
Harrisburg, Pennsylvania, USA

Acknowledgements

Editors who made this publication possible:

The Rt Revd J. Mark Dyer, *Chair*
The Rt Revd Dr Emmanuel Gbonigi
The Rt Revd Mano Rumalshah
Dr Ruth Etchells
The Revd Canon Roger Symon
Miss Elizabeth Gordon Clark, *Secretary*

Morehouse Publishing
P.O. Box 1321
Harrisburg, PA 17105

Morehouse Publishing is a division of the Morehouse Group.

Printed in the United States of America

Cover design by Corey Kent

Lambeth Conference photos: *Anglican World* photos by Jeff Sells, Lynn Ross, Anne Wetzel, William Killough, and Harriet Long. Anglican Communion photos by Jim Rosenthal. Special thanks to Marcus Perkins for permitting use of his Lambeth 1998 photos.

Lambeth Conference (13th : 1998 : Canterbury, England)
The official report of the Lambeth Conference 1998 : July 18–August 9, 1998, Lambeth Palace; Canterbury, England.
p. cm.
ISBN 0-8192-1797-2 (pbk.)
1. Anglican Communion Congresses. I. Title.
BX5021.L6 1998c
262'.53—dc21 99–12950
CIP

Contents

Introduction

The 1998 Lambeth Conference was the largest-ever gathering of Anglican bishops. Between 18 July and 9 August, some 750 bishops met together to worship and pray, to talk and to study the Bible together. Those have been the very simple aims of Lambeth Conferences ever since 1867, when 76 bishops met together at Lambeth Palace at the invitation of Archbishop Longley. In suggesting a meeting, Longley wrote to his colleagues:

> Such a meeting would not be competent to make declarations or lay down definitions on points of doctrine. But united worship and common counsels would greatly tend to maintain practically the unity of faith; whilst they would bind us in straiter bonds of peace and brotherly charity. (R. Davidson, ed.: *The Lambeth Conferences of 1867, 1878 and 1888.* SPCK 1896)

Although Archbishop Longley was correct in his observation that the Lambeth Conference of Bishops was not empowered to 'lay down definitions or points of doctrine', their decisions and resolutions have always been taken most seriously as expressing 'defining moments' in the life of our Communion.

Indeed, that first Conference was called primarily because of widespread concerns over the Colenzo Affair in South Africa, and it is probably true to say that most Conferences since have found themselves, willingly or unwillingly, some 'great matter' which has challenged the unity of the Anglican Communion at that time. To recognise this fact is not, however, to negate the fundamental reason for meeting, which is to build up the fellowship of the bishops, and through them, to build up that sense of unity throughout the Communion, and with our fellow Christians of other traditions, without which our common witness to the Gospel is badly flawed.

This volume, for which I am enormously grateful to Bishop Mark Dyer, Canon Roger Symon and all members of the Editorial Team, records much of the written material of the 1998 Lambeth Conference. I believe it will go a long way towards recording for posterity much of the substance of the Conference; and I am particularly glad that this time the official record includes some of the major plenary addresses, sermons and special addresses such as that by the British Prime Minister, who spoke at Lambeth Palace during the lunch which Eileen and I hosted midway through the Conference. It also includes, very significantly, a report of the Spouses' Conference, which was held alongside the Bishops' Conference, and which made a quite unique contribution to the three weeks in Canterbury.

I hope very much that this volume will become a basic text, not just for students of history, but also for all those who seek to guide the life of the Anglican Communion at every level over the next decade. The resolutions of the Conference give us a significant word picture of how the Anglican episcopate is thinking on a wide variety of issues, some of them, like international debt, of enormous significance to the world at large at this moment. But equally important are the four section reports, for they give a more substantial taste of the progress of the Conference, and of the nature of the debates which took place among bishops on some really quite difficult issues. Perhaps I could draw attention especially to the report of Section II, *Called to Live and Proclaim the Good News*, which not only records the Section's work, but also gives us an excellent model for mission and evangelism, by imaginatively mixing personal stories with theological reflection.

But I return to where I started. The heart of the 1998 Lambeth Conference, as with its predecessors, was its worship, its prayer, its Bible study and its fellowship. These elements of common life cannot be captured in printed form. They are what make our Communion what it is, a vibrant, faithful Christ-centred community, seeking fallibly, humbly, but with great courage and steadfastness, to live and preach the Gospel of Christ crucified and risen. And those gifts are not gifts restricted to bishops in or out of Conference. They are the gifts we all share, and I thank God for that. So long as they are the heartbeat of our life in Communion, I am confident that God will lead us through the maze of challenges and opportunities to a still stronger oneness in Christ.

So, as you delve into this volume, I hope you will do so prayerfully, and remember the spirit in which the words came into being. I am so grateful to all who worked so hard to make this Conference happen, and if I single out David Long, the Conference Manager, and his staff, it is only because without his constant attention to detail at every level that essential spirit which filled the gathering would never have been free to work.

+George Cantaur
Archbishop of Canterbury

Editors' Preface

This volume does not seek to convey the essence of the Thirteenth Lambeth Conference, but to record its resolutions, reports and principal addresses.

When the Archbishop of Canterbury convened the Conference in September 1994, he invited the bishops "to strengthen the theological, spiritual and personal bonds of the Communion". That was their first objective, and its success would have to be gauged by their personal testimonies. The strengthening of friendship and understanding, and the deepening of spirituality, are not immediately visible or easy to measure. They grow slowly and patiently, and the primary purpose of Lambeth '98 was to foster them.

Nor is there any attempt here to convey the impact of the worship, offered each day by a different Province, or the shared intimacy of the daily Bible Study Groups and the short videos *Leadership under Pressure*, or the excitement of the great occasions. These experiences, central though they were to Lambeth '98, lie outside the scope of this book, and their value will emerge in the hearts and minds of the bishops as they look back on what they learned from Lambeth '98.

This book has another purpose. It represents the first response to the Archbishop's other objectives: to encourage the bishops in their ministry of interpreting the Church's faith, leading the Church's mission, and clarifying their minds on certain designated issues.

This was the framework in which the preparation was designed, and the agenda was formed. Over the course of three years, and nine Regional Meetings, Provinces and Dioceses met to identify their critical concerns, often with surprising unanimity. These were then sifted and refined by the Editorial Committee, and referred to the Design Group and Consultants at the St. Augustine's Seminar in April 1997. There they were grouped together into the Section themes and along with supporting study papers, sent out as the agenda in October 1997.

The Conference Section Reports, together with the *Virginia Report*, form the main substance of the Conference, and the main part of this volume. The *Virginia Report* on the nature and meaning of Communion was commissioned by a resolution of the Lambeth Conference of 1988, and was therefore submitted and warmly received as a foundation document for the whole Conference. The Reports, which were received by the Conference, have the authority of the Sections that produced them. The *Virginia Report*, by way of Resolution, has the authority of the whole Conference.

In addition among the Reports is the Inter-Faith Report. This dimension of Anglican experience was high among the Regional priorities. In the Report Bishop Michael Nazir Ali of Rochester, England, summarises the high profile of Inter-Faith events during the Conference; his essay on 'Christians and Other Faiths' and the speeches of six other bishops at the Plenary Presentation on Islam are included here.

Certain themes were chosen for presentation to the whole Conference. These Plenary Presentations took different forms, and included video, discussion, drama, music and addresses. The principal addresses are recorded here. Conspicuous among them was the Presentation on International Debt on 24 July. It began with a video prepared by Christian Aid to which the President of the World Bank, James Wolfensohn, responded. His speech, the address of the Archbishop of Cape Town, Chair of Section 1, and the response of the Bishop of Worcester, Chair of the Sub-Section on Debt, are included. The theme was further treated at the London Day, 28 July, when a group of bishops met two Ministers of the British Government, the Chancellor of the Exchequer, Gordon Brown, and the Secretary of State for International Development, Clare Short, together with diplomats and bankers, for a private meeting at Lambeth Palace under the chairmanship of the Archbishop of Canterbury and Baroness Linda Chalker. At the Lunch for the whole Conference that followed in Lambeth Palace Garden, the Prime Minister, the Right Honourable Tony Blair, addressed the guests on 'Global Poverty and Unpayable Debt'.

Dr. David Ford, Regius Professor of Divinity at the University of Cambridge, led two Plenaries on 'The Bible, the World and the Church', one at the beginning, and one at the end of the Conference. The Presentations incorporated video and a performance of *Wrestling with Angels* by the Riding Lights Theatre Company, telling the story of the encounters of Jacob with God and Esau recorded in Genesis 33; but Professor Ford's addresses stand on their own as compelling examples of how Anglicans approach Holy Scripture.

Every day the Bishops listened to the Word of God expounded in the Conference worship. The sermons on five special occasions stand out, and are reprinted here—the Opening and Closing Services, Ecumenical Vespers, the Feast of the Transfiguration on Hiroshima Day, and the Vigil of Meditation and Prayer.

Finally we include the Archbishop of Canterbury's Pastoral Letter sent to all Churches as the Conference closed, and the Report to the Bishops on the Spouses' Programme by Mrs. Eileen Carey.

The Rt Revd J. Mark Dyer, *Chair*
The Rt Revd Dr Emmanuel Gbonigi
The Rt Revd Mano Rumalshah
Dr Ruth Etchells
The Revd Canon Roger Symon
Miss Elizabeth Gordon Clark (Secretary)

PRESIDENTIAL ADDRESS

photo: *Anglican World*

Archbishop Carey—president of Lambeth Conference 1998.

Presidential Address
The Most Revd and Rt Hon George L. Carey
Archbishop of Canterbury

Transformation and Renewal

After all the planning of the last few years it was wonderful for me to stand in the Cathedral yesterday morning and to be able to say with you all 'Yes, our thirteenth Lambeth Conference is now under way'. I am frequently asked: 'What is the point of it'? and you will recall that the very first Lambeth Conference began with that criticism. There was a certain coolness within the Church of England when Archbishop Longley first broached the subject. A number of senior bishops declared their opposition and the Archbishop felt the cold shoulder of Westminster Abbey when Dean Stanley would not allow the Conference to have the final service in the Abbey.

Outside the Church there were those who couldn't see the point of it. The *Times'* comment was: 'This sort of ecclesiastical tea party at which some 70-year-old gentlemen would indulge in a mild chat about religious politics… was… frittering away their time and energy on impractical dreams'. *Punch* had a cartoon of bishops washing their dirty linen in public. The *Daily Telegraph* read the Pastoral Letter with 'respectful melancholy'.

So you see some things like criticism never change. I guess many whose opinions of the first Conference were so negative would be astounded to see us gathered today. Over 700 bishops from 36 different Provinces with over 600 spouses, who will share their own separate Programme. Such is the growth of our Communion. They would also be surprised to see women bishops among that number for the first time. And I want to say how glad I am to welcome them.

As we gather, then, I want to share with you my personal hope and longing that all of us may be led into a more radical discipleship shaped by God's transforming power through the renewal of our lives.

For many months now there has been only one biblical image in my mind that I have wanted to share with you. It is the penultimate chapter of the Revelation of St John where John describes the Christian vision of God. A glorious picture of the city of God—Alpha and Omega—in the midst of his people with the triumphant cry: 'Behold, I make all things new!'

And there is an extraordinary irony about it that we can all recognise and appreciate. There is John on the island of Patmos, surrounded by an uncrossable sea—at least for him, in enforced exile—given such visions of the grandeur and holiness of God with the fierce denunciations of all that opposes the rule and reign of God. No doubt, as with us, there was much to encourage him. God was at work in the world, the Church was growing, the faithfulness of people was extraordinary and the grace of God at times almost palpably present. But there were also discouragements and disappointments. He was in prison, after all. He knew all about the discouragement of persecution, the disappointment when people let you down, and when God himself seems at times remote.

And we can identify with this theme of blessing and disappointment. Since we met ten years ago there have been many blessings we can recount. Who could have forecast in 1988 that within eighteen months European Communism as a great ideological power would come to a crushing end with the toppling of the Berlin Wall? Who could have foreseen then that within a few years the political reality of apartheid in South Africa would cease, without civil war? Who would have believed that even now, amidst all that still threatens it, they could be on the verge of peace in Northern Ireland? Who would have believed that one of the results of the last Conference, the call to make the 90s a 'Decade of Evangelism,' could in so many Provinces have been so effective? We have been blessed and we have been surprised by the goodness and generosity of God.

Yet, there have been many disappointments as well. We have seen the country of Rwanda broken through bitter racial conflict and our own Church there sadly torn in two. Though we are delighted that our Church in Rwanda is now whole, we mourn the 800,000 murdered in that genocide. The war in the Sudan continues to rage and as a result the land of Sudan has too many widows and too many orphans. We are glad to note the ceasefire which was agreed last week to allow aid to reach the suffering people of Bakr El Gazel. But what is required is an end to the war and a lasting peace based on justice and freedom for all. I hope this Conference will send a strong message to the Sudanese Government and to the SPLA.

Poverty and starvation stalk too many of the lands where Anglicans serve; the AIDS virus is a curse in too many countries and blights the lives of millions. Ignorance and lack of educational opportunities hold back millions of young people. We are told by the President of the World Bank that 'three billion people live on under two dollars a day. One billion three hundred million live on under one dollar a day. One hundred million go hungry every day. One hundred and fifty million never get the chance to go to school'. They are the awful statistics behind the issue of the relief of the burden of unpayable debt on which we will focus as a major element in this Conference.

This is our world. This is the world in which we work and to which we are called to serve and witness.

And who has not known discouragement and disappointment not only in the world in which we work, but in doing the tasks we have been set? Even when our circumstances are undramatic, so often we seem to see so little for our toil. We can feel marginalised, especially if our declaration of God's love and sovereignty of God is ignored or brushed aside.

These experiences are ones that all Christians of every generation must in honesty wrestle with. None of us is immune from them and to those who have come to this Conference worn out physically, mentally or spiritually, may I encourage you to use this time for personal refreshment through worship, through silence, through conversations and through prayer. Don't spend so much of your time rushing from one activity to another that you miss out on what God wants most to give you. Spiritual health, my brothers and sisters, is just as vital to seek as physical health.

Yet, if the experience of disappointment and discouragement is part of our Christian vocation, and one which I hope we will honestly share one with the other, woe betide us if we confine ourselves over the next three weeks to self-pity or mere introspection. Even when evil seems to prevail in so many places, and in so many ways, the challenge before us is to bring to the world an authoritative vision of the God of love and justice who is the beginning and end of all things. The God who declares: 'Behold, I make all things new,' is the same Lord who called an earnest, searching Rabbi called Saul, to say to the Roman Christians after his conversion: 'Be transformed by the renewal of your mind'. He is the same Lord who is the unseen President of our Conference and who calls us to be transformed people with a vision for renewal.

So what will this mean in practical terms for those of us gathered here? May I suggest there are four main areas on which we need to focus: The Renewal of our Vision, our Church, our Mission and our Vocation as Bishops.

First is required the *Renewal of our Vision.* Irenaeus, the great second-century bishop and theologian, had a wonderful vision of God and his activity in the World. It is one we should foster too. For him Christ had redeemed all things. All things were reaching forward to their consummation when 'God will be all in all.' That is a breathtaking vision when one recalls that Irenaeus was the Bishop of tiny Christian congregations in what is now southern France, in the midst of great hostility and, at times, persecution. Faced with such trials, Irenaeus' response was not to surrender to despair or disappointment but rather to go deeper into an understanding of God whose will it is to 'gather into one' all things in heaven and on earth. Irenaeus' ministry, in spite of the truly awful context in which it was set, is a challenge to us in our own day, with its unmistakable optimism in God. He wrote:

> For just as God is always the same, so the human being who is found in God always progresses towards God. Nor shall God at any time cease from bestowing benefits and riches on humankind; nor

> shall humankind cease from receiving these benefits and from being enriched by God. For the human being which is grateful to its creator is the vessel of his goodness and the instrument of his glorification. (*AH* IV. 11.1–2)

What a mind-stretching vision of God's generosity and goodness! And in it he gives us a key to how we, in this Conference, a family of Christian leaders, may be transformed in our ministry together and in our ministry individually. That key is a heartfelt, simple gratitude to our God: gratitude practised daily, gratitude practised hourly; gratitude which becomes living praise. For it makes us—even us!—'vessels of God's goodness' and 'instruments' by which God will be glorified. That is the first—wonderful—task of this Conference: to be a place of transformation and of renewed vision, for the sake both of God's Church and, still more importantly, of the world.

It is all too easy to lose the big picture in the detail of busy ministries. In one of Alec Vidler's books he comments: 'Men connect the church, not with the disturbing and renewing encounter of a Holy God, but, as someone has said, with "unattractive services, tedious homilies, the smell of hymn books, the petty round of ecclesiastical functions, the collection bag, an oppression due to lack of oxygen and memories of Sunday school"'.

And, so often, that narrow kind of experience has cut people off from the powerful reality of the Christian faith. Here in this Conference, we have the opportunity to bring and share with each other all the distresses, as well as the joys, of the cultures from which we come; all the different understandings and divisions of the Anglican Communion, as well as all that unites us. All these we can bring to be transformed by the power of the God and Father of our Lord Jesus Christ, which we celebrate in gratitude; gratitude to our Sovereign God who makes of it all something quite new, something which declares his goodness.

So, it is my hope that we too will talk about our theology as much as the issues that confront us because solutions will only emerge from a real encounter in gratitude with our living God.

And isn't this a particular challenge for Section One with its gaze on 'Being fully Human?' This Section will have a particularly busy time with so many controversial issues: the environment, freedom, and international debt—to say nothing of human sexuality!

I hope, of course, that we will see real progress being made over the three weeks as we seek to listen carefully to what the Spirit is saying to the Churches. The danger may be, however, of a too rapid immersion in the issues with the result that the true scale of divine reality is forgotten as we focus on the detail. May I urge us all to spend as much time on a truly grand theology of the awesome beauty, might and wonder of God as we will on the relatively minor questions we constantly ask about the way that we should behave in relation to his glory and goodness. The many world problems we face will be discovered in their true perspective only if we look at them steadily in the context of our grateful certainty of God's sovereign love; the God who can transform what is deathly and death-dealing within us; the God who is 'working his purposes out as year succeeds to year'.

Which leads me to my second point. For as well as the Renewal of our Vision we must determine to seek the *Renewal of our Church*. Here we need, I believe, to begin with a glad acknowledgement of, and deep gratitude for, the goodness of the Church and the grace of God brought to us through her. The missionary to India, E. Stanley Jones, used to say: 'I love my mother in spite of her wrinkles!' And we love the Church because through her we found faith in Christ, hope, blessing and renewal. We must not number ourselves among those who despise her, denigrate her or speak ill of her. I am sometimes very sad when fellow Anglicans mock our Church publicly and criticise her unfairly. When we do so we are not following our Lord who 'loved the Church and gave himself for her'. She is indeed, 'that stretched magnificence' in Edwin Muir's tribute to the Church through the centuries.

And from that context of love for God's Church and through our theological wrestling, working with those of different traditions to our own, we shall, I believe, discover new and unexpected riches. It was Archibald Tait, Bishop of London and later Archbishop of Canterbury, who commented ironically just over a century ago in the midst of the disputes surrounding the publication of a book entitled *Essays and Reviews*: 'The great evil is that the liberals are deficient in religion, and the religious are deficient in liberality. Let us pray for an outpouring of the very spirit of truth'.

And let us also pray for the renewal of the Church through an outpouring of that same Spirit. In a world where so many people talk in extreme terms, and claim that their perception of the truth is the only one that counts, let us remember that we have always been a Communion where diversity and difference has been cherished and, indeed, celebrated. Brian Davis, formerly Archbishop of Aotearoa New Zealand and Polynesia, who died just a few weeks ago, and is greatly missed by us all, wrote these splendid words in his book *The Way Ahead*: 'The Anglican Church, whilst not claiming to be the definitive form of Christianity, has the advantage of maintaining the faith and order of the ancient Catholic tradition, as well as the freedom and evangelical spirit of the Protestant tradition. The Anglican *via media*, or middle way, has encouraged the growth of tolerance, freedom and generosity of spirit. We are not a coercive institution but depend on friendly persuasion. Within our decision-making structures we know, most of the time, how to argue and fight fairly. We are also an inclusive church, welcoming those whose faith is fragile and uncertain, as well as those whose faith is strong and heroic'.

But, lest I should be misunderstood, I am not arguing for some kind of Anglican comprehensiveness that is vague and woolly or is uncertain about the foundations of our faith. Indeed not. We have a firm hold on a historic credal faith, earthed in Holy Scripture. This is primary and pivotal and there are boundaries to our faith and morals which we cross at our peril. In the splendid words of our *Virginia Report:* 'Anglicans affirm the sovereign authority of the Holy Scriptures as the medium through which God by the Holy Spirit communicates his word in the Church and thus enables people to respond with understanding and faith. The scriptures are "uniquely inspired witness to divine revelation" and "the primary norm for Christian faith and life."'

But it is important to go on to the next Section of the *Virginia Report:* 'The scriptures, however, must be translated, read, and understood, and their meaning grasped through a continuing process of interpretation. Since the seventeenth century, Anglicans have held that scripture is to be understood and read in the light afforded by the twin contexts of tradition and reason'.

And, of course, that doesn't mean that we use terms like 'tradition' and 'reason' as 'cop-outs' to do whatever we want! What it does mean is that there is an interplay of Bible, tradition and reason which never undermines the primacy and authority of scripture.

A theology which wrestles with the text of scripture in the light of the faith of the Church through the ages, the scrutiny of reason and the experience of Christians in the Church and world today, is what I believe we should be working at over these next three weeks. And wherever those discussions may take us, let us never forget that it is people, our brothers and sisters in Christ, who will be deeply affected by whatever stance we take.

Now, I have said already that there are boundaries beyond which we cannot stray if we are to be true to all we have received and to ourselves as Anglicans today. But, saying that is to invite the question: 'If the Anglican Communion is a family of interdependent churches, and the Lambeth Conference has no binding doctrinal force, in what sense can we speak of the Anglican Communion?'

And here we will need to face head on both the strength and the weakness of our form of ecclesial structure. Its perceived weakness in the eyes of some is that it is not a hierarchical, monarchical form of 'top-down' authority. In the absence of any universal structures of collegiality that could determine how each Province should act, there are those consequently who want to give the Archbishop of Canterbury a more monarchical role. Now, not only has our Communion rejected this option firmly, but so has every Archbishop of Canterbury in recent years! But if we shy away from such centralising authority in the See of Canterbury, we also tend to shy away from the empowering of the other bonds of unity—the Anglican Consultative Council, the Primates Meeting and the Lambeth Conference. In them we have structures for consultation but not for making juridical decisions that are binding on the Communion as a whole.

Thus, if we meet as a fellowship of self-governing, national churches, in what realistic form can we claim to be a 'Communion'?

The answer is found, I believe, in what we share and hold in common: a common heritage of doctrine, faith, liturgy and spirituality; an understanding of authority as expressed through a 'dispersed,' rather than centralised authority; and episcopal leadership exercised in conjunction with synodical government. We make no apology for this form of polity which has real strengths because the conciliar forms of consultation are strong and rich.

In the closing words of his excellent book *Unashamed Anglicanism,* Bishop Stephen Sykes states that: 'The natural mode of (Anglican) ecclesiology is to allow debate, disagreement, and conflict as a normal part of its life. It will provide a structure for the God-given gift of insight and leadership and for understanding and consent; and that structure will be appropriate to differing patterns of authority in different cultures at various times'.

Yes, this is open to the charges of 'untidiness' and 'incoherence'. Nevertheless we can defend our position proudly because the alternatives remain authoritarianism and the stifling of individual conscience. And if, as John Henry Newman once remarked, 'every organisation seemed to start with a prophet and end up with a policeman,' it seems we have successfully avoided this criticism.

Nonetheless, we need to treasure our Communion as a gift from God and also to pay attention to the tension between the local and the universal. To be in communion means that the 'local church' both expresses and encompasses the faith of the universal church. Indeed, that is exactly what it means to be 'catholic'. And for Dioceses, Provinces and the Communion itself, it means to keep in step; to maintain unity at all times. To quote Dr Paul Avis in the current edition of *Theology*: 'To practice the grace of walking together without coercive constraints is the special vocation of Anglicanism in our pluralistic world'.

In the light of these reflections there are many practical questions we need to address if we are to be open to God's renewing Spirit. How may we stay together when difficult decisions threaten to divide us? How may we be more effective leaders of our Provinces, Dioceses and Churches? Again, the *Virginia Report* asks searching theological and practical questions about our structures that I trust this Conference will address properly and responsibly.

As we do so, we need to remind ourselves that Anglicanism has never regarded itself as a final form of Christianity. As with many Churches, we look ahead to God's promise of a transformed and renewed Church when we shall all be, visibly, One, Holy, Catholic and Apostolic. That destiny beckons us on even if we cannot yet see the character of that unity and the programme it will take. Over the last ten years much progress has been made both in our theological conversations with other churches and in the deepening of lived relationships. The Resolution in 1988 to deepen our dialogue with the Lutheran Churches has led to the Porvöo Agreement between the Lutheran Churches of the Nordic and Baltic region and the Anglican churches of these islands. We thank God for that and are so pleased to have a number of Lutheran bishops from those Churches with us. We rejoice too at the continuing theological dialogue between ECUSA and the Evangelical Lutheran Church of America and we are pleased to note as well the movements towards unity between Lutherans and Anglicans in Africa and Canada. Indeed, whether one looks internationally to our relationships with the Roman Catholic Church and the Orthodox or, in this country, to those with the Moravians and the Methodists, there is much to celebrate in the ecumenical journey of closer co-operation, deepening friendship, frank consultations and creative theological dialogue and convergence. Much needs to be done, but none can deny the progress we have made together. It is a mark of the power of God's Spirit at work among us.

But, and this is my third main point, there also needs to be a *Renewal of our Mission.* Ten years ago, this Conference issued the invitation to make the 90s a decade of evangelism. It was an inspiring and necessary call in the main directed by our African brothers. Now as I travel the Communion it is clear that many Provinces have responded to that invitation brilliantly, with energy and enthusiasm and we can chalk up some significant successes as we have opened ourselves to a process of renewal.

For instance, we have at last put an end to the puzzling divide espoused by some of forcing a choice between mission or evangelism. We are clear now there is no 'or.' It is mission and evangelism. We are called to proclaim Christ and we exist for mission. The narrower task of making disciples and leading them to baptism is well and truly placed within the task of sharing God's mission to the entire world. How my heart was moved three years ago by one of the Sudanese bishops here with us today, who spoke of the problem of preaching the Gospel in the refugee camps outside Khartoum, which my wife and I were visiting with him: 'You see, Archbishop,' he said hesitantly, 'We have a saying, "empty stomachs have no ears."' That kind of compassion is central to any vision of the mission of a transformed church. People need to be fed physically as well as spiritually, and a Church that exists for God in his world must be prepared not only to spread the Gospel but also to press for action on the great issues confronting our world, whether they are to do with International Debt or the Environment. That is part of what it is to be involved in God's mission and it is something we neglect at our peril.

But evangelism must not to be avoided either, even if, as Anglicans, we have often found it quite difficult in the past. We are called to be evangelists in the line of Augustine, the first Archbishop of Canterbury who came to this country in such fear and humility 1400 years ago. Our apostolic message, in the words of Paul in 2 Corinthians, is to say to all people: 'Be reconciled to God'.

So too we have been learning that it is love that is the most important ingredient if we wish to be effective missionaries and evangelists. There are techniques of evangelism, to be sure, but the 'charism' of love is the main channel through which the majority of converts will come. They will come through the devotion of worship; through the love and graciousness we offer those searching hesitantly for faith. As the former Primate of Canada, Ted Scott, wrote: 'Nothing is really true unless love is involved in it'. Words echoed by the Welsh Anglican poet, R.S. Thomas, who, reflecting on the dangers of loveless evangelism, wrote:

> They listened to me preaching the unique Gospel
> Of love, but our eyes never met.

Aggressive, insensitive evangelism or prosyletism has never been our style, and God forbid that we should ever adopt it; but love for others is surely where true discipling begins. And if we are hesitant evangelists, then let us begin with loving the world for Christ's sake, and let that lead us to sharing what that love means in a world hungry for it.

Let me also stress the importance of the local in the task of mission and evangelism. I want to affirm and encourage Provinces in continuing to develop their own traditions and express worship and faith in their own culture. I have often said, jokingly of course, to those Provinces influenced by the English Church in the last century: 'Be less English! Be more African or Asian or South American. Let your own traditions, music, and ways of devotion enrich your life!' And I am so delighted that this is happening and we, here in the more established parts of the world where Anglican Christianity first took root, are beginning to learn from your experiences, as we see your faith, your joy and your love for our Lord. By empowering and celebrating the local, we enrich the whole.

I believe that we are also beginning to learn as a Communion that evangelism and dialogue belong together. For the first time in the history of Lambeth Conferences there will be a Plenary specifically given over to our relations with Islam and I was delighted that representatives of other faiths were present at our Opening Service. There can be no doubting the importance of inter-faith dialogue and co-operation for the peace and well-being of the world. It is important, too, as a number here will remind us from their own experience, for those Provinces where Christians are in a minority and where, sometimes, to be a Christian is to face persecution.

But dialogue, co-operation and friendship with those of other faiths need not deaden the nerve of mission. My personal journey in inter-faith relations in recent years has yielded a rich harvest of appreciation of what we have in common with people of other faiths. I count many of them as friends. But this does not compromise the specificity of the Christian revelation. We hold Jesus Christ as the one Saviour of the world and we invite all to honour him as Lord for it is a faith given to us to share with all. We are called to be unapologetic about the claims of Christ. That is our message and that is the transforming heart of the Church's teaching.

Of course, the way we witness to our Lord is very dependent on the context we are in, but fundamental to all contexts must be an invitation to consider the claims of Christ and to respect and dialogue with those with whom we disagree.

There will be no transformed Church and no renewed Mission if, to echo R.S. Thomas once again, eyes do not meet in friendship, welcome, understanding and kindness. Indeed, it did not escape several of the early Church Fathers that 'Chrestos'—kindness—was but a vowel difference from 'Christos'—Christ, the anointed one. Respect, courtesy, kindness and gentleness are part of the true structures of faith through which the grace of God comes shining through.

But my fourth and final point is this. As people called by God to hold a particular office in his Church we must seek the *Renewal of our Vocation as Bishops*. For as leaders, we can function either as a barrier or as a channel. If we are not transformed, corporately and individually, through that constant practice of gratitude for a loving, sovereign Lord, his vision for his Church and his people will never become a reality. Ten days ago I had the immense privilege of unveiling the statues of ten twentieth-century martyrs which now form part of the West Front of Westminster Abbey. Some like Janani Luwum, Martin Luther King and Oscar Romero exercised leadership on behalf of many. Others like Esther John, Manche Masemola, Wang Zhiming or Lucian Tapiedi are little-known outside their own countries and churches. Yet all died a martyr's death, and all knew what it was to be a servant of Christ and an effective channel for his Spirit.

One of my hopes for this Conference is that through mutual counsel, spiritual encouragement and the sharing of visions for the advancement of Christ's kingdom, we will become more effective channels for God's Spirit to work through. And that means facing up to the challenge of renewal and transformation for ourselves. Ours is to be a ministry of service, following the pattern laid down by Our Lord in washing his disciples' feet. Now at times we can be tempted by an office dignified by the trappings of robes and ornate pageantry. Some have further identified episcopacy with a lofty style of autocratic leadership. But we must never avoid the real challenges of episcopal leadership. For that challenge is to follow our Lord in such simplicity of discipleship that our goodness, our holiness, our humility is there for all to see.

I noticed that, in the regional response from the Province of Central Africa, this statement of Bishop Michael Nazir-Ali is quoted: 'We need to pray earnestly that humble men and women of God will emerge as Christian leaders—leaders whose authority derives from their humility and service; who persuade but do not coerce; who free Christians to exercise the gifts which the Holy Spirit has given them; who make the gospel attractive to the millions who need to believe but are sceptical of the church's structures'.

Together at this Conference let us seek a fresh vision of Christ-centred leadership. For there is a true glory in such leadership—and I have seen it again and again as I have travelled the Anglican Communion. Humble, sacrificial, devoted service continues. On behalf of the whole Anglican Communion I want to say to you, my fellow Bishops: Thank you. Thank you for giving yourselves so fully and completely to God. Thank you for the ways in which you serve his people. May the example of those martyrs, and the many others through the centuries who have given their lives to, and for Christ, continue to inspire us.

So, my brothers and sisters, this theme of transformation whether of our Vision, our Church, our Mission or our Vocation must be central to all we shall be doing together here in this place. I thank God for the gift of communion and especially for the Gift of our Communion. With so many threatening divisions in our world and the anger, hatred, distrust and cynicism which erodes real community, let us enjoy our fellowship and life as a gift from the gracious and generous God we worship. Let us treasure it and put it to good use these precious three weeks.

Beyond all the excellent elements that will make up our Conference and the Spouses' Programme—worship, bible study, group work, seminars, Section work, friendships, plenaries, meetings and eating and drinking—there rests and remains the ultimate victory that *God is,* and in him is the triumph and the victory. Sadly, the world, and even some parts of the Church, have lost sight of that ultimate mobilising vision; that we, and all things, are not the random pawns of a futile universe which will come to an end either in a big bang or a whimper. Rather, we need to remind ourselves constantly, that one day, as in Irenaus' Vision, Christ will be all in all.

The Gospel is about new and certain life; about the power which created the universe and raised Christ from the dead; about the power which promises transformation of our world, our church and all of us gathered here. This is the fundamental conviction on which this Conference rests. That is the certainty in which we shall do all our work in these next three weeks. That is the glorious power in which we shall go back to our churches and in the world in which we live. And may we look forward with expectancy and declare with John that God does and will 'make all things new'. May that vision transform and inspire us.

THE VIRGINIA REPORT

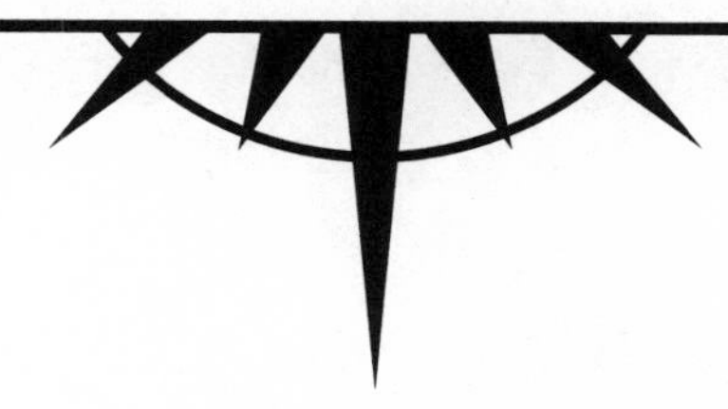

The Report
of the Inter-Anglican Theological
and Doctrinal Commission

photo: *Anglican World*

The Rt Revd Simon Chiwanga joins the procession.

Members of the Inter-Anglican Theological and Doctrinal Commission

The Revd Victor R. Atta-Baffoe, The Church of West Africa
The Rt Revd Colin Bazley, Iglesia Anglicana del Cono Sur de America
The Most Revd Peter F. Carnley, Anglican Church of Australia
The Rt Revd J. Mark Dyer, The Episcopal Church, USA
The Revd Dr Milton B. Efthimiou, Orthodox Participant
The Rt Revd Penelope A. B. Jamieson, Church of Aotearoa, New Zealand & Polynesia
The Very Revd Colin Jones, The Church of Southern Africa
The Rt Revd Dr Samuel B. Joshua, The Church of North India (United)
The Revd Dr Patricia G. Kirkpatrick, Anglican Church of Canada
The Revd Samuel I. Koshiishi, Nippon Sei Ko Kai
Professor Dr Michael Root, Lutheran Participant
The Rt Revd Stanford S. Shauri, Church of Tanzania
The Rt Revd Stephen Sykes, The Church of England
Dr Mary Tanner, The Church of England
Dr Fredrica Harris Thompsett, The Episcopal Church, USA
The Most Revd Robert H. A. Eames, The Church of Ireland (Chairman)
The Revd Dr Donald Anderson, Anglican Communion Office (Secretary to November 1996)
The Revd Canon David Hamid, Anglican Communion Office (Secretary from November 1996)
Mrs Christine Codner, Anglican Communion Office (Administrative Secretary)
The Revd Professor David Scott, Virginia Theological Seminary (Observer)

Preface

This Report is the work of the Inter-Anglican Theological and Doctrinal Commission which comprises theologians and church leaders who themselves represent the diversities of the Anglican Communion. Their task was to respond to the call of the Lambeth Conference of 1988 to consider in some depth the meaning and nature of communion. This response was to be set within the context of the doctrine of the Trinity, the unity and order of the Church and the unity and community of humanity. At the heart and centre of the Anglican pilgrimage lies the concept of communion. From it we derive so much of our belief and practice. It is not itself a static concept. It has become with our pilgrimage a living and developing reality. Yet that fact alone demands understanding which cannot be tied to any one period of our history or to any single cultural approach.

This Report is offered to the Anglican Communion as one more step in the process of seeking greater understanding of what communion means to the Body of Christ. In particular it seeks to suggest ways in which our Communion can respond in practical ways which touch and concern how we order our corporate life and lives as individuals.

I wish to acknowledge with sincere gratitude the generosity and support given to the Commission by the Right Reverend Peter Lee, Bishop of Virginia, the Diocese of Virginia and the staff of the Virginia Theological Seminary. Their practical assistance and encouragement made the production of this Report possible.

It has been a great privilege to chair the Commission and I acknowledge the support and work of all its members.

+Robert Eames
Archbishop of Armagh

Introduction

Origin and Mandate of the Commission

In 1988 the Lambeth Conference was faced with a question that challenged the unity of the Communion: the proposal by the Episcopal Church of the United States of America to consecrate a woman to the episcopate. In the light of its deliberations the Lambeth Conference passed resolution 1 on the ordination or consecration of women to the episcopate. In response to this resolution of the Conference the Archbishop of Canterbury, in consultation with the Primates, established a Commission on Communion and Women in the Episcopate under the leadership of the Most Reverend Robert Eames, Archbishop of Armagh:

(a) to provide for an examination of the relationships between Provinces of the Anglican Communion and ensure that the process of reception includes continuing consultation with other Churches as well; and

(b) to monitor and encourage the process of consultation within the Communion and to offer further pastoral guidelines (*The Truth Shall Make You Free*, The Lambeth Conference 1988. Resolution 1, page 201).

The Eames Commission, as it came to be known, met five times and produced four reports which were published together in December 1994. Its last meeting was in December 1993 and its report will be presented to the 1998 Lambeth Conference. During its lifetime the Commission engaged in theological reflection on the nature of *koinonia*. It offered guidelines on how Anglicans might live together in the highest degree of communion possible while different views and practices concerning the ordination of women continued to be held within the Communion. The Eames Commission saw this as a way of enabling an ongoing process of reception both within the Anglican Communion and the wider ecumenical fellowship. Its guidelines are intended to support graceful and charitable relationships and to ensure proper pastoral care for one another. Before its last meeting, five women had been consecrated as bishops. Also in that period the ordination of women to the priesthood had received the necessary consents in the Church of England and over one thousand women were ordained as priests, and by then women had also been ordained as priests in Australia, Aotearoa, New Zealand and Polynesia, Brazil, Burundi, Canada, Hong Kong and Macao, Ireland, Kenya, the Philippines, Scotland, Southern Africa, Uganda, the USA and West Africa.

The Eames Commission between 1988 and 1993 provided a model of how Anglicans can remain together in the highest degree of communion possible while endeavouring to come to a common mind on a matter which touches the fundamental unity of the Communion.

The 1988 Conference recognised that there was a need to describe how the Anglican Communion makes authoritative decisions while maintaining unity and interdependence in the light of the many theological issues that arise from its diversity. To address this need, the Conference resolved that there should be:

> As a matter of urgency further exploration of the meaning and nature of communion with particular reference to the doctrine of the Trinity, the unity and order of the Church, and the unity and community of humanity (Lambeth Conference 1988, Resolution 18, page 216. See Appendix I).

Resolution 8 on the Final Report of the Anglican Roman Catholic International Commission also had a direct bearing on the exercise of authority in the Church. It encouraged ARCIC to explore the basis in Scripture and Tradition of the concept of a universal primacy, in conjunction with collegiality, as an instrument of unity, the character of such primacy in practice, and to draw upon the experience of other Christian Churches in exercising primacy, collegiality and conciliarity.

In implementing Resolution 18 of Lambeth 1988, and at the request of the Primates of the Communion, the Archbishop of Canterbury invited a group of representative church leaders and theologians to meet in December 1991 at the Virginia Theological Seminary at Alexandria, USA to begin the exploration. The Consultation's report was called *Belonging Together.* The Report was circulated widely within the Communion between 1992 and 1994 with a request for critical comment. A number of Anglican member churches responded officially. There were also responses from theological institutions and individuals.

All the responses were considered by the Inter-Anglican Theological and Doctrinal Commission, the successor of the 1991 Consultation, when it met in December 1994, and again in January 1996, on both occasions at the Virginia Theological Seminary. This report is the product of its consideration and further reflection on the issues.

Chapter 1
The Context

Our Lord Jesus Christ prayed that his followers might be one, as He and the Father are one, so that the world might believe (John 17:20–21). Christians of every tradition struggle to respond in faith, life and witness, to the vision of unity expressed in the prayer of Jesus. At every level of Christian life, the call to graceful interdependence and unity in faith and doctrine challenge us.

From the earliest time in the history of the Christian community, an admonishing voice has been heard exhorting believers to maintain agreement with one another and thereby to avert divisions. From an almost equally early date they have found consensus, even on apparently major matters, singularly difficult to achieve. When the second-century Churches evolved a collection of early Christian documents which came to be called the New Testament, they had a few documents which did not attest and reflect deep disagreements, and the formation of the collection itself was the product of controversies. Nevertheless the controversies themselves were stages on a road towards greater consensus.

What makes unity and interdependence particularly difficult today? In the last 200 years the world has seen extraordinary development in the political, scientific, economic and psychological spheres. These developments have brought many blessings to the peoples of the world. At the same time there has been the disintegration of traditional cultures, values and social structures and unprecedented threats to the environment. The tension between blessing and disintegration creates a challenge to the unity and interdependence that the peoples of the world face.

The authority of nineteenth- and twentieth-century notions of progress, economic growth and the free market economy, the omnipotence of scientific method and technology, and competitive individualism are no longer accepted without question. In many places there is a search for cultural, personal and social identity which honours the integrity and value of cultural roots.

Within this context Anglicans strive to be faithful to the Gospel in their particular cultural contexts, and to face moral, doctrinal, social and economic exigencies which demand discernment and response if identity as the Christian community is to be maintained. For example, issues of justice and human rights including human sexuality, the family and the status of women, racial equality, religious freedom and the use and distribution of resources demand attention. Our response to these issues is conditioned by our particular cultural context, our way of interpreting the Bible, our degree of awareness of being part of a wider human community and our attentiveness to the response of other ecumenical partners, and to the concerns of those of other faiths.

The churches of the Anglican Communion struggle with these concerns within a life of communion and interdependence. Discernment has to be exercised about which concerns are best addressed by the local church, which provincially, and which by the whole Communion. An added burden is placed on decision making when churches are separated from one another.

New challenges to unity press impatiently upon all churches, not least those of the Anglican Communion. Today we might cite divisive issues in, for example, the Indian Ocean and Europe, Rwanda, Northern Ireland, Nigeria and the Middle East, the United States, Australia and South East Asia.

When Christians find themselves passionately engaged in the midst of complex and explosive situations, how do they avoid alienation from those who by baptism are their brothers and sisters in Christ, who are embraced in the communion of God the Holy Trinity, but who disagree? How do they stay in communion with God and each other; how do they behave towards each other in the face of disagreement and conflict? What are the limits of diversity if the Gospel imperative of unity and communion are to be maintained?

In addressing issues raised by the complexities of contemporary life, solutions will in some cases be necessarily provisional. There are times when the path ahead is insufficiently clear for categorical claims to be made. Forming a mind entails learning from those within the Anglican Communion and being in partnership and dialogue with ecumenical and interfaith colleagues. There is merit in the Anglican approach of listening to others, of holding each other in the highest degree of communion possible with tolerance for deeply held differences of conviction and practice.

While we are aware of significant challenges to our unity as a Communion we recognise that we have received the gracious gift of God the Holy Trinity, the resources of our life in Christ in word and sacrament and the determination to develop appropriate and more effective structures for maintaining unity in service and mission.

The Commission has centred its study on the understanding of trinitarian faith. It believes that the unity of the Anglican Communion derives from the unity given in the triune God, whose inner personal and relational nature is communion. This is our centre. This mystery of God's life calls us to communion in visible form. This is why the Church is called again and again to review and to reform the structures of its life together so that they nurture and enable the life of communion in God and serve God's mission in the world.

The references in the Lambeth resolution to the trinitarian doctrine and the unity and community of the whole human family make it clear that the concern of the Lambeth Conference was not simply for strengthening the peace and unity of the Anglican Communion, but also for the faithful and effective engagement of the Communion in God's mission of love and reconciliation in the world.

The mission and ministry of reconciliation entrusted by God to the Church are given in baptism to the whole people of God, the *laos*. While this report necessarily dwells on the structures of ministry in the processes of oversight, their interdependence and accountability, it does so in the conviction and hope that this reflection will open up the possibility of creative change which will strengthen the ministry and mission of the whole people of God.

The instruments of communion which are a gift of God to the Church help to hold us in the life of the triune God. These are the instruments which we seek to renew within the Anglican Communion. They are also the structures we seek to share with all those who have been baptised into the life of the Triune God. Our hope is that this theological reflection may contribute not only to the Anglican Communion but to the ecumenical goal of full visible unity.

In reflecting on the structures of Anglican unity and authority, we are aware that discernment, decision making and teaching with authority are today, sadly, in the context of separated Churches, and are therefore only partial reflections of the One, Holy Catholic and Apostolic Church. This requires Anglicans to listen to the experience of other ecclesial communities and to continue to deepen the work of ecumenical dialogue on the nature of authority and its exercise in the Church and to renew our Anglican structures in line with the emerging ecumenical convergence.

Having referred in this chapter to the context and the challenges that face Christians today, the report goes on in Chapter 2 to a theological reflection on the gracious gift of love in the triune God and how the Church responds to that gift in the ministry that the Church has received from Christ. Chapter 3 examines the bonds of interdependence: what holds Anglicans together. Chapter 4 explores the principle of subsidiarity, identifying the ways in which the bonds of unity are appropriately expressed at the different levels the Church's life. Chapter 5 identifies the principles which undergird our life together and Chapter 6 offers some observations about how Anglican international institutions of unity might be strengthened and improved in order to strengthen our life together for the sake of God's mission in the world.

Chapter 2

Theology of God's Gracious Gift: the Communion of the Trinity and the Church

The Understanding of God's Gracious Gift

God's gracious gift of steadfast loving-kindness was from the beginning known by the people of God in the form of covenant. From the prophets came the conviction that God's faithfulness was never ending even when God's people were forgetful and betrayed the divine trust.

God's love and faithfulness was understood as having been an act of creation. God's promise to remember the everlasting covenant between God and every living creature on the earth (Gen. 9:17) was a promise which was renewed again and again through the ages.

God's word to Moses in Exodus 3:14 expresses the divine promise which forever grounds the hope of inter-relational communion between God and the people of God in an everlasting and personal relationship even in the midst of tragedy.

The people of God interpreted the memory of the Sinai Covenant in words remembered as spoken by Moses, words which would forever define God's sacred relationship with his chosen people:

> For you are a people holy to the LORD your God; the LORD your God has chosen you out of all the peoples on earth to be his people, his treasured possession. It was not because you were more numerous than any other people that the LORD set his heart on you and chose you—for you were the fewest of all peoples. It was because the LORD loved you and kept the oath that he swore to your ancestors. (Deut. 7:6–8a)

God's chosen, the people of Israel, would tell the story of God's never-failing love in intimate longing and passion. So the prophet is moved to proclaim:

> You shall no more be termed Forsaken, and your land shall no more be termed Desolate; but you shall be called My Delight is in Her, and your land Married; for the LORD delights in you, and your land shall be married.
>
> For as a young man marries a young woman, so shall your builder marry you, and as the bridegroom rejoices over the bride, so shall your God rejoice over you (Is. 62:4–5).

And in the midst of despair and anguish Jeremiah speaks of God's loving act of restoration:

> But this is the covenant that I will make with the house of Israel after those days, says the LORD: I will put my law within them, and I will write it on their hearts; and I will be their God, and they shall be my people (Jer. 31:33).

Jesus spoke of this God of steadfast loving-kindness and faithfulness, as his Father. He prayed: "I thank you, Father, Lord of heaven and earth, because you have hidden these things from the wise and the intelligent and have revealed them to infants; yes, Father, for such was your gracious will. All things have been handed over to me by my Father; and no one knows the Son except the Father, and no one knows the Father except the Son and anyone to whom the Son chooses to reveal him" (Matt. 11:25–27).

The good news of the Christian Gospel is that Jesus' life among us is God's life—God breaking down the barriers of our bondage and sinfulness. In Jesus, God is with us in all our human helplessness; with us in our life and in our death. In Jesus, God is faithful to us even on a cross. In the risen Jesus, God is with us to transfigure and set free all those who are bound by fear and sin. Jesus is God with us, and to know Jesus is to be with God. God has shared our human world with us, and through the great events of cross and resurrection we are empowered and invited to share God's life, to share God's glory and freedom, to proclaim God's holiness and mercy in word and act. We know God as we live with Jesus: so that we can and must say that Jesus' life is the act and expression of God (*The Lambeth Conference 1988*, page 82).

The climax of the Son's revelation of the Father occurs in the passion, death and resurrection of Jesus. On the night before he died Jesus revealed that the communion of love he shared with the Father would be shared by the community of his disciples. John's Gospel remembers the intimate moment of God's gracious gift of love.

> As the Father has loved me, so I have loved you; abide in my love. No one has greater love than this, to lay down one's life for one's friends. I have called you friends, because I have made known to you everything I have heard from my Father. You did not choose me but I chose you. And I appointed you to go and bear fruit, fruit that will last, so that the Father will give you whatever you ask him in my name. I am giving you these commands so that you may love one another (John 15, 9, 13, 15–17).

The love with which the Father loves Jesus is the love with which Jesus loves us. On the night before he died Jesus prayed (John 17) that all who follow him should be drawn into that love and unity which exists between the Father and the Son. Thus our unity with one another is grounded in the life of love, unity and communion of the Godhead. The eternal, mutual self-giving and receiving love of the three persons of the Trinity is the source and ground of our communion, of our fellowship with God and one another. Through the power of the Holy Spirit we are drawn into a divine fellowship of love and unity. Further, it is because the Holy Trinity is a unique unity of purpose, and at the same time a diversity of ways of being and function, that the Church is called to express diversity in its own life, a diversity held together in God's unity and love (The Lambeth Conference 1988, page 130).

At the Last Supper with his disciples, Jesus promised the outpouring of God's Holy Spirit. He prayed that God would come to the community as the gift of the Holy Spirit. The Spirit would bear witness to the truth of all that Jesus said and did.

> I will ask the Father, and he will give you another Advocate, to be with you forever. This is the Spirit of truth, whom the world cannot receive, because it neither sees him nor knows him. You know him, because he abides in you, and he will be in you.

Jesus goes on,

> On that day you will know that I am in my Father, and you in me, and I in you. They who have my commandments and keep them are those who love me; and those who love me will be loved by my Father, and I will love them and reveal myself to them (John 14:16–17; 20–21).

The sending of the Holy Spirit at Pentecost created the Church, the community of Jesus Christ. The Holy Spirit lifted up the community into the very life of God: Father, Son and Holy Spirit. The Spirit empowered the community to pray "Abba, Father" as free, adopted, children of God (Rom. 8:15–17, Gal. 4:4–7). "Clothed with power from on high" (Luke 24:49), the community is empowered to go forth to proclaim the Good News of God to all peoples and nations. The Holy Spirit is the unifying force of God in the community. The unity of the Church which is given, and yet which it seeks to deepen, is grounded in the very unity of God, Father, Son and Holy Spirit (Eph. 1:3–14, 4:1–6).

Every act of God is an act of the undivided Holy Trinity. The very being of the Church is thus dependent upon the outpouring of God's gracious love, the love of Father, Son and Holy Spirit. The experience of the truth of the revelation of God in Jesus Christ came to the disciples as a gracious gift. What the disciples experienced at Pentecost in Jesus Christ was that communion of life with God which was present at creation and which will be perfected in the fullness of time.

The Communion of the Trinity and the Life of the Church

By the power of the Holy Spirit the Church is born into history as the Body of Christ (1 Cor. 12:27). The Church is called the temple of God (1 Cor. 3:16), a chosen race, a royal priesthood, a holy nation, a people God claims as his own (1 Pet. 2:9). These images of the Church speak of a communion with God: Father, Son, and Holy Spirit; Christians are participants in the divine nature. This communion also determines our relationship with one another. "We declare to you what we have seen and heard so that you also may have fellowship with us; and truly our fellowship is with the Father, and with his Son, Jesus Christ" (1 John 1:3). Communion with God and one another is both gift and divine expectation for the Church (Eames I, *Koinonia and the Mystery of God*, 21–22).

Because the Church as communion participates in God's communion of Father, Son and Holy Spirit, it has an eschatological reality and significance. The Church is the advent, in history, of God's final will being done "on earth as it is in heaven." That will was revealed in the life and ministry of Jesus Christ and is continually inspired by the work of the Spirit in the life and mission of the Church. The Church is the icon of the future toward which God is directing the history of the world. A faithful church signifies by its life that it is the living promise of God's purpose in the midst of today's history. The Church lives in the present, remembering again and again (making *anamnesis*) the Christ event and receiving in hope the promise of the Kingdom. In this way, the saving events of Christ's death and resurrection and the foretaste of the Kingdom are brought into the present experience of the Church.

The Church looks forward in Christ, through the power of the Holy Spirit, to that day when God's name will be made holy, God's Kingdom come, when God's will is done on earth as it is in heaven. The seventh-century theologian St. Maximus the Confessor put it this way: "The things of the past are shadow; those of the present icon; the truth is to be found in the things of the future" (Scolion on the ecclesiastical hierarchy, 3,3:2). Faithful Christian community with God, the Holy Trinity, is focused in a vision of the final and ultimate reign of God. Its mission is to be the living and visible sign of that divine reign, when He will dwell with them as their God; "they will be his people, and God himself will be with them; he will wipe every tear from their eyes. Death will be no more; mourning and crying and pain will be no more; for the first things have passed away (Rev. 21:3–4).

The Communion of the Trinity and Mission and Ministry

A living faith in the God of Jesus Christ draws us into the life of the Holy Trinity. This means living as Jesus understood and lived his life, empowered by God's Spirit:

> The Spirit of the Lord is upon me, because he has anointed me to bring good news to the poor. He has sent me to proclaim release to the captives and recovery of sight to the blind, to let the oppressed go free, to proclaim the year of the Lord's favour (Luke 4:18–19).

The same Spirit of the Lord rests upon the Church and dwells in the hearts of the believers, empowering the community to go forth as Christ did to proclaim the reign of God. The mission of the Church is to be the icon of God's life. By prayer and praise, mercy and peace, justice and love, constantly welcoming the sinner, the outcast, the marginalised into her sanctuary, the Church is revealed as communion and is faithful to its mission. As Body of Christ (1 Cor. 12:27), Temple of the Holy Spirit (1 Cor. 1:16), God's own people (1 Pet. 2:9) the Church lives in mutual love and is sent forth as a missionary community to gather all of creation into God's reconciling love, restore and renew it in the life of the triune God (Rom. 8:19–25).

The mission of Christ and the Church is celebrated and proclaimed in the liturgy which shapes the trinitarian faith of the people of God and empowers them for a life of ministry and mission. This is especially true of Holy Baptism and Holy Eucharist.

As the sacrament of initiation into the life of the Church, baptism is related not only to a single experience, but to lifelong growth in Christ and participation in his ministry. Those who are baptized are called upon to reflect the glory of the Lord with ever increasing splendour as they are transformed by the power of the Holy Spirit into his likeness. As they grow in the Christian life of faith, baptized believers demonstrate that humanity can be regenerated and liberated. They have a common responsibility to bear witness in the Church and the world to the Gospel of Christ, "the Liberator of all human beings." (*BEM*, Baptism 9,10).

The eucharist also embraces all aspects of life. It is a representative act of thanksgiving and offering on behalf of the whole world. The eucharistic celebration demands reconciliation and sharing among those who are brothers and sisters in the one family of God, and constantly challenges those who participate to search for appropriate relationships in social, economic and political life (Matt. 5:23f.; 1 Cor. 10:16f.; 11:20–22. Gal. 3:28). All injustice, racism, separation and denial of freedom are radically challenged when Christians share in the body and blood of Christ. Through the eucharist the grace of God penetrates, restores and renews human personality and dignity. The eucharist involves believers in the central event of the world's history, the passion, death and resurrection of Christ, and sends them into the world in peace to love and serve the Lord (*BEM*, Eucharist 20).

Jesus Christ manifests and carries out for us God's creative, reconciling and perfecting mission and ministry to the world. All Christian ministry is rooted in that unique ministry of Jesus Christ. The centre of Jesus's ministry is his self-offering on the cross for the reconciliation of God and humanity and the healing of the whole human family (Col. 1:19; 2 Cor. 5:19). Christ's passion, death and resurrection brings into relationship those who had become alienated, both individually and corporately. The reconciling work of Christ, the very heart of the Christian good news, brings those who receive him into the trinitarian life of sharing and interrelationship.

Christ calls human beings to share in that loving and redeeming work of God and empowers them for that ministry with his Spirit. Jesus prayed, "As you have sent me into the world, so I have sent them into the world" (John 17:18). Christ called and equipped his disciples and sent them to reflect his own ministry of healing, teaching, leading, feeding and proclaiming. Through the varied aspects of the Church's one ministry, the Kingdom which Jesus proclaimed is brought into historical expression.

To be baptized and to participate at the Table of the Lord is to be entrusted with Christ's one, continuing mission through the Church. The baptised are called to unity and interdependence. United to Christ, each member of the Body relates to the other members; they are interdependent with and through Christ. To celebrate the eucharist together reveals and builds this mutuality. "We who are many are one body for we all partake of the one bread." In eucharist the Spirit affirms and renews communion in Christ and the gifts given us to participate in the divine mission.

The Holy Spirit bestows on the community diverse and complimentary gifts. (cf.*BEM*, Ministry 5) God the Creator blesses people with many talents and abilities. The Holy Spirit graces individuals with special gifts. The outworking of one person's gift in the Church is unthinkable apart from all the others. The mutuality and interdependence of each member and each part of the Church is essential for the fulfilment of the Church's mission. In the early Church, those who spoke in tongues needed interpreters of tongues; Paul's mission to the Gentiles complemented Peter's mission to the Jews. The ministry of serving tables in the early Church freed the other disciples to preach God's word. The gifts of all contribute to the building up of the community and the fulfilment of its calling.

But the one mission of the Church, the Body of Christ, must always find its motivation, its intelligibility and its integrity in the one ministry of the Church's Lord, Jesus Christ. The variety and difference among Christian charisms would quickly become incoherent and disabling if it were to become eccentric, without a reference to its centre in Christ. An important function of life in communion is always to remain attentive to one another, particularly when conflict arises, so that the centre may never be forgotten. Seen in the framework of God's mission of love in Christ and the Spirit, the variety of gifts, which may appear to be potentially divisive, is seen to be necessary, mutually enriching, and a cause for thanks and praise to God.

God invites his people to enjoy diversity. As Christ's body, the Church must affirm that variety of gifts and use them faithfully both for the building up of the body "until all of us come to the unity of the faith and of the knowledge of the Son of God, to maturity to the measure of the full stature of Christ" and "to equip the saints for the work of ministry" (Eph. 4:12–13).

Chapter 3

Belonging Together in the Anglican Communion

Anglicans are held together in a life of visible communion. Baptism is God's gift of unity, the means by which an individual participates in the life of God, Father, Son and Holy Spirit and is brought into a living community of faith. The confession of a common faith, the celebration of the eucharist, a life of common prayer, the service of an ordered ministry, conciliar structures, shared service and mission sustain a life of Anglican belonging. These elements belong to the universal Church and are not unique to Anglicans. They are nevertheless, lived out in a recognisable and characteristically Anglican way.

In the sixteenth century, members of the Church of England continued to understand themselves as the local embodiment of the Catholic Church, continuing to live in England with the same faith, sacraments and ministry of the Church through the ages. And yet they developed a family likeness which today characterises Anglicans who live not only in England but in the thirty-six provinces of the Anglican Communion.

One feature of Anglican life is the way it holds together diversities of many kinds. From the Reformation Anglicans endeavoured to hold together people of different temperaments, convictions and insights: the puritans who wanted more radical reform and the conservatives who emphasized their continuity with the pre-reformation Church. Today, for example, evangelicals, catholics, liberals, and charismatics bring a diversity of insights and perspectives as Anglicans struggle to respond to the contemporary challenges to faith, order and moral teaching. Bound up with these groupings are the differences which arise from a variety of reactions to critical study of the Bible, particular cultural contexts, different schools of philosophical thought and scientific theory. The Reformation insistence on providing the Scriptures in the vernacular opened the possibility that the faith is expressed in the language, symbols and imagery of the different cultural contexts.

At best the Anglican way is characterised by generosity and tolerance to those of different views. It also entails a willingness to contain difference and live with tension, even conflict, as the Church seeks a common mind on controversial issues. The comprehensiveness that marks the Anglican Communion is not a sign of weakness or uncertainty about the central truths of the faith. Neither does it mean that Anglicans accept that there are no limits to diversity.

The Anglican Way: Scripture, Tradition and Reason

Anglicans are held together by the characteristic way in which they use Scripture, tradition and reason in discerning afresh the mind of Christ for the Church in each generation. This was well-described in the *Report of the Pastoral and Dogmatic Concerns* section of Lambeth 1988.

Anglicans affirm the sovereign authority of the Holy Scriptures as the medium through which God by the Spirit communicates his word in the Church and thus enables people to respond with understanding and faith. The Scriptures are "uniquely inspired witness to divine revelation," and "the primary norm for Christian faith and life."

The Scriptures, however, must be translated, read, and understood, and their meaning grasped through a continuing process of interpretation. Since the seventeenth century, Anglicans have held that Scripture is to be understood and read in the light afforded by the contexts of "tradition" and "reason."

In one sense tradition denotes the Scriptures themselves, in that they embody 'the tradition,' 'the message,' 'the faith once delivered to the saints.' Tradition refers to the ongoing Spirit-guided life of the Church which receives, and in receiving interprets afresh God's abiding message. The living tradition embraces the ecumenical creeds, the classical eucharistic prayers, which belong with the Scriptures as forming their essential message. Tradition is not to be understood as an accumulation of formulae and texts but the living mind, the nerve centre of the Church. Anglican appeal to tradition is the appeal to this mind of the Church carried by the worship, teaching and the Spirit-filled life of the Church.

Properly speaking "reason" means simply the human being's capacity to symbolise, and so to order, share and communicate experience. It is the divine gift in virtue of which human persons respond and act with awareness in relation to their world and to God, and are opened up to that which is true for every time and every place. Reason cannot be divorced either from Scripture or tradition, since neither is conceivable apart from the working of reason. In another perspective reason means not so much the capacity to make sense of things as it does "that which makes sense," or "that which is reasonable." The appeal to reason then becomes what people—and that means people in a given time and place—take as good sense or "common" sense. It refers to what can be called "the mind of a particular culture," with its characteristic ways of seeing things, asking about them, and explaining them. If tradition is the mind that Christians share as believers and members of the Church, reason is the mind they share as participants in a particular culture.

Anglicanism sees reason in the sense of the "mind" of the culture in which the Church lives and the Gospel is proclaimed, as a legitimate and necessary instrument for the interpretation of God's message in the Scriptures. Sometimes Scriptures affirm the new insights of a particular age or culture, sometimes they challenge or contradict those insights. The Word of God is addressed to the Church as it is part of the world. The Gospel borne by the Scriptures must be heard and interpreted in the language that bears the "mind" and distills the experience of the world. Tradition and reason are therefore in the Anglican way two distinct contexts in which Scriptures speak and out of which they are interpreted.

The characteristic Anglican way of living with a constant dynamic interplay of Scripture, tradition and reason means that the mind of God has constantly to be discerned afresh, not only in every age, but in each and every context. Moreover, the experience of the Church as it is lived in different places has something to contribute to the discernment of the mind of Christ for the Church. No one culture, no one period of history has a monopoly of insight into the truth of the Gospel. It is essential for the fullest apprehension of truth that context is in dialogue with context. Sometimes the lived experience of a particular community enables Christian truth to be perceived afresh for the whole community. At other times a desire for change or restatement of the faith in one place provokes a crisis within the whole Church. In order to keep the Anglican Communion living as a dynamic community of faith, exploring and making relevant the understanding of the faith, structures for taking counsel and deciding are an essential part of the life of the Communion.

The Anglican Way: Sacrament and Worship

Fundamental to the Anglican way of living with and responding to diversity is the constant interplay and influence of Scripture, tradition and reason. The Scriptures are read and interpreted in the round of common daily prayer and in the celebration of the sacraments. In worship the faith is encountered in the hearing of the word and in the experience of the sacrament. In the sacrament of baptism Christians die and rise again with Christ through the waters of baptism to new life in him. In the eucharist they encounter the central mysteries of the faith in the anamnesis, the making present of those past events and the experience of future glory, through the power of the Holy Spirit. Word and sacrament are fundamental to the life of the Anglican Communion as it seeks to teach the faith and to give guidance for the right conduct in human life, expressing this in doctrine and moral guidance. A family likeness in common prayer expressed in many languages is a precious heritage which is significant in forming Anglican identity and maintaining unity. A commitment to daily prayer, to systematic scripture reading, to praying the psalms and canticles, to regular credal confession of the faith, and to intercessory prayer for one another and for the needs of the world is an integral part of Anglican belonging.

All of these resources keep Anglicans living together in fidelity to the memory and hope of Jesus under the guidance of the Holy Spirit, who leads into all truth. In the present they are bound together as they remember the past and anticipate the reconciliation of all things in Christ at the end of time.

Interdependence of Charisms in the Life of the Church

All who are baptised into the life of God and live out their calling as members of the Anglican Communion are given a charism of the Holy Spirit for the life of the Communion and for the service of others. The vocation of the *laos* is exercised in a broad context of social and communal life in civil society, at work and in recreation and within the family, as well as within the life of the community of the Church. By virtue of their baptism all members are called to confess their faith and to give account of their hope in what they do and what they say.

The calling of lay persons is to represent Christ and his Church; to bear witness to him wherever they may be; according to the gifts given to them, to carry out Christ's work of reconciliation in the world; and to take their place in the life, worship and governance of the Church.

To enable the community of faith to respond to Christ's call God has given to the Church the charism of ordered ministry: the episcopate, the presbyterate, and the diaconate. The ordained ministry is exercised with, in, and among the whole people of God.

The calling of a bishop is to represent Christ and his Church, particularly as apostle, chief priest, teacher and pastor of a diocese; to guard the faith, unity and discipline of the whole Church; to proclaim the word of God; to act in Christ's name for the reconciliation of the world and the building up of the Church; and to ordain others to continue Christ's ministry.

The calling of a priest or presbyter is to represent Christ and his Church, particularly as pastor to the people; to share with the bishops in the overseeing of the Church; to proclaim the gospel; to administer the sacraments; and to bless and declare pardon in the name of God.

The calling of a deacon is to represent Christ and his Church, particularly as a servant to those in need; and to assist bishops and priests in the proclamation of the Gospel and the administration of the sacraments (ECUSA, *BCP*, page 855–856).

The complementary gifts bestowed by the Holy Spirit on the community are for the common good and for the building up of the Church and for the service of the world to which the Church is sent.

The Ministry of Oversight

The continuation of a ministry of oversight (*episkopé*) at the Reformation exercised by bishops, by bishops in college and by bishops in council is what is referred to in the current ecumenical writing as "the personal, collegial and communal" ways of exercising the ministry of oversight. These forms of ministry help to hold Anglicans together in a community of discernment and reflection. Every diocese in the Anglican Communion knows something of the exercise of the personal ministry of oversight of the bishop (or bishops); of collegiality in the coming together of bishops and clergy; and of the communal dimension of oversight which brings together the bishop with clergy and laity in the meeting of synods. These dimensions of the ministry of oversight are expressed in different ways in the different regions of the world and are affected by local circumstance and custom.

The bishop presides over the gatherings, collegial and communal in the diocese. Sometimes the bishop shares the presiding over meetings with a member of the laity. In most places at the level of a Province, the collegial and synodical gatherings are presided over by an archbishop or presiding bishop. Collegiality and primacy are thus part of the Anglican experience at diocesan, Provincial and Communion wide levels. Within the Communion, Provincial primacy, influenced by the different cultural contexts, varies in perception and practice.

Structures of Interdependence

The life of belonging together with its characteristic ethos within the Anglican Communion is supported by a web of structures which hold together and guide a common life of belonging. These structures owe something to their continuity with the western Catholic Church and also to the Reformation of the sixteenth century. They have undergone considerable development since the sixteenth century and continue to be subject to change and development today.

At the Reformation the Church of England maintained the threefold order of ministry in continuity with the early Church. Bishops in their dioceses continued to be the personal focus of the continuity and unity of the Church. There was no attempt to minimise the role of bishops as ministers of word and sacrament nor to stop a collegial relation between bishops and presbyters in the diocese or bishops together at the level of Province. Conciliar life continued to be part of the Church of England's experience. The role of Parliament and the Royal Supremacy ensured that the role and place of the laity were embedded in the structuring of the life of the Church of England. In time this developed into synodical structures which bring together ordained and lay for discernment, decision making and authoritative teaching.

The expansion of the Church of England as a result of British colonisation led to the formation of Provinces each with its own episcopal and synodical structures for maintaining the life of the Church. In the post-colonial period of the twentieth century the various independent Anglican Churches are governed by synods which recognise bishops' authority in some form as crucial and distinct, but which include, not only presbyterial representation, but also lay representation. Each Province too has developed some form of primatial office in the role of archbishop or presiding bishop.

The expression of episcopacy and the form of synodical and collegial government are not identical in each place. The experience and exercise of authority in the local context has played a part in shaping the different Provincial structures and processes. In some places the increasing emphasis on democratic forms of representation in modern secular governments has also affected church government.

In the development of the Anglican Communion there is no legislative authority above the Provincial level. (How far this is a result of the Royal Supremacy in the Church of England is a matter for reflection. Other historical factors in other Provinces have also affected the question of autonomy and interdependence.) There has been an insistence upon the autonomy of the Provinces of the Anglican Communion. However, while autonomy entails the legal and juridical right of each Province to govern its way of life, in practice autonomy has never been the sole criterion for understanding the relation of Provinces to one another. There has generally been an implicit understanding of belonging together and interdependence. The life of the Communion is held together in the creative tension of Provincial autonomy and interdependence. There are some signs that the Provinces are coming to a greater realisation that they need each other's spiritual, intellectual and material resources in order to fulfil their task of mission. Each Province has something distinctive to offer the others, and needs them in turn to be able to witness to Christ effectively in its own context. Questions are asked about whether we can go on as a world Communion with morally authoritative but not juridically binding decision-making structures at the international level. A further question is the relationship between the autonomy of a Province and the theological importance of a diocese which is reckoned to be the basic unit of Anglicanism.

The interdependence of the Provinces has come to be maintained by certain ministries, structures and relationships which continue to develop. The first of these is the Archbishop of Canterbury.

While the request for the first Lambeth Conference in 1867 came from the Communion and not from Canterbury, it assembled at the invitation of the Archbishop of Canterbury, who also presided over it. The continuing role of Canterbury, as a focus of the unity of the Anglican Communion and the "first among equals" in the Anglican college of bishops, came to clear expression in this way. The primacy of Canterbury and the international collegiality and conciliarity of Anglicanism are inextricably interrelated.

The primacy of the See of Canterbury and its key role in the Communion clearly emerged in many of the resolutions of the first Lambeth Conference. However, at the Conference of 1897 the role of the Archbishop of Canterbury in gathering the Communion was explicitly acknowledged and affirmed when he was urged to foster the maintenance and development of the Communion by calling the Conference of bishops every ten years.

Today Anglican identity and authenticity of belonging is generally determined by the outward and visible test of communion with the See of Canterbury. The 1930 Lambeth Conference explicitly defined Anglicanism in this way:

> It is part of the Holy Catholic and Apostolic Church. Its centre of unity is the See of Canterbury. To be Anglican it is necessary to be in communion with that See.

Resolution 49 added further:

> The Anglican Communion is a fellowship, with One, Holy, Catholic and Apostolic Church… in communion with the See of Canterbury… (Lambeth Conference 1930, Resolution 49)

Lambeth 1968 described the role of the Archbishop of Canterbury in more detail:

> Within the college of bishops it is evident that there must be a president. In the Anglican Communion this position is at present held by the occupant of the historic See of Canterbury, who enjoys a primacy of honour, not of jurisdiction. This primacy is found to involve, in a particular way, that care of all the churches which is shared by all the bishops.

The Lambeth Conference of 1978 in a further statement on the basis of Anglican unity said, *inter alia*:

> Its [unity] is personally grounded in the loyal relationship of each of the churches to the Archbishop of Canterbury who is freely recognised as the focus of unity.

Being in communion with the See and Archbishop of Canterbury has been a visible sign of the membership of bishops and of their Churches in the Anglican Communion. The Archbishop of Canterbury's task has been described as involving "in a particular way, that care of all the churches which is shared by all the bishops", and also as a task "not to command but to gather" the Communion. Clearly, the emphasis is upon service and caring and not upon coercive power.

The Lambeth Conference of bishops first met in 1867. It arose from the missionary concern of the Provinces, particularly the bishops of Canada, but the first moves to establish a meeting of all bishops of the Anglican Communion did not go unopposed. What was said about the identity and role of the first Lambeth Conference in 1867 was cautious:

> It has never been contemplated that we should assume the functions of a general synod of all the Churches in full communion with the Church of England, and take upon ourselves to enact canons that should be binding upon those represented. We merely propose to discuss matters of practical interest and pronounce what we deem expedient in resolutions which may serve as safe guides (*Lambeth Conferences 1867–1930*, SPCK (1948), page 9).

The consultative rather than legislative role of the Conference was reiterated clearly in 1920:

> The Lambeth Conference does not claim to exercise any powers of control. It stands for the far more spiritual and more Christian principle of loyalty to the fellowship. The Churches represented in it are indeed independent, but independent with the Christian freedom which recognizes the restraints of truth and love. They are not free to ignore the fellowship… the Conference is a fellowship in the Spirit (*Lambeth Conference 1920*, SPCK (1920), Evangelical Letter, page 14).

A balance is held between denying any power of compliance or control while upholding the need for loyalty to the fellowship expressed in restraint imposed by virtue of belonging to the Communion. No one part should act without regard for the others.

In 1958 the Lambeth Conference recognised the need for an executive officer who would serve both the Lambeth Consultative Body and the Advisory Council on Missionary Strategy. It was out of the tireless efforts of the Right Reverend Stephen F. Bayne Jr. that communication within the Communion was strengthened and a new vision of interdependence and mutual accountability in Anglicanism was shaped. From his work, and that of his successor, Archbishop Ralph Dean, came the vision of a Consultative Council.

The Anglican Consultative Council (ACC) was established by a resolution of the 1968 Lambeth Conference. The Conference recognised that there was a need for more contact between the Churches of the Anglican Communion than that provided by the Lambeth Conference every ten years by bringing together bishops, presbyters and laity, under the presidency of the Archbishop of Canterbury, to work on common concerns. The Council met for the first time at Limuru, Kenya in 1971.

Resolution 69 of the 1968 Lambeth Conference set out eight areas of ministry belonging to the Anglican Consultative Council:

1. To share information about developments in one or more provinces with the other parts of the Communion and to serve as needed as an instrument of common action.

2. To advise on inter-Anglican, provincial, and diocesan relationships, including the division of provinces, the information of new provinces and of regional councils, and the problems of extra-provincial dioceses.

3. To develop as far as possible agreed Anglican policies in the world mission of the Church and to encourage national and regional Churches to engage together in developing and implementing such policies by sharing their resources of manpower, money, and experience to the best advantage of all.

4. To keep before national and regional Churches the importance of the fullest possible Anglican collaboration with other Christian Churches.

5. To encourage and guide Anglican participation in the ecumenical movement and the ecumenical organisations; to co-operate with the World Council of Churches and the world confessional bodies on behalf of the Anglican Communion; and to make arrangements for the conduct of pan-Anglican conversations with the Roman Catholic Church, the Orthodox Churches, and other Churches.

6. To advise on matters arising out of national or regional Church union negotiations or conversations and on subsequent relations with united Churches.

7. To advise on problems of inter-Anglican communication and to help in the dissemination of Anglican and ecumenical information.

8. To keep in review the needs that may arise for further study and, where necessary, to promote inquiry and research.

The Anglican Consultative Council meets every three years and its Standing Committee annually. Its constitution and functions have been clearly set out and agreed to by the Provinces, and it has been incorporated as the legal entity for the Communion. In 1988 the members of the ACC were invited participants without vote at the Lambeth Conference. They have been invited to Lambeth 1998.

Its most vital purpose, however, like the Lambeth Conference, is to establish a communion of mutual attentiveness, interdependence and accountability to serve the unity and interdependence in mission of the Anglican Communion. The mutual attentiveness required when members from various parts of the Communion share the richness of their experiences also helps to form the mind of the Communion and is a reminder of the rich diversity of gifts which God has given us. The sharing of stories enhances and deepens the Communion's experience of interdependence at all levels.

Important to this process are representatives who are able not only to bring the concerns and stories of their Provinces with them but carry the proceedings of the council back to their communities, at the Provincial, national and diocesan levels. Only this constant interchange will provide the basis on which member Churches are able to develop and maintain constant relations and full communion with their sisters and brothers around the world. Each Provincial Church has a responsibility to assist their representatives to carry out this task.

The gathering of bishops, priests and laity at the meetings of the Anglican Consultative Council since Kenya 1971 provides a much needed opportunity for the opinions and experiences of the Communion to be shared.

The 1978 Lambeth Conference approved a proposal that the Archbishop of Canterbury convene a regular Meeting of the Primates. At that Conference Archbishop Coggan said:

> ...I am coming to believe that the way forward in the coming years—and it may be a slow process—will be along two lines: first, to have meetings of the Primates of the Communion reasonably often, for leisurely thought, prayer and deep consultation. There have been such meetings, but on very informal and rare bases. I believe they should be held perhaps as frequently as once in two years. But if that meeting now on some fairly regular basis is to be fruitful, those primates would have to come to such meetings well informed with a knowledge of the mind and will of their brothers whom they represent. Then they would be channels through which the voice of the member Churches would be heard, and real interchange of mind and will and heart could take place. That's the first thing.

> The second line, I think, on which we might make progress would be to see that the body of Primates, as they meet, should be in the very closest and most intimate contact with the ACC.

The minutes of the 1979 Meeting of the Primates comment that:

> The role of a Primates' meeting could not be, and was not desired as a higher synod... Rather it was a clearing house for ideas and experience through free expression, the fruits of which the Primates might convey to their Churches.

Since then, meetings of the Primates have become occasions of debate and discussion of personal and Provincial matters in the context of eucharist, prayer and study, in which the primates have achieved, in spite of the constantly changing membership of the group, a deep sense of fraternity that has nourished the unity of the Communion. At a meeting of the Primates at Newcastle, Northern Ireland in 1991, the Primates considered that the primary importance of meeting is the building and maintenance of personal relationships:

(a) as a sign of the unity and catholicity of the Church;
(b) to give high profile to important issues;
(c) for mutual support and counsel.

The Primates also expressed the opinion that there appears to be no issue which is the exclusive preserve of the Primates alone; all issues, doctrinal, ecclesial and moral, are the concern of the whole baptised community.

What has yet to be given serious consideration is Resolution 18 Section 2(a) of Lambeth 1988:

> This conference urges that encouragement be given to a developing collegial role for the Primates' Meeting under the Presidency of the Archbishop of Canterbury, so that the Primates' meeting is able to exercise an enhanced responsibility in offering guidance on doctrinal, moral and pastoral matters.

The episcopate is the primary instrument of Anglican unity, but episcopé is exercised personally, collegially and communally. The emergence of the Lambeth Conference and more recently, the Primates' Meeting and the Anglican Consultative Council, together with the primacy of the Archbishop of Canterbury, have become effective means of keeping the Provinces in touch with each other and of binding the Anglican Communion together. Apart from the episcopate these instruments were not given from the beginning but have gradually developed and are still developing. The instruments, while having no legislative authority, provide the means of consultation and go some way to helping to form a Communion-wide mind on issues that affect the whole Communion. In these developments we see the conciliar nature of modern Anglicanism which is one of its least recognised yet most characteristic features. However, the Provinces remain autonomous. They are governed and regulated by synods which recognize the authority of bishops in some form as crucial and distinct, but which also include representation from the ordained clergy and the laity.

This complex and still-evolving network of structures within Anglicanism has developed and serves to keep Anglicans in a life of belonging together, a life of relationship. These structures are both formal and informal and interrelate and affect one another in subtle ways. They involve personal, collegial and communal relationships at the parochial, diocesan, regional and international levels. Each contributes towards a web of interdependence and serves to guard against isolation.

This complex network of structures gives expression to the fundamental bond of Anglican life which is that unity given in the life of God, Father, Son and Holy Spirit. That life of divine communion is made visible in a characteristic way within the ordered life of the Anglican Communion. The combination of allegiance to Scripture, tradition and reason, the life lived within the gifts of Scripture, creeds, sacraments, and ordained ministry, the essential inter-relatedness of lay and ordained and the structured, conciliar life contribute each in their particular way to a life of interdependence and belonging. The life of the Communion is dynamic as the fellowship seeks to respond to new insights, challenges and threats.

At the end of the decade one question for Anglicans is whether their bonds of interdependence are strong enough to hold them together embracing tension and conflict while answers are sought to seemingly intractable problems. In particular the call for more effective structures of communion at a world level will need to be faced at Lambeth 1998 for the strengthening of the Anglican Communion and its unity into the next millennium. A further question concerns the wider ecumenical community. Is there a need for a universal primacy exercised collegially and respecting the role of the laity in decision-making within the Church? This question was referred to the Anglican-Roman Catholic International Commission (ARCIC) by Lambeth 1988 and is also raised by the Bishop of Rome's invitation in *Ut Unum Sint.*

Chapter 4

Levels of Communion: Subsidiarity and Interdependence

The Churches of the Anglican Communion belong to the one, holy, catholic and apostolic Church. That is to say, they understand themselves as an integral part of the mystery of God's reconciling work and an embodiment of the presence of God in the world. The task and aims of the Church are given by divine commission. The Church is commanded to go to all nations and make them disciples of the Lord (Matt. 28: 19f.). His followers are sent by Christ into the world, as he was sent by the Father into the world (John 17). God has entrusted the Church's ministers with the task of being ambassadors, and makes an appeal for reconciliation through them (2 Cor. 5:18f.). In the most fundamental way, therefore, the Church is for mission, by commission.

As the Church reflected on the nature of this mission it formulated four classic "marks" or "attributes" which ought to characterise its life at all times, and in all places. These it confesses in the words of the Nicene Creed. It is to be one, as the Body of Christ, to proclaim and to embody the reconciliation of all things in Christ. It is to be holy, that is, to have about it the marks of the sanctifying presence of the Holy Spirit; it is to be catholic, that is, to be, as Christ was, for all people, at all times, in all places; and it is to be apostolic, to witness courageously and unceasingly to the authentic and liberating gospel of Christ, as taught by the apostles.

Together with these marks goes the presupposition that the Church must be a receptive and learning community. It can manifest none of these attributes unless Christians are encouraged corporately "to go to school" with Christ, to be nourished by teaching and the sacraments, and to grow up into his likeness (Eph. 4:11–16). So the Church is a school in which the gift of teaching is acknowledged, but in which all the teachers are themselves learners, enjoying mutuality of encouragement and correction. This enables the Church to be a teaching community not simply for its own sake, but for the sake of its mission to the world.

Although the aims of the Church have been given to it, nonetheless the Church has continually to formulate and reformulate its specific objectives with a view to their being consistent with these fundamental aims, and also appropriate and relevant to the given conditions of a particular place and time. The gospel has to be proclaimed afresh in each generation. New challenges and opportunities constantly arise to be addressed; new threats have to be resisted.

The Levels of the Church's Life

This raises the question of where and at what levels decisions are to be made. Characteristically, questions arise in the Communion in a particular place at a particular time. To respond appropriately and effectively the Church needs to be clear that there is a diversity of levels on which the God-given mission of the Church is carried out. The word "level" is used in this context neutrally; the more local is not "lower" in a pejorative sense, nor is the more international "higher" and for that reason more important. Each level has its own integrity and its own demands. Some matters concern a single parish; some relate to a diocese; some would be appropriately addressed by a national or Provincial assembly; a very few would be better approached at a regional or international level; and some are matters for the Communion as a whole as a part of the universal Church.

There is no simple way of separating levels, or of assigning the consideration of particular matters to particular levels without controversy. An ethnic matter, for example, may be divisive at parish level, and be relevant at every intermediate stage to the international level. No one guideline can be invoked to determine where responsibility for a decision lies.

The character of the Christian faith from its early days has given it a profound investment in the quality of personal, face-to-face relationships. Christians are called to embody in daily life God's reconciliation of all things in Christ, living newly in the light of God's justice and forgiveness. It is through the personal witness of Christians to the reality of that new life that the attractiveness of the gospel becomes apparent. And the gifts of the Holy Spirit, which are various to different people, are given precisely so that used together in humility and love and with attentiveness to one another's interests, they may contribute to the building up of the whole body.

The Principle of Subsidiarity

The principle of "subsidiarity" has been formulated to express this investment in the local and face-to-face. Properly used, subsidiarity means that "a central authority should have a subsidiary function, performing only those tasks which cannot be performed effectively at a more immediate or local level" (*Oxford English Dictionary*).

Subsidiarity may properly be applied to the life of the Church in order to resist the temptation of centralism. But in the life of the Church the local level was never seen as simply autonomous. Because the work of Christ was itself a reconciliation of humanity, there is evidence from the first days of the churches of concern for the unity of the communities, both in their internal relationships and in their inter-relationships. St. Paul, for example, writes of his anxiety for the continuity of preaching and teaching the authentic apostolic gospel, and for the effectiveness of the united witness of the Church to the gospel of reconciliation. Care was taken, as the Church grew, to preserve the continuity of its witness across time and its coherence and effectiveness in different places.

It is important to clarify the principles which should govern the relationship of the different levels of the life of the Church to one another. Clarity on this matter makes for creative, sustainable and transparent partnerships in the Body of Christ. Every "higher" authority ought to encourage the free use of God's gifts at "lower" levels. There must be clarity on what has to be observed and carried out at that level, and also on the limits of its competence. As much space as possible should be given to personal initiative and responsibility. For example, in the relationship between a bishop and a parish priest and congregation, there is initially a giving of responsibility to the latter for the task of worship, witness and service within its geographical boundaries or area of immediate influence. The priest and parish will be given a set of tasks which they are obliged to fulfill. These will be few in number and general in character. The limits of their authority and responsibility will also be explained to priest and parish. These will essentially reflect agreements made previously by church synods, and expressed in canons and other ways. They will be honoured by all unless and until they are changed by the due processes of agreement. Subject to such boundaries the priest and parish will be encouraged to use all their gifts, energy and commitment to enable the gospel to go forward in that area. The bishop and parish priest will maintain the highest level of communication possible so that encouragement, advice, and, where necessary, correction can be given, together with new tasks as occasion arises.

Anglicans may properly claim that the observation of different levels and the granting of considerable freedom to the lowest possible level has been a feature of their polity. In Anglicanism today canonically binding decisions can only be made at the level of a Province or in some Provinces at the level of a diocese. Decision-making by Provinces on appropriate matters has proved a source of strength to the Anglican Communion. Thereby, Provinces take responsibility in clear and bold ways for what they do.

However, when decisions are taken by Provinces on matters which touch the life of the whole Communion without consultation, they may give rise to tension as other Provinces or other Christian traditions reject what has been decided elsewhere. The Eames Commission has stressed the need for consultation prior to action, and for charity and patience in this situation, insisting that discernment and "reception is a continuing process in the life of the Church, which cannot be hurried" (Eames III, Reception 43–4).

The proclamation of the gospel to all humanity must embody its universal coherence. Care needs to be taken to prevent a Province from becoming bound by its culture. The corrosive effects of particular environments are often not perceptible to those who are immersed in them. The principle articulated here of a relationship between Provinces and the world-wide Communion applies at other levels also. At each interface the aim is to free the people of God to use their God-given gifts responsibly and co-operatively, in every way compatible with the gospel and its effective proclamation in word and deed.

The move to ordain women to the priesthood and the episcopate provides a recent example of the process by which Anglicans have struggled together to form a mind on a matter which affects the ministry and therefore the unity of the Communion. It is a story which throws into sharp relief some of the emerging questions concerning both the structures of Anglican interdependence and the processes by which we come to take decisions together.

The story illustrates, for particular historical reasons, how binding decisions can only be made at the level of a Province or in some places at the level of a diocese. However, it also reveals a struggle to honour the interdependence of Anglicans through reference to the international organs of consultation. When, in the 1960s, the matter of the ordination of women became urgent for the mission of the Church in Hong Kong, Hong Kong first brought the matter to the Lambeth Conference. The Conference asked that every regional church should study the matter. In this way consultation was initiated. But in spite of an attempt to listen to one another, in fact no written responses had been received by the time the Provincial representatives met for the first meeting of the Anglican Consultative Council. The Council adopted the following resolution:

> In reply to the request of the Council of the Church of South-East Asia, this Council advises the Bishop of Hong Kong, acting with the approval of his Synod, and any bishop of the Anglican Communion acting with the approval of his Province, that, if he decides to ordain women to the priesthood, his action will be acceptable to this Council; and that this Council will use its good offices to encourage all Provinces of the Anglican Communion to continue in communion with these dioceses. (Resolution 28(b), *The Time is Now,* Anglican Consultative Council First Meeting, Limuru, Kenya, 23 February–5 March 1971. London: SPCK (1971), page 39).

In a similar way in 1985, after the General Convention of ECUSA had expressed its intention not to withhold consent to the election of a bishop on the grounds of gender, it also sought the advice of the newly created Primates Meeting. Through its working party the Primates sought the advice of Provinces. It was that Communion-wide reflection from 17 provinces that formed the background to resolution 1 of Lambeth 1988:

> That each province should respect the decision and attitudes of other provinces... without such respect necessarily indicating acceptance of the principles involved, maintaining the highest degree of communion with the provinces that differ.

In much the same way as a juridical decision made at Provincial level has to be received, so the expressed 'mind of the Communion' given in resolutions of Lambeth Conferences, still has to undergo a process of 'open reception' in the life of the Anglican Communion and the whole Church. Much emphasis was placed by the Eames Commission on the need for an open process of reception following the Lambeth 1988 Resolution.

There has been an increasing awareness that certain issues arise that affect the unity of the universal Church. Issues of faith, the sacraments, the ordering of the ministry, fundamental changes in relationships with another World Communion and ethical issues have implications for the life of communion. These need a Communion-wide mind if a life of interdependence is to be preserved.

Matters which touch the unity of the whole Communion can rarely be decided without argument and therefore must always be brought to the life of prayer. The Church needs to be tolerant and open enough to conduct its arguments with charity and attentiveness to the wisdom and guidance of the Holy Spirit. Care needs to be taken to ensure that complex matters are fairly and appropriately considered. Different cultures have differing traditions in the matter of consultation and decision-making.

Anglican theologians, such as Richard Hooker, have spoken of the need for consent, without which the mere exercise of authority can amount to tyranny. But there is no one way of establishing what constitutes consent. Where there is disparity and diversity of traditions there is need for great care with communication. As long ago as 1888 the Chicago-Lambeth Quadrilateral asserted the appropriateness of different styles of episcopal authority, appropriate to different cultures: "The Historic Episcopate, locally adapted in the methods of its administration to the varying needs of the nations and peoples called of God into the Unity of His Church" (*Report on Home Reunion*, Article 4, pages 159f.).

The Particular Church and the Church Catholic

The life and mission of the Church is at its most authentic and vibrant in a particular context, that is a cohesive geographical region or an area covered by a people, tribe or group with its own traditions and customs. 'Local' can mean different things in different places. A single parish can be a locality, and that place can be as small as a village, or as big as a city. A cohesive geographical region can be a local entity, or an area covered by a people, tribe or group with its own traditions and customs. Styles and ways of living, received wisdom, social customs or rituals, clan structures and inter-relationships can all contribute to a sense of particularity. The Church is effective when it is embedded in a local place, challenging wrongs, healing relationships, standing with the vulnerable and marginalized, and opening up new possibilities for mutual service, respect and love. In such a context what the word "church" stands for is a rich, many-sided reality embodying God's saving and reconciling presence within a particular context. It is a richly referential term, culturally resonant, and locked into an established symbolic system or network of meanings.

It is important that the Church in its particular embodiment is not the 'translation' of an abstract ideal into a merely temporary or transitory vehicle. The life of the Church, particularly developed, would show respect for the history of the Church of past centuries, including the early centuries and the biblical communities, noting both their failings and faithfulness. It would also be ready to be helped and challenged by the contemporary Church in other places, and use the experience of fellow Christians as a way of discerning truth within the ambiguities of local tradition and culture.

Dependent upon such embodied ecclesiologies is the expression of a catholic doctrine of the Church, which attempts to express what is, or should be, true of the Church in all places. Our trinitarian theology (chapter 2) provides the basis of such an ecclesiology. It is no accident that it is rooted not just in the doctrines and experiences of the churches of the Anglican Communion, but in the convictions of the vast preponderance of Christians who have ever lived, and of the public witness of their churches. In no sense is this ecclesiology untried or flimsy. Like certain forms of highly sophisticated modern metals, it is thin and exceptionally tough, proved in vast numbers of stresses. It is a vital resource, and to draw upon it is to show a wholly appropriate respect for the Church catholic. We have also spoken of the "marks" or "attributes" of the Church as providing its general aims. These are true, but likewise unspecific. Nor do they prevent disputes from breaking out as to their precise interpretation. What, for example, does it mean to be a "holy" Church in the context of a hedonistic culture? St. Paul himself had to work hard to interpret the Christian's responsibility in relation to the ramifications of idolatry in pagan society.

At all times the theological reflection and *praxis* of the local church must be consistent with the truth of the gospel which belongs to the universal Church. The universal doctrine of the Church is important especially when particular practices or theories are locally developed which lead to disputes. In some cases it may be possible and necessary for the universal Church to say with firmness that a particular local practice or theory is incompatible with Christian faith. This was said, for example, to those churches in South Africa which practised and justified racial discrimination at the eucharist. Similarly if a church were to develop a different baptismal formula than that delivered in Scripture and used throughout the world, a comparable situation would arise. The Chicago-Lambeth Quadrilateral is a list of norms and practices which must characterise the Church at all times everywhere. However, it is not a complete ecclesiology; nor is it free from interpretative ambiguity.

Elizabethan Anglican ecclesiology, for example as developed by Richard Hooker (c.1544–1600) or Richard Field (1561–1616), is a locally embodied ecclesiology for a particular time and place. It is not a 'translation' of a universal ecclesiology, which can then be (as it were) 'retranslated' into different times and places. It is, as ecclesiologies should be, a whole-hearted attempt to embody the saving presence of God in a given culture. It is a rendering of biblical ecclesiology, which is itself particular and local. Elizabethan Anglicans, however, acknowledged the authority of the Nicene Creed and sought to show how the Church of England belonged to the one, holy, catholic and apostolic Church. The contemporary churches of the Anglican Communion also need locally embodied ecclesiologies, not pale imitations of Elizabethan Anglicanism, but full, rich, and relevant embodiments of God's saving presence within a locality. Nor will they be mere 'translations' of a universal ecclesiology, but a confident and whole-hearted seeking of God's way for the Church in transforming relationships with particular traditions, structures and institutions.

But no local embodiment of the Church is simply autonomous and it is plain from the history of the Church that local churches can make mistakes. A care for reconciliation and unity is implicit in the catholicity of Jesus' unique, atoning work. The apostolicity of a particular church is measured by its consonance with the living elements of apostolic succession and unity: baptism and eucharist, the Nicene and Apostles' Creeds, the ordered ministry and the canon of Scripture. These living elements of apostolic succession serve the authentic succession of the gospel and serve to keep the various levels of the Church in a communion of truth and life.

Chapter 5

Koinonia: Purpose and Principles for Developing Structures

The purpose of all structures and processes of the Church is to serve the *koinonia*, the trinitarian life of God in the Church, and to help all the baptised embrace and live out Christ's mission and ministry in the world. Through baptism each person is called to live the new life in Christ in the power of the Holy Spirit and is anointed with grace to do so in communion with all members of the same Body of Christ.

As we have seen in the Anglican Communion today the structures of unity and communion at a world level are still developing. This development needs now to be inspired by a renewed understanding of the Church as *koinonia*; a recognition of God's gift to the whole people of God of a ministry of *episcopé*, exercised in personal, collegial and communal ways within and by the whole company of the baptised; by principles of subsidiarity, accountability and interdependence; and by an understanding of the Spirit led processes of discernment and reception.

The Communion of the Trinity

In chapter two we explored an understanding of the Church as communion, participating in and called to manifest in its own life, the life of God, Father, Son and Holy Spirit. Those who are baptised, through the power of the Holy Spirit, die with Christ and rise to new life in him and are joined with all the baptised in the communion of God's own life and love. Through baptism and through participation at the Table of the Lord the baptised are called to a life of unity and interdependence and using all their diverse charisms entrusted with carrying out God's mission in the world. The structures of the Church, at every level, are to serve this vocation of the Church. In the way they are ordered as well as in the way they inter-relate and function they are to reflect and embody the fundamental reality of the Church's life—its communion in the life and love of God, Father, Son and Holy Spirit.

This means that the personal and relational life of the Church is always prior to the structural. But without enabling structures the Church's life is weakened and the relational and personal life unsupported. Right structures and right ordering provide channels by which, through the power of the Holy Spirit, the mind of Christ is discerned, the right conduct of the Church encouraged and the gift of the many are drawn upon in the service and mission of the Church.

Episcopé, Personal, Collegial and Communal

A ministry of oversight (*episcopé*) of interdependence, accountability and discernment is essential at all levels of the Church's mission and ministry, and for the sake of the Church's wellbeing, must be exercised at every level in a way that is personal, collegial and communal. A bishop's authority is never isolated from the community; both the community of the Church and the community and unity of all humankind.

Personal

The ministry of oversight should be personal because the presence of Christ among his people can most effectively be pointed to by the person ordained to proclaim the gospel and to call the community to serve the Lord in a unity of faith and witness. Bishops have a special responsibility for maintaining and focusing the internal unity and communion of the local Church. In the diocese where they have oversight they represent, focus and have a care for the unity of the Church. Bishops also relate the local church to the wider Church and the wider Church back to the local church.

Bishops are called by God, in and through the community of the faithful, to personify the tradition of the gospel and the mission of the Church. As the one with special responsibility to ensure that the proclamation of the word and the celebration of the sacraments is faithful to the gospel and the tradition of the Church, the bishop has specific responsibilities for the calling of all humanity into the unity of the Church. This specific responsibility is exercised in partnership with other bishops, clergy and laity, with members of other ecclesial bodies and leaders of the local community. Thus episcopal ministry is no authoritarian ministry above and separate from the community, but is a ministry, based in the grace of God, always exercised in relation to the community and always subject to the word of God.

By virtue of ordination, bishops are called and empowered to represent Christ to the community of the faithful and to the wider local community. This is the personal ministry of *episcopé*. While this is the unique responsibility of the diocesan bishop, it is at the same time always shared with others. At a regional level Primates exercise a personal ministry of oversight and at the level of the whole Communion the Archbishop of Canterbury exercises a personal ministry of *episcopé*.

Collegial

Bishops share in a collegial relation with those whom they commission to serve with them in the diocese, in the priestly ministry of word and sacrament and in the pastoral work of the Church. Bishops also share collegially with other bishops of the same Province representing the concerns of the local church and community to the wider Church, and bringing back the concerns and decisions of the wider Church to their local community. The Lambeth Conference and the Primates' Meeting are wider expressions of collegiality.

Communal

Bishops exercise their office communally. The community's effective participation is necessary in the discovery of God's will, under the guidance of the Spirit. In their communal relationships, bishops meet with representatives of those who hold office, or those who exercise responsibility within the community of the local churches. This accords with the principle of subsidiarity, keeping the bishop in touch with the concerns and decisions which belong properly to the more parochial levels of diocesan life. As representative persons, bishops have a moral duty to reflect the concerns of the whole community, especially those whom society pushes to the margins.

The practical expression of the personal, collegial and communal ministry of the bishop is to be seen in synodical government. The churches of the Anglican Communion may be said to be episcopally led and synodically governed. The task of synods is properly consultation, deliberation and legislation. Episcopal leadership is, however, always in accountable relation to the whole Church, both local and universal.

There is a proper place for the communal expression of the Church's life and ministry at levels other than the diocesan. Every Province has its communal synodical gathering. At the world level the Anglican Consultative Council (ACC) currently embodies the communal dimension of the church life, reminding the Communion of the shared episcopal, presbyterial, diaconal, and lay vocation in the discovery of the mind of Jesus Christ. At the world level, however, the meetings of the Anglican Consultative Council (ACC) are consultative, not legislative in character.

Primacy and collegiality are complementary elements within the exercise of *episcopé*. One cannot be exercised without reference to the other in critical and creative balance. Further, both in turn must be open to the Christian community in a way that is both transparent and accountable, and in the decision-making of the Church, upholds a reception process in which critique, affirmation and rejection are possible.

The role of primacy is to foster the communion by helping the bishops in their task of apostolic leadership both in their local church and in the Church universal. A Primate's particular role in *episcopé* is to help churches to listen to one another, to grow in love and unity, and to strive together towards the fullness of

Christian life and witness. A Primate respects and promotes Christian freedom and spontaneity; does not seek uniformity where diversity is legitimate, or centralize administration to the detriment of local churches.

A Primate exercises ministry not in isolation but in collegial association with other bishops. If there is a need to intervene in the affairs of a diocese within the Province, the Primate will consult with other bishops, and if possible act through the normal structures of consultation and decision-making. The Primate will strive never to bypass or usurp the proper responsibility of the local church. ARCIC I spoke of the ministry of primacy in this way:

> Primacy fulfils its purpose by helping the churches to listen to one another, to grow in love and unity, and to strive together towards the fullness of Christian life and witness; it respects and promotes Christian freedom and spontaneity; it does not seek uniformity where diversity is legitimate, or centralise administration to the detriment of local churches. (*The Final Report*, Authority I, para. 21)

The primacy of the Archbishop of Canterbury and the meeting of Primates reflects at the Anglican Communion level the primacy and collegiality exercised at Provincial level. There is a difference, however, in that distance and infrequency of meeting add difficulty to the process of consultation and decision. Discernment, decision and action at this level will normally depend only upon the consensus of the Primates' meeting or a part of it and demands great sensitivity.

Subsidiarity, Accountability and Interdependence

The Holy Catholic Church is fully present in each of its local embodiments. Decisions about the life and mission of the Church should be made in that place and need only be referred to wider councils if the matter threatens the unity and the faithfulness of teaching or practice of the Church catholic, or where the local church encounters genuinely new circumstances and wishes advice about how to respond.

The various levels of the Church are accountable to each other. This will be expressed by openness to dialogue, by attentiveness to the particularity of people, times and places, by acceptance of interdependence on both the personal and corporate levels and by honouring plurality and diversity as gifts of God.

Attentiveness, in the Christian community, is a specific quality of interacting among members of Christ's body. Christian attentiveness means deciding to place the understanding of others ahead of being understood. It means listening and responding to the needs and the hopes of others, especially when these differ from one's own needs, agendas and hopes. Further, Christian attentiveness means keeping these needs and agendas in mind when making one's own decisions and developing one's own practices. Such attentiveness is consonant, we said, with the quality of God's love known in Christ and shared in the Holy Spirit. This divine love is imaged beautifully in John's Gospel, where the Father and Son glorify and affirm the identity of one another. It is mirrored further in our Lord's acute awareness of and compassionate responsiveness to the needs of others.

The world-wide Anglican assemblies are consultative and not legislative in character. There is a question to be asked whether this is satisfactory if the Anglican Communion is to be held together in hard times as well as in good ones. Indeed there is a question as to whether effective communion, at all levels, does not require appropriate instruments, with due safeguards, not only for legislation, but also for oversight. Is not universal authority a necessary corollary of universal communion? This is a matter currently under discussion with our ecumenical partners. It relates not only to our understanding of the exercise of authority in the Anglican Communion, but also to the kind of unity and communion we look for in a visibly united Church.

Discernment and Reception

The faith of the Church is always in need of fresh interpretation, so that the living Christ can be realised in the lives of contemporary men and women. Discerning the mind of Christ for the Church is the task of the whole people of God, with those ordained for a ministry of oversight guiding and leading the community. Authority is relational. Some matters are properly determined at a local or regional level, others which touch the unity in faith need to be determined in the communion of all the churches.

When a matter is raised by a local church processes of discernment, decision making and reception all have their part to play. It is the responsibility of the local church to consider the implication of taking decisions for the wider Communion. Anglicans agree that the Great Ecumenical Councils of the fourth and fifth centuries were the highest conciliar authority. However, no ecumenical council possesses final authority simply as an institution. Even with these early councils there was no guarantee that the guidance of a council was free from error of judgement or distortion of the truth. Its words were accepted as true and binding, not because a particular council spoke, nor because it has been convened by a particular authority, but because its decisions came to be received and recognised by the faithful in the local churches as expressing the truth of the gospel. This is not to say that certain councils of the Church in the past and in the Anglican Communion today should not command the respect of the faithful and be taken with all due seriousness in the response and discernment process.

Anglicans hold that the universal Church will not ultimately fail. Through the leading of the Holy Spirit, truth is gradually discerned. However the discernment of truth is never an uncomplicated and straightforward matter. There are always setbacks along the way.

Within the Anglican Communion matters which touch the communion of all the churches need to be discerned and tested within the life of the interdependence of the Provinces, through the meeting of bishops in the Lambeth Conference and through the consultative process of the Anglican Consultative Council and the Primates' Meeting. Beyond that lies the process of open reception within the life of the local churches. The maintenance of communion both within and between churches, in the process of testing the truth of a decision needs great sensitivity, and adequate space needs to be found for clearly expressed dissent in testing and refining truth. In the process of discernment and reception relationships need to be maintained, for only in fellowship is there opportunity for correcting one-sidedness or ignorance. Though some of the means by which communion is expressed may be strained, the need for courtesy, tolerance, mutual respect, prayer for one another and a continuing desire to know and be with one another, remain binding upon us as Christians. The reception process involves the preparation of appropriate and informative study materials and the preparation of occasions for conversations, bringing together those on both sides of the particular issue.

In a divided Christendom there is no possibility of making decisions today in a General Council. Nevertheless, at this stage of the ecumenical movement any decisions which touch the faith or order of the universal Church need to be offered for testing within the wider ecumenical fellowship.

In the matter of discussing the mind of Christ for the Church, under the guidance of the Holy Spirit, discernment, conciliar debate and decision making followed by a process of reception each have a part to play. It is not a matter of weakness that the Church is unable to make instant decisions in relation to the complex matters of faith, order and morals which come before it, but the way it lives in the process of discernment, decision making and reception may give profound witness and provide a model for other communities.

Theological Coherence

The mission of the Church is to embody and proclaim Christ's gospel of love and reconciliation, healing and freedom. This must be transparent not only in the words it speaks and in its advocacy of justice and peace, but also in its visible structures and processes. The theology implicit in the Church's structures and processes must be one with the explicit theology of its words.

It is with the principles we have explored in this chapter that we turn now to reconsider the instruments of Anglican belonging at a world level and raise questions about how they might develop in the light of these principles.

Chapter 6
The Worldwide Instruments of Communion: Structures and Processes

In this chapter we raise a number of questions about the future development of the world-wide instruments of communion, the way they function and their inter-relation, one with the other. The Commission was not asked to give specific proposals for future developments. It simply seeks to ask questions which the bishops at Lambeth will need to address if they are to give direction for the future interdependence and coherence of the Anglican Communion.

The Archbishop of Canterbury

In our historical section we noted that to be in communion with the See of Canterbury is an important ingredient of Anglican interdependence, yet each of the Provinces is autonomous. The Archbishop of Canterbury is neither a supreme legislator nor a personification of central administrative power, but as a pastor in the service of unity, offers a ministry of service, care and support to the Communion. The interdependence of the Anglican Communion becomes most clearly visible when the Archbishop of Canterbury exercises his primatial office as an enabler of mission, pastoral care and healing in those situations of need to which he is called. This pastoral service of unity is exercised by invitation. For example, at the request of Provincial leaders, the Archbishop has exercised a pastoral role and mediation in the Sudan and Rwanda.

The Archbishop of Canterbury exercises his ministry in relationship with his fellow Primates. In considering how to respond to a request for assistance from a Province, he wisely consults all the appropriate resources in the region, the Province and the local diocese. Here, as elsewhere in the exercise of primacy, subsidiarity is important. So too is the exercise of an *episcopé* in which personal, collegial and communal elements are held together.

Together with a ministry of presence and teaching, there is also a certain administrative primacy. Historically this has found its unique expression when the Archbishop of Canterbury calls and presides at the Lambeth Conference, where the relationship of the Archbishop of Canterbury to the Communion, and the bishops to each other, is most clearly seen. It is also visible in his chairmanship of the regular meetings of the Primates, and also exercised within the life of the Anglican Consultative Council where the Archbishop of Canterbury acts as its president and as an active participant in its meetings.

It is nevertheless most often the personal pastoral element in the exercise of this office which has become the most visible evidence of the Archbishop of

Canterbury as an instrument of unity. Given the magnitude of this ministry, there must be concern that pastoral and spiritual care, beyond the prayers of the Communion, be made available to the Archbishop.

The special position of the Archbishop of Canterbury in the Communion raises questions that need to be addressed. Are there mechanisms by which tasks may be shared within the fellowship of the Primates, without weakening the symbol of unity provided by one person? Is the Archbishop of Canterbury adequately resourced as Primate of the Communion? Is there sufficient coherence and consultation between the Anglican Communion Secretariat and the staff of Lambeth Palace? Does the role of the Archbishop mean that the Church of England must be more cautious in its decisions than other Provinces? Does an Archbishop of Canterbury necessarily have to be a member of the Church of England? Does the Primate of the Anglican Communion need to be the occupant of the see of Canterbury?

The Lambeth Conference

The Lambeth Conference plays an important role in strengthening the unity of the Anglican Communion by expressing the collegiality of bishops in a clear and concrete way at the international level and in symbolising the relatedness in bonds of spiritual communion of each of the dioceses from which the bishops come.

Though the Conference is not legislative it offers the opportunity to bishops who come from churches in different cultures and social and political contexts, and with different agendas and problems, to live together, to worship together, to join in Bible study together and to listen to each other. Through these means each bishop may share the difficulties and joys of every other church. This indicates that each church in the Anglican Communion is a partner in mission and a part of the body of Christ. In this way the Conference embodies the Pauline concept of the Church as a body. As Paul writes, "when one part of the body suffers the rest of the body suffers." Each part of the body is different, but every part is necessary to the body.

The Conference also signifies the fundamental importance of face to face communication for the healthy life of the Communion. The personal encounters that it facilitates and the relationships that grow from them signify one aspect of the servanthood of bishops who bring the reality of each diocese to the whole Communion as a whole back to their own diocese.

The Lambeth Conference thus helps to define the bishop's role as one who represents the part to the whole and the whole to the part, the particularity of each diocese to the whole Communion and the Communion to each diocese.

Attentiveness at the Lambeth Conference

In the context of the Lambeth Conference, Christian attentiveness entails in the first place that individual bishops and groups of bishops will heed the voice of other bishops when these express the needs and hopes of the Church in their place. Such respecting of the voice of others, especially when such respect requires taking into account needs and agendas that are not one's own, can mean that bishops from one part of the world make their own an agenda they did not bring originally to Lambeth. And this can result in a bishop or group of bishops leaving the Lambeth Conference committed to a quite new programme.

A special concern of Lambeth 1998 will need to be how the college is attentive to, and integrates the insights of women bishops attending the Conference for the first time.

Christian attentiveness at Lambeth should mean giving special heed to those bishops whose first language is not English, and to those bishops who do not come from politically, culturally and economically powerful Provinces in the Communion. Attentiveness becomes distinctively Christian when the bishops assembled give ear to, and make space for, the voices of those Christians who are seldom, if ever, heard.

One example of such Christian attentiveness in the past is western bishops' heeding of, and being responsive to, the deep concern of African bishops regarding polygamy. A second example, from the Lambeth Conference, 1988, is western bishops acknowledging the legitimacy of a call from Asian and African bishops for a renewed commitment to evangelism. All the bishops left Lambeth 1988 committed to a Decade of Evangelism which they had not anticipated before the Lambeth Conference process began.

Increasing the opportunities for, and occasions of, Christian attentiveness should be promoted and protected at the Lambeth Conference. This will allow the bishops gathered at Lambeth to share in, to be shaped by, and to show forth, the attentiveness of God the Father's love as we know it in Jesus Christ through the Holy Spirit.

Interdependence at the Lambeth Conference

The principle of communal interdependence, if brought to bear on the Lambeth Conference, might be thought to demand its reform so as to introduce priests and deacons and lay people into its structure. This was in fact suggested in 1871 before the second Lambeth Conference, when the presiding bishop of the Episcopal Church, USA suggested that the Lambeth Conference should be transformed into a "Patriarchal Conference" of world bishops, representative clergy and laity, under the presidency of the Archbishop of Canterbury. This would tend, however, to confuse Lambeth with the synodical structures of the local and national churches and move it in the direction of a "world synod." The calling of a World Anglican Congress from time to time may be a more appropriate opportunity for presbyters, deacons and lay people to meet together with bishops at an international forum. We explore this proposal in Appendix II.

An alternative approach would be to suggest that the gathering of bishops should continue to be seen collegially, but in the context of the life of the Church as a whole. Insofar as bishops are representative persons they should understand Lambeth as an opportunity to bring the issues and concerns of their own dioceses to the consideration of brother and sister bishops. Few issues are entirely peculiar to a particular diocese, and the sharing of experiences and approaches to the resolution of difficulties makes for the easing of the burden of decision making.

At the last Lambeth Conference the Archbishop of Canterbury invited participating bishops "to bring their dioceses with them." At the same Lambeth Conference bishops voted on resolutions in the light of a preceding consultative process that had already occurred in their home dioceses and Provinces and at ACC-7. One obvious example was the resolution on the *Final Report of ARCIC I* which expressed a "Communion-wide mind" on the consonance of ARCIC with the faith of Anglicans. This resolution did not just express the mind of the bishops acting entirely alone, but as spokespersons who reflected the mind of their Provinces and were together expressing the mind of the Communion.

The bishops acting collegially can speak prophetically to the Church and to the world. On some issues such as, for example, ordination, the Church itself should expect the advice of those to whom the responsibility to ordain has been given. When the bishops speak to the Church, however, this should not be in an autocratic way, but in a manner that makes a positive contribution to, and stimulates, a continuing conversation in the wider life of the Church. True leadership demands consultation and partnership.

Accountability at the Lambeth Conference

Bishops are accountable for their words and actions at Lambeth, before God and the whole Church. The bishops at Lambeth are to represent those who have no voice: those who can rely on no one else to tell their story and plead their case; those whose concerns society and/or the Church have chosen, sometimes deliberately, sometimes forgetfully to address. It is when the bishops consider themselves to be accountable to those who have the least that they discover the way of God's Kingdom.

The diocese is to be brought with the bishop to Lambeth, and Lambeth through the bishop back to the diocese. It is an important way of involving the entire membership of the people of God in the concerns and thinking of the world-wide communion. Post-Lambeth educational programs may dictate that, in addition to the usual publication of a report of its proceedings, educational resources, audiotapes and videos should be made available so as to assist the bishops in the sharing of the Lambeth experience.

There are again questions worth asking. Is a Conference every ten years too frequent to allow for adequate preparation, consultation and reception? What is the nature of the authority of the Conference? How binding are the resolutions of the Conference? How should issues be selected and prepared; what concerns should be addressed? What form of report or pastoral letter would best strengthen the communion of the Church? If the Lambeth Conference is an effective instrument of unity of the Anglican Communion, what is its special vocation in relation to the movement for the visible unity of the Church? What part should ecumenical participants play? How might the Lambeth Conference encourage the development of shared oversight with other Christian traditions? How does the authority of the Lambeth Conference relate to the authority of other churches, in particular to those churches which claim to be the Church?

The Anglican Consultative Council

Unique among the international Anglican instruments of unity, the ACC includes laity among its members. The inclusion of the laity in decision-making bodies has long been a principle of Anglican life. Thus, the royal priesthood of the entire people of God (1 Pet. 2:9), and the mutuality and interdependence of the various ministries within the Church, are witnessed to and affirmed. Means must be found to honour the specific experience and expertise that various lay members bring and also to provide them with whatever further resources and experiences they might need to participate fully and responsibly in the life of God's Church.

It is important that these rich experiences of being in community not be lost through either infrequency of meeting or too large a gathering. Significant too is the participation of members from the two-thirds world who represent a growing majority in the Communion and whose issues increasingly occupy the Communion's concern. Every effort needs to be made to enable people whose first language is not English to communicate freely and effectively so that there be no feeling of exclusion.

The mission of the Anglican Consultative Council is to represent the concerns of the Communion, in the Communion and for the Communion. Most of this work is effected day by day through the General Secretary and the Secretariat. However, to be effective and credible, the Secretariat must be governed by a reference group which is informed, has continuity and is also representative of the Communion's diversity. It must be adequately staffed.

There are two possible ways in which change might be effected in order to enhance the representative nature of the ACC and its effectiveness: first, by creating a smaller council which would meet more frequently, or alternatively, by enlarging the Standing Committee and leaving the size and frequency of the ACC as it presently is. It is important that the representation be balanced between laity and clergy, with greater continuity of membership than at present. Representatives should have entrée to the councils of their own church and be knowledgeable about its concerns and interests.

The existence of the Anglican Consultative Council raises questions of a general nature. What is the relationship of this body to the Lambeth Conference and to the Primates' Meeting? What part should the ACC play in contributing to the major issues that are to come before the Lambeth Conference and the reception of the Lambeth resolutions? Should the on-going tasks of the Communion be done by an expanded secretariat, or through meetings of the ACC, or a combination of both? Who is responsible for the continuity of membership in the ACC; is it the members themselves, is it the Primates, who makes this decision? What is the nature of the responsibility and accountability of those elected to serve on the ACC?

The Primates' Meeting

The Primates' Meeting provides the opportunity for mutual counsel and pastoral care and support of one another and of the Archbishop of Canterbury. Their meetings have an inherent authority by virtue of the office which they hold as chief pastors. The Meeting provides a place between Lambeth Conferences for each to share the burning or persistent issues of their Province and their own primatial ministry. It is the context in which Primates can identify common issues and resolve outstanding concerns. It also provides for a broader horizon than the Provincial which makes it possible for a Primate to consider a regional matter in a world-wide context. There is an opportunity to take responsibility together in the concern for the wellbeing of all the churches.

The Primates have in fact found it easier to affirm collegiality for the sake of consultation, study and mutual support than for the exercise of pastoral, moral and doctrinal guidance. This experience raises in yet another context the theological and practical importance of holding together the personal, collegial and communal modes of *episcopé*.

Each Primate exercises his personal primatial ministry with fellow bishops and the synod of his Province. Similarly, the Archbishop of Canterbury exercises this Communion wide ministry both collegially and communally. In the same way, the collegiality of the Primates' Meeting is exercised in relation to the personal and communal elements of the *episcopé* at the Communion-wide level.

The exercise of collegiality with one another and with the Archbishop of Canterbury, as well as the exercise of collegiality with all the bishops at the Lambeth Conference, raises the question of the relation of the Primates' Meeting to the communal gatherings of the Anglican Consultative Council. It is to be noted that while the Standing Committee of the Primates' Meeting meets with the Standing Committee of the ACC, this has hardly enhanced relations with the ACC. As an instrument of world-wide unity within the Communion, the Primates' Meeting has responsibility to maintain a living relationship with the ACC, so that the collegial and communal exercise of oversight are held together. Archbishop Donald Coggan commented at the 1978 Lambeth Conference that the Primates' Meeting should be in the very closest and most intimate contact with the ACC. What in fact this would mean in practice still has to be worked out.

How far should the task of the Primates' Meeting be that of responsibility for monitoring the progress of recommendations and resolutions which come from the Lambeth Conference in the interim between Conferences? For example, in the period following Lambeth 1988, the Primates received and promulgated the recommendations of the Eames' Commission to the Communion. The Primates' Meeting also referred to the Provinces the *Porvöo Common Statement* and the *Concordat of Agreement.*

In chapter 3 it was noted that the Primates have been reluctant to give serious consideration to resolution 18 Section 2(a) of Lambeth 1988 which asks the Primates to exercise greater responsibility in offering guidance on doctrinal, moral and pastoral matters. Should Primates be expected to make authoritative statements, or should the Primates' Meeting be encouraged to exercise a primarily pastoral role, both for their own numbers, but also for the Communion? What is the relationship of the Primates' Meeting to the Lambeth Conference and the Anglican Consultative Council? Do the Primates have sufficient resources for their ministry?

The Inter-relation of the Instruments of Communion

In reviewing the world-wide instruments of communion this report has at times commented on the relationship of one to the other and on their interconnectedness with structures at other levels of the Church's life. Three instruments, the ACC, the Primates' Meeting and the Lambeth Conference have their own distinctive characteristics and potentially hold in balance and tension three aspects of the life of the Communion. Lambeth focuses the relation of bishops to bishops and therefore dioceses to dioceses. The Primates' Meeting focuses the relation of Primates to Primates, and therefore Provinces to Provinces. The ACC, which is the most comprehensive gathering, represents the voice of the inner life of the Provinces, with representatives of laity, clergy and bishops. These three instruments of interdependence are presided over by the Archbishop of Canterbury, thus focusing the unity and diversity of the Communion.

At the present time the formal structural and continuing relations between the Lambeth Conference, the Anglican Consultative council and the Primates' Meeting is the responsibility of the Secretary General and the Anglican Communion Secretariat which staffs all three bodies. Greater clarity on the relations between the instruments of communion themselves would make for creative, effective and sustainable relations within the Anglican Communion. It is urgent that ways be found to strengthen the resourcing of the ACC Secretariat if it is to serve effectively the world-wide structures of Anglican belonging.

Final Reflections

A deeper understanding of the instruments of communion at a world-level, their relationship one to another and to the other levels of the Church's life should lead to a more coherent and inclusive functioning of oversight in the service of the *koinonia* of the Church. When the ministry of oversight is exercised in a personal, collegial and communal way, imbued with the principles of subsidiarity, accountability and interdependence then the community is protected from authoritarianism, structures serve the personal and relational life of the Church and the diverse gift of all is encouraged in the service of all. The Church is thus opened up to receive the gifts of the Holy Spirit for mission and ministry and enabled to serve more effectively the unity and community of humanity.

We have necessarily concentrated in the report on the world wide instruments of the Anglican Communion. However, by virtue of our baptism we have in a communion in the Holy Trinity and therefore with the universal Church. The long history of ecumenical involvement, both locally and internationally, has shown us that Anglican discernment and decision making must take account of the insights into truth and the Spirit-led wisdom of our ecumenical partners. Moreover, any decisions we take must be offered for the discernment of the universal Church.

Appendix I

Lambeth Conference 1988 Resolution 18

The Anglican Communion: Identity and Authority

This Conference:

1. Resolves that the new Inter-Anglican Theological and Doctrinal Commission (or a specially appointed inter-Anglican commission) be asked to undertake as a matter of urgency a further exploration of the meaning and nature of communion; with particular reference to the doctrine of the Trinity, the unity and order of the Church, and the unity and community of humanity.

2. (a) Urges that encouragement be given to a developing collegial role for the Primates' Meeting under the presidency of the Archbishop of Canterbury, so that the Primates' Meeting is able to exercise an enhanced responsibility in offering guidance on doctrinal, moral and pastoral matters.

(b) Recommends that in the appointment of any future Archbishop of Canterbury, the Crown Appointments Commission be asked to bring the Primates of the Communion into the process of consultation.

3. Resolves that the Lambeth Conference as a conference of bishops of the Anglican Communion should continue in the future, at appropriate intervals.

4. Recommends that regional conferences of the Anglican Communion should meet between Lambeth Conferences as and when the region concerned believes it to be appropriate; and in the event of these regional conferences being called, it should be open to the region concerned to make them representative of clergy and laity as well as bishops.

5. Recommends that the ACC continue to fulfil the functions defined in its Constitution (developed as a consequence of Resolution 69 of the 1968 Lambeth Conference) and affirmed by the evaluation process reported to ACC-6 (see Bonds of Affection, pp 23–27); in particular to continue its consultative, advisory, liaison and communication roles within the Communion and to do so in close co-operation with the Primates' Meeting.

6. Requests the Archbishop of Canterbury, with all the Primates of the Anglican Communion, to appoint an advisory body on Prayer Books of the Anglican Communion. The body should be entrusted with the task of offering encouragement, support and advice to Churches of the Communion in

their work of liturgical revision as well as facilitating mutual consultation concerning, and review of, their Prayer Books as they are developed with a view to ensuring:

(a) the public reading of the Scriptures in a language understood by the people and instruction of the whole people of God in the scriptural faith by means of sermons and catechisms;

(b) the use of the two sacraments ordained by Christ, Baptism with water in the threefold name, and Holy Communion with bread and wine and explicit intention to obey our Lord's command;

(c) the use of forms of episcopal ordination to each of the three orders by prayer with the laying-on of hands;

(d) the public recitation and teaching of the Apostles' and Nicene Creeds; and

(e) the use of other liturgical expressions of unity in faith and life by which the whole people of God is nurtured and upheld, with continuing awareness of ecumenical liturgical developments.

Explanatory Note

On 1 above: If there is the possibility of ordination of women bishops in some provinces, it will throw into sharper focus the present impaired nature of communion. It is a matter of urgency that we have a further theological enquiry into and reflection on the meaning of communion in a trinitarian context for the Anglican Communion. Such an enquiry should relate to ecumenical discussions exploring similar issues. This, more than structures, will provide a theological framework in which differences can be handled.

On 2 above: We see an enhanced role for primates as a key to a growth of interdependence within the Communion. We do not see any inter-Anglican jurisdiction as possible or desirable, an inter-Anglican synodical structure would be virtually unworkable and highly expensive. A collegial role for the primates by contrast could easily be developed, and their collective judgment and advice would carry considerable weight.

If this is so, it is neither improper nor out of place to suggest that part of the consultative process prior to the appointment of a future Archbishop of Canterbury should be in consultation with the primates.

On 3 above: We are convinced that there is considerable value in the bishops of the Anglican Communion meeting as bishops, both in terms of mutual understanding and as an effective agent of interdependence.

On 4 above: Regional issues need regional solutions. Regional confeences can also provide for wider representation.

On 5 above: We value the present work of the ACC. We do not see, however, that it ought to move beyond its present advisory role.

On 6 above: Concern for how the Church celebrates the sacraments of unity and with what consequences is a central expression of episcopal care and pastoral oversight in the Church of God. As bishops of the Anglican Communion we have a particular responsibility for securing those elements in worship which nurture our identity and unity in Christ and which therefore have an authority for us as Anglicans. (A parallel but significantly different resolution has been proposed by the Anglican Consultative Council: Resolution 12 of ACC-7.)

(See further paras. 113–152 of the Report on 'Dogmatic and Pastoral Concerns'.*)*

Appendix II

An Anglican Congress

In considering the world-wide instruments of Anglican unity the Commission considered what role and contribution an Anglican Congress might make in the future. The Commission did not see a Congress as becoming a fifth instrument of unity for the Anglican Communion. Nevertheless, it did acknowledge the creative opportunity a Congress might, from time to time, offer the Communion, for the renewal of its life, witness and mission. At the same time the Commission was aware that, at a time of economic pressure on all institutions, the calling of a Congress would put additional financial strain upon the Communion.

The following paragraphs begin to explore some of the issues that would need to be considered if it were thought the time was right for calling for an Anglican Congress.

Local congregations and communities are strongest when there are regular opportunities to come together for worship, social gatherings and other festivals. The ties of friendship between individuals and families are strengthened when they share their joys and sorrows. Similar occasions offered to Anglicans on Provincial, regional and world-wide levels, could also develop and strengthen ties of affection within the Communion.

A World Anglican Congress held perhaps once every ten years might provide an opportunity to bring together representatives from various vocations and spheres of life. It would provide an occasion for conversation, and for sharing of needs and opportunity for prayer and worship.

In the planning of the Congress, Provinces and dioceses should be explicitly invited to propose participants who have a variety of God-given gifts to offer, and a capacity to receive the gifts of others and to be enriched by them. It would be of the essence of such a Congress that the diversity of cultural contexts in which the Anglican Church has taken root, should be visible.

The Congress would need to be planned in such a way that mutual cross-cultural communication could take place. Even if there were a small number of official conference languages, attention needs to be paid to the mode and style of communication, so as to facilitate genuine giving and receiving. A premium should be set upon face-to-face contact, as distinct from amplified addresses inhibiting response and dialogue. Nor should mutual communication be regarded as an end in itself, but as governed by and serving the goal of the universal mission of the Church, under the guidance of the Holy Spirit. A Congress should not be so tightly structured and organised as to inhibit the freedom of the Spirit and the fruit of new discovery and infectious insights and joy.

The Congress would need to be attentive to particularity of context and life and an effort would made to avoid misty generalities. The stress would be laid on quality and depth, not quantity and superficiality. The Congress would avoid global tourism, and vague or fashionable international rhetoric, and give the opportunity for the exploration of complexity in depth.

If it is to be a proper reflection of the life of the Anglican Communion it would be essential that participants be full-hearted participants in the mission of the local church, and understand and accept the responsibility of accountability to that church, both in preparation for the Congress and following the Congress. Membership of the Congress should include laity, deacons, priests and bishops. The Archbishop of Canterbury would preside, and be accompanied by a number of Primates, as well as by other bishops. Efforts should be made to symbolize the personal, collegial and communal aspects of the ministry of the Archbishop. At the same time as the unity of the Church is made visible, the recognition of the diversity of God's gifts should also be expressed. There should be opportunity to show how plurality and unity are held together within the one fellowship.

As an international Congress, it would not be appropriate for decisions or resolutions to be taken. A message to the Communion might be an appropriate form of communication.

THE REPORTS

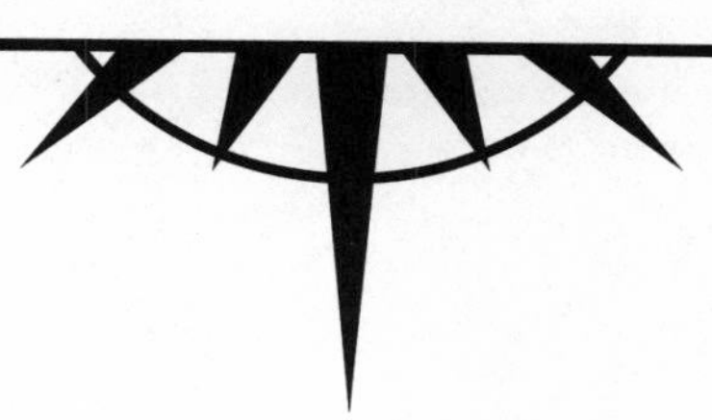

photo: *Anglican World*

A baptism performed by Archbishop Carey in Mozambique.

Preface

Since its inception in 1867, the Lambeth Conference has had a powerful influence on the life of the Anglican Communion. Much of that influence has been intangible and unseen. Bishops have found that the experience of praying and consulting together has enlarged their vision of the Church, deepened their understanding of the faith, and encouraged them in their personal vocation. In this way their dioceses have benefited from their participation.

The subjects debated at Lambeth emerged from a long series of preparatory meetings in all Regions of the Communion. Every Region was asked to identify their priorities for discussion, and these priorities were then grouped together in one of the four Sections: Called to Full Humanity, Called to Live and Proclaim the Good News, Called to Be a Faithful Church in a Plural World and Called to Be One.

One concern has been common to every Lambeth Conference, and that is the nature of the Anglican Communion itself. What is its authority, and the meaning of Communion? What are the limits to its diversity of beliefs and practices and what holds the Provinces of the Communion together? It was to pursue these questions more deeply that Lambeth 1988 asked the Archbishop of Canterbury to call together a commission. The Commission's Report (called the *Virginia Report*, after the Virginia Theological Seminary USA, where it met) was received at the Conference. Its concerns are fundamental to our understanding of the Anglican Church.

One other theme was given such widespread importance in all Regions that it was decided to give it a special place—the encounter with Other Faiths, particularly Islam. The Inter-Faith Report records the way the Conference responded.

The reports have the authority of the Sections that produced them, but the Resolutions were adopted by the whole Conference. It is now for the Provinces to receive them, study them and respond appropriately. The Bishops have spoken but the Church as a whole must decide. This volume is intended to help all Anglicans to play an informed and responsible part in the life of their Church as it seeks to respond faithfully to God's call in our day.

Rt Revd Dr J Mark Dyer, Chair
Rt Revd Dr Emmanuel Gbonigi
Rt Revd Mano Rumalshah
Dr Ruth Etchells
Revd Canon Roger Symon
Miss Elizabeth Gordon Clark (Secretary)

Called to Full Humanity
Section I Report

Introduction

Successive Lambeth Conferences have found moral, social and pastoral issues are matters of central concern to bishops gathering from many parts of the world. Our contexts and cultures are different, but many of the issues we face in a fast-changing world are similar. International communication, travel and trade have brought many benefits to the world. Yet they have also brought many problems. Globalisation affects us all for better and for worse. A Lambeth Conference is a major opportunity to reflect upon shared issues. It is an opportunity to do this sharing in a context of joint worship, Bible study and pastoral and theological reflection.

The title of this section is 'Called to Full Humanity.' Each of these words is important. Our concern is about 'humanity' within and beyond the Church. The Anglican Communion throughout the world has a broad and challenging social agenda. Our concern has always been both for people as individuals and for the wider societies in which they live. In the Anglican tradition the pastoral care of individuals is bound up with action for social and economic justice. The needs of the poor and the marginalised in the world require nothing less. A major theme of this conference will be the international debt crisis which is having such a devastating effect upon the poor in many countries.

Our concern is with 'full humanity'. As Christians full humanity is expressed finally in Jesus Christ. In Christ we encounter humanity in all its fullness. Our relationship to God in Christ is finally what makes us fully human. Life in Christ now offers us a vision of what human life in all its fullness will be later.

We are being 'called' to full humanity. We do not claim that we have achieved full humanity. Our own sins, weaknesses and frailties are only too evident to us. Rather we are called by Christ as bishops to serve, oversee and guide communities that have already experienced the first fruits of the Kingdom but long for more. As a pilgrim Church we are called to follow Christ and to attempt to live more Christ-like lives in the world.

The Lambeth Conference in 1988 offered an important reminder:

> A Lambeth Conference cannot lay down guidelines about what all Churches should be doing in every place. But it can assert on behalf of all that no part of human life is excluded from God's care and concern. It can reaffirm moral principles for the guidance of communities

> and peoples, as well as for individuals. It can remind the world that there is much to be concerned about in the way human beings hurt each other and exploit God's creation. It can go on asserting, in the face of so much which seems to deny it, that the reconciling power of Christ's love and the motivating power of the Holy Spirit are available to heal, restore and renew a world in which we are promised that 'sin shall not have dominion over you' (Rom. 6:14).[1]

Under the rubric of "The Call to Full Humanity," Section One of the 13th Lambeth Conference set out to debate and reflect on a number of seemingly disparate themes: Human Rights and Human Dignity, the Environment, Human Sexuality, Modern Technology, Euthanasia, and International Debt and Economic Justice. Despite their apparent different areas of interests, these themes are all linked by the fact that they encompass areas in which we, as the Anglican Communion, are compelled to examine our ethical and moral views and our actions as we seek our full humanity as Christian people.

At the beginning of our deliberations, Professor Denise Ackermann delivered the Section's plenary address in which she sought to lay theological guidelines for our deliberations. Beginning with the question: "What does it mean to be truly human, as an individual, in a community of faith, in this world?" she explained that the theme of her paper would be the search for an ethic of relationship in difference and otherness. In other words, how we can live respectfully, lovingly and creatively across our differences, in communion with one another.

The 'problem of difference' lies at the heart of our inability to live together in justice, freedom and peace. Otherness and difference are feared or ignored, or used as reasons for exercising unjust power in relationships, such as the apartheid policies implemented in South Africa. Speaking of 'the other', according to Professor Ackermann, is to speak of poverty, justice, of human sexuality, of gender, race and class. To speak of the other is to acknowledge that difference is problematic, often threatening, even alienating and that we do not live easily or well with it. This is so in the church, the Body of Christ made up of a great diversity of peoples, attempting to live in communion with one another, and yet no longer having "one language and the same words" (Gen. 11:1). How do we, therefore, live with otherness and difference?

We must also ask, what are the obstacles to a creative living within difference? How do we cope with the ways in which 'difference' becomes the basis for the unequal distribution of resources? How does a globalised market with the rapid transmission of huge sums of money relate to the quest for justice and for a creative living with difference?

Professor Ackermann suggested that the notion of mutuality in relationship should lie at the heart of our efforts to achieve our full humanity. In order to live in relationships which are based on the reciprocal interdependence of equals and which lie at the heart of true community, we draw on our tradition of a Trinity which is in relation with itself and with the whole of creation, through God's covenanting love for us which culminated in the life, death and resurrection of Jesus Christ.

The practice of Christian relationship begins with confessing and lamenting our unwillingness to deal lovingly with those who are different. This, according to our speaker, requires an epiphany which moves from abstract theological truths to the actual practice of relationship. In his sermon at the opening service of the Lambeth Conference, Bishop Simon Chiwanga spoke in similar vein of our need for 'awareness' of one another. The key moments of an epiphany of awareness begin with looking into the face of the other, seeing the other as an authentic reflection of the image of God while at the same time seeing oneself in the face of the other. The other becomes the mirror of oneself. There is no relationship possible if, in the words of the poet R. S. Thomas quoted by Archbishop George Carey in his presidential address, "our eyes don't meet."

Having seen and been seen, we are moved to hear the story of the other, no matter how much it may differ from our own story or evoke dangerous memories. Truly hearing the story of the other changes one's own story forever. This is the preamble to ongoing conversation, in which differences can be acknowledged and common ground sought. Hearing and speaking do not imply agreement. They demand responsibility. An ethic of relationship in difference and otherness is born out of the claims those who are other and different make on one. In his plenary address to the Conference on Making Moral Decisions, Bishop Rowan Williams, spoke movingly about our struggles to know ourselves, as such knowing is fundamental to our moral choices. This we learnt, often with pain but with gratitude, as our deliberations proceeded.

The One who knows our differences calls us to the Table, asks us to make peace with one another and knows full well how difficult that can be. The call to full humanity is nothing less, Professor Ackermann concluded, than the call to grapple daily with the challenges, implications and surprises of seeking to be in relationship with each other in all our difference and otherness.

Theological Method

With this in mind, what can be achieved in this Section? Some way of ordering our deliberations was thought to be important and a four-stage method was devised to be applied to six themes. Theology increasingly stresses the need for clarity about how we are doing theology. A characteristic of much Anglican theology is that it is grounded in first-hand experience and practice. Theology seeks a two-way process, with faith informing practice and practice informing faith. It is this style of theology which sets the four-stage method that follows:

The Situation

A feature of this Lambeth Conference is that regions have been consulted widely and have already reported back the moral, social and pastoral issues that affect them most strongly. From these reports a number of key issues emerge that are of major concern to many Provinces. Six broad themes which cluster these issues have been identified: Human Rights and Human Dignity; The Environment; Human Sexuality; Modern Technology; Euthanasia; and International Debt and Economic Justice.

Sometimes Anglicans are accused of letting sociology dictate theology. The focus here is quite different. The primary resource in depicting each situation is the pastoral voice of the different regions of the Anglican Communion. The very exercise of bringing dioceses to Lambeth means that bishops become aware of the social reality that confronts the whole Church and shapes mission and ministry. The differing pastoral situations challenge the way we live our faith. Many positive, but often complex, developments as well as many pressing problems that close this century challenge us to examine our call to full humanity, in Christ Jesus.

Theological Reflection

The situation inevitably raises questions of faith and the resources available to us as Christians, and specifically as Anglican Christians. Lambeth 1988 and more recently the Virginia Report have articulated well how Anglicans approach the questions that life-situations ask: it is by the proper use of Scripture, Tradition and Reason in the context of prayer and worship.

For the writers of the Virginia Report "Anglicans are held together by the characteristic way in which they use Scripture, tradition and reason in discerning afresh the mind of Christ for the Church in each generation." This Report affirms that the Scriptures "must be translated, read, and understood, and their meaning grasped through a continuing process of interpretation." It affirms that "tradition refers to the on-going Spirit-guided life of the Church which receives, and in receiving interprets afresh God's abiding message." And it affirms that 'reason' means simply the human being's capacity to symbolise, and so to order, share and communicate experience. It is the divine gift in virtue of which human persons respond and act with awareness in relation to their world and to God, and are opened up to that which is true for every time and every place."

Scripture, Tradition and Reason determine the way we view the world, and how we respond to the questions that culture and context raise for the faith. This is a mutual process. It is never simple or uniform since we bring into the process of theological reflection our distinctive insights and cultural differences.

There are many features of the modern world for which to give thanks. Sometimes theological reflection moves us to be critical of some developments in the modern world, and it also helps us to receive its unexpected gifts. Modern medicine, for example, has proved to be a blessing.

Putting into Context

The question to be answered here is: What insights arise when we apply this process of theological reflection in our own local context? In this process there is a need to be defined and specific and also to allow diverse voices and contexts to speak. Difference is to be respected and context is to be humbly honoured. The Gospel speaks to all situations and local traditions and the place of culture in the church and provides the context for a faithful response.

Practical Application

The product of theological reflection and the examination of the context leads to a consideration of how the situation may faithfully be changed for the better. This is how the Christian vision gives faithful substance to the given context. This is how we seek to be faithful Christians expressing our full humanity in a diverse and changing world.

Theme 1
Human Rights and Human Dignity

Situation

In this fiftieth anniversary year of the United Nations Declaration on Human Rights we, as bishops meeting at the 1998 Lambeth Conference, have heard stories of the continued abuse of these rights and the attack on human dignity in our world today. Some of the stories are particularly dreadful. Millions of people across the world are the victims of war and violence, sectarian and racist strife, the abuse of political and economic power and the intolerance of the different faces of religious fundamentalism and exclusions. We have been shocked by the way these attacks on human rights have victimised women and children. The face of poverty and of the pain of abuse is all too often to be seen in the lives of women and children.

Our comments affect many situations in the world. But we have been especially moved by the terrible stories coming from the Sudan and Rwanda. In Rwanda the genocide which began in 1959 has claimed more than one million lives. We are told by our brothers and sisters that many people have been cut limb from limb, others buried alive, and still others wounded and left to die. The women often fared the worst, being raped, and if pregnant, their wombs slashed open so that mother and child would both bleed to death. The number of orphans and of disabled persons has risen drastically. The resolutions we present highlight these particular situations as well as the issues cutting across so many communities.

Our report can be summarised under seven broad headings:

The Widening Gap between Rich and Poor

Here we cannot but make the link with the concern of the whole conference on the impact of International Debt. Many reported on the crippling effect of such debt on their capacity to begin to deliver even the most basic service to their people (e.g. Tanzania, Zaire, Zambia etc). Children go without education. The elderly, disabled and sick persons go without even the most basic medical care. Millions are hungry and without paid work. Those who do have work are often exploited and badly remunerated. We heard of the state of collapse of the economy in Zaire, following years of dictatorships and the abuse of power by Mobuto Sese Seko's regime (supported economically by loans from the West). Even nations whose Governments are working to improve matters, find their endeavours hindered by the effects of debt. The message is the same whether it comes from Central or West Africa, South America or Asia. From prosperous nations e.g. the UK and the United States, we hear too of the same widening gap between rich and poor. Poverty has not only become highly feminised, but is also a special burden for persons of colour.

The Violation of Women and Children

Stories of the rape of women, the abduction of children (North Uganda) and their enslavement (Sudan), the abuse of children for economic gain through prostitution in sex tourism (South East Asia), and the grinding face of poverty experienced by women struggling to meet the needs of their families, were heard from the Sudan, Uganda, the countries of South East Asia, Sri Lanka and across the countries of the "South." From these countries as well as others, come accounts of the sexual torture and genital mutilation of women, and the inability or unwillingness of people to fight for its elimination. In many countries of the world children are denied education and are often exploited at an early age in the workplace. Without exception we heard of the exploitation of women who, when they are employed, are paid less than men are for the same work. These abuses of basic rights and dignity of people loved by God and created in God's image, bring shame on the whole human community.

Effect of the Global Economy

The internationalising of our economy and its financial system may have advantages. The downside is experienced in the poorest nations of the world. We have already spoken of debt. The privatisation of significant sections of economic life has meant that ownership and control of major agricultural and production enterprises has been put into the hands of international companies controlled in the West. From the West Indies we hear concern over the precarious state of their banana industry due to unfavourable rulings on free trade by the World Trade Organisation. Instead of concentrating on the production of food, clothing and shelter for the local community, economies are having to satisfy the needs of international markets. This has increased the division between rich and poor, between the nations, and within nations.

Human rights must include economic fairness and equity, and enable local economies to gain greater control over their own affairs.

War, Guns and Landmines

The devastating effect of war cannot be overstated. In Mozambique, Rwanda, Sri Lanka, Sudan, Uganda, Zaire and NW India we heard of the effects of persistent conflict and violence. The terrible loss of life, the destruction to families, and the appalling effect on people who have lost limbs to landmines, let alone the destruction of property, cattle and the order of local community life, is manifest in these situations of violence and war. Bishop Ochola shared with us the tragic story of his wife Winnie, who died as a result of a landmine explosion that brought the personal pain of the effects of war into our midst. We must commit ourselves above all to peace. We must resist the temptation to support the production and sale of arms that feed these conflicts for economic gain. The Christian Church struggles, at great cost to itself, to keep alive the vision of peace in the midst of historic conflicts over land that have been the cause of so much devastation in our world. The resolution we bring on this issue seeks to invite a faithful response to the evil of war.

Racial and Caste Discrimination

From both the developed and developing countries we have heard of the persistence of racism, of ethnic struggle and of cultural division marked by caste systems. Whether it is the needs of African Americans and of minority ethnic peoples in Britain, the Dalits in India, the Buraku-min of Japan, or all people suffering from genocide in Rwanda, we have to recognise the sinful consequence of these racist and cultural divisions. They lead to many human rights abuses. People's rights are not protected by legal systems, whole communities are driven off their land and excluded from power, and others are threatened with annihilation.

In Texas, USA, a black man was recently dragged to his death behind a truck being driven by several white men. The Klu Klux Klan still gathers throughout the USA, and the burning of a number of Black churches has been attributed to similar hate groups. It has been said that the most segregated time of the week is Sunday morning, when races worship apart from one another.

In Sri Lanka people frequently disappear, or are arrested and held for long periods of time without being charged with any offence. The continuing ethnic conflicts there have resulted in increasing numbers of orphans.

Religious Extremism and Nationalism

These deep and excluding cultural forces feed nationalism and violence and cause profound injustices. The powerful forces of religious extremism have served to feed conflict and violence. We have heard of the effect of these forces in Islamic and Hindu contexts—in Sudan and India and Pakistan. We are aware that the history of the Church is not without its moments of similar abuse. Religion can be a powerful force for good. It can also be a powerful force for evil, feeding intolerance and the resultant abuse of human rights. One bishop shared the story of young people who came to Sudan from Uganda to be present for his consecration. On their return they were arrested and their left ears cut off because they were not "listening to the words of the Qur'an." Before they were released they were forced to eat their own ears. Our resolutions commit us to renewed endeavours to preserve the rights of all people to freedom of belief and conscience. It is clear from the experience of the victims of religious extremism and nationalism that this is an urgent need.

Refugee Migration, Asylum Seekers and Uprooted and Displaced People

Millions of people being driven from their homes, forced to live either as refugees in other countries or as displaced and uprooted people within their own countries. Across our world people are suffering in refugee camps, in villages for displaced persons or as asylum seekers waiting upon others to find a welcome in another country.

Again, it is the women, children and the elderly who suffer the most as a consequence. People have a right to live in peace within their own communities and to support and sustain their families in freedom. The evidence of such a huge and unsolved refugee problem in our world is testimony to how far those in power and those caught up in the sectarian struggles of our world have abandoned any sense of moral obligation to uphold human rights. Our resolutions call for a renewed endeavour by the Christian community to tackle this evil and respond to the needs of its victims.

Indigenous Peoples

Indigenous peoples all over the world are in need of advocacy. In Northern Argentina, the Mataco, Chorote, and other tribal people are denied rights over their lands. The Khoisan people of South Africa are vulnerable to extinction in that country. They were forced by the apartheid regime to serve as trackers to trace freedom fighters, and have not yet been recognised or given the protection they require to survive in the new South Africa, as their traditions, languages, and customs are in danger of extinction. Recent reports from Australian government sources reveal that thousands of aboriginal children were forcibly removed from their parents and families and placed in foster homes for decades up until the 1970s, in order to eliminate the separate existence of indigenous people. In North America, the Native Americans still struggle to gain the rights of hunting, fishing and land use guaranteed in treaties with the governments which confiscated their lands and displaced them, as well as the right to engage in religious rites and ceremonies.

In every case indigenous peoples are disproportionately poor, have little access to a good education and health care, suffer from higher death rates, and in Australia and the United States are often prone to alcohol and other drug abuse. In every case, the plight of these people is given a very low profile. They are ignored, and their needs are given low priority. They are not treated as 'neighbours' let alone 'brothers or sisters.'

Throughout these harrowing stories we have heard of the costly courage of many within the church and outside who have worked tirelessly for peace and justice, providing help and protection to the victims of human rights abuses, and the hope of a better and different future. The commitment of the church to the world-wide enforcement of the UN Universal Declaration on Human Rights is but one way we can stand with them and affirm the universal dignity of all people in our world.

Theological Reflection

Our understanding of relationships is rooted in the doctrine of the Triune God; Father, Son and Holy Spirit. The Trinity models the community of love into which we are incorporated.

The Christian tradition compels us to accept that every person, believer and non-believer alike, reflects the image of God. To be made in the image of God is to share in God's personal nature. Our God who is in relationship with each one of us requires from us that we be in relationship with one another. From the beginning of creation, humanity is called in freedom to be members of God's family. For Christians the justification of respect for human rights and freedom is extremely personal. Our common sharing in the image of God requires that our relationships with one another be based on mutual respect, dignity, freedom and ethical responsibility. Every person's humanity, integrity and rights are to be respected because: Jesus Christ, the Son of God, has given every person the promise of freedom; the Spirit of God is within each created being; the Father has loved each one of us first. Thus to be made in the image of God is a sign of God's presence in us. To respect one another is to respond not just to one's equals but also to God.

The revelation of God in Christ shows us love that is limitless and boundless. Out of God's boundless love, we are called into a covenant relationship. The promise of the covenant is a promise of ongoing mutual relationship, in which unconditional love, presence, justice, peace and wholeness will flourish.

Translating what "covenant" means into ethical and moral guidelines for human behaviour needs a thorough understanding of the nature of human relationships in God's created human family. Aspiring to the fullness of our humanity requires the understanding that such fullness cannot be achieved alone. We are made for relationships— with God, ourselves, others and creation—and the quality of our relationships is the touchstone for ethical actions.

The New Covenant is confirmed by our baptism into the suffering, death and resurrection of Jesus Christ, and incorporation into the Body of Christ, in which there is neither Jew nor Greek, slave nor free, male nor female (Gal. 3:28). St. Paul challenges us to eschew all discrimination: "When Christ who is your life is revealed then you will also be revealed with him in glory. In that renewal there is no longer Greek and Jew, circumcised and uncircumcised, barbarian, Sythian, slave and free; but Christ is all and in all!" (Col. 3:4,11).

The Church therefore judges no one by human standards. The Church is called to be, in the highest measure possible, an instrument, a sign and a foretaste of the unity of humankind, a fellowship around a common table. The Eucharist is the covenant meal of the Christian community that represents Christ's gift of unity to which it aspires. In the Trinity, the Church finds the source and inspiration for its unity in God the Holy Trinity. In spite of our failures, the Church witnesses to the abundant life that human beings can discover through the love of God made known in Christ.

Human community is built out of an intricate and mutually sustaining web of relationships with one another and with God (c.f. the Virginia Report, chapter 2). By the power of the Holy Spirit the Church discovers and re-discovers its communion with the Holy Trinity and builds its fellowship in acts of truth and love. For Christians this communion is lived in the Church. But many societies, cultures and religions also seek unity in community of love, care and interdependence. Some African cultures express this communion as *ubuntu. Ubuntu* means that persons are human to the extent that they are in relationship with others and that one's humanity is given value by the humanity of others. The shared humanity of *ubuntu* can serve as a vivid example to the whole Church as it seeks to witness to its life of communion in God.

Christian morality is deeply concerned with the human good of the world in a distinctively religious way because the Christian concern for moral actions and ethical principles derives from our deep awareness of and gratitude for God's creative and redemptive acts. In this sense the Christian concern for human rights transcends the fundamental humanistic reasons which are common to all people of good will. The concern of Christians comes from our deep awareness of and gratitude for God's creative and redemptive acts.

When Christians reflect on human rights we are faced with a fundamental ambiguity. On the one hand, our history and our scriptures abound with stories about the abuse of human rights. On the other hand, the present culture of human rights has its origins in the Jewish and Christian traditions of the inviolable dignity of each human being as created by God. We need, therefore, to reflect with humility on our own shortcomings in terms of our human rights practices while, at the same time, holding to the certainty that the language and practice of human rights are grounded in our belief in a God who created all of humanity of equal worth.

Sin, the separation from God, is all that prevents, impairs and destroys our relationships. Conversely, we damage and destroy the other when we refuse to be in relationship with her or him. Thus the infringement, abuse or denial of the dignity and worth of people by violating their human rights is evil and sinful.

In spite of their brokenness and shattered relationships, as well as the denial of God's presence in all of creation, Christians celebrate and live in the power of the Resurrection and the gift of the Holy Spirit. We are called and empowered by the God of Creation, Christ Jesus and the Holy Spirit to be messengers and the embodiment of the freedom, peace, healing, love and compassion which God has for the broken world and its inhabitants. In spite of the horrific stories that have been shared and through which we have become united, the witness of faith, courage and compassion has signaled the presence and power of God. Ours is the task of continuing the presence and power of God to heal and to reconcile.

Context

In 1998 throughout the world we are observing a declared International Human Rights Year in celebration of the 50th anniversary of the adoption of the Universal Declaration of Human Rights (UDHR). Throughout these fifty years the UDHR has served as a principal standard for human rights policy and practice. The UDHR together with the international Covenant on Civil and Political Rights (1966) and the Covenant of Social, Economic and Cultural Rights (1966) form the body of international common law in the field of human rights. Also 1998 represents the midpoint of the United Nations Third Decade for the Elimination of All Forms of Racism (1993–2003), and the final year of the Ecumenical Decade of Churches in Solidarity with Women. These decades represents yet another call from the community of nations to take determined action to eliminate racism and sexism.

The Vienna Declaration and Programme of Action (1993) states that human rights are universal, interdependent and interrelated. This declaration maintains that human rights must be viewed as a whole and that they apply to all situations. Much emphasis has been given to individual rights and freedoms. However appropriate this emphasis may be, we must not lose sight of the fact that there are rights which are held in common. This is recognised, for example, in the rights of indigenous peoples, the rights of the child and the rights of women. The African Charter of Human and Peoples' Rights has led the way in recognising communal rights. Intrinsic to the meaning of rights is a set of corresponding duties and responsibilities. Rights have no meaning unless they are exercised with the understanding that they bestow a duty to respect the rights of another. The 1988 Lambeth Conference resolved that the work of international human rights organisations be commended. In particular, Lambeth 1988 endorsed the UDHR and asked provinces "to support all who are working for its implementation" (Resolution No 33).

It is against this background that we at the Lambeth Conference 1998 have examined the issues of racism, ethnicity and nationalism. Racism has been defined as any attitude which encourages and supports discrimination on the basis of visible characteristics like colour of the skin. These are unalterable characteristics given by God in Creation. In political terms, racism is an ideology of control, exclusion and subjugation. So understood, racism determines who has power to make and enforce decisions, as well as whose destiny such decisions affect. Racism controls access to resources and it sets standards for acceptable behaviour based on a set of values and a cultural system of the dominant group. Racism is a threat to peace. It imposes its will by violence and it gives rise to resistance and struggle. Racism is a blasphemous ideology; it denies God's intention in Creation. Racism distorts human value and its anthropology is partial and false.

Ethnicity and nationalism are descriptive terms. Ethnicity is a given fact of the human situation like race, tribe or language. There is nothing intrinsically wrong with them. Instead, they should be joyfully acknowledged and recognised by others. Ethnicity and nationalism are marks of human identity. They cause problems, however, when they become sources of pride and bigotry, when they lead to blind allegiance and when they become barriers to relationships between neighbours and are used to justify conflict. When this happens, Christians living in such contexts must re-examine their allegiance and submit themselves to the authority of Christ.

Nowhere do Anglicans live in isolation. We live in neighbourhoods. Our daily lives intersect with and are affected by the lives of others who belong to other faiths. The religious plurality in the midst of which we live and move and have our being obliges the Church to relate to other faith communities. Some Anglicans live among Islamic, Hindu and Buddhist communities. In some parts of the world, Christians suffer the widespread denial of human rights based on religious discrimination. As a result of the rise of extremist religious communities, Christians must be careful not to descend into militancy themselves. Where possible, it is important to seek to understand the faith of our neighbours in order to enter into meaningful dialogue with them and to work together for peace and well being in our communities.

Many bishops, clergy and laymen and laywomen have made great contributions to peacemaking throughout the world. Some have been and are being martyred. We think of the martyrdom of the late Archbishop Janani Luwum of Uganda, and the faithful witness of Archbishop George Browne at the height of the civil war in Liberia. We also recognise the prophetic witness of Archbishop Desmond Tutu in opposition to apartheid in South Africa.

Practical Application

As Christians we hold in tension realism about human limitations as well as hope in the power of God's transcending love. Thus, the suggestions that follow are both a challenge and an invitation.

In the Church

The Church as a Model Community: Every Christian community should be a model of mutual love, acceptance and reconciliation. Whenever Christians gather they should examine their lifestyles critically and seek to develop honest and affirming relations with one another. In recognition that the Church is the Body of Christ efforts should be made to encourage participation by all and the acknowledgement of distinctive gifts, ministries, cultures and other qualities. To achieve this goal, the Church discerns and identifies all discriminatory practices in its structures, images and symbols, and commits itself to reform and renewal.

The Church as a Moral Community: The Christian community should lay the foundations for moral values that mark the character of a truly human community. Efforts should be made to avoid too close an identification with particular tribal, ethnic or national consciousness but should seek as wide and genuine a catholicity as possible. Renewed attention must be paid to the family so as to create an environment where all children can be loved, nurtured and protected from the effects of family violence, especially in this age of widespread social breakdown. Children should be protected from conscription in war and unjust employment practices, and special measures should be taken to meet the needs of unaccompanied child refugees.

In The World

In obedience to the teachings of Christ, the Church is obliged to live and proclaim the gospel and to promote and protect human rights. The Church has a responsibility to contribute to the promotion of just societies, and is called to prophetic witness where human rights violations occur, and where corruption and nepotism threaten public trust.

Theme 2
The Environment

Preface

The whole creation is an act of Divine love. Every part from the smallest to the largest is intended to be beautiful, both for itself and in its relationships with the whole. However, creation as we experience it is disordered. It is also only in recent years that we have begun to understand the enormous scale of the damage humanity has caused and is causing to the created order; and the consequences of this for the earth itself (land, water and air), for all living things and not least for the human species itself.

It is our contention that environmental issues are of primary importance within the Section entitled 'Called to Full Humanity.' Ecological concerns are central to our discussions on all the other themes in Section One, as our relationship to the created order is fundamental to human well being.

We therefore claim for environmental issues pre-eminence in time, energy and prayer. The matter is even more serious because of the relative lack of priority given to it at this conference. There is little time. World governments will not prioritise these issues because of perceived political cost.

This then becomes a challenge for the world's faith communities. It is a challenge for those of us who inherit the Biblical story. Our gospel is not anthropocentric, it is God-centred, it is life-centred, it is Logos-centred and it is Jesus Christ-centred. May our worship, witness and service immerse us in praise and thanksgiving for the creation which God has so wonderfully fashioned and which yet awaits with agony its own redemption.

Situation

As Christians we need to be aware of our responsibility and accountability for the destruction of the natural environment and should seek to question, personally and collectively, the use of resources which uphold iniquitous systems. World-wide public awareness now exists that the environment is being devastated by pollution, deforestation, desertification, ozone depletion and global warming. It is also clear that the consequences of these ecological changes fall disproportionately upon the poor of the world. Yet despite this awareness, the social and political resolve to create a more ecologically sustainable way of life has not materialised.

Lambeth Bishops Voice Their Concerns

"Poverty still remains one of the most serious problems in the world. Already there are around a quarter of the developing world's population living in extreme poverty. This figure is increasing with 77 per cent of the world's population earning only 15 per cent of total income. Every day over 800 million people go hungry, many of them children. Per capita income of rich nations is 65 times greater than that of the poorest nations. Poverty is both a cause and a result of environmental problems. In African countries such as Uganda, a specific link is identified between poverty and environmental problems.

"Industrialised countries although comprising only 24 per cent of the total world population account for over 75 per cent of consumption of commercial energy, metal and mineral resources. Over 90 per cent of all industrial and hazardous waste and industrial effluence are generated by developed countries. In the two thirds world both deforestation and the dumping of toxic waste are typical examples of squandering and abuse of natural resources. From Southern Africa it is noted that war, poverty and apartheid have had devastating effects on the environment. These effects are inter-linked and multiple and range from deforestation and overgrazing of land to population growth, the dumping of toxic wastes and hazardous pollution. Tropical rain forests are being cleared at the rate of 15.4 million hectares per year. Some countries like the Philippines have lost some 80 per cent of their forests. Most of Latin America's rain forests have been destroyed to make way for multinational projects like production for fast-food chains. The current crisis of international debt puts enormous pressure on the environment in the two thirds world as these countries often resort to the growing of cash crops and destruction of forests in order to earn foreign exchange to pay their debts. Under the new Intellectual Property Rights (IPR's), there is a growing tendency towards patenting of seeds and plants which results in a reduction in the diversity of crops that farmers in the two thirds world can plant. Developmental projects that do not consider the environmental impacts also cause large-scale displacement of people from their land. For example, some one million people face displacement from their homeland in Central India to make way for a mega-hydro-electric project. (In this connection this conference commends the booklet, *Save our Future* to members of the Lambeth Conference.)"

Today's environmental problems are a by-product of an integrated economic system in which millions of people and commercial entities are involved. The sheer complexity of the system and the attendant ethical issues can be immobilising. All forms of globalisation often exclude concern for human values. Social trends such as the destruction of communities and ways of life are assimilated as inevitable consequences of economic laws that only a sentimentalist would dare to question. Christians in common with other people concerned with environmental issues face the intellectual challenge of developing a wholistic view of nature, humanity and God, in which economic processes have their part, but in which limits are recognised. These limits flow from a reverence for human life and the integrity of the whole creation.

In these circumstances some environmentalists have come to believe that the necessary changes will only be brought about by a profound shift of consciousness rooted in some kind of religious or spiritual renewal:

"I think of religion, or more specifically the Church… engaging in discourse about their responsibilities to care for creation within the context of their traditions of faith, as being more important in the effort to conserve life on earth than all the politicians and experts put together. The Church may be in fact our last best chance."[2]

"Environment is the stuff of religion, and religion is the stuff of the environment. Yet we are schizophrenic about them."[3]

Given that there are such expectations outside the Church, it is not surprising that some environmentalists express their frustration at the apparent complacency and lack of vision regarding ecological issues within the Church:

"I can't help but be astonished at the sheer lack of urgency among Church leaders today; ours is a world crying out for leadership, for some kind of spiritual guidance. And yet as the winds of change whistle up their richly caparisoned copes, where on earth are they?... It seems to me so obvious that without some groundswell of spiritual concern, the transition to a more sustainable way of life remains utterly improbable."[4]

Solemn declarations have been made in the past. Lambeth X in 1968 inveighed against pollution. Lambeth XI in 1978 addressed an appeal to leaders and governments of the world on environmental issues conscious "that time is running short." Lambeth XII in 1988 also passed a resolution on the environment in which the Bishops called upon each province and diocese "as a matter of urgency" to inform the faithful about "what is happening to our environment and to encourage them to see stewardship of God's earth for the care of our neighbours as a necessary part of Christian discipleship."[5]

Lambeth XIII must translate these aspirations into action.

The Archbishop of Canterbury has stated that ecological challenges are "unlikely to be met satisfactorily without the moral and spiritual motivation nurtured by the churches." But he has also acknowledged that, with a few exceptions, "our contributions to public debate about environmental responsibility have often been patchy and undistinguished."[6]

An Eco-Theology for Lambeth XIII

Plainly a great challenge and opportunity lies before the Church. Yet if that challenge is to be met, a widespread spiritual renewal and conversion must be experienced within the Church. There is also an urgent need for the Church to reflect on Scripture and Christian tradition in the light of the ecological crisis and consequently to bring their faith into an effective engagement with the pursuit of a more sustainable way of life.

The gravity of the present challenge to the global ecosystem arises from the technologically enhanced impact of human intervention on our planet. Scripture was inspired in a different world but biblical insights into the nature of the God-human-world relation provide a firm foundation for a contemporary ecological theology.

The Creation Covenant

The foundations of an ecological theology can be found in the ancient biblical notion of the creation covenant. Whilst only implicit in the accounts of creation in the Book of Genesis, the creation covenant is made explicit after the flood. The relevant texts are to be found in Genesis 9 and also in Isaiah 11, 24, 32, and

55 and Hosea 2. In these passages God is pictured binding together all living beings, and the earth itself, into a web of inter-relatedness. The effects of this covenant can be seen in the interdependence of the natural order. Thus creation was established in a divinely intended state of *shalom*, usually translated 'peace' but also incorporating ideas of harmony, justice and integrity.

Furthermore, whilst the creation covenant is founded upon God's 'rainbow' promises, like all covenants in scripture, it also assumes human moral responsibilities, including ecological responsibilities. While the covenant in no way legitimises a crude anthropocentrism, human beings are given a special place in mediating the divine promise and intention to other human beings, to future generations, to other living creatures and to the earth as a whole. Contempt for creation is therefore sin, a betrayal of the covenant and the trust reposed in human beings to 'till' the earth but also to 'keep' it (Gen. 2:15). It is in this context that human dominion, *radah*, is to be exercised (Gen. 1:26).

In Jesus Christ the Creation Covenant is renewed. "When anyone is in Christ there is a new creation" (2 Cor. 5:17). The redemptive purpose of God for a created order that has fallen into bondage and decay becomes a reality. The Logos theology of St. John in the first chapter of his gospel is well known but its application to the created order is sometimes neglected. All things were made through Him and all things find their fulfillment in Him. The Logos became flesh dwelt among us and in his life, death and resurrection reveals that to be fully human is to be in communion with God and the created order.

The Sacrament of Creation

Ecological theology is also founded on the belief that a deep communion exists between God and creation. In this sacramental sense, a distinction is maintained and affirmed between the natural and the divine.

Christian doctrine preserves the necessary tension between divine immanence (God present in creation) and divine transcendence (God above and beyond creation). According to St. Basil and the Nicene Creed each person of the Trinity relates to creation in a different way. The Father as the original cause is the 'Creator of all things.' The Son as the creative cause is the One 'through whom all things were made.' The Spirit as implementing cause is the 'Creator of life'.

Sacramental theology does not divinise nature but affirms the Trinitarian presence of God in creation and points to the natural world and matter itself as an effective medium of divine revelation, a means of communion with God. Nature is 'sacred by association.'[7] By the sacramental presence of the Spirit, creation is endowed with sacred value and dignity. It is to be cared for and loved as a vehicle of God's own presence and revelation.

Priests for Creation

Far from granting a mandate for human beings to do as they please with the earth, the divine bidding that they should have dominion over creation actually implies a solemn responsibility on the part of humans to treat the earth with reverence and respect. As the divine image-bearers, humans are uniquely called to embody and express God's will and purpose for all creation, a vocation which clearly excludes its abuse and wanton destruction.

First and foremost human beings should be understood as biologically and ontologically part of nature and as partners with every other creature on earth. This is implied in the symbolism of Genesis 2 where God forms "adam," the first earth creature out of the very dust *(ha'adam)*. In an evolutionary perspective we have come to see human beings as the embodiment of a line of development which incorporates a number of simpler forms of life. This finds its theological expression in the teaching of St. Maximus the Confessor that the human being is the microcosm of creation, the crown of the whole creation.

God also ordained, however, that human beings should be his fellow workers. Whereas other creatures adjust to the given world, the human being desires to create its own world, transforming raw materials into new realities. Nevertheless this 'subduing' of the natural world for human purpose and creativity was never intended to be to creation's detriment but rather the way in which it was to find its fulfillment. Human beings are called to be priests and pastors of creation, living bridges between heaven and earth. They are to pronounce God's blessing on creation and they are also the means of expressing creation's praise and longing to God.

Nowhere is the priestly ministry of humanity brought more clearly into focus than in the Eucharistic feast, which is indeed, "the Eucharist for all things."[8]

The Eucharist embodies the conviction, not only that elements of earthly reality—bread and wine—can become means of grace for human beings, but that also, as they are offered up to God by human beings, the elements themselves receive new meaning and status. The offertory prayer declares:

"Blessed be God through whom we have this bread to offer which earth has given and human hands have made. It will become for us the bread of life."

The prayer is a subtle balance between recognising God's gift while acknowledging our human role in developing and using it rightly, and accepting its potential as a communication of God's own reality.[9]

The priestly offering of bread and wine in the Eucharist, then, is itself a microcosm of the wider priestly ministry which human beings exercise in relation to creation as a whole. Human beings may legitimately transform nature, but only in the context of recognising the natural world as a gift from God, blessed with the capacity to be a sign and means of the divine presence and therefore to be treated with reverence and respect.

Human beings must neither disappear into the community of creation, nor must they be detached from that community. They are called at once to be *imago mundi* and *imago Dei*, and to stand before God on behalf of creation and before creation on behalf of God. Though they may enhance creation by skill and technology, this is only in order to offer it once again to the Creator. As servant-priests, they must be willing to make personal and corporate sacrifices for the common good of creation.

The model for this sacrificial service is provided by the *kenosis* of Jesus Christ who emptied himself of 'dominion' and sacrificed himself for the world. No ecological theology is complete if social justice is not a part of it. "Jesus self emptied his power and dominion for the sake of both human and non-human creation."[10]

Sabbath Feast of 'Enoughness'

The whole idea of the Sabbath is rich with ecological significance, not least because it points away from anthropocentric interpretations of creation. This is achieved in two ways. Firstly, the Genesis narrative emphasises that creation reaches its crown and consummation not in the creation of humankind on the sixth day but in the peace of the Sabbath on the seventh day. Secondly the Sabbath concept when related to the fallow season for the earth introduces a constraint on human intervention in nature and thus sets limits to the human exploitation of the natural order.

Rather than being simply a pause between bouts of activity, the Sabbath was to be an occasion for celebration and thanksgiving, a feast of contentment and 'enoughness.' The rhythm of Sabbath days and Sabbath years reclaims time from a mere succession of passing moments and gives life a shape which flows from the recognition that creation was brought into being not to serve any transient human purpose but to be material for the praise and glory of the Creator.

Yet today, creation "wears man's smudge and shares man's smell;" it is "seared with trade and smeared with toil,"[11] knowing no respite from the demands of human beings addicted to a cult of "more." The Sabbath then must be reinvigorated, not as nostalgic symbol of a religious past, but as a feast of redemption and an anticipation of the ecological harmony and sustainable equilibrium of Christ's Kingdom.

Theme 3
Human Sexuality

Human sexuality is the gift of a loving God. It is a gift to be honoured and cherished by all people. As a means for the expression of the deepest human love and intimacy, sexuality has great power.

The Holy Scriptures and Christian tradition teach that human sexuality is intended by God to find its rightful and full expression between a man and a woman in the covenant of marriage, established by God in creation, and affirmed by our Lord Jesus Christ. Holy Matrimony is, by intention and divine purpose, to be a life-long, monogamous and unconditional commitment between a woman and a man. The Lambeth Conference 1978 and 1988 both affirmed "marriage to be sacred, instituted by God and blessed by our Lord Jesus Christ."

The New Testament and Christian history identify singleness and dedicated celibacy as Christ-like ways of living. The Church needs to recognise the demands and pressures upon both single and married people. Human beings define themselves by relationships with God and other persons. Churches need to find effective ways of encouraging Christ-like living, as well as providing opportunities for the flourishing of friendship, and the building of supportive community life.

We also recognise that there are among us persons who experience themselves as having a homosexual orientation. Many of these are members of the Church and are seeking the pastoral care, moral direction of the Church, and God's transforming power for the living of their lives and the ordering of relationships. We wish to assure them that they are loved by God and that all baptised, believing and faithful persons, regardless of sexual orientation, are full members of the Body of Christ. We call upon the Church and all its members to work to end any discrimination on the basis of sexual orientation, and to oppose homophobia.

Clearly some expressions of sexuality are inherently contrary to the Christian way and are sinful. Such unacceptable expressions of sexuality include promiscuity, prostitution, incest, pornography, paedophilia, predatory sexual behaviour, and sadomasochism (all of which may be heterosexual and homosexual), adultery, violence against women and in families, rape and female circumcision. From a Christian perspective these forms of sexual expression remain sinful in any context. We are particularly concerned about the pressures on young people to engage in sexual activity at an early age, and we urge our churches to teach the virtue of abstinence.

All human relationships need the transforming power of Christ which is available to all, and particularly when we fall short of biblical norms.

We must confess that we are not of one mind about homosexuality. Our variety of understanding encompasses:

- those who believe that homosexual orientation is a disorder, but that through the grace of Christ people can be changed, although not without pain and struggle;

- those who believe that relationships between people of the same gender should not include genital expression, that this is the clear teaching of the Bible and of the Church universal, and that such activity (if unrepented of) is a barrier to the Kingdom of God;

- those who believe that committed homosexual relationships fall short of the biblical norm, but are to be preferred to relationships that are anonymous and transient;

- those who believe that the Church should accept and support or bless monogamous covenant relationships between homosexual people and that they may be ordained.

It appears that a majority of bishops is not prepared to bless same sex unions or to ordain active homosexuals. Furthermore many believe there should be a moratorium on such practices.

We have prayed, studied and discussed these issues, and we are unable to reach a common mind on the scriptural, theological, historical, and scientific questions that are raised. There is much that we do not yet understand. We request the Primates and the Anglican Consultative Council to establish a means of monitoring work done in the Communion on these issues and to share statements and resources among us.

The challenge to our Church is to maintain its unity while we seek, under the guidance of the Holy Spirit, to discern the way of Christ for the world today with respect to human sexuality. To do so will require sacrifice, trust, and charity towards one another, remembering that ultimately the identity of each person is defined in Christ.

There can be no description of human reality, in general or in particular, outside the reality of Christ. We must be on guard, therefore, against constructing any other ground for our identities than the redeemed humanity given us in him. Those who understand themselves as homosexuals, no more and no less than those who do not, are liable to false understandings based on personal or family histories, emotional dispositions, social settings and solidarities formed by common experiences or ambitions. Our sexual affections can no more define who we are than can our class, race or nationality. At the deepest ontological level, therefore, there is no such thing as "a" homosexual or "a" heterosexual; there are human beings, male and female, called to redeemed humanity in Christ, endowed with a complex variety of emotional potentialities and threatened by a complex variety of forms of alienation.[12]

Theme 4
Modern Technology

Technology and the Quest for Full Humanity

'God blessed them, and God said to them, "Be fruitful and multiply, and fill the earth and subdue it; and have dominion over the fish of the sea and over the birds of the air and over every living thing that moves upon the earth."' (Gen 1:28)

'The LORD God took the man and put him in the Garden of Eden to till it and keep it.' (Gen 2:15)

What Price This Gift?

Technology is the means by which human beings exercise dominion, but rather than crush and subdue creation, we are created to tend the gift of dominion and preserve creation for God. We cannot talk about dominion except with reference to the Lordship (dominion) of Jesus Christ who came not to be served but to serve, and who is exalted because he humbled himself and became obedient. We cannot talk about technology without also talking about stewardship.

Human beings by nature make and use tools. They are extensions of ourselves by which we seek to alter our environment to secure a better life for ourselves and for future generations. A sword is an extension of our arm—as is an atomic bomb; an automobile is an extension of our feet, television extends our sight, a computer our memory; medical science extends the life of the biological organism; and through genetic engineering it is now possible to re-programme the genetic codes of life and create new life forms.

Ian Barbour argues that initially technology was viewed as "liberation," then it was viewed as "demonic," but now it is increasingly viewed as power which can be used responsibly or irresponsibly. A word of caution is due. Technology, as the historian Arnold Toynbee noted over forty years ago, is not merely a surface phenomenon. It is not merely an external appendage or tool.

The truth seems to be that all the different elements in a culture-pattern have an inner connection with each other so that if one abandons one's own traditional technology and adopts a foreign technology instead, the effect of this change on the technological surface of life will not remain confined to the surface, but will gradually work its way down to the depths till the whole of one's traditional culture has been undermined and the whole foreign culture has been given entry, bit by bit, through the gap made in the outer ring of one's cultural defences by the foreign technology's entering wedge.[13]

Everyone wants technology because it brings with it the promise of a better life, but technology also brings with it a particular worldview and is fed and sustained by market forces. Technology brings with it not just the surface enhancement of life, but it moves inward and shapes our understanding of ourselves, our relationships and our world.

Global Perspectives

We have heard accounts of both the promise and danger of technology, and we are aware that the focus of concern is often different between the two-thirds world and the West. The West might be more immediately concerned about cloning or the effect of Y2K (the Millennium Bug—the malfunctioning of computers programmed to recognise the year in two digits [e.g. 98] in the year 2000) which will affect banking, the food industry, military and security organisations, communication and the entire world-wide technological infrastructure. The two-thirds world might be more concerned about the technology of food production and the impact of technology on employment, the creation and depletion of jobs.

Modern technology can save lives, cure disease, increase productivity, connect people globally, free them from menial drudgery and make it possible to access an infinite store of knowledge which was not previously available.

Technology is also gadgetry. There is a bumper sticker on some American cars which says, "He who has the most toys wins." Technology is a toy. However, it often delivers less than it promises: a cure for cancer, a paperless society, or a more cost efficient business. Cures remain elusive, paper consumption increases, and costs continue to go up to buy replacements for obsolete equipment and highly trained technicians. Technological tools can be addictive and an end in themselves. They can alienate and isolate people, even kill and dehumanise. Yet, we want these tools. We marvel at what they can do. This theme of "Yes, but..." will recur time and again in this report.

Some of the poorest parts of the Anglican Communion appear to be most concerned about the harmful effects of modern technology. Anxieties were expressed at the Lambeth Conference 1988 where it was argued that the Church "has a responsibility to see that people do not become alienated from the life of God and his world by the misuse of technology."

We are concerned for the lack of technological accessibility in many countries. In South Africa computers could be used for "distance learning," to help supplement the short supply of teachers, but computers and other forms of technology largely remain unaffordable. As a result many people in the developing world do not share fully in the positive changes in communication such as easy means of travel, telephones, televisions and communication via the Internet. Technology can have a negative impact: the destructive influence of globalisation on local cultures and the division between the rich and the poor, are trenchant examples. In the United States it is becoming increasingly clear that the economic gap will be determined in large part by those who can manipulate this technology and those who cannot. Those who can will have jobs in the 21st century. Those who cannot—mostly the poor—will continue in the cycle of poverty and unemployment.

At the Southern Africa Regional meeting, bishops from Madagascar expressed concern about the double-edged nature of this technology: "In some instances modern technology is seen as an aid to development. Its employment within the Malagasy world of business, finance and industry should enable the country to integrate into the modern world, to the ultimate benefit of its citizens. The other side of the coin, however, is the fact that advances due to the introduction of modern technology will inevitably lead to job losses, which exacerbate the problems of a country already suffering from chronic unemployment."

The Province of Uganda, also, noted this double-edged nature of modern technology, citing the example of television, which can "inform, educate and entertain" but which can also cause harm. For Uganda "technology in general can have good effects, but it can also be destructive. Tea picking machines make people jobless. Computers and new information technology bring about loss of neighbourliness, and can reduce humanity, since human beings are meant to relate to human beings not to machines."

The Episcopal Church of the Sudan noticed this double-edged characteristic in the application of genetics to medical experimentation and believes these practices to be potentially immoral in that they manipulate human life, but also potentially useful in the sense that they facilitate human discoveries and scientific achievements.

In East Asia—Japan, China, Hong Kong and Taiwan—there are benefits similar to those in the West, but in a global economy there are also financial crises brought on by technology when investors can move in and out of markets quickly leaving workers without jobs. On the parish level, however, the use of computers and the Internet have been beneficial. Information is immediately accessible, and e-mail has enabled people from all corners of the diocese and the world to communicate.

In India half the population cannot read and write. Technology is language specific, which means that this half of the population is left out. Yet, with the onslaught of satellite communications, people in the most conservative rural areas are impacted by the values of the West. Eighty per cent of the people who live in villages are bombarded with western values in life-styles that undercut their traditions, and there is no way to control what is received. At the same time this pervasive presence of information can also be liberating. New ideas cannot be kept out, and this has served to promote and extend democratic ideals. Tyrants and dictators can no longer carry out their totalitarian rule in secret. The news media can gather and disseminate information instantly. It is inevitable that this information will be reduced to 'sound bites.' Such information is always selected and can be inaccurate. The media are market driven and exist to sell newspapers and capture the viewing audience. Ordinary, good news is rarely reported.

When technology is received from the West it is often obsolete, making competition difficult in the market place. There is a tendency to dump waste on the two-thirds world, not only values but also products no longer used or acceptable in the West, e.g. DDT, which, although it does ecological damage, is in demand because it works.

The primary challenge is the responsible appropriation of technology. The startling developments in biotechnology that have resulted from genetic science in the last two decades suggest the prospect of enormous changes in agriculture and in the treatment of human disease and incapacity. Many fear that these biotechnological developments could also reduce bio-diversity, risk harmful mutations and manipulate human destinies by genetically eliminating those traits that we do not consider desirable.

Magicians do not tell their secrets. Likewise technocrats guard their knowledge well. Since more and more research and development is in the hands of corporations for profit, and less and less is done by educational and governmental institutions, there is a positive disincentive to share technological information. There is also a concern that more and more technological power is being concentrated in the hands of fewer and fewer people. They are not politicians but technocrats. For instance, the Microsoft Corporation dominates the computer world. This is made possible in publishing, agriculture, banking, health care and other areas. The term "globalisation" might well be replaced by the term "new colonialism."

We are concerned about the varieties of biogenetic engineering and their effect. Cloning has already been accomplished in animals and it is certainly possible with human beings. Do we want to create drones without brain stems and sustain them artificially so that we can harvest their organs as needed? We cannot afford to leave these questions to be answered only by science and industry. The church has a word to say about the uniqueness of each person and the sacredness of life.

The Technology of War

There is ongoing concern about the technology of war. The sale and deployment of arms serves only to impoverish and kill populations. Nations that sell arms often do business with both sides of a conflict.

Atomic testing in Pakistan, India and other places in the world is of deep concern, as is the continuing existence of landmines in Mozambique, Sudan, Bosnia and in many other countries. Yet, for every landmine dismantled, twenty are planted. We urge the United States and all other nations that have not signed the Ottawa Accords to do so immediately. In addition we urge all nations to cease the production, testing and deployment of nuclear weapons, and "to beat their spears into ploughshares."

It is possible to learn how to make an atom bomb on the Internet. There is a fear that the nuclear stand-off can escalate and that, with readily available technology and the right ingredients, a bomb can be in the hands of those nations most prone to violence. While nuclear energy promised to be an efficient alternative to fossil fuels, it is becoming more and more clear to many that all forms of nuclear power, whether for peace or war, have the potential to inflict more harm than good. There is the ever-present danger of nuclear meltdown, and damage to the environment from radioactive waste. More nations now have access to the nuclear knowledge that can lead to the further development and deployment of biological weapons and poison gas.

There is also great concern that with this new knowledge even small nations now have the capability of developing and deploying biological weapons and poison gas.

Technology and Theology

In naming the creatures Adam was invited to share with God in the shaping of creation, but the temptation of Adam and Eve was to go beyond this and to strive to be like God, to know good and evil and possess all knowledge. We are called to extend our knowledge but to do so in obedience to God with humility. We are made in God's image, and there is within us, therefore, the urge to create. God loves to create for God creates to love. So it is with us. We are created and we create for relationship. That is what it is to be fully human.

Human beings are called to be co-creators, continuously seeking to create a world suitable for human needs, unlike the rest of the created order which adjusts to the given world. The exercise of human transforming power should contribute to the fulfilment of creation rather than to its detriment. In this sense, human beings are to be seen as the pronouncement of God's blessing on creation, the vehicle through which the whole of creation's worship and longing for God is expressed.

The temptation of technology is the same as it was for Adam and Eve. We want to know it all, or, as in the Tower of Babel story, to "make a name for ourselves." Scientists seek the "god particle." It is easy to forget that God is God.

We are naïve if we think that technology is morally neutral. As Jeremy Rifkin says:

"...for in the act of utilising the power inherent in each new tool we fashion, someone or something in the environment is compromised, diminished, or exploited to enhance or secure our own well-being. The point is; power is never neutral. There are always winners and losers whenever power is applied."[14]

From the perspective of the Gospel, effectiveness is judged by whether the poorest end up with jobs, food, and water. Paul reminds us: "If one member suffers, all suffer together with it; if one member is honoured, all rejoice together with it. Now you are the body of Christ and individually members of it" (1 Cor. 12:26–27). If that does not happen there is good cause for suspicion.

The Church needs to be informed enough to know the difference between technology as technique (manipulating development gene by gene or electron by electron) and the effect of technology within the context of a whole ecosystem. We are more than the sum of our parts. We have been consistently saying that to be fully human is to be in relationship. That is what it means to be a part of a body; no member is less important or more essential to the working of the body than any other, whether it be the human body, the body politic, corporate bodies, or this body-universe.

There are questions to ask and alternatives to choose from. First, what of the long-accepted medical axiom to "do no harm"? Second, is the power appropriate? Does it preserve and enhance or does it destabilise? Is it ultimately manageable and controllable? Is it accessible to all and does it produce benefits available to all?

We tend to feel helpless in the face of so much inevitable technological development, but the truth is that much of this development is consumer driven. The marketplace now determines what technology is developed. Consumers do have a voice in determining where and how development occurs. The anti-impotence drug Viagra had the largest initial sales of any drug ever produced. It was developed because there is a market for it. Manufacturers will continue to develop what consumers will buy.

The role of a bishop, as one ordination rite declares, is to stir up the conscience of the people and to help those who have no helper. The leaders of this worldwide communion need to be informed because we are in communion, because we have heard the deep suffering of those in our midst, and because some of us have access to the power and wealth which can serve our fellow human beings in carrying out God's work on earth.

A Call

We are aware that unprecedented technological changes will take place in our world in the next decade. Unimaginable technological changes have taken place since we assembled for the Lambeth Conference ten years ago. Who could have imagined the computer revolution, the Internet, the information age, the unravelling of the genetic code, cloning and cross-species genetic mutations? We as leaders need to keep abreast of these developments and speak about their ethical implications in the decade ahead.

Therefore, we call for the establishment of a commission through the Anglican Consultative Council to track these developments, to reflect on them theologically and ethically, and to keep bishops and other church leaders informed of new developments. We believe that it is possible for this commission to do its work and inform the church through the use of the very technologies we have been discussing: e-mail and Internet conferencing.

God has blessed us with memory, reason and skill. We are called to use God's gifts to care for God's creation, God's creatures and one another.

Theme 5
Euthanasia

Situation

As bishops of the Anglican Communion, part of the one, holy, catholic and apostolic Church, we believe that there are five bedrock principles upon which the discussion of euthanasia and related issues rest:

- life is God-given and therefore has intrinsic sanctity, significance and worth;

- human beings are in relationship with the created order and that relationship is characterised by such words as respect, enjoyment and responsibility;

- human beings, while flawed by sin, nevertheless have the capacity to make free and responsible moral choices;
- human meaning and purpose is found in our relationship with God, in the exercise of freedom, critical self-knowledge, and in our relationships with one another and the wider community;
- this life is not the sum total of human existence; we find our ultimate fulfilment in eternity with God through Christ.

In the debate on euthanasia, these five principles have to be kept in constructive tension with one another. To promote one principle above another leads to serious distortions in making moral choices.

The debate about euthanasia has thus far been dominated by the West. Our discussion here has been enriched by the spirituality and theology of ancestral and indigenous peoples that call the Church to new understandings of the "fullness of humanity."

Theological Reflection

The manner in which human beings treat one another should be a reflection of the dignity which God in Christ has conferred upon them. That dignity may be cherished as much in the way we care for the dying as in the preservation and well being of the living. This is also why intentionally foreshortening another person's life is so alien to the Christian position.

It is because Christians recognise the sanctity and dignity of human life, one of the sharpest theological questions we face in the euthanasia debate is the problem of suffering. Put starkly; how can the idea that God is a God of love be consonant with a world in which there is so much suffering? The problem of theodicy has taxed the Church since its earliest days. This is not the place to attempt a comprehensive review of all the possible answers to this question. We do however want to draw attention to one profound Christian insight: God suffers in Christ within our own suffering and ultimately redeems and transforms it upon the Cross, giving us new life and unending hope.

In Christian theology, the sovereignty of God is not found in divine impassivity or indifference. Rather it is expressed when God as divine love enters into our suffering. As the prophet Isaiah has said, "He was wounded for our transgressions, he was bruised for our iniquities: the chastisement of our peace was upon him and with his stripes we are healed" (Isaiah 53:5). To try to think of God as a wounded healer is to reach that point of understanding where language bends and fractures under the strain of what it is trying to convey. This is not a puzzle that we can solve, but a mystery that is only understood as we enter it and live within it.

The belief in a sovereign but suffering God who redeems, a theology of God's sovereignty which contains suffering, and the mystery of redemption, is expressed through the care which all Christian people are called to offer to those in need. Despite our failures, we are compelled through God's love in Christ to try to live with open and compassionate hearts.

The other major theological problem is the question of personal autonomy. As bishops, we believe that humanity is created in the image of God, and that personal autonomy and freedom, are gifts of God to be cherished and advanced. In euthanasia, however, where life is terminated intentionally, the exercise of personal autonomy is precluded by two things. Firstly, it is precluded by the acknowledgement that God alone has sovereignty over life and death, and secondly, by our recognition that personal, moral autonomy is inextricably bound up with the autonomy, rights and responsibilities of others. Moral decisions are not made in a vacuum, they are always made in a communal context; personal choices have social consequences.

In the debate on euthanasia, it is the duty of the Church to ensure that its theology of God, of suffering and of personal autonomy, is explored with intellectual rigour and seriousness by everyone involved. It is also our duty to ensure that the most compassionate and Christ-like care is given to those facing death or making life and death decisions.

Context

In societies where a high level of medical facilities and advanced technology are widely available, questions raised by euthanasia are increasingly acute. In Europe, North America and Australia, for example, there is continuous popular and ethical debate about the subject. It is mistaken, however, to assume that the ethical problems surrounding death and dying are solely a western phenomenon. Every society has had rules and norms about these matters.

The current debate is frequently confused because the word euthanasia contains a broad range of meanings. Popularly the word is used to identify a range of behaviours from suicide to so-called 'mercy killing.' In order to clarify the debate we believe that careful distinctions need to be made. Literally translated, the Greek word *euthanasia* means a 'good death.' In this paper we take it to mean the act by which one person intentionally causes or assists in causing the death of another who is terminally or seriously ill in order to end the other's pain and suffering. Following very largely the definitions of the Washington Report,[15] we distinguish between two different kinds of euthanasia, voluntary and non-voluntary.

Voluntary euthanasia is that in which a competent, informed person asks another to end his or her life and is not coerced into doing so. For example, if a terminally ill, competent man who is under no compulsion asks his wife or a nurse to give him a lethal injection in order to end his life, this will amount to voluntary euthanasia.

Non-voluntary euthanasia is that in which a person who does not have the capacity for informed choice is killed. For example, if a woman with senile dementia and in great pain and suffering has her life taken by her daughter, this is non-voluntary euthanasia.

In both of these cases there is clear, purposeful activity. In each case there is the intention that death should be immediate or follow very rapidly. It is important to distinguish these two categories from the withdrawal or withholding of medical help when someone is *in extremis*. A legitimate moral distinction can be drawn between allowing someone to die and causing that person to die.

We have reached substantial agreement that the following measures are permissible and consonant with Christian faith:

- to withhold or withdraw excessive medical treatment or intervention (e.g. life support) may be appropriate where there is no reasonable prospect of recovery;

- when the primary intent is to relieve suffering and not to bring about death, to provide supportive care for the alleviation of intolerable pain and suffering (e.g. analgesics) may be appropriate even if the side effect of that care is to hasten the dying process;

- to refuse or terminate medical treatment (such as declining to undertake a course of chemotherapy for cancer) is a legitimate individual moral choice;

- when a person is in a permanent vegetative state, to sustain him or her with artificial nutrition and hydration may indeed be seen as constituting medical intervention.

The dying process itself has the potential for personal and spiritual transformation, reconciliation and healing for the dying person and his or her loved ones. The Church in partnership with other caring agencies needs to foster openness of communication between the dying persons, their families, and loved ones and members of the medical community. Pastoral care for dying persons and their loved ones is, in part, preparation for the life to come.

Practical Applications

As bishops, we have a great deal of experience in providing pastoral and spiritual care for the sick, the dying and their loved ones. This ministry includes counselling, prayer, the provision of sacraments and the preparation of funeral services. Christian funeral liturgies, among other things, stress the continuing dignity and value of a person after death, illustrating that life in its fullness is not simply to be equated with physical existence. We share deeply in the lives of those who suffer and those who mourn, often receiving from them as much or more than we give.

Ministering to the dying and their loved ones is a fundamental pastoral duty of the Church and should include the ministry of the lay and ordained members.

As Anglican bishops, we have reached the following conclusion about euthanasia:

- We cannot under any circumstances endorse euthanasia as a means of ending pain and suffering when defined as 'the act by which one person intentionally causes, or assists to cause, the death of another who is seriously or terminally ill.'

- We recognise, nevertheless, that some people appear to hold a different point of view. This may in part be due to a difference of definition and we want to make clear that euthanasia is *not* to be equated with such actions as declining or terminating medical treatment where excessive intervention would lead to further or increased suffering and the outcome would be futile.

- We believe that in many societies where there is apparent strong support for euthanasia there is considerable confusion between declining or terminating treatment (*permissible*) and the intentional act of causing the death of another by positive means other than declining or terminating treatment (*impermissible*).

- We believe that the mistake of describing euthanasia (properly defined as above) by the term 'mercy killing' adds to confusion about what is and what is not permissible. To kill, or to assist in the killing, of another person who is terminally or seriously ill is, in our view, to act in the place of God; to arrogate to human autonomy that which properly belongs only to God's sovereignty.

In those societies where there is growing concern about the pain and suffering of the dying, very often drawn out by excessive medical intervention, the means to relieve pain and suffering (palliative care) are, or should be, made widely available.

As well as rejecting euthanasia as an impermissible appropriation by human beings of God's sovereignty, we are aware of many dangers that will arise should any society seek to make euthanasia lawful.

Among such dangers are:

- the virtual impossibility of framing and implementing legislation that would prevent abuse by the unscrupulous;
- a diminution of respect for all human life, especially of the marginalised and those who may be regarded as 'unproductive' members of society;
- the potential devaluing of worth, in their own eyes, of the elderly, the sick and of those who are dependent on others for their well being;
- the potential destruction of the important and delicate trust of the doctor/patient relationship.

As bishops, we believe that a clear line needs to be drawn between what is permissible and what is impermissible both in the sight of God and in the human laws of society.

Though we recognise that declining, withholding or terminating medical treatment may be morally appropriate in certain circumstances to enable some people to die with dignity (and want to insist that that lies outside our precise definition of 'euthanasia'), we hold that whoever has the final responsibility for making those decisions should make them:

- with careful, open and just consultation with family members, loved ones and medical experts, regarding all the possible consequences;
- with prayerful and spiritual understanding for the consequences of one's relationship with God and with others.

As bishops, we are committed to fostering among the members of our Church a clear and deep understanding of the ethical, spiritual, theological and legal implications arising from the debate about euthanasia that is taking place in many countries of the world. We hold that proper decisions must be made to ensure respect for human rights and human dignity throughout the world, including those countries where there is only limited, if any, advanced medical technology available. We are also committed to doing all in our power to ensure that those who are terminally or seriously ill receive the best possible pastoral and medical care, including palliative care.

Theme 6
International Debt and Economic Justice

Process

We have told stories from our own countries, heard again of the suffering and waste that we, as Bishops, have seen personally.

We have reflected on a theological presentation on the theme of difference. We have wept at the imposed and accumulated difference in resources available to our different peoples. We have seen how this gulf destroys what God intends for the invaluable encounter between diverse cultures and peoples.

We have engaged, and continue to engage with professionals in the field—economists, including two from the IMF and World Bank, and aid agencies—to consider questions like:

- What would the substantial debt reduction we seek cost and who would bear that cost?
- Which debts can and should be written off, or substantially reduced?
- What are the criteria for deciding this?
- Are there debts that should be declared not to be debts at all (because of the way in which, or the purposes for which, they were incurred)?
- Are there conditions which should be required for the cancellation of some debts?
- Above all, who is to make decisions about all these questions to assure mutuality and justice?

Theological Considerations

As members of the world-wide Anglican Communion drawn from rich and poor nations, we believe that God created a good world for all persons. It is a world in which we are bound together in our common humanity, formed in God's image, and in which each person has equal dignity and value. With immeasurable generosity, God has given bountiful resources for all to share. We are responsible to hold God's gifts in trust for one another seeking the good of all.

Globalisation has made us more interrelated than ever before. While offering enormous opportunities for the development of human well being, it has, in fact, magnified the injustice of a world of inequality, where the strong pursue their interests to the detriment of the weak. Sin has always been with us. Globalisation magnifies its effects through the power of governments and financial institutions.

The financial structures and agreements we create for exchange and development must serve the common good. They may not take the place of God and become the criteria by which all must act morally. We believe that amongst nations and between nations and financial institutions only those agreements which serve the good of all are recognised by God as legitimate and, therefore, as true credit and debt.

We believe that the same generosity of God that was manifested in Jesus Christ is apparent in the liberation of the world. It is a liberation of all aspects of our humanity; it brings freedom from all that destroys healthy human life. Following the pattern of our Lord Jesus and his compassion, we cannot stand by while developing nations represented among us pay up to ten times as much each year in debt repayments as they receive in aid from the wealthier nations, and while up to 40 per cent of a nation's income is spent in debt servicing instead of basic needs such as food, health, and education. This is a scandal, a grave moral wrong. Hearing one another's stories, we are deeply affected by the enormous weight of human suffering, seriously compounded in many countries by the burden of debt.

We feel compelled to speak out against this suffering. Through our baptism into Christ we are one body in him and are called to be in relationship with one another. When one member of the body suffers, all suffer. If my bowl is full and yours is empty, I must share what I have.

The generosity of God does not leave humanity with a debt that cannot be paid. On the contrary, through the release accomplished for us in the Cross of Christ, we are called to stand before God in full dignity. We are fully justified and are being changed into the people God made us to be. In a similar way, as human beings, we must seek to release each other from exploitative relationships of debtor and creditor into the freedom to be equal persons to one another.

Our Lord Jesus came from heaven to earth as a vulnerable baby. As Anglican leaders, we know that to follow in his steps is to face the challenge to our own lifestyles and those of our churches. Those from the richer nations recognise that we are poor when we trust in our many possessions and institutions rather than in God. Our giving and receiving expresses the nature of God who gives abundantly. Such a theology of giving and receiving within a common humanity causes us to challenge a process of decision-making in which the power lies with the creditor nations.

In Christ Jesus we hope for a kingdom of justice and love, the power of which is already present through the Spirit of God in the world. The vision God has given us is of a world in unity and peace, a world transformed by love.

The International Financial Context

The crisis of indebtedness faced by the poorest nations must be placed in the context of decisions by western banks in the 1970s to disburse, rapidly and widely, "petrodollar" loans, as a way of averting a crisis of inflation in the West. These decisions were followed by a period (during the 1980s and 1990s) when interest rates were, and continue to be, at historically high levels. Over the same period, falling prices for key export commodities made it difficult for indebted nations to raise the hard currency (US dollars, yen or sterling) needed to repay debts.[16]

At the same time the cost of imports from the West rose—worsening the terms of trade between rich and poor nations.[17]

Against this backdrop, the IMF and World Bank, on behalf of their member governments, have encouraged the de-regulation of capital flows, in particular the removal of exchange controls over movements of capital in and out of countries. This facilitates the availability of foreign credit, and enables foreign investors to repatriate capital and profits more easily from developing countries. However as foreign loans and profits by foreign investors have to be repaid in hard currencies, developing country governments have increasingly faced difficulties as profits or earnings in local currencies have been converted into hard currencies, draining their central banks of foreign reserves. Repaying foreign debt and repatriating profits to foreign investors become particularly difficult for governments when local currencies are devalued relative to the currency in which the debts have to be repaid. This is a marked feature of the current debt crisis in South East Asia.

Debt and Economic Degradation

As the debt crisis in the countries of Asia, Africa and Latin America worsened in the 1980s, the IMF and World Bank[18] stepped in and began offering concessional or "soft" loans[19] to help in the repayment of old loans. By the mid 1990s it had become clear that these loans, far from resolving the debt crisis, were adding to the problem. Even "soft" loans become expensive to repay when a country's means of repayment (revenues from export sales) falls, or when currency fluctuations increase the cost of repayment.

As these countries became more indebted so social and economic conditions deteriorated. Most indebted nations have suffered economic and social degradation, civil war and the spread of previously unknown diseases. Poor people in countries whose commodities lost value would often turn to the export of drugs like coca which appear to be more valued in the West than say, coffee or cocoa. Poor country governments have stripped hardwood timber forests to raise hard currency to pay debts, thereby damaging the environment further.

High levels of indebtedness led in effect to insolvency, even though there is no recognition in international financial law of insolvency by a sovereign government. However, *de facto* insolvency exists, and can best be illustrated by the failure of sovereign governments to repay debts. In 1995, despite high and rising actual debt service, at least 43 per cent of scheduled repayments by sub-Saharan governments went unpaid.[20]

Such "non-performing loans" lead to breakdown in debtor/creditor relationships—and undermine the international lending system.

The Heavily Indebted Poor Country Initiative (HIPC)

Finally in the late 1990s creditors recognised that their own financial systems were being discredited. In 1996, in a historic agreement, a group of the most important creditors, the World Bank, the IMF and the Paris Club of bilateral creditors, agreed on a new initiative for writing off some of the debts of some of the poorest countries, the so-called Heavily Indebted Poor Country Initiative (HIPC).

The HIPC Initiative had a number of good points, as Professor Sir Hans Singer has pointed out.

"It was agreed at a time when special action was badly needed. It departs from the established habit of merely rescheduling debt, recognising the situation of insolvency in which many poor developing countries find themselves. It embraces the principle of debt cancellation... and thus implicitly accepts joint responsibility for the accumulated debt burden. It addresses the problem of multilateral debt... and there is some flexibility" in its application. Its weaknesses are that "debt stock reduction may only become applicable after six years... the process is long-winded and laborious... the criteria by which debt sustainability is judged are exclusively financial ones. They should be supplemented with development criteria... (its) still seen as too much of a concession by creditor countries, which impose conditions on relief."[21]

In practice, HIPC is not providing highly indebted countries with an exit from the burden of debt. At the time of going to press (July 1998) only six countries (Uganda, Bolivia, Cote d'Ivoires, Burkina Faso, Mozambique and Guyana) are expected to benefit (in other words to gain actual relief) from HIPC by the end of the year 2000. Benin will have to wait, as will Senegal, Mali, Guinea-Bissau, Ethiopia, Tanzania, Zambia, Nicaragua, Bangladesh, Vietnam, Laos—all highly indebted countries—all with clearly unsustainable debts.

At a meeting held at Lambeth Palace on the 28 July 1998, the British Chancellor expressed the hope that twenty countries "would have entered the HIPC process" by the year 2000. They can then expect to have a long period of conforming to IMF economic conditions, before obtaining relief.

So HIPC, as presently constituted, is not a sufficient mechanism for relief. We believe creditor nations, for the health of the world economy, for simple justice, and for their own self-interest need a much greater sense of urgency in dealing with the debt crisis.

Mozambique and Uganda are both countries that have had relief under HIPC. Mozambique is defined by the World Bank as the poorest country in the world. After protracted and difficult negotiations with creditors, including the Russian government, the Mozambique government will make a saving of US$13 million a year on debt service under HIPC. Instead of paying US$113 million in debt service, Mozambique will be paying US$100 million in debt service to her much richer creditors. Uganda, in contrast, saves only US$1 million per year—after HIPC. Before HIPC, average debt service between 1994/5 and 1996/7 was US$118 million per year. Between 1999 and the years 2002/3 debt service is due to fall to an average of US$117 million per year.[22]

So HIPC is not delivering relief. On the contrary it demonstrates that creditor nations lack any sense of urgency in attending to the crisis facing the poorest countries. This should not surprise us, as since the 1982 Mexico crisis creditors have balked at debt re-scheduling and debt cancellation.

Debt and Poverty

Highly indebted countries can only repay their debts at great human cost. This is because these countries are obliged by their creditors, or by pressure to raise capital in foreign markets, to prioritise debt repayment over expenditure on health, clean water and sanitation. By doing so, governments put the lives of their poorest people at risk.

While some governments may care little about the quality of life of their people, many would wish to concentrate spending on these areas of development. However their debts, and pressure from their creditors, means expenditure on infrastructure and development has to be subordinated to foreign debt repayment.

Debt, Democracy and Corruption

Once governments become deeply indebted, international financial creditors play a much larger part in the determination of government policy. Fragile democratic structures and accountability are undermined.

In countries led by dictators, it is invariably ordinary local people who eventually challenge and remove corrupt dictators. This happened in Zaire, in Indonesia, in Haiti, in the Philippines and in South Africa. However it is more difficult for the people of developing countries to challenge their corrupt leaders, if they receive financial backing from the West and from international financial institutions, like the IMF and World Bank. Some of the world's most corrupt leaders have also been recipients of large loans and substantial debt relief. Most notable amongst these are the recently deposed Presidents Suharto of Indonesia and Mobutu of Zaire.

These debts are regarded by many as "odious," an international legal doctrine first used by the US when it took Cuba from Spain at the turn of the century.[23] What many Bishops from countries with such debts have asserted is that it is particularly "odious" that the children of the new Philippines, or the new Democratic Republic of the Congo or of the new South Africa should be expected to pay the debts of previous corrupt regimes.

Lack of Discipline in International Lending

Unlike domestic creditors, international creditors are not subject to the discipline imposed by bankruptcy or insolvency statutes, which could subject them to losses. In the absence of international bankruptcy laws, a line cannot be drawn under debts, at a given point of indebtedness, and the debts brought to an end. Instead debts are allowed to grow inexorably. Because they are debts that have to be repaid in foreign currency, these debts increase when local currencies are devalued. The creditor's right to be repaid becomes paramount. When countries get into arrears, as many of the poorest do, then interest on unpaid debts is compounded. In any pyramid of creditors, the IMF and World Bank occupy the apex, as "preferred" creditors that must be repaid before all others. The IMF also acts, in effect, as a "gatekeeper" to international capital markets, denying access to funds if countries do not keep up with debt repayments, or if they fail fully to implement conditions such as IMF economic Structural Adjustment Programmes.

Under international financial relationships, creditors play a dominant role. They are both active in promoting lending, pre-eminent in setting conditions for the granting of such loans, and play a dominant role in determining whether debt relief should be granted, and on what terms. In particular creditors can insist on the appropriation of government resources for the repayments of debts, and for these repayments to take priority over other spending. In this respect they differ from domestic creditors, who are subject to the disciplines of an independent arbitrator or receiver. In international financial relations, creditors play the role of plaintiff, judge and jury in relation to loans and debts.

On the other hand, political leaders and government officials in developing countries have an in-built bias towards borrowing. This is because loans to governments have often to be repaid over much longer periods than a government official or politician can expect to remain in office. Loans are often agreed in secret, between local elites and international financial elites, and are seldom subject to public scrutiny. This absence of accountability to citizens of a country encourages corruption by both lenders and borrowers.

Lending as an Arm of Foreign Policy and Export Promotion

Western nations increasingly use taxpayer-subsidised lending as a way of encouraging poor countries to buy western exports. This export promotion helps maintain employment in western countries, and stabilises the balance of payments. In the increasingly competitive global market, loans, particularly subsidised (or concessional) loans, are a form of inducement to purchase one western export or project over another. Publicly supported Export Credit and Investment Insurance Agencies are supporting some US$432 billion in trade and investment, accounting for more than 10.4 per cent of world exports. Of this amount, over US$70 billion a year is for long-term loans and guarantees for investments and projects in developing countries. These often have significant adverse environmental and social impacts. Long-term loans from these agencies account for more than 20 per cent of developing country debt, and 37 per cent of developing country debt owed to official, publicly financed agencies. Ninety-five per cent of debts owed to the UK by developing countries is owed to the Export Credit Guarantee Department of the Department of Trade and Industry, similarly for Canada (74 per cent) and the US (50 per cent).[24]

Furthermore, unlike domestic creditors, international creditors can avoid the harmful effects of market forces. At the heart of the western system is the precondition that economic decisions must also carry financial risks. Where the link between economic decisions and risk is severed, economic efficiency, it is argued, is endangered. This link is often severed for international lenders, in particular the state-backed multilateral creditors, the IMF and World Bank. They take economic decisions, but the international financial framework protects them from the risk of losses on bad loans.

When bad lending decisions turn into major financial crises, as in Latin America in the 1980s, Mexico in 1995 and now in South East Asia, the IMF and

World Bank are brought under pressure by western governments, and by the threat of systemic financial breakdown, to bail out international lenders.

It is against this background that bad and often "odious" loans have been made by creditors, that bad debts have been accumulated by unwise borrowers, and that losses and costs have been transferred to many of the poorest taxpayers and citizens in the poorest countries.

Examples

PHILIPPINES

The Philippines' debt provides an example of loans made to support a western ally, and to promote western projects and exports.

The Philippines now has a debt of US$41 billion and was expected to pay nearly US$6 billion in debt service (interest plus principal repayments) in 1996. Two-thirds of this debt—US$27 billion—was lent to the Philippines during the Marcos dictatorship. It is estimated that Ferdinand Marcos and his wife Imelda pocketed one-third of the entire borrowing of the country during the period of his rule. The World Bank estimated the loss to the country as US$2.5 billion per year during this era. Marcos's personal wealth when he was overthrown was estimated at US$10 billion.

Western banks, international financial agencies such as the World Bank, and Western "aid" agencies all lent massively to the Philippines under Marcos, despite saying publicly that the regime was corrupt and was siphoning off huge commissions and kick-backs into foreign bank accounts. Nearly 10 per cent of the Marcos debt is accounted for by a single project—a nuclear reactor built by the US company Westinghouse on a site of a volcano, against the advice of local people.

There is a moral issue here. The children of the Philippines, who were not even born when Marcos was in power, cannot be asked to repay money lent to the Marcos family to be squandered. This was immoral and "odious" lending. It is the lending agencies—not the children of the Philippines—who must bear the moral and financial responsibility for scandalous and immoral lending.

There is another important moral issue here. What lesson do we teach? If the banks, aid agencies and international financial institutions are allowed to enforce the collection of loans made to "odious" and corrupt dictators like Marcos, we will never again be able to argue for morality in lending. However if these loans are declared "odious" and invalid, this sets a precedent which will govern future lending—that the lender must oversee what the recipient does with the money, and if the people who must ultimately repay the loan agree with the way that money is being used.

Mozambique

Mozambique is an example of the role that creditors play in showering a country with loans and in imposing conditions for the repayment of loans (Mozambique has been implementing IMF programmes for more than ten years).

Under the HIPC Initiative (Heavily Indebted Poor Countries), the international community has cancelled substantial amounts of Mozambican debt. Yet ordinary Mozambicans gained nothing. What went wrong?

The answer is that international creditors only cancelled debts which Mozambique would never pay anyway. According to the International Monetary Fund, Mozambique paid US$113 million per year in debt service before HIPC and will pay US$100 million per year after HIPC.

Of course, Mozambique is grateful for this saving of US$13 million per year, but it is not enough. Mozambique will still pay as much in debt service as it spends on health and education. Mozambique will still spend more than 5 per cent of its GDP on debt service, at a time when it has one of the highest rates of maternal and child mortality in the world. The introduction of primary education for all children has had to be delayed due to lack of money. According to estimates from the United Nations Development Programme (UNDP), if half the debt service was cancelled and the money applied to health and education, it would save the lives each year of 115,000 children and of 6,000 mothers who now die while giving birth.

Finally, it must be asked why Mozambique has this debt. Nearly all was incurred during the 1980s, when Mozambique was in the midst of a civil war, with parties supported by the Soviet Union and the South African government. These loans were given in "solidarity" by the old Soviet Union to help Mozambique government survive the onslaught of a rebel army supported by the apartheid regime and its allies. The Civil War devastated the economy and one million Mozambicans were killed. It is now over, but Mozambicans are still paying the price—in the lives of the mothers and babies who die (Mozambique has one of the highest maternal and infant mortality rates in the world) because the government is obliged by creditors to divert resources from health care and sanitation into debt repayment.

What Will It Cost?

Total low-income-country debt is US$540 billion, but because some of that is concessional[25] it is necessary to define that debt in terms of its net present value[26] of around US$410 billion. In practice, Jubilee 2000 and other campaigns are not talking about all low income countries (e.g., China) receiving debt relief. They refer to "severely indebted low income countries" whose present value of debt is US$185 billion. Adding on the "moderately indebted low income countries" would take that to US$280 billion or (excluding India) US$210 billion.

So, we should recognise we are not calling for the complete cancellation of all the debt, but rather the unpayable amount, or that amount which can only be repaid at great cost to human life.

We should note that there is only an additional cost, if the debt which is cancelled would otherwise have been paid. This means reduction beyond existing arrangements and beyond the level defined by the World Bank as "sustainable."

Given the high level of uncertainty about the cost of existing arrangements, it is difficult to estimate precise costs. This probably would involve debt reduction of about US$100 billion or, if middle income countries like the Philippines, Jamaica and Peru are included, US$150 billion.

These numbers have to be placed in context. They are a small proportion of the total debt owed by developing countries in 1997—US$2.17 trillion.[27]

Compare these sums to the foreign exchange trades settled each day on the international currency markets—US$3.5 trillion. (Daily London *Financial Times*, forex trades.) Each day, developing countries transfer debt repayments to their creditors which amount to US$740 million. This is equivalent to 0.02 per cent of all foreign exchange transactions.

The sum of US$150 billion should also be compared to the sums paid in annual debt service. For example, in 1997, US$270 billion was paid by developing countries to creditors in richer nations.[28]

In the same year, developing countries received US$25 billion in aid. So for each US$1 received in aid, US$11 was sent back in the form of debt service.[29]

On the 27th of April 1998 "blue chip" shares on the London Stock Exchange fell in value by US$41 billion.[30]

This one-day fall would pay the debt service for all developing countries in two months.

Who Would Bear the Cost?

The cost of debt relief would be borne by three types of creditors: private creditors (commercial banks and public companies), governments (bilateral creditors) and multilateral banks (such as the World Bank, the IMF and the African Development Bank, which are owned jointly by a range of governments).

The issue of cost only comes to the fore if creditors can reasonably expect debts to be paid in the future. If there is no such expectation, then there is no cost to be compensated for. In cases of bilateral debt, taxpayers have already borne the cost of loans when their funds were used to underwrite loans and compensate lenders.[31]

In many cases private banks have already made provision for expected losses, and in some countries have received, or can expect to receive, tax relief on these losses. The true value of sovereign government debt can sometimes be determined by the international debt markets, where poor countries' debts may be traded. Often the value of these debts is discounted to around 10 per cent or so of the nominal value.

Multilateral creditors could raise funds to finance their expected losses on future debt service in a number of ways. First by drawing on the net income (profits) of their lending. As these sums could otherwise be used for future lending to developing countries, there is some resistance to this proposal. Secondly, they could appeal for taxpayer funds to be made available bilaterally by member governments. Thirdly, the IMF could draw on the sale of IMF gold reserves to fund part of the cost. This proposal was made in 1996 by the British Chancellor of the Exchequer, but strongly resisted by Germany and her allies on the board of the IMF. At the time gold was valued on international markets at US$400 per ounce. Today the price is in the region of US$250 per ounce. Hundreds of millions, if not billions, of dollars that could have been used for debt relief have been lost by that decision. Sale of IMF gold at today's prices (July 1998) could raise US$25 billion.

Conclusion

The proposal to write off those debts whose repayment can only be guaranteed at great cost to human life is a humane proposal, intended to give the children of developing nations a future. While there may be costs to creditors in the North, they should be balanced by the following benefits.

First, poorer countries would be in a stronger position to attract investment and to trade. This would benefit those in the North who have lost markets in countries which have become degraded by high levels of debt.

Second, by lifting countries out of the mire of endless international debt repayments, there will be a chance to stop the drain of resources to unproductive purposes and to restore economic stability to the poorest countries. This in turn will enable countries to emerge from the social chaos and civil war that so often follows economic disintegration.

Third, social and economic degradation is a direct cause of the displacement of whole peoples to neighbouring countries and further afield. The restoration of economic stability is known to attract people back to the country of their birth, to their homes and communities.

Fourth, it is well known that countries desperate to raise hard currency to pay off international debts are forced to exploit their environment for this purpose. Hardwood forests are stripped, land is over-used and the effect is damaging to the environment as a whole.

Finally, the production and export of drugs is often the most lucrative source of income for people of the poorest countries. Debt cancellation would restore some economic stability to the poorest countries and offer them the opportunity to diversify trade and increase opportunities for their people.

All these benefits accrue to people in both the North and South and should be seen alongside the potential costs of our proposal.

Notes

1. Lambeth Report 1988, p. 159, para. 20.
2. Max Oelshlaeger, *Caring for Creation* (New Haven: Yale University Press, 1994).
3. Address by Sir Crispin Tickell, Lambeth Conference, Religion and the Environment, University of Kent at Canterbury, 29 July 1998.
4. Jonathan Porritt, *Seeing Green* (London: Blackwell, 1984).
5. Roger Coleman, ed., *Resolutions of the Twelve Lambeth Conferences* (Toronto: Anglican Book Centre, 1992).
6. Quoted from a Christian Ecology Link Seminar, October 1996.
7. James Nash, *Loving Nature: Ecological Integrity and Christian Responsibility* (Nashville: Abingdon Press, 1991).
8. "Apostolic Constitutions in Louis Bouyer's *Eucharist,* Notre Dame 1968," quoted in Andrew Linzey and Dan Cohn-Sherbok, *After Noah* (London: Mowbray, 1997).
9. *See* J. Habgood, "A Sacramental Approach" in Charles Birch (ed.) *Liberating Life: Contemporary Approaches to Ecological Theology* (Maryknoll: Orbis, 1990).
10. George Mathew at Lambeth XIII.
11. Gerard Manley Hopkins, *God's Grandeur.*
12. *An Examination of the Theological Principles Affecting the Homosexual Debate,* St. Andrew's Day Statement, 1995.
13. Arnold Toynbee, *The World and the West.*
14. Jeremy Rifkin, *The Biotech Century: Harnessing the Gene & Remaking the World* (New York: Putnam, Jeremy Taucher, 1998).
15. Committee on Medical Ethics, Episcopal Diocese of Washington, D.C., *Assisted Suicide and Euthanasia: Christian Moral Perspectives* (The Washington Report) (Harrisburg, Pennsylvania: Morehouse Publishing, 1997).
16. "If Africa's export prices had kept pace with import prices since 1980, African governments could have repaid all their debts one and a half times over."

World Bank, African Development Indicators, 1997, p. 87. From Adrian Lovett, *Chains Around Africa* April 1998, published by the Jubilee 2000 Coalition, UK.

17. The deteriorating terms of trade of the poorest nations have benefited those in the industrial countries as importers. They have been one element in helping to reduce and contain inflation.

18. Known as the "multilateral financial institutions" because they are funded and backed by a range of governments. "Bilateral financial institutions" are individual government financial institutions.

19. Loans offered at lower interest rates than current market interest rates, with longer repayment periods and longer periods of "grace."

20. World Bank, *Global Development Finance* 1998.

21. "Debt Relief for the Heavily Indebted Poor Countries: the HIPC Initiative" in *Proclaim Liberty—Reflections on Theology and Debt,* produced by Christian Aid, for the Lambeth Conference July 1998.

22. *See* correspondence between the IMF and Jubilee 2000 Coalition UK, June 1998. *See also* Joseph Hanlon, "HIPC Heresies and the Flat Earth Response," *Jubilee 2000 Coalition,* April, 1998. *See also* IMF World Bank, *Uganda HIPC Completion Point Document,* 20 March 1998.

23. The US argued that Cuba's debts were not the island's responsibility. They had, Washington insisted, been "created by the government of Spain, for its own purposes and through its own agents, in whose creation Cuba had no voice." Moreover the US insisted that the borrowed funds had been spent in ways contrary to Cuba's interest. The debts were never assumed by Cuba or the US, nor did their holders collect fully on their claims. (*See* Patricia Adams, "Odious Debts—loose lending, corruption and two thirds world environmental legacy," *Earthscan,* 1991.)

24. Michael G. Kuhn et al., *Officially Supported Export Credits—Recent Developments and Prospects* (IMF: March 1995). *See also* EURODAD Creditor Profiles, to be published in *Taking Stock of Debt,* September 1998.

25. Low cost loans, offered at lower interest and over longer repayment periods than market rates.

26. The present value is the amount of money the debtor would need to have in a bank account accumulating interest at the market rate, such that all the debt service payments due could be met by that account, and the final payment would reduce the balance of that account to exactly zero.

27. World Bank, *Global Development Finance,* 1998.

28. Ibid.

29. Ibid.

30. London *Independent,* 28 April 1998.

31. *See* Mick Hillyard, *Third World Debt Cancellation and Its Effect on the UK Exchequer.* (London: House of Commons Library, Summer 1997), p. 22. "Overall there is no effect on public spending totals, the Public Sector Borrowing Requirement, or the UK Exchequer when unpayable debt, on which there is no prospect of receiving payment of principal, is cancelled. The adverse effect on UK public finances occurred when the debts were created. In short, the Exchequer cost has already been paid."

Called to Live and Proclaim the Good News
Section II Report

Introduction

God has spoken to us and challenged us. We try here to share what we have heard him and each other saying.

Four major challenges have confronted us and form the burden of our report.

First, God is calling us at this moment. God is working in the world today quite beyond the limits of our budgets, structures and expectations. The gospel has the power to transform our individual and corporate lives, our families, communities and nations. It has the power to break beyond our timidity, insufficiency and aspirations.

Second, since the last Lambeth Conference, the greatest single new force shaping the world in which we do mission is the globalisation of the market economy. This is bringing rapid change. The groups most affected by these changes yet least equipped to deal with them are our children and young people. They live in a world where nothing is certain. They are offered only opinions, not truth. Among the most visible effects of this globalisation is the flight to the cities of people absorbed into the market culture.

Third, the globalisation of the market economy is threatening the identity and life of nations and communities. They often respond with the aggressive assertion of national and religious identity. In many countries this brings increased pressure on and persecution to Christian and other religious minorities.

Fourth, increased mobility in our world has brought people of different faiths and cultures to live side by side. This presents Christians with the challenge of affirming such plurality and remaining faithful to the distinctiveness of the Gospel.

We need and want to support each other in mission in the world today. Current structures of support derived from an earlier era for different tasks are proving inadequate. We have begun the process of providing such support in new and direct ways.

We have considered how to respond to these challenges by considering:

Sub-Section One	God's Call to Mission
Sub-Section Two	The Church as God's Partner in Mission
Sub-Section Three	The World God Loves
Sub-Section Four	The Missionary Congregation
Sub-Section Five	The Missionary Diocese
Sub-Section Six	Being a Missionary Bishop in a Missionary Church
Sub-Section Seven	How to Support Each Other in Mission
Sub-Section Eight	Resources for Mission

Editorial Introduction

The Section has received and approved the text of the report. Groups in the Section identified important stories from among those that they shared during their time together to be included as enrichment material. These are included as separate items, set apart from the regular text.

Sub-Section 1
God's Call to Mission

Mission goes out from God. Mission is God's way of loving and saving the world.

God calls his creatures to a future greater than they could ever make for themselves. From the beginning of the Biblical record, the voice of God is active, provoking human beings to move, change, and recognise who they are and what—by God's help—they can become. The very name of the church, *ecclesia,* means a community that has been summoned, not one that chooses to bring itself into being. *Ecclesia* is a word whose roots are in the secular world of the Greek and Roman Empires. Within the Roman Empire, *ecclesia* meant "a group of free citizens gathered to deliberate" and those who were to seek the welfare of their neighbours. It was a political and social concept. The early Christians, with the authority of Jesus Christ as their inspiration, believed themselves to be "free citizens" of a new order, an emerging, coming Kingdom. *Ecclesia* also means called out and called together; so Christians perceive themselves summoned and chosen by God. This ought to affect our worship, our evangelism and our response to the social, political and economic realities.

But the deeper we go into the meaning of God's call as it is recorded for us, the more we see that it tells us something of what God is. God does not simply call; God sends. God expresses and makes real the call to us in the lives, in the historical reality, of particular persons touched by God. The 'call' of Moses or of Isaiah is more than just a summons to be with God or to live by God's laws. It is a sending to others. The life of the prophet must itself become a message.

And at the climax of biblical history, 'God sent his Son.' God's very being—beyond the world and its history—is involved in an act of sending. And God the Son, God the Word, appears on earth, his whole existence being a mission: all that he is, is what God speaks and gives; he is God moving towards us, God's voice made into a human life. As he draws human beings around him in trust and friendship, he equips them in turn to call and communicate through the gift of his own vital reality—through his Holy Spirit.

God's Ears

Twelve people of different shapes and sizes, different colours and cultures and languages came together and began to talk, not with the Bible or with prayer, but with their own stories: what was good for them, what was difficult or hurtful or worrying, what they needed prayer over, what it was like to live where they lived. And they all listened carefully to one another. And bit by bit, they brought in the Scriptures, and made connections.

And even though it's only ten days later—because you will have guessed, I'm talking about here, about Lambeth—I have to say I think some healing and some hope has begun to be generated, certainly in myself, and I sense it in you.

I think that in the listening has been the Lord. And I go away with it, back to Tasmania, and it is going to be very important to me, what we've done for each other, and full of hope. A study of twelve people—it's a very interesting number.

Our calling is from God the Father, the source of everything. God calls us out of darkness into the Kingdom of his Son and sends us out in the power of the Holy Spirit to live and proclaim the Good News of the Kingdom. Our call and our sending do not depend on our resources or lack of them. All are called and all are sent.

The Church, as one body, holy in communion, catholic in pilgrimage and apostolic in proclamation, is called to worship and witness. To offer "spiritual sacrifices acceptable to God through Jesus Christ" (1 Peter 2:5); that is our worship, the sacrifice of persons (Rom. 12:1), the sacrifice of praise (Heb. 13:15) and the sacrifice of possessions (Heb. 13:16). To "declare the wonderful deeds of him who called you out of darkness into his marvellous light" (1 Peter 2:9).

Witness is people telling the story in word and deed of their experience of the liberating power of the Good News of God in Jesus Christ. In our report many bishops bear witness of the wonderful work of God among their people. Worship and witness, both in the power of the Holy Spirit, are the two most vital functions of the Christian Church.

We believe in a God who is completely engaged in mission and whose very life is a movement outwards, giving and sharing divine life and joy. One of the most distinctive things about Christian faith is that we believe in a God who has undertaken a mission from all eternity.

So mission is never our invention or choice. It has always started already. We have been caught up in God's own movement of love by being called to be with Jesus. To be with or 'in' Jesus is never to enjoy some static or private relationship with him; it is to be moving with him from the heart of God to the ends of the earth. "As the Father has sent me, so I send you," says Jesus. And just as being sent lies at the centre of who Jesus is, so it lies at the heart of who we are as Christians.

The Doors of Heaven

After the last of our white bishops made the last of his trips to see us just before he died, the village catechist said that the doors of heaven were going to open and close around him for the last time and then no one else would get in. The few remaining non-Christians quickly sought baptism.

This is mass conversion, and the motives are dubious. But the acceptance is there. And I believe the Holy Spirit can purify the motives. You, come and visit us in Melanesia! Send us your missionaries so our people can hear again: it's not colour that matters, but the liberating love of God.

Two things follow. Mission is not an option for Christians; it is simply part of being in Christ. And mission and evangelism are not two things but one: to be sent is to carry transforming life—the Good News. It is to be alive with the life of Jesus, which communicates both grace and truth. Sharing good news is always the goal and focus of the Christian's journey with Jesus Christ. As the Archbishop of Canterbury said to the Anglican Communion's Global Conference on Dynamic Evangelism Beyond 2000 (Mid-point Review of the Decade of Evangelism in the Communion):

> Mission which does not have evangelism as a focus is not Christian mission, and evangelism which keeps itself aloof from matters of

> justice and human welfare does not reflect adequately the biblical revelation. We must insist on the seamless character of mission and evangelism.[1]

What exactly is the Good News? It is that God's everlasting will is that we should share God's divine joy. This will is so strong and faithful that God is always free to forgive our sin, overcome our slavery and create for us a new beginning. And this news comes to us through the life of Jesus, through his death (in which he bears the consequences of our sin for us) and through his resurrection, which demonstrates that the divine will can bring life out of death (2 Cor. 4:7–12; 5:16–21). It is for us to respond to the invitation God gives us in Jesus. We hear and receive it when we are touched by the Holy Spirit. It is, therefore, never just information but a movement into new possibilities of living with God, with ourselves, with each other and with the rest of creation.

Since baptism is the beginning of our journey with Christ, mission is to be the concern of all the baptised. The Great Commission of Matthew 28 to baptise and make disciples is not given to a few specialists, but to all who were gathered in the presence of the risen Christ. The whole Church, the *ecclesia*, the assembly summoned by God, is sent with and in Christ, in the power of Christ's resurrection. This is why we must think very hard indeed about how all God's people are to be equipped for mission. The people of God are equipped principally by the gifts of the Holy Spirit and there is renewed awareness today of their depth and power in the life of the church. One implication worth noting is that Christian mission is always a mutual service within the Church as well as outreach beyond it; it cannot ever be identified simply with the flow of agenda and resources from the privileged to the underprivileged.

If being baptised means being drawn into God's own act of mission, then that divine mission is going on in all of us constantly. The more we let this divine action through, in our plans, our words and acts, the more it will achieve its purpose. God's Word does not return empty; it accomplishes its purpose. So we can say with Paul that the One who calls is faithful, and that the One who calls equips us with what we need; and we can rely on the promise of Jesus as he sends his followers on his business, that he will be with them always.

Scripture read in the context of our lives is a place where we expect to encounter a God who calls. In the community of those called to walk with Jesus, the call is constantly renewed by exposure to the Bible. Churches that are really on the move, throughout the world, are churches listening gratefully and joyfully to Scripture. Here the voice of God, made real in the history of the people of Israel and the life of Jesus and the witness of the early communities of believers, becomes immediate to us. We discover afresh that we are already objects of God's mission even before we know we are subjects or agents. We remember that God's mission has been on its way to us since before the world was made. Mission demands faithfulness to the Bible as a living challenge, and as a promise of transformation.

Sub-Section 2
The Church as God's Partner in Mission

We welcome and have been stimulated by the theology of mission presented by Missio (the Anglican Communion Mission Commission) in 1996 in 'Sing a New Song.' We have built on it as we share our understanding of the Church as God's Partner in Mission.

A Transforming Church

God is moving in history right now. As always, such movement requires the eyes of the discerning and the ears of the listening. Our Communion is called as part of the universal Church to be a sign of God's presence and grace-full activity among the nations. To be a sign of 'the Kingdom come on earth as it is in heaven,' (Matt. 6:10) we need to 'set our hearts on God's Kingdom first, and his saving justice' (Matt. 6:33). Such a sign requires not only a theology of abundant grace, but also one that demonstrates a communal ethic of the re-distribution of wealth and the practice of Jubilee. 'Unlike our society, the Gospels see sin and debt as fundamentally inter-related.'[2]

We must pay increasing attention to culture and mission developing 'a more integrated understanding of the relationship between justice and the Gospel and show awareness of the reality of structural sin as well as personal sin.'[3]

We cannot absolve ourselves from the vision of social and economic justice that the prophets, the Saviour and the apostles announced.

The task of mission has at its heart the recognition that the earth is the Lord's; the task is the transformation of the life, not only of individuals, but also of society, nations and the created order (cf. John 10:10).

The Cost of Taxis

Where I live in the Province of Southern Africa, we have had taxi wars: huge mini-bus operations, lethally competitive and responsible for much bloodshed including innocent bystanders and passengers—thirty-six people killed in the latter half of 1997 alone. Nobody could intervene. Politicians had tried, parties had tried, government had tried. Damage mounted.

The church leaders decided it was time they tried. Through personal contacts, they brought the various executive members of the rival associations together in the City Hall on December 16, 1997. It was tense. We waited for them. They were late.

We insisted that we start with prayer. There followed a sermon—very powerful. We then broke them into small groups, with questions to respond to concerning God's word. Hours passed. At last the executives came out, and this is what they said: "We believe God's word to us this morning is that we must seek peace."

Of course it was a long hard haul. But on December 24 an agreement was signed, with structures in place for arbitration. One executive stood up. "The reason this has worked is that God's Word and God's leaders were in it." God can speak into situations of conflict. God brings life out of death. Thanks be to God.

Effective mission entails a clear witness to the presence of God in all creation and the responsibility of the human race as a steward of the created order. This is especially important in the present century with its all-too-frequent abuses of natural resources and other living creatures in our world. All our work in evangelism must include this theme: in Christ the possibility is given of a right relationship to the whole creation; in Christ we are called to seek justice for all creation.

Such transformation does not come without cost. For many within the Communion, following the example of Jesus has meant laying down life because of the sins of the world. God's love for the world, revealed in the self-giving, sacrificial death of Christ, continues to be enacted today, and for the sake of the world we are invited to walk the way of the Christ of the Cross. The Scriptures provide us with abundant evidence that God's purpose is the redemption of the world through our Lord Jesus Christ. Scriptures therefore challenge us to live and work so that the just and compassionate reign of God will be the common experience of all humanity. In the face of the challenge which the Risen Lord has set before her, the Church must change under the Holy Spirit's power so as to become:

A Church Rooted in Community

The first Christians marked their commitment by locating in the community as well as being community. They were called out of the world but not removed from it: redemptively immersed in and aware of the agony and pain that characterise a fallen world, but not moulded by it. While in that state of redemptive witness or *marturia*, 'they were looked up to by everyone' as they were learning and worshipping together where the grace of the Holy Spirit was visible in their prayer and praise. They practised benevolence, sharing their goods with the needy, breaking bread together, and undertaking their daily tasks with joy and patience, striving not to be anxious about tomorrow. It was the discipline of this common courtesy and gracious behaviour that marked them out as people having something worth embracing, so that 'day by day the Lord added to their community' (cf. Acts 2:42–47). The Spirit of God, who gives gifts to God's people to offer in the service of God and each other, has called the Church to such a life since she is the agent for reaching the world with the life and love of God.

The Church we long to see is therefore a network of worshipping communities, both great and small, which are rooted in context, living out God's vocation to live in love (John: 15:12–17), seeking the welfare of all God's people irrespective of racial or cultural differences, and living in forgiveness and generosity in the spirit of Jubilee (Lev. 25, Luke 4:18–19).

We look for episcopal and diocesan structures to take the form of a servant, focused on local communities of faith, and broad in vision. They will facilitate the witness of a world-wide communion to the unity of the Godhead in their own oneness in Spirit, while celebrating their enriching diversity and catholicity.

The Head of the Body

They tried to stop my enthronement as bishop. This is in western Kenya. They tried to scare me off with threats, with letters to the police, they chased the people from the church where they were getting ready for the service, they brought petrol, they set fire to it, they told their men, "Come back with his head!" But you see I'm not headless.

The congregation called me, said, "It's very, very bad here; don't come." But I said, "If it's bad, that's where the bishop should be. I'm coming; don't leave." I didn't tell my wife the whole phone message!

The man who called for my head was running to jump on their pick-up truck, he slipped, fell, and died there, just like that! I got there, we prayed in the church and I said, "React to nothing, but be still and see what the Lord is going to do for us."

A Church of Jubilee

Private wealth, meritocracy, the temptation to centralised power together with debt slavery are documented in the Bible in both testaments. Alongside the betrayal of the most vulnerable, the poor and excluded lies a prophetic tradition which criticises national political and religious leadership which allows such iniquity and sets forth a Sabbath or Jubilee vision of social and economic justice. Such a vision was seen as central to Israel's identity as chosen people, and became integral to Jesus' own proclamation of Sabbath, "the year of the Lord's favour"(Luke 4:18–19; cf. Isa. 61:1–2). It is significant that Luke records this text from Isaiah as the one by which Jesus both defines and inaugurates his mission in his first sermon.

By so defining his mission, Jesus exposes (both through parable and miracle) the centrality of Jubilee and seeks its practice as a continuous reality in the Kingdom of God, loosed from the legalism of the fiftieth year. We may reflect that Jesus' primary confrontations were with those who had the power to release from debt, and who refused so to do. If we are to avoid spiritualising the 'Good News for the poor' then it must reflect actual debt cancellation and the return of property and persons to their rightful place.

Jubilee was practised, albeit infrequently, and the prophets, notably Isaiah (3:14–15), Hosea (2:5) and Amos (8:5–6), were chief among the critics when the nation's leadership resisted and refused so to do. Both Jeremiah and Ezekiel indicate some practice of Jubilee, albeit intermittent. Jeremiah criticises one of the kings for reneging on his Jubilee commitment (Jer. 34:14–16). Ezekiel holds the vision of Jubilee economics and re-distribution. (Ezek. 45:7–8; 46:17–18; 47:13–23)

Cut to the Quick

It was how the missionaries lived and worked, sacrificially and humbly: that was what converted. My own father was converted from animism—the African traditional religions—to Christianity in a way that was very similar to what I'm going to tell you.

A missionary was cleaning a very bad sore on a woman, and the scissors he used slipped and hurt her. She slapped him. She was just reacting to the pain. He didn't get mad; he apologized to her. The head chief was there, watching. He said, "You! You European. You have been telling us stories of Jesus, how he lived, what he did, you said thousands of years ago. You didn't tell us you are this Jesus!" The missionary said, "No, no! I'm not Jesus. I've simply come to tell you of him. We try to be as like him as we can, and to do what he did when he came."

It's the life lived that is the language of mission. My own father knows.

The New Testament pictures examples of the re-distribution of wealth and the return of lands, not just in the stories of Jesus, but the actions of notable disciples Levi (Luke 5:27–31) and Zacchaeus (Luke 19:1–10). By following Jesus, the fishermen made an economic choice to leave behind one of the staples of living in a peasant society 'house, family or fields'—for nets! (Mark 1:18–20; Luke 5:28; Mark 10:29–30).

It is easy to dismiss as heroic idealism the practice of Sabbath or Jubilee economics in the early church (Acts 2:45; 4.35), or St. Paul's plea in 2 Corinthians to work for communities in which 'those who had much did not have too much; and those who had little did not have too little' (2 Cor. 8:14–15). However, the challenge to the Communion comes as starkly as the question posed to Jesus by the disciples, 'Who, then, can be saved?' (Mark 10:26). Imagining a world in which those who have resources share in such a way that St. Paul's minimalist position is met, requires the practice of *koinonia* on a scale so far unimagined. Only one reality is more unimaginable: a world in which there are no rich and poor. Jesus had such an imagination. When the disciples expressed their incredulity as we do ours, his response was stark and simple—'By human resources it is impossible, but not for God: because for God everything is possible' (Mark 10:27).

We long for a church that will live in the spirit of Jubilee—the *now* of the 'acceptable year of the Lord'. We will work for a Church that sees the Gospel as embracing all things, including economics. We will commit ourselves afresh to being a Church that brings healing to a wounded humanity, speaking, acting for and being in solidarity with the vulnerable and excluded. We shall promote the spirit of Jubilee by working for the cancellation of unrepayable debt of the world's poorest nations by the year 2000, and for the freeing of all prisoners of conscience. We shall commit ourselves to becoming a transforming church through repentance of our failure to practise Jubilee, and to seek a future in which such practice is integral to the whole life of our Communion in its mission in and to the world.

Furthermore, we suggest that the churches of the Communion be strongly encouraged to set aside a regular proportion of their income for mission, as a witness to the importance of sharing resources for the sake of the Kingdom of God. Evidence from history shows that the power for mission is more than economic power but that our giving can be a measure of our commitment to God's mission.

A Revitalised Church Living in the Simplicity of God's Love

Ours is a Trinitarian faith: We believe in God as Father, Son and Holy Spirit, one God in Three Persons, who in the eternal communion of his love creates, recreates and transforms us. We are a community of the baptised, called to faith and hope. We are to shine as lights in the world to the glory of God, preparing the way for God's order of freedom and love to be revealed among us.

Any vision of the future of Christian mission within the Anglican Communion needs to hold at its centre the simplicity of God's gift of love, which is given to be shared. Our vision of mission must offer the profound hope that the chief end of humanity is to give glory to God and to enjoy God forever. Mission is love, the supreme fulfilment of the new commandment (John 13:34, 35).

However, our structures rarely provide an environment of loving joy which transforms people and the communities or neighbourhoods in which they live. Our prayer and vision is for a revitalised Church which, in witness and communion, is a true sign of God's Kingdom in context: celebrating God's faithfulness; rooted in biblical faith; dynamic in mission and evangelism; creative and joyful in worship; caring in fellowship; generous in giving for mission; committed to social transformation through transformed people.

We recognise that to be revitalised in this way, our Church will need in many places to change its way of being Church, change attitudes, and welcome and nurture people. All this implies 'transformation.'

Conversion Factors

'When I preach, when I break open the Gospel for the people of our great city of New York, I never fail to be surprised at how I re-convert myself.'

'We've lived for almost thirty years with the killings in Northern Ireland. A woman let her husband out of the car in their farmyard, he took a few paces, and was gunned down by the Republican Army. He'd been a church warden. After the funeral, the woman decided she'd continue his work as church warden. Her fidelity to her faith despite what she'd seen has had a tremendous effect on the parish and the locality. I meet her often.'

'Do you remember the film of the life of Jesus? We had it dubbed in Swahili. One of our women came up to me after. "Bishop!" she said. "I didn't know Jesus wasn't a white man! But he was speaking our language. I saw the words coming from his mouth!"'

Personal Transformation

What sort of people must we be in order to be part of such a community? We need to meet the risen Lord Jesus in repentance and faith, continually turning to him and away from the ever-present calls to self-love. By turning to Christ we find our true identity as children of God and our true calling as servants of God and one another. This is true freedom, in Christ, from sin and the power of evil.

This is full humanity, as members of his Body, indwelt by his Spirit. As we have turned to Christ and call others so to do, we are all being transformed from one degree of glory to another, and we are turned to the world God sent his Son to save.

Sub-Section 3
The World God Loves

The world God loves is a world of diverse cultures in which many religions are active. These present various challenges to which the church is to proclaim Good News. We identify four in particular: globalisation and urbanisation, children and youth, religious pluralism, and communication.

Globalisation and Urbanisation

Our concern for mission and evangelism has made us aware that whereas the most rapid growth of our church is in the rural areas of the developing world, the most urgent challenge to Christian belief and belonging is to be found in the cities. By the year 2000, over 50 per cent of the world's population will be living in cities. The number of cities with populations of more than 13 million is growing. The real challenge to Christian mission in the twenty-first century will be that of urban mission.

The urbanisation of the world's population is a consequence of globalisation. Globalisation is itself being given both power and shape by the triumph of late twentieth century liberal capitalism with its consequence of a global market and a parallel revolution in communication technology. The development of ever faster and increasingly sophisticated means of transferring information and assets has contributed to a consolidation of the power of the market and turning all aspects of human life into commodities to be sold.

However, we do not say that urbanisation and globalisation are wrong in themselves, or can or should be resisted. We recognise that throughout human history it is in cities that human societies and cultures have expressed their highest aspirations and celebrated their greatest cultural achievements. We are mindful too that the Book of Revelation sees human destiny fulfilled in a city—the New Jerusalem.

We *do* say that both urbanisation and globalisation are now out of control and are failing more and more human beings and human communities. They are in danger of destroying the very idea of the city, where all have a place, where the majority can find fulfilment, and where a society's cultural and spiritual achievements can be celebrated. The sight of children picking over the rubbish tips of Buenos Aires and Mumbai (Bombay), whilst the rich of those cities lock themselves into their fortified ghettos for protection, are graphic reminders of the increasing failure of our cities. The recent flight of capital from countries in South East Asia, with the consequent collapse of their economies, and the devastating effects of the poorest nations of the world struggling to service unrepayable debts, are symptomatic of uncontrollable globalisation.

One of the characteristics of urbanisation is the loss of community. People secure themselves from outsiders by their housing arrangements. Residential areas are simply dormitories. Life is lived at the workplace or in recreational areas. People have become 'displaced' persons who are essentially rootless; their places of living are marginal to their places of meaning.

The groups most influenced by these changes, and least equipped to deal with them, are our children and young people. To them we now turn.

Stations of the Bus

I wanted it to be fun. I wanted to have a bus. I'm bishop of a large episcopal area in West London short of resources for mission. I very much wanted to do mission, but already our clergy are fewer than our 107 churches and I didn't want to ask the parishes for any more support. So I went to the deaneries and prayed with them, praying for inspiration—and for mission funds. On the second occasion, a woman I'd never met came up to me and said, "I'll buy the bus," and she did: a double-decker.

We call it the Mission Bus. Down its side is painted "2000 Years since What? "—our bit towards reclaiming the birth of our Saviour in the imagination of the world, and in this case, the children in the schools. For the bus goes into the schools, and me with it, holding parties on the bus, celebrating Jesus with music, drama, dance, balloons and badges, and on the upper level is our final station: Resurrection. We all end up experiencing resurrection.

Children and Young People

The encounter with young people is an experience of cross-cultural mission within our societies and our churches. As we review past reports, we note a constant call to understand, recognise, include and change our churches in response to the concerns of young people. Each generation of bishops faces a new challenge of a new youth culture. This is one way in which societies and churches renew themselves. We were the youth of the 50s and 60s.

But the rate of change in youth culture is becoming ever more rapid. We have found helpful the notion that in culture we live both in a background (what can be taken for granted) and a foreground (what requires current choice). Young people live with little background and a large foreground—they take little for granted. In the foreground today we see the myths of the market telling us that self-fulfilment, self-gratification and self-development are our highest goals. In many traditional societies the culture's name for God is being forgotten in modernising, urban cultures. The church must address this foreground of fantasy with the eternal reality of the Kingdom of God. But our struggle is to discern when the Kingdom of God may affirm and embrace changes in cultures and express gospel values in inculturation, and when the Kingdom of God would show a better way. We need the help of Christian young people in exercising this discernment. Such discernment will be critical for evangelism in the youth culture.

Youth culture is now a global culture. Because of the wide use of electronic communication, they are often called the 'connected generation.' Youth culture is marked by African rhythms, Asian symbols, and a sense of solidarity with the environment and recognition of the immensity of the cosmos. Young people in many parts of our world are also at great risk from violence, prostitution, drugs, pornography and demonic powers. And there is a new facet to youth. While Christians in Africa have grown from 60 million to 330 million since the end of the colonial era in 1960, over half the population of some African countries is now under sixteen. In Latin America most of the members of churches are under forty. For many of us, youth are our nation and Christian youth are our Church.

Young people can be enthusiastic and caring, but like people of all ages they can also be rash and judgmental. In some cultures, Christian young people may be isolated from the mainstream of their peers. As such, they can find themselves struggling to survive in an alien context.

The concept of youth and youth culture is itself a fairly recent creation. While we need to attend to youth culture, we must do so informed by biblical perspectives. We must bring to youth culture a critique from our biblical perspective. The Bible speaks both about God's call to young people and the wisdom he offers them (Samuel, Mary, Timothy). The Bible also speaks about God's infinite care for children. (Deut. 24:17, 27:19; Matt. 18:6). It would direct our attention, then, to ministry to children as the indispensable pre-requisite for ministry to young people. Many of our problems with young people are the fruit of our neglect of children.

Concern for children is an authenticating mark of the Church. "The Kingdom of God belongs to them." It is right that every child should have the chance to discover that they have a loving heavenly Father. To deny that possibility is a type of abuse. Work with children can help create that proper childlikeness in the Christian community for which Christ called.

The Bubble Boy

A young man who is a priest in our diocese, Chilean-born, son of a miner, was eight years old when he reached the breaking point watching the fights between his mother and drunken father. He ran out of the house and called upon God to give him a way out. He was led to a church, was converted, and later on was instrumental in bringing his whole family to God.

At twenty, he emigrated to the USA with a diagnosis of leukemia. He was given a 25 per cent chance of survival. He went to Los Angeles with his sister; he was an illegal immigrant—but he worked anyway, any menial job he could get, and his health suffered the more. Two years later, he got the chance of a bone marrow transplant operation. He stayed one year in a bubble, and survived. He's a composer and a guitar player. In the bubble, he could listen to music. He began composing again—so many beautiful songs, praise songs.

He heard a call to the ministry after his ordeal. He entered a programme with the Lutheran Church, won his accreditation while working to support himself, was brought to our diocese and was ordained deacon, and is a tremendous testimony to the healing power of the Lord. He is a man full of joy, and of compassion for the poor. His congregation is growing by leaps and bounds. It's a wonderful thing to see how the Lord raises up young people today, calls them to discipleship, calls them to ministry—and empowers them to do it.

If this concern is to be translated into action, there will need to be a significant change in the attitudes and priorities in many congregations and among many church leaders. All too often, children's work is seen to be a low priority, and many of those who work amongst children feel discouragingly unaffirmed. And yet the truth is that in many congregations the majority of their members have come to faith or made significant steps on their faith journeys before the age of thirteen.

Christian parents look to the churches for help with the formation of their children. They must not look in vain. However, we need to look beyond our congregations also. In many places there is the opportunity to reach out with the Gospel to the children of the wider community. In nominal Christian cultures, non-churchgoing parents often positively welcome such ministry from the churches and seek out church schools for the education of their children.

We are aware that many societies are properly concerned that their children should be protected from abuse and manipulation. Children's evangelism does not have to be, indeed must not be, manipulative. The best examples of children's evangelism known to us always seek the involvement and support of parents. Evangelism among children is essentially an exercise in introducing them to the story of Jesus Christ and to the community that seeks to live out that story.

Leaders of Good Cheer

They're called the Ascension Eagles. They are cheerleaders. This is very much a 'foreground' example of mission. They're all from a very poor area in East London. Their leader is the wife of one of our priests; she comes from America. She found the girls tremendously interested in cheerleading from what they'd seen on television and films. The girls are very proud to be the Ascension Eagles, and they are very proud to be coming to the Lambeth Conference. It's been one way of bringing young people together.

But the point is that they recently performed at a major Christian service at Coventry Cathedral, and this is what I noticed: they were very professional in their presentation, but the group that followed them was in some ways a rather sad little group from another inner-city church. The Ascension Eagles, for all their own professionalism, were cheering on this second-rate little group for all they were worth. It was such generosity! And I saw in that a sign of the grace of God.

Last Easter, they were asked to compete on Easter Sunday. They said no. They were begged. They prayed about it, and decided they would accept on condition that they were allowed to conduct Easter worship on site. They put it all together themselves, and two other whole teams of competitors, with their parents, joined them in the arena. We're not certain yet how many of them will come to be committed Christians, but I see it as a major initiative in bringing inner-city young people together in the mission of the Church, and I'm excited by it. And as a bishop I want to encourage it.

We need to remember that there are plenty of others who have no scruples about seeking to influence the minds and affections of children. In some parts of the world, children are drawn into fighting for revolutionary causes, in others children are drawn into prostitution, while increasingly our globalised, secular and materialistic culture seduces the minds of us all. Millions of children around the world have access to television, videos and even the Internet. If churches fail to teach children about a loving heavenly Father, revealed in Jesus Christ, other values will flood into their lives. We do not live in value-neutral societies anywhere in our world.

At Lambeth we heard of many cases where work amongst children is seriously hampered for lack of committed helpers. There can surely be no more noble a calling than to help young lives step out on the Christian pilgrimage. Ministry among children is not about 'babysitting' so that adults can worship. God not only works in children; he can and does work through children. It is indeed true that God has ordained that his praises shall come from the mouths of the very young.

Evangelism among young people can often seem to be a higher priority than that amongst children. The problems and evidence of alienation from the Gospel may seem more stark. We cannot help wondering, however, whether these problems and challenges are more serious because the Churches failed those young people much earlier in the years of their own childhood.

The True Church Strong and Free

I do want it to be known that we perceive ourselves in the Dominican Republic as being the recipient, with other Protestant Churches, of a certain level of persecution. Our church is open to all who want to come. Unfortunately, that sometimes means people baptised in the Roman Catholic Church who have ceased to have any links with their mother church. We are then accused of stealing parishioners, but we don't proselytise.

The local Roman priest puts up signs in the supermarket saying, "The Anglican Church is a false church. It is not valid." The Cardinal replies to my letter of protest with, "I am told some of your people pretend to be Roman Catholic priests."

I assure him this is not so. But we are, I'm afraid, quite a missionary diocese. Our work thrives. We are one of the most active in the Caribbean. What are we to do?

Evangelism among children—especially among the many accessible but unchurched children—is likely to be more effective if conducted at peer-group level. Some churches in the United States have established parallel 'children's churches.' Others speak of the value of children's Christian clubs linked to schools as well as churches, and to weeknights as opposed to Sunday activities. Again we were told of the value of Holiday Clubs and summer camps as enjoyable formats where children were imaginatively introduced to the Good News. Clearly, great thought must be given to how such children can experience a sense of belonging to the whole people of God. This proper concern, however, must not deter us from seeking to reach out to those many children who are open to us and to the Good News that we have to share.

There is as much the need to demonstrate the love of God to children as there is to talk of it. Increasingly children are the victims of civil wars, family breakdowns, and the effects of prostitution. HIV/AIDS is affecting not only young people, but creating a generation of orphans whose parents have died of AIDS. The tragic phenomenon of 'street children' is to be found in many cities. We do well to remember the sternness of our Lord's words concerning those who allow his 'little ones' to suffer. There is a need for the abandoned children of our world to find compassion and practical help offered in the name of Christ.

Religious Pluralism

The increasing connectedness of the world is bringing closer contact between people of different religions. Religion is often presented as a cause of conflict. So secular media and others teach children and young people that religion is only a matter of opinion, not truth. How may we Christians, committed to truth, combine witness and hospitality to people of Other Faiths?

Dialogue

The word 'dialogue' expresses well the kind of positive and open attitude to Other Faiths which has been widely accepted in recent Christian writing on this subject. It is understood as one mode of mission alongside other modes such as service, proclamation and witness. But the word has certain limitations:

- It tends to be associated with formal dialogue for specialists at a more academic and intellectual level. But we would not normally refer to a conversation between two neighbours as 'dialogue.'

- Some people associate it with a view of Other Faiths which discourages evangelism. So an unhelpful polarisation develops between 'mission and evangelism' on the one hand and 'dialogue' on the other, apparently incompatible approaches.

- Dialogue becomes unnatural and one-sided when one party takes all the initiatives and the other is reluctant or unwilling to join in. We are frequently told, for example, that Muslims are not generally interested in dialogue.

- When Christians live under governments that seem openly hostile to the Christian community, much of their energy is spent on the struggle for survival. Some bishops asked, 'How can you have dialogue with people who are trying to wipe you out?'

- In some situations dialogue has not worked. In the Sudan it is claimed that the Christian Kingdoms of Meroe and Axun were able to resist the spread of Islam to the south for a considerable length of time, but then gradually came under Muslim control after beginning to enter into dialogue with the Muslims.

In spite of all the limitations in the word, we want to affirm our commitment to dialogue because it expresses a readiness to listen to followers of Other Faiths in a friendly spirit. It does not rule out witness and proclamation, but is an important element in the mission of the Church. Bishop Michael Nazir-Ali's Conference paper "Embassy, Hospitality and Dialogue: Christians and People of Other Faiths" (cf. Interfaith Report, Lambeth 1998) explores the historical, theological and biblical basis for this understanding of dialogue. What it is likely to mean in practice in different situations, however, is worked out in greater detail in the remainder of this section of the report. Many of the examples come from the Muslim world because of the particular focus on Muslim-Christian relations at the Conference.

Thirty Theses on Christian Responses to People of Other Faiths

In what follows we have sought to expand the four principles of dialogue which were published by the WCC in 1979 and commended by the Lambeth Conference in 1988 (Resolution 20, p. 218) into a fuller statement which covers basic attitudes, relationships, theology, practical responses and methods in mission, and finally calls for some immediate action. Because of the polarisation between different positions in discussions about Other Faiths, we have deliberately tried to use the words 'dialogue,' 'mission' and 'evangelism' as little as possible, and have tried to elaborate all that is valuable in the approaches with which these words are associated.

Boundless

A year after my consecration, the Archbishop of Canterbury was asked, by the Home Secretary, whether I would be willing to serve on a judicial inquiry into the matter arising from the racist, unprovoked murder of a black teenager, Stephen Lawrence, in South London—a murder whose perpetrators have never been brought to book. The British government wanted a black bishop who had good standing with the police and with the black community, although the murdered teenager was a Methodist.

So I attend public hearings four days a week and somehow see to my episcopal duties (by the sheer grace of God!) on the other three days. My role has been one of peace-maker—especially when the five suspects appeared before us—and reconciler and advocate for truth and justice, deeply rooted in community and the Gospel. I have come to realise the truth of the words of St. Francis to his friars: "Go and preach the Gospel to everyone—and use words if you must." The prayers of all Christians in England and especially my Christian community in Stepney, London, have been overwhelming.

The ministry of reconciliation is given to us as a way of living and proclaiming the Good News. But the cost in prayers and time has no bounds.

Basic Attitudes

1. *We must have a real desire to listen to people whose faith and world-view are different from ours.* Our haste in speaking often means that our words are not understood, and there is no real meeting of hearts and minds.

2. *Respect for the faith of others should not allow us to mock the beliefs and practices of others.* However much we disagree, we should resist the temptation to disparage convictions that are precious to others. There is no place for the kind of polemic which seeks to destroy the beliefs of others, or makes fun of their practices.

3. *We should be determined to believe the best about others.* This may mean, for example, recognising the differences between Islam at its best and the actions of particular Muslims, or challenging popular parodies of Buddhism. It may also mean a willingness to believe that others can change.

4. *We will want to recognise gladly all the common ground that we can find, and at the same time all the differences.* If we concentrate only on differences or insist on minimising differences, pretending that they do not exist, we cannot begin to understand each other.

5. *There needs to be a spirit of repentance which arises out of an awareness of the genuine wrongs and even crimes that Christians have committed in the past.* These have sometimes been the result of zeal and sometimes of cowardice. This should not indulge in feelings of guilt over our missionary past. Professor Lamin Sanneh of Yale University, in an overview of the history of Christian mission (particularly in the modern period), strongly argues that the overall effect of mission has been to affirm local cultures throughout the world. But because of the Christian contribution to anti-semitism, for example, and the practice of slavery, we need to be willing to say, 'Both we and our fathers have sinned' (Ps. 106:6).

6. *We need to recover the right kind of confidence in the message of the gospel.* This will not be a brash or proud arrogance, but a humble recognition that there is something distinctive about the message concerning Jesus for people of all faiths, and it will spring at its best from a spontaneous desire to share what we know of Christ. The Apostle Peter and the early Christians in a situation of real difficulty prayed for boldness, courage and confidence (*parresia*); and Paul asked others to pray that he might 'fearlessly make known (*parresiasomai*) the mystery of the Gospel' (Eph. 6:19–20). Perhaps Christians today, especially in the West, need to pray in similar terms!

Relationships

7. *Christians need to work as far as possible for genuinely open and loving human relationships with people of Other Faiths.* This call will inevitably sound unrealistic to Christians who are suffering at the hands of others. In situations where tensions of these kinds do not exist, it should hardly be necessary to make such a statement. But differences of race, culture and belief often make it difficult for Christians to establish warm and natural relationships with people of Other Faiths. There can sometimes be similarities with the kind of relations that existed between Jews and Samaritans at the time of Christ: 'Jews do not associate with Samaritans' (John 4:9).

On the Rock

One of our priests in the Sudan had a problem when he came to the point of completing the call of his vocation to the priesthood. His marriage was breaking up! He and his wife had held their wedding in our church. It seemed a good marriage. They had three children. But then, Susan had an affair, and their life was on the rocks. This was a real problem for the Church. The bishop decided to have Susan and Samson attend a counselling and healing ministry. It worked. Susan had been ashamed of being the wife of a pastor! But she is willing to give it a go. They renewed their marriage vows, and have revitalised their life together as husband and wife. They have forgiven each other, that's the point, and are reconciled to God the Father, Son and Holy Spirit. All glory goes to Almighty God.

---

8. *Generalisations based on one situation cannot easily be applied in another, since political and social contexts vary so much from one part of the world to another.* We are told that Muslims behave in a particular way when they are in a minority, but in a completely different way when they are in the majority. This is probably also true of Christians! There are significant differences between the three regions of Nigeria, and these situations are very different from those in North America

and Europe. We therefore need to understand the special dynamic which affects relationships between different faith communities in our own situation, and at the same time recognise the enormous diversity in other situations. We need the humility to be challenged and informed by the experience of the Body of Christ in other parts of the world.

9. *Christians need to be willing and able to talk about anything that is of interest and concern to people of Other Faiths (the dialogue of life!).* It is a mistake to think that Christians should always be talking about what they believe. We may be able to communicate more about our world-view by talking about issues in everyday life than by talking about religious subjects. While some are good at talking about dialogue, others are better at actually practising it!

10. *Even in situations where dialogue seems impossible, there should be a real desire for face-to-face meeting, frank exchange of opinion and peace-making.* A Northern Nigerian bishop believes that in his difficult situation the alternatives to dialogue are far more frightening: "If we don't engage in dialogue, we will eat each other up." A Pakistani bishop says that "no matter how difficult the situation is, dialogue is the only way."

11. *The way religious communities relate to each other in one part of the world can have immediate and far-reaching effects on communities in other parts of the world.* The protest of Muslims in Bradford to Salman Rushdie's *The Satanic Verses* had serious consequences in Islamabad. Muslims of Birmingham, England, fear that before long they could be treated as badly as Muslims of Bosnia. Because we live in a global village with instant electronic communication, conflict in one context can quickly create conflict in another.

12. *In the context of genuine relationships, it is entirely natural for Christians to share their deepest convictions.* If a Christian is not offended by a devout Hindu who speaks about his/her way of life, the Hindu probably expects Christians to speak in the same way. If shyness in speaking about faith is a part of Western culture, it is not so common in the rest of the world. People of Other Faiths often do not understand the reluctance of Western Christians to speak about their faith.

Theology

13. *The content of the Christian message is likely to focus on the person of Christ.* Some Christians speak of the 'uniqueness of Christ' or the 'normative' nature of his being and work, while others speak of the 'distinctiveness' or the 'finality' of Christ. In each of these phrases Christians are attempting to articulate their conviction that in Jesus Christ God's love for humankind is fully revealed. But Christian convictions about the divinity of Christ also have to do with belief in Christ as the incarnation of God's eternal Word and Wisdom, and many

Christians have spoken of how Other Faiths have received some vision of this Word and Wisdom. Our imperative is not only to take the Good News of Christ to those who have never heard it, but also to seek to show how Christ, the Desire of all nations, can be recognised by them as the fullness of what has been glimpsed.

14. *Our approaches to people of Other Faiths are likely to be influenced profoundly by our understanding of salvation.* Because of convictions about how God works within the religions of the world, some are critical of the idea of mission to people of Other Faiths; some reject it completely. Others may affirm the appropriateness of mission among people of Other Faiths, but differ radically in their views about the need and urgency for taking initiatives to make Christ known, and about how mission should be carried out. The diversity of views among Anglicans on this issue needs to be recognised with frankness, since it frequently affects decisions about what mission should mean in practice.

The Cost of Mission

In Algeria there were two branches to the Worker Youth Movement. A young lady who was a leader among the youth there was a Muslim, but in the movement she discovered Christ and wanted to become Christian. She applied for baptism. The assistant for Action Catholique was wracked with indecision. If she converts, he thought, she will be perceived as a traitor by her people, the people she now leads. And she will cease to lead them, and that will be a great loss of a force for good here. And he applied to his Cardinal—a great man, much loved of the Algerian people, though he was a Frenchman, and there was war.

This good man gave sober thought and prayer to the problem. He came to the same conclusion: that the girl would lose her leadership ability, and be perceived as a traitor to Algeria into the bargain. Now this was before Vatican II. What he asked of that young woman was this: that she renounce baptism, for the good of the people—that she live on the outside of the faith she loved and that that should be her cross.

This is the cost of mission: this is the way of the cross.

Practical Responses

15. *Christians need to know more about Other Faiths and to develop an understanding of them.* Far too many Christians are ignorant about the faith and life of their neighbours. This ignorance breeds fear, prejudice and misunderstanding.

Empathy with people of Other Faiths does not mean agreeing with them or compromising one's Christian convictions, but leads to a more genuine human relationship and to mutual understanding, enabling both parties to communicate more faithfully what they believe and what they feel. It is important that Christians appreciate the difference between the beliefs and practices of Other Faiths at their best and at their worst and learn not to compare the best in their own tradition with the worst in the other. Not everything that Muslims do can be attributed to Islam!

16. *Christians will want to seek the total well-being of others.* They should see people of Other Faiths as neighbours to be loved (Luke 10:27), and should have a wholistic approach which addresses the community as much as the individual, and the material and physical as much as the spiritual. On the basis of such an approach to the Muslim community in Bradford, the bishop is able to say, "We seek to commend our faith by our care and love and concern. In the name of Christ we declare the love God has for you."

17. *Christians should be willing to work as far as possible in co-operation with people of Other Faiths in addressing human concerns and working for justice, human rights, and the environment.* For example, in working for conservation of the environment with indigenous peoples in Australia, Christians find that they are dealing with deeply-held religious beliefs about the natural world. Christians and Muslims have worked side by side in the struggle against apartheid in South Africa. We believe that in many of the issues addressed in Section I (Called to Full Humanity), Christians can and should be seeking to work as closely as possible with other faith communities.

The Gift of the Wise Men

Some years ago, a group of church leaders in Israel/Palestine had a meeting with Yasir Arafat, the head of the PLO. They thought they should give him a gift, and they decided on a presentation copy of the Qur'an. And to their surprise, instead of welcoming it, he scolded them. "What are you doing giving me a copy of the Qur'an?" he said. "These are my scriptures. Why did you not give me your scriptures? " And one of the bishops who was in that group said to a friend of mine afterwards, "He shamed us."

---

18. *Situations where Christians feel that there is no prospect of co-existence call for special attitudes of patience and perseverance.* In the Sudan some Christians have felt that there is no alternative to joining the armed struggle. Where this is rejected, there still are other options, including service to the community through institutions like hospitals and schools, finding allies within the country who have some sympathy for the Christian community, and entering into dialogue with

the government through the National Council of Churches. When none of these options is open, the local church can still by its presence and worship be an oasis in what appears to be a desert. And martyrdom, far from being the end of the road, can be a means of grace. Christians should know from the history of the Church right up to the present time that "the blood of the martyrs is the seed of the Church."

19. *Christians must be prepared to engage in advocacy on behalf of fellow Christians in difficult situations.* The visits of the Archbishop of Canterbury to the Sudan and Pakistan in recent years have brought enormous encouragement to the Christian communities in these countries, not only through the visits themselves, but also through continuing relationships with governments and religious leaders.

20. *Churches in situations where these difficulties do not exist have a special obligation to support suffering churches in other parts of the world.* "If one member suffers, the whole body suffers" (1 Cor. 12:26). Support through prayer and encouragement often needs to be expressed also in practical and economic assistance.

21. *Many of the most difficult issues in inter-faith relations today are caused by the rise of 'fundamentalisms' of different kinds.* The term 'fundamentalism' was first used in a Christian context in North America in the early twentieth century, but has now come to be used to describe a complex phenomenon which has emerged in recent years in the context of several other world religions, especially Judaism, Islam, Hinduism and Sikhism. These different 'fundamentalisms' represent responses to a wide variety of causes, including resentment over past colonialism and continuing economic and cultural imperialism; protest against corrupt regimes; millennial hopes in situations of economic hardship; disillusionment with the failures of capitalism and socialism; and the search for cultural, religious and national identity in the face of globalisation and modernity. Christians need to appreciate the complexity of these different causes and understand how the 'fundamentalist' faces of the different faiths should be related to the 'ideal' and historical expressions of the different faiths.

22. *Christians must be able and willing to present the Gospel in ways that are culturally appropriate.* Working in the context of Other Faiths and cultures demands special attention to the issues involved in inculturation or contextualization. The advice of Pope Gregory the Great, who wrote a manual about the bishop's teaching and pastoral office, to Augustine of Canterbury, himself a missionary bishop in a missionary diocese, was not to destroy all the artifacts and practices of pagan religion, but to transform at least some of them by giving them a Christian content. This approach provides a clear example of a serious attempt to find appropriate ways of enabling the Gospel to take root in a particular cultural context and can still be applied today in working with primal religions.

23. *We cannot avoid the difficulties associated with people of Other Faiths becoming disciples of Christ and accepting baptism.* It is possible to argue that the Qur'an itself

does not require the death penalty for apostates. The reality is, however, that in many parts of the world Muslim communities and their leaders frequently act on the assumption that Islamic theology and tradition require capital punishment for those who convert to another faith. One bishop says frankly that in his situation 'conversion spells death.'

24. *There are situations where clear pastoral guidance is needed by Christian congregations.* In many countries, for example, Christian girls are advised not to marry Muslims, while in others clergy do not feel they can be so directive. In many countries there are expectations and requests that Christians will join with people of Other Faiths in some kind of worship on civic occasions or at times of national celebration, remembrance or mourning.

Methods

25. *In many situations Christians feel that they can and should appeal to the principle of reciprocity.* This does not mean a kind of 'tit for tat' response which says 'We will treat you badly here because people of your community treat us badly there'. Rather it is an attempt to put into practice the Golden Rule "do to others what you would have them do to you" (Matt. 7:12). Because of his involvement with the Muslim community in Bradford the bishop believes he can say, "In the name of God, we seek to care for you here in Bradford. Can you join with us in caring for the Christian minority in Pakistan? We are caring for your rights here. Can you care for the rights of Christians in Pakistan?" In some situations, however, Christians have reservations about appealing to the principle of reciprocity, since it could mean that if Muslims can demonstrate that they are treated unjustly in Europe, they have no obligation to support the cause of Christians elsewhere. And good, open relationships cannot be built on the basis of any kind of bargaining.

26. *Christians want to make Christ known and give others the opportunity of following him.* They are not 'seeking to convert' or 'in the business of conversion' in the sense that their sole aim is to make the other person change his/her belief. They should not be concerned about 'the game of numbers.' Generally, however, they will want to share with others what is most precious to themselves, wanting for all people a clearer understanding of the Christian Gospel. The Apostle Paul expresses this genuine desire to communicate the faith in the words: "Since... we know what it is to fear the Lord, we try to persuade others... We are... Christ's ambassadors, as though God were making his appeal through us—we implore you on Christ's behalf: Be reconciled to God" (2 Cor. 5:11, 20). This kind of desire, however, must be distinguished sharply from 'proselytising.'

27. *The word 'proselytising' refers to seeking to make converts by methods that are not appropriate.* We believe that methods which are not appropriate for Christians include bullying or manipulation; using of material resources to win converts;

seeking to win converts who will be carbon copies of ourselves or of our form of Christianity; misusing power and privilege; and targeting vulnerable individuals or groups in insensitive ways. Some are calling for an agreed 'Code of Conduct' which rules out methods of these kinds which should not be used either by Christians or by other faith communities.

'Uncles and Aunties'

When we look around in our churches in Rwanda, two-thirds of the congregation are younger people. That's on Sundays. This has been a challenge to the Church—how to nurture these young people. At the end of the day, when you look at registrations for weddings in the church, you see maybe two or three people are celebrating their marriages in the church. You have this paradox: you see many young people coming to the church, but few of them are having a traditional Christian marriage.

So as a response to this challenge to the Church, we see being developed a kind of 'uncle and auntie' approach which we have borrowed from our culture. We have a list of uncles and aunties, and they meet young people every Tuesday of every week, and one Saturday a month. This has led to a kind of outreach to people in the town and the rural area. We have outreach which has embraced street children. The results are there: two of the street children are now members of our choir. The results are the offspring of the uncles-aunties approach which is proving so fruitful in our Church.

---

28. *An ecumenical approach is needed in developing our response to people of Other Faiths.* Anglicans need to work closely with other Christian communities in developing their theology of religions and exploring appropriate action in different situations. The Pontifical Council for Inter-Religious Dialogue, for example, in its document Dialogue and Proclamation (1992), called the church to "witness and the dialogue of salvation" with all men and women, insisting that dialogue does not constitute the whole mission of the church, and that it cannot replace proclamation. Similarly the World Council of Churches at its sixth Assembly in 1983 appealed for both witness and dialogue, adding that dialogue is not a device for Christian witness nor a denial of Christian witness.

We turn then to consider how we may communicate the Good News in our urbanized, young and religiously plural world.

Immediate Needs

29. *We need to find the most appropriate structures to facilitate the sharing of news, information, ideas and resources relating to inter-faith concerns.* It is hoped that the

Lambeth Conference will recognise the potential of the ACC's Network for Inter-Faith Concerns (NIFCON) to meet this need.

30. *In addition to the kind of sharing we propose, there may be a need to find ways of developing specific strategies throughout the Communion.* We trust that all bishops will find particular means by which they can lead their churches in mission in these areas, both at diocesan and provincial levels.

The Challenges of Communication

How can we make our voices heard above the Babel of sounds in our cities and on our media? This is increasingly important when locality is not where people's lives are lived. They live in a "virtual" community, held together by newspapers, television, electronic communication and transport. These are the modern sinews of public society.

How can we speak a language of the people? Should we formulate our faith in more Buddhist or Islamic terms according to the context? Or should we use non-religious terms? How may we convey the experience behind the language?

How do we make our voice heard when it disturbs society; when the channels of communication are controlled by the rich who do not like a faith which proposes changes in society but prefer an individual Christianity in a secular paradigm; when the messages of the media get direct to our members and draw them away to the sound of a different drum?

These are the questions that perplex us. But we know that the most effective communication of the Gospel is a local congregation that believes and practices it. Local congregations exist in a vast number of human communities, and mean the Churches of all denominations are recognised as the largest NGO on earth. To the calling of the congregation we therefore turn.

Sub-Section 4
The Missionary Congregation

It is completely clear to us that the local congregation is the fundamental unit for the proclamation of the Gospel, the discipling and nurturing of believers and the service of the community. For it to do its work well, it may well need to work in cells or small community groups. The touchstone by which all other activity in the wider church is measured is whether it is perceived as supporting and encouraging the local congregation in mission.

We refer to a "missionary" congregation. We recognise that the term "missionary" carries negative connotations for some. But we want to recover the sense that each congregation, diocese and bishop is called by God to mission, and find good precedents in the bold use of the term by missionary dioceses in Nigeria and England.

Congregations in some areas may not be based on locality. People who work in a particular section such as business, finance or education may form small cells or communities in their work place, or come together to address particular fields of concern such as the ethics of a multinational company.

As the gospel is set forth by communities of faith and individuals:

- in the witness of their lives;
- in the proclaiming and preaching of the word; and
- in acts of loving service and mercy, men, women and children, by God's grace, come to repentance and faith in Jesus Christ.

An essential part of finding new life in Christ is:

- becoming part of a community of faith;
- receiving nurture and teaching;
- learning to pray and worship; and
- becoming involved in service and witness.

The church into which Christians come is to be a welcoming, loving, praying, serving community. The Christian community must be built up and placed at the service of God in the world he loves. Pastoral care is itself an evangelistic tool. Baptisms, marriages and funerals are important evangelistic opportunities in many situations. In some situations pastoral care needs to extend beyond the community of the faithful to attend to the needs of the excluded and marginalised.

We urge a renewed emphasis on the implications of our baptismal covenant. To achieve this, we need to commit ourselves to:

- renewal of worship to be lively and accessible;
- renewal of regular personal prayer;
- building confidence among the laity to tell their own story and share responsibility with bishops and clergy; and

- developing vocations for all forms of ministry, including the ordained ministry.

Spitoon Chaplain

In Singapore we had a prison chaplain who did wonders. I thought of him when we read Paul together this morning: "Therefore I am content with weakness, insults, hardships, persecutions and calamities." And so I shared it with the group, and they suggested I tell it.

Every day this chaplain would pass the cell of a particular hard-core criminal; every day he would say, "John, the Lord Jesus loves you, and I love you." Every day the prisoner would spit in his face. The chaplain would stop, wipe the spittle from his glasses, his face, and walk on. Every day the same, day after day. Until one day, the prisoner was in great trouble, and he called for the chaplain.

The chaplain was fetched. "What's wrong with you?" John shrieked. "Are you crazy? Every time I spit at you, it's the same words! 'The Lord Jesus loves you, and I love you.' And you don't get mad. Are you crazy?"

This was the opportunity the chaplain had waited for. Bit by bit he opened the Gospel to John, and bit by bit John committed his life to the Lord. He studied theology in prison, got ordained when he left, and became a pastor, first in Singapore, then in America. When the old chaplain died, he came over for the funeral. He hugged the coffin and wept. "This man gave his life for me. This man was like the Lord."

This means there must be:

Ministry to the flock of Christ:

- pastoring, nurturing, praying and praising;
- teaching, training, equipping;
- administering gifts and resources; and
- organising, presiding and leading.

Mission to the broken world of which we are a part—in the five marks of mission as identified in our communion:

- to proclaim the Good News of the Kingdom;
- to teach, baptise and nurture new believers (incorporating them into the body of Christ);
- to respond to human need by loving service;
- to seek to transform the unjust structures of society; and
- to strive to safeguard the integrity of creation and sustain and renew the life of earth.

While we are firm in our commitment to the local congregation, that does not make us congregational. We recognise the many pressures, particularly in western society, to develop congregational autonomy. The surrounding culture of selfishness and "what's in it for me" conspires with an unbiblical overemphasis on the local church to produce congregations who lack any sense of communion or responsibility with other congregations in their locality (ecumenism), their diocese, or other parts of the world. Local congregations become wealthy while the means of connecting them with others are starved of resources.

The Congregation's Worship and Reading of Scripture

The congregation's life is to be wrapped up in and flow out of prayer and the worship of God, who calls us and gives us life, and to whom all glory and praise is given. This life is especially nourished by our study of scripture, which is the source of our strength and our impulse to mission.

Our daily life and service, our engagement in the world so that it may be transformed in solidarity with God's justice and love, our personal prayer and the liturgy of the Church are all together our worship—they are our offering of love to the God of life.

In liturgy, the work of the people is the moment of revelation, which reveals to us God present in the world and in our lives, above all in the body. There is an embodied character of worship, God-given, whose active memory needs to be recovered where it is lost. God in Christ reveals the pattern of reality for us; the order of the world is shaped by the dying and rising of Christ.

Lacrima Christi

People tend to assume I have the most enviable position in the Anglican Communion, short of the Archbishop of Canterbury. That may be so: New York is a very complex, very exciting city, but it is as bewildering for me, sometimes, as it is for them. I find often that my ministry of evangelism to this great city is simply one of presence.

Some time ago I read in the newspaper, as I frequently do, that a child had been abused by a man who was the live-in partner of a woman. The child had been killed. The woman was a convert to the Pentecostal Church and had a very strong faith in God. I visited her high-rise apartment to speak with her, and as she described for me what had happened, she got hysterical and she cried out, "Where was God in all of this? How can I believe in such a God? "

How do you reply to that? What can satisfy the heart on that score? I didn't have an answer. My only response was to hold her, hold her and then turn away in my own grief. She looked at me, and I burst into tears. I said nothing.

I left, and after a few weeks made a few calls and then nothing happened. Several months later, she turned up at the Cathedral of St. John the Divine in New York City on Sunday when I was celebrating and preaching. After the service she came up to me, gave me a hug and said, "Do you remember me?" and I said no. And she repeated the incident of her child's death, and my visit. And then she said to me, "I had decided I could never continue to worship a God who had allowed such a tragedy in my life." And she said, "I was prepared to do that—until I asked you the question, 'Where was God in all of this?' And instead of giving me some glib answer, you simply held me, and you wept." And she said, "Nobody ever wept for me before. I knew those were tears of compassion and love. It transformed my life, and I'm here to tell you 'Thanks'."

So worship is integral to Christ's mission. We bring our stories, our experience of sin and desolation, of suffering and struggle, of grace and forgiveness, all that we have and all that we are, and we long for the Word of life that brings judgement and salvation. We offer ourselves not as we ought but as we are able through the work of Christ, and we anticipate the fulfillment of all things, above all in the hearing and proclaiming of the gospel, and in the sacraments, which are visible proclamations of the gospel message of Cross and resurrection, repentance and faith, echoed in our lives.

In all parts of the world, and from widely different contexts, we seek ways of speaking and symbols of celebrating that we are in right relationship with God and with one another. We are people in history, both corporate and personal. This means among many other things, that we have our own stories to tell, and the narratives of our communities. In telling our stories and in celebrating our narratives, we want to bring symbols of hurt and hope, which include histories and unreconciled memories to be redeemed by the continuing work of God in Christ. We are people within culture. We bring our languages, our song, our symbolism and art, that these too may serve the mission of God. We are people who long for the presence and mystery of God to transform the things of everyday life; our homes and families, our work, our social and political relations, that they may also bear witness to our hope.

These forms of the Christian narrative grow and change at the periphery, but their heart is set on the cross of Christ which is both historical event and eternal reality. As part of the Catholic church we live in communion with those who have gone before us in the faith—as well as those yet to come. Whatever its context, it is the work of worship to allow the offering of all of these to God whose grace gives us back our lives with Good News to proclaim in prophetic word and deed.

A Small Blessing

I sense that if we paid more attention to our mission and ministry of nurture in the faith to children, we would have less trouble with our youth ministries. This is a story of the potential of children. It moved me very deeply. I was attending a service in another diocese, not my own, and the pastor had asked the congregation to pray for each other. Out of nowhere, a little boy tugged at my jacket and asked me if there was anything I had for him to pray for. I said that as a matter of fact there was. I had knelt down to be near his face, and I told him of a problem in my own diocese—nothing this seven- or eight-year-old could know about.

With the most natural gesture in the world, this small boy reached out his hands and placed them on my shoulders. He prayed with great simplicity and concern. Oh, I was truly prayed for, truly blessed.

In all parts of the world, we see and affirm many common strands of renewal:

- among indigenous people in Paraguay, new ways of reading the Bible and building liturgy from the ground up;

- the emergence of young people and their music in liturgical leadership in the urban South American context;

- in Kenya, the development of liturgies of blessing of the home continuous with the history of the people and based on Scripture;

- in Europe, the rediscovery and re-valuing of the rich spiritual resources of our Christian tradition—in pilgrimage, in the benediction of God the Creator, in the Epiphany tradition of gift, in the sacramental understanding of hospitality;

- in Australia, the bringing of the experience of the people to the Bible, to seek out priorities for church and community in the twenty-first century; and

- in England, in a recovery of joy and thanksgiving in liturgy, and in a recovered emphasis on reconciliation and witness in the Peace and the Dismissal.

We see a continuing need:

- for the recovery of confession and absolution as a life-giving moment, both in helping us to examine our everyday lives in the light of the Gospel, and in hearing the word of grace that enables us to live as forgiven people;

- to resist the privatisation of spirituality in parts of the world where communities of belonging, e.g. family, neighbourhood or work, are rapidly fragmenting;

- to engage creatively with the Lectionary, by publishing resource material based on the common Lectionary to enable connections between the Sunday homily and the development of the Christian community, so that the theology and spirituality of the traditions of Anglicanism are not a chain to imprison us but a discipline to strengthen us;

- to connect the dedication of our pastoral work with Word and Sacrament; and

- to engage honestly and openly with the human need for touch as an expression of the Word made flesh, especially in contexts where past abuse and concealment have made this an issue of sensitivity.

We recognise that in mission and evangelism, we can only plant seeds, and that it is important to allow space and silence and patience for these to take root and grow; to wait faithfully upon the Lord.

We seek to encourage:

- the development of small groups of people as missionary communities, whose lifestyle, behaviour and reflection on scripture will lead to the transformation of both persons and communities;

- popular reading of scripture as a resource of the people rather than for the people, both in small groups and in personal Bible reading;

- the development of contextual theological education that includes community development and empowerment; and

- dialogue between popular and scientific modes of scriptural interpretation as one informs the other.

The Missionary Congregation and Reconciliation

Although globalisation has brought people together through technology and communication, people are still unable to live together as communities. The Church has to build bridges of reconciliation through mission and evangelism, reconcile people to God through Jesus Christ and people to people. The church has to live and be alive to preaching the Good News of the Prince of Peace when addressing tribalism, sectarianism, racism, discrimination, regionalism and war. We experience these both in the household of God and in society as a whole. The bishops, as chief teachers of the church, must lead a change of attitude within the Christian community by repentance, forgiveness and healing. We therefore recommend that the Anglican Communion strengthens its commitment to reconciliation as a major focus of its mission.

Abundance

This is about how, out of their sufferings, people are empowered to react positively as Christians. The world knows about the genocide in Rwanda in 1994. During the genocide, I was supposed to be killed. Many times over, they tried to take my life. Many times God made miracles and I survived. And God said to me, "Look here, you are alive, even your wife and children are alive." This was very unusual, to have the whole household survive, though of course my parents and brothers and sisters had been killed. And here I was, rethinking my vocation, and God was talking to me. "You are the father of the fatherless." That was clear. It was clear that my vocation was John 10:10—to bring life and bring it more abundantly. And it is what led me to help found a charity for orphans—the Archbishop of Canterbury visited it in 1995. We have 8000 orphans.

Our system is to try to find families for these orphans—not necessarily a man and a wife, we just need to see there's a grownup, capable of taking charge of these children. Then we assist the families. What we find is that there are people whose children have been killed, and we help them to answer evil with good, by taking in other children. And what we find is that in some cases, parents who have lost four children, say, would take in eight children! And they would love them! Their lives change; they are transformed. They are

> helped by helping. I tell the orphans even, to pray for their killers, the killers of their parents. And that helps in the process of reconciliation. I could have reacted differently, they could have reacted differently, all of us bitter and angry. But that's not what the scripture says. Abundant life is the teaching and the theme of our life.

A major area that remains unreconciled is our economic relations. The overwhelming, and in some cases unrepayable debt owed by poorer nations has turned out to be a form of economic slavery, which has had a crushing effect on the health, education and well-being of people living in poverty. The church recommends to governments and lending institutions that this debt be cancelled, with proper evaluation, policies and safeguards put in place which prevent the poor paying the price. Furthermore, government and lending institutions should guarantee national collateral to ensure that such cancellation is made with appropriate controls to give the poorest the best chance of improving their situations. Equity, fairness and representation are the best medicine against poverty and corruption. The critical question is who should make the decisions as to whether acceptable progress has been made in developing governance. The best answer is for them to form arbitration panels in each country and/or region of the judiciary, education, and community leaders and religious leaders and thus strengthen the 'civil society'. This would put in place a process of accountability. New loans should be made only to countries with democratic constitutions that guarantee the rights and welfare of the people. In national budgetary priorities military spending should not be given priority over economic and social welfare and the granting of loans. International debt is a complex economic dilemma.

The Anglican Communion needs to initiate:

- greater awareness as to the condition of the people carrying its burden;
- greater awareness of the circumstances of corruption and lack of safeguards in international development lending; and
- meetings of economists and secular leaders who are people of faith to negotiate and pursue practical and acceptable solutions and new initiatives.

Urban Churches

The processes of globalisation and urbanisation present two complementary tasks for mission and evangelism as we move into the twenty-first century. The first is to make the processes of globalisation and urbanisation work to the good of humanity where possible and resist them where necessary; to join with others to tame, humanise and redeem the processes, which are proving so destructive to human beings including the wealthy and the powerful. These processes are not serving the majority of citizens in every country, poor or wealthy. As part of setting up an urban mission network, we therefore envisage a sharing of how the church is collaborating with others in making the processes of urbanisation and globalisation serve humankind more effectively.

Soul Food

In my diocese in the Province of the Congo in Zaire, I leave home quite commonly for five or six months at a time. It takes me that long to get around my parishes. I don't have my own transport. So I sit at the side of the road and wait for an empty lorry. Often they're full. Sometimes I wait for five days before I get a lift. So I get to the next village. Sometimes they're waiting for me, and have been waiting for days. But sometimes they've had no word of my coming—we have little means of communication—and so I wait while they let people know I've arrived. They walk from 20 kilometres away. So I wait a long time.

Then we have a good long service, several hours. We don't eat much, one meal a day, maybe every other day. That's what there is. But this is evangelism in our diocese. We have big confirmations! I confirm up to 100, 150, 200 at a time. Our Bible study group here wanted me to tell you about this—my way of life.

This is a particular responsibility of the church in the wealthy nations. Part of urban mission must be to make the connections between the inordinate power of financial markets and the fundamental purpose of God for his creation. Many Christians in the industrial, commercial and financial world find little in common between their faith and the kinds of decisions they find themselves making in their working lives. This loss of connection needs to be addressed as part of what it means to proclaim Jesus Christ today.

The second task for mission and evangelism is to help, particularly the poor, the marginalised, and those who are the victims of the processes of globalisation and urbanisation to discover the grace, goodness, and new life to be found in the living God through Jesus Christ.

The processes of globalisation and urbanisation do not have the last word. The proclaiming of the Good News in the contexts of increasing urbanisation require first a prophetic challenge in the public arena of the human costs of this process. Cities have been places of rich culture and human fulfillment. Many urban residents now find their lives characterised by isolation, insecurity and frustration.

The Good News is first encountered in Christian congregations who celebrate their humanity within the story of Jesus Christ, communities which offer understanding, love, support and acceptance. Such congregations address, through thoughtful action, these issues which erode possibilities of human fulfilment.

The Good News becomes visible as congregations respond from the richness of the Gospel tradition to identified local issues of human community so that people can believe there is a future for them.

At the local level, the task of mission and evangelism is to create communities of memory, meaning, celebration and hope. Such communities were described thirteen years ago in the Church of England's report "Faith in the City" as being local (focused on the neighbourhood), outward- looking (serving the neighbourhood) and participating (collaborating with others in justice and service). There is growing evidence that this model is enabling the urban church "To Live and Proclaim the Good News" in ways that are welcomed by the disadvantaged.

The Good News has to attend to the rootlessness of people in our cities. Local congregations are not always able to do this. There is a social marginalisation of the Church in our urban cultures. Some of our urban churches need to develop involvement with the surrounding community. It is in the public arena in our cities that people derive their identity, source of meaning and value system. To do this we will need to address the Gospel more intentionally to displaced people in the public arena.

In an increasingly secularised society in Africa where people are being urbanised, with a consequent lack of corporate identity, i.e. family and tribe, the African concept of *Ubuntu*, which sees a person as a person in the full sense only in relation to others, provides the basis of a model. This concept of interdependence is at the heart of *koinonia*.

The task of addressing urban cultures is beyond the capacity of single congregations. It requires the collaboration of a number of local churches, Christian communities and agencies.

In an urban diocese in the USA the thrust in urban ministry has been to work to minimise the resources expended on buildings while at the same time maximising those resources for mission and evangelism.

Strategies include:

- bringing smaller congregations together which cannot support their buildings and developing a new congregation from their numbers (in some cases this means building a new, larger, more cost-effective church than any of their present ones);

- developing an area ministry to share the resources of all the churches in a geographical area for the expansion of mission; and
- establishing Community Development Corporations, owned by local churches, though incorporated separately, for the purpose of receiving governmental, corporate and foundation monies to expand mission and ministries.

We must learn from all these models as we face the challenge of urban mission and ministry in the new millennium, or else people living in the urban world will desert the Anglican Communion looking for a form of Christian faith or other faith which satisfies their longing for acceptance, wholeness and justice.

The Missionary Congregation, Children and Young People

We need transformation within our Anglican churches, to meet the challenge of young people. We need to create a sense of belonging in our churches for them; give them reasons for faith and hope by clear teaching and nurture, and engage in ministry partnership with young people, sharing with them our joy in the life of Christ.

Youth ministry already exists in our Communion and the Christian Churches all over the world. There is much diversity throughout our Communion. In some situations young people keep their links with the church, in others they are conspicuous by their absence. In parts of Africa young people remain committed Christians but move on to other denominations.

The Time of Trial

My diocese is in the capital city of Madagascar, which has four dioceses. I'm going to tell you the story of a young boy called Sedra—the name itself means 'trial,' which I trust is just a coincidence. Madagascar is very big; I'm not sure which part he came from. I do know there were four children in the family. The mother and her children did not and do not know where the father is. The woman had been married, but the husband had disappeared. No doubt he was still alive somewhere, probably with a new family.

The mother and her children never went to church; they had no church. But it happened that the children went to an Anglican school. There were some Scouts and Guides among the students. These Scouts and Guides were very gifted at getting in touch with new young people, befriending them, and they took Sedra under their wing. Slowly, they drew him into the Scouts at the Cathedral.

He really didn't know what to expect. He liked games, and singing, and learning skills. But the Scouts are a Christian affiliation, and it's the custom, besides all the other activities, to worship together, to have Bible studies together, to recite some prayers together. And Sedra had to do his duty in this. And when they go camping, they learn something very fundamental and deep about the Christian faith. Little by little, Sedra was receiving the faith, and becoming a Christian.

To round out the story, the mother, who'd never been to church in her life, is now a staunch member of the Mothers' Union and has three of her four children confirmed. The other is on the way. Sedra is now at military academy, and hopes to become an officer. He attracts others to the faith. This is how it works.

In the UK, young people often drift away from the church after their student years. But we have been heartened by stories and examples of effective work with young people and children in many parts of our Communion. Examples include new initiatives in community building among young people in England and Wales through out-of-school clubs and activities; contemporary worship in Nigeria and the Americas; and other situations where the church has prioritised the reaching of young people, especially non-literate young people, in ways that are consistent with local cultures. These include:

- A ministry called "The Learning Place" in the inner city of Jacksonville, Florida (Diocese of Florida, ECUSA), which has focused its task to reach young children age 5–8 who are already falling through the cracks in the educational system and failing at basic literacy skills such as reading and arithmetic. Making use of tutors from parochial school systems in the Diocese, other children are helping these children to keep up to speed in their homework assignments under the guidance of trained adult teachers. Other adult leaders bring exposure to arts, sciences, and simple chapel worship to help the children express themselves freely and with disciplined skills.

- In the Churches of India and Pakistan it has been found particularly beneficial to use the local dialects of the various areas of the Church in order to simplify the task of communication in the various places where the Church must reach the population.

- In Uganda and Kenya, and many other African nations, young people are graduating from schools, or have left schools, without having mastered the necessary skills. They are thus easily vulnerable to emotional and manipulative appeals from politicians.

- As a result the Church in many areas has started to teach basic civics to young people in order to educate them on their rights and the ways of government, so that they cannot so easily be influenced by emotional appeals that may be harmful to them. In Nigeria, a major problem has been the 'absence' of parents because of work in their early years of child raising, with the result of a population of children who lack values. This also happens in the UK where both parents usually need to generate income to pay for home. The Church must help parents once again to raise their children, and to teach fundamentals of faith to the children. Congregations can assist with this latter ministry.

Youth cultures around the world have started to move from linear to non-linear thinking, from rational thought to feeling responses, from intellectual pondering to action-based efforts to change things. The Church must seek to understand this shift and find ways to use its understanding to enhance the communication of the Gospel to those young people who have never heard the Good News.

In all cultures, in order more effectively to reach young people, including non-literate young people, and communicate the Good News to them, the Churches must seek to make effective use of the arts, of music, dance and story-telling, and to initiate projects that challenge their capacity for idealism. The Church must train and equip believing young people to be the evangelists to other young people, their peers, who do not yet know the Gospel. The Church must engage young people as members of the Church now, not just the Church of the future. They are the leaders of the future, but members now. Young people should be involved creatively in all aspects of Church life, in liturgy, in structures, in decision-making and in many forms of ministry to others. They have the energy and the desire, and need only the guidance and training of the elders of their community of faith.

We must create a culture in our churches in which young people and children feel comfortable and at home. They have often been regarded as a complex problem rather than a God-given asset for the enrichment and revitalisation of the church. Young people want to be accepted, respected and given their rightful place in the congregation. This will require flexibility, changed attitudes and generosity of spirit among older parishioners. It may require alternative worship, styles of ministry and congregations. It will involve recognising their search for spirituality; creating opportunities for young people to take greater responsibility in the life of the church and make their mistakes as we make ours; being open to young people in need; encouraging and supporting the service of young people to others; using and encouraging the work of existing youth organisations. Where Anglican churches are losing their young people to other churches, it is often because the Anglican churches are unwilling to be open and flexible enough to embrace the culture of their young.

An Old Story from Wales

I see the black cloud now about to flee,
and the wind from the north is veering just a little.
After a great storm, there will shortly come
pleasant weather upon my poor soul.
Nothing will remain long of the black stormy night.

Long ages have not been appointed
for anyone to carry the cross.
The glad dawn that shines yonder says that
a fine morning is on the way.

I can see the sunlight on the hills of my Father's house,
showing me the foundation of my free salvation,
that my name is up there on the books of heaven
and that there is nothing that can blot it out.

Sweet as the honeycomb, and nourishing, and healing
are all heaven's chastisements, and
the strokes of my Father's rod.
Each cross, each woe, each strong wind
ripens saints for heaven.

From *Selected Verses from Pantycelyn*, Llyfr Emynau a Thonau
(trans. H. A. Hodges)

So the Anglican Church must be focused and intentional about its commitment to ministries with and by young persons. Youth ministry needs to be appropriately supported, affirmed and resourced. Resources in both personnel and finance must be provided and shared for youth ministry. This applies locally in parishes and dioceses, and in mission partnership with other provinces. The need to assist in providing church schools and the means to attend them is crucial in some of our African provinces and in other parts of the world. In many cases the best practice in youth ministry is in inter-denominational youth ministries. Anglicans often have a high involvement in these and have much to draw from them and to contribute to them.

Our own young people tell us that they would welcome more local and personal interest and support from their own bishops. They would welcome more face to face encounter and opportunity for conversation and sharing. This cannot be replaced by others. Bishops must take the initiative in this. We must take a leadership role in making a deeper commitment to bringing this vital, growing majority of the world the truth of the Gospel of Jesus Christ in ways that are relevant, exciting, transforming and life-giving. To do this we must take time to understand the culture of young people and communicate appropriately with them. The culture of a bishop is far removed from the culture of youth. It is not easily bridged. Training courses may be needed for bishops and clergy to understand young people and their culture and bishops need to encourage churches to be patient when youth ministries do not immediately produce conventional church members.

Begging for Brigades

In the area in which I work, there is a shortage of priests, so I look for priests from other dioceses. I asked for a particular priest, Ajulo, from the diocese where I myself had been appointed. I put him to work in a certain parish and when he got there, he found hardly anyone, and no young people. He went around the village, asking, "Why? Why are the young people not coming?" Somebody told him, "We had the Brigade before. Now we don't, and there's no club, nothing. That's why."

So he went round the adults, collecting, begging for money. He got enough to go to Lagos, and bought a band set and brought it home. He appointed a captain, and they started Bible study, drill, learning how to beat the drums. Within a month, the church was packed! From that station, they went from station to station inaugurating the Boys' Brigade. Since then we've had new life in that area.

This does not mean, however, that all Bishops and clergy are expected to be expert in youth culture and youth ministry. Those with special gifts at every level (bishops, clergy, layworkers and young people themselves) need to be identified and assisted in forwarding this ministry. Sometimes cross-fertilisation of experience with other continents, cultures and spiritualities can release and empower new life. Young people are not afraid of a challenge, and they are quite ready in many cases to face the realities of life and its hardships in areas of deprivation. At the heart of effective ministry with, among and by young people are relationships of mutual honesty, openness, trust and respect. Superficial assumptions, putting on airs and above all hypocrisy will negate effective youth ministry at any level. Young people today do not take easily to our structures, nor are they eager to organise or be organised.

Our traditional ministries to young people through Church schools still have a very significant role to play. Church schools are an important tool in evangelism in some cultures. Christian schools play a critical role when Christians find themselves discriminated against in the education programmes of some nations. In a church school, it is possible to talk about vision. We must both preserve and extend church schools and encourage the vocations of chaplains and teachers. Our work in schools, colleges and universities is often done ecumenically.

In some places, after-school and holiday clubs, summer camps with games, competitions and Bible teaching and friendly outreach attract a large proportion of children with no connection to the church, who thereby gain a memory of God which they carry into young adulthood.

In many situations, the establishment of youth organisations, church choirs, Scouts and Guides, Girls Friendly Society, Young People's Brigades, Bands and Cheerleaders, etc. in connection with the Church in recent years has proved highly successful in channelling young people's energies and giving them a sense of self-worth.

Recipe from Recife

There are some kids who lived on a rubbish dump in Recife in the north of Brazil. They were drawn to the dump looking for things to recycle. That was how they subsisted. At one point it was discovered that they were eating human remains, dumped there from a nearby hospital. Of course, as you can imagine, it made the newspapers.

An Anglican woman priest read about it and got involved, and so did others. First she started a new parish beside the dump, a ministry to these young people. Then she went to the town council and hassled them for support. She's quite a woman. And because of the nature of their need, more than the town council got involved—and as well, other town councils. There has been a big housing appeal, and a farm has been donated, which has been converted into workshops for the young people; they learn trades there, and teams of other young people from various countries, including the UK, come out to visit the area and to help with the training and the running.

It is an international enterprise. There's such an acute need.

In other contexts young people do not want so much to be entertained as to be valued and listened to. In one US diocese, churches have established small groups of about ten each where they can tell the story of what is going on in their lives, request prayer for their concerns and those of their friends, pour out the needs of their hearts and study scripture together. The young people are bringing their unchurched friends with them. In the USA a programme based on Cursillo, 'Happening,' helps young people to make the transition from family faith to adult faith and so encourages them to continue in worship.

To facilitate the full participation of young people will require:

- At the level of the prime unit for youth evangelism and ministry—the congregation—the training of clergy and laity, and openness by congregations to the presence and input of young people.

- At the level of the diocese to support the local congregation through training leaders, encouraging and stimulating ideas and events. At a worldwide level The Anglican Youth Network has been in existence for over ten years and has organised two World Conferences of Young Adults, as well as seeking to develop better links among young people in the Anglican Communion. In affirming this work, we would wish to see a greater implementation of a liaison with the Network on the part of Bishops. We would suggest that each province has a liaison bishop with the network.

Churches and dioceses have also held Young Adult Forums with the church being challenged by the young people themselves about new developments in worship, the identification and nurturing youth skills, and about the need for reconciliation both inside and outside the church.

We raise the following issues:

- Young people need to draw on the resources of religion. What changes are needed in our worship, styles of ministry and congregations to encourage the full participation of our young people?

- Should worship be on a day other than Sunday?

- Since so much family time is undermined by TV and other outside forces, should the Anglican church consider producing liturgies for use in the home to build up the spirituality of Christian family life?

Men and women in mission and evangelism

We believe that men and women have equal and often differing contributions to make to evangelism. Many women are primary evangelists, as mothers of children, friends to their neighbours, and as givers of hospitality.

Many women missionaries have played and continue to play a very significant part in our churches. We salute the work of the Mothers' Union and other organisations and commit ourselves to training women and men to enable them to play their full part in mission and evangelism. We recognise that we still need to listen to the voices of women about evangelism and to encourage and empower them to be equal partners with men in the mission structures of our dioceses.

Children and family

We cannot consider evangelism and ministry among children and young people without considering the way in which our churches nurture the family.

A living church will nurture covenanted relationships in the family—husband and wife, children and parents, learning how to listen to each other and grow with each other. Parents are our first teachers of the faith.

Knock, Knock

This happened in my diocese of southwestern Brazil. A man knocked on the door of the priest's house. "I need money." The priest was a little circumspect. "What do you want the money for?" "To buy medicine for my child." The priest had heard that one before. "Do you have the prescription? " The man showed the prescription. The priest said, "Come back in one hour." He took the prescription, went and bought the medicine, and was waiting for the man. "Thank you very much! God bless you!" "No, no, no, I want to go with you to your home." This was a very circumspect priest. "He could still sell the medicine, get the money and buy drink, or drugs, or...," he thought to himself. "But it's so far from here." "That's all right."

They drove in the priest's car to a very poor village of about fifty families, no white, no indigenous, just poor mixed, despised by either side, many children, no employment, no electricity, no water, no sanitation. The priest returned many times to that village, he taught them to bake bread, to plant a kitchen garden, to petition city hall, to found a school; he changed the life of that village. Recently I received nearly forty of their adults into the Church and they've got a church school going. This is mission: answering a knock on the door.

The Congregation and Communication

In a world where communication by print and by electronic means is sophisticated, rapid and controlled by few people, it is essential for the Church to observe the media closely and stringently, whilst cultivating positive and truthful relationships with journalists and seeing the media as potential means of sharing the Gospel with others. In our dealings with the media we must be professional in putting over our Christian view. In answering a question on a given issue we can make an honest point about the faith by introducing it in such terms as "This is what really matters to me as a Christian and this is what I would like to say."

The Anglican Communion does not have one mind on many subjects and is not in a position to speak with one voice. The Anglican Communion should affirm that bishops in different dioceses in different cultures have a right to speak in respect of ministering the apostolic faith in their own particular circumstances and cultures. Some degree of disagreement on aspects of interpretation and activity of the faith may occur but their fundamental fellowship in the larger Anglican Communion remains.

While *Anglican World* magazine is greatly valued across the Communion, it would benefit from more material that reflects the world-wide nature of the Communion.

All Christian communication is by way of explaining Christian presence and witness through the Christian Community. But our confidence is not finally in our ability to communicate. In all we have said and will say about the Church's mission our confidence for our congregations' witness is in God's power to transform through the Gospel, empowerment by his Holy Spirit, and the spiritual disciplines of faithful prayer and Bible reading.

Missionary congregations do not stand alone. In our Anglican Communion they are part of missionary dioceses.

Sub-Section 5
The Missionary Diocese

"We are all missionary dioceses now."

Since the last gathering of bishops at the Lambeth Conference, we are beginning to see God changing the emphasis of the Communion from maintenance to mission. We rejoice in this move of the Spirit and reaffirm that *every diocese is called to be a missionary diocese.*

Already some long-established dioceses are coming to recognise this in a new way and now refer to themselves as "missionary dioceses." This is the case with the Diocese of Wakefield in the north of England: it courageously came to recognise the magnitude of the challenge facing it, as, for example, the number of teenage young people throughout the Diocese attending church on a Sunday was only 360 out of a population of one million.

Music That Speaks

Many years ago, I was a curate in south London, in a parish with a lot of Afro-Caribbean people, and I oversaw the youth work. We had camps in East Grinstead, we had discos, we had Bible studies, I prepared them for confirmation. The girls were in the Brownies and the Guides, but there wasn't much for the boys. I've never been a Boy Scout, so I organised a servers' guild and a choir. But I can't sing! And I know nothing about music. So I needed a choir master. This proved difficult, because the kids were, shall we say, very lively. We went through quite a few organists.

So in despair, we put an advert in The Church Times: 'small inner-city parish looking for dedicated organist.' A man in his early seventies arrived, an ex-civil servant in the Ministry of Labour, had earned a doctorate of music in his spare time, very devout, also very gentle and very patient. And to my amazement, he won the love and affection of these rough boys. He'd bring them marshmallows, he'd take an interest in them, but he also taught them to sing. He made them into a very good choir.

When he died, I learned his story. We were surprised to discover that the preacher at his requiem would be the then Bishop of St. Alban's, Robert Runcie. Runcie told us that the man's only son had been one of his best friends; they'd served together in the army. When the son had died, the man had resolved that he would not be bitter, not ever blame God for this, but see it as a challenge to him to work with young people in deprived parishes—which he did for the rest of his life. And of course, Robert Runcie was inspired by the man who died to have a vocation himself.

New Dioceses

New dioceses, however, can have special reason to call themselves "missionary dioceses;" we are thinking of those starting from the smallest beginnings. They have no option about mission and must go out to proclaim the Gospel or die. We give thanks that since the Decade of Evangelism began, God has called many new dioceses into being and we have been learning how he blesses the growth of his Church in this way.

From one diocese which covered the whole of the northern part of Nigeria, eighteen new dioceses have been formed. Where this one diocese was unable to evangelise the area effectively before, the Word of God is now spreading and very many people have come to faith in Jesus Christ and been built into his Church. This is a key example and gift of God to our Communion.

In many parts of the Communion we see clearly that where the prompting of the Spirit is followed and the responsibility for forming a new missionary diocese given, sometimes to only a few Christians under the leadership of a missionary bishop, the proclamation of the Gospel has moved forward significantly and the Church grown. There are examples of this not only in Nigeria, but also in Uganda, Zambia, Uruguay, Peru and Bolivia among others.

Two Ways of Beginning a New Diocese

By dividing an existing diocese:

In Uganda, where one bishop has 8,000 confirmations in a year, it is being proposed that the diocese be divided. In another area one bishop is unable to reach a region of his diocese for geographical and political reasons and another diocese is urged.

By starting in a new geographical area where no significant presence has existed before:

The new dioceses of Nigeria are one single instance, as given above. The Diocese of Uruguay, originally part of the Diocese of Argentina, grew from the remnants of a chaplaincy ministry to English expatriates and an earlier initiative by a neighbouring parish in South Western Brazil. And in the Dominican Republic, the present Diocese is soon to be divided so that mission to the remoter parts of the island can more effectively be carried out.

Funding

Lack of funding and facilities is a common factor. In almost all cases funding has been vastly insufficient and continues to be a major headache for bishops at a time when they already have much responsibility on their heads.

Bishops find they have to dedicate a disproportionate amount of their time to fund raising, and in one case the bishop did not even have a stipend, house or transport to begin with. Many have raised funding through personal contacts, as in two cases of bishops whose family and friends got together to provide them with transport. "Christians should be taught to give so that the work of bringing people to faith can go on."

In Nigeria, each new missionary diocese is linked with a wealthy parish in one of the big cities to provide funding on a decreasing scale over the first five years. This was seen as a positive strategy which also involved Christians in established parts of the Church with the missionary enterprise.

Raising money for development projects is much easier than raising money for the beginning of new dioceses. We must wake up the churches and people of the

Anglican Communion to support this work and ask the Bishops to remind their people of the responsibility to this particular work of primary mission and evangelism.

We need resources for evangelism and mission work. Travelling, training, literature, translating and communication are expensive, but necessary.

In some cases there were strong voices against the forming of a new diocese, usually for financial reasons. "But we can't control the Spirit in that way; rather we must respond to the Holy Spirit's initiative in mission."

Clear Mission Strategy

It is especially important for a new diocese to have a clear and simple mission strategy, so that all pull together in unity.

In nearly all cases, the approach of the new dioceses to mission has been "integral," and the proclamation of the word has gone hand in hand with works of mercy and social concern and development.

Structures

Structures and order are important in a missionary diocese and for the emerging Christian community. However, they must be appropriate and enable mission rather than putting it in a straitjacket. When David went to fight Goliath he had the wisdom to leave aside Saul's armour; he knew he needed flexibility to fight the way he knew best (1 Sam. 17:39).

The Bishop as Missionary

Our experience affirms the role of the bishop as missionary, given authority by the Church to go and exercise the apostolic gifts and to raise up a local church, the diocese.

This was the case in the early centuries of the Christian Church and notably the tradition of our Celtic heritage. In a new diocese, the role of the bishop as a leader in mission is clear and essential.

A missionary bishop must:

- have a strong love of God and people;
- be passionate about mission and have a vision for it;

- love the Church and be well formed in the identity of Anglicanism;
- be sensitive to the culture of the people to whom he/she is sent;
- be willing to start in the most humble and simple way; and
- be a person of courage.

A Waste of Shame

We don't know how to make reconciliation. We are in desperate need of finding ways of moving into its enlarged space before it is too late. A church warden became the treasurer of his family church, stole £50,000 and went to prison for it—two and a half years. He committed himself to pay back the theft in full, and he did. When he went to return to the church he'd been in all his life, he found himself unwelcome. So he attended a nearby church. It took him two years to find a job. On the day he landed it, his wife was blinded. Soon after he began work, he was diagnosed with cancer; he died within a few months.

At the funeral, held, of course, at the nearby church, most of those attending came from his family parish. These are the people who could not find a way of forgiving and receiving back into the church a penitent before it was too late. God have mercy: how do we find a way forward? How do we learn acceptance?

Bishops who start new dioceses often find it a lonely experience, out on their own, with little support and can become discouraged because things are so small. Yet at other times there are moments of exhilaration and a sense of privilege.

Clergy

All bishops spoke of the difficulty of finding clergy and the difficulties of training new clergy. In one new diocese, a seminary was founded in the second year, and although progress was slow to begin with, there is now a strong and growing national clergy and lay leadership. Training is not an option for when we are well established, but should begin with the new diocese. Jesus called the apostles right at the beginning of his ministry (Matt. 4:18–22) and trained them as he went along. We need to re-evaluate our training programmes to ensure they are training people for the real ministry that exists and will exist in the context of mission.

God's Vision for the Church's Continuing Mission

God continues his work of mission and it is our privilege to "work together with Him" (2 Cor. 6:1). We want to encourage provinces in appropriate areas to take the risk and we believe that the forming of a new diocese can be a powerful means of expanding the mission work of the Church. The decision to start a new diocese should come out of a process centred in prayer, discernment and waiting on God. We believe such a decision will always correspond with the Church's primary function of mission.

While it is the ecclesiastical responsibility of provinces to start new dioceses in their area, it is, nevertheless, part of the Church's common mission. The worldwide Communion therefore has a responsibility to offer support and make resources available in whatever ways are appropriate, and we ask the ACC and Primates Meeting to consider how this can be done more effectively.

At the same time there are regions of the world where the message of Jesus Christ has not yet been proclaimed, areas outside the present jurisdiction of our provinces. While the great commission of our Lord Jesus Christ to "go and make disciples of all nations" (Matt. 28:19) still stands, the Anglican Communion must urgently consider how initiatives in mission to such areas should be organised and resourced. We ask that the Archbishop of Canterbury, the Primates and the ACC look at this and do all in their power to enable an appropriate response.

It is important that in fulfilling its calling the Anglican Communion gather information and experience about beginning new missionary dioceses. We request the Mission and Evangelism Desk in the ACC to gather and share information about the work of beginning new dioceses and to keep it before the Communion as an important dimension of our missionary enterprise.

Missionary Dioceses in Contexts of Persecution

We heard stories from a wide variety of situations in which Christians are relating to people of Other Faiths. We reflected on these experiences in the light of scripture and of our understanding of Christian mission. Some of these stories were from situations of cordial relationships between people of different faith communities. But stories from Nigeria, Sudan, Iran, and Pakistan have described situations of tension and sometimes of open conflict. In several cases Christians feel themselves under considerable pressure from governments motivated by particular kinds of Islamic ideology.

Iran

This small church would like to feel that it is part of the whole life of Iran, but is made to feel an unwanted minority. Before the revolution the work of the Church initiated by missionaries included health and education. Muslims gradually accepted these services. The revolution meant that missionaries had to leave, and Christian institutions were closed or taken over. Before the revolution the Anglican Church was small but forward-looking and active. It made a great impact. It was the Church which suffered most in the revolution. Its bishop was nearly killed and had to leave the country. His son was murdered. The present bishop was as a priest imprisoned for a while. His wife's property has been confiscated and sold. The Government uses the Armenian Orthodox Church to say that there is no discrimination. But the Armenian Orthodox do not normally seek converts. Conversion from Islam and baptism into the Christian Church are not permited. There is no equality under the law for Muslims and Christians.

Jail Break I

I got to know Ben Jones when I started chaplaincy work in a penitentiary in Central Florida (my home was Cuba, but that's another story). Ben was a prisoner. He played the piano for the other prisoners, and had formed a group around himself, a small Christian community of prisoners who cared for each other.

Ben was amazing. The warmth that came from that man! He's in for a sexual offense which he denies committing, and he gets moved from prison to prison, usually maximum security, and now that he's converted, he converts others to the love of the Lord and creates Christian fellowship in every prison he's in. That is his mission. When I left to be bishop, he thrust this ring into my hand; he said, "It's all I have of value." He was thanking me for the work we did together in that prison we met in. I wear it always. It says "Jesus lives."

The bishop is encouraged by signs that the relationship between the government and the church is improving, and believes that the time is right for the world-wide community to encourage this building on the 1988 resolution on Iran. The Archbishop of Canterbury has received an invitation to visit the diocese.

Sudan

The truth about the situation in all parts of Sudan is becoming more widely known. A racist government is in power and is waging war to subdue the South. The government is Arab Muslim. Much of the South is Christian. This has an economic as well as a tribal and religious dimension. There is no health or education provision, and no currency.

Nigeria

Military rule is in place. This means Muslim rule, although Christians are in a majority in two regions out of three. Christians therefore have no place in government, or government service. Contracts are given to Muslims. Some Christians compromise and take Muslim names in order to put bread on their tables. Christians are liable to lose their jobs. What is needed is a return to democratic government.

Jail Break II

I learned Ben's story. He'd been a professor; he was framed, he says, on a harassment charge, sentenced, imprisoned; ostracized by his family, he became bitter and violent in prison, until somehow, somebody reached him with the Gospel. His missioning began.

Ben was kept on the move, from one maximum security to another. On one of his moves, which always terrified him, the driver of the van stopped, got out, opened the back of the van and said to him alone among the inmates, "You. Get out. Come over here." Ben was quaking. "Do not be afraid," whispered the driver. "I too am a Christian, and the Holy Spirit has moved me to instruct you: very soon you are going to be in the midst of the divine appointment, and I must anoint you." This was all new stuff for Ben. But later that night, a young man was admitted, headed for Death Row, kicking and screaming. Ben recognized his former self. He also recognized his divine appointment. He didn't feel adequate to it, but he did what he could, helping that teenager to reconciliation with God before his date with Death Row.

And that's how Ben lives now: moved from prison to prison, playing the piano for the inmates, gathering Christian companionship around him, and aspiring to live like a real monk in real community. If he ever gets out, that's where he would choose to go—a monastery—if anyone would have him.

These stories have in common the fact that persecution is directed against Christians. In each case the government is Islamic. The stories envisage different hopes for an outcome: in Iran, recognition of the right of the Church to exist: in Nigeria and the Sudan a democratic government.

The following questions are raised:

- Is a secular democracy the only structure within which minorities can be protected? Or is it possible to have a religious state with a proper place and care for minorities? If it is the first, are we not giving in to the privatising of religion?

- What can be said or done to or within a religious state where conversion is forbidden, especially from Muslim to Christian? Is the concept of the "secret believer" one way forward? Or does this deny confessing the faith?

- How do we challenge the adherents of a religion whom we believe are not living to the highest teachings of their faith (and how do we allow ourselves to be challenged)? Do we need to listen to and make use of voices from among those within a faith community who are criticising it?

- Does the concept of universal human rights give any protection to those being persecuted, and how can such rights be claimed in a state where they are not recognised? What measure of protection does solidarity in the Anglican Communion give to persecuted minorities?

The work of new dioceses, and experience of dioceses under pressure, highlights the importance of mutual support in the Communion.

Companion Link Relationships

The Missio Report and material requested a list of companion relationships between dioceses to be prepared for Lambeth. This list reveals that many dioceses have no companion relationships. For example, only two of the twenty-two dioceses of the Church of South India have such relationships.

An example of a very fruitful new companion relationship is that between the Diocese of Uruguay and the Diocese of South Western Brazil, who have developed an important joint mission initiative on the shared borders of their dioceses. One diocese provides personnel while the other provides accommodation and resources.

While dioceses in England often have more than one companion relationship, it is time within the next ten years to take a significant initiative encouraging all dioceses to develop companion relationships; these should straddle provinces as part of the process of developing the cross-cultural nature of the Communion.

While helpful guidelines for forming links exist, we wish to establish as a goal to be achieved by the next Lambeth Conference the forming of a companion link for every diocese.

Sub-Section 6
Being a Missionary Bishop in a Missionary Church

God calls us all to meet the enormous opportunity offered through Jesus Christ, in the power of the Holy Spirit, to transform lives and societies. What is more, God has placed us in a time of great and universal spiritual hunger as the third millennium arrives.

At the Right Hand of God

Confirmation visits in southwest Rwanda involve travelling through the natural forest where militia have been operating since the genocide. The army commanding officer gives me three armed soldiers to accompany me in the Land Rover. For two and a half hours, we discuss the gospel. I ask the officer what I should do if the militia shoot from the forest. "You stop the car, my soldiers get out, and you back off." "What if they have laid a land mine in the road?" "That's easy. Bishop and soldiers go to heaven together." Then we have two-and-a-half hours discussing who goes to heaven and who doesn't!

Having recognised here, with thanksgiving, the encouragement received from the witness of those parts of our Communion that are growing, and also having explored ways in which all dioceses need to transform their lives, structures and use of diocesan resources against a yardstick of missionary effectiveness, we look next at the pattern of the bishop's own life in this light.

Two pictures to begin with:

We heard the story of a Nigerian bishop consecrated to serve a diocese governed and populated by a very large Muslim majority. He inherited seven congregations and four clergy. Two years later, there are ten congregations and eight clergy. He sees himself primarily as an evangelist, and defined his priorities as:

- prayer, worship and the study of the Bible;
- helping congregations identify and reach out to areas ready for evangelism;
- preaching for commitment;
- training clergy and people to nurture new believers; and
- using his resources for mission.

We heard from an English bishop about the expectations of his diocese, expectations that do not release the bishop to be a leader/servant in mission. These demands and expectations were identified as:

- prayer, worship and the study of the Bible;
- engaging with local and national authorities;
- the care, nurture, encouragement and discipline of the clergy; and
- the management of structures and personnel.

The pastoral care of the clergy and the responsible management of structures are proper and necessary concerns. But the challenge we must face is whether they can be so exclusively the focus of the bishop's responsibilities that the priority of proclaiming good news to all is pushed to the margin of the bishop's timetable.

A Church that is being renewed along the lines we have been sketching will prompt and encourage a shift of emphasis. The bishop whose ministry grows from, works with and is addressed to such a Church will have a new sense of the opportunities opened up for leading and encouraging a diocese in mission by first attending to and serving the vision of the church as a whole. We have repeatedly seen the importance in the bishop's ministry of direct involvement with persons and congregations, standing with them and among them. As St. Augustine said: "For you I am a bishop; with you I am a Christian." The bishop is first and foremost a baptized Christian, and must struggle to be a model of Christian faithfulness. The bishop's life must be marked by prayer, self-offering and apostolic zeal, so that it offers direction and inspiration to the community of believers. The bishop is in a special position to show the Church what its possibilities and expectations might be—just as the bishop is always learning from the community about those possibilities in concrete situations.

- Do we make visible to our people the vitality of Christian hope?
- Do we help create an environment in which the growth and deepening of Christian life is expected?

The bishop is also a servant (deacon), and must always be at the disposal of the Church, ready to assist in local situations and perform practical tasks. The bishop models the service of Christ to the Church and the world.

The bishop, in modeling such service, should never be reluctant to go directly to places of need and neglect (for example, prisons, refugee camps, places where living conditions are wretched) and being seen alongside the suffering and rejected, victims of persecutions or prejudice, people with HIV/AIDS, those with physical and mental hurts. The bishop's service is in both listening to such people and helping their voices to be heard.

- Do we show a readiness to be present with our people in humble and practical ways?
- Do we show a readiness to be where need is most acute and to speak for and with the needy?

The Grateful Dead

Twelve years ago when I was a priest in Panama, there was a man who played the organ and I asked for his help in my church. He would say "yes" but never show up. Yet we stayed in touch. One night he had a car accident and I was called to the hospital. "Sorry, Father. You've come too late. He died!" I said, "I need to see the body," but I was told it was ready for the morgue. "It goes in five minutes." "I only need two: I must pray." They let me.

The body was covered with a blanket. I pulled it back. The corpse sat up. It said, "What are you doing here, Father?" "I'm looking for you," I said. "They thought you'd died. The doctor's report has gone in already." But the corpse, of course, lived. "Father, now you have an organist for your church." And we did. That man went on to get a music degree and to teach kids lots of instruments. He always says, "I died. But I got born again."

The bishop is still an elder (presbyter), to whom is committed the task of praying in the name of the community and of making the love of Jesus Christ real and specific for the community—and especially for other pastors. The bishop models the pastoral role, teaching, preaching, and holding up a common vision. The bishop will not see pastoral concern as an alternative to prophetic or missionary witness, but will always seek by practical pastoral love to draw persons and communities into the full freedom of Christian maturity, into active love, transforming prayer and grateful witness.

- Do we show to other pastors care and concern in small things, encouragement and openness?
- Do we ever use the imperative of care and concern as something to protect us from challenging and being challenged?

A Little Trust

I'm someone whose parents did not go to church much themselves but who was caught up in Sunday school in an age when 70 per cent of English children were in Sunday schools. And that custom has long since gone. A recent survey showed that only about 15 per cent of English children have any contact with the Church, and many of them are children of adult attenders.

One of the things that encourages me in Maidstone is that a little Trust was formed a few years ago to try and reach the children whose parents don't go anywhere near a church. Their main focus of activity is in the day schools, in setting up clubs after school hours, where they can get permission from the staffs. They've set up a number of these King's Kids Clubs, I think they call them, in schools around Maidstone. They try to work on the basis of one leader for fifteen children. Some are struggling, but some are flourishing; the numbers are quite encouraging.

Every summer, they run three weeks of summer camps. About fifty children come for each of the three weeks; I've been to one myself, and it's very exciting to see the numbers—even more exciting to find, in well over half the children who come, that they have no outside connection with the Church. The whole formula, for camps and for clubs, is a mixture of games and lots of fun competitions that kids enjoy, plus simple Bible teaching, and above all, good friendship. And I believe that this may well be, in our situation in England, the sort of format we have to explore in the future if we're to be trying to get a memory of God in the children and young adults of our country for the future.

But the bishop is, *distinctively,* someone to whom apostolic authority is given. The bishop is a witness to the resurrection and to the hope of Christ's coming, above all in the context of the Church's eucharistic worship, and to take the news of the resurrection to places where it has not been heard. The bishop is a guardian of the faith received from earlier generations and which is now to be passed on gratefully and hopefully to the bishop's successors. Apostolic succession is not only a matter of formal historical continuity, but a responsibility to receive and transmit this gift. Thus, too, the bishop seeks to work from and with a community eager to share this news. As a public figure in many cultural and social contexts, the bishop has the opportunity of addressing large gatherings in the Church and in the wider community and of interacting with people in industry, commerce, government and education, with leaders of other religious communities and with those who form opinion in society. It is vital that these opportunities be seen in an apostolic light, as part of an intentional series of strategic actions flowing into the mission of God, not as signs of status. And in the Church, the bishop must foster the same sense of purpose and coherence, taking every opening to name the vision, articulate common goals and cultivate purposeful reflection about mission at every level in a diocese. The bishop will be at the heart of a team of pastors and servants—from archdeacons to intercessors to lay office-holders and administrators in the parish—holding this vision and purpose together, a corporate witness to the resurrection. In many contexts, though, the bishop's task is not to control but to recognise, affirm and give room for new initiatives coming from local communities, naming the gracious presence of Christ, who renews the Church in ways that are always unexpected.

- Do we use our opportunities in the wider community for apostolic witness?

- Do we seek to give common purpose to all the worshipping communities we serve?

Bishops, then, have to look hard at the schedule they work with. Just as they will seek to direct the resources of a diocese towards the priorities of mission, the priorities of the Kingdom, so they have to reflect on the stewardship of their own time and resources for the sake of the Kingdom. They will identify openings for enlarging a diocese's vision (parish conferences, retreats and consultations for pastors, large gatherings and celebrations); they will look at their wider involvement in public life with an eye to using the opportunities there; they will not be too shy or too proud to do ordinary tasks among ordinary people. Bishops should therefore determine, and be encouraged by their dioceses and national churches, to give priority in their lives to spending substantial and quality time among people in all parts of the church's life, encouraging them to look outwards and upwards. The bishop's primary ministry is as a servant-leader among the people of God, sharing his/her vision, and working and living out with the baptised what it means to be a holy people in the place and time where they are set. So the bishop should seek to build up the congregation as part of the universal Church, with them becoming a holy worshipping community:

- seeking to learn and grow with them as teachers and as disciples; and

- reaching out with them in the work of mission and evangelism.

We recognise that bishops and dioceses work in radically different contexts. Nevertheless we believe that, whatever the context, the challenge to transform our life and work remains the same. Above all, bishops must keep clear and fresh their own vision of the Risen Lord. Desmond Tutu said that he was too busy to pray for less than two hours a day! They must themselves first be receivers of grace and Good News from God. "Who is sufficient for these things?"

Sub-Section 7
How to Support Each Other in Mission

We need and want to support each other in mission in the world today. Current structures of support derived from an earlier era for different tasks are proving inadequate. We want to begin a process of support in new and direct ways. We are called to live and proclaim the Good News enfleshed in our different cultures but not made captive to them. To do this we need the encouragement, critique and perspectives that we can offer each other from our different cultural perspectives. We also need to consider ways in which aid can be co-ordinated across the Communion.

Pit Terror

We had a civil war in Nigeria in 1968. I was a churchgoer then, but not a Christian. When I went to the front in the war, my uncle persuaded me to carry certain charms to keep me safe. The night before the attack, I had a dream. I wondered what it meant. I dreamt a bullet passed through my head and out the other side, and I lived. And a second bullet went through my stomach and out the other side, and I lived. I asked one of my leaders about it. He put to me a question which I will never forget. "Are you a true Christian?" At that point I wasn't. But I thought about it, and said 'yes'. He said, "It means if you are a true Christian, you will survive, if you are not, you are dead."

Going into the attack, a very strong voice told me to leave those charms behind, in the trench. I took instead my pocket Bible. People were killed, four to my right, four to my left, but not me. The same on the way back from the front. People with mightier charms than mine had been killed. So I prayed to God, "Please show me the way; let me know; do I use these charms or not, believe you wholly or not?"

In the morning I had a very sore throat. Going for medical treatment, we were bombed. Three people were killed, but not me. Again near the medical centre. There was no medicine, so we had to go to another centre. And a very strong voice said to me, "Now carry those charms." So I did. In the ambulance we had an accident. I was the last one to get free of the wreck. This was totally against what the charms had promised me. Now a very big voice said inside me, "Now, have you seen what has happened to you? These charms are useless to you. Believe in me only."

So I looked for a leaf to wrap them in, and the voice said, "Now go to the pit toilet, drop them in, pray over them, and then pass your excreta over them." I did as the voice told me. The joy I came out from that toilet with—I've never had such joy, it was greater than I have ever experienced since! That day made me a Christian. And here I am a bishop. Praise the Lord.

Bishops, clergy and laity are called by God to live the whole Gospel so that lives and cultures are transformed. So the Anglican Communion needs to be transformed with a clear and renewed strategy for mission and evangelism.

In several dioceses in the United States, structural renewal has been accomplished to make missionary activity more viable in the lives of local congregations. The basic principle at work here is that the Bishop's office must be viewed as a servanthood ministry to the several congregations of the Diocese, rather than the centre of power and decision making.

Restructuring some dioceses according to this primary value has resulted in the elimination of many diocesan committees that in the past had held responsibility for accomplishment of mission and ministry within the Diocese. These responsibilities and decision-making authorities are now located in regional groupings of local congregations, much closer to the people who bear the responsibility to accomplish and fund the ministries they engage.

Principles which guide the implementation of this restructuring for mission and servanthood ministry are that:

- Christ's ministry in the world is most effective when carried out by people equipped in local Christian communities;

- the administrative structures of the Diocese exist to serve the local communities of faith; and

- the role of leadership in congregations is to educate, equip and empower the ministries of the members.

Diocesan structures must allow for the possibility of delegating not only responsibility, but also authority for decision-making to the lowest possible levels, and the structure must also allow for ways to some diocesan funding to the local regions in order to enable the more effective results.

In the language of the corporate world this is known as "inverting the pyramid" of organisational structures in order to affirm and maximise the contribution of the individual members of the organisation. In the Church, this is understood to be a way of releasing the power of the Holy Spirit in the lives of many people whom God has called in Christ to carry out mission and ministry in their local congregations, and through them to the Church throughout the world. In this form, the Bishop is no longer the hierarch, but rather the servant of all, in the name of Jesus Christ.

Episcopal leadership needs to be transformed so that we are seen to be servants of God's mission in Christ to his world. Leaders at every level should be appointed who are committed to mission and evangelism, proclamation and social action.

Lay people must be encouraged and empowered to be the forefront church's mission. The dependence of a congregation on one pastor often inhibits the growth of the congregation. When energies go into exclusively sustaining the congregation, there are no energies left for outreach. Pastoring structures are needed which share this responsibility throughout the congregation. The criteria for the value of any structure wider than the local congregation is to what extent and how effectively is this serving the mission of the local congregation.

Forward to the Millennium

The forthcoming millennial year bears witness to the formative effect of Christianity upon many of the cultures and countries of our world. It will provide a remarkable opportunity for churches and individual Christians to witness to Jesus.

In those countries with a long established Christian tradition the Millennium could provide an opportunity to reawaken the cultural and spiritual memory of society.

Power in a Basket

Some visitors of Bishop Newton's in Papua New Guinea went down to the village of Weddau near the Mission station, where they met an old blind priest of the pagan religion. He had in his keeping a very precious stone. They got it from him (by paying his relatives perhaps) and took it back to the Mission house. The old pagan priest was grief-stricken. Newton heard about this escapade, and he went and took the stone from the visitors, placed it in a traditional basket, and carried it back to the pagan priest. The priest was overjoyed. After the priest's death, his relatives gave the stone to be placed in the wall of the Anglican cathedral at Dogura.

Missiologists writing about the preaching of the Gospel in the Pacific have often talked about the need for power encounters: they mean the Christian destruction of pagan charms and fetishes. I think the power of the Gospel is in love, in healing, not in wounding or destroying. In Newton's story we see a real power encounter; this is the Gospel of Christ.

We welcome the Pope's call for the year 2000 to be seen as a Jubilee when the creditor nations and agencies should take positive steps towards remitting the unrepayable international debts of many impoverished countries in the developing world. We note that, together with its ecumenical partners, the Church of England is promoting the year as a year of "New Start"—a new start for the world's poor, a new start at home, a new start with God.

2000 A.D. will also see the completion of the ten years of the Decade of Evangelism, ten years of changing the way of life of the Communion to a "dynamic missionary emphasis going beyond care and nurture to proclamation and service" (LC88 Resolution 44).

We need to continue what we have begun to do here at Lambeth in learning lessons of good practice in mission and evangelism from one another in our experience of the Decade of Evangelism. We have spent our time together sharing what God has been doing in our dioceses and the ministry of our congregations. Our evaluation at this point can only be "It is the Lord's doing and is marvellous in our eyes" (Ps. 118: 23). We are firmly set on our task of putting a dynamic missionary emphasis at the heart of our life as a Communion. We therefore hope that the best is yet to come.

Sub-Section 8
Resources for Mission

We note and identify the following resources for mission:

"Mission and Ministry" in *The Truth Shall Make You Free: The Report of the 1988 Lambeth Conference*

"Sing a New Song" (Missio, 1996)

The Cutting Edge of Mission—a Report of the Mid-Point Review of the Decade of Evangelism. Ed. Cyril Okorocha (Anglican Communion Publications, 1996)

Vision Bearers by Richard Kew and Cyril Okorocha (Mowbray, 1997)

Encountering the West by Lamin Sanneh

From Everywhere to Everywhere by Michael Nazir-Ali (Collins)

Faith in the City—The Archbishop of Canterbury's Commission on Urban Priority Areas (1985)

Anglican Life and Witness. Ed. by Vinay Samuel and Chris Sugden (SPCK, 1997)

Transformation Journal—issues on "Youth Ministry and World Mission," March 1994 "Children at Risk,"April 1997 "Called to Full Humanity," January 1998 (OCMS)

Notes

1. The Most Reverend George L. Carey
2. Ched Myers, *New Economy of Grace*, Sojourners, July/Aug 1998.
3. Mary Motte, *The Missionary Imperative in Western Culture*, Thinking Mission, USPG 1995.

Called to Be a Faithful Church in a Plural World Section III Report

Prologue: A Vision

St. John, the visionary on the Isle of Patmos, gives a captivating picture of the new order of God's reign:

> I saw no temple in the city, for its temple is the Lord God the Almighty and the Lamb. And the city has no need of sun or moon to shine on it, for the glory of God is its light, and its lamp is the Lamb. The nations will walk by its light, and the kings of the earth will bring their glory into it. Its gates will never be shut by day—and there will be no night there. People will bring into it the glory and the honour of the nations (Rev. 21:22–26).

The vision speaks of God's purpose for the whole of creation. Peoples of diverse cultures and nations dwell together in the unity of God's reign. God is their light. There is community with God and each other. No longer is there any fragmentation that tears apart humanity or a global drive that destroys local identities. There is unity in diversity; all are embraced in God's love. Nothing that harms even the weakest will have any place or power there. Finally, God is glorified as the nations offer to God and share within their common life the heritages and honour of their diverse cultures. What a vision—human beings and all of creation reflecting the splendour of the inner communion of the triune God—'otherness in communion'!

The story of Pentecost tells of a new stage in the understanding of this yet-to-be-fulfilled vision. By the outpouring of the Holy Spirit the Church was called into being as the sign and instrument of God's work of drawing all things into unity in Christ Jesus. The miracle of Pentecost lies precisely in the juxtaposition of 'each' and 'all'. Each hears in their own language and yet all are bound together in the Spirit. The same Spirit who enables each local church to be rooted in its culture also draws it to be in communion with all other local churches across other cultures. Thus diversity and unity, local identity and universal *koinonia*, contextuality and catholicity, are hallmarks of the Church.

The call to be a faithful Church in a plural world, to be the first fruits of a new creation in which the rich diversity of all God's people is held together in unity, comes to us afresh and with a sense of urgency today. For the world in which the Church is called to live and witness at the eve of the new millennium is increasingly plural and fragmented, yet at the same time drawn into a 'global village.'

Sub-Section 1
A Plural World

The Context

The world today is characterised by two opposing forces. The first is an increasing process of fragmentation of the world, a testing of human community everywhere through the struggles for particular cultural, ethnic or religious identities; the second is a process of globalisation. In almost every part of the world, we find a search for cultural roots and tradition, a stress on cultural uniqueness, an insistence on 'difference' and the right of each group to its own specific way of being and development. The positive value of this trend can be seen in the new self-awareness of indigenous peoples as well as other minority groups in different parts of the world. The search for cultural identity frees and builds up a people. But the same trend often also has a far more powerful negative effect. The demands for ethnic and cultural identity frequently lead to violent separatist tendencies and conflicts between cultural minorities. At times this process is manifested in forms of militant religious particularism, the formation of new nation-states, and conflicts based on ethnicity, religion and language within a single state. What is important too is that many of these conflicts which appear to be economic, political or social are sustained by cultural factors and religious symbols. In many instances religion is used to legitimate and support inter-ethnic conflicts; hence we witness a process of increasing politicisation of religion or sacralisation of politics. When different religious communities co-exist in a single state, relations between them are often strained. This suggests a need to continue to examine the cultures in which Christians find themselves, to see where they resonate with the Gospel and where the Gospel is their critique. Conversely, Christians also need to examine the way the Gospel is being proclaimed, to see whether it is disabling or fruitfully challenging its cultural contexts.

The second trend is toward the uniformity of various social-units of the world such as nation-states, cultures or ethnic groups, drawing them into an all-encompassing world system. The twin forces of the world market and the media of mass communication, the two most powerful engines of this global process, stand over against the inter-ethnic, religiously militant and local struggles for identity. Across the world, human beings are caught between a process of globalisation which promises community for 'all' but allows no room for the local identity of 'each', and the centrifugal forces of localisation that struggle for the identity of 'each' at the expense of the community of 'all'.

It is also clear that on the eve of a new century and millennium, peoples everywhere have been affected by the emergence of a global dimension to human culture. Developments in technology, especially in the area of communication, have created a true 'global village' in which geographical distance is less important than at any time in human history. One consequence of this is that ancient longings for freedom and newly-awakened hopes for justice are fed by the experience of people in other parts of the world as ideas flow from one corner of the planet to another.

Women, more than half the human race, are often excluded from this emerging global consciousness as was highlighted at the world-wide gathering of Anglican women in Brazil in 1992 and the Beijing conference of women in 1995. Incidents of domestic, governmental and religious violence against women and the sexual exploitation of women and girls are experienced around the world. Women and girls in many cultures continue to be routinely denied access to education, technology and economic opportunities that will enable them to become full citizens of this 'global village'.

Enormous social and political changes have re-drawn the map of the earth and made millions of people into refugees. In many countries, great numbers of people once dispersed over large regions have migrated to urban areas, creating vast multi-cultural cities. The urban environment is a meeting-place for a broad plurality of cultures, lifestyles, choices and faiths.

But this multiplicity of sub-cultures is accompanied by a drab urban sameness as each city begins to look much like the next. Hence the urban is characterised by both cultural plurality and global conformity. The effects of urbanisation reach beyond the suburbs and the shanty-towns to even the most rural villages and islands.

In many cases the urban environment, economically over-extended, is marked by a breakdown of law and order, the collapse of health care and education, loss of identity and traditions and the clash of contradictory expectations.

An emerging economic order which makes extensive use of technology is being shaped by largely unaccountable multi-cultural entities. Issues of poverty now have global, not just national, dimensions. The dangerous division continue to widen between a wealthy minority who usurp the use of the world's diminishing resources and the masses of the world's poor for whom misery, hunger and death are constant threats. Changes in the global workplace have created a new environment for human labour in which the application of economic criteria ignores human values; and millions have little or no work.

The power of the media to shape perceptions about the world influences how human diversity is perceived, and can heighten the stresses of living with others who are different. Some dominant cultures continue to exercise enormous influence over, and even threaten the survival of, other cultures, both within a single state, and between nations. One effect of this, in some parts of the world, is perceptible in the way relationships between church and state affect how people live together in one society. Some Christians must practice their faith in settings where they are a small and persecuted minority, or where civil authority is hostile to them. Every culture and society is clearly affected in some way by issues related to diversity. But whether those effects are perceived as blessing or curse depends very much on the historical conjuncture of forces and currents unleashed in our own time.

People in the West are experiencing a rapid change from modernity to post-modernity. Modernity has had both positive and negative effects in for church and society. Positively, the rise of modern science from the soil of Christian Europe, combined with that movement of thought known as the Enlightenment, has made possible an ongoing technological revolution which impacts on many aspects of our lives. The enormous potential for good contained in these changes can be seen in the development of rapid travel and communications as well as the successes associated with modern medicine. However, modernity has also led to an exaggerated emphasis on the autonomous individual over against the dependent community; and thus contributed to the destruction of the environment and the exploitation of earth's non-replenishable resources in the short-term 'human' interest. In a variety of ways it has gradually led the West into an ideology that seems to generate injustice and spiritual emptiness.

In reaction to the excess of modernity, the West also has begun to experience a counter trend of post-modernity. This is characterized by a loss of confidence in human progress, and by caution over the powers of reason exercised in isolation. It has also caused suspicion over all claims to know truth and to explain the world in terms of any single overarching vision or truth-claim. Its emphasis upon difference and upon the part over against the whole, or the local against the universal, has become pervasive. We observe a weakening of traditional truth-claims both in church and society; in many instances, as a result, Christian faith in the West has abdicated the public arena and retreated into the private sphere.

Anglican Christians experience this reality of human diversity in a variety of ways. For some, it describes the society in which they live, made up of people of many ethnic backgrounds and faiths as well as those who affirm no religious faith. For others, it is part of the legacy of the colonial past which they are still struggling to overcome. For yet others, it is an aspect of their experience of the Church itself as it attempts to bring into one communion people of differing backgrounds, tribes, races, languages, or social classes. Within the life of the Church, Anglicans have become accustomed to differences in emphasis on varying aspects of our tradition, reflected in our varied styles of worship, prayer, and the ways we understand the Church. In addition, in many cultures the values, customs and assumptions of young people are so different from those of previous generations that we must speak of a separate 'youth culture' within the Church as well as within the larger society.

At the same time we celebrate the growing confidence in the gospel and the vitality of the churches in the two-thirds world. There is a wholistic world-view which underlies the vision of the Church and its mission in many parts of the churches in the South. It will be significant therefore to make conscious connection between this emphasis and experience of wholism and the emerging post-modern mood in the contemporary Western world.

It is in this context that we hear the call afresh to be a faithful church renewed in faith, worship and witness to be the sign and foretaste of a God-intended human community affirming our particular identities and yet united in a common sharing of the Spirit. It is the call to live in the spirit of Pentecost today, for it is on the day of Pentecost that God reverses the chaos symbolised by Babel, which attempted to unify through one language and which allowed no room for human diversity. Pentecost inaugurates a new humanity where local cultures are drawn together by God's redeeming and inclusive love. The Church is the first fruits of this new creation in which 'all' and 'each' are held together.

At the heart of the Christian tradition through the centuries lies the emphasis upon both the contextuality and catholicity of the gospel. They are in tandem and inseparable. The Anglican Communion has consistently stressed both the one and the many, held together within the sacramental life of the Church. In our tradition, Anglicans are united by the sacrament of the Eucharist, where the diversity of the many are brought together in unity in the body of Christ.

The Task

The work of Section III explored the calling of the Church to be faithful in a plural world, dealing particularly with issues upon which the regional meetings of the Communion asked Section III to reflect. We have done this at three levels. Our report examines the question of how each local church can live and witness to God's liberating and uniting love in a plural world by being both rooted in its cultural milieu and in communion with the Church universal. It seeks to understand how the Church in each place can be through its faithfulness to worship, the scriptures and prayer, both genuinely contextual and truly catholic, particular and universal. It affirms that it is in *koinonia* shaped by Christian spirituality, nurtured by the Eucharist, that fragmentation is healed and diversity is made enriching.

The report also seeks to understand how as a Communion we may wrestle with our differences as well as celebrate what unites us. How may we understand and exhibit the nature of our faith, and the relationship between faith and the many cultures we represent, so that our witness is truly faithful? How may our differences contribute to our unity and our sense of common identity? How may we embrace our membership in one Communion when our differences seem to threaten our common witness?

Finally, the report seeks to explore how our experience of unity in diversity, both within and between the member churches of the Anglican Communion, affects our discussions and relationships with other people, not least those of other denominations of the Christian Church, of Other Faiths and of no faith.

Sub-Section 2
A Faithful Church

As a Communion which identifies itself as part of Christ's one, holy, catholic and apostolic Church, Anglicans claim to embody in our own time and in our diverse settings the faith of the apostles as it is transmitted through the New Testament. Like the first Christians, Anglicans have been called 'from every nation, tribe, people and language' (Rev. 7:9). Like the disciples at Pentecost, we marvel to hear the Gospel, each in our own language (Acts 2:11). And like the early followers of Jesus who struggled to live united with each other in faithful response to their experience of being saved by a crucified and risen Lord, we seek a life together that affirms a common faith even while it recognizes the differences among us.

The book of Acts reminds us that when the disciples received the Holy Spirit at Pentecost, they were forged into a united people that proclaimed the gospel of Christ with persuasion, passion and signs. The power of their witness depended upon the gift of God's Spirit to a community united by faithfulness to 'the apostles' teaching, and to the fellowship (*koinonia*), to the breaking of bread and to prayer' (Acts 2:42). Those marks of faithfulness held by the first Christians remain to challenge and call us to be a faithful church in our own time.

Called to Be a Church Faithful in Koinonia

As the *Virginia Report* of the Inter-Anglican Theological and Doctrinal Commission reminds us, the Christian doctrine of the Trinity declares that the communion (*koinonia*) of three Persons in the One God expresses the very reality of the divine Being in terms of diversity and unity. The mutual self-giving and receiving of love of the three persons of the Trinity are the source and ground of our communion and fellowship with God and with one another. Because the Holy Trinity is a unity of being and at the same time a relationship of persons, the Church is called to express its diversity in truth, unity and love.

Koinonia (communion) literally means 'holding a common life together.' All humanity shares in common the potential to respond to the life of God. The

Church holds in common that this life is revealed and offered to the world by Jesus Christ. Within the Anglican Communion, this experience of a common life has traditionally been expressed in our use of Scripture, the Apostles' and Nicene Creeds, Baptism and the Eucharist, and the historic Episcopate, and in the formularies and constitutions of the difference provinces which spell out the doctrinal and structural features of Anglicanism.

In the words of the WCC Commission on Faith and Order, the *koinonia* which God intends for humankind is 'a participation in the life of God through [the Word] in the Holy Spirit, a shared life within communion in unity and diversity'[1] which draws us into the mystery of love which is God's very being. We perceive the reality of God in a number of ways. We meet God through our participation in the creation. God is also revealed in the experience of human relationships. And God encounters us through the structures by which our relationships with others and the rest of creation are ordered and transmitted from generation to generation, both within the Church and in its cultural contexts.

All Christians are called to share in God's reconciling work, through the Church. In every time and culture, this mission reminds each of Christ's disciples that theirs is the same calling Paul recognised as his own: "God, who reconciled us to himself through Jesus Christ, has given us the ministry of reconciliation... entrusting the message of reconciliation to us. So we are ambassadors for Christ, since God is making his appeal through us" (2 Cor. 5:18–20). It is in this way that God's own purposes are carried forward, however imperfectly, through the church's own mission. Although "we have this treasure in earthen vessels" (2 Cor. 4:7), the task entrusted to us is to seek, in the words of the Catechism of one of our member churches, "to restore all people to unity with God and each other in Christ."

This is the work of the whole people of God: "You are a chosen race, a royal priesthood, a holy nation, God's own people, in order that you may proclaim the mighty acts of him who called you out of darkness into his marvelous light. Once you were not a people, but now you are God's people" (1 Pet. 2:9–10a).

As the people of God, Christians are built up in the Body of Christ, 'until all of us come to the unity of the faith and of the knowledge of the Son of God, to maturity, to the measure of the full stature of Christ' (Eph. 4:12–13). While the New Testament and Christian tradition offer many images and models of the Church, this particular model of the Church as the Body of Christ is of special value because it clearly identifies the work of the church with Christ's own ministry, and because it encourages us to identify and affirm the charism of each.

Paul reminds us, 'we have gifts that differ according to the grace given us' and 'not all members have the same function' (Rom. 12:4–8; see 1 Cor. 12:4–26). Nevertheless, we are interdependent participants in the same body as we continue to share in Christ's work in the world. Though we fulfil a variety of functions within the body, there remains a fundamental unity and equality in the one body into which 'we were baptized—Jews or Greeks, slaves or free—and we were all made to drink of one Spirit' (1 Cor. 12:13). In Paul's words, 'in Christ Jesus you are all children of God through faith. As many of you as were baptized into Christ have clothed yourself with Christ. There is no longer Jew or Greek, there is no longer slave or free, there is no longer male and female; for all of you are one in Christ Jesus' (Gal. 3:26–28).

In such unity in Christ we find our freedom to serve—and God's service is perfect freedom. This freedom is not anarchic or indiscriminate. It requires the gifts of order and discipline so as to ensure that ministry and mission are exercised with efficiency and effectiveness, and in obedience to the will of God, who orders all things well. The orders of bishops, presbyter and deacons are effective ministers of God's grace working through the whole body of baptized Christians. Such orders are necessary to the well-being of God's Church as are the means whereby all Christians are equipped and empowered to exercise their gifts of the Spirit.

Baptism into the death and resurrection of Christ is the foundation of all Christian ministry. Through baptism, each follower of Christ is called into that ministry and the Holy Spirit gives the gifts necessary to carry it out. Paul's celebration of the variety of the Spirit's gifts and their usefulness in accomplishing God's purposes (1 Cor. 12:8–10) is echoed in the document *Baptism, Eucharist and Ministry:*

> All members are called to discover, with the help of the community, the gifts they have received and to use them for the building up of the church and for the service of the world to which the church is sent.[2]

The baptized and empowered community is also a eucharistic community, in prayer, praise and worship, receiving ongoing strengthening and nourishment for mission and ministry from the body and blood—the very life—of its self-giving and risen Lord. Nourishment in the Eucharist is the foundation of the energy that sustains the Church in its mission.

The Church is most faithful to its calling when all its members recognise their vocation as disciples of Christ and that they received their vocation in baptism, whatever form of ministry they might exercise. It is important that this be emphasised in our baptismal preparation and liturgies. This dramatic life-changing event should be accompanied by the full use of such powerful symbols as water, light, clothing, and an authentic welcome by the people of God.

While the specific words of the baptismal promises differ among the churches of the Communion, their content highlights five commitments understood broadly as directly related to the ministry of the whole people of God, none of which can be said to be more important than the others. These are worship, proclamation or evangelization, forgiveness or reconciliation, service and working for justice.

Within the Body of Christ, all Christians are called to worship, to know and share forgiveness, to share through word and action the stories of their faith in God's reconciling work in Jesus, to be people of compassion in love and service, and to hunger and thirst for righteousness, fairness and peace.

All the baptised are to be equipped to perform their ministries in accordance with their gifts and 'to give a reason for the hope that is in us' (1 Pet. 3:15). As in the days of the early Church, we live in a pluralistic society. The demands of the Gospel are many. We believe member Churches may need to develop or strengthen models of adult catechetical practice leading up to adult Christian initiation which stress both God's grace and the full demands of the Gospel as they accept and practise a new way of life. All Christians who would respond faithfully to their baptism deserve and need continuous formation in the biblical story, the faith of the Church, the ways in which the values of God's reign shape our living, the practice of prayer, as *koinonia* with God, the church's worship and its call to serve the world.

The varied gifts and skills which women bring to the Body of Christ have enhanced its ministry in word and deed and sacrament. The vows made in Baptism call us to a vision of the Church as a safe, sacred and healthy place for all people. If the Church is to embody the *koinonia* of God the Holy Trinity fully, the fear and denial which prevent its transformation must be confronted by the following principles:

- all people are equal in God's eyes and have equal access to the community of faith;

- the Church is called to strive for justice for all human beings and especially for those who are most vulnerable;

- the Church is called to oppose all forms of violence against women and children, both within and beyond the community of faith; and,

- the Church is called to empower women to develop and use their God-given gifts within their own cultural contexts.

By their Baptism, all the members of the *laos* as Body of Christ commit themselves to its ministry in the world. This ministry may take place within the context of the family or household, the village, neigbourhood or community, the school, workplace or the arena of civil authority, and through volunteer service. It is not limited by age, education, social status or any other criterion by which people sometimes seek to devalue the work of others. The world needs the gifts of *all* the members of the Body, seeing their work as an opportunity for service, offering care and compassion, struggling against poverty and oppression, striving for fairness and God's peace in their own lives and the lives of others. Furthermore, it is important to recall that the Body gathers together in worship in order to be strengthened for ministry in the world. The term 'lay ministry' can be misunderstood as referring primarily to work within the Christian community and so runs the risk of ignoring much of the ministry to which Christians are called. There is an equal danger in assuming that laity are in the world and ordained ministers are not.

However, gifts shared amongst the baptised are also meant to be used within the Body for the building up of the Church. This vocation is fulfilled in a variety of ministries, such as those of teachers and catechists, musicians, readers, pastors, visitors, leaders of prayer, discerners of others' ministries, administrators and organisers, counsellors and in the ministry of healing. Some are ordained to the church's ministry of word and sacrament as bishops, presbyter and deacons to focus the ministry of oversight, sacramental presence and service which properly belongs to the whole Christian community. In more and more provinces of the Communion, disciples work together in teams locally adapted to their specific context for the building up of the Body. We rejoice in these developments, including the recovery of diaconal ministry as belonging to the whole people of God and focused in both lay ministry and in a reinvigorated diaconate.

The theological basis for an understanding of Church and ministry affirms the calling of all to service through Baptism in accordance with the gifts bestowed on each. Furthermore, this calling is true of the local church in relation to the whole. For the doctrine of the Church undergirding this approach to unity and diversity in the people of God gives due weight to the local church as the whole Church of God in that place, rather than an incomplete fragment of a whole with a centre elsewhere.

It must always, therefore, be a distortion of what it means to share in the body of Christ when some ministries are exercised in such a way as to diminish the full significance of others. Many churches from across the Communion report that in the temporary absence of an ordained minister or when ordained ministry has been withdrawn, congregations discover and mobilize valuable lay resources from their own number. This suggests that sometimes the style of a particular ordained ministry, especially when seen locally as the primary ministry within the Church, can be a hindrance to the development of the whole people of God. However, many churches also witness to the effective ways by which ordained ministers support, enable and accompany lay people who are coming to realize their full potential as members of the Body of Christ.

Similarly, lay ministries are sometimes exploited and oppressed by a hierarchical style or structures; in some cultures women are particularly vulnerable in this respect. But the Communion also offers many examples of creative partnerships in shared leadership where the ministry of the ordained helps the whole body to express its vocation to a ministry of oversight, sacramental presence and service.

Because our worship should signal and celebrate the kind of Church and people we are by the grace of God, we urge all the member churches of the Anglican Communion to review their liturgies of ordination and commissioning to ensure that the interdependence and wholeness of the ministry of all the baptized is affirmed and celebrated.

The stories told by Anglicans from across the worldwide Communion describe the historical circumstances which have brought us by the action of God to this point in our shared pilgrimage of faith. Wherever we look in the Anglican Communion it is evident that the laity have played a vital part alongside the ordained in the mission of the Church. We are confident that the shared insight and common purpose evident in these developments are signs of the Spirit of God moving across the face of the earth. We seek now to build on this inheritance which is ours by God's grace, and to glorify God and build God's reign through the diverse but equal ministries to which all are called.

Called to Be a Church Faithful to the Apostles' Teaching

For more than a century, Anglicans have referred to Resolution 11 of the Lambeth Conference of 1888 (the so-called "Chicago-Lambeth Quadrilateral") as defining the principles on which the unity of a faithful church is based. The first of those principles affirms 'the Holy Scriptures of the Old and New Testaments, as "containing all things necessary to salvation," and as being the rule and ultimate standard of faith.'

The diverse situations in which the New Testament took shape meant that its writers were challenged to express the truth of the gospel faithfully in their own contexts. The book of Acts, for example, recalls the efforts of Paul and the other apostolic missionaries to proclaim the gospel in ways that addressed the specific needs and understanding of their hearers in different places and cultures. The four gospels also demonstrate clear differences of emphasis as the evangelists sought to understand and express their faith in the Word, made flesh in Jesus, to different audiences.

Anglicans have consistently asserted that if the Word of God is to continue to be proclaimed in our own time, the scripture must be interpreted in ways that both address its hearers and appropriate the teaching of the whole Bible, not setting one text against another but reading its parts in the light of the whole. In doing so, we make use of both tradition (as discovered in the Creeds and the teaching of the Church through the ages) and reason to interpret the scriptures, which retain their priority within the community of faith. Some Anglicans, following Hooker, believe that some elements of Christian faith form an essential part of our response to God's word, while others are non-essentials and reflect particular circumstances and cultural differences.

The Bible must be understood in the context of those to whom it was written and its abiding principles then interpreted for us in our own time and culture. In order to do this, we must recognise the cultural presuppositions which we ourselves bring to the Bible and the value of seeing it through the eyes of people of other times and cultures. This recognition of the effect of culture on our understanding of Scripture in no way diminishes its ultimate authority for our faith and the outworking of that faith in our lives.

Allowing the Word of God to judge us through the Scriptures permits us to see the ways in which we fall short of God's demands. In some cultures, the Scripture has been used to buttress unjust and corrupt behaviour: examples of this abound, as when the Bible was used to support doctrines of *apartheid* in South Africa and racial segregation in other parts of the world. The authentic interpretation of the Bible was a major contribution to the over-turning of the doctrine of *apartheid.*

As Anglicans, we accept that the Bible is binding on us. As we keep it, so it keeps us. We believe there is great need for the teaching of the actual text of scripture rather than theories about the text. Good scholarship is essential, as are teachers who can faithfully interpret and expound scripture. However, it is also true that some of those who understanding scripture best, and can help us to apply its meaning, are people who have had very little theological training.

We acknowledge that within our traditions there are differing approaches to Scripture. But these are not necessarily mutually exclusive. Rather at best they are richly complementary, and those of each tradition should seek to learn from the others. For some, the Bible speaks immediately to them; stories from Scripture speak to stories in their lives. For others, the Biblical Word of God comes through the process of critical scholarship. Each needs the other, if Scripture is to be experienced in its fullness. So while we honour the diversity of approaches we look for a unity of attitude towards Biblical authority and a unity of expectation towards it revelatory power.

Called to Be a Church Faithful in the Breaking of Bread

The reference in Acts 2:42 to 'the breaking of the bread' reveals the first believers as faithful in their meeting together for the meal at which the worship-event we call the 'Eucharist' was shared. Here in embryo is both the substance and the symbol of the Church's life in the world, gathering in the presence of Christ to share a meal with each other, engaging in that central act of worship by which they responded to the Lord's command to 'do this in remembrance of me', and from it bearing witness to Christ in the world. Our concern has been to trace the full implications of the worship which was to grow from that starting point as the characteristic distinguishing action of the church, by which the people of God are constituted and sustained as the Church.

We begin with a note of the significance of worship in a plural church. In its fullest sense worship is living in Christ, presenting our bodies as 'a living sacrifice, holy and acceptable to God' (Rom. 12:1) living in love and open to the unity God wills for our diverse humanity. But holy living is focused and sustained in regular corporate worship, as, developing the patterns of those early disciples, we follow the shape of the liturgy. Such worship is central to our lives as Christians, and by it we are to be renewed for God's mission to a broken humanity.

Our theology is reflected in our liturgy: we pray as we believe and come to believe as we pray. The structure of the Bible itself reflects an arrangement for reading in the assembly, and is best understood in the context of worship. Liturgical worship is the 'inner surface' of all ministry. It embraces, expresses and empowers the life and mission of the church—or it is a vanity, a nothing (Amos 5:21–24). So we dare not isolate it as an activity on its own. Rather it is a key to our grasping all the rest, including our unity in spite of diversity, the various ministries through which we function as a community, and the importance of daily life, in all its cultural expressions, as the sphere of our spiritual worship.

As the 1988 Lambeth Conference declared, culture is the context in which people find their identity. We believe the issues of liturgical inculturation is of crucial contemporary significance and affirm the continuing importance of Resolutions 22 and 47 of the 1988 Lambeth Conference. Resolution 22 noted that "God's love extends to people of every culture and (that) the Gospel judges every culture according to the Gospel's own criteria of truth, challenging some aspects of culture while endorsing others for the benefit of the Church and society." It further urged "the Church everywhere to work at expressing the unchanging Gospel of Christ in words, actions, names, customs, liturgies, which communicate relevantly in each contemporary society." Resolution 47 declared that each member church of the Anglican Communion is free, "subject to essential universal Anglican norms of worship, and to a valuing of traditional liturgical materials, to seek that expression of worship which is appropriate to its Christian people in their cultural context." Resolution 4.12 of Lambeth Conference 1998 clarifies this, urging that new Provincial liturgical texts and practices be consonant with accepted ecumenical agreements reached in multilateral and bilateral dialogues.

Sub-Section 3
Unity and Diversity in the Anglican Communion

The member churches of the Anglican Communion are bound to each other by a common spiritual ancestry and by the common faith we share. At times, our differing perceptions of the gospel and the varied ways in which we seek to be faithful in different contexts may challenge and even impair that communion. But the transcendent nature of the reign of God reminds us that no culture completely embodies the gospel, just as no culture is left without any sign of God's presence.

Because Christians are called to serve and embody the values and aspirations of the reign of God in specific contexts, they are always in creative dialogue and tension with whatever culture they call their own. Faithful witness requires us to examine critically the assumptions and values of that culture in the light of the reign of God, noting that some will be evident in the life of the church itself. For Christians, such reflection is part of the on-going process of repentance and conversion demanded by the Gospel.

The Anglican Communion offers a forum in which that process of reflection and transformation can take place. Dialogue with Christians of other cultures can provide the prophetic challenge to transform whatever might be alien or even hostile to the values of the Gospel of God's reign. Sharing the stories of God's presence among us in our many contexts can strengthen our faith and give us new insights and courage to sing the Lord's song in our own land.

Anglican Christians, bound to each other in a worldwide Communion, can, if they will, draw upon their diversity to develop and broaden an understanding of the gospel and the promises made by God to the whole creation. We can hear from one another both a word of judgment and a word of hope. As the *Virginia Report* reminds us, the diversity of the Anglican Communion is neither an accident nor a cause for regret. On the contrary, it is a way of experiencing the reality of God and God's purposes for humankind. Indeed, the diversity through which we experience our unity is God's gracious gift to us.

The report of the Inter-Anglican Theological and Doctrinal Commission, *For the Sake of the Kingdom* (1985), which was received by the last Lambeth Conference, began to grapple with the issue of what it might mean for Anglicans to live faithfully in a world increasingly aware of its diversity. It made an important distinction between two approaches to diversity.[3]

First is noted an ideological reading of diversity, in which all differences are of equal value and therefore not accessible to evaluation, or critique from a contrary point of view. While this 'ideological pluralism' does avoid conflict, it does so by relativising all faith, though it does offer some ground for dialogue between those who disagree with each other. At the same time, faith is marginalised from public life and its specific forms appeal only to those who are already in agreement with it.

Although this extreme perception of pluralism is increasingly encountered in different forms throughout the world, the Inter-Anglican Theological and Doctrinal Commission was careful to distinguish it from an alternative view of diversity more congruent with the gospel. That viewpoint affirms that the gospel is one, though the Church hears and responds to it in multiple forms.

The encounter with diverse understandings of the gospel and responses to it can breed conflict among Christians today. As in other times and places, this conflict can be the source of theological controversy and ecclesiastical division. But we should also recall that such incidents have often provided the occasion for the Church's renewal and growth, even when factors other than the strictly doctrinal are involved.

We can also rejoice at the determination of successive generations of Christians to understand and to declare their faith, and we can receive their testimony with humility and gratitude. We receive that testimony not only because of what it meant to those whose witness it was, but because of what it has made us and how it has enriched us all. We are not observers of the Church's story but participants in it. As we are called upon to make choices, we observe how those who have gone before us have made similar choices, often at great cost, about how the message of Christ is to be heard and proclaimed. We receive and tell the story of how for two millennia Christian people and communities have sought to be faithful to God amidst the many alternatives which called for their allegiance and understanding. In telling their story, we tell our own. Just as they were required in word and deed to hold the vision of God's reign and proclaim its presence among them, we too are called to be faithful in our own times and places.

We can honour, value and make our own the story we have received, but we cannot expect those who have gone before us to bear the witness that only we can make. That task is ours alone. We are shaped by our past, and our thoughts will be constrained by the limits of our own perceptions and possibilities, even if we are now aware of those limitations. But in spite of them, our testimony must become part of the Church's story in our own time and in the many contexts in which we live.

Anglican Christians are united in their belief that all Christians should encounter and express the faith in the words and ideas of their own culture. But our history also tells us that this principle has not always been put into practice. In those places where Anglican mission took place in close association with the colonization of some peoples by others, particular cultural expressions of Christianity have sometimes been considered as especially privileged or even necessary to preserve the authentic nature of Christian faith. This attitude has often gone unexamined because culture traditions normally carry with them the force of apparent truth. This has led to negative judgements about another culture, as inappropriate contexts for the Christian faith, making the expression of faith within these cultures more difficult.

Nor has the belief that faith may and indeed should be expressed in a variety of cultures prevented controversy with regard to the acceptable limits of diversity within the Christian community. While many would agree that faith can be distorted by cultural attitudes, beliefs and traditions, Christians often disagree about the criteria for avoiding such distortion. Furthermore, the presence of different ideas, customs and values within the household of faith is sometimes perceived as a threat to the integrity of the gospel. Throughout Christian history these disagreements, penetrating into important matters of faith, have led to breaks in communion. But especially in the early centuries, such controversy also brought about the development of important statements of the faith. In our time insistence on the co-existence of divergent opinions and practices within the Anglican Communion is sometimes considered to foster relativism and lack of clarity with regard to the acceptable limits of diversity.

Our Communion has grown from a church shaped by English culture, history and institutions. Because English Christians expressed their faith in their own culture, that same faithfulness to this practice of inculturation is reflected when Christians of whatever culture tell the gospel story in their own particular setting.

As this inculturation has been practised by Anglicans around the globe, our churches have come to exhibit a great variety of liturgies and vestures, of pastoral and spiritual practices, and missionary strategies. The Anglican story now highlights not only the great figures of its English past; it also honours countless men and women, lay and ordained, whose lives have enriched our witness in many cultures and across the whole earth.

The Anglican Communion has developed an ecclesiology without a centralized authority which acts juridically on behalf of all its member churches. No single Province or group of Provinces has the right to arbitrate on behalf of other Anglican Provinces, or determine the shape of their faithful discipleship. Rather, the future of Anglicanism must draw on the resources of the whole Communion. On the other hand, without any sense of connectedness or accountability to the wider Communion, individual churches will lose touch, not only with each other, but with the Anglican and Christian tradition from which they took their origin. They could then cease to be churches incarnating the gospel within their own culture, and become prisoners of that culture or to their own past. Their life will be static and fixed, rather than responding to a dynamic and living tradition.

The measure to which the Anglican Communion can be faithful to its *koinonia* will determine whether local churches can claim to incarnate the universal Church in their own life. It will also determine its capacity to retain its own integrity as a tradition, as well as its ability to walk together with other Christian communions on the shared pilgrimage towards visible unity and the reign of God.

The Church's life is never wholly private. Because Christian mission and ministry are carried out within the context of a given society, therefore the ways the Church is related to its society are of crucial importance for that mission and ministry.

Ordained Ministry: The Three-Fold Order

Among the baptised the three-fold ministry of deacon, presbyter, and bishop orders the ministering community of God's people. The ordained ministry is never separate from or independent of that community. Indeed, the ordained ministry receives its authority from Christ by the Holy Spirit within the whole Body. Certain developments in ministry within the three-fold orders were brought to our attention. These included ordained local ministries, and a re-discovering of the diaconate as a 'separate and equal order' rather than a transitional one.

Ordained Local Ministries

Since the Lambeth Conference of 1988, a number of churches have developed and now offer to the Communion a pattern of ministry variously described as 'total ministry' or 'mutual ministry' or 'ministering communities.' This pattern of team ministry is still evolving and its form varies from place to place. A significant aspect of this development is the ordination of clergy (who may be non-stipendiary or supported by the community) licensed specifically for local service as priests or deacons. These local clergy work with a team of authorized laypersons under the oversight of an experienced priest who has special responsibility to provide resources and support for the local team. We rejoice in the growing number of dioceses and provinces which encourage the ordination of persons as priests and deacons to serve the Church, as did Paul, at their own cost. We thank God for their contribution in building up and sustaining the life and witness of God's people across the globe. We encourage bishops and dioceses to ensure that they are enabled to play their full part at all levels of diocesan life.

In some places the shortage of financial resources has been the catalyst for the church to develop lay ministry and new forms of partnership between clergy and laity. In other situations such developments have emerged from awareness that a new approach to mission and ministry is needed. This movement is one result of the deepening understanding of the relationship between baptism and the ministry of the whole people of God; as well as of the complementary relationship between ordained and lay ministry.

This pattern of ministry requires the commitment of the bishop and diocese in providing the necessary resources for the training and formation of both lay and ordained members of 'ministering communities.' These teams provide sacramental ministry, pastoral care and proclamation and teaching of the Word. While ordained ministry always includes teaching and pastoral care as well as a sacramental ministry, in these ministering communities much of the teaching and pastoring will be shared by lay people.

It is important to affirm in the face of these developments that there is only one order of diaconate and one order of priesthood. The ordination and licensing of self-supported and/or local priests in no way implies establishing another order of diaconate or priesthood. The ways in which particular clergy exercise ministry is determined by the bishop's license. The formation of 'local clergy' is of great importance and must address the local context and the importance of a collaborative approach to ministry. Ongoing training should be required for all authorised ministers, whether ordained or lay, stipendiary or non-stipendiary.

In some situations, under the direction of the bishop, deacons or licensed lay ministers lead the liturgy of the word and administer the eucharistic elements which have been previously consecrated by a priest. There may be occasions when this is the only means by which people can receive Holy Communion; nevertheless, it deprives them of participation in the central action of the Eucharist and should only be allowed in the absence of a priest or bishop.

In some parts of the Communion it has been proposed that deacons or lay people be licensed to preside at the Eucharist. Such a development would challenge the tradition of the church catholic that ordained ministry serves the church by uniting word and sacrament, pastoral care and oversight of the Christian community. Presiding at the Eucharist is the most obvious expression of this unity. Lay presidency would also create major difficulties with many of our ecumenical partners as well as within the Anglican Communion. We are not able to endorse this proposal.

The Diaconate as a Distinct Order of Ministry

As the Body of Christ, the Church as a whole is called and empowered to make God's compassion, care and justice tangible and visible in each generation. Through this ministry, God's reign draws near to people whatever their circumstances or condition. In the early centuries of the Church's life, the diaconate provided focus and inspiration for this ministry of all God's people. Today, in a number of dioceses the renewal of the diaconate helps the whole people of God to be more effectively not only the servant Church ministering to human need.

Like the ministries of oversight and priesthood, the ministry of service and the proclamation of the Word traditionally associated with the diaconate, belongs to the whole Body of Christ. Where deacons exercise their special ministry within the Church, they do so by illuminating and holding up the servant ministry of the whole Church and calling all its members to that ministry.

All the churches of the Anglican Communion embrace servant-ministry as an integral part of their life. However, not all have chosen to restore the diaconate to its more traditional form as a distinct order. Nevertheless in some places within the Anglican Communion the diaconate has re-emerged as a separate and distinct order, and not as a transitional ministry leading to the priesthood. The re-establishment of the diaconate in this form liberates bishops and presbyters to exercise their complementary and distinctive tasks, a process hinted at in Acts 6. All God's people are called to exercise their ministry in the spirit of servanthood.

The significance given to *diakonia*, as a servant ministry of love and justice, in ecumenical discussion and common action is a positive and encouraging development, but more attention is still needed because not all churches accept it as a distinct order.

Active servant ministry in relation to human need within and beyond the Church, and a visible diaconal presence in the liturgical life of the community, are essential features of the diaconate. The traditional liturgical functions of the deacon are reading the gospel, overseeing the intercessions, setting the table for the eucharistic celebration and leading the dismissal.

Fears are sometimes expressed that a renewed diaconate may take away from the laity their God-given ministry. While this remains a possibility, the experience of many dioceses indicates that the appropriate training and oversight of deacons at work in dioceses, congregations and agencies of care, advocacy and justice will ensure that more, not less, lay participation in servant-ministry will occur. Dioceses and churches where the diaconate has not been established as a distinct order are invited to explore this ministry with those dioceses where this has taken place. This may lead to a fresh discovery of the value of the diaconate in strengthening and renewing the ministry of the whole people of God.

The relationship of deacons to their bishop and other diocesan and local leaders may need clarification and strengthening. Ongoing discussion and consultation with the appropriate bodies within the Anglican Communion would help to clarify the specific vocation, ministry and place of the deacon within the life of the church. There is urgent need for worldwide consultation among Anglicans already engaged in the renewal of the diaconate.

Servant-ministry belongs to all the people of God, including bishops, presbyters and deacons. While deacons have a special role and responsibility with respect to the servant life of the community, all share in this ministry. For this reason, some have asked that the 'direct ordination' of those clearly called to a priestly ministry (without prior ordination to the diaconate) be considered by representative Anglican theologians in consultation with the wider ecumenical community, and that the practice of transitional diaconate be reviewed. The separate ordination of those called to the distinctive or vocational diaconate may help clarify the significance and focus of their ministry to the people of God and the world.

All the ministries undertaken by deacons are performed on behalf of the whole Body of Christ in each place. They are called and ordained as the go-between servants, to bring the needs of the world to the people of God, and to enable, lead and encourage the faithful response of the whole people of God.

The Presbyterate

With the servant ministry of the diaconate, the ministry of presbyters is found at the heart of the community of faith in each place. Entrusted by the bishop with the presidency of the Eucharist, presbyters share in many aspects of the bishop's ministry, providing leadership to the whole people of God in worship, proclamation and community.

Presbyters are called in their community to encourage the people of God, as members of the Body of Christ, to the fullness of their baptismal ministry in a scriptural Church marked by unity, holiness, catholicity and apostolicity. Presbyters assist all God's people to discover and use to God's glory the gifts and ministries given to them by God.

In promoting unity, they call together the people's diversity of gifts into the service of the one Body of Christ, enabling pastoral care, healing and reconciliation. In exemplifying holiness, they seek to serve a holy church marked by compassion, justice and generosity. In promoting catholicity, they call the people of God to responsibility for the whole community in which they live, regardless of divisions of race, gender, privilege and wealth. In faithfulness to the teaching and mission of the apostles, they call the whole Church to ministry and mission. This demanding calling requires intensive and continuing training and formation within a faithful worshipping community.

The Episcopate, Collegiality and Conciliarity

In common with historic Christianity, the Anglican Communion considers the episcopate to be one of the defining elements of its life together. Rooted in apostolic ministry, bishops symbolise and guard the unity of the church as a whole, and within a diocese represent its coherence in the faith. The bishop is the link between the local and the wider church, and serves as an advocate of justice and reconciliation in the wider society. The bishop also serves as the historical embodiment of our faithful ancestors who have gone before and the faithful yet to come.

Bishops exercise their leadership in a wide variety of styles, reflecting widely diverse gifts and cultural contexts. These styles are influenced by personal gifts but are most often shaped by the discerned need and mission of a diocese at a particular time. Therefore the ministry of a bishop may be predominantly pastoral, missionary, educational, prophetic or collegial. Diverse understandings of the nature of power, authority, responsibility, and accountability shape the practice of *episcopé* among the churches of the Anglican Communion (cf. *Virginia Report—Episcopé:* Personal, Collegial and Communal).

In Anglican tradition, the authority of the bishop is always exercised within a synodical framework of church government. The exact ways in which this relationship is structured—by each church's constitution, by the needs of the diocese, and by local cultural traditions that influence them—varies from one Province to another. Whatever these circumstances, the authority given to a bishop is neither for the sake of personal power nor for pride of place, but in the service of the Gospel for the people of God.

Successive Lambeth Conferences have specifically rejected the possibility that the Anglican Communion might be linked by any centralised government or jurisdiction. For example, the 1920 Lambeth Conference, speaking about the spirit of Anglicanism, stated:

> It stands for the far more spiritual and more Christian principle of loyalty to the fellowship. The Churches are indeed independent, but independent with the Christian freedom that recognizes the restraints of truth and love. They are not free to deny the truth. They are not free to ignore the fellowship.[4]

The 1930 Lambeth Conference noted the vulnerability which such an ideal might entail, without faltering in the conviction that the 1920 Conference has discerned the right way forward for Anglicanism:

> Freedom naturally and necessarily carries with it the risk of divergence to the point even of disruption. In case any such risk should actually arise, it is clear that the Lambeth Conference as such could not take any disciplinary action. Formal action would belong to the several Churches of the Anglican Communion individually; but the life of the Lambeth Conference, sought before executive action is taken by the constituent Churches, would carry very great moral

> weight. And we believe in the Holy Spirit. (*Lambeth Conference* 1930, p. 153).

The form in which Anglican structures had developed offers resources for responding to the problems raised by the Communion's ever-increasing diversity. The development of episcopal leadership within a structure of synodical government emerged in several parts of the world in the context of their local cultures. Yet, this framework of government still appears to some to reflect the influence of Western parliamentary democracy, and more collaborative and consensual structures may be needed. However, we should not underestimate the significance of synodical government as an expression of *koinonia* for Anglican churches. In Anglicanism, episcopacy and conciliarity are combined in such a way that the whole people of God, clergy and laity together, are brought into a fellowship in which decisions about common life could be made. Differing gifts of discernment and ministry within the Body were linked together in a common purpose. The mind of Christ is discerned by the faithful consent of the whole Church.

Synodical government is based on the belief that attentive and reasonable debate about the true meaning of Scripture and the Christian tradition will focus our discernment of the mind of Christ. This conviction is of special importance when the Church lacks clarity about a particular aspect of its common life. Paul reminds us that all Christians see 'through a glass darkly' (1 Cor. 13:12) but when there is prolonged difficulty in achieving consensus over difficult issues, such as the ordination of women to the priesthood and episcopate, then the pressure on our synodical structures becomes intense.[5]

In resolving that it was within the authority of each Province of the Anglican Communion to make its own decision concerning the ordination of women to the episcopate, the 1988 Lambeth Conference expressed the hope that the highest possible degree of communion would be maintained between the Provinces, especially between those Provinces who differed from one another. This principle of seeking the deepest level of communion also relates to differences within dioceses and Provinces and serves as a guide to their decision-making and life together.

Both the Eames Commission on Women in the Episcopate and the Inter-Anglican Theological and Doctrinal Commission have responded to the challenge of maintaining the deepest possible communion in the midst of disagreement. Both stress the nature and gift of the *koinonia* of the Holy Trinity as the framework for communion among Christians. The Eames Commission's 1994 Report stressed that our communion is established in baptism and that therefore differences over ministerial order might impair but could not destroy communion among Christians. It reminded us that all ordinations within a divided Christianity are 'provisional,' until such time as they are all received as one within the Church Universal. However, if all Christians are united in Christ, then no single act can completely destroy the *koinonia* given in baptism. In order to safeguard the communion already achieved, the Eames Commission Report proposed guidelines encouraging mutual understanding and respect during this period of reception.

Belonging Together, an interim study document issued by the Theological and Doctrinal Commission in 1992, sought ways in which Provinces could embrace a positive sense of interdependence rather than a mere process of consultation, which it feared might produce either 'fragmentation' or 'artificial uniformity.'[6] In the previously-cited *Virginia Report*, the Commission sought to describe the marks of our unity (scripture, tradition and reason; sacraments and worship; mutuality of gifts within the church; episcopal oversight) by which Anglicans are identified despite their differences. Its primary emphasis is on the gift of God's gracious love, *koinonia* and the Holy Trinity, as the context for those instruments which seek to maintain the coherence of the Anglican Communion: the Archbishop of Canterbury; the Lambeth Conference; the Anglican Consultative Council, and the Primates' Meeting.[7]

The Virginia Report also emphasises the principle of subsidiarity which, according to the Oxford English Dictionary, means that 'a central authority should have a subsidiary function, performing only those tasks which cannot be performed effectively at a more immediate or local level.'[8] This principle, which aided the churches in their decision about the ordination of women, recognizes that member churches should decide how to order ministry, leadership and worship to their own setting; but as the *Virginia Report* observes,

> in the life of the Church the local level was never seen as simply autonomous. Because the work of Christ was itself a reconciliation of humanity, there is evidence from the first days of the churches of concern for the unity of the communities, both in their internal relationships and in their inter-relationships.[9]

For this reason, it goes on,

> the Eames Commission has stressed the need for consultation prior to action, and for charity and patience…, insisting that discernment and reception is a continuing process in the life of the Church, and cannot be hurried.[10]

The Virginia Report further expounds the principle of 'open reception.' It states that churches continue to remain in communion with each other while allowing that important differences may exist between them. This process of 'open reception' gives time for the whole Communion to recognise whether or not such differences remain within the limits of acceptable diversity. This was the principle proposed by Gamaliel when the Jewish authorities were deciding what to do about the apostles at the beginning of their ministry; see Acts 5:33–39.

The Pauline theology of the church as the Body of Christ provides a framework for a wholistic understanding of the way Christians receive and pass on a tradition. From the reading of Scripture and by reflection on the Church's tradition, the whole Church is involved in discerning the meaning of the Gospel. Bishops have a distinctive role in focusing, guarding and proclaiming the faith, but they do so on behalf of the people of God. Because the Church experiences its common life through a whole web of relationships and across a broad range of ministries, *koinonia* can be sustained even as some elements of the tradition are challenged and developed. Specific differences need not break communion; they may clarify both the nature of the communion we already share and the vision of communion which has yet to be achieved.

The faith we share not only looks back to its origins, it also points forward to the time when God will be 'all in all' (1 Cor. 15:28). Meanwhile, the Church has the responsibility to ground its hopes and incarnate its faith in the diverse realities of its own generation. The Chicago-Lambeth Quadrilateral's insistence on the historic episcopate affirms an episcopate which witnesses both to the Church's beginnings and to its ultimate fulfillment in Christ. It speaks of the historic episcopate as one which is to be "locally adapted in the method of its administration to the varying needs of the nations and peoples called by God into the unity of His Church."[11]

Because the Church prays for and looks forward to the final reign of God, its life and ministry in the present is meant to anticipate that truth. The *Virginia Report* cites the Archbishop of Canterbury, the Lambeth Conference and the Primates' Meeting as examples of episcopal ministry which can work together for effective participation in the discovery of God's will and the guidance of the Spirit in the present age. There are also other expressions of Anglican unity; such as the Anglican Consultative Council, exchange visits, companion diocesan links, Partners in Mission consultations. These are supported a life of common prayer, the Anglican Cycle of Prayer and the bonds developed through theological education. Together these structures help us discover ways in which the different parts of the body can deepen the *koinonia* which is our mission and purpose as we continue the work of discernment in the face of the differences which we face on the eve of a new millennium.

Sub-Section 4
A Faithful Church in a Plural World

The member churches of the Anglican Communion rejoice in the faith we proclaim in so many cultures around the globe. We give thanks to God for calling us into the Body of Christ which continues in the apostles' teaching and fellowship, in the breaking of the bread and the prayers. And our hearts are grateful for the many bonds we share with others in situations far different from our own.

But like Jesus and his disciples, churches find themselves surrounded by nameless masses, many of whom struggle to find their identity in a world that has little use for them. The New Testament knew them as the *ochlos*, the faceless crowd drawn to the promise of the good news they heard from Jesus. In our time they often have no one to defend them or plead their cause, and remain as marginalised victims of a world which has no need or care for them. In our time, as in the time of Jesus, they meet us hungry for acceptance, thirsty for dignity, longing for hope. They stand before us as images of the multi-faceted and complex world the people of God are called to serve.

How are we to embrace this diverse world of which we are a part? Its challenge demands that we encourage and develop strategies and networks which seek to empower human community, help groups to rediscover their identity and celebrate their diversity. It is important that the Church be seen to welcome a multi-ethnic, multi-cultural setting for its witness to glory in the diversity of God's creation, rather than a grudging and reluctant tolerance.

Furthermore, it should be noted that in many places there is an unresolved tension between generations about cultural elements that have served previous generations well in their struggle for survival and self-respect, but which may be less appreciated by the young. Moreover, in many cases the cultures among which Christians live and minister represent a heritage which predates by many centuries the arrival of Anglican Christianity. Witness in such situations, as indeed in every situation, demands sensitivity and respect for the traditions and values of those among whom we live.

Marriage, Family, and Sexual Relations

One example of the clash of cultures is found in sexual relationships, and the value given to marriage and family life. Faithful patterns of marriage and family life reflect the love of God in Christ for humankind (Eph. 5:31–32). Those patterns can be severely tested not only by the different values between generations but by powerful cultural forces which preach an exaggerated individualism. These forces attacks the heart of human community and erodes the commitments and mutual self-sacrifice which are at the centre of the Church's teaching about marriage. This is heightened by the harsh realities of want, violence, HIV/AIDS, social dislocation and rapid social changes. The victims of this crisis include most especially the young, the old, and the economically marginalized, all of whom may suffer from loneliness, neglect, economic and sexual exploitation.

Cultural traditions influence the beliefs which Christians in different settings bring to the understanding of human sexuality, marriage and family life. Indeed, Christians in different parts of the world often have very different understandings of the family. The positive aspects of such differences are to be accepted as reflecting the diversity of God's good creation.

The Gospel sheds the light of God's judgement and mercy all our human patterns of living. In witnessing to God's holy love, the Church has the blessed task of remaining faithful to the clear New Testament standard of marriage, and of love, faithfulness and integrity in family life, friendship and social relationships. While at the same time, the Church also embraces those who have different lifestyles but are seeking God's mercy and love as part of our common repentance and forgiveness.

The New Testament provides not only a norm of loving faithfulness, but also a source of renewal which can transform our family relationships. It reminds us that Christians understand sexuality as a unique gift of God which is deeply personal. Hence Christians reject all that depersonalizes or idolizes human sexuality, such as pornography.

It is important for the Church to provide support for family life, and to ensure that congregations provide skilled and compassionate guidance in preparing people of all ages to live out their family commitments in the light of their faith. In many parts of the world, the Church has a long history of engagement in women's issues. The circumstances of our world now call for similar attention to the special needs of men, children and the elderly. For example, in many different ways around the globe men are also experiencing new pressures on personal identity and crises in employment and family roles. The Gospel challenges the Church to support men in renewing their parental and family commitments and in discovering the reality of the new creation in Christ.

Relations between Church and State

Our Anglican tradition presents many different examples of relations between Church and State. While the Church of England remains established by law, other churches of the Anglican Communion have different relationships to the governments under which they live. In some countries the church is recognised as one religious body among many; in others, there are serious limits on the church's mission and ministry because of hostile governmental attitudes or actions. Some churches are the focus of conscientious opposition to government policy, corruption or injustice. In other places the church or its leaders play an important role as peace-makers in the face of civil disorder and its aftermath. For some parts of the church, simply continuing to believe and practise the faith is an act of resistance.

Thus Christians make judgments about the appropriate relationship between church and state in particular and different circumstances. The role of the church in the struggle in South Africa during the last twenty-five years is a good example of such judgements. In every judgment, the church is called to embody and witness to the lordship of Christ and to seek how it can best serve the interests of society as it witnesses to the values of the reign of God.

Church and Urbanisation

The Church has an important role to play in helping individuals and communities come to terms with the global changes which urbanisation demands of them. Although the modern 'mega-city' would be unrecognisable to any biblical writer, the New Testament nevertheless addresses the people of our contemporary cities as authoritatively as it first addressed the world of the early Church. So the Church is called to develop forms of evangelism and pastoral care which speak to our contemporary urbanised cultures. Laity and clergy need to be trained to analyse and engage these cultures from the viewpoint of their Christian faith and to challenge the exploitation and spirit of competition they espouse.

Global Economics and Attitudes to Money

The global economic changes shaping our world bring benefits to many by making available employment, goods and services. But developing nations, often rich in resources, can, and in many cases have, become dependent on foreign capital and expertise and lose their resources to foreign owners. Environmental damage wrought by trans-national enterprises and fluctuating prices can further diminish the wellbeing of peoples for whom survival itself is a struggle.

Money in itself is morally neutral. It is socially useful as a means of exchange by which our primary needs are satisfied. The current dominant global culture tends to reduce all values to the economic and fosters an uncontrolled avarice that feeds personal selfishness and idolises wealth. The people of God are called to value love and service and to affirm the absolute dignity of the human over against the reduction of all value to the purely economic.

As individuals and in local churches, we are called to cultivate an appropriate simplicity of living that exercises a responsible stewardship of the earth's resources.

The member churches of the Anglican Communion have a role to play in seeking to moderate the negative impact of global economic forces, and to develop partnerships that share resources and both encourage self-sufficiency and interdependence. Grassroots initiatives which foster small business enterprises among the poor and unemployed, and projects that improve health, education, job skills, housing, and food and water supply, are concrete means by which our churches can contribute to the healing of a deeply divided world.

Interfaith Relations

Many aspects of the plurality we have noted arise from a widespread loss of any kind of religious faith. But there is also a pluralism of religious faiths in the diverse world in which we live. So being "Called to be a faithful Church in a plural world" also means being a sign of God's promise to restore the human community in Christ even in a context of increasing religious plurality.

In the New Testament Jesus' public ministry begins with a reference to the acts of God on behalf of the Gentile world, with the story of the widow of Zarephath and Naaman, the leper (Luke 4:26–27). The young Church is led by the Spirit to struggle with the conversion of the Gentiles. The story of Peter and Cornelius (Acts 10:22–11:18) underlines the fact that God's love reaches out beyond the known boundaries of race and religion and that God has no favourites. How can the Church be faithful to the example of Christ in the face of increased tensions between people of different faiths?

Stories shared at the 1998 Lambeth Conference indicate that within the Anglican Communion relationships with people of Other Faiths vary widely. In some places those relationships are characterised by cordiality and cooperation in nation-building and struggles for justice. In other places, relationships are competitive and Christians face hostility, oppression and martyrdom.

Social and political realities necessarily shape the nature and form of Christian response to people of Other Faiths. Where there is open conflict, it is often the case that factors other than religion or theology are involved. In such situations there are no simple solutions. But in the light of our call to be a faithful church witnessing to the reconciled humanity that God intends in Christ, we are constrained to strive for community with our neighbours of Other Faiths and of no faith, however difficult and costly it may be.

On the basis of the revelation of God in Jesus Christ, we affirm that salvation has been offered to all people through Christ. The gift and claim of Christ is what we want to share with people of Other Faiths. We also acknowledge that there are aspects of truth about God and creation which are present in Other Faiths. As the 1989 World Council of Churches' conference on mission and evangelism in San Antonio expressed, 'We cannot point to any other way of salvation than Jesus Christ; at the same time we cannot set limits to the saving power of God.' As humble recipients of the salvation that God offers in Christ, we are called to witness unequivocally to that gift and its giver, recognising that at no point can those who have been called to witness take the place of judge, who is God and God alone.

An appreciation of the gracefulness of our God, who has never left any time or place without witnesses, should move us to humility in any personal claim to understand the fullness of the truth about the God of all creation. We note too that a renewed understanding of the Triune God's ways with humans helps many Christians to be open to persons of Other Faiths as well.

Furthermore, interfaith dialogue is not conducted only between two or more religious systems but between persons who live by different faith-commitments. Relationships between Christians and people of Other Faiths should therefore be founded on mutual respect, sensitivity to their deepest faith commitments and experiences, and a willingness to be their servants for Christ's sake. Where local circumstances allow, relationship should issue in dialogue that searches for common beliefs, acknowledges honest differences, and enable us to work together in service to the world. Such a dialogue has, in the words of the San Antonio report referred to above, 'its own place and integrity and is neither opposed to nor incompatible with witness or proclamation.... Witness does not preclude dialogue but invites it, and... dialogue does not preclude witness but extends and deepens it.' It is appropriate therefore that member churches invest time and resources to equip the faithful for dialogue, noting that in order to engage in dialogue they need to know the teaching and practice of both their own faith and at least of one other faith.

The Lambeth Conference 1998 has noted the increasing tension between religious traditions in several parts of the Communion, in particular the tension between Islam and Christianity in some places. We are aware that many people are discriminated against, harassed and even persecuted for their faith. In some countries there is an unhealthy alliance between a single religious tradition and political powers: in others laws prohibit the practice of one's faith, and religious conversions. We call upon all peoples of faith to deplore all manifestations of religious intolerance and ideological fanaticism and to affirm in clear terms the principle and practice of religious freedom.

The Anglican Communion as a world fellowship of churches is placed in a position to share instances of religious persecution and intolerance, and to provide the international support and solidarity needed by those who suffer because of their faith-commitments.

Sub-Section 5
Conclusion

Within a short time after the conclusion of the 1998 Lambeth Conference, the whole world will embark on the commemoration of a new millennium. For many, it will be a time of awakened hope for humankind and the earth we share. For others, it will be time of crisis as the seemingly insuperable problems faced by the human race continue to take their toll of misery and death. For Christians, it will mark the climax of twenty centuries of mission and ministry, and point us both backward towards the One whose birth is the turning point of history and forward towards the yet-to-be-fulfilled promises of God's reign.

Perhaps no generation of Christians has had a clearer global sense of the depth of the differences that can separate peoples from one another. Nor has there ever been a time when the unity of faith we share has been so important for the survival of our witness and the healing of the nations.

The God who 'made of one blood all the nations that dwell on the face of the earth' is the same Lord whose divine Word 'came to preach peace to those who were far off and to those who were near.' 'In him the whole building is joined together and rises to become a holy temple in the Lord. And in him you too are being built together to become a dwelling in which God lives by his Spirit.' (Acts 17:26; Eph. 2:17, 21–22)

In spite of the tensions and conflicts that divide our world and even challenge the unity of the Body of Christ, participants in the 1998 Lambeth Conference powerfully affirmed the unity in word and sacrament we share around the Lord's table, of which the diverse worship which united us daily was a powerful witness and sign.

May our unity in faith in the Lord Jesus be a source of blessing to the whole earth. Though we are many we are one, for we all share in the one Bread of life.

Notes

1. *Towards Koinonia in Faith, Life and Witness: draft of a working document,* prepared in Dublin, April 1992. (WCC Commission on Faith and Order, 1992; FO/92:9).

2. *Baptism, Eucharist and Ministry* (WCC, Geneva, 1982).

3. See also the discussion of culture and the faith at the Lambeth Conference 1988, as noted in *Dogmatic and Pastoral Concerns,* paras. 23–40, pp. 87–92, "The Truth Will Set You Free."

4. *Lambeth Conference* 1920, Encyclical Letter, p. 14.

5. In 1971, the Anglican Consultative Council held that there were no essential theological obstacles to the ordination of women to the priesthood, and that therefore each church could make its own decision. A similar judgment was reached by the Primates' Meeting and the 1988 Lambeth Conference with regard to the ordination of women to the episcopate.

6. *Belonging Together,* p. 4.

7. The *Virginia Report* discusses primacy in chapter 5. 'A Primate exercises ministry not in isolation but in collegial association with other bishops. If there is a need to intervene in the affairs of a diocese within the Province, the Primate will consult with other bishops, and if possible act through the normal structures of consultation and decision-making. The Primate will strive never to bypass or usurp the proper responsibility of the local church. ARCIC I spoke of the ministry of primacy in this way: "Primacy fulfills its purpose by helping the churches to listen to one another, to grow in love and unity, and to strive together towards the fullness of Christian life and witness; it respects and promotes Christian freedom and spontaneity; it does not seek uniformity where diversity is legitimate, or centralise administration to the detriment of local churches." (*The Final Report,* Authority I, para 21.)'

8. *The Virginia Report,* Inter-Anglican Theological and Doctrinal Commission, 1997, p. 29.

9. *The Virginia Report,* p. 29.

10. *The Virginia Report,* p. 30.

11. Lambeth Conference 1888, Resolution 2, p. 122.

Called to Be One
Section IV Report

Introduction

For many centuries Anglicans have prayed the deliberately inclusive prayer that 'all who profess and call themselves Christians may be led into the way of truth, and hold the faith in unity of spirit, in the bond of peace and in righteousness of life' (Church of England, Book of Common Prayer, 1662). This prayer notably combines a love of truth, a concern for fellowship, and a readiness to recognise the claims of morality and justice. Every Lambeth Conference has had a deep concern for unity, both the unity of the Church and the unity of human community, at the heart of its agenda.

In responding yet again to our Lord's great intercessory prayer (John 17), that his disciples might be one as he and the Father are one, we acknowledge first of all that we are called—called by God to be saints (1 Cor. 1:2), and called by God to be one (Eph. 4:1–6). Humility, gentleness, patience and loving tolerance are intrinsic parts of that vocation. We are summoned to make

> every effort to maintain the unity of the Spirit in the bond of peace. There is one body and one Spirit, just as you were called to the one hope of your calling, one Lord, one faith, one baptism, one God and Father of all, who is above all and through all and in all (Eph. 4:3–6).

As bishops we have in particular heard God's word to us through our study of Paul's Second Letter to the Corinthians. Here we read that God has committed to us (by which we understand Paul and his close collaborators) the ministry of reconciliation (or *at-one-ment*, as the early translation of William Tyndale rendered it in English). This reconciliation is, in the first place, God's own act in Jesus Christ. It involves a reconciliation between those who are estranged from each other, a reconciliation which should be manifest in the words and structures of the Church.

Embodying God's reconciling love in the relationship of historically divided churches involves much painstaking and detailed work, supported by the apostolic virtue of patience. Three main themes had been identified by the preparatory enquiries as strongly supported by the regions. They emerged directly from the experience of contemporary ecumenical engagement.

- The first theme reviewed the complex ecumenical scene with its mixture of signs of hope on the one hand and setbacks on the other. Do Anglicans still share a common commitment to visible unity and is there behind the many ecumenical endeavours a shared vision of that unity which is God's gift to us and our vocation to play our part in bringing into being?

- The second theme reviewed the progress made in bilateral and multilateral conversations at international and national levels and reflected on some of the issues concerning coherence, common vision, response and reception.

- The third theme took the Conference into uncharted waters with a consideration of the pastoral and ecumenical issues which arise out of Anglican experience of New Churches and Independent Christian Groups.

In each theme we were aware that our ecumenical vocation is carried out in the context of the encounter with people of other faiths and none. If our witness is to be credible it requires that Christians are united. Moreover, the attitudes and methods used in dialogue with other Christians, provide models for our engagement with people of other faiths—the need for patient and attentive listening and authentic witness to the Gospel of Christ.

The work of the three themes brought together reflection on the experience of growing together with other Christians locally, regionally and internationally with the theological work of the dialogue. There emerged from our work an unmistakable call for the bishops, as promoters and guardians of unity, to:

- recommit themselves to the goal of full, visible unity;

- claim together a common portrait of the unity to which God calls his Church;

- renew an understanding of the Chicago-Lambeth Quadrilateral in the light of the insights of ecumenical dialogue and experience;

- strengthen Anglican structures of unity and coherence;

- reflect upon the implications of the growing fellowship of the Anglican Communion as it embraces and is embraced by the United Churches and Churches in Communion;

- engage more intentionally with New Churches and Independent Christian Groups;

- receive the fruits of ecumenical dialogue into changed relationships;

- continue in ecumenical conversations and promote their results; and

- maintain consistency and coherence in ecumenical advances without being afraid of legitimate anomalies on the way to visible unity.

Throughout the work of the Section the presence of bishops and other leaders from the United Churches, the Churches in Communion and from Ecumenical Participants reminded us that friendships are the soil in which unity grows. They offered us insights from their traditions and helped us to look beyond the confines of the Anglican Communion and to glimpse a wider and richer communion. As we receive God's gift and respond to God's call our mission will be more credible and the praise of God become a united chorus increasing thanksgiving to the glory of God, Father, Son and Holy Spirit.

Sub-Section 1
Receiving the Gift: Towards a Vision of the Unity to Which We are Called

What is the unity to which we are called?

God has entrusted the Church with the task of proclaiming the everlasting Gospel of reconciliation, in the power of the Holy Spirit. The ecumenical question remains, however: what sort of unity would speak to the world of the God in whom we believe and the Kingdom to which God invites us? A portrait of unity would provide a vision to guide us on the way. It can be no more than a portrayal, with broad brush strokes, of the unity with rich diversity to which God calls us. It would however guide us both in developing the unity and identity of the Anglican Communion and also in our pilgrimage with other Christians towards the full visible unity of the one, holy, catholic and apostolic Church, as a sign, instrument and foretaste of God's Kingdom.

In the decade since Lambeth 1988 the ecumenical scene has developed in complex and sometimes apparently untidy ways. The experience of those gathered at this Conference testifies to impressive progress as well as at times to an increasing recognition of some of the hard questions and even in places a cooling of relationships. Nevertheless, through this complex scene emerges a strong commitment to visible unity and a common conviction, shared with many other Christians, of the shape of the unity to which God calls us. The experience of developing relationships with churches of different traditions and at different levels of the Church's life has brought into the open a number of aspects of unity of which we were previously only dimly aware and a number of issues which require further exploration.

What are Anglicans learning from ecumenical experience?

United Churches and Churches in Communion

As a result of Resolution 12 of the 1988 Lambeth Conference the bishops of the

Churches of North India, South India, Pakistan and Bangladesh are present at the Lambeth Conference for the first time as full members. Their presence here, as well as in the Primates' Meeting and the Anglican Consultative Council, enriches our fellowship and is a reminder of our commitment to work for the full visible unity of the Church. These Churches spoke to us of the joys of a unity expressed in a common liturgy and the use of a common lectionary, with the opportunity for all to participate in decision-making and social service. Common theological education has been an important factor in uniting the previously separate churches, giving ordinands an experience of one another's traditions at the level of initial ministerial formation. The process of uniting is not, however, without difficulties. Property disputes, especially over Anglican and Presbyterian property and the merger of denominational trusts have involved bishops and diocesan officials in complex and time-consuming lawsuits with new divisions over the possession of property. This adversely affects the credibility of the mission of the Church in some parts of India. The Churches of North and South India look forward to a wider unity with the Mar Thoma Church, a hope which is already symbolised each year in a concelebrated and shared Eucharist on 'Unity Sunday.' Prior to the founding of the Church of South India the Mar Thoma Church was already in communion with Anglicans in South India.

The Mar Thoma Syrian Church of India and the churches of the Anglican Communion are churches in communion. In the United States of America and in Canada there are now formal agreements for the oversight of Mar Thoma congregations. In Sydney, Australia, a priest is shared between Anglicans and members of the Mar Thoma Church. In England, Australia, the USA and Canada, congregations use Anglican buildings.

A more long-standing relationship of communion is that with the Old Catholic Churches of the Union of Utrecht, based on the Bonn Agreement (1931). Visits, shared sacramental fellowship and pastoral care, mutual participation in episcopal ordinations and, in some places, consultation over mission and pastoral strategy continue to nurture the relationship of communion. However, subsequent developments and more recent agreements, particularly the Porvöo Agreement, point to a richer vision of the full, visible unity of the Church. These encourage Anglicans and Old Catholics to reconsider their relationship. In particular we should search for ways to take counsel and make decisions together, address the anomaly of overlapping jurisdictions and consider the implications of wider ecumenical relationships particularly with the Roman Catholic, Orthodox and Lutheran Churches.

In 1997 a *Common Declaration* was signed between the Philippine Independent Church and the Philippine Episcopal Church. Through this *Common Declaration the Concordat of Full Communion,* first approved between the Philippine Independent Church and the Episcopal Church of the USA in 1962 (the Philippine Episcopal Church being then a missionary district of ECUSA), was reaffirmed. Both churches in the Philippines are now committed to discussions about the establishment of a single non-overlapping jurisdiction, making more real and manifest the unity established in this historic agreement. The Philippine Independent Church also has relations with a number of other Anglican provinces and companion relationships with some Old Catholic Churches of the Union of Utrecht and with the Church of Sweden.

In response to Resolution 4.5 of the 1988 Lambeth Conference, the Anglican Churches of Great Britain and Ireland and most of the Nordic and Baltic Lutheran churches signed the *Porvöo Declaration* in 1996, bringing these churches into a relationship of visible unity with an interchangeable ministry, all in communion with the See of Canterbury. The impetus for this agreement came from changes taking place in northern Europe after the collapse of communism and the perceived need for a credible united witness in a Europe seeking its own unity and identity. This agreement deepened the existing fellowship between Anglicans and some of these national Lutheran churches, and established communion where it had not previously existed. This agreement gives grounds for great rejoicing. Although the Anglican Churches of Great Britain and Ireland referred the agreement to the Primates' Meeting, which in turn consulted the Provinces, some other Anglicans felt that the Anglican Consultative Council ought also to have been consulted, and even that the matter should not have been acted upon before it had been considered by the Lambeth Conference. The question has also been raised about the compatibility of approaches to Anglican-Lutheran unity in the Porvöo Common Statement, and the Lutheran-Episcopal *Concordat of Agreement* in the USA and the Waterloo Declaration in Canada. These questions reinforce the desirability of the proposal in the *Agros Report*[1] for the establishment of an Inter-Anglican Standing Commission on Ecumenical Relations *inter alia* to review such regional proposals in order to ensure that they are consonant with an overall agreed vision of the goal of unity. (See Resolution IV.3, p. 69.)

Now that the Lutheran Porvöo churches are in communion with the See of Canterbury, representative bishops of these churches are present at the Lambeth Conference as members. A contact group oversees and monitors the implementation of the Agreement. Meetings of bishops and other synodical leaders are held every four years to explore common issues of mission and service. A meeting of the Primates was held in 1996 and another is to be held in 1999. There is regular participation in the consecration of bishops and an interchange of clergy has begun. Partnerships and exchanges are developing. Where the jurisdictions overlap, expatriate clergy and other congregations are welcomed into the life of the local dioceses. It is intended that episcopal oversight will come to be shared, as a further stage towards the resolution of the anomaly of overlapping jurisdictions. The Porvöo Agreement has also enabled traditionalist groups in Anglican and Lutheran churches to consult and support one another.

The presence and active participation in the Lambeth Conference of these Churches in Communion is a sign of the growing diversity and richness of a communion of churches which extends beyond that previously experienced in the Anglican Communion. This gives a glimpse of a future 'beyond Anglicanism' in which the full, visible unity of all Christians may become a reality.

The joys of our fellowship with churches in communion and the sorrows of limitations to that wider fellowship alike witness to a commitment to overcome the divisions of the past. They challenge us to live a life of visible unity, both as a more faithful response to God's gift in answer to the prayer of Jesus and for the sake of more effective and credible mission. We need to continue to reflect together on this experience in order to see how best to strengthen our life of communion and to address issues which are posed by the experience. These include: the strain placed on the United Churches because of their membership of more than one denominational fellowship or Christian World Communion; the need to develop more effective structures of mutual accountability, common discernment and decision making; anomalies arising out of parallel and overlapping jurisdictions; and the implication of regional relationships of communion like that inaugurated by the Porvöo Agreement for other regional developments. It is anomalous for churches to be in communion with some Provinces of the Anglican Communion, but not with others. Nevertheless, the juridical autonomy of the churches of the Anglican Communion means that each church has finally to make its own decisions about entering into a relationship of communion.

The increasing number of churches in communion raises questions about the nature of the Anglican Communion. By entering into communion with Anglicans other churches do not themselves become Anglican. Rather, they bring the treasures of their own inheritance with them and enrich our common life. At the same time their identity will also be enriched. Life in communion will bring changes to both of us, making for a more diverse communion.

Local experience

Every bishop has stories to tell of ecumenical engagement at diocesan level. In many places the desire for unity comes from the grass roots and gives strong support to common prayer, partnerships in theological education, common witness on matters of social concern, chaplaincy work in schools, hospitals, prisons and the armed forces, the sharing of buildings and other resources and joint participation in inter-faith dialogue. Everywhere these relationships are affected by the particular context: for example, the presence of other faith communities, the relation of the state to the church, or the pressures of war and deprivation.

Two concerns were reported. The first relates to the challenges posed to the historic churches by new churches and independent Christian groups, often of a literalist character. In many places these groups seem to want to have little to do with formal ecumenical structures: sometimes they work against the witness of other churches. Nevertheless, we believe that we have much to learn from their strength of biblical teaching, their desire to evangelise, their awareness of the power of the Holy Spirit among them, their determined training of every member of the congregation, their enthusiasm, and their trust in the power of the Holy Spirit to heal broken lives. These things contribute to our understanding of the life of visible unity. We note the interest of some of these groups in exploring forms of church life and ministry that would link their churches to a wider fellowship; this is sometimes expressed in the form of a desire for some form of association with the wider episcopal tradition. Further attention is given to this in Sub-Section 2 of this report.

A second concern expressed by many is the current state of relationships with the Roman Catholic Church. In many parts of the world Anglicans enjoy a great warmth of fellowship and common witness with Roman Catholics. We heard good stories of co-operation in matters of social concern: the Anglican–Roman Catholic Dialogue of Canada has issued a joint statement and study guide on seeking and building the common good in society; the House of Bishops of the Church of England and the Roman Catholic Bishops' Conference of England and Wales have issued a joint statement on euthanasia; we were especially moved by what we heard of solidarity between Anglican and Roman Catholic bishops in the face of persecution in the Sudan. The Ecumenical Directory[2] is imaginatively applied by a number of episcopal conferences, and in some places pastoral and sacramental sharing goes far beyond what is commonly regarded as possible. We welcome the widespread co-operation between Anglicans and Roman Catholics in theological formation. The 1997 Guidelines for Ecumenical Formation[3] contain an outstanding commitment to visible unity and impressive directions for the curriculum. Anglicans should seek to match this commitment in their programmes for pastoral formation. Anglican and Roman Catholic religious communities often have close relationships, and there is much sharing by both individuals and communities, including through participation in the Consultation of Religious Superiors. They have also benefited from the generous advice and support of Roman Catholic Communities.

Elsewhere, however, the relationship seems less easy, and we learned that the agreed statements of the Anglican Roman Catholic International Commission (henceforth 'ARCIC'), like other ecumenical texts, are not as well known as they should be. The lack of translations into various languages needs attention, but it seems that sometimes the lack of translations is not so much due to the shortage of resources as to the absence of any real local relationship demanding such provision. There are places where the Ecumenical Directory seems unknown and we also heard of situations in which there are continuing pastoral problems, especially over interchurch families.

The differences between the official Anglican and Roman Catholic rules concerning eucharistic sharing are both well known and widely misunderstood. There is much need for patient mutual explanation of the ecclesial integrity of the policies and practices of both churches. At the same time we note that in many parts of the world the faithful in both churches do not observe the strict letter of the canonical regulations of their own Communions. While we do not seek to encourage such actions, we want to understand the theological and ecclesial significance of the widespread feeling by Christian people that it is the Lord of the eucharist who invites to his table.

All this calls for a reflection on the experience of shared life at the local level in the light of the theological consensus and convergence expressed in the ARCIC agreed statements. These statements themselves contain a challenge to a more committed and intentional sharing of common life and witness as a stage on the way to organic union, the expressed goal of the Anglican-Roman Catholic dialogue. (Resolution IV.23) Neither Church seems really to have faced the question posed by the first ARCIC Commission—'what are the next concrete steps that can be taken on the basis of the ARCIC Agreement?'

Among many local developments, we noted with interest the proposal in Wales for the appointment of an 'ecumenical bishop' for the Covenanting Churches in Wales to share oversight with the Anglican bishops and with the leadership of the Methodist and Reformed churches, particularly in relation to local ecumenical projects. (Resolution IV.4) This imaginative proposal illustrates how those who share a common life in a local context come to feel the need to be served by a common ministry of oversight of a personal and collegial pattern. This confirms the Anglican understanding that a common ministry of oversight is needed to serve the visible unity of the Church. Such a development is to be seen as a stage on the way to the reconciliation of churches and ministries.

Regional and national advances

In many parts of the world Anglicans are moving into formally committed relations with other churches as steps on the way to visible unity. In Southern Africa Anglicans have entered into a covenant relationship with Reformed and Methodist churches which includes mutual eucharistic sharing and mutual acceptance of ministries, with the possibility of an ordained minister of one church being authorised to serve in one of the other participating churches.[4] The Church Unity Commission has begun an exploration of the ministry of *episcopé*, to seek a form of *episcopé* that would help the South African Church to fulfil its own mission in the church of the twenty-first century and also be helpful to the Church at large. In England Anglicans and Moravians have signed the Fetter Lane Agreement, which commits them to sharing together wherever

Anglican and Moravian congregations exist side by side. The Church of Ireland has also signed the agreement.

In other areas, proposals are under discussion. In the USA and Canada proposals are well advanced for establishing relations of 'full communion' with the main Lutheran churches. The Canadian Anglican-Lutheran *Waterloo Declaration*, which would bring the two churches into full communion, will be voted on in 2001. Preliminary decisions relating to the *Waterloo Declaration* are already being made. The American Episcopal-Lutheran *Concordat of Agreement* was overwhelmingly approved in 1997 by the Episcopal Church USA, but narrowly failed to gain the necessary two-thirds majority in the Lutheran Churchwide Assembly. A revision of the Concordat is now being prepared by the Lutherans, in consultation with representatives of the Episcopal Church, for consideration by the two churches in 1999 and 2000. In Papua New Guinea there has been a strong desire to find a way of developing Anglican-Roman Catholic relations at a regional level. In Scotland, at the Scottish Episcopal Church's invitation, multilateral conversations have been reopened as the Scottish Churches' Initiative for Union. An interim report was published in 1998 and it is intended to offer a final report to individual churches by 2002.

These developments and many others illustrate the commitment to move towards visible unity by steps and stages. They increasingly raise questions of coherence and consistency between different regional agreements and indeed with the international dialogues. An important theological question is whether all are committed to the same vision of full, visible unity. In moving from our present divisions towards visible unity we recognise that anomalies are likely to arise. These anomalies are rooted in the greatest anomaly, which is division within the Body of Christ. We must learn to distinguish between anomalies which are 'bearable,' because they are evidence of untidiness on the way to an agreed vision of visible unity, and those which are 'unbearable' because they indicate radically different understandings of the nature and unity of the Church. More work will be needed on which anomalies are tolerable and which are not in the move to visible unity.

National and regional councils of churches and the WWC

National and regional councils of churches and the World Council of Churches are valuable and in some cases indispensable forums and instruments for common witness and shared mission, for the exploration and development of relations with other faiths and for the multilateral examination of matters of faith and order. It is frequently national and regional councils of churches which enable Christians to speak to governments on issues which affect the daily lives of people: human rights, environmental concerns, health policy and social welfare. Councils of churches help to keep the development of bilateral relations in the widest multilateral context. Many regional councils have in recent years restructured themselves and reviewed the basis of membership and styles of working. There was great appreciation expressed of the fact that the Roman Catholic Church is a full member of an increasing number of national and regional councils of churches. In the Middle East this has led to a radical examination of the criteria for membership which is now based on the concept of 'families of churches.'

On the eve of the celebration of the fiftieth anniversary of the World Council of Churches, the Lambeth Conference, acknowledges with gratitude the work of churches together at the world level. By its support of the work of mission and evangelism, of interfaith relations, of justice, peace and the integrity of creation, of the community of women and men in the Ecumenical Decade of Churches in Solidarity with Women, and especially the work of the Faith and Order Commission, the World Council of Churches has made a significant contribution to the understanding of unity. In this it has held together the unity of the Church and the unity of the human community. The World Council of Churches provides an invaluable ministry of *diakonia* by co-ordinating the relief and development efforts of the churches and responding quickly to natural disasters through its ability to connect directly with member churches in the areas affected.

The statement on visible unity adopted by the Seventh Assembly in Canberra, *The Unity of the Church as Koinonia: Gift and Calling*,[5] was particularly important for Anglicans in deepening the vision of unity. Not only is it consistent with our Anglican understanding, but it challenges us to go on taking bold steps in partnerships with others on the basis of explicit agreements in faith.

We remain convinced of the potential of the World Council as 'a privileged instrument' of the ecumenical movement to help the churches respond together to God's call to the goal of visible unity 'in one faith and one eucharistic fellowship expressed in worship and common life in Christ, and to advance towards that unity in order that the world may believe.'

It is for these reasons that we value the move as we enter a new millennium to restate a common vision and understanding of the World Council of Churches within the Common Understanding and Vision (CUV) process.[6] Within the broadest multilateral explication of a common vision, Anglicans will be helped to reflect upon, and to be challenged about, their own commitment to unity.

At the same time as expressing gratitude for the work of the Council, concern was expressed by bishops at the Lambeth Conference about the next stage of the Council's life. It is not clear that some of the crucial issues raised in the CUV process have as yet been fully explored: what is the vision of the goal of visible unity that will motivate the Council in the next years? How will new programmes and the structures of the Council contribute to that end? What is the nature of the fellowship churches enjoy as members of the Council? What is the basis for membership of the Council that would most faithfully represent where the ecumenical movement has reached as it enters a new millennium?

Many Anglicans and others continue to ask what changes in the World Council of Churches would be required to make it possible for the Roman Catholic Church to be not only a member of the Faith and Order Commission but also a full member of the Council itself. At the same time we are disturbed to hear of the problems the present working of the World Council creates for some Orthodox churches.

These questions highlight the necessity for some radical new thinking about the basis and aims of the Council and lead us to ask how far other churches will be willing to go in making the necessary changes. We cannot ourselves envisage a credible future for a council of churches at the world level in which the voices of the Roman Catholic and Orthodox Churches are not fully represented.

We believe it is vital to re-form and renew the World Council of Churches. For fifty years the Council has provided the most inclusive experience of ecclesial sharing at the world level. It is now time to try to understand the nature of the fellowship we experience and its ecclesial significance. This challenge has also been identified by the Ecumenical Patriarchate.

Sharing in common witness

During the last decade Anglicans have co-operated with other Christians, as well as with members of other faiths and none, in movements of justice and peace and in the care of creation: in Southern Africa in the struggles against apartheid; in Tanzania in the struggle to feed the hungry and respond to the needs of refugees; in Australia among aboriginal people; and in the base communities of Latin America as agents of hope and empowerment; in the work of the Middle East Council of Churches for peace, justice and human rights. Initiatives often come from the local level. In many places in the world Anglicans work with others to confront the threat of weapons of mass destruction, to search for global economic justice, to stand against the ravaging of creation and to work for the equality of women and men. Injustice is too strong for a divided Church. A profound unity in communion is experienced in struggling together for justice and peace but that in its turn exposes the need for full sacramental communion and structures of mutual accountability.

Increasingly it is acknowledged that there can be no separation between the search for the unity of the Church and the engagement in struggles for justice and peace. The ecumenical quest must unite concern for the oneness of the Church with the issues concerning full humanity which touch the lives of all people in God's world. The unity of the Church entails the acceptance of the same basic moral values, the sharing of a common vision of humanity created in the image of God and re-created in Christ. This has been emphasised by the report of ARCIC, *Life in Christ* (1994), and the reports of the World Council of Churches, *Church and World* (1990), *Costly Unity* 1993), *Costly Commitment* (1995), and *Costly Obedience* (1996).

Moral values also concern matters of personal conduct. These too bear strongly upon our ecumenical relationships, both with the Orthodox and Roman Catholic Churches on the one hand, and with New Churches and Independent Christian Groups on the other. We acknowledge the concern expressed by those who warn us to maintain the traditional biblical teaching on matters of human sexuality as affirmed by the Lambeth Conference of 1978.[7] This question is dealt with at greater length in the Report from Section I of this Lambeth Conference and is the subject of Resolution I.10.

The experience of sharing together in the last decade has resulted in an emphasis on the unity of the Church understood as 'moral community'—the Church called to reveal justice and peace in its own life as it carries out its sacred obligation to work for the full humanity of all people and the preservation of God's creation. At the same time, given the ambiguity and complexity of so many moral challenges, the issue of the formation of a common mind in response to the complex ethical challenges sends us back to questions of unity: the need to be formed together in the faith of the Church; the need to be nourished and sustained in a single sacramental life as well as the need for structures of mutual accountability, discernment and decision-making.

The Anglican experience of living with difference

Our experience of a growing unity with other Christians is matched by increasing concern for the unity and identity of the Anglican Communion and the bonds which hold Anglicans together.

In recent years a number of developments have strained the ability of Anglicans to maintain their unity in diversity. For example: the desire for more inculturated worship has raised questions about liturgical unity; different views and practices concerning the ordination of women have restricted the interchangeability of ministry within the Communion; some proposed unity agreements in different regions have appeared to be based on divergent understanding of historic episcopal succession. In endeavouring to come to a common mind on these issues, there is a dynamic tension between the desire for provincial autonomy and the desire for responsible oversight of such developments in the interests of interdependence at the level of the Communion as a whole.

This highlights for us the importance of the proposals in the *Virginia*[8] and *Agros Reports* concerning instruments of unity at the world level. Already the *Eames Commission*[9] has offered a credible model for maintaining as high a degree as possible of common life and sacramental sharing, when disputed questions threaten the communion of the Church and the mind of Christ for the Church is being discerned. We believe this approach contains creative possibilities for the future, not only for the unity of Anglicans but may also be a gift we can make to others. This raises two closely related issues. On the one hand there is the question of how the legitimate limits of diversity are to be identified and protected. On the other hand, when disputed questions touching important matters of faith and order threaten the communion of the Church there is a need for means to maintain unity while God's will is conscientiously sought by people who cannot at present accept each other's positions.

Over the past 150 years, various small groups have separated themselves from the Church of England and other churches of the Anglican Communion over particular matters of faith and order. These include the Free Church of England, the Reformed Episcopal Church and the Church of England in South Africa. In recent discussions between these churches and the respective Provinces of the Anglican Communion, it has become clear that however much we have in common, the restoration of communion will be hard to achieve.

More recently, as a consequence of a number of developments, and especially the decision of a number of Provinces of the Anglican Communion to ordain women to the priesthood and episcopate, some further separations have occurred. The resulting bodies, some of which claim the title 'Continuing Anglican Churches,' share many features of the church from which they emerged, claim continuing fidelity to an Anglican inheritance, and are sometimes served by former Anglican priests and bishops. Nevertheless they are not in communion with the See of Canterbury.

Although the overall numbers of people involved in these groups are relatively small, this fragmentation is a cause of great sadness. Nevertheless, the fact that after many years of separation it has recently been possible to hold discussions with the Free Church of England gives us hope that in time steps can be taken towards reconciliation with other churches of broadly Anglican tradition from whom we have become divided. It is desirable for those Provinces of the Anglican Communion where congregations of these churches are present to try to open dialogue with a view to reconciliation, endeavouring to consult more widely within the Anglican Communion on the issues of faith and order involved.

Reflection: implications for visible unity

We have reflected on stories from around the world, on the experience of ecumenical partnerships of many kinds. This reflection reveals a diverse and complex situation in which there are both joys and sorrows. We detect in many places a movement from competition through coexistence and co-operation, to commitment, convergence and communion. The stages are not like a straight road; they are more like a winding river, being joined by many streams each of which is itself winding. What may look like progress from one point of view may, from another point of view, actually carry one further from the mouth of the river.

Even where we are not yet 'in communion,' we recognise that we are not 'out of communion,' but already experience a considerable degree of communion grounded in a common baptism and shared faith. We have acknowledged some hardening of attitudes and frustration with what to some is slowness of progress. Nevertheless, we find no evidence of an 'ecumenical winter,' but much which speaks of a maturing of the ecumenical movement. This is creating a situation in which differences and difficulties can be faced frankly and to some extent even be owned together in committed relationships. When differences between two churches are seen as problems for them to resolve together, they are more likely to see which differences are matters of legitimate diversity and which can have no lasting place in the fully reconciled life of the Church.

Our experience is helping us to understand new things in the unity Anglicans are called to share with their Christian brothers and sisters as a credible witness to the unity of God's kingdom. We glimpse a vision of a unity of the one, holy, catholic and apostolic Church beyond the Anglican Communion. At the same time this experience demonstrates the desirability of articulating a portrait of visible unity so that the different endeavours are oriented towards a recognisably common goal. The acceptance of a common portrait of visible unity by the many different partnerships in the different regions of the world would strengthen Anglican unity and also help to maintain a coherence and consistency and thus be reassuring to our ecumenical partners. We know that as we move together new dimensions will be seen in the unity to which God calls us.

Visible unity, koinonia *and friendship: towards a portrait*

There are already things we can say about a portrait of visible unity. In St. John's account of the farewell discourse of Jesus, the Lord says to his disciples, 'I do not call you servants any longer, for a servant does not know what his master is doing; I call you friends because I have revealed to you everything I heard from my Father' (John 15:15). Jesus also made a direct link between his disciples' friendship with himself and the love they should have for one another. In turn he linked their love for one another both to his own unity with his Father and to the credibility of their witness in the world. One of the conclusions we draw from what we have heard in the present situation of the ecumenical movement is that friendship is not only a critical means for advancing on the path to unity, but is itself an essential part of the unity to which we are called.

The basic meaning of the word *koinonia* refers to what is held in common, and to what holds us in common. Most fundamentally it points us to the Trinitarian life of God and the mutual love and action of Father, Son, and Holy Spirit. At the centre of the communion of the Church 'is life with the Father, through Christ, in the Spirit. Through the sending of his Son the living God has revealed that love is at the heart of the divine life. Those who abide in love abide in God and God in them; if we, in communion with him, love one another, he abides in us and his love is perfected in us (cf. 1 John 4:7–21). Through love God communicates his life. He causes those who accept the light of the truth revealed in Christ rather than the darkness of this world to become his children. This is the most profound communion possible for any of his creatures.'[10]

The emphasis on the reality of *koinonia* makes us order our priorities: God, the world, the Church. It reminds us that the unity of the Church is grounded in the divine life and builds upon and transforms communion given in creation, realised in part in the natural relationships of family and kinship, tribe and people. Visible unity is to point to the sort of life God intends for the whole of humanity, a foretaste of God's Kingdom. This divine intention forms the context for our search for Christian unity. We regret that it was not possible to explore the relationship between Christian ecumenism and this wider context, especially in relation to dialogue with people of other faiths.

The *Canberra Statement* of the Seventh Assembly of the World Council of Churches (1991) said that 'The purpose of God according to Holy Scripture is to gather the whole of creation under the Lordship of Christ Jesus in whom, by the power of the Holy Spirit, all are brought into communion with God. The Church is a foretaste of this communion with God and with one another.' This calling undergirds the responsibility of the Church 'to proclaim reconciliation and provide healing, to overcome divisions based on race, gender, age, culture, colour and to bring all people into communion with God.' It follows that the divisions within and between churches are a hindrance to the Church's mission of reconciliation as well as an affront 'to its very nature.' In other words, they are all limitations of communion.

The 'elements' or 'characteristics' of visible unity are described in the *Canberra Statement* as:

- the common confession of the apostolic faith;
- a common sacramental life entered by the one baptism and celebrated together in one eucharistic fellowship;
- a common life in which members and ministries are mutually recognised and reconciled; and

- a common mission witnessing to all people to the Gospel of God's grace and serving the whole of creation.

The statement adds:

'The goal of the search for full communion is realised when all the churches are able to recognise in one another the one, holy, catholic and apostolic Church in its fullness. This full communion will be expressed on the local and universal levels through conciliar forms of life and action.'

Among the achievements of ecumenical dialogue has been increasing agreement about the marks of the full, visible unity which is the expression of the *koinonia* of the Church. This is no innovation; Acts 2:42 is an early description 'They devoted themselves to the apostles' teaching and fellowship (*koinonia*), to the breaking of bread and the prayers.' Another list is found in the Creed: 'one, holy, catholic and apostolic.' There are various ways in which these aspects of the Church can be described: theological, juridical, missiological, sociological and so on. Such approaches are necessary and helpful up to a point, but they can serve to highlight the differences between the churches and draw attention to the different emphases that keep them apart rather than to the vision which seeks to bring them together.

For this reason, some recent statements have sought rather to 'offer a portrait of a church living wholeheartedly in the light of the Gospel.' A typical example is the *Porvöo Common Statement,* which puts it like this:

- it is a Church rooted and grounded in the love and grace of the Lord Christ;

- it is a Church always joyful, praying continually and giving thanks even in the midst of suffering;

- it is a pilgrim Church, a people of God with a new heavenly citizenship, a holy nation and a royal priesthood;

- it is a Church which makes common confession of the apostolic faith in word and in life, the faith common to the whole Church everywhere and at all times;

- it is a Church with a mission to all in every race and nation, preaching the gospel, proclaiming the forgiveness of sins, baptising and celebrating the eucharist;

- it is a Church which is served by an ordained apostolic ministry, sent by God to gather and nourish the people of God in each place, uniting and linking them with the Church universal within the whole communion of saints;

- it is a Church which manifests through its visible communion the healing and uniting power of God amidst the divisions of humankind;

- it is a Church in which the bonds of communion are strong enough to enable it to bear effective witness in the world, to guard and interpret the apostolic faith, to take decisions, to teach authoritatively, and to share its goods with those in need; and

- it is a Church alive and responsive to the hope which God has set before it, to the wealth and glory of the share God has offered it in the heritage of his people, and to the vastness of the resources of God's power open to those who trust in him.[11]

In summary, Porvöo concludes: visible unity 'entails agreement in faith together with the common celebration of the sacraments, supported by a united ministry and forms of collegial and conciliar consultation in matters of faith, life and witness. For the fullness of communion all these visible aspects of the life of the Church require to be permeated by a profound spiritual communion, a growing together in a common mind, mutual concern and a care for unity (Phil. 2:2).'[12]

Whatever form visible unity is to take, a portrait must communicate a picture of diversity given in creation, inspired continually through the gift of the Holy Spirit, and which is the result of the Gospel lived out in the specificity of cultural and the particularity of historical contexts expressing the richness of those specificities and particularities. The Church on earth, as the Church *in via,* remains marked by the sins of humankind and by its solidarity with the sufferings of the world. If visible unity is about living in the world the communion of God's own life then our portrait of visible unity must show that tension, even conflict, will always be part of life this side of the kingdom. 'Sharp things that divide us can paradoxically turn out to be gifts.... The world with all its divisions is not used to such a possibility as this: that those on opposing sides should stay together, should remain in dialogue, bearing each other's burdens, even entering one another's pain.'[13]

These last words, about one another's pain, take us to the heart of *koinonia,* understood as a participation in Christ who 'though he was in the form of God, did not cling to equality with God, but emptied himself, assuming the condition of a slave. And being found in human form he humbled himself and became obedient to death, death on a cross' (Phil. 2:6–8). The extent to which the Church is and is seen to be one with human suffering is one of the most telling of all signs of its identity as the Body of Christ.

A rich portrait of visible unity is emerging in ecumenical conversations. It would be an ecumenical advance if the churches together could own such a portrait and confirm a common commitment to visible unity as the goal.

The Chicago-Lambeth Quadrilateral: a dynamic for unity

Over a hundred years ago a classic attempt was made in the Chicago-Lambeth Quadrilateral to give a brief, shorthand expression of the features necessary for visible unity. This has served Anglicans well as a basis for ecumenical conversations and also for understanding their own unity and identity. It was resolved by the Lambeth Conference of 1888:

> That, in the opinion of this Conference, the following Articles supply a basis on which approach may be by God's blessing made towards Home Reunion:
>
> (a) The Holy Scriptures of the Old and New Testaments, as 'containing all things necessary to salvation,' and as being the rule and ultimate standard of faith.
>
> (b) The Apostles' Creed, as the Baptismal Symbol; and the Nicene Creed, as the sufficient statement of the Christian faith.
>
> (c) The two Sacraments ordained by Christ Himself—Baptism and the Supper of the Lord—ministered with unfailing use of Christ's words of Institution, and of the elements ordained by Him.
>
> (d) The Historic Episcopate, locally adapted in the methods of its administration to the varying needs of the nations and peoples called of God into the Unity of His Church.

The Quadrilateral is not to be thought of as a list of unrelated and static items, but as a skeletal framework, which if it is to live needs to be embodied in a community and breathed upon by the Spirit in a life of fellowship in worship and service. Subsequent Lambeth Conferences have explicated the Quadrilateral within particular historical contexts and in the light of the ecumenical movement. The interpretations of the Quadrilateral have gone through a series of 'precisions and distinctions.' There are certain clear lines of development. For example, the Lambeth Conferences of 1920 and 1948 placed a greater emphasis on the historic episcopate in the work of the reunion of the Church.

Those things of which the Quadrilateral speaks are gifts for sustaining and nurturing a life of unity, God's gifts of Christian connectedness. As Anglicans, deeply involved in ecumenical relations, we need now to refresh our understanding of the Quadrilateral in the light of what we have learnt on the ecumenical journey and re-commit ourselves to the Quadrilateral both as an outline of the characteristics of the visible unity of the one, holy, catholic and apostolic Church and also as a means of undergirding our own internal unity. (Resolution IV.2) The significance of the Quadrilateral for relationships with New Churches and Independent Christian Groups is further explored in Sub-Section 2 of this Report.

The study of the Faith and Order Commission of the World Council of Churches on the common confession of the apostolic faith seeks to unite Christians in the faith of Christ, uniquely revealed in the Scriptures and focused in the Nicene-Constantinopolitan Creed.[14] It aims to help divided churches, by means of an ecumenical explication of the faith, to recognise the faith of the Church in their own lives and practices; to repent and renew their lives where they are not faithful; and to recognise other churches as churches where the same faith is proclaimed and confessed. Recognition is an essential step on the way to common confession. This ecumenical exploration has opened up questions. What are the tolerable limits to diversity in confessing the faith? What is the role of, and the relation between, Scripture, Tradition and traditions in seeking to re-express the faith for today? The study holds together confession in word and confession in life. Christians witness to their faith as they respond to the world's needs and seek answers to complex ethical questions. The questions raised in this ecumenical exploration are also relevant to internal discussion as Anglicans seek to live out the faith in different cultural contexts and as they respond to criticisms that we have departed from the fundamentals of the Gospel. This criticism comes from internal sources, from ecumenical partners and members of other faiths. It is raised acutely by some New Churches and Independent Christian Groups whose presence and challenge is more keenly felt in some Provinces than others.

Ecumenical dialogue continues concerning the sacraments of baptism and the eucharist, building upon the convergences of *Baptism, Eucharist and Ministry* (henceforth 'BEM') and ARCIC. A common understanding and practice of baptism now unites a wide range of churches. Nevertheless, some traditional controversies over baptism have resisted solution, and rebaptism continues to be a problem in relation to a number of churches, including some of the New Churches and Independent Christian Groups. Much convergence has been achieved on the sacrament of the eucharist, particularly in the areas of eucharistic sacrifice and the presence of Christ in the eucharist. The integral relation of sacramental life and ethical witness has also been fundamental for ecumenical agreement:

> The eucharistic celebration demands reconciliation and sharing among all those regarded as brothers and sisters in the one family of God and is a constant challenge in the search for appropriate

> relationships in social, economic life. As participants in the eucharist, therefore, we prove inconsistent if we are not actively participating in this ongoing restoration of the world's situation and the human condition.[15]

It is on the fourth item of the Quadrilateral that much ecumenical debate still turns and where greater convergence is still needed. There is general agreement on the need for a personal ministry of oversight (*episcopê*), but much more exploration is needed, especially with those of the Reformed tradition, on the ministry of bishops. *The Niagara Report*[16] has already made an important contribution to this. The Quadrilateral takes a firm stand on historic episcopal succession. Since Lambeth 1988 the ecumenical debate has led Anglicans to locate historic episcopal succession firmly within the apostolicity of the whole Church, the Church living in fidelity to apostolic faith and mission. Historic episcopal succession is seen as sign—effective sign—first of God's promise to be with the Church and also of the Church's intention to remain faithful to God's promise and command. This has enabled the ecumenical discussion to take place in a more healing context, but it has at the same time sharpened some of the issues. What is the relationship of the apostolicity of the whole Church to the sign of apostolicity in the historic episcopal succession? How can Anglicans move from acknowledging the authenticity and fruitfulness of the ministries of other Christian communities and enter with them into a reconciled life, served by a reconciled ministry, without seeming either to deny the fruitfulness of the ministry of partner churches or the gift of God to the Church in the sign of historic episcopal succession? It has become clear that there are differences of emphases, and different language used, in the different parts of the Anglican Communion in speaking about recognition and reconciliation of ministries. This causes bewilderment in our ecumenical partners faced with apparently different Anglican responses. Further work is needed by Anglicans, together with ecumenical partners, on the fourth item of the Quadrilateral, including a fresh exploration of what was intended in the phrase 'locally adapted in the methods of its administration' and what it might imply for today.

Clarification is needed not only about the precise definition of theological terms which cause difficulties in ecumenical dialogue, but also about matters of fact about power in the Church, including how decisions are reached, by what processes and involving what persons. In clarifying these issues it is important to remember that the Church, which is under God's grace and a sign of God's kingdom, is also a natural human organisation, subject to the same constraints as any other. How authority is exercised in the church is an integral part of the further interpretation of the fourth article of the Quadrilateral which needs to be conducted as an collaborative venture between Anglicans and their ecumenical partners.

The Quadrilateral provides a statement of Anglican unity as well as a basis for ecumenical dialogue. It raises questions both for Anglicans and for the ecumenical future. Given that the unity of the Church will always be threatened when new knowledge poses perplexing questions to the faith, order and moral life of the Church, how are Christians to be held together in unity? What ecclesial structures would best sustain unity, and enable those entrusted with oversight to lead the faithful in the discernment and reception of the truth? The *Virginia Report* suggests the need to strengthen bonds of communion. It is important to stress that this is not merely a structural agenda. Appropriate enabling structures are fundamental to the dynamic and faithful life of the Church as it discerns the truth and embodies it in its life.

In *BEM*, para. 26, *Ministry*, we read that ministry should be exercised in *personal*, collegial and communal ways at every level of the Church's life. 'It should be personal because the presence of Christ among his people can most effectively be pointed to by the person ordained to proclaim the Gospel and to call the community to serve the Lord in unity of life and witness. It should be *collegial*, for there is a need for a college of ordained ministers sharing in the common task of representing the concerns of the community. Finally, the intimate relationship between the ordained ministry and the community should find expression in a communal dimension where the exercise of the ordained ministry is rooted in the life of the community and requires the community's effective participation in the discovery of God's will and the guidance of the Spirit.'

This insight is already widely embodied in the life of the Anglican Communion and is expressed in the *Virginia Report*, which comments, "These dimensions of the ministry of oversight are expressed in different ways in the different regions of the world and are affected by local circumstance and custom."

Some have even suggested that it would now be appropriate to include as a fifth item a statement about the ministry of oversight exercised in personal, collegial and communal ways at every level of the Church's life. Whether or not there is support for this suggestion, there seems to be general agreement that there is a need for more developed structures of communion to maintain unity with diversity and to sustain Christians in a dynamic life, as they engage with differences on the way to discovering the mind of Christ for the Church.

Sub-Section 2
New Churches and Independent Christian Groups

Introduction

When the agenda for the Lambeth Conference was being formulated the responses from the regions indicated that there was a difficulty in almost every part of the Anglican Communion in establishing good and constructive relations with some of the newer Pentecostal and fundamentalist churches. The forms taken by these churches are diverse, and were spoken of in different ways.

'The growth of Pentecostalism in the area influences issues regarding baptism and charismatic renewal. Fundamentalism (often imported from northern media), is an issue: scripture is often used to support ideologies.' (West Indies)

'Fundamentalism which is narrow, divisive, exclusive and unaccommodating is a major threat to unity. The state of transition through which Southern Africa is going results in feelings of deep insecurity on the part of many who then seek the certainty offered by fundamentalist faiths. This retreat into fundamentalism is in itself a threat to unity and peace and is a destabilising factor. The fundamentalist churches challenge the Church of the Province of Southern Africa, however, offering as they do an enthusiasm, a measure of community support, and a degree of biblical teaching not often found in Anglican churches.' (Southern Africa)

'This topic has a particular West African manifestation in the rise of the charismatic movement and the proliferation of African Independent and Sectarian Churches. What is the Anglican response as regards: (a) ecumenism and (b) church order?' (West Africa)

'Concern was expressed over the development of the work and mission of mainly African Independent and Sectarian Churches. They operated very independently and gave a bad image to the rest of the world.' (East Africa)

'The fundamentalist movements tend to emphasise the differences between themselves and ourselves, rather than reaching towards ecumenism. Because of their lively interpretation of the Bible, they tend to be attractive to younger people and are thus seen to be a threat to the Anglican church and other established churches, and also to ecumenism.' (Indian Ocean)

'We noted the presence of fundamentalist Churches and parachurch organisations in our region and their often damaging impact, in relation to them we need to ask what we mean by Christian fundamentalism and to determine criteria for engaging in dialogue and co-operation with them. The criteria we would recommend are: Trinitarian belief, mutual recognition of baptism, affirmation of the two natures of Christ.' (West Asia and the Middle East)

Apart from these specific responses it is generally acknowledged by the churches in Western cultures that fundamentalist and pentecostal churches and groups play a significant and growing part in religious and public life.

The sheer scale of the pentecostal/charismatic movement should not take us by surprise. David B. Barrett estimates that there are nearly 480 million such persons, making it the second largest Christian movement in the world today after the Roman Catholic Church.[17] All the main world Christian families are involved in relationships with these churches and groups, and not infrequently these relationships contain difficulties. Some Pentecostal Churches have rejected the ecumenical movement, preferring associations of evangelical churches where these exist. In 1993 the General Council of the Assemblies of God adopted a by-law disapproving of its ministers or churches engaging in the promotion of the ecumenical movement. At the same time attempts have been made from time to time to establish a constructive dialogue. From 1972–1976 a dialogue was held between the Secretariat (now Pontifical Council) for Promoting Christian Unity of the Roman Catholic Church and leaders of some pentecostal churches and participants in the Charismatic Movement within Protestant and Anglican churches. In its Final Report a large number of topics were identified for further consideration. Dialogue between Roman Catholics and Classical Pentecostals took place from 1977 to 1982 and from 1985 to 1989, issuing in the publication of the agreed statement *Perspectives on Koinonia.* There have also been other dialogues between Pentecostal churches and the Reformed and Baptist Christian World Communions. In 1997 a meeting was held by the WCC for representatives of its member churches with representatives of Pentecostal churches.

In taking up these subjects for special consideration, it should be noted that New Churches and Independent Christian Groups have never previously been directly addressed at a Lambeth Conference. At the same time, issues to do with biblical inspiration, in connection with biblical study and criticism, have repeatedly been addressed as an internal Anglican matter (see, for example, the *Report of the Committee on the Critical Study of Holy Scripture,* 1897, and Resolutions 1–12 of the Lambeth Conference of 1958). The Lambeth Conference has also addressed issues concerning the charismatic movements, most recently in 1988. Particular attention was paid to the subject of charismatic experience in the life of many Anglicans and to the collected work *Open to the Spirit* (1987), prepared for the Anglican Consultative Council. In one of the Resolutions the conference noted the rapid growth of Pentecostal Churches in many parts of the world, and encouraged Anglicans to engage in personal contact and theological dialogue where possible.

Definition

We adopt the title 'New Churches and Independent Christian Groups,' rather than 'Fundamentalist and Pentecostal Churches,' out of a desire to be as comprehensive and descriptive as possible. We set aside from the start any definition of the diverse churches and movements as aspects of a single 'fundamentalism.' Some 'pentecostal' churches are not 'fundamentalist,' and some 'fundamentalist' churches are not 'pentecostal.' We are also very cautious about the precise definition of 'fundamentalism,' which is sometimes identified in a hostile and confrontational way. The word 'fundamentalism' derives from a series of tracts entitled *The Fundamentals*, produced in the United States of America in the early part of the twentieth century. Written by eminent Evangelical leaders, they were widely distributed in the English-speaking world. They were intended to reinforce five principal doctrines in opposition to Liberal Protestantism: the verbal inerrancy of Scripture, the divinity of Jesus Christ, the Virgin Birth, a physical resurrection and the bodily return of Christ, and a substitutionary view of the atonement.

'Fundamentalism' is a term now more widely used to refer to conservative or ultra-conservative forms of Christianity. It is also applied, misleadingly, to other faiths. In not beginning with 'fundamentalism' as the defining category, as though what we are talking about is merely external to Anglicanism, we are acknowledging that how the Holy Scriptures are to be interpreted is a question that is also internal to Anglican churches, and arguments about biblical study and criticism have been, and are normal and common between Anglicans. We are also aware that some of the churches involved are not 'new' in the sense of being completely unrelated to any of the Christian World Communions. The holiness churches and movements of the late nineteenth and early twentieth centuries are also hardly 'new'; and there are charismatic developments in and offshoots from the classical post-Reformation Christian traditions.

We are clear that a study of New Churches and Independent Christian Groups does not include groups which are not specifically Christian, such as the Jehovah's Witnesses, the Church of the Latter Day Saints (Mormons), or the 'Children of God' ('The Family'). Nor, for the purpose of this report, have we focused on the more longstanding churches in the pentecostal and evangelical traditions, such as the Assemblies of God, the Elim Pentecostal Church, the Brethren, the Seventh Day Adventists and the Kimbangist Church in the Congo.

New Churches and Independent Christian Groups can be understood as occupying a place on a series of alternative positions.

The Pentecostal/Charismatic—Literalist

Although all these churches and groups hold a high view of Scripture, pentecostal or charismatic churches tend to focus more upon contemporary experience in their interpretation than those who place emphasis on a strongly literal interpretation of the Scriptures. Moreover, even within the former group there is a distinction between classical pentecostal and neo-charismatic forms of churches.

The Local—World-wide

Many New Churches and Independent Christian Groups arise from local needs, in a particular local culture and with local leadership. They are grass-roots churches, earthed in their own time and place. Others are part of a world-wide network, and may even be supervised, planted and funded from outside. Many of the latter are groups based in the USA, which import an American culture into other countries, with very little sense of the need for inculturation.

The Independent—Connexional

Many New Churches and Independent Christian Groups are fiercely independent, sometimes with a congregational polity, but more often with a local charismatic leader who has given time and energy to establishing his own 'church.' Some of these have a 'pure church' theology, and have arisen as breakaway groups from other churches. Others have a strong need for a wider identity, and come out of or enter into a 'connexion' with other similar groups. This connexion may be expressed by using a similar title for the group of New Churches and Independent Christian Groups; by attending similar conferences or 'get-togethers,' by having oversight or 'covering' from leaders outside of themselves or by sharing some agreed basis of faith and commitment.

Characteristics of New Churches and Independent Christian Groups

A very substantial amount of work has already been done on a number of the churches or groups with which we are concerned. In addition to this, and drawing on our own experience we observe a set of characteristics which often apply to New Churches and Independent Christian Groups, although not all of these will apply to every group.

(a) Are generally strong on the Bible.

Teaching and preaching is given priority. They are often selective in the parts of the Bible they use in worship and teaching, but the people are generally enthusiastic about discovering the truth of Scripture and are often thoroughly familiar with large parts of the Bible. Some veer towards extreme fundamentalism and biblical literalism, while others do not.

(b) Are generally assured about their faith, and keen to evangelise others.

In many cases they are passionate about conversion, and make clear to enquirers what they must do to become Christians.

(c) Are generally focused on a key charismatic leader.

In some cases it may be a group of leaders. Many have in fact arisen out of the vision of one particular person. The leader is usually given a position of authority and respect, and in some cases the leadership may even be passed on in the family to a son.

(d) Train up and deploy every member of the congregation.

In the case of charismatic churches, this may focus on identifying and releasing the 'the gifts of the Spirit' among God's people. There is often a strength of commitment demanded by these churches, and a sense of being honoured by being given a position of responsibility.

(e) Generally teach clear traditional moral values especially with regard to sexuality and family life.

People are not left in any shadow of doubt about moral absolutes. However, such churches may at times have 'blind spots' about issues such as materialism.

(f) Express their worship with freedom and enthusiasm.

Often the quality of music is excellent, there is freedom to dance, clap or raise hands, speak and sing in tongues, and be expressive and even emotional in worship. The worship is perceived as being free-flowing, spontaneous and joyful.

(g) Often offer healing and wholeness to those whose lives are broken.

This may be through laying-on-of hands, individual prayer ministry, counselling, or meeting their practical needs.

(h) Believe in tithing.

Most such groups affirm the biblical principle of tithing. There are New Churches and Independent Christian Groups which engage in 'prosperity teaching,' but this is not true of all.

Relationships with Anglicans

The story here is one of a wide variety of experiences. One of the first responses by many Anglicans to New Churches and Independent Christian Groups is a sense of threat, and we must be honest about this. The reasons for this sense of threat are many and various and often particular to the situation, but some emerge as common. For example:

'They have taken Anglicans away from their own church'

It would appear that a large part of the growth of New Churches and Independent Christian Groups, especially at the initial stages of their existence, is 'transfer growth.' There can be a resentment among Anglicans that some New Churches and Independent Christian Groups do not engage adequately with evangelism where it is difficult, but rather may appear to 'prey on' the already converted in the established denominations.

'They attract young people'

Many such groups attract young people. Others focus on families or young adults; others still on elderly people. But, with lively music, good sound systems, and challenging worship, they sometimes may be felt to drain the established churches of the youth generations.

'They get commitment'

In these new churches and independent groups people often suddenly come alive in their faith, speak out their faith to others, tithe their money and become enthused about bible study and prayer. We note with concern that this often goes alongside a kind of 'looking down' on the established churches as being 'dead,' 'formal,' 'rigid,' 'old-fashioned' or even barely Christian at all. It is noted in several cultures that members of New Churches and Independent Christian Groups will often return to the established churches for marriages or funerals, which can make the established Church feel as though it is being 'used.'

'They re-baptise'

The whole question of New Churches and Independent Christian Groups and sacraments is difficult to chart. In some cases, they appear to have no sacraments; in other cases they appear to have quasi-sacramental signs (e.g. blessed handkerchiefs for healing); and some of them appear to be traditional in practising the sacraments of Baptism and the Lord's Supper. With regard to baptism, many do not baptise infants, although this is not true of all. It can be very difficult for Anglicans when some of these groups deny our baptism as valid and persuade people to be baptised again as adults.

What Anglicans might learn

Having mentioned these negative responses, it is important to note that it is only in going beyond these to build up relationships, to take the initiative to visit and get to know such New Churches and Independent Christian Groups, to pray and to enter into dialogue, and if possible, to engage in common service or witness, that we will be able to develop this area. Not all experiences of New Churches and Independent Christian Groups have been negative. Many are very open to relationships with Anglicans; some have even joined local ecumenical councils of churches; some have reached a point where they themselves have become established, and some embrace aspects of Anglican liturgy in their worship or hanker for deeper roots in their spirituality or their theological understanding of the Church.

All relationships with fellow Christians of different traditions are rooted in God's call to us to be one. This call is articulated with clarity in various places in Scripture (John 17, 1 Cor. 12, Eph. 4); our movement towards another church or group is motivated, therefore, not by a desire to retain one's own church members, or to weaken or eliminate competition, or to bolster one's own 'market share,' but by a readiness to be obedient to God's will for the Church as taught in the New Testament. The modern world presents the church leader with many temptations to think and act on the assumption that the principles of the market apply to the founding and flourishing of churches, rewarding entrepreneurial flair and attention to the consumers' needs. Moreover all of this can be presented as responsiveness to divine guidance and the enjoyment of spiritual victory. For the mission of the New Testament churches, however there was no place for such competitiveness. Nor is the unity of the Church an optional extra; 'make every effort to maintain a unity of the Spirit in the bond of peace' (Eph. 4.3). It is in such a spirit that we call on all leaders of Anglican churches, having attempted to discern the nature of local New Churches and Independent Christian Groups, in a spirit of penitence for our own failures, to seek to understand by personal contact what might be learned from these churches or groups. For example:

We should learn to plan for and expect growth.

Many of these churches plan towards, pray for and expect growth to take place. In some places this is done through cell groups (e.g. in Singapore) in others, through seeker-friendly services (e.g. in Willow Creek, Chicago). Some Anglican churches have successfully embraced methods of growth which have come from their churches. But we need a mindset which expects growth.

We might learn to offer 'freer' styles of worship.

We are by nature a liturgical church, and much of our church teaching is conveyed in a liturgy which is rich in scriptural reference. There is a place, however, for freedom within a liturgical framework. Certain provinces have already developed 'a Service of the Word,' with both fixed and flexible elements. Other provinces have experimented with 'free' services alongside, but separate from, the traditional services.

We should learn to give greater weight to teaching and proclaiming the Scriptures.

Although we have a good framework for reading the Scriptures in our lectionaries, our teaching is often perceived as shallow, brief and unrelated to life. We need to take greater care to train people in the knowledge of the Scriptures and to help them to live under the authority of the Word of God in practical ways. Emphasis should be given to Bible study groups and passing on the Scriptures to the next generation.

We should be clear about our moral teaching.

In the context of considerable public uncertainty about moral standards, not least about sexual morality, there is great merit in teaching a biblically based moral code as a guide to conduct in public and private life, together with sensitive pastoral provision for those who fall short of the ideal. In this connection, this Section receives and recognises the Kuala Lumpur Statement on Human Sexuality as a contribution from the Anglican leaders present at the Second South to South Encounter (1997) to the Anglican Communion.

We should train our people to evangelise (and enthuse them about evangelism).

We must find ways of enabling new converts to express and witness to their new found faith. Some Anglican provinces are giving particular and renewed attention to confirmation as an act of public adult commitment, and are developing the renewal of baptismal vows as a means of public testimony.

Future ecumenical relationships with New Churches and Independent Christian Groups

This section of the Lambeth Conference believes that this growing part of the world-wide Church needs and deserves a new degree of sympathetic attention by Anglicans, specifically as a new development of their ecumenical vocation. At the same time the variety of forms of New Churches and Independent Christian Groups is simply bewildering, varying both from province to province and, internally, within a given province. The foundations of research into some of these churches and groups have already been laid, and some Anglican scholars are prominent in their interpretation. Relations with these churches and groups are, in certain parts of the Anglican Communion, vital and reliable information difficult to acquire. For this reason we ask the Primates to explore ways in which the fruits of relevant research and enquiry can be made available to provinces and dioceses.

The Chicago-Lambeth Quadrilateral

For many years Anglicans have taken their guidance in ecumenical relationships from the Chicago-Lambeth Quadrilateral (see Sub-Section 1 of this Report). We believe that the articles of the Quadrilateral are illuminating and helpful for our future contacts with New Churches and Independent Christian Groups of all kinds. As the section on Ecumenical Relations of the Report of the 1988 Lambeth Conference noted:

> The Quadrilateral... is an attempt to describe four interrelated elements used by the Spirit of God to hold together a body of diverse men and women in Christ... If it is to live, [it] needs to be embodied in a community and breathed on by the Spirit in a life of fellowship in worship and service. (sec. 55–7, p. 137)

Used in this manner, the Chicago-Lambeth Quadrilateral may form a generous and open way of recognising and rejoicing in genuinely common features belonging to the life of God's Church, professed by ourselves and fellow Christians in New Churches and Independent Christian Groups.

At the same time, if any elements are lacking in the witness of New Churches and Independent Christian Groups, then the Quadrilateral may help Anglicans at every level to understand why we urge caution or even dissent from their teachings.

Perhaps the most difficult area in our relationships with New Churches and Independent Christian Groups is that of authority in the interpretation of the Scriptures. It is the Anglican tradition to acknowledge the fact of diversity of interpretation, and Anglicans commonly do all in their power to contain disagreement within the worshipping and learning Christian community. But the Church uses the Apostles' and Nicene Creeds to indicate that there is a boundary between what is true and what is false or heretical in the interpretation of Scripture (see the discussion in the section on Dogmatic and Pastoral Concerns of the Lambeth Conference 1988 [sec. 70–91]). The fact that difficulties may arise in determining where the boundary lies does not mean that there are no boundaries. And on certain occasions it belongs to the leadership of the church to declare where it judges the truth to lie; any such judgement needs to be in a process of reception by the whole body of believers to whom it is addressed, as consonant with Scripture and tradition. In this way there is a check upon interpretations of Scripture of a purely local or individual character.

The fourth element of the Quadrilateral relates to authoritative leadership in the church. Occasionally this is perceived by these churches and groups to be authoritarian and overbearing; at other times the importance of the office and work of a bishop, exercised as a service to the unity of the church, becomes apparent in the midst of conflicts or the threat of schism. Moreover, the Anglican tradition of episcopacy is strongly pastoral in character, in accordance with the model of leadership in the Pastoral Epistles. It is notable that the episcopate acquired its form at much the same time that the Canon of the Scriptures of the New Testament was determined.

Sub-Section 3
Convergence in Faith and Order—Dialogues with Other Churches

The ecumenical task is to receive the gift of oneness in Christ and, through the confession of a common faith and a common life in worship, mission, witness and service, to make ever more manifest and visible the unity of Christ's Church. Theological dialogue with Christians of other churches is part of our faithful response to Christ's prayer for unity (John 17:20–24). Dialogue with other churches on matters of faith and order has become an important instrument within the wider Ecumenical Movement. In recent years moral, ethical and social justice issues have rightly been added to the classical faith and order agenda, for God's plan is nothing less than the gathering of all things in Christ (Eph. 1:10). As well as the international dialogues, a number of national or regional conversations were reported to this Conference. This has inevitably and rightly led to an emphasis on the particular historical and social context of the relationships concerned. All dialogues, however, continue to seek a balance and harmony between the fundamentals of Christ's revelation and the social and cultural context in which we find ourselves. It is here that a dynamic, pneumatological perspective is so important. The Spirit is given to teach and to bring to remembrance all that is of Christ (John 14:26). It is the Spirit also who will lead us into all truth (John 16:13). Our ecumenical dialogues are not only concerned with the past, with the historical and theological causes of our unhappy divisions; they are equally concerned with a faithful vision of the configuration of Christ's future Church: one, holy, catholic, and apostolic.

Bilateral, International and Regional Dialogues

The Assyrian Church of the East

The relationship with the Assyrian Church of the East has been cordial and close since the nineteenth century. In the early years of this century the Patriarch studied at St. Augustine's College, Canterbury. It is a distinct church with its own very ancient traditions and a long history of mission. Though not a member of the Oriental Orthodox family of churches, it has suffered in a similar way to other ancient Christian churches through upheavals, persecution and migration in the Middle East. This has resulted in large diaspora communities in North America and Australia, as well as a smaller community in Great Britain. A Christological agreement has been signed by Their Holinesses Mar Dinkha IV of the Assyrian Church of the East and Pope John Paul II. An official dialogue has also been renewed (1998) with the Syrian Orthodox Church for the discussion of Christological issues, pastoral matters, the sacraments, and the common Syriac culture shared by the two churches. Past Lambeth Conferences had already concluded that there is no longer a major Christological obstacle preventing closer relations with Anglicans (cf. *LC1908 and 1920 Reports and Resolutions 08.63/64 and 20.21*). It is therefore hoped that where communities live side by side, encouragement should be given to regional conversations.

The Baptist Churches

Resolution 10(3) of Lambeth 1988 called for dialogue between the Anglican Communion and the Baptist World Alliance. Because of lack of resources, it has regrettably not been possible to implement this. Nonetheless, many contacts between Anglicans and Baptists take place in the context of multilateral conversations and in councils of churches. Informal conversations have also been held between the Church of England and the Baptist Union of Great Britain; these have discussed the goal of visible unity and have examined both our mutual histories and contemporary examples of shared life in local ecumenical partnerships.

An informal meeting in September 1997 outlined possible ways forward. A welcome suggestion has been that an initial core group (possibly two Anglican and two Baptist theologians or historians) could meet Anglicans and Baptists in different regions for a first quinquennium with a view to the identification of issues for study in an international forum in a second quinquennium.

The Lutheran Churches

Anglican-Lutheran dialogues are taking place in many parts of the world, as well as through the Anglican-Lutheran International Commission. They are coming to share in a common vision and a common concern for the mission of the Church, which has proved to be their motivation and strength: God's purpose for creation and God's call to obedience. The dialogues have been further strengthened by the fact that Lutherans and Anglicans are re-discovering substantial doctrinal agreement and, sometimes with surprise, a similarity in worship, mission and ministry. We have a familial likeness.

Since the last Lambeth Conference, which welcomed and commended the *Niagara Report (LC88.4)*, the International Commission has published *The Diaconate as Ecumenical Opportunity* (1996), which contributes to the ecumenical discussion about the different experiences of 'diaconate' in the two traditions, pointing towards the renewal of a vocational diaconate. Regional or national dialogues have continued to flourish or have developed in Africa, Australia, Britain and Ireland, Canada, and the USA. In Africa two official consultations have taken place, and a Continuation Committee has been established to explore paths towards greater unity and to develop collaboration for justice and human rights and for the pastoral care of scattered Christian communities. In Australia official conversations are continuing and developing. In Canada both churches have committed themselves to seeking full communion; the Anglican Church of Canada and the Evangelical Lutheran Church in Canada are now examining the *Waterloo Declaration*. The British and Irish Anglican churches have already signed the *Porvöo Declaration*, recommended in the *Porvöo Common Statement*, which also contains an agreed portrait of full, visible unity. The agreement establishes communion between these Anglican churches and the majority of the Nordic and Baltic Lutheran churches. In the USA the proposed *Concordat of Agreement* between the Episcopal Church and the Evangelical Lutheran Church in America (henceforth 'ELCA'), the result of many years' work, was narrowly defeated by six votes short of the required two-thirds majority in the Churchwide Assembly of the ELCA, after securing agreement at the Episcopal Church's General Convention one month earlier. A preliminary draft revision of the *Concordat* prepared by the ELCA with the assistance of representatives from the Episcopal Church has been proposed. A revision is due to be resubmitted to the Churchwide Assembly in 1999. If accepted, it will then be considered by the General Convention of 2000.

In all of these regional dialogues substantial agreement has been recorded, though there are still issues remaining to be addressed. These include differences in terminology; issues connected with the threefold ministry; the status of our foundational documents; and church-state relations. Some Anglicans and Lutherans are opposed to the ordination of women. In neither Communion is there yet complete consensus about our existing agreements. There is also a need to clarify further the meaning of 'apostolic succession' and its implications for unity. The *Niagara Report* (1987) drew on an important insight from the Lutheran-Roman Catholic dialogue, namely that 'apostolic succession in the episcopal office does not consist primarily in an unbroken chain of those ordaining to those ordained, but in a succession in the presiding ministry of a church which stands in the continuity of apostolic faith and which is overseen by a bishop…' (Lutheran Roman Catholic Joint Commission, '*The Ministry in the Church*,' para. 62)

On this basis Anglican churches were asked to take the necessary steps to acknowledge the authenticity of the existing ministries of Lutheran churches with which they are in dialogue (cf. *Niagara Report* paras. 53 and 94). This far-reaching principle was subsequently applied in varying degrees in three regional agreements: in the *Porvöo Declaration*, in the proposed *Waterloo Declaration* and in the *Concordat of Agreement.* In northern Europe (*Porvöo Declaration*) the intention to maintain succession in the historic sees and the continuity of the 'folk-churches' with the pre-Reformation Church were decisive factors and many of the churches concerned had in any case retained or regained the historic episcopal succession; the interchangeability of ordained ministers does not apply to those ordained other than by bishops. The *Concordat* and *Waterloo,* located in different North American contexts, extended this principle, and, especially in the *Concordat,* emphasised the apostolicity of the Church as a whole. In each case, the interchangeability of existing ordained ministers is seen in the framework of a commitment to value and maintain and value the historic episcopate in the future.

The changed relationships envisaged or achieved involve definite commitments. These include a mutual welcoming of each other to sacramental and pastoral ministrations, mutual participation in episcopal ordinations, and the interchangeability of ordained ministers. They also include forms of collegial and conciliar consultation.[18] A lived example of the latter is the happy presence of bishops of the Lutheran Porvöo churches at this Lambeth Conference as members of the Conference. The interchangeability of liturgies has also been proposed.[19]

The Malabar Independent Syrian Church

The Malabar Independent Syrian Church,[20] coming from the Syro-Malankar Orthodox tradition in India, affords eucharistic hospitality to Anglicans. Good relations have continued to develop with the churches of the Anglican Communion in recent years. The Malabar Independent Syrian Church would welcome an agreement on Christology with the churches of the Anglican Communion.

The Methodist Churches

The last Lambeth Conference called for an international Anglican-Methodist dialogue (Lambeth Conference 1988, Resolution 9). The Report of the Anglican-Methodist International Commission to the World Methodist Council and the Lambeth Conference, *Sharing in the Apostolic Communion* (1996), contained an agreed statement clearing the historical ground between Anglicans and Methodists, as well as proposals to enable Anglicans and Methodists to grow together in worship, mutual care and mission, and to affirm and recognise one another as churches. It recommends that a working group should encourage action in each place leading to full, visible unity. *Sharing the Apostolic Communion* is addressed to the Lambeth Conference as well as the World Methodist Council, so it is a matter of regret that it was not sent to the bishops of the Lambeth Conference before the Conference, which would have made possible its evaluation within a process of reception. The Report was, however, sent to the Provinces for information and to the tenth meeting of the Anglican Consultative Council at Panama (1996).

The founders of Methodism, John and Charles Wesley, were and remained Anglicans: the goal of Anglican-Methodist dialogue is, therefore, the restoration of a broken unity rather than the establishment of a fresh relationship.

Above all, mission motivates this dialogue. The acceptance of a stage-by-stage approach is also a characteristic of the Report. The Commission calls for the threefold ministry to be renewed by both Communions together. This would include both churches reconsidering their understanding of the diaconate and the incorporation of the historic episcopate into Methodism It is the Commission's hope that the historic episcopate will become again for all a gracious sign of the unity and continuity of Christ's Church.

The Commission strongly believes that the ministry of those already ordained should not be called into question. Outstanding issues remain, in particular how the ministries can be made interchangeable within the context of the restoration of ecclesial communion. Structures for decision-making at local, provincial and global levels would need to be established. Questions relating to decisions about the ordination of women also need to be addressed.

We have noted with hope and gratitude the unanimous adoption of paragraph 95 of *Sharing in the Apostolic Communion* by the World Methodist Council at Rio de Janeiro (1996). This contains two proposals to enable our two communions to grow together in worship, mutual care and mission. In the light of their positive adoption by World Methodist Council, Anglicans should now also consider these two proposals in the light of the whole Report. This would first involve the mutual acknowledgement that:

- both churches belong to the one, holy, catholic and apostolic Church of Jesus Christ and participate in the apostolic mission of the whole people of God;
- in the churches of our two communions, the Word of God is authentically preached and the Sacraments instituted by Christ are duly administered; and
- our churches share in the common confession and heritage of the apostolic faith.

The Conference has felt it right to adapt the wording of the proposed resolution from *Sharing in the Apostolic Communion* for the sake of a consistency with other dialogues. Following other regional models, the Conference believes that emphasis should now be placed in Anglican-Methodist relations in regions, in which the relative development of relationships between Anglicans and Methodists vary very considerably from one another. But in each case developments should be based on the insights of *Sharing in the Apostolic Communion* and made relevant to specific contexts.

On the basis of the above acknowledgements, the second proposal recommends the establishment of a Joint Working Group to consider ways of celebrating this mutual acknowledgement and to prepare, in full accordance with the principles accepted in the Report, guidelines for moving beyond acknowledgement to the reconciliation of churches and, within that, the reconciliation of ordained ministries, including structures for common decision-making. There is also a need to monitor regional developments, such as the welcome agreement of the Conference of the Methodist Church of Great Britain and the General Synod of the Church of England to enter into formal conversations following the informal conversations (*Commitment to Mission and Unity* [1997]). A Working Group could first promote, encourage and monitor regional or national developments and offer guidelines for further developments as and when regional and local developments made this necessary. There would also be an important role here for the proposed Inter-Anglican Standing Commission on Ecumenical Relations.

The Moravian Church

The Moravian Church or *Unitas Fratrum* is a single international church, whose Unity Church Order, agreed by the Unity Synod, binds its provinces.

Ecumenical dialogue between the Moravian Church and the Anglican episcopate took place in the 1740s, and the question of Anglican-Moravian relations was first raised at a Lambeth Conference as early as 1878, appearing on the agenda of each subsequent Conference until that of 1948 accepted the end of specific Anglican-Moravian conversations.[21] These were taken up again in England in 1989, resulting in the Fetter Lane Agreement between the Church of England and the Moravian Church in Great Britain and Ireland. The Fetter Lane Declaration has subsequently been adopted by the Church of Ireland, and will be signed by representatives of all three churches in November 1998.

The Declaration contains a mutual acknowledgement of churches and ministries and commits the signatory churches to take all steps towards visible unity which are currently possible. There is a particular emphasis on unity at the local level, with a commitment to encourage the establishment of a Local Ecumenical Partnership wherever a Moravian and an Anglican congregation live in the same community. The Common Statement also lists five issues on which further convergence would be required before visible unity between

Anglicans and Moravians could be attained, including the role of the episcopate within a united church, and the process of formally reconciling our two ministries.

Moravians and Anglicans also live alongside each other in other parts of the world, including North America, South Africa, Tanzania and the West Indies. In all of these areas, Moravians are more numerous than they are in Britain and Ireland, and Anglican-Moravian relations are generally good. The *Fetter Lane Declaration* commits the signatories 'to share the insights of our Common Statement with Anglicans and Moravians in other parts of the world, and to invite our international bodies to consider the implications of this Agreement for their consultative processes.' (para. 55 b[ix]) This would be an early task for the proposed Inter-Anglican Standing Commission on Ecumenical Relations.

The Oriental Orthodox Churches

The Oriental Orthodox Churches are a family in communion with one another. Historically, the relationship of the Anglican Communion with the Oriental Orthodox Churches has always been one of support and assistance. The Anglican/Oriental Orthodox International Forum has built on this historic relationship in the development of dialogue on matters of common theological interest and concern.

Oriental Orthodox theologians have already agreed to a short unofficial statement on Christology with the Roman Catholic Church, a brief official agreement on Christology with the Reformed World Alliance and a much fuller official one with the Byzantine Orthodox. The official agreements still await ratification by Orthodox and Oriental Orthodox synods. The Oriental Orthodox family of churches would welcome an agreement on Christology and other theological and ecclesial issues with the Anglican Communion. At the same time, they are uneasy about what may lie ahead in the Anglican Communion. In addition to the new context brought about by the ordination of women in many Anglican provinces, they are concerned about current Anglican debates concerning homosexuality, abortion and other ethical issues.

Recent historical developments have posed new problems for the Oriental Orthodox churches. In Armenia, for example, the collapse of the Soviet Union has provided many opportunities for the Armenian Orthodox Church, and there are good examples of partnership and co-operation with other Christian churches, but there has also been an influx of Western 'missionaries' seeking to proselytise. Another development affecting these Churches is the resurgence of Islam. Islamic and Hindu nationalism can create serious pressures on Christians in particular regions.

In spite of these problems and continuing questions between Oriental Orthodox and Anglicans, there is a real commitment to deepening the dialogue. As the 1988 Lambeth Conference stated (Resolution 5[9]), the time is right for the Anglican-Orthodox Forum to be upgraded to an International Theological Commission and among other ecclesial and theological issues to seek a formal agreement on Christology. It is also opportune to encourage bilateral discussions with individual Oriental Orthodox Churches on a regional basis.

The Orthodox Churches

We give thanks for and continue to support the resumption of the work of the International Commission of the Anglican-Orthodox Dialogue, the formal means of international dialogue between the Orthodox churches and the churches of the Anglican Communion. Over the last ten years the work of this Commission has produced interim agreed statements addressing fundamental aspects of ecclesiology:

- The Trinity and the Church
- Christ, the Spirit and the Church
- Christ, Humanity and the Church

These interim statements are commended to the bishops of the Anglican Communion and their theological advisors for study. The Commission looks forward to receiving responses to the interim statements by the end of 1999.

Progress continues to be made in relation to the *filioque* clause in the Western version of the Nicene-Constantinopolitan Creed. *The Dublin Agreed Statement* (1984) recommended the restoration of the original form of the Creed as authorised by the Councils of Nicaea (325) and Constantinople (381), without prejudice to the Augustinian and Western theology of the Holy Spirit. The restoration of the original form of the creed was approved by the Lambeth Conferences of 1978 and 1988 and by subsequent meetings of the Anglican Consultative Council and the Primates. A number of churches of the Anglican Communion have responded. The Episcopal Church in the USA has decided to remove the clause in future Prayer Books, as have the Scottish Episcopal Church, the Anglican Church of Aotearoa, New Zealand, and Polynesia, the Anglican Church of Canada, the Church of the Province of Central Africa, and the Anglican Church in Wales. The Church of England has agreed that in all future publications of revised eucharistic rites the original form of the creed will be recommended for use on appropriate occasions. It was omitted at the opening Eucharist of the 1998 Lambeth Conference, following the precedent of the last Lambeth Conference.

In response to resolution 6.7 of the 1988 Lambeth Conference, the Lambeth Conference acknowledges with gratitude the initiative of His Holiness Patriarch Alexei II of Moscow and All Russia to both the Church of England and the Episcopal Church in the USA to enter into what the last Lambeth Conference called an exploration of 'increased contact, co-operation and exchanges' (LC88.6.7). There has been extensive development of this relationship and a warm and friendly bond has been established between the churches concerned. These relationships are to be commended and new ones encouraged. However, such provincial relationships need to be developed in such a way as to complement rather than duplicate the important work of the International Anglican-Orthodox Dialogue.

The Reformed Churches

After the publication of the Report of the Anglican-Reformed International Commission, *God's Reign and Our Unity* (1984), Resolution 7 of the Lambeth Conference 1988 recommended that the Anglican Consultative Council collect from the Provinces responses to the dialogue and any consequences that have resulted. It also requested the Anglican Consultative Council to consult with the World Alliance of Reformed Churches (WARC) about the possibility of establishing a small continuation committee to encourage a wider study and implementation of the insights of this dialogue as a contribution towards growth in unity.

A small exploratory committee met in March 1995. After a review of Anglican-Reformed relations in the USA, South Africa, Canada, the United Kingdom, and the Netherlands, the committee recommended that WARC and the Anglican Consultative Council establish a small Joint Working Group with a mandate to:

- monitor Anglican-Reformed relationships;
- sponsor joint studies in appropriate areas, particularly as proposed in *God's Reign and Our Unity;* and
- encourage co-operative projects which would lead to greater understanding.

The establishment of a second Anglican-Reformed bilateral theological dialogue was not recommended.

The Joint Working Group met for the first time in June 1996. It surveyed bilateral Anglican-Reformed relations, as well as relationships in wider contexts in different parts of the world. It recommended research projects on fuller participation in movements leading to full, visible unity and a study of the exercise of personal episcopacy in the Reformed tradition, together with case studies of local Anglican-Reformed sharing in mission, justice issues, and congregational life.

We also note with interest the Meissen Agreement between British and Irish Anglican churches and the Evangelical Church in Germany, which includes Reformed as well as Lutheran and United churches. This agreement was inspired by the vision of the Church as sign, foretaste and instrument of God's Kingdom set out in *God's Reign and Our Unity* and built upon the convergences recorded in that report. We look forward to the forthcoming report of the conversations between the British and Irish Anglican churches and the French Lutheran and Reformed churches, and to the developing Scottish Churches' Initiative for Unity, in which the Scottish Episcopal Church and the Church of Scotland are major partners.

The Roman Catholic Church

The results of Anglican-Roman Catholic dialogue are being communicated and received in the various provinces of the Anglican Communion, though somewhat unevenly. Theological reflection and joint study continue and are essential for the reception of the results of the dialogue. It was noted that more work is being done at the local or missionary level but that the reception of Anglican-Roman Catholic consensus was not consistent throughout the Anglican Communion and that much depended on individual personalities and the particular characteristics of the churches at the local level. In some places the local identity of either church is defined negatively: that is to say, membership of one church is defined by not being a member of the other church. There is also a considerable difference of 'ecclesial culture' between Anglicans and Roman Catholics, which often results in the misunderstanding of actions or statements by leaders of one church by members of the other.

To assist the reception process, we re-affirm the importance of the ARCIC Statements. The necessity of ensuring that the Statements are translated and made available for study is strongly emphasised, as are the Report and Resolution of the last Lambeth Conference on the Final Report (1982). Inasmuch as *Eucharistic Doctrine and Ministry and Ordination*, together with their *Elucidations*, were affirmed by Lambeth 1988 as 'consonant in substance with the faith of Anglicans,' we believe there is a need for them to be known as such at provincial and diocesan levels. These agreements ought to be respected and regarded as 'consonant in substance with faith of Anglicans' and be received into the lives of the Provinces.

We also urge that the Provinces consider subsequent Statements for discussion, evaluation, and eventual reception: *Salvation and the Church* (1987), *Church as*

Communion (1991), *Life in Christ* (1994). The bishop's role as teacher is crucial in the reception of these, as in that of all other ecumenical agreements, particularly when agreed statements achieve a level of ecclesial endorsement and so potentially become a common part of the teaching tradition of two or more churches.

We look forward to the completion of the work of ARCIC II on authority, while noting that the work requested by Lambeth 1988 on primacy and collegiality is still continuing. Relevant to this continuing work is the Encyclical Letter of Pope John Paul II *Ut unum sint* (1995), inviting all Christians to reflect with him on the ministry of unity of the Bishop of Rome as a service for the universal church. The Provinces are urged to consider this letter and respond to it.

We commend and support the work of the Anglican Centre in Rome, especially at the time of its move to a more accessible location. The Anglican Centre continues to play an integral part in our continuing journey towards full, visible unity.

Of particular importance for the Anglican-Roman Catholic dialogue for the future is the meeting spoken of in the *Common Declaration* of Pope John Paul II and the Archbishop of Canterbury (December 1996). We commend this meeting, now proposed for the year 2000, and encourage Provinces to respond to the invitation of the Archbishop of Canterbury to submit items for its agenda. Among them consideration should be given to matters of difficulty on either side, for example inter-church marriages and the consequences for the dialogue of the ordination of women, as well as guidelines to facilitate the transfer of clergy from one communion to the other (noting that useful and working models of good practice already exist). But above all the proposed meeting should look at the overall future of the dialogue, its purpose, direction and shape, its priorities and its methodology in the light of many graces and advances, as well as some set-backs, since its inauguration by Pope Paul VI and Archbishop Michael Ramsey in 1966, which 'founded on the Gospels and on the ancient common traditions may lead to that unity in truth, for which Christ prayed' (*Common Declaration*, 1966).

The Faith and Order Commission of the World Council of Churches

The work of the Faith and Order Commission of the World Council of Churches continues to provide an important multilateral framework in which to reflect upon the work of the bilateral dialogues. The six volumes of the responses of the churches to '*Baptism, Eucharist and Ministry*' and '*The Responses to the Responses, 1982–1990*' have provided a vital ecumenical resource. Despite this the findings of these documents have clearly not informed the practice of a number of provinces. While many bishops reported a lack of knowledge of most of the publications of the Commission on Faith and Order, their reflection on the central themes which the Commission had addressed were uniformly positive.

An example of the way in which the practice of some provinces showed no knowledge of *BEM* is in the area of Christian Initiation. Differences in practice and discipline include the shift in some provinces (England and Australia) towards more adults and fewer young people seeking confirmation. This contrasts with the situation in Nigeria and Zambia where the norm continues to be confirmation at the age of twelve. In the latter cases, as in the West Indies, confirmation continues to be required for admission to communion. In England and Australia two practices continue in parallel: baptism, admission to communion, confirmation; or baptism, confirmation, admission to communion. In the West Indies the discipline is complicated by many visitors from North America where young children are admitted to the eucharist before confirmation and thus expect and receive the same hospitality in the West Indies.

The issue surrounding Christian Initiation highlights the need for more efficient means for the distribution of and response to ecumenical reports so that they may be received into the life and practice of the churches. We therefore endorse the recommendation of the *Agros Report* (para 185–6) (see also Sub-Section 4 regarding Response and Reception).

The Canberra Statement: The Unity of the Church as Koinonia: Gift and Calling (WCC, 1991) was endorsed by the 1991 General Assembly of the World Council of Churches meeting in Canberra. It describes the unity of the Church which God gives and to which God calls us. It outlines the marks of that unity, and suggests steps on the way to making that unity visible. It speaks of:

- the common confession of apostolic faith;

- a common sacramental life entered by baptism and celebrated together in one Eucharistic fellowship;

- a common life in which members and ministries are mutually recognized and reconciled;

- such a communion will be expressed on the local and universal levels through conciliar forms of life and action; and

- in such a communion churches are bound together confessing the one faith and engaging in worship and witness, deliberation and action.

The Canberra Statement adopts a positive attitude towards diversity while recognising that there are limits to legitimate diversity, and begins to explore what those limits are. We commend the statement to the Lambeth Conference as a creative description of the nature of the unity of the Church and the steps for making that unity visible.

The Faith and Order Commission has made a useful contribution to the churches in their bilateral dialogues in its work on the common confession of the apostolic faith. The Commission has published a study guide, *Towards Sharing the One Faith*, which might be particularly helpful for Anglicans in discussion with New Churches and Independent Christian Groups (see Sub-Section 2).

The report *Towards a Common Date for Easter* (WCC, Middle East Council of Churches Consultation in Aleppo, Syria, 5–10 March 1997) provides a useful and thorough examination of the issues, the historical background to the present different practices and the continuing relevance of the canons of Nicaea. We welcome the report as a basis for a major ecumenical agreement on a common date for the celebration of the resurrection, noting that in 2001 all the existing traditions will be celebrating Easter on 15 April.

We note the recent work of Faith and Order in the area of worship and spirituality. *So We Believe, So We Pray* (1993) explores the significance of an *ordo* or pattern of Christian worship and how shared worship is a contribution to the search for unity. A further contribution on the baptismal *ordo* and questions of the ethical implications of baptism was published in 1997.

The major event since the last Lambeth Conference was the Fifth World Conference on Faith and Order, held in Santiago de Compostela, Spain in 1993.[22] The theme of the Conference, 'Towards *Koinonia* in Faith, Life and Witness,' was Faith and Order's answer to the question, 'Where are we going in the ecumenical movement?' Under this theme the Conference considered the results of the three major studies: *Confessing the One Faith; Baptism, Eucharist and Ministry;* and *Church* and *World*.[23] We note that the Fifth World Conference gave a clear message with which we concur:

> We say to the churches: there is no turning back, either from the goal of visible unity or from the single ecumenical movement that unites concern for the unity of the Church and concern for engagement in struggles of the world.

We welcome the fact that the World Conference took note of the guidelines for inter-faith dialogue proposed by the World Council of Churches in 1979:

- dialogue begins when people meet each other;
- dialogue depends upon mutual trust and understanding;
- dialogue should lead to common service to the community; and
- dialogue includes authentic witness.

Some bishops were very concerned about the relationship between dialogue and evangelism, but this topic was considered more fully in another section of the Conference. We commend these guidelines for use in the Provinces of the Anglican Communion, noting that, while such dialogue always gives an opportunity for authentic witness, it is primarily about seeking peace and unity between communities.

The World Conference in 1993 called for further work on ecclesiology and on ecumenical method. Later in 1998 the Commission will publish three major reports:

- *A Treasure in Earthen Vessels: An Instrument for an Ecumenical Reflection on Hermeneutics.*
- *Episcopé and Episcopacy and the Quest for Visible Unity.*
- *The Nature and Purpose of the Church: A Stage on the Way to a Common Statement.*

These will provide important resources for Anglicans in international and regional bilateral conversations.

Sub-Section 4:
Consistency and Coherence—Response and Reception

Consistency and Coherence

As we reviewed the vision of the unity to which we are called and the complex network of bilateral and multilateral dialogues in which Anglicans are engaged at international, regional and national levels, we became more and more conscious of a series of questions relating to consistency and coherence which affect the process of response and reception.

The description of the goal in different dialogues

Anglicans have used a variety of words and phrases to describe the unity to which we are called, e.g. organic unity, visible unity, full communion. Terms such as full communion have not always been used consistently (cf. LC88 Section Report, 'Ecumenical Relations,' 94–99). Until the Lambeth Conference of 1958, full communion was usually used to describe a relationship found within a single confessional family. It came to be applied to wider ecclesial relationships in which there is a mutual interchangeability of ministers or members. More recently, this definition has itself been questioned by some, though not all, Anglicans, who ask 'Does full communion imply more than sacramental interchangeability? Does it not also imply mutual interdependence and an ecclesial commitment to take counsel together in all matters affecting each other?' In some ways this is a reversion to an earlier understanding of the meaning of full communion, in which being in communion implied structures for common decision-making as well as mutual support and common witness. It has been argued that communion is in fact a closer relationship between churches than any other description. Behind divergences of terminology may lie different visions of the unity to which we are called. So it has become important to include within a given ecumenical dialogue some description of the unity we seek. The different understandings of the same terms make even more urgent the need for a common description of our vision of visible unity.

Consistency between international dialogues

Dialogues with different partners at the international level raise issues of consistency and coherence. Do Anglicans say consistent things to each of their ecumenical partners? The work of the Bilateral Forum convened every two years by the Faith and Order Commission of the World Council of Churches on behalf of the Christian World Communions provides a useful context for reviewing matters of consistency between all of the dialogues.

Consistency between regional dialogues

Dialogues with the same confessional partner at regional levels raise questions of consistency. A case in point is the remarkable regional progress made in Anglican-Lutheran relations since the last Lambeth Conference. In the USA, longstanding discussion with Lutherans has resulted in the proposal for a *Concordat*, the goal of which is described as 'full communion.' In Europe the British and Irish Anglican churches have signed the *Porvöo Declaration* with Nordic and Baltic Lutheran churches in which the stated goal is visible unity which entails 'agreement in faith with the common celebration of the sacraments, supported by a united ministry and forms of collegial conciliar consultation in matters of faith, life and witness.' (*Porvöo Common Statement*, para. 28) In the USA, the Evangelical Lutheran Church in America and the Episcopal Church are frequently alongside each other in the same territory. In Europe, Anglicans and Lutherans have historically been largely separated by the North Sea. Do we, and should we, have the same ultimate goal of unity? What is the significance of the different terms used in these and other regional dialogues?

Temporary anomalies

In moving towards visible unity we recognize that temporary anomalies are likely to arise. *The Porvöo Declaration* and the proposed *Concordat* offer different ways for Anglicans to accept the ministries of those ordained in churches in which the historic episcopal succession has at some time been disrupted or in which the office of bishop has only recently been introduced. In both cases there will eventually be a full acceptance of the historic episcopate as sign of the apostolicity of the whole Church. This understanding of apostolicity and succession, derived from the multilateral agreement *Baptism, Eucharist and Ministry* (1982), deepened and clarified in the *Niagara Report* (1987), can be seen as being worked out in two very different geographical, cultural and ecclesial contexts. The complexity can cause uncertainty; however, a temporary anomaly is bearable if there is an overall agreed goal of visible unity.

Extended implications of specific relationships

Another question arises when agreements are accepted. What, for example, does the *Porvöo Agreement* do to the relations between Anglicans and Lutherans elsewhere in the world? 'Are your friends (necessarily or automatically) my friends?' This untidiness and these questions of relationship are inescapable given a step-by-step, stage-by-stage advance to Christian unity.

Consultation

Increasingly, we need to ask when we are considering entering a relationship of communion with a partner church whether we are obliged to consult with other churches with which we are in a relationship of communion. Similarly, do we not have an obligation to consult with ecumenical partners, preferably by including them in the conversations?

Extending agreement

How do churches which were not a party to an original ecumenical dialogue come into an existing ecumenical agreement? Is it a matter of merely signing on? Should a new dialogue begin? Or should we find ways of extending agreement which take into account the particularities of the relationship, bearing in mind that there are finite limits to the number of people and the financial resources available?

Ecumenical method

Churches are often divided because of the different ways in which they express the faith. Their official statements were frequently composed in separation at times of controversy and were designed in part to deny what others were saying. Ecumenical method involves going back together to the Scriptures and ancient common tradition of the faith and then, avoiding polemical language, re-expressing the common faith in fresh ways. Problems may be created when people expect to find in ecumenical texts the specific formulations with which they are familiar from their own confessional traditions.

These new and puzzling questions—and they are not exhaustive!—bear testimony to the progress and growth of the ecumenical movement. God not only calls us to a vision of unity. God also answers Christ's prayer for unity (John 17) into which we are drawn whenever we pray and labour for unity. These complexities arise because we have reached a new stage in the ecumenical movement. Some regional dialogues have borne fruit in actual agreements, which have led to changed relationships. This is cause for rejoicing. Even if the present ecumenical map is complex and difficult to read, we have moved on from academic dialogue to real relationships between the churches.

These questions of consistency and coherence lead us to support the suggestion made originally by the meeting of the Ecumenical Advisory Group in Agros, Cyprus and endorsed by the Anglican Consultative Council at Panama in 1996, that there should be established (in place of the existing Ecumenical Advisory Group), an Inter-Anglican Standing Commission on Ecumenical Relations.

Its tasks would include the monitoring and encouraging of multilateral and bilateral dialogues, both regional and international, including the process of response to the dialogues, decisions about them and reception. It would be asked to review and ensure consistency in ecumenical conversations. When a potential agreement would in its judgement affect the life of the Anglican Communion as a whole, in consultation with the Anglican Consultative Council, it would refer the matter to the Primates' Meeting, which might itself seek the guidance of the Lambeth Conference before encouraging the Province to enter into the relationship proposed. It would also give particular attention to anomalies which arise in proposals, with a view to discerning whether they may be bearable in the light of progress towards an agreed goal of visible unity, and perhaps offer advice as to their resolution. It would further assist the Communion should another Province consider a particular regional agreement for adoption. It could also address issues of terminology and facilitate the circulation of ecumenical documents and other resources, where possible in the languages of the Communion. It would also be able to assist the Provinces as they develop relationships with New Churches and Independent Christian Groups, both by circulating relevant studies of these very different Christian communities and by helping Provinces to understand their own identity in a way which would give them confidence to approach such new communities. Reflection on the Lambeth Quadrilateral and New Churches and Independent Christian Groups might be fruitfully assisted by the proposed Inter-Anglican Standing Commission on Ecumenical Relations (see Sub-Section 2).

To be effective in carrying out its work and responsibility, its membership would need to include:

- Anglicans who are familiar with the work of the Faith and Order Commission of the World Council of Churches, and of Anglican international bilateral dialogues:
- Theologians with appropriate expertise and experience;
- Those involved in regional relationships;
- Those who can link with the Inter-Anglican Doctrinal Commission and the International Anglican Liturgical Consultation; and
- Persons skilled in adult education and communication.

It is proposed that its staff would be the Director of Ecumenical Affairs and Relations of the Anglican Communion, assisted where appropriate by the Secretary for Ecumenical Affairs of the Archbishop of Canterbury. The members should be appointed by the Archbishop of Canterbury after consultation with the Primates and the Secretary General of the Anglican Communion. The chairperson should be a Primate similarly appointed.

Response and Reception

The reports of the bishops were very mixed. Some reported 'little response to' or reception of ecumenical texts. Some provinces have little or no knowledge of *Baptism, Eucharist and Ministry*, the most widely circulated ecumenical report. This text was widely discussed in the synods of the Communion and formally accepted by the Lambeth Conference 1988. Similarly, the bishops reported a limited knowledge of the ARCIC *Final Report*, and the *Niagara Report* of the Anglican-Lutheran International Commission, which were commended by the last Lambeth Conference. When the Lambeth Conference has articulated the mind of the provinces that an agreed statement is consonant with the faith of Anglicans, these agreements need to be received into the life of the church. Reception into the life of the church would assist Anglican cohesiveness and help us to grow in communion with our ecumenical partners. For example, the incorporation of the convergences on the eucharist in *BEM* into liturgical revision would assist the provinces and give them assurance that with increasing liturgical inculturation they still retain the classical elements of the Christian eucharist. *BEM* recommends that the churches test their liturgies in the light of ecumenical eucharistic agreement. This would be an excellent example of reception of ecumenical agreement into the life of the Church.

One reason why the process of the reception of ecumenical agreement is so slow is a lack of understanding of ecumenical method and process. At the preliminary stage of response more attention needs to be given to communication and to the questions which accompany any ecumenical agreement as it is sent to the churches. Texts must also be translated and in many instances be accompanied by study material. More investigation needs to be given to the needs of provinces where printed material and other means of communication are not easily available for many people. How do we communicate the fruits of ecumenical agreement in provinces where the ecumenical agenda is more likely to be centred on cooperation in witness and social justice issues?

Official response to texts comes through synods and other official organs of the church, and the process differs according to the structures of authority that exist in each province. The reception process has raised questions for all churches, not only those of the Anglican Communion, about ecclesiology, including structures of authority and where authority lies.

The Report on Dogmatic and Pastoral Concerns to Lambeth 1988 helpfully clarified the process of reception in the following way:

> What is it that constitutes the mind of a Province, Communion or the whole Church? On the one hand the expression of 'consensus' will involve the achieving of certain thought out and stipulated majorities in synods at the appropriate level: discerning the mind of a Province, in provincial synod, discerning the mind of the Communion, at the Lambeth Conference, in the Primates' Meeting and in the meetings of the Anglican Consultative Council; and in the context of the whole Church, at a truly ecumenical council. A synodical majority on its own, however, cannot be deemed to constitute the mind of a Province or Communion or of the whole Church. (*Lambeth 1988, Dogmatic and Pastoral Concerns,* page 117f.)

This quotation makes clear that reception does not mean automatic acceptance of a matter. It refers to an 'open process' of discernment in which a matter may be accepted or rejected over a period of time. To this we would add a quotation from the Grindrod Report (which lay behind the Lambeth Conference 1988 resolution on Women in the Episcopate) and which is quoted by the Eames Commission Monitoring Group Report in preparation for this conference:

> 'Reception' is a long and spiritual process involving both official response by the synods and councils of the Church 'at the highest level of authority'. It also involves a longer and more widespread process of reception. Conciliar or synodical decisions, themselves emerging from widespread consultation and episcopal guidance, have to be received. If in the course of time the Church as a whole

> receives a synodical decision this would be an additional or final sign that it may be judged to be in accordance with God's will for the Church (Final Report of ARCIC, *Authority I*, para. 6; *Elucidation* para. 3; Authority II, para. 25). The people of God, under the guidance of the Holy Spirit, have to be involved in forming the mind of the Church in matters affecting the faith of the Church. Within this process the authority of those exercising leadership, individually, and corporately, is not a formal or imposed one. It is an authority supported and accepted by the involvement of the whole fellowship. (*Women in the Anglican Episcopate* [Toronto: ACC, 1998], p. 115.)

This gives each bishop both the mandate and the context in which to lead and to teach in accordance with Christ's prayer for unity and God's plan for the unity of all things in Christ: the unity to which we are called.

Conclusion

'There can be no ecumenism worthy of the name without conversion of heart.'[24] This is true both for individuals and for communities. The ecumenical movement is about conversion to Christ and to one another in Christ. The nearer we come to Christ, the nearer we come to one another. We as bishops are pledged to lead our churches and dioceses in penitence for past attitudes of pride and self-sufficiency. We should re-direct ourselves with patient attentiveness to our brothers and sisters of other traditions in order to receive from them the gifts they have to offer.

As bishops we have a particular responsibility to lead in the search for visible unity, which arises directly from our responsibility to foster unity among those whom we serve. There should be no distinction between our care for the unity of our dioceses and our care for the unity of Christ's universal church. If we as bishops have heard God's call to unity, we should be obedient to it in the depths of our being.

At the Ecumenical Vespers which formed one of the high points of our time together at the 1998 Lambeth Conference, we expressed our commitment in prayer:

> O God, holy and eternal Trinity,
> We pray for your Church in all the world.
> Sanctify its life; renew its worship;
> Empower its witness; heal its divisions;
> Make visible its unity.
> Lead us, with all our brothers and sisters

Towards communion in faith, life and witness
So that, united in one body by the one Spirit,
We may together witness to the perfect unity
Of your love. Amen.[25]

Notes

1. *A Report of the Ecumenical Advisory Group of the Anglican Communion*, 1997, Appendix 1, pp. 59ff.

2. Pontifical Council for Promoting Christian Unity, *Directory for the Application of Principles and Norms on Ecumenism* (Vatican City, 1993).

3. *The Ecumenical Dimension in the Formation of Those Engaged in Pastoral Work*, Pontifical Council for Promoting Christian Unity.

4. *Statement on the Mutual Recognition of Ministries*, Church Unity Commission, 1994.

5. *Signs of the Spirit. Official Report, WCC Seventh Assembly*, ed. M. Kinnaman (Geneva, 1991), pp. 172 ff.

6. *Toward a Common Understanding and Vision of the World Council of Churches: A Policy Statement*, WCC, 1997.

7. Resolution 10.

8. *The Report of the Inter-Anglican Theological and Doctrinal Commission*, 1997.

9. *Women in the Anglican Episcopate: Theology, Guidelines and Practice. The Eames Commission and the Monitoring Group Reports* (Toronto, 1998).

10. ARCIC, *Church as Communion* (London, 1991), para. 15.

11. *The Porvöo Common Statement in Together in Mission and Ministry. The Porvöo Common Statement with Essays on Church and Ministry in Northern Europe* (London, 1993), para. 20.

12. Ibid., para. 28.

13. Response to the Archbishop of Canterbury, Lambeth Conference 1988, p. 292.

14. *Confessing the One Faith*, Faith and Order Paper no. 153 (WCC, 1991).

15. *Baptism, Eucharist and Ministry* (WCC Faith and Order Paper no. 111, 1982), *Ministry*, para. 20.

16. Anglican-Lutheran International Continuation Committee, *The Niagara Report. Report of the Anglican-Lutheran Consultation* on *episcopé*. Niagara Falls, September 1987 (London, 1988).

17. David B. Barrett, 'Annual Statistical Table on Global Mission 1994,' *International Bulletin of Missionary Research* 20: 1 [January, 1996] 24–5.

18. See the *Porvöo Common Statement* (London: Council for Christian Unity Occasional Paper no. 3, 1993), para. 58.b.i–x.

19. See *Joint Working Group of the Anglican Church of Canada and the Evangelical Lutheran Church in Canada, Called to Full Communion: A Study Resource for Lutheran-Anglican Relations, Including the Waterloo Declaration* (Toronto: Anglican Book Centre 1998), question 7.d, p. 19.

20. See J.R. Fenwick, *The Malabar Independent Syrian Church* (Nottingham, 1992).

21. C. J. Podmore, "The *Unitas Fratrum* and the Church of England," in *Anglican-Moravian Conversations: The Fetter Lane Common Statement with Essays in Moravian and Anglican History* (London: Council for Christian Unity Occasional Paper no. 5, 1996), pp. 72–82.

22. *On the Way to Fuller Koinonia,* the Official Report of the Fifth World Conference, Faith and Order Paper no. 166, (WCC, 1993).

23. *Confessing the One Faith,* Faith and Order Paper no. 153, (WCC, 1991); *Baptism, Eucharist and Ministry,* Faith and Order Paper no. 111, (WCC, 1982); *Church and World,* Faith and Order Paper no. 152, (WCC, 1990).

24. Second Vatican Ecumenical Council, Decree on Ecumenism, *Unitatis Redintegratio,* 7.

25. *On the Way to Fuller Koinonia: Official Report of the Fifth World* Conference on Faith and Order, Santiago de Compostela, Faith and Order Paper no. 166 (WCC, 1994).

Inter-Faith Report

Introduction

Relations with people of Other Faiths came high on the agenda of nearly every pre-Lambeth regional meeting. The Rt Revd Dr. Michael Nazir-Ali, Bishop of Rochester (England), was appointed Coordinator of the inter-faith work of the Conference. He invited four people to work with him as an Inter-Faith Team. Their names and individual roles are in paragraph 3.3. The Team has been well-placed to hear and report the stories which the bishops have brought to the Conference from a wide variety of inter-faith situations, from co-operation to conflict.

Inter-Faith concerns were, therefore, more visible at this Conference than at any previous Lambeth Conference. A few members of Other Faiths, while not participants, took some visible part in the events of the Conference.

Inter-Faith Events During the Conference

Opening Service

Invited representatives of five world faiths were in Canterbury Cathedral for the Opening Service, and had their own place in the procession. Jews, Muslims, Hindus, Buddhists and Sikhs were represented.

Presidential Address

The next day, the Archbishop of Canterbury said in his Presidential Address to the Conference, "I was delighted that representatives of Other Faiths were present at our Opening Service. There can be no doubting the importance of inter-faith dialogue and co-operation, for the peace and well-being of the World." He went on to speak of both dialogue and Christian witness in his personal journey in inter-faith relations in recent years.

Market Place

An evening 'Market Place' meeting was arranged by NIFCON (the Anglican Communion Network for Inter-Faith Concerns) on the first Wednesday of the Conference. The bishops had the opportunity to meet a Muslim, a Buddhist, a Sikh and two Christians, all from Birmingham. It went very well and after a lively evening of inter-faith storytelling, the Buddhist visitor said, "Next time we really need a whole day for this."

CCJ Evening

On the same evening, about twenty-five people attended the Market Place evening of the Council for Christians and Jews (CCJ), regarding the Arab Palestinian Christians. There were four visiting speakers including one from Israel. After some challenging exchanges, all sides and parties were agreed that they were 'for peace.'

NIFCON

NIFCON also used its 'Market Place' meeting to launch a leaflet that asked every bishop to tell his or her inter-faith story during the Conference. NIFCON had a stall in the Market Place marquee throughout the Conference, as the focus for hearing these stories.

Plenary

The biggest inter-faith event was the Plenary Presentation to the whole Conference on Muslim-Christian Relations and the Anglican Communion on Monday 27 July 1998. Bishop Michael Nazir-Ali, as Moderator, gave a brief Introduction on the history of Muslim-Christian relations. He then introduced three pairs of bishops, who gave their own perspectives on Muslim-Christian relations, both positive and negative: first from the Gambia and Nigeria, then from Jerusalem and Pakistan, finally from Egypt and England. At the end the Moderator summed up the major issues which had emerged and which hopefully would be taken up in the sectional and regional meetings.

Follow-up

To give the bishops an opportunity to discuss the plenary theme, an extra meeting was arranged for the same evening. This was well attended, with eighty people present and contributions from many parts of the world. This ended memorably when a postgraduate Muslim student from the University of Kent at Canterbury spoke from his heart and many bishops responded to his plea for dialogue and understanding.

Media

Media interest was very strong in the days leading up to and following the Plenary. Following the Plenary on Islam, BBC Radio's 'Sunday' programme had contributions from five or six bishops. The Chairman of the Team, the Bishop of Rochester, spoke several times on the radio and to journalists. On the day of the Islam plenary, three members of the Inter-Faith Team, Bishop Michael Nazir-Ali, Colin Chapman and John Sargant, together with Bishop Josiah Idowu-Fearon from Nigeria gave the Conference's daily Press Briefing, and faced about seventy reporters. The reports next day were mostly from Bishop Josiah's stories, but the varied range of situations between Muslim and Christians in the Anglican Communion was well conveyed by the Plenary, and by most reports of it.

Buckingham Palace

On the London Day, representatives of the same five world faiths as were at the Opening Service, and of Baha'is, Jains and Zoroastrians, were invited to join the Conference members at the Garden Party in Buckingham Palace. Also invited were the Director of the Inter-Faith Network for the United Kingdom and the Secretary of the Church's Commission for Inter-faith Relations, the principal ecumenical body for inter-faith work by the British and Irish churches.

Other Meetings

Other meetings around the Conference had strong inter-faith implications. The Pakistani bishops were invited to meet local Christians in Canterbury after the Plenary, with the title "Christians under Threat in Pakistan." Another evening, arranged by the Church in India, Pakistan and Bangladesh, was entitled "Mission and Leadership under the Shadow of Growing Religious Fundamentalism," though only one of the speakers focused on that theme. And there were several private meetings of bishops from particular areas who have had urgent inter-faith concerns.

Perhaps it was also significant that that, as the Conference went on, inter-faith concerns surfaced of their own accord, in all sorts of places. Prime Minister Tony Blair prefaced his speech to the Bishops' Lunch at Lambeth Palace with particular mention of other religions, and aspects of the value systems which they and Christians share. "One of the great things that a gathering like this can do, is not just to send an international signal, but also to send a signal of openness from the Churches themselves towards people of other religions."

It seemed quite natural when Jean Vanier, leading the Vigil in the second week, gave an example from Calcutta of Christians living on the dividing line between

Hindus and Muslims, all three working together for peace and reconciliation, "for we are all children of God."

Major Issues That Have Emerged

The Team identified and examined some of the theological themes which have arisen during the Conference. We were conscious that many of these themes had already been explored in Sectional and Regional meetings. Here we have outlined some of these themes in this Report. It is our sincere hope that these themes and issues will provide a framework for further discussion and action during the next decade.

Storytelling

More than at any previous Lambeth Conference, members of this Conference have heard accounts of the difficulties which exist between Christians and people of Other Faiths. In spite of this, and perhaps because of it, they have also realised that Christians and people of Other Faiths must continue to listen to one another and remain open to the possibility of peaceful co-existence and even friendship.

Dialogue

The much-used term 'dialogue' signals a willingness to remain open and to listen to the other. It is sometimes thought that 'dialogue' refers only to formal, structured meetings of religious leaders and that ordinary people have no access to it. This is certainly not the case as dialogue can take place at any level and in a number of ways.

In the New Testament, and in the early history of the Church, terms like *dialegomai* and *dialogizomai* have the sense of a discussion which aims to persuade. This dimension of bearing witness to all that God has done for us in Christ remains important today, even as we listen to the story others have to tell. As Christians, we do not simply share our beliefs and experiences, we want others also to have 'the knowledge of the glory of God in the face of Jesus Christ' (2 Cor. 4:6).

In order to do this effectively, however, we need not only to listen to our partners but also to understand their world-view and systems of belief. We need to appreciate their patterns of spirituality and worship. In other words, without dialogue of this kind we will not be able to bear witness in a way that is meaningful for our partners.

Dialogue can certainly be an occasion for witness but Christians may also engage in dialogue with others to promote some common aim, such as respect for basic human freedom, including freedom of religion. Again, although friendship and communication between neighbours or colleagues at work may not always be seen as dialogue, it is in fact the dialogue of life, which is very significant in terms of promoting mutual understanding and respect and in the building up of a community.

Conversion

Christians bear witness; it is God who converts, and people are converted to God. Such conversion conforms to God's revelation in Christ. The way in which we live, as well as our words, should lead to a continual conversion to God, both for us and our neighbours. Conversion is a process and, at some point, leads to baptism and membership of the Church, the Body of Christ. An initial act of witness is not enough, people need to be supported and nurtured in their spiritual pilgrimage. Local Christian communities and pastors should be equipped for such support and nurture.

While Christians will always seek their own and others' conversion to God, this is not the same as proselytising. There is no place in our strategies of mission for material inducements, psychological pressure or the targeting of vulnerable individuals or groups. The integrity of individuals and groups must be respected, even as we witness to Christ in their midst.

Basic Freedoms

It has been said already that Christians should be committed to basic freedoms, including the freedom to believe, to practise one's faith and to propagate it. The idea of reciprocity in terms of our relations with people of Other Faiths is about the expectation that the followers of each faith will be committed to such freedoms wherever they are and whenever they happen to have influence or power.

This Conference has had a particular concern for faith-communities which are also minorities in certain contexts. Where Christians have access to decision-making bodies, they will encourage the participation of such minorities in national and civic life. They will seek to ensure that such communities are not discriminated against in the areas of employment, housing or access to community services. Naturally, Christians expect their partners in dialogue to have a similar commitment where they have power or influence. Such treatment of religious minorities is especially important in states where one faith has a privileged position in relation to the social and political order.

Working Ecumenically

We recognise that a great deal of our inter-faith work is done ecumenically. Anglicans should always be prepared to work with other churches in this area and to learn from their experience. Experience in ecumenical dialogue can sometimes be helpful in inter-faith dialogue. A common study of the Bible, for example, has sometimes helped Christians to see controversial matters among them in a new light and to develop new ways of speaking about beliefs which have highlighted areas of agreement among them. In a similar way, a common study of the scriptures of two faiths can lead to a better appreciation of both scriptures and to mutual learning and enrichment.

Monitoring

Plenaries, Sections and Bible Study groups at the Conference have all emphasised both the opportunities for inter-faith encounter and the difficulties. So that both the positive and the negative aspects of our relations with people of Other Faiths can be monitored and good practice encouraged, it has been suggested that the work of the Network for Inter-Faith Concerns be strengthened and that the Network be given special responsibility for monitoring Christian-Muslim relations as they affect the different provinces of the Anglican Communion.

Plenary Presentation: Monday, 27 July 1998
Muslim-Christian Relations and the Anglican Communion

An Introduction by the Bishop of Rochester, the Rt Revd Dr. Michael Nazir-Ali.

When the Design Group for this Lambeth Conference began its work, it asked the different Provinces of the Anglican Communion to suggest matters that could be on our agenda and nearly every part of the Anglican Communion, every province, said that relations with people of Other Faiths were very important for them. Now because this is a very diffuse and scattered Communion of Churches, people said this for a variety of reasons. Some wanted to know, for example, how Christians and people of other faiths could co-operate together for the reduction of international debt, and you will have heard more of this at this Conference. Others wondered whether a common position on the environment could be adopted, and yet others were concerned about basic human freedoms in different parts of the world. There was also a concern that while the Communion should participate in and encourage dialogue, at the same time the question of Christian witness and how that relates to dialogue was also important. People were conscious that the different religions have formed the various cultures in which we live, and Anglicans wonder about the extent to which they can accommodate to those cultures and where they must bear a distinctive witness as Christians.

On the question of unity, while people were clear that the priorities in this Conference would be about the unity of Christians, they were aware, nevertheless, that human unity, the unity of all humankind, is also a Biblical imperative, and they could not ignore this. Relations with Other Faiths is relevant in this context also. And so we realised in the Design Group very quickly that we could not limit the question of relations with people of other faiths to one section or another. These matters had to be discussed in every Section as indeed they are being discussed. That is good, that is how it was intended to be. Also, because we are such a widely dispersed Communion, we have relationships with people of different faiths. In the Middle East, for example, these are triangular among Jews, Christians and Muslims. In India, there is a new Hindu nationalist Government that will be raising its own questions for Christians in India. But we were also aware that Islam and Christianity are both missionary faiths and they find themselves in the same place and at the same time sometimes in competition with one another, particularly in Africa and East Asia, but in nearly every part of the world. And so relations with Islam, relations between Muslims and Christians were regarded as very important for the work of this Conference.

This session is about relations with Muslims and I suppose we have to begin by saying that relationships with Muslims have existed for as long as Islam has been a historical religion. The prophet himself had very close relationships with Christians and Jews, some were among his closest friends and colleagues; the Qur'an, the Holy Book of the Muslims, is full of references to figures in the Bible and to figures in Christian history. When the prophet was persecuted in Mecca by the pagans, he sent his closest followers to other Christians, to the Christian kingdom of Ethiopia, and these people were given refuge by the Ethiopian king as fellow believers, after some theological dialogue had taken place! When the prophet of Islam acquired temporal power, when he became ruler of Medina, one of his first acts was to promulgate the so-called constitution of Medina, which recognised the rights of Jews, Christians and other groups as equal citizens in Medina. Later on he concluded friendly treaties with the Jews of Khaibar and with the Christians of Najran and with the latter, particularly, on an equal basis. So during the lifetime of the prophet of Islam there were Jews and Christians in what we now call the *Khalij*, peninsular Arabia. It is only later that people of faiths other than Islam were expelled from peninsular Arabia on the basis of a rather dubious tradition that the prophet himself had said this. We know from history that the prophet never did this. After his lifetime, Islam, of course, spread very rapidly in the Christian East, in the countries of Syria, Palestine, Egypt, Mesopotamia (now Iraq) and in some of the territories of Byzantium itself. We need to recognise that many of the great cities of the Christian East, which capitulated to the Muslims did so because they felt the oppression of Byzantium. And so very quickly the cities of Jerusalem, Damascus and Alexandria had capitulated to the Muslim rulers because they felt they were going to get a better deal under them. Islam also, as you know, spread to North Africa, another great Christian centre, and even to Spain and Southern France.

As Islam spread into these countries which until then had been Christian, there was of course the necessity of coming to some kind of accommodation with the non-Muslim subjects, whether Christians or Jews, and sometimes Zoroastrians. And so the idea of the *Dhimmi* evolved, that is to say protected religious minorities that had certain rights but also suffered from certain disabilities. We know that for the time this was quite an enlightened system because in Western Europe, for example, at that time, there was very little tolerance of any kind of dissent, so even the limited arrangements that were available under the *Dhimmi* system were better than nothing at all. More importantly, perhaps, we know that Christians and Jews made notable contributions to the development of what we now call Islamic civilisation. The translation of Greek works into Arabic either directly from the Greek or from the Syriac were mainly carried out by Christians and very often Christian clergy. Christians made an important contribution in medicine, in the other sciences, and later on the mediation of this learning to Western Europe brought about the Renaissance. So there is a long history of living together, not without its problems but also with many notable achievements, and these need to be recognised this afternoon.

In the nineteenth century, under the influence of certain Western powers, the Ottoman and then other Muslim states began to remove the disabilities from which Christians and Jews had suffered until then. This gave rise in the Middle East for example to what is now called the Nahda, or Arab nationalism, which brought Christians particularly into the mainstream of political and economic life. So the modern states of Syria, Iraq, Egypt and certainly the Palestinian Liberation Organisation are informed by this non-confessional view of citizens of all faiths living together and working together for the good of their country. This was a notable development, I feel, in the Islamic world, but it happened outside the Middle East as well. In Pakistan, for instance, the founders of the country felt that, while they had been or felt an oppressed minority in undivided India, they wanted to ensure that the minorities in Pakistan did not feel similarly oppressed. That is not how it has turned out but this was the will of the Quaid-i-Azam, Muhammad Ali Jinnah, and his colleagues. In Indonesia, the Panchasila system ensured full participation for Christians and Hindus and other minorities in the life of the nation. We may ask therefore: if there has been such a long history of co-existence and co-operation in culture and learning and political life, what then has gone wrong? And I think here we have to note, as I am sure the speakers later on will, the emergence of Islamism or fundamentalism or whatever term you want to use for it. There are many complex social, political and indeed economic reasons for the emergence of these movements, and it is not one movement, it is many different movements. The reaction first of all to colonialism: people who wanted to establish their own identity, national and religious, were drawn to looking back at their history. The corruption of their own rulers meant that they were looking for a way of life that was not corrupt where they could live according to a religious code that made sense to them. The failure of both capitalism and of the command socialist economies in the Muslim countries meant that people were looking for a third way, especially in the economic sense. Civil wars, where Muslim countries and elements within Muslim countries fought proxy wars on behalf of the superpowers, is another reason for the rise of Islamism or fundamentalism. Afghanistan as a theatre for war, where many of these movements were nurtured, is a good example.

Where do we go from here? Well, this afternoon we have arranged for three pairs of speakers, one from the continent of Africa, one from Asia, and one from Europe and North Africa, to share with you where their churches are today.

Christian Relations—With Islam: The Gambia
by the Bishop of Gambia, The Rt Revd V. S. Tilewa Johnson

Introduction

The Republic of The Gambia is a strip of land which extends horizontally from the west coast of West Africa inland. With the exception of the coastal border, the country is surrounded by Senegal. The population of The Gambia, around 1.3 million, is approximately 95 per cent Muslim and 3 per cent Christian, with the remainder being mainly of African traditional religion. Not only is The Gambia a predominantly Muslim country, but it is also situated in a strongly Muslim region. The population of Senegal is 95 per cent Muslim, with 5 per cent being adherents to the Christian and African traditional faiths. Other strongly Muslim populations in the region are found in countries such as Mauritania, Mali and Burkina Faso. The influence of Islam in West Africa can be dated back as far as the seventh century A.D., when the Berbers of North Africa became Muslim and frequented West Africa for trading purposes. As noted by L. K. Fuller in his book *Going to the Nation* (1993), "What happened in North Africa was a tragedy for West Africa. The Berbers became Muslims, and they were the ones who came as traders across the Sahara to West Africa and brought Islam with them. If they had been Christians they would have brought Christianity in those early years instead." From the fourteenth century onwards a constant Muslim presence could be seen in West Africa, and Islamisation took place after that—particularly through the eighteenth and nineteenth century jihads, when Islam became popularised.

Christianity was first brought to The Gambia in the fifteenth century, through Portuguese traders. However, it did not last, and it was not until the first half of the last century that Christianity returned to stay. The Christian population of The Gambia is concentrated mainly in the coastal urban area, and originally comprised the Krio-speaking population who migrated to The Gambia from the population of freed slaves in Freetown. Since that time the other ethnic group which has contributed to the urban Christian population is the Wollof. In the rural areas the main adherents to the Christian faith are those who were previously of the African traditional religion, such as the Manjagos, Balanta and Karoninka, who have migrated to The Gambia from Guinea Bissau. The population of the provinces is at least 99 per cent Muslim. The Gambia is a secular state, with freedom of religion enshrined in the constitution.

Christian Relations With Islam

In The Gambia relations with Islam are part of daily life. Since the return of Christianity to The Gambia, during the first half of the last century, there has been close interaction in social life, in the workplace and within the educational system. Christians and Muslims attend each other's wedding ceremonies and funerals, there is intermarriage and, within the extended family, there can be both Christians and Muslims. All State functions are preceded with prayers by leaders of both religious communities. However, mutual invitations to religious occasions are rare. Each New Year leaders of both religious communities visit the State House together to offer greetings to the President. Immediately following the *coup d'état* of 22nd July 1994, religious leaders of both communities were invited to the State House by the Head of State; where he informed them that they are seen as 'torch bearers of morals and ethics' in the nations, and were free to address any issue with his government in the future. Since that time, the leaders of both religious communities have joined voices to point out wrongs in society. Each Christmas, New Year and Easter Church leaders broadcast messages to the nation on radio and television.

During the process of transition to democratic civilian rule in The Gambia following the 1994 bloodless *coup d'état*, a number of commissions were established to facilitate this process. The Christian community was represented by a Church leader on each of these institutions, as follows: the National Consultative Council—the Catholic Bishop; the Constitutional Review Commission—the Anglican Bishop; the Panel for Civic Education—the Methodist Chairman; and the Provisional Independent Electoral Commission (PIEC)—the Anglican Bishop (Vice Chairman). The PIEC was responsible for implementing and coordinating all activities for the Presidential and National Assembly Elections, which brought in the democratic civilian government of the Second Republic. Subsequently, an Independent Electoral Commission

(IEC) has been set up to organise all national and local government and traditional leader elections. The Anglican Bishop was privileged to be appointed as Chairman of the IEC by the President of The Gambia.

Christians and Muslims work closely together, particularly in areas of common social concern and in development work. This is both at an individual level and at an institutional level where Christian and Islamic NGOs (Non-Governmental Organisations) operate side by side.

Since the ingression of Christianity to The Gambia, a social priority of the Christian missions has been the establishments of schools. Therefore, many Muslims have passed through Christian schools—taking part in religion classes and acquiring a knowledge of the Bible and a deep understanding of the Christian tradition. The renowned Gambian scholar, Lamin Sanneh, in his book West African Christianity (1983) states "...in 1955 the Methodist Boys High School [in The Gambia] had 140 pupils on its books. Of these, 29 were Methodist, 24 Anglican and 87 Muslim. In 1956 the Scripture Prize was won by a Muslim boy." However, conversely, Christian children, raised in a mainly Christian environment, did not have the same experience with regard to Islam and the Qur'an.

The ecumenical movement of The Gambia, the Gambia Christian Council (GCC), established in the sixties by the Roman Catholic, Anglican and Methodist Churches, has long since had a committee which deals with inter-Church and interfaith matters. However, interfaith relations did not receive any priority on the GCC agenda until 1982. After the attempted *coup d'état* of 1981 the World Council of Churches (WCC) offered aid to the GCC for a programme of "national reconstruction," with the proviso that the programme should be carried out in collaboration with the Muslim community. From that time onward GCC organised seminars to study inter-faith issues, stressing the importance of an ecumenical approach to relations with Islam. This situation was consolidated in 1986 with the formation of a PROCMURA (Project for Christian Muslim Relations in Africa) Area Committee and the posting of an Area Adviser to world with the GCC. Regular seminars continue, with themes covered including *shariah* law, marriage, prayer and fasting. Initially seminars involved only Christians in order that their initial questions and feelings may be aired openly, but later also included Muslims (seminars then called 'Building Bridges of Friendship'). Intensive courses in Islamic Studies have been organised for catechists, lay preachers, evangelists, etc, throughout the country, and the Catholic, Anglican and Methodist Churches all include a component of 'Christian approaches to other faiths' in their lay training courses. The Catholic Church already has a developed theology of religions, and interest in dialogue with Other Faiths has received a renewed emphasis following the African Synod of Catholic Bishops in Rome, during which interfaith dialogue was identified as one of the main themes for the churches of Africa.

PROCMURA Women's Wing (PWW) is active in The Gambia, with regular meetings of a group of Christian women who have a particular concern for Christian-Muslim relations. The group is also associated with a group of committed Muslim women, who share similar concerns on problems in society. In the same spirit of Christian Muslim co-existence, and arising out of a Youth Conference in Nigeria, PROCMURA contacted various youth groups with the view to setting up a Youth Wing. The response has so far included only Christian youth. Therefore, the time is being spent on educating these Christian youths on Islam and Christian Muslim relations. Drama is found to be a powerful medium to illustrate this. The Christian youth experience peer pressure where religion is concerned, particularly in school where their faith is constantly challenged.

The Roman Catholic community is by far the largest Christian denomination in The Gambia. A visit to The Gambia in 1992 by Pope John Paul gave further impetus to the interest in Christian Muslim relations within the Catholic community. The Pope stressed the importance of the good relations existing between the two religious traditions, and noted similarities between the two. He stated that "we are all pilgrims on the path of seeking to do God's will in everything. Although we differ in many ways, there are important elements of our respective faiths which can serve as a basis for fruitful dialogue and a strengthening of the Spirit of tolerance and mutual help." He met with leaders of the Muslim community, and Muslims were present at the Mass he celebrated at the Independence Stadium whilst in The Gambia.

The Evangelical Fellowship of The Gambia have the aim of evangelising the country. Therefore, the issue of Christian Muslim relations is discussed at a different level. However, experience has shown that it is essential to have a knowledge of Islam in order to share the Christian faith effectively with Muslims.

Conclusion

The Christian Church is a presence in The Gambia, which is very predominantly Muslim. Aggressive evangelism is uncommon, and not encouraged by the mainline churches. There are remarkably peaceful relations between the two faiths, and interaction at all levels. Genuine conversions from Islam to Christianity are not common, and rapid conversions following intensive evangelism have been shown to evaporate over time. Conversion through material incentives have also proved not to last. However, there are signs that the constant Christian presence can have a gradual, but profound, effect. This is particularly by bearing witness through service to those in need and development work, the interaction between the people of both faiths, and the exposure of a large part of the population to Christianity through mission schools, as well as a tradition of rural Muslim children being sent to urban Christian families for upbringing and formal education. Although, as noted, open declarations of conversion are rare, it is quite possible, or even likely, that hearts can be turned quietly but surely. Although the situation is one of religious tolerance and co-existence, with the Church operating as a presence, together with formal efforts at interfaith dialogue and Islamic instruction for churches, it must also be emphasised that this does not imply any degree of compromise on the part of the Church. We proclaim the Gospel of our Lord and Saviour Jesus Christ daily—in action and word—leaving the job of conversion to the Holy Spirit of God. Any compromise in our own faith would not bring us closer to our Muslim brothers and sisters, but further away, as they lose respect for a weak faith—whether their own or another.

We continue to give almighty God all the thanks and praise for the peace we experience in The Gambia.

Relationship between Muslims and Christians in Nigeria by the Bishop of Kaduna, Nigeria, The Rt Revd Josiah Idowu-Fearon

A Brief Historical Background

The modern state of Nigeria originated with the arrival of British traders on the southern coast called the Bight of Benin. In 1861 a British colony was established centred at the seaport of Lagos. From here the British extended their influence and created two protectorates: the Western protectorate comprising the Yoruba people to the west and north of Lagos; and the Oil Rivers protectorate, which included the eastern regions as far as the Cameroon. These two protectorates were then united into the single Niger Coast protectorate. In 1903 the Northern protectorate was formed after the defeat of the Hausa and Fulani peoples.

In 1914, the British established a central government in Lagos for the two protectorates, and the colony and protectorates of Nigeria evolved. However, no effort was made to encourage the country to become united. At the amalgamation, the system of government in the North based on Islamic law was retained and a separate form of government was adopted in the South. From the outset, therefore, Nigeria had two sets of government with two sets of values, and a rather confused system in the middle part of the new country where the inhabitants were predominantly pagan.

The Root of the Crisis in Nigeria

In the northern parts of Nigeria, Lord Lugard pursued a policy of favouring Muslims in administrative matters. For instance, he appointed Muslims as judges of courts in non-Muslim areas. Though he insisted that Muslims in such positions should not see themselves as missionaries, nothing was done to ensure that they did not behave so. Furthermore, Sir Perry Girouard introduced an administrative system that marginalised non-Muslims in the middle belt of Nigeria by the division of the north into districts under fief holders.

This policy made no provision for the administration of non-Muslim territories that constituted about one-half of the protectorate of Northern Nigeria. The policy was applied indiscriminately without regard to the indigenous forms of administration. Given a Fulani and Muslim district head, it is clear that the general tenor of the administration would be based on Islam as understood in Hausa-Fulani culture modified to some extent by the presence of the British. Mosques were erected wherever Muslim officials were stationed and Muslim courts naturally followed. There were bound to be some local people who wished to be associated with the new ruling class which was prepared to reward them with material benefits. Hausa language and Islamic religion therefore became attractive.

Lugard's Political Memoranda required that an Islamic or alkali court be established at the headquarters of every district. In theory the law to be administered was "native law and custom," but in practice this meant Islamic law, *shariah.* Other legal tribunals and processes were forbidden, and this meant the abolition of the legal system of non-Muslims. For Lord Lugard, the emirships, the Islamic courts and the fiscal system were the cornerstones of his Indirect Rule policy. This was inherited and continued by his successors. The most seriously affected of the non-Muslim territories were those surrounded by the emirates; these are in what is today referred to as the political middle belt region of Nigeria and where over 90 per cent of the crises between the Christians and Muslims have taken place.

Islam and Christianity in Nigeria

Islam arrived in Nigeria in the tenth century from North Africa, via the trade routes to the old Kanem Bornu Empire. From there it spread, culminating in the emergence of the Sokoto Caliphate in the nineteenth century. Christianity, on the other hand, first came through the early efforts of the Capuchin Fathers from Portugal in the fifteenth century, but it made little or no impact on the old Benin Kingdom. It was the missionaries who accompanied the British merchants who introduced the Christian faith to Nigeria successfully in the nineteenth century, starting in the Western part of the present Nigeria via Badagry, Abeokuta and Lagos. From there the Christian faith began its northward advance across the country, where there were some encounters between the faiths. However, it was with the amalgamation of the Northern and Southern Protectorates that the formal incorporation of the two religions within a single political entity occurred.

At present, the country can be divided into three sections:

- the "far north," comprising the following states: Kebbi, Sokoto, Katsina, Kano, Adamawa, Yobe, Jigawa, Bornu, and Dutse;
- the "middle belt," comprising Niger, Kwara, Kogi, Plateau, Kaduna, Bauchi, Gombe, Benue, and Jalingo; and
- the "southern states," comprising Lagos, Ogun, Oyo, Oshun, Ondo, Ekiti, Edo, Asaba, Imo, Abia, Enugu, Cross-River, Rivers, Aqua-lbom and Anambra.

In the "far north," Islam comprises about 80 per cent of the population, compared with 10 per cent being Christians. Islam and its culture dominates the entire society. Christians do not have the same rights as their Muslim neighbours: no provision is made for Christian state education; public propagation of Christianity is prohibited; leaders of the Christian community are ignored; converts from Islam are threatened and attacked; inter-marriage is prohibited, unless between a Muslim man and a Christian woman, with the hope that he would convert her; it is difficult for Christians businesses to get government patronage; burial grounds are denied; and, it is extremely difficult to get approval for the erection of places of worship. These experiences may vary, but generally Christians are treated as second-class citizens.

The situation in the "middle belt" is very different. Here the Christian and Muslim populations are almost balanced, Christians making up 60 per cent of the population. In this region it is not unusual to find mixed marriages, Muslims and Christians in the same family sharing in religious celebrations. In general terms, there is religious tolerance and almost equal treatment for all irrespective of religious affiliation.

Turning to the "southern states," the picture is the same as in the "middle belt," though the Christians make up over 80 per cent of the population. The relationship is so cordial that apart from some misunderstanding in Ibadan very recently, we have never had any major Muslim-Christian crisis in this part of Nigeria.

Some Major Religious Conflicts

Below are set out some of the major religious conflicts in the past few years:

December 1980: Maitatsine religious uprising, Kano, 4177 died.

December 1982: Followers of Maitatsine in Bulunkutu, Kaduna, over 100 died.

February 1984: Followers of Maitatsine in Jimeta, Yola, 763 died, 5913 displaced.

April 1985: Followers of Maitatsine in Gombe, over 100 died.

May 1986: Religious fanatics attacked the wooden sculpture of Jesus Christ in the University of Ibadan Chapel and set it ablaze.

March 1987: Religious riots in Kafanchan, Kaduna and Zaria, over 100 died.

March 1991: Shiite Muslims rioted in Katsina and Daura.

April 1991: An ethnic misunderstanding in Bauchi degenerated into a full-blown religious war between Muslims and Christians; thousands died.

October 1991: Religious riots in Kano in protest against the Crusade of Reinhard Bonnke, 1000 died.

March 1992: Muslim and Christian students rioted in Jalingo, over 100 died.

May 1992: Another ethnic misunderstanding in Zangon-Kataf degenerated into a full-blown war between Muslims and their Christian neighbours which spread to Kaduna and Zaria, over 3000 died.

We have also within the last four years had major religious crises in Jos, Bauchi and Potiskum, which led to hundreds of deaths and the loss of millions of dollars worth of property.

Efforts at Finding Solutions

The government has ignored this situation, despite the incessant calls of Christian leaders and other concerned figures. However, in 1987, after a major disturbance in Kafanchan, the Federal government set up a body called the Advisory Council on Religious Affairs (ACRA). The committee was made up of an equal number of Christians and Muslims representing all the states in the "far north" and the "middle belt." The Council met and deliberated on three occasions and then faded out because the Christian representatives felt the Muslims were not sincere.

In the same year a group of intellectuals came together to found what they called the National Association for Religious and Ethnic Tolerance (NARETO) with the aim of "launching intellectual battles against odds for a new society based on religious harmony and ethnic equity."

In 1991 the Federal government again made an effort by asking its Directorate for Social Mobilisation (MAMSER) to gather together 30 leaders from the "far north" and the "middle belt" to investigate the causes of the frequent crises. This body met and made certain recommendations, but a change of government meant that their recommendations were not implemented. The present government has implemented a part of the recommendations in some parts of the "middle belt" and the result is indicative of the bright future Nigeria has a nation.

In July 1992, NARETO held a seminar in the city of Abuja, after which the Federal government announced that a new body called "Centre for Propagation of Religious and Ethnic Tolerance" (CENPRETO) was to be set up. According to government directives, the body should take "the onus of propagating those things that unite us as a people, sensitise the citizenry to the positive value of ethnic and religious tolerance." Sadly, nothing came out of this.

A former military Head of State, General Olusegun Obasanjo set up a programme called the "Farm House Dialogue" on issues of national and international interests. The body has had about three programmes on the theme of Religious Pluralism and Democracy. The findings if implemented could foster peaceful coexistence in the country but the General is now in prison and the organisation has died.

Why Religion Became an Important Factor in the Politics of Nigeria

Before 1967 when the first set of states were created out of the existing four regions that made up Nigeria, the "far north" and the "middle belt" were taken as one homogeneous political entity, giving that part of the country a larger population than that of the "southern states." In political terms, this meant that whatever was shared in the country, the northern part had the greater portion! During this period there was some solidarity and the northerners from the middle belt, though not well catered for, accepted the situation.

But with the creation of the states in 1967, the hegemony of the north began to give way to a feeling of independence within each of the newly created states. Each state began to develop at its own pace; indigenes from the "middle belt" who had been working in frustrating conditions in northern Nigeria began to seek transfers to their home states. Those who still chose to continue working in the "far north" began to do so on contractual terms.

The result of this loss of hegemony was a search for an alternative, and religion filled this hiatus. Now that the unity of the north was gone, an alternative source of unity was found in Islam with its very strong concept of the *umma.* Religion began to play a vital role in the political life of Nigerians, especially those from the northern states, immediately after the creation of the first set of states in the country. From then, appointments began to be made on the basis of one's religious affiliation. This affected the armed forces with non-Muslims complaining that top military, air force, navy and police officers, were drawn from the Muslim *umma.*

Another explanation for the prominence of the role of religion and the religious crises in the north, in particular, is due to an evangelical form of the Christian faith that began to gain ground from the late 1960s. Before then the Muslims accepted and tolerated the very small Christian presence in places such as Fagge in Kano State. As long as the Christian communities remained a small community without active evangelism, they were accepted and allowed to live within their domains. From the early 1970s, the Christian presence in most parts of the north began to spread and evangelism actively took place among the animists, some even 'daring' to take the gospel to the Muslims! This was seen as a threat to the *umma*.

The surreptitious manner in which the government of the country registered Nigeria as a member of the Organisation of Islamic Congress (OIC) and some other Islamic religious organisations without the consent of all Nigerians has led to suspicion of government motives and fear of Muslim domination. This also has brought religion to the forefront of Nigerian politics.

In addition, Christians have become more aggressive and courageous in their confrontations with Muslims (Kafanchan and Zangon Kataf). Constant violent attacks by Muslims in the North has led to campaigns among Christians to stand their ground and, if possible, fight back, especially in cases where the destruction of Christian lives and property is not punished by the government of the area.

How Lambeth Can Help the Nigerian Religious Situation

Although the sudden preoccupation with issues of religion in Nigeria was directly linked to political calculations, it is also the case that religion, when properly managed, can serve as an integrating factor for achieving unity, cohesion, and national integration, especially in a pluralistic nation such as Nigeria. As large as the Anglican Communion is on the continent of Africa, there does not exist any Centre solely owned by the Anglican Communion for documentation and research on the relationship between Islam and Christianity. We are aware of such Centres owned by the Roman Catholic Church and this has helped in their relationship with Muslims on the continent. A Centre of this nature would certainly encourage mutual relationship further and educate the millions of Anglicans in Africa who are currently being fed with unbalanced and confrontational literature. Our approach must be eirenic because it is the way of the cross.

A recent study shows that the Christians are opposed to the *Shari'a* being enshrined into the Constitution because of the fear that this will infringe upon the religious freedom of the Christians. One is reminded of a similar attempt in the Sudan in 1971 when that country was contemplating introducing comprehensive *Shari'a* into their Constitution. Well-meaning people and countries cautioned against such a move because of the grave implications. They carried the day and the idea was dropped. Ten years later, *Shari'a* was introduced into the Constitution of Sudan governing the Muslims and the Christians alike. The result is the civil war in which the Sudan is still embroiled. The humiliating and pathetic condition of the Christian communities in Pakistan is also worth some sober reflection. A few people have tried to draw the attention of those in power in Nigeria to the consequences of allowing the Shari'a to apply to every facet of the country but it seems the Muslims are having their way. A cautionary voice from Lambeth may prove helpful. The Anglican Church in Nigeria needs this support.

Relations With Islam in the Middle East
by the Bishop of Jerusalem, The Rt Revd Riah Abu El-Assal

Introduction

This is an attempt to confront an issue that will continue to address itself to us as long as we continue to live in the Middle East. This is also true in many parts of our globe. No one with enough common sense will either pretend as if it is not there, or belittle the impact and the potential that lies within it. Islam is recognised as one of the three monotheistic religions, and Muslims form one-fifth of the population of the world.

Statistics

A United Nations department on statistics estimated that by the year 2025, the number of Muslims in the world would reach two billion, 600 million of whom would be Arabs, with 60 per cent below the age of 25. In the year 2050, the number will reach four billion, of whom one billion would be Arabs. The same source shows that by the year 2040 the number of Arabs in the Holy Land will become equal to that of the Jews, and will exceed it in less than a generation.

Arab Christians

We Arab Christians trace our origin to the first Pentecost. We were the tail-end of the list of seventeen nationalities present then (Acts 2:11).

Our roots go deep into the soil of a region where, despite all difficulties and the fact that we have been buried beneath a superimposed western veneer, the legacy of nearly 150 years when the faith was closely aligned with European imperial power, we have survived for 2000 years: nothing less than an awesome achievement.

Today we make up 16 million out of 250 million Arabs. Some 150,000 remain in the birthplace of our faith, Israel and Palestine, hardly 1.5 per cent of the population. Our mere physical presence is at stake. This too demands our attention lest the Holy Land become a museum of holy stones.

Our history is complex, mingling alienation and hope. Not only were we among the 3,000 converts of that first Pentecost, our numbers swelled when the Apostle Thomas reached Arabia on his way to India.

In our first five centuries, the Church expanded throughout the Middle East and North Africa. The Gospel profoundly influenced all the peoples of the region, including the founder of Islam, Mohammed himself. From among our own were martyrs and saints. The Patron Saint of England, St. George, is but one: a Palestinian from Lydda.

The historical events of the seventh century—schisms, the monopoly of Byzantium over the Church in the Middle East, the superstitions that replaced true faith, heresies, and the like—caused many to leave the Church and join Islam. In other words, it was the failure of the Church caused the rise of Islam. Christians in the West and the East would not preach the Gospel of reconciliation to those who drifted away. They counted them as worthy of the fire of hell rather than the salvation of a loving forgiving God. The majority became the minority. The whole region was lost to Islam. Then followed the Crusades, the missionary enterprise, the fall of Constantinople to the Muslims in 1453, the arrival of European colonial powers. And, last but not least, the coming of the State of Israel, which many evangelical Christians view as a fulfillment of Old Testament prophecies, thus causing us Middle East Christians a real embarrassment and placing us on the side of collaborators against the majority of our own people. Such factors and others, both local and international, shaped the kind of relations we have with Islam today.

For 1,300 years we have been co-living and having daily living dialogue with Muslims. We had our problems and difficulties. In some countries we were discriminated against, denied equal rights, attacked, persecuted and rejected, not allowed to build or renovate churches, viewed as not 100 per cent Arab, and as collaborators with the Christian West. Foreign rule in the Middle East, especially Ottoman, caused us real pain. In other areas such practices, as mentioned above, were not welcomed at all. Despite all this, we became accustomed to live with them, and they learned to appreciate our presence among them. An indigenous Arab Christian Church has survived. Muslims recognise the great contribution we have made to the awakening of the Arab nation.

Islam

Whatever the views Christians, more specifically Western Christians, have of Islam, no one can deny that it was an essential aspect in the history of humankind. Many Orientalists viewed it with suspicion and caused many to fear and misunderstand it. No wonder many of us relate to it today as a problem rather than as a challenge. Muslims are human beings, created by the same God who created all of us, not by a semi-god. They are part of the world that God so loved and desires to save through His only son Jesus Christ. There are some in the world who cannot live without enemies. If they cannot find them, they create them. With the collapse of communism many wish us to view Islam as the new enemy number one.

Generally speaking, people are scared and suspicious of what they are ignorant of. True Islam is not known to the many in the West. Hence the suspicion, the bias and prejudice against it and against its adherents. It may be useful to point at this juncture that Muslim power structures that were indigenous to our region, rooted in its customs and mores, were generally more tolerant of religious pluralism than their European counterparts. Until the time of the Ottoman Turks, the ascendancy of Arab Islam heralded periods of greater peace and tolerance than what ensued under western Christian or Jewish rule. Having said this, one needs to point out that Islamic fundamentalism and fanaticism caused more harm to Islam and to the Muslims than it did to others.

Personal Experience

I am but one of over a thousand Arab Palestinian Christian Anglican Israelis. I dare say that I speak for the greater majority of them, if not for the majority of all Arab Christians in Israel. Our experience with Islam has been one of mutual respect, and mutual trust.

At Christ Church School in Nazareth, we have over 600 students; 65 per cent are Muslims. We keep our good Anglican tradition of having Chapel services every morning. All attend. All take Christian Education classes and Muslims do better than our own in their exams. Only once or twice in thirty years have I encountered problems. The real problem that I had over the years came round Christmas. Most parents think their children qualify to be shepherds, kings, Mary etc. etc. It is very difficult to place 600 students on a small stage inside our Church. We share our faith. We do not impose it. We share it in the spirit of truth and love.

Another example: I ran twice for parliament in Israel (the Knesset). The Progressive List for Peace party, assigned me the Triangle area, totally Muslim. Muslims of other parties tried to discourage what they thought of as their own from voting for this "not only Christian, but also a priest!!" The response of the masses was heart-lifting: "With Muslim votes, we will bring the first Christian priest into the Jewish Knesset." They did extremely well. Palestinian history testifies to the good relations that prevailed over the years.

Conclusion

To conclude, before we judge others, we need to examine where we have failed locally and internationally. How much of the negative recent developments are the result of the double standard policies some governments in the West played in the Arab Israeli conflict? And how much were economic interests a part of the dirty game of international politics?

Finally I need to remark that the intellectual and doctrinal differences between Islam and Christianity show mere diversity of thinking, which bears in it the enrichment of the human civilisation that brings them together. The aim of history is not that a certain nation should impose itself on other nations, but it is to seek harmony and co-existence. Respect for the human experience, viewing the other compassionately, knowledge gained through moral and intellectual honesty: surely these are better if not easier goals at present than confrontation and hostility. And if in the process we can dispose finally of the residual hatred, the offensive generality of labels and stereotypes, as well as the myths of the past, then so much the better.

Islam and Christian Response in the Present-Day World
by The Bishop of Lahore, Pakistan, The Rt Revd Alexander John Malik

Islam in the Present-Day World

The Spread of Islam

Islam is not an unknown entity in the present-day world. It makes headline news in today's world. When one looks at the world map, one cannot help but be impressed by the extent of the spread of Islam all over the world. It originated in Saudi Arabia, but soon it spread to neighbouring countries and within a century it touched other continents like Europe, the Indo-Pakistani subcontinent and China. Right from its inception it kept its pace of expansion, influence and vitality. It had great empires like the Ummayids, the Ottomans and the Moghuls. No one can deny the contribution of these empires in the fields of science, art, literature and architecture. Even in today's world its spread is most noticeable. Right from West Africa to the whole of North Africa and parts of Central and Eastern Africa, it has spread through the whole of the Middle East to South East Asia and parts of China. A number of newly independent states of the former

Soviet Union like Uzbekistan, Turkmenistan, Azerbijan, Kazakstan are all Muslim. There are sizeable contingents of Muslims in Europe, North America, South Africa and Australia. Black Muslims and immigrants from Islamic countries form a sizable group of Muslims in Western countries. According to one estimation there are about 1000 million Muslims all over the world. The Muslim growth in numbers is mainly due to their biological growth. This fact is most apparent when one compares the population growth rate of some of the Islamic countries with some of the Western countries. The fertility rate (children per woman) further authenticates this fact.

Population Growth Rate

ISLAMIC COUNTRIES

Afghanistan 5.8 per cent, Jordan 4.9 per cent, Oman 4.2 per cent, Libya 3.5 per cent, Syria 3.4 per cent, Pakistan 2.8 per cent, Indonesia 2.6 per cent, Iran 2.5 per cent, Saudi Arabia 2.2 per cent, Egypt 2.2 per cent

WESTERN COUNTRIES

Italy 0.1 per cent, England 0.3 per cent, France 0.4 per cent, Finland 0.5 per cent, Estonia 0.6 per cent, Germany 0.6 per cent, Austria 0.7 per cent, USA 1 per cent, Canada 1.2 per cent, Australia 1.4 per cent

Fertility Rate (Children per Woman)

ISLAMIC COUNTRIES

Afghanistan 7, Nigeria 7, Oman 7, Pakistan 7, Saudi Arabia 7, Senegal 7, Dibouti 7, Ethiopia 7, Egypt 5, Algeria 5

WESTERN COUNTRIES

Austria 1, Italy 1, Australia 2, UK 2, USA 2, Canada 2, Sweden 2, Switzerland 2, France 2, Denmark 2

The Economist in its article "Living with Islam" writes, "Islam at its most ferocious is cutting a blood stained path to the front of the world's attention. Insurgents in Algeria slash the throat of anyone who has the temerity to disagree with them. Islamic gangs are out for blood in Turkey and Pakistan: in the latter, blasphemers face a legal death. Anarchy reigns in Afghanistan. Suicide bombers are happy to die for Allah so long as they can take Israelis with them. Christians are threatened by Guerillas in Egypt, by the regime in Sudan. Free thinkers begin to bend to the Islamic wind."[1]

Religion and Politics Are One in Islam

Right from the beginning one has to grasp one thing: that Islam is not only a religious faith but a political ideology as well. In Islam religion and politics are intertwined, they go hand in hand. There is no division of Church and state as there is in most of the western countries. Muslims proudly say that Islam is a perfect code of life (*Al-Din*). It is a system which integrates all religious, social, economic, and political institutions on the foundation of faith (*iman*), the conviction and commitment to accept God as the sovereign Lord and to submit and surrender (*Aslama*) completely to His will (*riza*) as revealed in the Qur'an and the tradition (*Sunnah*) and codified by different *Madahibs* (Schools of Islamic jurisprudence) in the form of *Shariah* (Law). Islamic community i.e. the people of Islam represents a social movement to actualise the ideal of Islamic life in time and space, here and now and not leave them for the hereafter. In other words, people of Islam endeavour to establish God's rule and reign on earth in the form of an "Islamic State," a sort of theocratic state. The reign of the first four caliphs (*Kulfa-e-Rashideen*) of Islamic history serve as a prototype and model.

This type of thinking is not new, one finds this combination of religion and politics even in the Old Testament. Moses was a prophet but also a political leader and statesman in the modern sense of the word. So also David was a king and a prophet. Prophet Muhammad (PBUH) was also a prophet and ruler of Arabia, and commander of his army. Religious and political powers were concentrated in one person. Thus, for a Muslim, establishment of an "Islamic State" represents to him the *summum bonum*, the highest bliss of the Islamic life and struggle in this world.

There are two Islamic concepts which help achieve this *summum bonum*, the highest bliss of Islamic life here on earth: one by which the whole world is divided on the basis of Islam i.e. *Dar-ul-Islam* and *Dar-ul-Harab* (world of Islam and world of war); and, second, *Jihad* (holy war). Both concepts are inter-linked and sustain each other. The Islamic concept of holy war encourages Muslims to accept martyrdom in the name of Allah (God) i.e. to kill and to be killed in the name of Allah and for the sake of Islam. About *Jihad*, the Qur'an says,

> Fight those who believe not in Allah, nor in the latter day... until they pay the tax in acknowledgement of superiority and they are in a state of subjection (Sura 9:29).
>
> Let those fight in the way of Allah who sell the life of this world for the other, who so fighteth in the way of Allah, be he slain or be he victorious, on him we shall bestow a vast reward (Sura 4:74).
>
> Fight in the way of Allah against those who fight against you, but begin not hostilities. Lo! Allah loveth not aggression. And slay them whenever ye find them (Sura 2: 190–193).

And there are others like Sura 2:216–218; 4:74–80, 89–91: 9–29. [2]

"Fighting," in a way, is a religious duty for the people of Islam. Militancy in a real way is part and parcel of the spirit of the religion of Islam. This, again, is not new. Much the similar notion one finds in the Old Testament, where Yahweh, the God of Israel in a special way, is pictured as commander of the Israeli armies. The Jews and the Muslims are very close to each other in this concept of Holy War. The concept of Jihad in Islam encourages the world of Islam (*Dar-ul-Islam*) to wage war against the rest of the world which is not within the fold of Islam:

> Fight those who believe not in Allah, nor in the latter day... until they pay the tax in acknowledgement of superiority and they are in a state of subjection (Sura 9:29).

This, at least, was the pattern and strategy, especially in the early history of Islam. Muslims were the first to conquer Spain, colonised and ruled it for almost 900 years. They did not stop here; the Islamic armies conquered parts of the African and Asian continent. No army could match the fighting prowess of the Islamic armies of that era. That era is considered to be the golden era of Islam by many Muslims and they still dream, long and struggle for such an era to dawn in the modern day world.

Struggle Between the Modernists and the Islamists

For this reason, the modern Muslims are really divided, torn apart between the modern, open, liberal, democratic form of government and the "Islamic state" run on the Islamic laws. The classic example of this is the situation in Algeria where the Islamists won the election but the army *junta* and the liberals blocked the way for the Islamists to come to power. Both sides are killing each other and the struggle continues. Turkey is another example where the Islamists once came to power but the advocates of a secular system of government did not let the Islamists remain in power. Egypt is yet another case of tension and strife between the Islamists and protectionists of modern, liberal, democratic form of government. Afghanistan which was liberated from the Russian occupation with a strong support from the western powers, finally succumbed to the Islamist forces known as Talibans but the civil war among themselves continues resulting in many casualties. The struggle of the Islamists to come to the portals of power has not diminished in any way throughout the Islamic world.

In the struggle between the Islamists and the liberals, one of the trends worth noticing is that wherever the Islamists are active or come in power, there the non-Muslim minorities are persecuted. For example, in Iran, soon after the Ayatollah Khomeini's revolution, Ba'ha'is were termed non-Muslims and were forced to leave Iran. The then-Bishop of Isphan's son and the then-General Secretary of the Iran Bible Society were murdered, supposedly by the Islamic guards. The Christian Church was just allowed to exist in Iran but not flourish. This, perhaps, is the general strategy throughout the Islamic world with regard to minorities. In Pakistan, too, before the late president and martial law administrator Zia-Ul-Haq's era, Christians and Muslims lived together with a fair amount of harmony and peace. But his introduction of the blasphemy law (295 C) has landed many in jail and some have been killed even before they were tried in court, e.g. Niamat Ahmar of Faisalabad, Manzoor Masih, Dr. Farooq of Gujranwala, etc. Even the judge who exonerated Salamat Masih, a teenage illiterate boy who was accused of blasphemy, was shot dead for doing his duty.

The whole Christian village of Shantinagar was burned by an unruly mob of thirty thousand who thought that the Qur'an was desecrated in that village. Blasphemy law is like a hanging sword for the minorities. Munir Khokhar, a local counsellor, was shot at for defending a Christian graveyard from being destroyed by a Muslims mob. Ayub Masih, an accused in a blasphemy case, was shot at while being brought for a court hearing in Sahiwal. There are similar examples of this sort of behaviour by the Islamists in Egypt, Indonesia and Nigeria but the outstanding ones are in Sudan and Saudi Arabia. Ralph Kinney Bennett, quoting Marshall, says:

> Since 1989 the Sudanese government has been engaged in a wholesale war against Christians, who constitute roughly one-fifth of the population. Marshall reports that the goal of the ruling National Islamic Front led by Hassan Al-Turabi who some consider the country's de facto leader is to 'eradicate non-Islamic religion.'
>
> In the North, Al-Turabi's forces control the necessities of life. 'Non-Muslims are given the choice of converting to Islam or being denied food, clothing and shelter,' Marshall says. Thousands of women and children have been sold into slavery to Muslim masters who force them to convert to Islam.
>
> Sudan's Nuba Mountains, where Christians have lived since the sixth century, are now a wasteland of mass graves, destroyed villages and camps filled with starving women and children. Half a million Nuba Christians, virtually all men, have been killed in the past decade. 'The word genocide is thrown around too frequently,' says Marshall. 'In the case of Sudan, however, it is a factual description.'
>
> American ally Saudi Arabia is another country where, Shea says, 'freedom of religion simply does not exist.' All citizens must be Muslims. Expressions of Christianity wearing a cross, reading a Bible or uttering a non-Muslim prayer-are prohibited.

> The Mutawwa'in, the Saudi religious police, search out hidden church services among the millions of Filipinos, Koreans, Indians and other foreign workers. In December 1992 two Filipino Christians arrested for allegedly preaching Christianity were sentenced to death on Christmas Day. After an international outcry, the sentence was commuted to deportation.

Strategy of Islamists

These may seem to some to be isolated events. But they are not. Rather they depict a pattern of Islamic strategy which is to harass and intimidate its minorities and get more and more where Islam itself is a minority especially in the western world. In Islam a Muslim can marry a Christian woman but a Christian is not allowed to marry a Muslim lady. Likewise, a Christian can convert to Islam but a Muslim is not allowed even if he wants to. Apostasy in Islam is a grave sin and an apostate is liable to be killed. There is no freedom of religion/conversion in Islam. A Muslim too, as a human, has the right to choose from amongst the different religious faiths, but that right is denied to him by the Islamists. A Muslim may criticise other religions but others are not allowed (by law) to say anything against Islam. Even the Islamic welfare fund (*Zakat*) is to be used only for the Muslims. Non-Muslims are not entitled to receive this fund. It is highly discriminatory even in the distribution of relief in a natural disaster. Such like defences are part and parcel of the Islamists' strategy to keep their people within their fold. Once freedom of conversion is given in Islam, it will be a different story. Islamists' strategy in this regard has won them successes of no mean nature. Arabic has, now, become an international language. Special Islamic meals (*halal* meat) are served on flights. Special Islamic attire/dress is allowed in schools. Islamic centres and mosques have been built practically in all of the Western countries. Provision of Islamic religious education has been made for Muslim students in England and some other European countries.

Islam as Religious Faith

Islam is not only a political ideology but also a religious faith that attracts millions of people to its fold. Millions of people bowing before Allah at the time of annual pilgrimage depicts a moving scene, highlighting their commitment to the Islamic way of life. Not only at the times of pilgrimage but even in their daily lives, their commitment to prayer five times a day, fasting during the month of Ramadhan and their effort to mould their lives according to the laws of Allah is remarkable. There are millions of people who quench their spiritual thirst by following the Islamic way of life and take prophet Muhammad (PBUH) as their model of life. People of Islam are ready to die to defend the honour and respect of their prophet. *Fatwas* against Sulman Rushdie and Taslima Nasreen should be seen in this light. Islam does not allow criticism of its Holy Book (the Qur'an) or its prophet. There is nothing like "form criticism." Only one version of the Qur'an was allowed to exist during the time of 3rd Caliph Uthman. For the Islamists everything is final: the Qur'an as the revealed book is the final revelation; Prophet Muhammad (PBUH) as the prophet is the final prophet, and *Shariah* as the divine law is the final code of ethics and morality. They strongly believe that *bab-ul-Ijitihad* (independent reasoning) is closed. So, in Islam, there is always an appeal to the past, to the Shariah, the laws which need to be followed. There is, however, a small minority of Muslims who believe that the *bab-ul-Ijitihad* needs to be opened to make Islam relevant to the modern day world. Islamic fundamentalism or as a matter of fact any fundamentalism in any religion is due to not being able to cope with the modern-day world. The struggle between the traditionalists and the modernists continues in Islam and at times gets very violent, a factor which needs to be controlled.

Missionary Zeal of Islam

Coupled with the desire to make Muslim countries Islamic states, another expression of Islam in the present-day world is the desire to convert the whole world to Islam. It is believed by the Muslims that Islam is the final and only true religion. Others like Judaism and Christianity, even though revealed through their respective prophets, i.e. Moses and Jesus, have been corrupted by the followers, with the result that only the Qur'an and Islam have to be trusted and accepted. Pakistan is commonly called the "fort of Islam" against which no forces would be able to stand. There are a number of Islamic evangelistic associations engaged in the propagation of Islam—commonly known as *Dawah*—both within and outside Pakistan. As state and religion are the same and Islam has been declared the state religion, it is incumbent on the state to make provisions for the spread of Islam. Islam is truly a "missionary" religion and the duty of evangelism is not only left to the individuals but the state is normally active and supportive of the Islamic evangelistic activities. Countries like Saudi Arabia, Libya, Malaysia, Pakistan and Indonesia are particularly active in this field.

Islamic Solidarity

In order to regain and re-capture the vision of the Islamic *umma* (the whole community of faith), a number of Pan-Islamic movements have been organised, i.e. The Organisation of Islamic Countries, The World Islamic Council, etc. There is a growing feeling that attack on one Islamic country is an attack on the whole Islamic *umma*. This trend is capturing the hearts and minds of many Muslims in spite of the many differences among themselves. I personally will not be surprised that soon Islamic countries might form a United Nations and Chamber of Commerce of Islamic countries.

Rejection of Western Civilisation and Culture

The most noticeable expression of Islam in the present-day world is the rejection of Western civilisation and culture. This rejection partly may be that the West is considered to be Christian and partly because of its modernist liberal and secular tendencies. On this, the educated Muslim is really torn. The West or the universal civilisation it leads is emotionally rejected. It undermines, it threatens, but at the same time it is needed, for its machines, goods, medicines, war planes, the remittances from emigrants the hospitals which might have a cure for calcium deficiency or the universities which will provide higher degrees. In this torn situation and failure to respond meaningfully to the modern world, Muslims commonly rely on Islamic fundamentalism. Therefore, slogans like "Nizam-i-Mustapha," "Enforcement of Shariah," "Islamisation of Banking and Education" or "Enforcement of Hadoods" are commonly heard and are used for popular election campaigns. Within this majority, there are some, though a small number, who feel that there could not be a truly "Islamic State" and one could not reverse the process of history. Such people are normally met by a taunt that they are corrupted by the liberal Western philosophies and are even termed *kafirs* (non-believers). People freely use religion to legalise their doings. Any attempt to criticise Islam or Prophet Muhammad (Peace be upon Him) is not only discouraged but also prohibited. Violation of this law would land one in jail and later be hanged. Islam is being imposed from outside and with force of the legal system. Freedom of speech is guaranteed in the Constitution but not applicable to religion. Thus, disciplines like form criticism or the application of scientific methods of study are resisted and rejected. People normally fear making any attempt of modern interpretation of Islam or the Qur'an unless it suits the already accepted one. Therefore, Islam is in a state of flux, torn by a desire to have an ideal Islamic state over and against the modern state between law and grace. The sum total of Islamisation in some Islamic countries so far have been the introduction of certain Islamic laws and not so much of renewing of "inner persons," where all legal systems are conquered and triumphed over by an experience of "new birth."

Christian Response

Rejection

Christians and their corporate body, i.e. the Church/ Churches, are quite confused and puzzled as how to respond to the growing challenge of Islam. Some even call it a "threat" to Christian Church and society. They become quite nervous when they see mosques and Islamic centres being built in great numbers in Western countries. According to Voice of America's survey, every other month a big Islamic centre or a mosque is being built in America. Westerners who are not used to this phenomenon find it very difficult to accept the situation. Their worry is amplified when they hear of Islamic organisations' involvement in terrorism hijackings and bomb blasts. The growing apathy of the Church further aggravates the situation. To them, it looks like Christianity is on the decline and Islam is on the rise. Faced with this situation, they develop quite an antagonistic attitude towards Islam and Islamic people. Thus their first response is usually negative towards Islam.

Accommodation

Not all the people subscribe to such a negative response. So they respond in a little more positive way, basing their rationale on the premise that all people have a right to subscribe to whatever faith or belief they want to. So they go out of the way to help, to be kind and considerate towards the people of Islam.

Diakonia (Service)

This diaconal response to the challenge of Islam is advocated both in the Western Churches where Muslims are in a minority and in the Churches in Islamic countries where Christians are in a minority. Like her Master and Lord, the Church has to engage herself in serving others: "The Son of Man has come not to be served but to serve (Matt. 20:28)." Service (*diakonia*) is a practical form of proclamation. Actions usually speak louder than words. Even in the life of Jesus, we see that practically every miracle of his aroused a response from his audience. The Church's different ministries such as education, health care, adult literacy, emergency help and drug prevention, are different forms of *diakonia* and are different forms of mission. ACC-6, while discussing "Mission and Ministry," rightly says:

> Just as Jesus was able to hold together proclamation and service, the Church must also hold the two together in the right balance. It is no longer necessary to put a wedge between evangelism and social responsibility and Christians should not be divided between those who see mission primarily as evangelism and those who identify mission with activities designed to relieve human suffering. Evangelism and social responsibility are partners. It is this vision of man as a social being as well as a psychosomatic being which obliges us to add a political dimension to our social concern (John Scott, Christian Mission in the Modern World, p. 29). Jesus did not only heal the sick; he also challenged scribes and Pharisees on issues of Sabbath law and fasting (Matt. 2:23–28), dietary laws and divorce (Mark 10:2–12). The healing of a man who was sick for 38 years and his commanding him to break the Sabbath was a challenge to the selfish structures of the society which put more emphasis on

> observing (unnecessary) Sabbath laws rather than seeing a man who had suffered for thirty-eight years healed. We are therefore called upon not only to do acts of mercy but to go to the root causes of human suffering and struggle for justice with hope of transforming the unjust structures which are by and large responsible for human suffering. Christ's followers are called in one way or another, not to conform to the values of this world but to be a transformed and transforming people (Rom. 12:1–2; Eph. 5:8–14).[3]

Dialogue

The fourth response is dialogue. Though dialogue is viewed by both the Christians and the Muslims with some apprehensions, His Excellency Sheik Zaki Yamani, the famed Saudi OPEC diplomat, in his foreword to Professor Montgomery Watt's *Islam and Christianity Today—A Contribution to Dialogue,* extols his approach, his attitude in challenging Christians and Muslims for a dialogue, and his "tireless persistence" which has "enhanced the chances of its ultimate success." But he bluntly warned,

> In the great debate between Christians and Muslims however, there are areas of fundamental principles where no amount of logical discourse can bring the two sides nearer to each other and therefore the existence of an impasse must be recognised. Issues like the Trinity, Divinity of Christ and the Crucifixion so central to Christian beliefs have no place in the Islamic faith, having been categorically refuted by the Qur'an, on the authenticity of which there is no discord among Muslims. The discussion in this book of the Crucifixion and the "Salvation" it represents therefore will not be very convincing to the Muslim scholar and the attempt to find real parallels to it in Islam will have dubious prospects of success.[4]

In an ecumenical context, inter-religious dialogue is one of the significant ways to engaging in mission. As the Church's mission is basically addressed to those who do not know Christ and his Gospel and how God in Christ calls all peoples to himself, inter-religious dialogue becomes a means to proclaim and present Christ. In the light of the economy of salvation, the Church sees no conflict between proclaiming Christ and engaging in inter-religious dialogue. Pope John Paul II, in an Encyclical, says that dialogue should not in any way detract from the fact "that salvation comes from Christ and that dialogue does not dispense with evangelisation." Watt goes on further to say:

> Although the Church gladly acknowledges whatever is true and holy in the religious traditions of Buddhism, Hinduism and Islam as a reflection of that truth which enlightens all men, this does

> not lessen her duty and resolve to proclaim, without fail, Jesus Christ who is the Way, the Truth and the Life. The fact that the followers of other religions can receive God's grace and be saved by Christ apart from the ordinary means which he has established does not thereby cancel the call to faith and baptism which God wills for all people.[5]

Dialogue of Life

In the Encyclical quoted above it is written:

> Dialogue should be conducted and implemented with the conviction that the Church is the ordinary means of salvation. Through dialogue, the Church seeks to uncover the 'Seeds of the Word,' a ray of that truth which enlightens all men; these are found in individuals and in religious traditions of mankind. Dialogue is based on hope and love and will bear fruit in the Spirit. Other religions constitute a positive challenge for the Church; they stimulate Her both to discover and acknowledge the signs of God's presence and of the working of the spirit, as well as to examine more deeply Her own identity and to hear witness to the fullness of Revelation which She has received for the good of all. This gives rise to the Spirit which must enliven dialogue in the context of mission. Those engaged in this dialogue must be consistent with their own religious traditions and convictions and be open to understand those of the other party without pretence or close-mindedness, but with truth, humility and frankness, knowing that dialogue can enrich each side. There must be no abandonment of principles nor false irenicism but instead a witness given and received for mutual advancement on the road to religious inquiry and experience and at the same time for the elimination of prejudice, intolerance and misunderstandings. Dialogue leads to inner purification with docility to the Holy Spirit, will be spiritually fruitful… dialogue can assume many forms and expressions from exchanges between experts in religious traditions or official representatives of those traditions to co-operation for integral development and the safeguarding of religious values; and from a sharing of their respective spiritual experiences to the so-called "dialogue of life," through which believers of different religions bear witness before each other in daily life to their own human and spiritual values and help each other to live according to those values in order to build a more just and fraternal society.[6]

In the present day multi-religious, multi-lingual, multi- racial, multi-cultural situation prevalent in most of the advanced countries, there could be no fixed or stereotyped Christian response to the challenge of Islam. There would be many and varied responses depending on the situation. The main point in this response is that it has to be open, liberal and flexible. This openness and flexibility does not mean that we should accept the ideology of Islam without its critical evaluation (1 John 4:1) or reject it without reason or compromise with it at the expense of Christian principles and "kingdom values". The presence of other religions or ideologies should not deter us from sharing our religion or faith with others, but it needs to be done with love and humility on the pattern of our Lord and Saviour Jesus Christ.

Islam in Egypt
by The Bishop of Egypt, The Most Revd Ghais Abdel Malik

Egypt has a strategic position in the Middle East, lying between Europe and Asia in the North of Africa. It has a population of 62 million, the majority being Sunni Muslims. There are ten million Christians and the Coptic Orthodox Church is the largest of the churches. Other than that there are Coptic Catholics, Roman Catholics, Greek Orthodox, Greek Catholics, Armenian Orthodox and sixteen within the Protestant denomination.

Throughout the centuries Christians and Muslims have lived together, during times of joy and times of trouble. They faced wars together, and so fought together, died together, and survived together. Their children are taught in schools together. Christian and Muslim are part of the one body of Egypt, drinking the same water, living together in towns, villages, living together in blocks of flats. As neighbours they visit each other and their children are friends. Someone once called them Coptic Christians and Coptic Muslims. Simply speaking, Coptic means Egyptian.

Egypt is a Muslim country and its constitution is based on Islamic Sharia. Most Muslims are open-minded pious people, following the teaching of their Holy Book, the Qur'an. They stand fast to the law of their religion, that is, prayer, fasting, tithing, the *Haj* (visiting their Holy Land of Mecca).

The media often use the word 'persecution'! Here we have to differentiate between 'persecution' and 'difficulties'.

Persecution is the word that is used when the government targets a minority group and wishes to dissolve that group, e.g., the Roman Empire and Christianity! But troubles and difficulties are started by blinked individuals with closed minds. They find others to follow them. I do not call this persecution.

During the past few years you will undoubtedly have heard about acts which have taken place in Upper Egypt. Churches were burnt down, Christians were killed,

Christian shops were raided and burgled. The cry was 'persecution' while in fact this was not a direct attack against the Christians for their own sake, but an attempt by the terrorists to shake the stability of the country hoping, thereby, to bring down the government and rule themselves. These terrorists convince themselves and try to convince others that they are following the Qur'an. Failing in their target they then tried another method of attack, this time against the tourists; after that, the police. These acts of violence alienated the majority of Muslims and those who had supported the fanatics stopped doing so and allied themselves with the authorities. At the present time the government have the situation under control.

Sometimes people ask how we see that we have freedom as Christians when we are not permitted to build churches. We have full freedom to worship in our churches and the freedom to carry out unrestricted our church activities. It so happens that the regulations concerning the building of churches date back to 1902 and a special permit is needed for permission to build. During the last year the President authorised eleven permits to the Evangelical Church. Additionally the President has given permission to the Governors to authorise church repairs. We see this as co-operative progress!

I am often asked, too, about proselytising. We are living in a country where this is against the law and so the answer has to be 'no, we cannot do this'. As a church we do not impose on others to accept what we believe, but rather show them how we live. It is our mission to love them and show them God's love through our work with our hospitals, social work, schools, etc., and through the way we conduct our daily lives. We show them how we face our problems and deal with them as God's people. This is the way, here in Egypt, that we share with them the good news.

I see a great need for Christian/Muslim dialogue. I recommend it and, indeed, it has already been started.

In October 1995 His Grace The Archbishop of Canterbury delivered a lecture at the Al Azhar University at which the Grand Mufti and the Grand Sheikh of Azhar were present. This was well received and there was an encouraging return address. A year later the Grand Sheikh visited the Archbishop in England and I was present at some of their talks which were greatly encouraging.

Meeting together builds trust, and when we were faced by the worst acts of violence by the blind fanatics there were Muslim-Christian gathers in church to demonstrate their solidity against such forces. They were together as one body of the country.

The visit of Bishop Kenneth Cragg in March of this year gave us additional opportunities for meetings and talks with the Muslim leaders and this proved to be extremely valuable towards strengthening dialogue. Whilst not myself an expert in Islam, I do all I can to encourage good relations and co-operation. I do hope this has given you a brief picture of how live Christians, as a minority group, live with Islam in Egypt, the progress that has been made and the goodwill we have received.

Muslim-Christian Relations in the Anglican Communion by the Bishop of Bradford, the Rt Revd David Smith

We move now into a very different world. The video came from Birmingham, but it could have been Bradford, Blackburn—it could have been many parts of this country.

I want to cover this from a slightly different angle, to talk about Bradford and to describe some of the things we have been trying to do for a very long time, beginning long before I came to Bradford, to develop links with people of other faiths and particularly with Muslims. As I tell our story, it may encourage and offer opportunity for challenge to others.

Bradford is a city in West Yorkshire with a reputation for warm hospitality. People from Ireland, Germany, Yugoslavia, Poland, Serbia, the Ukraine, the Caribbean and India and Pakistan are among those who have now made their home in our city. In the 1960s people came from Pakistan to work in the then-flourishing textile industry. Most have now moved away from the idea of a return to Pakistan. They have settled, they declare themselves to be British, and they are nearly all Muslims. We have a population of somewhere around 55,000 Muslims out of a total population of some 455,000 or more people. Ten thousand Sikhs, ten thousand Hindus and a very very tiny Jewish community. I do not wish to ignore the Hindus and the Sikhs and the Jews for we work with them closely, but I do intend obviously today to concentrate on the Muslims.

Over the past decade or two, a number of crises have arisen. A headmaster called Ray Honeyford made remarks which caused deep hurt and dissent in the Muslim community, and the then Bishop of Bradford and Muslim leaders met together to see how they could deal with the unrest which had been stirred up. Later, Salman Rushdie's book *The Satanic Verses* was publicly burned, again amidst signs of great distress and anger. This again brought Anglican and other Christian leaders together with Muslim leaders to say "How can we together deal with this situation?" And then in 1995, there were the disturbances which became known as the Manningham riots, in which a small number of Muslim youths ran amok and caused enormous damage, largely in the part of Bradford known as Manningham. And on that occasion too, we met together to say "How can we deal with this unrest, how can we build up relationships for the good of the community, how can we begin to repair the damage that has been done?"

Working together in order to overcome a crisis has built up a sense of trust between very different leaders in the Muslim and Christian communities. But do please remember we are talking about a country and a city in which Muslims are a minority, in which they are still trying to work out what it means to be a Muslim in a modern Western city like Bradford. Most have come from very rural parts of Pakistan, from Milapur, Attok and so on. The Muslims have a sense of being in a strange land, they often have a sense of being a minority that is discriminated against and they are fearful for their future. This is almost a complete reversal of roles from the other parts of the world, which we have considered this afternoon. And they look to the Bishop of Bradford as being in one sense and one sense only their spiritual leader. He is in their view the senior spiritual leader in Bradford, and it is his responsibility, although he is a Christian, to ensure that minorities have their rights respected and can practise their faith in peace. That has a very interesting consequence, which I shall seek to stress a little later on.

But now let us be very down-to-earth and very simple. What are the kind of policies we are seeking to follow to develop and foster good and positive relations between Christians and Muslims in Bradford?

Well, the first one is so obvious it ought not to be mentioned: it is to encourage people to meet. But there are parts of Bradford which are almost exclusively dwelt in by people from Pakistan, or Bangladesh. They have their own shops. There is the mosque. They frequently speak Punjabi, Urdu or whatever. And they may have very little contact with what you might call the broadly white Bradfordian population. It is only when people can begin to meet each other, and to discover in each other human beings that progress can be made. We then seek to build up a sense of trust and respect for those who are different. Listen and learn—don't go charging in to talk about your agenda, but listen, learn, respect. And that will breed tolerance. We fight as hard as we can against the phenomenon called Islamophobia in which Islam is not infrequently misrepresented. But we also seek to be honest about the situation, which we find. And as Bishop Johnson said so eloquently earlier, the people who really can enter into dialogue in Bradford are those Christians of a strong faith, with Muslims of a strong faith. If people amongst the Muslim community feel that you care little about your religion, they simply do not want to know.

And so what do we as a missionary faith, what attitude do we take? And the answer is simply this: we seek to commend our faith, and I do underline that verb. We seek to commend our faith by the care and love and concern we show for those of other faiths, and in so doing we say "In the name of Jesus Christ we declare to you the love that God has for you." But it may be done in very simple and practical ways.

For example, unemployment. Youths from a background of Pakistan and Bangladesh are usually much more involved in the unemployment figures than their white peers. At one stage, something like three times as many were unemployed. In the world of education, I had supported very strongly the desire for a voluntary-aided Muslim school in Bradford. Many Muslim children go to Church of England-aided schools, indeed we have some where more than 95 per cent of the pupils are Muslim. But their parents want them to go there because they say these are places of spiritual value, and they know their children will be cared for and respected. That is supported by the Inter-Faith Education Centre, which is a unique place and organisation. There you will find teachers authenticated by the world faiths in Bradford, materials for use in schools, and the best assurance we can offer that religion will be taught properly by people who are respected as true teachers of that faith. In some parts of West Yorkshire, Muslim parents withdrew their children from religious education in schools. In Bradford they said "We want them there." They have produced in Bradford a religious education syllabus which has been approved by all the representatives of the world faiths, and indeed was produced by those representatives. This is not syncretism; this is not watering down faith; this is enabling children to learn about other faiths first-hand from people authorised to teach them.

I have regular meetings with people of other faiths and leaders, off the record, no minutes kept, in order that we may just keep an eye on what is happening in Bradford, see if we can foresee problems and tension points and try to reduce that possibility of conflict. We welcomed a year or so ago the Sheikh of Alazar, from Egypt, that very distinguished Muslim scholar. And he came to us and spoke about the importance of tolerance and respect and understanding. And if I may give you a very simple example of the lack of understanding, I had been to speak to some girls in the Islamic Society in one of our high schools. During lunch with their Imam present, one of the girls protested strongly that Christians misunderstood what we regard as arranged marriages, and then she came back with the charge "And you Christians send young girls into convents to become nuns against their will." I can think of one or two nuns not a million miles from this Hall who might not necessarily agree with that! But it seems ridiculous that this is the kind of misconception with which young people so easily grow up, and later in life it can fester and turn into something that is not comical, but very threatening.

The other dimension of life in Bradford for Anglicans is very interesting. We within the Anglican Communion are linked with four dioceses in Sudan. So we cannot be cosy about what is happening in Bradford. My wife and I were in Sudan this last January and February; we were also in Sudan two years ago. I spent a week with the Sudanese House of Bishops in Nairobi in February, and more recently, with the Bishop of Salisbury, down in Salisbury. We are very very well aware of the suffering and discrimination, which is the lot of our brothers and sisters in a country which has a National Islamic Front government. And so we say to our fellow Muslims in Bradford, "Look! In the name of God we seek to care for you! Can you not see how you now are invited to join with us in caring for Christians who are in a minority in Muslim countries?" Last October I went to Pakistan with a Muslim, a very great friend in Bradford, Ishtiaq Ahmed, Director of the Racial Equality Council. We went in partnership—a Muslim and a Christian leader. We took two ladies with us, and BBC Radio Leeds sent a reporter for the whole trip who turned out to be a practising Hindu. And we said, "The medium is the message. Look at us! See who we are. We trust each other, we respect each other, we do not compromise our faiths but we work together for the common good." In Pakistan I sat at the feet of some of the bishops here, and so did Ishtiaq. We went to Chantinagar to see the devastation there. We went to the grave in Lahore of the young man who had been shot dead outside court when he had been acquitted under blasphemy law. We listened to Muslims in the Islamic University in Islamabad. We went to learn and understand a little more, so we could go back and say to our Muslim brothers and sisters, "Look! We are doing our utmost to care for your rights. Can you join us in caring for the rights of our Christian brothers and sisters in a minority?" After Shantinagar, the Council for Mosques in Bradford joined with the Christian leaders in issuing a public statement deploring all violence anywhere against religious minorities. After the return from Pakistan, I spoke to the Council for Mosques about the abuse of the blasphemy law. When I had gone they discussed it, and wrote to the Prime Minister of Pakistan expressing their concern and distress at the abuse of the blasphemy law when applied to Christians or others. A very, very modest beginning, but there are courageous Muslims who are prepared to stand up and be counted and to work for peace and reconciliation, not only in our country but in other parts of the world.

And that is my final theme. Two days ago, one of my Pakistani brother bishops said "Peace and reconciliation." My Sudanese brother bishops say "Peace and reconciliation." We have shown that in little ways, Christians and Muslims in Bradford can work for peace and reconciliation. My prayer is that the whole Anglican Communion will keep in touch with what is happening in those countries where Christians and Muslims are face to face; that we shall support our brothers and sisters and that we too will work for peace and reconciliation amongst Christians and Muslims wherever we may be. An encouraging start, a tremendous challenge, and I invite you all to join in. Thank you.

Embassy, Hospitality and Dialogue: Christians and People of Other Faiths by the Bishop of Rochester, The Rt Revd Michael Nazir-Ali

Christian engagement with people of other faiths goes back to the very origins of Christianity. The Christian faith was born in a plural environment and had to relate not only to Judaism and to 'classical' Graeco-Roman religion but also to the various 'mystery' cults of the Mediterranean world as well as state religions such as Zoroastrianism in the Persian Empire.[7]

As an historical religion, Islam took its rise not only in the seventh century of the Christian era but in an environment heavily influenced by Judaism and

Christianity. From the very beginning, there was considerable social and religious (even theological!) interaction with Christianity.[8]

In India, too, the Church has been present from the earliest centuries and Christians have had to find a place for themselves in a largely Hindu social and religious context.[9]

Chasms and Bridges in the Early Years

Not surprisingly, then, Christians have had to reflect on the place of other faiths and people of other faiths within the divine economy. We know that many early Christian writers were aware not only of the challenge posed by these religions but also of the possibility of building bridges between the followers of these religions and Christians so that Christians might share their good news in a way that made sense to their hearers. At the same time, Christianity came to be deeply influenced by the language, ethics and iconography of at least some of these other traditions.[10]

Bishop W. G. Young tells us of an early dialogue that the mystic Bar-Daisan (Bardesanes) is supposed to have had with a Zoroastrian towards the end of the second-century. In classical theology, Bar-Daisan is often regarded as a heretic, particularly because of his supposed belief in 'astrological fatalism.' Here, however, we see him defending human freedom as a gift from God! In whatever country or culture we may find them, Christians can be distinguished because of their behaviour which is a result of obeying the law of Christ.[11]

Several centuries later, John of Damascus was a great defender of Christian Orthodoxy within the Islamic world. His work, *De Fide Orthodoxa,* was not only a summing-up of earlier patristic teaching; it was to become hugely influential in the development of both Western and Eastern theology. He is also supposed to have influenced the development of formal, or *Kalam,* theology in the Islamic world. John was the chief representative of the Christians in Damascus to the Caliph but was compelled, for reasons of his faith, to give up his office and to retire to a monastery near Jerusalem. His two dialogues with a Muslim interlocutor are well-known. In them John discusses with his Muslim partner the nature of God and of his Word. The dialogue is vigorous, at times even polemical, yet it also assumes a certain common basis from which the argument can be conducted. For instance, it is implicitly acknowledged that the partners in dialogue are talking about the same God, however differently they may understand him. Such a style of argument is characteristic of Christians within the Muslim world who do not display the hostility of Byzantium or, indeed, of the West.[12]

Medieval Interaction

In the West, too, it is not too much of an exaggeration to say that Christian theology in the Middle Ages was largely shaped by the need to respond to the so-called Islamic philosophers who were re-interpreting both Neo-Platonism and Aristotle, on the one hand, and the Quran, on the other. It is to the great credit of St. Thomas Aquinas that he not only provided an apologetic against such tendencies in his *Summa Contra Gentiles* but that he was also able to learn from these philosophers and to express the Christian faith in terms of this 'new learning'.[13]

In spite of the Crusades, both the Dominicans and the Franciscans were developing a peaceful approach to Islam and Judaism. The missionaries were expected to immerse themselves in the culture to which they were sent and to serve those in need. This 'witness of life' provided a basis for preaching the Gospel. Francis of Assisi certainly set the tone of this new approach in his visit to the Sultan Al-Malik, Al-Kamil at Damietta in Egypt. He was followed by many Franciscan missionaries, not all of whom had his wisdom. Raymond Lull was a layman who had been inspired by Francis and who sought to put his teaching into practice. He was able to persuade the Church to establish centres for missionary education and he, himself, undertook many missionary journeys. During the last of these he was beaten and expelled and probably died of his injuries. The Dominicans, too, had scholars like Raymond Marti who were well-acquainted with contemporary Judaism and Islam and who developed a Christian apologetic in relation to both.

It has to be acknowledged, however, that often this 'peaceful' approach meant no more than a renunciation of armed combat. The polemical spirit was still there and the atmosphere was one of argument and counter-argument. Although these missionaries had often studied the languages of the people to whom they were sent, they lacked the sympathy and friendship which might have deepened their dialogue and enabled them to get beyond mere controversy. The Roman Catholic scholar, Jean-Marie Gaudeul, remarks of Raymond Lull that he never seemed to have any Muslim friends, only interlocutors and opponents![14]

Reformation and Counter-Reformation

Curiously enough, the Reformation did not result in much cross-cultural missionary activity. The reasons for this are complex but have to do with the close relationship to the state which many churches of the Reformation enjoyed and with a curiously dispensationalist theology: God was sovereign and could reach people if that was his will—he did not need our co-operation in this! The Great Commission, moreover, had been fulfilled by the early Church and people who remained non-Christian did so because of heedlessness and ingratitude not ignorance.[15]

The Counter-Reformation in the Roman Catholic Church, on the other hand, was very missionary-minded. The newly acquired dominance of the sea-routes, wrested from the Arabs by Spain and Portugal, provided the spur to cross-cultural missionary work. The development, by the Jesuits, of the so-called Indian and Chinese 'rites' was an attempt to contextualise the Gospel, not only in terms of Indian or Chinese culture but also in terms of religious terminology and symbolism. The failure of these experiments is a witness of the obduracy of Christian bureaucracies in the face of the missionary task.[16]

The Modern Missionary Movement

It was not until the modern period of mission history, i.e. from the end of the eighteenth century onwards, that missionaries from the West began to take an interest, once again, in the language, literature and beliefs of other peoples and religions. Many of the earliest translations of the sacred books of these religions into European languages were made for missionary reasons. Increased knowledge of and familiarity with these traditions, however, often forced a re-evaluation of their relationship to Christianity. Missionaries like Temple Gardiner in Egypt and W. D. P. Hill in India spent long periods of time learning about the culture of a particular people before they felt able to witness to them as Christians. Such exposure led them, sometimes, to acknowledge truth in other faiths as well as devotion and moral awareness. A question that arose then had to do with the way in which such truth was related to Christ and to Christianity. This question remains with us today and is answered differently by different people. Many nineteenth-century missionaries, however, began to see other faiths as a sort of *praeparatio evangelica* (a preparation for the Gospel) in the same way as the early fathers had seen not only Judaism but also aspects of classical philosophy, poetry and religion. If other faiths are a preparation for the Gospel, then the latter is a fulfilment of the former. Missionaries, such as J. N. Farquhar, summed up this attitude when they were able to discern themes and concerns in another faith which pointed to a fulfilment in Christ. Such thinking drew on the Irenaean tradition of *anakephalaiosis*, or recapitulation, which sees all human history with its hopes and aspirations summed up in Christ (Eph. 1:10)[17]

The Oriental Experience

We should not forget, of course, that while Western missionaries were engaging with people of other faiths, perhaps for the first time, Christians of the ancient

Oriental, Orthodox and Eastern Rite Catholic Churches in the Middle East, Central Asia, India and Ethiopia continued to be witnesses to the Gospel among their neighbours of other faiths. There is much to learn from their history.[18]

In the same way, many indigenous Christians from Churches founded by Western missions were also engaging with their compatriots of another faith. The long history of Indian Christian theologians and their approaches to Hinduism is a case in point.[19]

Another example is that of theologians from a Muslim background in North India and what is now Pakistan. Even though their approach was somewhat polemical, they were able to engage with Islam at a fairly deep level.[20]

Ecumenical Consciousness and Interfaith Questions

The modern ecumenical movement began because there was a desire to bear a united witness to Christ in a world that was being recognised as increasingly plural. Since one third world missionary conference, which was also the first ecumenical conference of its kind, Edinburgh 1910, there has been a concern to relate the Christian message to people of other faiths. This concern has been expressed with increasing urgency throughout the twentieth century, not least because relations between the different religions are seen as crucial, not only to world peace but to peace regionally and even locally.[21]

Different conferences have called for a serious study of the world's religions, and engagement with them while recognising the distinctive nature of Gospel and dialogue to promote mutual understanding and respect.

The Second Vatican Council heralded the arrival of ecumenism in the Roman Catholic Church. The Council was aware, however, that its agenda could not be limited to the renewal of that Church and the beginning of dialogue with other Churches and ecclesial bodies. A truly universal Church must recognise the presence of other faiths in the world. It appears that, at first, there were no plans to issue a document on non-Christian religions. Pope John XXIII was keen, however, to heal the wounds of anti-Semitism and wanted the Council to develop a more positive view of Jewish-Christian relations. It was realised very quickly, however, that it would be difficult to address Judaism without also relating to Islam. This led to the rewriting of the document in such a way that all the great religions of the world were included. Michael Barnes comments that the document, *Nostra Aetate*, appears to be rather brief with bland statements about the world's religions. According to him, nothing very remarkable is said. What is remarkable is that anything is said at all.

Such a judgment is, perhaps, too harsh. The document attempts to set out a history of salvation which certainly recognises God's acts among his Chosen People and, specifically, in Christ as central, but it also attempts to find a place for other religious traditions within such a scheme. God's saving design is revealed in Christ but extends to all. Other religions may display knowledge of God derived not only from creation and from conscience but also from their particular religious experience. The Church should reject nothing which is true and holy in these religions. This truth and holiness are related to Christ as the Eternal Logos who is definitively revealed in Jesus of Nazareth but who also enlightens all human beings.[22]

Regarding the Jewish people, the Council and succeeding documents are at pains to emphasise the organic relation to the Church to Judaism. The 'mystery of the Church' involves the 'mystery of Israel.' The scriptures, liturgy and history have all to be understood in the light of this relationship. The special relationship is symbolised by joining the Commission on Religious Relations with the Jews to the Secretariat for Promoting Christian Unity, and the hope is expressed that these relations will be strengthened in collaboration with other Christians.[23]

The Anglican Communion and People of Other Faiths

Within the Anglican Communion, too, Lambeth Conferences since 1897 have considered the question of relations with people of other faiths. Sometimes their concern has been the preparation of Churches for the fulfilment of their missionary obligations. At other times it has been to uphold some principle of freedom of religion or of access to holy places.[24]

In more recent years, the Conferences have given particular attention to the question of dialogue between people of different faiths. In 1988 the Conference not only agreed a resolution on Inter-Faith dialogue which reflected the concerns of various ecumenical statements on the subject, but also commended a document, *Jews, Christians and Muslims: The Way of Dialogue*, written during the Conference, for study and action in the Churches of the Anglican Communion.[25]

Preparations for the 1998 Conference have suggested so far that this is an issue for nearly every 'cluster' of provinces which has met to highlight important elements in the agenda for the Conference. The reasons for this phenomenon are very complex and have to do with a world of increasing mobility as well as of many conflicts, local, regional and global in which religion plays a part.

The Need for Dialogue

In some parts of the world, Christians have lived 'cheek by jowl' with people of other faiths for centuries. The need for greater national integration and harmony has, however, made the task of dialogue even more urgent. On the one hand, Christians have realised that they need to learn from people of other faiths if they are to express their faith, in terms of worship and witness, in ways that are authentic to the culture and the idiom in which they live. Jyoti Sahi is an Indian Christian artist who attempts to convey insights of the Gospel in ways which draw upon Indian (even Hindu) themes. In a book (with Paul Middleton), he has also provided a study of how 'sacred space' is being understood by the churches in India in relation to the cultural and religious values of the people of India. In particular these have to do with holy places being, what Michael Ipgrave has called, 'places of mystery, memory and meeting.' It is interesting, in this connection, to note that the desire to 'contextualise' in this way is not just a concern of those churches in India which have their origins in the Western tradition, but also of those which spring from an ancient oriental background.[26]

It is not only Christians, however, who have felt the need to learn from others. Dr. M. M. Thomas, the doyen of Indian theologians, has drawn our attention to the acknowledged Christ of the Indian Renaissance. According to him, although this recognition is partial and inadequate, it is important, for the sake of the Church's mission, that it should be understood and evaluated. In his work he has tried to engage with leading Hindu reformers, such as Raja Ram Mohan Roy, Rabindranath Tagore and Mahatma Gandhi, especially in relation to their understanding of the meaning of Jesus Christ and of Christianity for religion and society in contemporary India. Dr. Thomas also discusses the response of leading Indian theologians to the ideas of these Hindu leaders and points out that the course of Indian Christian theology has been definitely affected by this acknowledgement of Christ within Hinduism itself.[27]

The Situation in the West

People of other faiths, especially Jews and Muslims, have lived in Western countries for a long time. This presence has, in recent years, been significantly augmented by immigration, whether for economic or political reasons. The second, and, in some cases, third-generation descendants of immigrants have, moreover, been born in the West and share its values and outlook in a number of ways.

Christians in Western countries have faced, therefore, a two-pronged situation: on the one hand, they have experienced other faiths as part of the 'strangeness' of their new neighbours. On the other, they are now experiencing it as the 'difference' of their friend at school or colleague at work with whom they have a great deal in common.

Since many people of other faiths are also ethnically different, this has sometimes caused confusion between race and faith: parents want their children educated in 'the white man's religion,' i.e. Christianity, and Asians, in particular, are assumed to belong to another faith. A bishop arriving from Pakistan for the last Lambeth Conference, for example, was asked if he was a 'Muslim' bishop!

Perhaps, more importantly, people identify culture with faith so that people belonging to a certain culture are also assumed to belong to a particular faith. The term 'multi-cultural' often means 'multi-faith' as well. The world-wide nature of the Christian Church and the fact that there are Christians of widely differing cultures often comes as a surprise.

In spite of such difficulties and confusions, however, Christians in the West have sought to relate to people of other faiths in a number of ways. There are several possible categories in which these different approaches can be classified. Bishop Kenneth Cragg has suggested that 'embassy' and 'hospitality' are two fundamental categories for thinking about mission. Hospitality has to do with welcoming people and meeting their needs. Embassy has to do with going out to them and sharing the Gospel with them.[28] Another way of thinking about mission has to do with witness, service and dialogue.

Christians in the West have tried to exercise a ministry of hospitality and service, for example, by opening up their homes and sharing skills needed in Western cultures with those of other faiths who have recently arrived in the country. Sometimes, they have made facilities, like church halls, available for social and educational purposes. The question of providing facilities for worship has been much more controversial and Christians have taken a range of positions on it. Some do not feel that any Christian premises should be made available for non-Christian worship, as, at the very least, it can confuse the wider community and make Christian identity less distinct. Others are willing for ancillary buildings, such as church halls, to be used for such worship and yet other will permit even the nave of a church to be used, but most of these would still not want the chancel and the sanctuary to be used.

The use of church buildings is a classic situation where Western Christians can learn from the history of Christianity elsewhere. In the early days of the expansion of Islam into the Christian countries of the Middle East, for example, the new rulers sometimes took over a part of a church for their worship, leaving the rest to the Christian community. In many cases, however, the whole building was eventually taken over. The second of the Righteous Caliphs, Umar, when invited by the Patriarch Sophronius to pray in the Holy Sepulchre at the time of the capitulation of Jerusalem to the Muslims, refused to do so on the grounds that if he did so, his fellow Muslims would use this as a pretext for converting the church into a mosque! Continuing questions about the precise identity of Hagia Sophia indicate the difficulties inherent in people of different faiths using the same building for their worship.[29]

In India there are one or two examples where the site of an ancient church is now used for interfaith meeting and dialogue.[30] There are other instances, however, of sites sacred to one faith being built upon by another which have caused hostility and even violence.

The history, then, is full of ambiguities and possible difficulties. Another issue has to do with the integrity of the Christian faith itself. Church buildings are often consecrated or dedicated for Christian worship and the canons or other rules of the Church require that nothing should be done in them which is contrary to the Christian faith or dishonouring to Christ.

If this rules out the regular use of a church building by another faith, what about the disposal of redundant churches to other faith-communities? If a building is surplus to requirements because the population has moved, or because there is ecumenical sharing, or because there are just too many buildings, is it permissible, or even preferable, to sell the building to another faith-community? Some denominations have clearly felt able to do this, sometimes on the grounds that this is better than seeing them turned into garages or warehouses. The Church of England, on the other hand, has been much more cautious. It has recognised, for example, the importance of 'sacred space' for a community. A building used for Christian worship has a certain character. This may be the physical shape of the building—many churches are cruciform in shape—or it may be the atmosphere conveyed by art or furniture or arrangements for music. Places of worship are also important as places of memory, not only for the worshipping congregation but often for the wider community also. The attachment of so many non-churchgoing folk to their parish church can only be explained if the church building is seen as focusing the collective memory of a community. The possibility that some churches are built on pre-Christian sites of worship only strengthens the argument about memory.

Many hold also that the sale of a church building signals a retreat from often the neediest communities which are deprived of an important symbol of their community life. Nor are such feelings of deprivation felt only locally. Internationally, too, there may be repercussions. Churches in minority situations, and under pressure from another dominant religious tradition, may feel betrayed by Churches in the West when they hear or read about the sale of churches in this way. It is certainly true that some people are only too willing to use such situations for anti-Christian propaganda.

For all of these reasons, Church authorities should think very carefully before disposing of church buildings which they do not need. They should explore, first of all, continued Christian use of such buildings, whether ecumenically or by sale or lease to another Christian denomination. If this is not possible, some community use should be sought. It has to be acknowledged that, in some cases, a building may have to be demolished. Only when these other options have been explored should the authorities consider disposal to another faith-community, and then only after the widest consultations in the community.[31]

One of the ways in which some Christians have tried to welcome people of other faiths in their midst has been to attend their worship and to learn from it. Other have found that their friendship has led them naturally to pray with their friends, especially at times of great need or rejoicing. Such experiences have gradually led to the demand for 'inter-faith' or 'multi-faith' worship. In using these expressions, people often mean different things by them. An event like the one arranged by the Vatican at Assisi, for example, involved the different faith-communities praying in their own groups but at the same time and in the same location. It is possible also to meditate together in silence. Then there are the gatherings of a 'serial' nature. In these each faith-community offers a reading or a prayer. There may be a common concern or theme but no attempt is made to suggest a common activity. As Marcus Braybrooke has pointed out, 'those present are in effect an audience listening to a religious anthology in which the distinctiveness of each tradition is clearly recognised.'[32] Finally, there are the services with a common order which has been agreed beforehand. Of necessity such services take place at the level of the lowest common denominator.

There are Christians who believe that it is never right to pray with someone of another faith as they may be praying to 'another god'. This may be true on some occasions, but, equally, at other times there may be an awareness on all sides of the one divine being who has created the world and ourselves and who is concerned for us. This divine being may be understood in different ways by the different traditions but, in spite of the differences, there is agreement that we are referring to the same God who has not left himself without witness anywhere (Acts 14:17).

Because Christian worship is Christ-centred, multi-faith worship of any kind can never become the regular, spiritual diet of Christians. It is possible, however, to pray with people of another faith at a critical moment in their lives. Indeed, sometimes they ask us to do this! In the same way, it may be possible to join people of another faith at times of national or local celebration or of crisis. National or local governments, embassies and voluntary organisations often organise such events (for example, on national days) and invite churches or individual Christians to participate. This is often an opportunity for witness and for dialogue. Should Christians agree to be present?

It is important that if Christians do take part in an event of this kind, they should be sure that nothing is done to dishonour Christ, or be contrary to the Christian faith. It is to be expected, of course, that representatives of other traditions will make sure that their beliefs are respected in a similar way.[33]

In many western countries, people of other faiths may still feel themselves at a distance from the centres of power and influence. At the time of writing, for example, there is only one Muslim Member of Parliament in Britain, in spite of the fact that Muslims constitute the most numerous religious minority in the country. Even his election has been attended by various difficulties. In a situation where people of other faiths may feel marginalised in national or local life, it is important for the Christian Churches to speak for them. Such a role of advocacy is even more necessary for a Church that is seen as a 'national' or 'established' Church. The Church of England, for instance, sees itself as an enabling agent for the greater participation of other churches and, indeed, other faiths in national life. This may take place at a country-wide level by making sure that other churches and representatives of other faiths are consulted, for example, about legislation relating to education or the social services. It also takes place in institutions like hospitals and prisons and universities where Anglican chaplains often make sure that chaplains from other Churches and now from other faith-communities have access to their people in such institutions. The Church of England, and other Christian Churches, are also making attempts to ensure that the other faith-communities are appropriately represented at civic events, both nationally and locally.[34]

While Churches in the West have been active in the 'hospitality' aspects of mission, serving the needs of people of other faiths and encouraging dialogue with them, it has to be admitted that the 'embassy' side of mission has not been greatly to the fore. There are some understandable reasons for this. Christians have often felt that they generally belonged to a privileged and affluent section of society and they should not be seen as 'preying' on those who were weak and vulnerable. Some have felt, rather, that their faith obliged them to struggle with people of other faiths to make sure they had the same freedoms and facilities which Christians themselves enjoyed. Others have wanted to learn more about the other traditions before they felt able to witness to them.[35]

The situation is changing, however, and many people of other faiths are now in influential positions in commerce, local government and the professions. Christians, also, have acquired some experience of what others believe. It is important, therefore, for the Church to make sure that, along with service and dialogue, the obligation to witness is not neglected. 'Hospitality' needs to be kept side by side with 'embassy'. Churches and Christians need to be equipped to witness sensitively, but boldly, of what God has done for us in Christ. Naturally, such witness should be in the spiritual 'idiom' of the one to whom we are witnessing. This requires patient listening and dialogue. Indeed, dialogue can be an occasion for authentic witness, and both service and dialogue need to take place alongside witness. It is important, however, to ensure that 'service' is not seen as proselytisation by our partners and that dialogue is not an occasion for preaching at them. Each activity has its own integrity but in the total policy of a Church, local, national or regional, all three should have a place.[36]

Christians in other parts of the world are, sometimes, a mirror image of other faith-communities in the Western world. In countries where Christians are a minority, they sometimes experience systematic discrimination in terms of education and employment. They are often marginalised from mainstream social and political life and, on occasions, they are even persecuted for their beliefs. Christians are not, of course, alone in facing such difficulties; other minority groups face them as well. It is here that the principle of 'reciprocity' can be put forward. It should be made clear straight away that this does not mean 'tit for tat'. Christians should not be saying that because people of other faiths have certain freedoms in the Western world, therefore Christians should have similar freedoms in countries where these other faiths are dominant. It is, perhaps, natural to feel like that but a more nuanced view is necessary. The principle of reciprocity should be seen as the commitment of each faith to fundamental human rights in every part of the world. Such a commitment should entail not just mental assent but active involvement in the promotion and defence of these rights. Respect for basic human freedoms and the rights of groups such as women and ethnic and religious minorities should be on the agenda of multilateral and bilateral dialogues.

Christian Faith in a Plural World

Awareness of the existence of faiths other than one's own has raised important questions about truth. Are all faiths a path to God? Do they all point to one transcendent reality even though the language they use to describe it is determined by their particular historical, cultural and social context? Is there anything unique and of universal importance in the Christian faith? There are many, of course, in all the faiths who do believe that the different faiths all lead to the ultimate reality in their own way and that the path taken by a particular person or group is most suitable for them because of who they are, where they have been born and how they have been brought up. It has to be acknowledged that there are some who see in a religiously plural situation an opportunity to relativise all of them in such a way that none can make a personal, social or political impact. A multi-faith context is taken, then, as an excuse for marginalising all spiritual and moral perspectives. It can also become an objection to believing at all: there are so many faiths, which one should I believe?

We have seen already that it is quite possible to acknowledge that God has revealed himself in the natural world (Acts 14:17), in people's consciences (Rom. 2:15) and even in their religiosity, however far removed that may seem from a Judeo-Christian point of view (Acts 17:22–31). At the same time, it is also possible to hold that we can recognise God's revelation in these other ways precisely because he has revealed himself definitively in the call, the liberation and the history of his chosen people and, supremely, of course, in the living, the dying and the rising again of Jesus of Nazareth. This history of God's judgement, as well as of his salvation, is the canon or the touchstone by which we are able to recognise God's revelation in other ways. As Bishop John Robinson once put it, to say that God is best defined by Christ is not to say that he is confined to Christ.[37]

What Does the Bible Say?

The Bible, as a record of God's dealings with the people of Israel, is mainly concerned, of course, with the experience of God's judgement and salvation among that people. It also has, however, a unique sense of the universality of Israel's God. Here is no mere tribal deity. The God of Israel is the Creator of Heaven and Earth and all that there is in them. He is the Creator of all the nations upon earth and is the directing force in their destinies. The election of Israel means, therefore, that God's purposes for all are especially focused and highlighted in Israel. The world, not Israel alone, is the stage of God's action. The Bible is a very complex and very diverse collection of documents which were originally composed for different reasons in a variety of contexts, cultures and languages. Although there is an underlying unity, there is also a great variety in the Bible's response to many questions, including that of relations with people of other faiths.[38]

Not all religion is good and in the Bible there is a negative response to bad religion. Those working on the sociology of the Bible tell us that early Israel was a 'flat,' non-hierarchical and egalitarian society. This was certainly because of their experience of God who had so dramatically freed them from slavery in Egypt, revealed his will for them in the desert and welded them into a nation during their years of wandering. When they entered Canaan, they encountered an oppressive and hierarchical society in which throne and temple collaborated. The defeat and destruction of the Canaanite city-states, at the time of the conquest, is seen as God's judgement on them. Equally, Israel is judged when she emulates their behaviour.[39]

Elijah's encounter with the prophets of Baal (1 Kings 18) is the climax of a long-running hostility in the Bible to the sexually permissive, even licentious, cult of the god Baal (of whom there were many local variants). Once again, such a negative response was needed if the moral fibre of the nation was not to be completely destroyed. After the Exile, there is the example of Ezra and Nehemiah refusing help for the rebuilding of the temple from those they perceived to have compromised themselves and attempting to purify the nation. In both of these responses there is a fear of syncretism; that the pure worship of God would somehow be mingled with beliefs and practices which were not consonant with the revelation received by the Jewish people.

These negative responses are there in the biblical material. They may have arisen because of an encounter with inauthentic, destructive or tyrannical religion. They could also have come about because of misunderstandings, political and military rivalry and just plain greed for land.

There are, however, positive approaches to those of other faiths as well. Consider the Canaanites, for instance; on the one hand, there is the rejection of an oppressive system based on elitism; on the other, there is gradual assimilation of Canaanite and other cultures and, in particular, their religious symbolism. Any fair reading of the account of the building of Solomon's temple will show the extent of such influence (1 Kings 6–9). The very building of the temple, and the placing of the ark in it, indicated a significant shift in Israel from being desert nomads to being a settled people like their neighbours.

A more positive relationship with the Canaanites is anticipated already in the Patriarchial narratives, in the story of Melchisedek, King of Salem, encountering Abraham, father of all the faithful. The story, as it has come to us, has been reflected on and redacted. Yet what we have clearly is a Canaanite priest-king, a symbol of all that early Israel was concerned to reject, bringing bread and wine to Abraham. We are then told that Abraham makes him an offering in recognition of this priestly service! Von Rad captures the element of surprise very well when he says, 'Melchisedek, in his veneration of "God most High, maker of heaven and earth," came close to believing in the one God of the world, whom Israel alone knew. This is surely the sense of the passage.... Such a positive, tolerant evaluation of a Canaanite cult outside Israel is unparalleled in the Old Testament.' He points out that the Melchisedek motif is related to the throne of David in Psalm 110. In the Christian tradition, this gives rise to reflection on the priesthood of Christ himself which is seen as being 'according to the order of Melchisedek' (Hebr. 6:20 ff.).[40]

Then there is the strange story of Balaam, the Mesopotamian prophet who is made to prophesy for Israel in the presence of their enemies (Num. 22–24). Was Balaam a saint or a sinner? In other parts of the Bible, he is shown in a very bad light and comes to a very sticky end (Num. 31:8, Deut. 23:4–5, 2 Peter 2:15, Jude 11, Rev. 2:14). Nothing can detract, however, from the fact that he was inspired by God's Spirit and prophesied in an authentic way.

In more political terms, there is Cyrus, who is called the Lord's anointed (or messiah!) to bring liberation to his people (Isa. 45:1–6). In the Pentateuchal and Historical Books there are other incidents, such as the meeting between Elisha and Naaman (2 Kings 5), which suggests a certain amount of tolerance and friendly interaction.

It is, however, in the writing of the Prophets that a more adequate theology of God's purposes for all people is being worked out. The Prophets tell us of how God has done this in the past, how he is doing it in the present and what he is to do in the future. Amos, for instance, declares that God has a purpose for and acts within the history of the various nations, both far and near. The language of the Exodus from Egypt is, moreover, used to describe God's 'saving plan' for these peoples (Amos 9:7). From the very beginning, God has worked in this way even if people have been unaware of it.[41]

Malachi, on the other hand, speaks of the ways in which God is recognised and worshipped, however inadequately, among the nations. In some cases, in ways that are worthier than the worship of Israel itself (Mal. 1:11). From the earliest times, attempts have been made to understand the text as referring to the future (in the Early Church the verse was regarded as a prophecy of the Eucharist). Even some Bible translations try to translate the verse as future but the plain sense seems to be that the prophet is referring to events that are contemporaneous with his activity.[42] In both Isaiah 19 and in the so-called Apocalypse of Isaiah (Chapters 24–27) there is a reference to a blessed community of nations. God's blessing no longer applies solely to Israel, the other nations are also blessed. Israel is the primary recipient of this blessing and also God's instrument in extending it to others. Otto Kaiser comments, 'To the extent to which people of different nations and religions are forced to become acquainted with each other and to live together, human relationships are set up which cannot and ought not to be ignored by an understanding of faith which is honest with itself.'[43] There is a reference here to the context in which the prophecy first arose, but there is also anticipation of a future which belongs to God.

Among the prophets there are different models of how God is fulfilling his purposes among the various people. There is, for example, the centripetal model where the nations all stream to Mount Zion to join in the Jewish cult (Is. 2:1–4, Micah 4:1–4). It has often been a temptation for the People of God, both Jewish and Christians, to think like that: God's purpose for the nations must be that they should become exactly like us! We have, however, seen already that God is working his purposes out in a variety of ways and that no one model is adequate in describing God's work.

Against the 'exclusion' of Ezra and Nehemiah, we have the more 'inclusive' approach of books such as Ruth, Jonah and Job. The ancient story of Ruth tells of how a Moabitess woman became the ancestress of David and thus of the Messiah himself (Ruth 4:17–22, Matthew 1:5, Luke 3:32). The Book of Job is not only located in the Arabian region but has many words of Arabic origin and Job himself is not, of course, a Jew but very probably an Arab. This echoes Jesus' reminder to the people of his home town that Elijah was sent to a widow in Zarephath, even though there were many widows in Israel, and that Elisha healed only Naaman the Syrian, even though there were many lepers in Israel at the time (Luke 4:24–27).

The universalism of the New Testament arises out of the response to the Gospel by the poor, the marginalised and the foreigners. We are told that the common people (*ochlos*) heard Jesus gladly (Mark 12:37). He keeps company with the sinners and outcasts of society (Matt. 9:10–13). Foreigners respond positively to the words and works of Jesus (Matt. 8:1–13, Mark 7:24–30, Luke 17:11–19, John 12:20–21). This is confirmed in the experience of the Early Church which is alerted to its world-wide mission by the response of those either on the margins of the synagogue or outside it altogether (Acts 13:44–48).[44]

Criteria and Basis for Dialogue

Why should Christians engage in dialogue with people of other faiths? Both Scripture and our experience provide criteria that God is working in the cultures and histories of all people. In different ways, people respond to this divine impulse and the Bible, as the inspired record of God's saving acts, provides us with a means of discerning how God has been working in the history, the culture and the spirituality of a particular people. Awareness of the divine need not be confined to the structures of institutional religion. Indeed, it may not be found there at all! It can be a very private affair and sometimes it may be found in counter-religious movements which set out to affirm human dignity and equality and which challenge oppressive social institutions.

The Trinity and Dialogue

Our basis for dialogue should be Trinitiarian. We enter into dialogue because we believe that all men and women have been made in God's image (Genesis 1:26–27). It is true that this image has been distorted by human sin and rebellion and stands in need of conversion (*metanoia*) but it has not been destroyed and it is possible for people to recall (*anamnesis*) something of God's intention for them and for the world even in this state. We may say that this possibility of discerning the signs of God in creation and conscience is the basis for natural theology.

In addition to this possibility, however, there is also general revelation: God has not left human beings on their own in trying to interpret the universe. The Logos, the Eternal Word of God, who provides coherence to the universe (makes it a universe), and who is incarnate in Jesus of Nazareth, also enlightens the hearts and minds of all human beings (John 1:9). The early Christian apologists identified the Logos with the divine Reason which holds the universe together and which provides order and stability to human societies. Its illumination may be seen in the work of those philosophers who sought to understand the world in a rational way and who taught that it was part of human destiny to use reason as a way of participating in the divine work. Although the poets were seen as obsessed with falsehood, nevertheless there were 'sparks of divine Reason' even among them, and the apologists follow Paul in trying to demonstrate the Christian God from the poetry of their time.

The morality of the Stoics and Platonists is also recognised as reflecting the light of the Eternal Word. Even the famed Sibylline Oracles are seen as witnessing to the truth revealed by Christ. This is not to say that these apologists were indifferent to the distinctiveness of the Christian faith or that they endorsed everything in Gentile religiosity. Far from it, in fact they were very critical of most popular and even philosophical religion. The apologists were, however, recognising the light of Christ wherever they saw it and used it to make their case.

The ubiquity of the Holy Spirit also makes dialogue possible. The Holy Spirit is not only the point of connection (*Anknupfungspunkt*) between God and the human being but is also the medium in whom and through whom human beings can communicate with one another regarding matters of ultimate concern.[45] The Johannine teaching that the Holy Spirit is in the world convincing it of sin, righteousness and judgement has been further developed in Orthodoxy. This is called the economy of the Holy Spirit. The Spirit is present everywhere and fills everything, inspiring people in their response to God and to Christ. For the Orthodox, this can include people of other faiths. The Spirit is leading all towards the final consummation, the recapitulation of all things in Christ.[46]

Reformed traditions, too, emphasise the prior work of the Holy Spirit in that renewal and recreation of the human personality which they understand as conversion. Such a view is based on the Pauline teaching that we can discern spiritual matters only because the Spirit is already at work in us (1 Cor. 2:14–16;12:3, 2 Cor. 3:4–6, Eph. 1:17–20; 3:14–19). In dialogue we must assume then that the Spirit is working to convert people to God. Signs of the Spirit's work will be discerned in their consonance with the Gospel, its teaching and values, but also by the fruit of love, joy and peace. In the same way, all that makes for human flourishing will be seen as a response to the Spirit's impulse and guidance. All that makes for strife, hatred, intolerance and greed is clearly not of the Spirit (Gal. 5:16–24). In spite of such criteria for discerning the presence and work of the Spirit, Christians will be surprised at the way in which the Spirit can be manifest and at the places of such manifestation. The Spirit blows in sovereignty and freedom. We may catch a glimpse of the work or hear the sound, but we do not fully understand the source (John 3:8).

How Does Dialogue Happen?

Dialogue happens when people who are neighbours or colleagues begin to talk to each other about their beliefs and spiritual experience. It can happen when people join together to struggle for freedom or human rights and discover that they are doing so because of their faith. Sometimes it comes about because people of different faiths are concerned about the moral and spiritual values influencing the communities in which they live. They discover that their different faiths both unite and divide them on a number of issues. From time to time people will want just to share spiritual experiences with one another. This is yet another form of dialogue.

Representatives of various faiths will sometimes arrange more formal dialogues between the leaders of the different communities or between scholars belonging to these communities. On occasions such dialogues will be limited to a specific issue or a cluster of issues. At other times they may be called to review the whole range of relations between two or more faiths. Dialogue may be bilateral, between representatives of two-faith communities, or multilateral, involving people from a number of such communities. The dialogue of specialists or scholars is very important, as crucial areas of agreement or difference can be clarified in this way. People can discover that their histories and beliefs are not as far apart as they thought and, even if they are, they begin to understand the reasons for the differences a little better. For this to happen, it is vitally important that scholars should share the results of their meetings with the people of their respective communities.[47]

Through careful listening to one another, people begin to understand the cherished beliefs of each side, even if they cannot agree with them. They begin to appreciate the spiritual wellsprings which motivate people's actions, even if they cannot endorse them. The German theologian, Hans Kung, in his project on The Religious Situation of Our Time, has pointed out that without peace between the religions, there will be war between nations and civilisations and even within nations and civilisations. Peace between religions will only come about as a result of a dialogue between religions and this must be based on a thorough investigation of the foundations of the religions. Indeed, we might say that such an investigation must be part of the dialogue.[48]

In Christian circles an important question that has arisen has to do with the appropriateness of witness in the context of dialogue. Some Christians have shied away from witnessing in a dialogical relationship because of fear that the partner may regard this as an abuse of dialogue and a covert way of proselytising. It is true that dialogue can be abused in this way by Christians as well as people of other faiths. At the same time, it has to be recognised that dialogue would not be authentic if people did not give an account of how their faith sustains and motivates them, how it comforts them at times of trial or sorrow and how it encourages them and gives them hope. Christians will want to listen respectfully and attentively to their partners' witness, but they will also want to witness to what God has done for them in Jesus Christ. It is perhaps worth quoting at length a statement from the World Council of Churches' Guidelines on Dialogue:

> ...We do not see dialogue and the giving of witness as standing in any contradiction to one another. Indeed, as Christians enter dialogue with their commitment to Jesus Christ, time and again the relationship of dialogue gives opportunity for authentic witness. Thus, to the member Churches of the WCC we feel able, with integrity, to commend the way of dialogue as one in which Jesus Christ can be confessed in the world today; at the same time, we feel

> able, with integrity, to assure our partners in dialogue that we come not as manipulators but as fellow pilgrims, to speak with them of what we believe God to have done in Jesus Christ who has gone before us, but whom we seek to meet anew in dialogue.[49]

Fundamentalism, Religion and Ideology

There are circumstances, of course, when dialogue is not possible or appropriate. Like other aspects of human life, religion can and does go wrong. Because of its importance to human culture and societies, such pathological religion can influence important areas of individual and social behaviour. Indeed, it can affect relations between communities and nations: one aspect of such behaviour, in recent times, has been the role of religion in resurgent ethnic or national chauvinism. Religions have been made part of, even basic to, ethnic or national identity from which others are excluded. This seems to be the case, for example, with those extremist Hindu organisations which want to identify being Indian with being Hindu, thus excluding large numbers of Muslims, Christians and others from participation in national life. Many of the ethnic conflicts in Eastern Europe or the Caucasus, for example, have a religious component. In many cases, both the oppressors and the oppressed understand themselves with reference to a religious tradition.

Often, chauvinistic manifestations of religion are confused with fundamentalism. It is true that there are some similarities. Both, for example, can function as ideologies for communal programmes and both share in some of the characteristics which Martyn Percy claims define fundamentalism. These include what he calls 'backward looking legitimation' of present practices or experience by an appeal to specific elements in the tradition, counter-cultural rather than culture-affirming attitudes and tendencies, or habits of mind, which tend to impose beliefs and values rather than share them with others.[50]

Fundamentalism, in the narrower sense, is, however, quite often a movement among 'people of the book.' Elsewhere, I have described it 'as a literal understanding of the primary documents of a faith and a desire to apply their moral, cultural and legal demands in their entirety without sufficient attention to the contexts in which believers have to live.'[51] It is interesting, in this connection, to observe that Judaism, Christianity and Islam all emerge as faiths which are experiencing a surge of fundamentalism at this time. In Christianity, fundamentalist movements have often emphasised personal piety and ethical behaviour in the light of what has been seen as biblical teaching. In some cases this has extended to social concern, but movements like 'the moral majority' in the United States of America and R. J. Rushdoony's 'reconstructionism' which have produced detailed political and legal programmes are comparatively rare and recent.[52] In Judaism, too, fundamentalists have concentrated on instruction and observance within the community and in families and individuals. In the State of Israel, however, fundamentalist attitudes have led to detailed political and social programmes. It is in Islam, though, that movements have emerged which have developed ideologies which are not only comprehensive but even coercive.

Such ideologies have either a conservative or a revolutionary basis. In some cases they legitimise an existing social and political order. In other cases they struggle against an allegedly corrupt or oppressive system. These ideologies not only see Islam as influencing every area of personal and social behaviour (other faiths also claim to do this), but they also seek to provide detailed legislation for such behaviour. This often results in the restriction of choice and the loss of flexibility for society as a whole and it seriously affects the freedom of groups such as women and religious minorities.

There are many complex reasons for the emergence of this phenomenon in the world of Islam at this time. They include a very large young population in many Muslim communities which is alienated from the mainstream in terms of education, employment and business opportunities. There is a continuing reaction to the experience of colonialism and neo-colonialism. The emergence of the state of Israel and the subsequent conflict with neighbouring peoples and countries are also factors, as are super-power politics in particular regions (e.g. in Central and South Asia). The failure of both 'command' and 'free-market' economies to delivery prosperous societies and accountable governments has contributed to the search for another, authentically Islamic, way. In countries where Muslims are a minority, they have often experienced marginalisation and even discrimination. This has sometimes had the effect of radicalising their politics in a fundamentalist direction. This has especially been the case with the young people who have lost confidence in existing systems and structures. Fundamentalist movements offer them community, hope and the possibility of a struggle to bring about change. They can also isolate them and make it more difficult for them to relate to the wider society around them.

It is often the case that dialogue, of a limited kind, can take place even with representatives of such movements. Christians will, however, need to relate to them in other ways as well. It may be possible, for example, for Christians or churches to act as mediators in the resolution of conflicts where such movements are a party to conflict. In some cases it has been shown that people in such movements have a certain respect for others with a religious commitment of their own. Christians may also find that they are advocates either for members of such movements, if their fundamental rights are being violated, or against these movements if they are violating the fundamental rights of others. It is important, also, to encourage people of all faiths to put their texts and traditions in historical and cultural contexts, while continuing to recognise them as authoritative. Legal and judicial traditions, similarly, should be seen as capable of reform and development in the light of authoritative texts. Failure to appreciate the need for this can result in great suffering for many. If a political, social or economic system is the cause of significant oppression, Christians should be prepared to bring this to the attention of local, national and international organisations, whatever the ideological basis of such a system.

We have seen then that the Church has a long history of relating to people of other faiths and that there are significant resources for such work. The history has both positive and negative aspects to it and critical reflection is necessary if it is to assist us in our task today. We have considered especially the witness of the Scriptures and of the Early Church and have sought to develop criteria and a basis for dialogue from these witnesses. The practice of dialogue and its appropriateness in various situations has also been discussed and we have ended with some reflection on religion as ideology. We have sought to rehearse briefly the theological and historical factors affecting the encounter between people of different faiths, but we have tried also to reflect a little on the programmatic aspects of this encounter.

+Michael Nazir-Ali
Bishop of Rochester
Lambeth 1998

Notes

1. *The Economist*, "Living with Islam," 18 March 1995.
2. Pickthall, M.M., "The Meaning of the Glorious Qur'an," Mentor Books, Chicago.
3. Anglican Consultative Council 6, "Mission and Ministry."
4. Watt, M., *Islam and Christianity Today—A Contribution to Dialogue*, p. 29.
5. Ibid.
6. *L'Osservatore Romano*, 28 January 1991, no. 4, p.13.
7. See further J. Stambaugh and D. Balch, *The Social World of the First Christians* (London: Society for Promoting Christian Knowledge, 1986) pp. 41 ff, 127 ff; W. G. Young, *Patriarch, Shah and Caliph* (Rawalpindi: CSC, 1974) pp. 3 ff.
8. R. Bell, *The Origin of Islam in its Christian Environment* (London: 1926) and M. Nazir-Ali, *Islam: A Christian Perspective* (Exeter: Paternoster, 1983).
9. A. Mar Thoma, *The Mar Thoma Church: Heritage and Mission,* (Tiruvalla: Ashram Press, 1985).
10. R.D. Sider, *The Gospel and its Proclamation: Message of the Fathers of the Church* (Wimington, Delaware: Glazier, 1983).
11. Young, op cit., pp. 15 f.
12. D. J. Sahas, *John of Damascus on Islam* (Leiden: Brill, 1972); M. S. Seale, *Muslim Theology* (London: 1964) and M. Nazir-Ali, *Frontiers in Muslim-Christian Encounter* (Oxford: Regnum, 1987) pp. 17 ff, 49.

13. See further, M.T. Clark (ed.), *An Aquinas Reader* (London: Hodder, 1972) pp. 15 ff.

14. In *Encounters and Clashes* (Rome: Pontifical Institute for the Study of Arabic and Islamics, 1984) pp. 161.

15. G. Warneck, *Protestant Missions* (Edinburgh: 1906); D. Bosch, *Transforming Mission* (New York: Orbis, 1992) pp. 239 ff; and M. Nazir-Ali, *From Everywhere to Everywhere* (London: Collins, 1990) pp. 42 ff.

16. See, for instance, S. Neill, *A History of Christian Missions* (London: Penguin, 1986) pp. 156 ff.

17. See further, J. N. Farquhar, *The Crown of Hinduism* (Oxford University Press, 1913). *See also* Michael Barnes, *Religions in Conversation* (London: Society for Promoting Christian Knowledge, 1989).

18. A. Atiya, *Eastern Christianity* (London: Methven, 1968); H. Hill (ed.), *Light from the East* (Toronto: Anglican Book Centre, 1988).

19. See, for example, J. C. England (ed.) *Living Theology of Asia* (London: SCM Press, 1981) pp. 191 ff.

20. Avril Powell, *Muslims and Missionaries in Pre-Mutiny India* (Richmond: Surrey, Curzon Press, 1993).

21. Hans Kung (ed.), *Christianity and the World Religions* (London: SCM Press, 1986).

22. *Nostra Aetate,* A. Flannery (ed.), *Documents of Vatican II* (New York: Costello, 1987) pp. 738 ff C.f. M. Barnes, *Religions in Conversation,* op cit., pp. 50 f.

23. *Guidelines on Religious Relations with the Jews* (CRRJ, 1974).

24. R. Coleman (ed.), *Resolutions of the Twelve Lambeth Conferences* (Toronto: Anglican Book Centre, 1992).

25. See further, *The Truth Shall Make You Free: The Lambeth Conference, 1988* (London: ACC, 1988), Resolutions 20 and 21 and Appendix 6. Also, the *World Council of Churches Guidelines on Dialogue* (Geneva: 1979) and *Council of Churches for Britain and Ireland, Christian Identity, Witness and Interfaith Dialogue* (London: 1991).

26. *Adisthan: Sacred Space* (Bangalore: BNCLC, 1993). See also *Communities and Buildings, A report of the Church of England's Inter-Faith Consultative Group* (London: CHP, 1996).

27. M. M. Thomas, *The Acknowledged Christ of the Indian Renaissance* (London: SCM Press, 1969).

28. K. Cragg, *To Meet and to Greet* (London: Epworth, 1992). See further C. Lamb, *A Call to Retrieval* (London: Grey Seal, 1997).

29. See the present writer's *Islam: A Christian Perspective* (Exeter: Paternoster, 1983) pp. 37, 86.

30. See A. Mar Thoma, *The Mar Thoma Church: Heritage and Mission,* op cit., pp. 2 f.

31. See further *Communities and Buildings,* op cit.

32. *In Many Mansions: Interfaith and Religious Intolerance* D. Cohn-Sherbok (ed.) (London: Canterbury Press) pp. 149 ff.

33. See further *Multi-faith Worship?* Interfaith Consultative Group (London: CHP, 1992).

34. J. A. Beckford and S. Gilliat, *The Church of England and Other Faiths in a Multi-Faith Society* (Coventry, 1996).

35. See further R. Hooker and C. Lamb, *Love the Stranger: Ministry in Multi-Faith Areas* (London: SPCK, 2nd ed., 1993).

36. *Christian Identity, Witness and Interfaith Dialogue,* op cit., pp. 5 f.

37. J. A. T. Robinson, *Truth is Two-Eyed* (London: SCM, 1979) p. 129 (quoting Sloane Coffin).

38. J. Goldingay, *Theological Diversity and the Authority of the Old Testament* (Grand Rapids: Eerdmans, 1987).

39. See further W. Brueggemann, *Trajectories in Old Testament Literature and the Sociology of Ancient Israel* (JBL, 1979) no. 98 pp. 161–85. Also M. H. Woudstra, *The Book of Joshua* (Grand Rapids: Eerdmans, 1981) pp. 37 f.

40. See G. von Rad's *Commentary on Genesis* (London: SCM, 1972) pp. 179 f.

41. See further J. Alberto Soggin, *The Prophet Amos* (London: SCM, 1987) pp. 142.

42. For an extended discussion see J. G. Baldwin, *Haggai, Zechariah and Malachi* (London: Tyndale, 1972) pp. 227 ff.

43. O. Kaiser, *Isaiah* 13–39 (London: SCM, 1974) pp. 111.

44. J. Stambaugh and D. Balch, *The Social World of the First Christians,* op cit., pp. 54 ff.

45. J. V. Taylor, *The Go-Between God* (London: SCM, 1972) pp. 42 f and 127 f.

46. G. Khodr, *Christianity in a Pluralistic World—The Economy of the Holy Spirit, in The Orthodox Church in the Ecumenical Movement* (C. G. Patelos ed.) (Geneva: World Council of Churches) pp. 297 ff.

47. *Dialogue and Proclamation,* Pontifical Council for Inter-Religious Dialogue (Rome: The Bulletin, May 1991); E. J. Sharpe, "The Goals of Inter-Religious Dialogue," in J. Hick (ed.), *Truth and Dialogue* (London: Society for Promoting Christian Knowledge, 1974) pp. 77 ff.

48. H. Kung (ed.) *Christianity and the World Religions* (London: SCM, 1993) pp. 440 ff. See also his Lambeth Interfaith Lecture, "World Politics and World Ethics as a Challenge to the Churches," November, 1994.

49. (Geneva: World Council of Churches, 1979) pp. 11. Such thinking is widespread in ecumenical documents and has, more recently, been reaffirmed by the Committee for Relations with People of Other Faiths of the Council of Churches for Britain and Ireland in Christian Identity—Witness and Interfaith Dialogue (London: CCBI, 1991).

50. M. Percy, *Words, Wonders and Power* (London: Society for Promoting Christian Knowledge, 1996) pp. 9 ff.

51. M. Nazir-Ali, *Mission and Dialogue* (London: Society for Promoting Christian Knowledge, 1995) pp. 85.

52. See, e.g. R. J. Rushdoony, *The Institutes of Biblical Law* (Phillipsburg, NJ: Presbyterian and Reformed, 1973). For a critique, see G. R. Fackre, *Ecumenical Faith in Evangelical Perspective* (Grand Rapids: Eerdmans, 1993).

PLENARY PRESENTATIONS

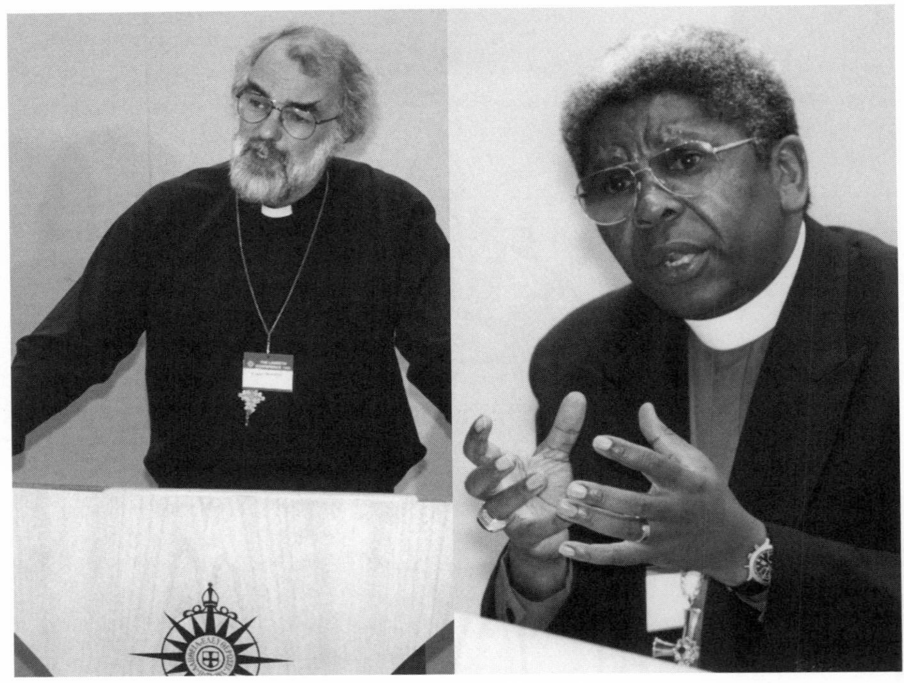

photos: *Anglican World*

The Rt Revd Rowan Williams (l) and the Most Revd Njongonkulu Ndungane (r)

The Bible, the World and the Church I
Dr David F. Ford, Regius Professor of Divinity, University of Cambridge, England

The Video

We have just been reading a living letter.

Five bishops and two spouses have spoken to us out of their biblical faith, their responsibilities in the Church, and their commitment to the flourishing of our world. We have seen in action what Bishop Tottenham called the living Church: people carrying on the living tradition in which the Bible lives.

Could anything more vividly picture biblical faith lived in the Church in this world of ours than Bishop Ochola from Uganda saying: 'My wife was killed by a landmine last May, and many of our clergy children have been abducted. They have done bad to us but we have to forgive in order to overcome the evil way of the world.'

What is at the heart of this faith? It is the vitality of the God who generates this forgiveness. This God also inspires remission of debt; reconciliation; generosity; vulnerable leadership; teaching and preaching; sexual morality; and the ordinary life of people in all our countries.

So this is what the Lambeth Conference is about: drawing on the 'new and certain life [of God]... the power which created the universe and raised Christ from the dead... the power which promises transformation of our world, our church and all of us gathered here'—as the Archbishop of Canterbury reminded us in his Presidential Address.

The Bible in the Conference

In the Conference Paul's Second Letter to the Corinthians is being studied every day in small groups, with face to face discussion and worship. This Presentation is happening now because the Archbishop of Canterbury and the Steering Committee also wanted the Bible to be the subject of a plenary session early in the Conference, so that the whole gathering could focus together on scripture in relation to the Church's life in the world. And the final plenary session will look again at how the Bible, the world and the Church have come together in this Conference.

We all know that drawing on the Bible for this Conference is not an easy matter. This is not surprising. The Bible is extraordinarily complex and multidimensional. How do we take account of dramatic narratives, of prophecies and radical questions, of passionate poetry and visions, of laws, teachings and letters, of cries and longings, of Abraham, Solomon, Ezekiel, Ruth, Job, Mary, Paul, and the angels of the seven churches? Who can do justice to them all? These writings had, as we know, a complex pre-history even before they became the Bible. Many were spoken, passed on, written down, edited, compiled, and interpreted over hundreds of years, and in many places and contexts.

And since the canon of scripture was fixed it has been translated and retranslated, and it has been interpreted generation after generation and all around the world. Those interpretations are not only in sermons, commentaries, teaching, creeds and academic studies. They are also in liturgies, prayers, hymns, music, art, architecture, poetry, novels, film, drama and the Panamanian dancing at our Opening Service in Canterbury Cathedral. The Bible lives in many ways, and is inevitably often immersed in contention and quarrelling.

How do we here approach the Bible?

It is taken for granted that we do not start from scratch. As members of this Conference most of us have studied the Bible over many years, we are aware of various academic approaches to it, and, most crucially, we have also lived in it, inhabited it, through worship, preaching, teaching and meditation. As Bishop Sykes said, 'We love God's word', and we do not ignore the problems this raises.

That inhabiting is a vital matter for the Bible in the Church. It is a book which is not so much to be applied, as if it were an instrument or a recipe, as to be lived in, indwelt—through worship, study and daily attentiveness.

The Bible in the Church is like a city we have lived in for a long time. Many of those who know this city well cannot say much about its history or the technicalities of its architecture. But they do know how to find their way about it, how to live a full life there, how to cope with many problems of this complex urban life, and how to pass on this vital understanding to family and strangers.

The Anglican tradition, which is so well portrayed in the Virginia Report that is being received by this Conference, is utterly clear about the primacy of God and of the worship of God which unites word and sacrament. The primary place of the Bible is therefore in the direct worship of God. In worship above all the living God of scripture meets us together and creates communion; the vitality of God finds us.

As the video we have just seen suggests, our chosen focus, 2 Corinthians, has immense potential here. Paul proclaims the utter primacy of God and the blessing of God; he sees Jesus Christ as central to the activity of God and the coming of God to the world; and he recognizes the horizon of the judgement of God within which his labour of discernment takes place.

So this plenary session asks this Conference, with all its complexity and diversity in theologies, countries of origin and concerns:

How do we move within the Biblical dynamic of God's life and blessing, in 'the light of the knowledge of the glory of God in the face of Jesus Christ' (2 Cor. 4.6)? And how is this formative and transformative in the Church for the world?

Making Moral Decisions
The Right Revd Rowan Williams
Bishop of Monmouth, Wales

What is it like to make a choice? The temptation we easily give way to is to think that it's always the same kind of thing; or that there's one kind of decision making that's serious and authentic, and all other kinds ought to be like this. In our modern climate, the tendency is to imagine that choices are made by something called the individual will, faced with a series of clear alternatives, as if we were standing in front of the supermarket shelf. There may still be disagreement about what the 'right' choice would be, but we'd know what making the choice was all about. Perhaps for some people the right choice would be the one that best expressed my own individual and independent preference: I'd be saying no to all attempts from outside to influence me or determine what I should do, so that my choice would really be mine. Or perhaps I'd be wondering which alternative was the one that best corresponded to a code of rules: somewhere there would be one thing I could do that would be in accord with the system, and the challenge would be to spot which one it was—though it might sometimes feel a bit like guessing which egg-cup had the coin under it in a game. But in any case the basic model would be much the same: the will looks hard at the range of options and settles for one.

But of course we don't spend all our lives in supermarkets. Some of us come from environments in which this kind of consumer choice is at best a remote dream, where it can sound like a cruel mockery to talk of such choices. And for the rest of us, the ones who do have the power to exercise such choices—is this model a sensible account of what it's like to make decisions in general?

Whom shall I marry? Shall I marry at all? Which charity shall I support this Christmas? Shall I resign from this political party, which is now committed to things I don't believe in—but is still better than the other parties in some ways? Should I become a vegetarian? Should I break the law and join an anti-government protest? Should I refuse to pay my taxes when I know they're partly used to buy weapons of mass destruction? How should I finish this poem or this novel? How should I finish my life if I know I'm dying? Think about these and choices like them. Each of them—even 'Which charity shall I support?'—is a decision that is coloured by the sort of person I am; the choice is not made by a will operating in the abstract, but by someone who is used to thinking and imagining in a certain way: someone who is the sort of person who finds an issue like this an issue of concern (another person might not be worried in the same way by the same question). And this means that an answer only in terms of the 'system', the catalogue of right answers, would help us not at all; what kind of code, we may well ask, would give us impersonally valid solutions to the dilemmas just listed? We believe that, in some contexts, we can say, 'You ought never to do that'; but there is no straightforward equivalent formula allowing us to say, 'You ought to do that'. As the Welsh philosopher Rush Rhees argues in an unpublished paper, telling someone else what they ought to do is as problematic as telling someone else what they want. There is a significant sense in which only I can answer the question, 'What ought I to do?' just as only I can answer, 'What do I want?'

But for me to answer either question is harder than at first it sounds. Rhees is careful to say that 'What ought I to do?' is drastically different from a question about my preferences, what I just happen to want (or think I want) at some specific moment. Herbert McCabe, a prominent British Catholic theologian and moralist, wrote many years ago—not without a touch of mischief—that 'ethics is entirely concerned with doing what you want'; going on to explain that our problem is that we live in a society, and indeed as part of a fallen humanity, that deceives us constantly about what we most deeply want. The point that both Rhees and McCabe are trying to make is emphatically not that ethics is a matter of the individual's likes or dislikes, but, on the contrary, that it is a difficult discovering of something about yourself, a discovering of what has already shaped the person you are and is moulding you in this or that direction. You might put it a bit differently by saying that you are trying to discover what is most 'natural' to you, though this begs too many questions for comfort. Rheas notes, very pertinently, that if I say I must discover something about myself in order to make certain kinds of decisions with honesty, this is not purely 'subjective': I am in pursuit of a truth that is not at my mercy, even if it is a truth about myself. And when the decision is made, I shall not at once know for certain that it is 'right'—in the sense that I might know if it were a matter of performing an action in accordance with certain rules: it may be that only as years pass shall I be able to assess something I have done as the 'natural', or truthful decision.

That too tells us something significant about our decision-making: we may in retrospect come to believe that—however difficult a decision seemed at the time—it was the only thing we could have done. We were less free to choose than we thought: or, we might say, we were more free (in a different sense) to do what was deepest in us. Some of our problems certainly arise from a very shallow idea of what freedom means, as if it were first and foremost a matter of consumer choice, being faced with a range of possibilities with no pressure to choose one rather than another. But we have to reckon with the freedom that comes in not being distracted from what we determine to do. The saint is often recognised by this freedom from distraction. They may not be—subjectively—eager to do what they are going to do, but they have a mature and direct discernment of what 'must' be done if they are to be faithful to the truth they acknowledge. And their confidence comes not from knowing a catalogue of recommended or proscribed actions, but from that knowledge of who or what they are that enables them to know what action will be an appropriate response to the truth of themselves and the world.

But it is time now to look harder at this matter of self-knowledge. We can easily misunderstand it of we think first and foremost of the self as a finished and self-contained reality, with its own fixed needs and dispositions. That, alas, is how the culture of the post-enlightenment world has more and more tended to see it. We romanticise the lonely self, we are fascinated by its pathos and its drama; we explore it in literature and psychological analysis, and treat its apparent requirements with reverence. None of this is wrong—though it may be risky and a courting of fantasy; but we have to think harder, in the 'Western' or North Atlantic world about the way the self is already shaped by the relations in which it stands. Long before we can have any intelligent account of our 'selfhood' in absolutely distinct terms, we already have identities we did not choose; others have entered into what we are—parents and neighbours, the inheritance of class and nation or tribe, all those around us who are speaking the language we are going to learn. To become a conscious self is not to say no to all this: that would be flatly impossible. It is to learn a way of making sense and communicating within an environment in which our options are already limited by what we have come into.

If this is so, self-knowledge is far more than lonely introspection. We discover who we are, in significant part, by meditating on the relations in which we already stand. We occupy a unique place in the whole network of human and other relations that makes up the world of language and culture; but that isn't at all the same as saying that we possess an identity that is fundamentally quite unlike that of others and uninvolved in the life of others—with its own given agenda. Thus the self-discovery we have been thinking about in the process of making certain kinds of decision is also a discovery of the world that shapes us. I spoke earlier of finding out what has shaped the person I now am; and this is always going to be more than the history of my own previous decisions.

And this is where we may begin to talk theologically (at last). How do Christians make moral decisions? In the same way as other people. That is to say, they don't automatically have more information about moral truth in the abstract than anyone else. What is different is the relations in which they are involved, relations that shape a particular kind of reaction to their environment and each other. If you want to say that they know more than other people, this can only be true in the sense that they are involved with more than others, with a larger reality, not that they have been given an extra set of instructions. The people of Israel in the Old Testament received the Law when God had already established relation with them, when they were already beginning to be a community bound by faithfulness to God and each other. The Law didn't come into a vacuum, but crystallises what has begun to exist through the action of God. When the Old Testament prophets announce God's judgement on the people, they don't primarily complain about the breaking of specific rules (though they can do this in some contexts) or about failure to live up to a moral ideal; they denounce those actions that signify a breaking of the covenant with God and so the breaking of the bonds of faithfulness that preserve Israel as a people to whom God has given a unique vocation—above all, actions such as idolatry and economic oppression. They denounce Israel for replacing the supremely active and transcendent God who brought them out of Egypt by local myths that will allow them to manage and contain the divine; and for creating or tolerating a social order that allows some among God's chosen nation to be enslaved by others because of poverty, and that is unworried by massive luxury and consumption, or sees its deepest safety in treaties with bloodthirsty superpowers. If you had asked one of the prophets about moral decision making, he might have responded (once you had explained what you meant to someone who wouldn't be starting with such categories) by saying, 'What we seek as we choose our path in life is what reflects the demands of the covenant, what is an appropriate response to the complete commitment of God to us. The Law tells me what kinds of action in themselves represent betrayal of God; but in deciding what, positively, I must do, I seek to show the character of the God who has called me through my people and its history'.

The truth sought by such a person would be a truth shared with the community of which they were part, the community that gave them their identity in a number of basic respects. When we turn to the New Testament, it is striking that the earliest attempts at Christian ethical thinking echo this so closely. We can watch St Paul in Romans 14 and 15 or I Corinthians 10 discussing what was in fact a profoundly serious dilemma for his converts: to abstain from meat sacrificed to pagan gods was regarded as one of the minimum requirements for fidelity to the true God by Jews of that age (as an aspect of the covenant with Noah, which was earlier and more comprehensive than the covenant made through Moses); and it had been reaffirmed by the most authoritative council we know of in the Church's first decades, the apostolic synod described in Acts 15. But the growing recognition that the sacrifice of Christ had put all the laws of ritual purity in question, combined with the practical complications of urban life in the Mediterranean cities, was obviously placing urban converts under strain. Paul is, it seems, fighting on two fronts at once. He warns, in Romans 14, of the risks of the 'pure', the ultra-conscientious, passing judgement on the less careful, at the same time as warning the less careful against causing pain to the scrupulous by flaunting their freedom in ways that provoke conflict or, worse, doubt. In the Corinthian text, he offers an even clearer theological rationale for his advice in arguing that any decision in this area should be guided by the priority of the other person's advantage and thus by the imperative of building the Body of Christ more securely. What will guide me is the need to show in my choices the character of the God who has called me and the character of the community I belong to; my God is a God whose concern for all is equal; my community is one in which all individual actions are measured by how securely they build up a pattern of selfless engagement with the interest of the other—which in itself (if we link it up to what else Paul has to say) is a manifestation of the completely costly directedness to the other that is shown in God's act in Christ.

So for the early Christian, as for the Jew, the self that must be discovered is a self already involved very specifically in this kind of community, in relation to this kind of God (the God of self-emptying). The goal of our decision-making is to show what God's selfless attention might mean in prosaic matters of everyday life—but also to show God's glory (look, for example, at Romans 15:7 or I Corinthian 10:31). What am I to do? I am to act in such a way that my action becomes something given into the life of the community and in such a way that what results is glory—the radiating, the visibility, of God's beauty in the world. The self that I am, the self that I have been made to be, is the self engaged by God in love and now in process of recreation through the community of Christ and the work of the Holy Spirit.

It's no use trying to answer the question about who I really am independently of this. There is no secret, detached, individual ego apart from these realities in which I am gracefully entangled. So perhaps the most important challenge to some of our conventional ways of talking about morality comes from the biblical principle that sees ethics as essentially part of our reflection on the nature of the Body of Christ.

What might this mean in more depth? The model of action which actively promotes the good of the other in the unqualified way depicted by Paul, and which reflects the self-emptying of God in Christ, presupposes that every action of the believer is in some sense designed as a gift to the Body. Gifts are, by definition, not what has been demanded, not the payment of a debt or the discharging of a definite duty. To borrow the terms of one of our most distinguished Anglican thinkers, John Milbank, a gift can't just be a 'repetition' of what's already there. At the same time, a gift has its place within a network of activities; it is prompted by a relationship and it affects that relationship and others; it may in its turn prompt further giving. But in this context it is important that a gift be the sort of thing that can be received, the sort of thing it makes sense to receive; something recognisable within the symbolic economy of the community, that speaks the language of the community. In the Christian context, what this means is that an action offered as gift to the life of the Body must be recognisable as an action that in some way or another manifests the character of the God who has called the community.

And this is where the pain and tension arises of Christian disagreement over moral questions. Decisions are made after some struggle and reflection, after some serious effort to discover what it means to be in Christ; they are made by people who are happy to make themselves accountable, in prayer and discussion and spiritual direction. Yet their decisions may be regarded by others as impossible to receive as a gift that speaks of Christ—by others who seek no less rigorously to become aware of who they are in Christ and who are equally concerned to be accountable for their Christian options. It would be simpler to resolve these matters if we were more abstract in our Christian learning and growing. But the truth is that we learn our faith in incarnate ways; Christ makes sense to us because of the specific Christian relationships in which we are involved—this community, this inspirational pastor or teacher, this experience of reading scripture with others. Of course (it ought not to need saying) such particularities are always challenged and summoned to move into the universal sphere, the catholic mind of the whole body. But this is what can be a struggle. If we learn our discipleship in specific contexts and relations, as we are bound to, our Christian identity will never be an abstract matter. We are slowly coming to acknowledge the role of cultural specificities in our Christian practice. But it's more than that, more than a matter of vague cultural relativity, let alone allowing the surrounding culture to dictate our priorities. It is that local Christian communities gradually and subtly come to take for granted slightly different things, to speak of God with a marked local accent. At a fairly simple level, we might think of different attitudes to the Christian use of alcohol in many African contexts as opposed to prevailing assumptions in the North Atlantic; or again we might think of differences as to who you might most immediately ask for help over matters of moral or even spiritual concern—a cleric or an elder in a community or a family council. At first sight, when you encounter a different 'accent', it can sound as though the whole of your Christian world is under attack or at least under question, precisely because no-one learns their Christianity without a local accent.

And it would be easy to resolve if we didn't care about Christian consistency if we didn't somehow share a conviction that the Church ought to speak coherently to its environment about discerning the difference between ways that lead to life and ways that lead to death. We want our faith to be more than just what we learn from those who are familiar and whom we instinctively trust, because we remember—or we should remember—how the faith moved out from the familiar territory of the Eastern Mediterranean to become 'naturalised' in other cultures. Tribalism is never enough. Yet when we begin to put our insights together, deep and sometimes agonising conflict appears. What are we to do?

So much is being said about issues of sexuality that I believe it is important to look seriously at some other matters also when we reflect on moral decision making and the character of our moral discernment. So let me take a different set of questions, one in which I have long been involved. I believe that it is impossible for a Christian to tolerate, let alone bless or even defend, the manufacture and retention of weapons of mass destruction by any political authority. And having said that I believe it is impossible, I at once have to recognise that Christians do it; not thoughtless, shallow, uninstructed Christians, but precisely those who make themselves accountable to the central truths of our faith in the ways I have described. I cannot at times believe that we are reading the same Bible; I cannot understand what it is that could conceivably speak of the nature of the Body of Christ in any defence of such strategy. But these are people I meet at the Lord's Table; I know they hear the scriptures I hear, and I am aware that they offer their discernment as a gift to the Body. At its most impressive, the kind of argument developed in defence of their stance reminds me that in a violent world the question of how we take responsibility for each other, how we avoid a bland and uncostly withdrawal from the realities of our environment, is not easily or quickly settled. In this argument, I hear something I need to hear something that, left to myself, I might not grasp. So I am left in perplexity. I cannot grasp how this reading of the Bible is possible; I want to go on arguing against it with all my powers, and I believe the Christian witness in the world is weakened by our failure to speak with one voice on the matter. Yet it seems I am forced to ask what there is in this position that I might recognise as a gift, as a showing of Christ.

It comes—for me—so near the edge of what I can make any sense of. I have to ask whether there is any point at which my inability to recognise anything of gift in another's policy, another's discernment, might make it a nonsense to pretend to stay in the same communion. It's finely balanced: I'm not a Mennonite or a Quaker. I can dimly see that the intention of my colleagues who see differently is also a kind of obedience, by their lights, to what we are all trying to look at. I see in them the signs of struggling with God's Word and with the nature of Christ's Body. Sixty years ago, Bonhoeffer and others broke the fragile communion of the German Protestant Churches over the issue of the anti-Jewish legislation of the Third Reich, convinced that this so cut at the heart of any imaginable notion of what Christ's Body might mean that it could only be empty to pretend that the same faith was still shared. How we get to such a recognition is perhaps harder than some enthusiasts imagine, and Bonhoeffer has some wise words about the dangers of deciding well in advance where the non-negotiable boundaries lie. Our task is rather to work at becoming a discerning community, ready to recognise a limit when it appears, a limit that will have a perfectly concrete and immediate character. For him, the limits are going to be set 'from outside': 'the boundaries are drawn arbitrarily by the world, which shuts itself off from the church by not hearing and believing' (*The Way to Freedom*, p.79). But of course the discernment of such boundaries has quite properly involved the Church in drawing boundaries 'from within', in the form of baptism and credal confession. To paraphrase Bonhoeffer: if we didn't have these markers of Christian identity, there would be no ground on which the Church as a community, a body with a common language, could discuss and discern a possible boundary being set by the world's refusal of the gospel.

The question is when and where the 'world' so invades the Church that the fundamental nature of the Church is destroyed; and to this question there is—by definition, Bonhoeffer would say—no general and abstract answer. Up to a certain point we struggle to keep the conversation alive, as long as we can recognise that our partners in this conversation are speaking the same language, wrestling with the same given data of faith. If I might put it in a formula that may sound too much like jargon, I suggest that what we are looking for in each other is the grammar of obedience: we watch to see if our partners take the same kind of time, sense that they are under the same sort of judgement or scrutiny, approach the issue with the same attempt to be dispossessed by the truth they are engaging with. This will not guarantee agreement; but it might explain why we should always first be hesitant and attentive to each other. Why might anyone think this might count as a gift of Christ to the Church? Well, to answer that I have a great deal of listening to do, even if my incomprehension remains.

And there is a further turn to this. When I reluctantly continue to share the Church's communion with someone whose moral judgement I deeply disagree with, I do so in the knowledge that for both of us part of the cost is that we have to sacrifice a straightforward confidence in our 'purity'. Being in the Body means that we are touched by one another's commitments and thus by one another's failures. If another Christian comes to a different conclusion and decides in different ways from myself, and if I can still recognise their discipline and practice as sufficiently like mine to sustain a conversation, this leaves my own decisions to some extent under question. I cannot have absolute subjective certainty that this is the only imaginable reading of the tradition; I need to keep my reflections under critical review. This, I must emphasise again, is not a form of relativism; it is a recognition of the element of putting oneself at risk that is involved in any serious decision making or any serious exercise of discernment (as any pastor or confessor will know). But this is only part of the implication of recognising the differences and risks of decision-making in the Body of Christ. If I conclude that my Christian brother or sister is deeply and damagingly mistaken in their decision, I accept for myself the brokenness in the Body that this entails. These are my wounds; just as the one who disagrees with me is wounded by what they consider my failure or even betrayal. So long as we still have a language in common and the 'grammar of obedience' in common, we have, I believe, to turn away from the temptation to seek the purity and assurance of a community speaking with only one voice and to embrace the reality of living in a communion that is fallible and divided. The communion's need for health and mercy is inseparable from my own need for health and mercy. To remain in communion is to remain in solidarity with those who I believe are wounded as well as wounding the Church, in the trust that in the Body of Christ the confronting of wounds is part of opening ourselves to healing.

This is hard to express. It may be clearer if we think for a moment of the past of our Church. In the Body of Christ, I am in communion with past Christians whom I regard as profoundly and damagingly in error—with those who justified slavery, torture or the execution of heretics on the basis of the same Bible as the one I read, who prayed probably more intensely than I ever shall. How do I relate to them? How much easier if I did not have to acknowledge that this is my community, the life I share; that these are consequences that may be drawn from the faith I hold along with them. I don't seek simply to condemn them but to stand alongside them in my own prayer, not knowing how, in the strange economy of the Body, their life and mine may work together for our common salvation. I don't think for a moment that they might be right on matters such as those I have mentioned. But I acknowledge that they 'knew' what their own concrete Christian communities taught them to know, just as I 'know' what I have learned in the same concrete and particular way. And when I stand in God's presence or at the Lord's Table, they are part of the company I belong to.

Living in the Body of Christ is, in fact, profoundly hard work. The modern liberal is embarrassed by belonging to a community whose history is infected by prejudice and cruelty (and so often tries to sanitise this history or silence it or distance themselves from it). The modern traditionalist is embarrassed by belonging to a community whose present is so muddled, secularised and fragmented (and longs for a renewed and purified Church where there are apparently clear rules for the making of moral decisions). If we cared less about the truth and objectivity of our moral commitments, this would matter infinitely less. But if I say that our moral decisions involve a risk, I don't mean by that to suggest that they have nothing to do with truth; they are risky precisely because we are trying to hear the truth—and to show the truth, the truth of God's character as uniquely revealed in Jesus Christ. And there are times when the risky decision called for is to recognise that we are no longer speaking the same language at all, no longer seeking to mean the same things, to symbolise or communicate the same vision of who God is. But that moment itself only emerges from the constantly self-critical struggle to find out who I am and who we are in and as the Body of Christ.

Can we then begin thinking about our ethical conflicts in terms of our understanding of the Body of Christ? The first implication, as I have suggested, is to do with how we actually decide what we are to do, what standard we appeal to. An ethic of the Body of Christ asks that we first examine how any proposed action or any proposed style or policy of action measures up to two concerns: how does it manifest the selfless holiness of God in Christ? And how can it serve as a gift that builds up the community called to show that holiness in its corporate life? What I have to discover as I try to form my mind and will is the nature of my pre-existing relation with God and with those others whom God has touched, with whom I share a life of listening for God and praising God. Self-discovery, yes; but the discovery of a self already shaped by these relations and these consequent responsibilities. And then, if I am serious about making a gift of what I do to the Body as a whole, I have to struggle to make sense of my decision in terms of the common language of the Faith, to demonstrate why this might be a way of speaking the language of the historic schema of Christian belief. This involves the processes of self-criticism and self-questioning in the presence of Scripture and tradition, as well as engagement with the wider community of believers. Equally, if I want to argue that something hitherto not problematic in Christian practice or discourse can no longer be regarded in this light, I have a comparable theological job in demonstrating why it cannot be a possible move on the basis of the shared commitments of the Church. I may understand at least in part why earlier generations considered slavery as compatible with the gospel or why they regarded any order of government other than monarchy to be incompatible with the gospel. I may thus see something of what Christ meant to them, and receive something of Christ from them, even as I conclude that they were dangerously deluded in their belief about what was involved in serving Christ.

I cannot escape the obligation of looking and listening for Christ in the acts of another Christian who is manifestly engaged, self-critically engaged, with the data of common belief and worship. But, as I have hinted, there are points when recognition fails. If someone no longer expressly brings their acts and projects before the criterion we look to together; if some one's conception of the Body of Christ is ultimately deficient, a conception only of a human society (that is, if they have no discernible commitment to the Risen Christ and the Spirit as active in the Church); if their actions systematically undermine the unconditionality of the gospel's offer (this was why justification by faith became the point of division for the Reformation churches, and why the anti-Jewish laws of the Third Reich became the point of division for the Confessing Church in 1935)—then the question arises of whether there is any reality left in maintaining communion. This is a serious matter, on which generalisations are useless. All we can do is be wary of self-dramatising, and of a broad-brush rhetoric about the abandonment of 'standards'. As the Confessing Church knew well, such a case requires detailed argument—and the sense also of a decision being forced, a limit being encountered, rather than a principle being enunciated in advance to legitimate divisions.

Unity at all costs is indeed not a Christian goal; our unity is 'Christ-shaped', or it is empty. Yet our first call, so long as we can think of ourselves as still speaking the same language, is to stay in engagement with those who decide differently. This, I have suggested, means living with the awareness that the Church, and I as part of it, share not only in grace but in failure; and thus staying alongside those on the 'other side', in the hope that we may still be exchanging gifts—the gift of Christ—in some ways, for one another's healing.

One of our problems, especially in our media-conscious age, is that we talk past each other and in each other's absence; and even when we speak face to face, it is often in a 'lock' of mutual suspicion and deep anxiety. But the Body of Christ requires more of us. It requires, I've suggested, staying alongside: which implies that the most profound service we can do for each other is to point to Christ; to turn from our confrontation in silence to the Christ we all try to look at; to say to one another, from time to time, hopefully and gently, 'Do you see that? This is how I see him; can you see too?' For many of us, the experience of ecumenical encounter is like this when it is doing its work. I wonder whether we are capable of a similar methodology when we divide over moral questions.

It does not preclude our saying—in the ecumenical context—'I can't see that; that sounds like error to me'; and in the ethical context, 'I can't see that; that sounds like sin to me'. It's what I want to say to those who defend certain kinds of defence policies, as I've noted. But what if I still have to reckon with my opponent's manifest commitment to the methods of attention to Christ in Word and worship? I risk an unresolvedness, which is not easy and may not be edifying, and trust that there may be light we can both acknowledge at some point.

And I am brought back to the fundamental question of where and who I am: a person moulded by a specific Christian community and its history and culture, for whom Christ has become real here with these people; but a person also committed, by my baptism, to belonging with Christian strangers (past, present and future—do we think often enough of our communion with Christians of the future? We are their tradition…). I am not sure what or how I can learn from them. They may frighten me by the difference of their priorities and their discernment. But because of where we all stand at the Lord's Table, in the Body, I have to listen to them and to struggle to make recognisable sense to them. If I have any grasp at all of what the life of the Body is about, I shall see to it that I spend time with them, doing nothing but sharing the contemplation of Christ. At the very least, it will refresh the only thing that can be a real and effective motive for the making of Christian moral decision: the vision of a living Lord whose glory I must strive to make visible.

International Debt I
Mr James Wolfensohn, President of the World Bank

It's rare that one gets two introductions that are so diverse. The introduction from the Archbishop of Canterbury was one of warmth and understanding and friendship in a joint endeavour to deal with the issues of poverty.

The other introduction was a 20-minute film which would have you believe that I rather like children dying, that I have no faith, that my interest is to collect debts, that I have no understanding of education or health, that I know nothing about the impact of payments imposed by governments, that would lead you think that I know nothing about the slums in Jamaica and know little about Tanzania. And all I can say to you is that I believe that each of those assertions is wrong.

It so happens that for the lady in the video who's not here is that two and half years ago I went to Seaview Gardens and Riverview City and unable to go in with police because they couldn't guarantee my security, I went in with Father Albert to the worst sections and segments of Jamaica and of Kingston.

And it was there that I met with the people, where I met with gang leaders who were armed, where I sat by the roadside, if I may say here, having a beer with some of the gang leaders, talking about how we could alleviate poverty, and where we as a Bank have put $200 million into Jamaica to try and make life more tolerable.

After an invitation to Tanzania I have met with President Mkapa more than once. We talked about issues of poverty. We talked about issues of corruption. Indeed the President was elected on a programme on corruption which arose out of a seminar which was given by the World Bank and where he took the seven items and used them as a basis for his election campaign. And where I had constant dialogue with him including about the issues of education where, contrary to the film, we are recommending communal financing of education, not individual financing, so that poor children can go to school.

I'm not angry about the film. I'm upset.

I'm upset because it paints a picture of our institution which is quite simply wrong. I work with 10,000 people in the Bank who are committed to poverty eradication. We do not get up every morning and think what we can do to ruin the world. I did not leave my business three years to come and work in the issue of poverty eradication and the issue of making the world freer, more equitable and safer for our children to be characterised as someone without a heart in a Christian Aid film. I find it difficult to take and very unattractive.

And maybe we should put out a film about what it is that we're doing. And maybe we should criticise NGOs and maybe we should criticise others who don't act. But we don't, and the reason we don't, ladies and gentlemen, is because we're too busy.

We have a problem not just of poor people in Jamaica, and not just of poor people in Tanzania and not just of poor people throughout Africa, we have a problem of three billion people in the world that live under $2 a day.

We have a problem of 500,000 children dying as a result of childbirth annually that could be saved. We have a problem of a billion, three hundred million people that do not have clean water. We have a problem of a billion and half people who do not have access to any form of house.

I have been to 83 countries. I do not go to the beaches as was suggested. I go to the slums and I go to the villages. And I yield the moral superiority to nobody. And nor do my people. I care. My people care. We work to try to make the world a better place.

And the characterisation of the Bank as the epicentre of debt problems which create all the problems of the world is neither fair nor correct.

I agree with the film on one thing, that there is a significant and overwhelming debt burden for many countries. I agree that if there was less debt we'd all be able to do much better in terms of poverty alleviation. I agree that if we were to alleviate debt there is a chance—a chance—that that money would go to education and health and the improvement of the lives of people.

I say "a chance," ladies and gentlemen, because it is a chance. I want to step back for two minutes and tell you what I do every day. What I think about every day. An organisation which is 54 years old, which is owned by 180 countries and which gets money from borrowing in the marketplace because the governments do not fund us more than the 20 million in equity that we have. Or the IDA funding which we give annually to poor countries, six billion a year, which we manage to get from those governments with enormous difficulty. Why do we get it from donor governments? Well, some governments give it voluntarily. Not all governments give it voluntarily.

And I spend an enormous amount of my time trying to convince governments that their responsibility to the poor of the world is not just to responsibility for charity, is not just a moral responsibility, but it is a responsibility to themselves in terms of interdependence with a world which has 4.7 billion people in development out of the total of 5.6 billion.

And I have troubles. I have troubles in the United States with Congress and I have troubles locally because you may or may not know that the level of overseas development assistance from those very governments in the last seven years has gone from 60 billion to 45 billion. That is not the World Bank. That is not the Monetary Fund. That is you. That is the people who are your parishioners and the governments you elect.

They are not giving the money for either debt relief or for overseas development assistance at the rate that it should be done, and people like me and in many cases people like you are giving pressure to the governments and should continue to give pressure to governments because they are the source of this Fund.

When I come to the office and I look at the range of issues to alleviate poverty, I reaffirm everyday that the issue which you are facing and that we are facing is the issue of poverty in a world which is inequitable and which, as I say, has three billion people under $2 a day.

Did you see headlines recently about Indonesia? Together with the Monetary Fund that is represented here, funds have been put together under their leadership to try and stabilise the financial situation in that country. Do you realise that 30 million more people are now living under a dollar a day than were living under a dollar a day five months ago? Thirty million more people. A total of 50 million people. And that 120 million people in that country of 200 million people are living under $2 a day? Some of those statistics get my attention. They get my attention in Korea, in Thailand, in Indonesia, in the Congo, in Bosnia, in Gaza.

I come in every day thinking of the proportions of this problem, which, ladies and gentlemen, are enormous.

We are losing the battle. It is not just the instances which you've seen here. I can tell you from my visit to over 80 countries harrowing stories, tear-jerking stories. Stories that I have seen with my own eyes that have caused me to break down. Not because I am a banker that has no feelings but because I do, I care. And so do my people.

And it is a grave injustice to put at the centre of the criticism the Bank and my friends at the Fund.

I have no doubt that we have made mistakes. It would be very difficult in the toughest business in the world, that of convincing governments not to be corrupt, to ensure that there is equity, to ensure that there is fair distribution of social resources, to ensure that rural communities get their fair share, and urban communities get their fair share. It would be impossible to wave a magic wand and cure that problem.

What I look at in terms of countries is that they should have some adequate form of government. That there should be fairness, and equity and representation. And in the last 10 years we've seen a move, happily, from a third of the countries in the world living under some form of democratic government to three-quarters.

But many of them are in transition. Many of them that were dictatorships do not have strong governments. Capacity is the limitation in many of these countries, and conditions of inequity and corruption are abounding everywhere.

I think about justice issues. If you don't have justice you cannot protect civil rights. If you don't have property rights you cannot have property. If you do not have bankruptcy laws, you cannot re-organise corporations and industry. If you don't have a functioning financial system you get the problems of Korea, Thailand and Indonesia.

These are not issues for professionals that are interested in macro theory. These are down-to-earth practical problems without which you cannot have alleviation of poverty.

The highest item on our agenda on which we're putting three billion dollars this year is education and health. If you want speeches on education and freedom on education, one of things you should do is come to the Bank. In terms of raising money I would love a dollar for every school I have visited under a tree in classrooms that do not have windows, no latrines, trying to bring new methods of education around the world.

We are the leaders in education, in health care. You talk about cholera. No one talks about River Blindness. We've eradicated River Blindness or nearly eradicated River Blindness in Africa for 30 million people in which by activities by the banks and by NGOs we have managed to clean up the water, kill the mosquitoes and restore people to arable land.

We're the major fighter in the world against AIDS. We're the major fighter in the world against malaria. None of that is in your film. None of it.

But look at the realities. We look beyond education and health and we say you cannot have a thriving country and poverty alleviation without communications.

President Museveni, whom we met, gives me lectures constantly on the issue or rural roads and rural communications and as you know, your Grace, you don't resist President Museveni. And so he is getting his rural roads. But it's not just in Uganda.

The issue of rural development in which in Africa 70 percent of the poor live, is a crucial element, an essential element in seeking to deal with the question of poverty and the one and a half billion people in the world that don't have clean water. We have a portfolio at the moment of 14 billion dollars in water projects. We are the leaders in trying to clean up water.

And whether it is the use of water for arable purposes, whether it is an initiative on the Nile that we're taking to the homes of the poor in which I have been to many times, seeing not just the water but the toilets which people are so proud to have because it gets rid of disease.

It is that that I worry about when I come to the Bank.

And I also worry about a broader range of issues. I worry about the rights of women. We are the leader in terms of putting money into issues of gender. I worry about the disabled. I'm worried about the elderly. I worry about social services.

And we at the Bank this year will put $18 billion into activities against poverty and with IDA another $6 billion a total of $24 billion going into projects of this nature.

That is why I get anxious. That is why I may sound defensive. I do not feel defensive. I feel that what we should get out of this Conference is not a sense of confrontation because I am doing many of the things that the Church wishes to do and should do itself. I am not putting out brochures or films about the inadequacies of the banks, or about the mistakes that have been made in various countries. About the lack of maximising your advantage in communities. I'm not putting out films about what you could do in terms of health and education and distribution because I don't believe in accusations. I believe in cooperation.

The reason that I have come to admire the Archbishop of Canterbury to such an enormous extent is that he has shown to me an openness to say, "We're both fighting poverty. Let's see what we can do together."

I urge you in your discussions not to focus on the Bank and Fund in terms of debt. And let me now deal in the last five or seven minutes with the debt issue. The debt issue is a very critical issue.

There is no doubt that in many countries the payment of debt is a principal reason that social and other services could not be provided. In the highly indebted countries the amount of debt is around $215 billion on present data, that is today's value of the future debt. In real terms it's probably between three and four hundred million dollars. But let's take the $215 billion figure that we've got. As the Archbishop said the total debt of the developing countries is 2 trillion dollars, 2 thousand billion dollars.

The HIPC initiative which was attacked interestingly by the representative of UNDP and I will refrain from commenting on those observations. The HIPC initiative was actually started by the Bank and the Fund. I visited Mali and I met a Moslem cleric wearing a white robe who said: "Mr. President, I must ask something about what you're doing. All I know is that with all the money coming in, my parishioners are not getting better off. He said I'm not an economist, but what I think happens is you put money in this pocket and you take it out of this pocket, and there's nothing left in the middle." And I thought that's a pretty good understanding of economics and I came back and decided to attack the unthinkable, the forgiveness of debt by the multi-lateral agencies along with the bi-laterals.

And let me just say to you that the 215 billion dollars, the World Bank has less than 9 percent. The Monetary Fund has less than five percent. Between 55 and 60 percent of that debt comes from individual creditor countries, many of whom are represented here. The United Kingdom, the United States, European countries have 55 percent of the debt and the rest are banks and various assorted creditors.

What we did in HIPC was to say let's attack that debt problem by getting every one together to try and relieve debt. We established one principle which is referred to here as "six years before you have to do it," before you begin the forgiveness. Again a fallacy.

Uganda was less than six months and indeed we started forms of debt relief as soon as we got the HIPC programme started, not in terms of the reduction of existing debt but helping to ensure that you do not accumulate additional debt. But that's by the way. Let us take the point in terms of this debt problem, as we have said that we're prepared to bear your full share. And we've done it on the basis of a very simple proposition, which you may understand in human terms.

First of all, most of you, although some may not, given this august body, most of you perhaps who are not in the Church, have some form of debt. You may have a credit card. You may have a mortgage. You have something with which you can live. It's part of life and there is a level where you can live with debt. That is part not only of an individual's life but it's also part of a country's life, so there is some sustainable level of debt.

The second thing to say is that if someone comes and says "Jim I'm in trouble. I've got all these debts and I can't send my kids to school and I can't do lots of things. Will you lend me or give me ten thousand dollars?" If the guy's a gambler or a womaniser or whatever or on drugs or has no sense of money the chances are you'll say, "Look I'll try and do something for your kids, but until you improve your ways I'm surely not going to give you $10 thousand because it will just go out the window."

Countries are the same. Corruption exists. Bad management exists. Inadequate assessment of social responsibilities exists. The purpose of the period of time so that countries can use their debt relief is simply for that purpose. It is to ensure there is sensible management and it can take six months, it can take two years, but at a point of three years a decision is taken and we start then in an alleviation programme. That is the reason for the time limit and it is not because of any reason to try and ruin the initiatives that we start.

And the last thing that I would like to say on this debt question is, insofar as the Bank is concerned and so far as the countries are concerned there is a limit to the extent that we and they are prepared to forgive debt.

But I have said on many occasions, and I repeat it to you now. If my owners who are the 180 countries want me to forgive debt, in the Bank which has a balance sheet of 150 billion dollars I can forgive 23 billion dollars. Why? Because the only capital I have is $23 billion. I have to borrow the other 130 billion so I can't repay the pension funds, the church commissioners, others who have invested I hope in World Bank bonds because they won't be very happy. I'm happy to do it, because I'm then out of business and I don't have to put up with these sort of videos.

The second thing I can do is to forgive the debt to IDA. IDA is the International Development Agency where we get funds from the governments given to us. We have 70 billion outstanding. I am very happy to forgive that but then how do I land further funds for countries to keep up IDA, unless the governments are prepared to fund it. And I can tell you from three years' experience, the governments are depending on the earnings of the Bank and the repayment of debt for between 50 and 60 percent for the funding of future IDA programmes.

Let me forgive it, let me forgive it. Get rid of the Bank. Get rid of IDA. Get rid of the fund. And then where are you? I have no objections. I'm 64 years old and I rather hanker for a little peace. But before you level your accusations against us, look at the economics. Look at the whether the government would give us additional moneys. Look at the realities of what you are suggesting.

If I forgive anything I have to halve the size of my balance sheet. I cannot do $75 billion worth of business because I cannot borrow the money because the money I can borrow depends on the capital I have. You would know that from simple 'Economics 1'. But I'll do it.

The more positive thing that I would suggest as I conclude is that instead of fighting each other and leveling accusations, we focus on the kids that are dying, and on the children who are not being educated and on the horrors of poverty together.

Together we can do a lot. We have expertise. You have expertise. We know a lot about development. You know a lot about people and communities. You have the best distribution system of any NGO in the world. You are out there in the field with your flocks, you and other religions. And we can both service the poor better together and we can influence governments better together and I believe we can make a real possibility that our children will have a better chance of living in peace and prosperity if we work together. That is the reason I flew over.

And I very much hope that in the subsequent discussions that you have on this subject you will recognise that I believe in God, secondly that I care and thirdly that our objectives are the same. Thank you.

International Debt II
The Most Revd Njongonkulu Ndungane
Archbishop of Cape Town

It is a great honour for me to have the privilege of leading the work of Section One of our Conference—Called to Full Humanity. I have come from Cape Town, the most beautiful city in the world—and I will tolerate no argument about that—at the southernmost tip of the continent of Africa.

Our continent is experiencing a new awakening in which its people are determined to take their destiny into their own hands. I come to this Conference as a Church leader whose jurisdiction covers South Africa, Mozambique, Lesotho, Swaziland, Namibia, Angola and the Island of St. Helena.

The Crisis of International Debt

All of the countries of my jurisdiction are affected and damaged by the crisis of international debt. It is a crisis of the first magnitude in the world. We here at the Lambeth Conference have a unique opportunity to address this crisis. I want to assert from the start, that this is not a financial crisis confined to Africa or Latin America. Countries that were until recently described as economic tigers, today find themselves toothless in the face of their own rising indebtedness. As we meet here in the peaceful surroundings of Canterbury, we should turn our minds to the struggling peoples of Indonesia, Thailand and South Korea. All are trying, and many are failing, to cope with the catastrophic consequences of reckless lending and borrowing and their nations' rising international debt. Severe indebtedness and turbulence in emerging markets are de-stabilising the economies of Russia and Brazil and impoverishing their people.

So let us be clear. The crisis of international debt that we are debating here today is not just a matter for the poorest countries. Nor is it a matter that only affects sovereign governments. It affects all of us everywhere, all of us who have become too dependent on credit cards. It affects those of us who struggle to repay loans to pay for the very roof over our heads,and those of us who live in fear of losing our jobs, and therefore our ability to repay our debts. Those of us in hock to the loan-sharks that prey on our poorest communities. We all live in the grip of an economy which encourages over-lending and over-borrowing. An economy which drives us relentlessly into debt. But the poorest, those with very little income to depend on, are not just in the grip of this economy. They are enslaved by it. They live in bondage to their creditors.

Our International Economy is Broken, is not Working

It is therefore opportune, that at this moment when the crisis of heavy indebtedness threatens to engulf not just the poorest countries, but also South East Asia, that we, a global communion of Anglicans, have gathered together in one place. We have an opportunity to address the issues faced by our broken world, to declare that our international economy is not working, to assert that it is not working because the global economy is not allowing God's people to achieve full humanity.

Jubilee and Release from Debt

We proclaim that the only economy that will work is one based on the beautiful vision of humanity which God in Jesus Christ came down to show us. It's a vision of love and grace, of compassion and equality. It's a vision, as the Archbishop of Canterbury reminded us, of the possibility of transformation and renewal. It's the vision of Jubilee, of the year of the Lord's favour, in which Jesus brings "good news to the poor", in which he proclaims "release to the captives and recovery of sight to the blind" and lets "the oppressed go free". It's a vision that releases the poor from the prison of indebtedness and dependent poverty. It's a vision where God's people have all that is necessary to live a human life—food, clothes, shelter, good health, and a chance to expand their opportunities through education.

But it's not just a vision for the poor. It's a vision for the rich too. It is a Jubilee for the powerful, who need a new vision of the proper use of riches, and the true value of all people. Through this vision we are called to our full humanity.

So let us rejoice in this gathering, and in the unique opportunity given to our Church, to proclaim our full humanity.

The Church Can Make the Poor Present

Let us remember above all that we are here to give a presence and a voice to the poor. The Church can make the poor present, can bring the voice of the poor into the room, can make the poor consequential. We are perhaps the only global, national and local institution that will give a presence and a voice to the poor, will defend the poor, will fight for the poor.

I have recently chaired the National Poverty hearings in South Africa—an initiative of the South African NGOs, the Human Rights Commission and the Commission on Gender Equality. We heard up to sixteen oral submissions each day of hearings over several weeks. During these hearings I came into contact in real terms with the many faces of poverty. For poverty is not just about low incomes; it is about loss of dignity, being treated as nothing, lack of access to basic needs. The faces of poverty can be found in women, children, the elderly and people with disability.

Listening to peoples' stories of survival amidst squalor and deprivation gave me a sense of the resilience of the human spirit. One story was of a boy aged 12 who looked after his brother of 7. They had no home and nothing to eat. They used dogs to sniff out food on a rubbish dump. And the older boy always made sure that his young brother had enough to eat before helping himself. One day they were found by a woman, who took them home, scrubbed them clean, gave them food and took them to a shelter, a modern version of the Good Samaritan. The young boy was like many others we heard. They spoke with the same voice: "We do not want hand-outs. We do not want charity. We have brains. We have hands—give us the skills. Give us the resources—give us the capacity to work out our own existence in order that we may have a fully human life."

Money Has More Powerful Rights than Human Rights

We live in a world in which it is not fashionable to speak of, or for, the poor. Political parties are proud to proclaim that they speak for business, enterprise and the free market; but embarrassed to speak of fairness, equity and justice for the poor. We live in a world where the human family has become increasingly divided—between the very few—those 20 per cent who take for themselves 83 per cent of the world's income, and the many who receive so little of the world's income. We live in a world in which money and riches are worshipped, a world in which money has more powerful rights than human rights. In a world governed and dominated by Mammon. Only amongst the faith communities does there seem to be any will to challenge Mammon, only in our churches, our synagogues, our mosques and our temples does it seem possible to envision a different world and a different economy.

The Church in all parts of the world, can make the poor present. I refer here not only to the Church in Africa, or Latin America, or South Asia; but also to the Church in America, in Canada and in Australia. For the world's broken economy is there too.

The Trickle-Up Effect

This is the opposite of trickle-down. This is the effect that defies gravity. It's the trickle-up effect. It's the transfer of wealth from the poor to the rich. And it's the same effect that lies at the heart of our broken international economy.

As this crisis has deepened, so poor indebted countries are increasingly transferring their tiny wealth to rich countries. They do this by paying interest, and then compound interest, on loans they have sometimes repaid several times over. They do this by using money given for aid and development to pay off debts. For every $1 that rich countries send to developing countries, $11 comes straight back in the form of repayment on debts owed to the richest countries.

So wealth is trickling up from the South to the North. Countries of the South find themselves giving away, virtually free, their precious commodities, like coffee, copper, tea and sugar. This is trickle-up, not trickle-down. This is a form of economics that denies us our humanity, rich and poor alike.

We are debating this issue today because trickle-up is not working, because enslaving the poor through debt is unjust, because each day the poorest countries transfer $717 million, to the richest creditor countries, because each year Africa transfer $12.5 billion to Western creditors.

Double Standards for Debtor Nations

Once in debt the poorest nations lose their economic independence, and have to bow to the advice of their Western creditors. Where Japanese farmers enjoy subsidies on their rice production, poor Zambian farmers are denied such support and protection. Where European textile industries are protected from competition, African and Indian textile industries are forced to compete with the richest nations. While South Africa's markets are opened up to the dumping of European beef, South African traders find there are no level playing fields in Europe. These are double standards—and their application is unjust.

Children in Debtor Nations Face Unlimited Liability

We are debating this issue, because these debts cannot be brought to an end. Because the children of indebted nations do not enjoy the protection of the law, or protection of the concept of "limited liability"—so that they are born into debt, and are forced to carry on paying the debts of previous generations. As we were reminded in our Section the other day, when a company like Eurotunnel gets into debt, and effectively becomes bankrupt, the burden of debt does not fall on the children of the managers or the workers. They are protected by the concept of limited liability. But not so for the children of the indebted nations. When Julius Nyerere asks, "shall we starve our children to pay our debts?"—the creditors, led by the IMF, say: "yes, you shall pay your debts before you feed your children. Yes, you shall prioritise repayment of debts over expenditure on health, education, clean water and sanitation. Yes, your children shall face unlimited liability for the debts of their governments."

Philippine Labor Exported to Help Pay Debts

We heard from our brothers, the bishops of the Philippines, that in their country, the repayment of debt has been written into the law—that 43 per cent of government revenues must be set aside by law, to repay debts, before the government can consider expenditure on other, more productive sectors. They told us of the human cost of this repayment. The human cost is the export of Philippine labour all over the world to earn hard currency to help repay their country's debts. So people of the Philippines can be found all over the world, being exploited as servants, sailors and prostitutes.

The law on debt repayment was, in effect, been written by Western creditors. Unlike the creditors of Eurotunnel, these creditors are not governed by a bankruptcy law, or by an independent receiver. They act as plaintiff, judge and jury when it comes to making loans, the repayment on debts owed to them, and the debt relief they might give. It is this unfairness, this imbalance, that lies at the heart of the injustice of international debt.

We are debating this issue because we are challenging "odious debts"—loans given to dictators like Marcos, Pinochet, Mobutu, or Suharto. These were loans made by Western governments that are quick to criticize corruption. Western governments that cannot see the mote in their own eye. The repayment of these odious loans and odious debts falls on the shoulders of their people once those corrupt dictators are dead and gone.

We must challenge the corruption at the heart of this lending and borrowing.

A Mediation Council

For all these reasons I am proposing a Mediation Council. We need a strict and neutral arbitration and monitoring process for agreeing debt relief for the poorest countries. Since 1982 and the Mexican crisis, there have been endless re-schedulings of debt; a growing number of initiatives by creditors—the Houston Terms, the Toronto Terms, the Trinidad Terms, the Naples Terms. Two years ago, creditors took another Initiative—the Heavily Indebted Poor Country (HIPC) Initiative. But these negotiations are dominated by creditors. We need an independent Mediation Council. More fairness. More transparency. More discipline The Mediation Council I propose would function as an international bankruptcy court. Its purpose would be to give countries that can no longer pay their debts, except at great human cost, a fresh start. The Court would call on local elites to explain why loans were taken out, how they were spent, and who benefited. It would call for greater transparency from Parliaments, both in the developed and developing world, and for have greater scrutiny of loan-giving and loan-taking. We would encourage governments to follow the example of Uganda, where no loans are sanctioned without the authority of Parliament.

The Mediation Council would challenge corruption, in both lending and borrowing. It would take evidence from experts. It would assess the country's capacity to pay. Above all it would seek to protect ordinary citizens of the country—men, women and children—from having to carry the full brunt of the country's debts and losses. Resources for human development—like clean water, sanitation, health provision and education—would have to be allocated before governments could divert funds to unproductive debt service.

Its purpose would be to give countries a fresh start—and by disciplining both debtors and creditors, to prevent countries from over-borrowing in the future, and to discourage lenders from making reckless loans. It would stop the poorest people of a country falling into a bottomless pit of debt in the future.

What I am saying here is that debt cancellation—far from being an unjustified and wasteful handout—is really an opportunity to return order, stability and discipline into the international financial system of lending and borrowing. It will make creditors think twice about making bad, and odious loans. It will make borrowers think twice about signing contracts for loans they know can only be repaid at a cost to the lives of their people.

The Heavily Indebted Poor Country Initiative (HIPC)

We recognise that the World Bank/IMF Initiative—HIPC the Heavily Indebted Poor Country Initiative, which offers limited debt relief to some of the poorest countries, was a historical break-through and a good beginning. But it is not enough. HIPC is a remedy for the lender's problems, for problems faced by the IMF, the World Bank and by OECD governments in getting their debts paid. It's not a remedy for the debtor nations. If you study the formulas it becomes clear that HIPC's present purpose is to make just enough adjustment in the debt burden, for debtor nations to repay their foreign creditors. That suits creditors, not debtors. But that should not surprise us, for it was designed by creditors, not by any independent body.

HIPC is not really going to be effective. We know, because we have seen how little it has done for a country in my region, Mozambique. Mozambique's debt relief under this scheme will make virtually no difference to her ability to reduce the appalling poverty in that country, which is still struggling to recover from the war fought against her people, by the apartheid regime and its allies.

Outright Cancellation Needed

Substantial and permanent debt relief, including outright cancellation, is a necessary and early part of the remedy which will enable these countries to thrive.

One consequence of changing the objective is that HIPC will cost the multilateral lenders more. At the moment the World Bank estimates that, by the time settlements are made, the total cost to all lenders in 1996 dollars will be only about $7.4 billion. Compare that to the $12.5 billion being promised to President Yeltsin. Compare that to the $60 billion that was found, almost overnight, to bail out bankers that had lent foolishly to South Korean private banks and companies. I know that the money for South East Asia is different, because it is new loans, to be repaid at high interest rates. Nevertheless, it is possible for the G8 countries to find such money, where there is the political will. What is lacking is the political will to find money to bail out the poorest people on earth.

Where We Stand Determines What We See

That is where we in the Anglican Communion and other faith communities come in. We know that where we stand determines what we see. In Section One, we have been hearing from each other about the effects of international debt on the poor and impoverished in our countries.

Observe, my brothers and sisters, that the world is waiting for a word of hope, of encouragement. The world longs to hear good news for the poor and recovery of sight to the blind, and to be told that now is the year of the Lord's favour. What will the Bishops give them? Bitter, distressing words of conflict over what it means to be human? The world already has more of that than it can bear.

What the bishops can give them is one voice, a voice strong in defence of the poor, bold in contradiction to the rule of money, and full of the love of God.

I invite you, my fellow bishops, to take this matter prayerfully into your own hearts. What is God calling you to say to the Church in your own country, to the members of your Diocese, and to the rich and powerful in your country?

In conclusion, the thought I would like to end on is that our primary concern must be for enhancement of the quality of peoples' lives. This can only be done by the mutual will and commitment of all institutions and interests, and by developing and developed countries together. And we need to recognise that what we are doing is constructing, not just a global economy, but a world community.

I have a dream. That we will celebrate the birth of Christ our Lord with a truly Jubilee celebration—by the cancellation of the unbearable debts of the poorest countries. That we will give a billion people a debt-free start. That the Third Millennium will be a new beginning for the Third World.

Help us realise that dream.

International Debt III
The Right Revd Peter Selby
Bishop of Worcester, England

I did not set out ever to be involved in the issue of debt. I set out on an exploration of the meaning of Jesus Christ for us today, and it was that exploration that led me to the issue of debt.

What upsets me is that we are not hearing from weak and helpless people asking for help from us. We are hearing about wasted resources, wasted capacities, undone expectations, disappointed hopes and all for a reason that I have come to understand is fundamentally an illusion for which human beings are being asked to sacrifice themselves.

My journey has also led me to a place of decision. I have to ask myself—and it's a very important question in relation to our modern economy—When is a debt a *debitum*, something that ought to be paid? Is there a debt for a tank that was used to attack your parents? Is that a debt? Is there a debt when what it is being used for is to pay interest rather than care for your children? Not, "Should this debt be forgiven?" Not, "should this debt be remitted?" But, "Is there a debt?"

I think that is the philosophical and the theological question to which this Conference is being required to give an answer.

My journey has also led me to ask questions about the institutions we have for dealing with debt. As you have heard here this afternoon, the World Bank and the International Monetary Fund are more than fifty years old. They were created to deal with problems of financial reconstruction after the Second World War, times that were utterly different. But we are relying on such institutions and the mechanisms of which they can avail themselves in this very different world, in a world where after the last twenty-five years, the amount of power and money has exploded in the world.

My journey has not only taken me to places of decision, decision about debt, decisions about the institutions that we have. I feel I have been taken on a journey to a temple. A temple now inhabited by a divinity that we all thought was an instrument, an instrument that served us. We have learned in these last twenty-five years that—by a series of progressive decisions—we serve it. It is, now, in charge. It has rights more than the rights of human beings. And, frankly, like many false divinities, it does not fail to ask for human sacrifice.

Earlier this week when we celebrated the liturgy of the Province of the West Indies and we were all invited to pray that we would not become slaves of money. When I hear the Church of the Province of the West Indies talking about slavery, I imagine that they do know what they are talking about. And if they see slavery as what money is about, not simply for the heavily indebted poor, but for us all, then we do well to pay attention. For what this divinity is doing is not simply impoverishing the poor, but fundamentally reshaping the lives of people along lines totally hostile to what we, as Christians, understand the shape of life is intended to be.

And to know that you do not have to travel very far, actually, you don't have to leave your own home. And I'm not keen that this Conference should pass any resolutions about world debt or demand that other people re-examine their activities and their beliefs if we don't re-examine them ourselves.

I have talked about some gloomy, sombre places but my journey has not only led me to sombre places. On May 16th it was my privilege in the company of a number of other bishops who are here to walk the line of human beings holding hands around the centre of the city of Birmingham as a call for Jubilee 2000, for the cancellation of unpayable debt. I saw in people's faces not just protest, not just outrage, but a glimpse of freedom, a glimpse of the possibility of a world in which the Christians' core teaching that we are justified by grace and not by debts and not controlled by money. I saw the faces of faith, of hope and of love.

When I look up now and I see the reference on the Compass Rose to the truth as our liberator, I want you to know that the call for Jubilee is now—as it was in the days of the Old Testament—primarily from our standpoint, a call to worship. It's a call to re-attune ourselves to the God we actually serve and away from the one that an absence of Jubilee and enslavement to debt requires us to serve.

It is to this call to worship that we are summoned. The details, the technicalities are things that will require our greatest ingenuity and our prayers. But let nobody use that as a reason not to attend to this primary call—a call for debt relief and cancellation. A call for debt release and cancellation is a call to worship, a call to honour the only truth which will set us free. Thank you.

A Youthful Spirit

The Right Revd David Moxon, Bishop of Waikato, New Zealand
The Right Revd Lindsay Urwin, Bishop of Horsham, England

In his presidential address at the beginning of the Lambeth Conference, the Archbishop of Canterbury placed a strong emphasis on encouraging the Communion in the work of renewal and mission. He stressed the importance of the 'local' in effective evangelisation, and affirmed and encouraged the Provinces to express worship and faith in ways which make connections with their own culture.

We are well used to speaking of the African, Asian or South American culture and in many communities we actively encourage and delight in the diversity of those who make up what Desmond Tutu delightfully describes as the 'rainbow people of God'. No one who shared in the daily pattern of eucharist and evening worship at the conference can have failed to marvel at the rich, even intriguing way various Provinces led us in the liturgy as they locally express it.

Within this cultural mix, there is also youth culture, which needs to be honoured and valued. In the discussions of the Section of the conference devoted to mission and evangelism, and within the small group charged with making a plenary presentation about youth ministry, we were refreshed and challenged by the sheer vitality and diversity of young people and their contribution to the life and witness of Anglicanism, whether it be as leaders in music ministry and worship in Paraguay, as evangelists in the diocese of Mt Kilimanjaro, or as part of the synodical process in South East Asia.

During the plenary presentation, participants experienced the giftedness of young people from a multi-ethnic parish in London's East End. This dynamic group exhausted the gathering with acrobatics and cheerleading. Led by the American-born wife of the parish priest, the young people not only learn skills and team-building, but also express their commitment by going out into the local community visiting and caring for older people. A small group drawn together for the Conference wrote and performed a dramatic presentation which told the tragic story of Dunblane, Scotland which saw the massacre of a group of children from a primary school, and the biblical story of the feeding of the five thousand. Youth leaders from the Holy Land and the Philippines shared their experiences as did five bishops.

As never before, young people are the 'connected generation'. Through the media and globally distributed entertainment, multi-national corporations and mass communications they are more aware of each other, and aspire not only to Western material values, but to be heard and participate in the formation of change in the life of our planet, and indeed, the life of the Church.

A video presentation during the plenary allowed young people from all over the Communion to speak to the bishops gathered in Canterbury. They testified to blessings received from their belonging, but also challenged the bishops to listen more to the voices of young people and address the pressing problems of our day, among them, drugs, poverty, debt and materialism. More than aware of the many voices and attractions offering alternatives to the Christian message, they called upon the bishops to help in focusing more energy in evangelising the unconnected young.

This call is reflected in a number of specific challenges made at the end of the plenary session. These echoed the resolutions prepared by the section and passed by the Conference, and so encouraged us to believe that they are timely and of the Lord. Specifically directed to the bishops, we pray that they will encourage a new wave of ministry among the young people of our world:

- We give thanks to God for the many young baptised believers throughout the world and especially those in our Anglican Communion.

- We salute those who encourage them in their faith and apostolic witness, and we salute young people themselves who in the midst of the many voices calling them have responded to the call of Jesus and are seeking to live his way.

- Brothers and sisters who have been called to walk in the footsteps of the apostles have a particular responsibility to nurture the young.

- Our Lord warned the first apostles not to hinder the young from finding a place in his arms, so we must look to our own lives, and the style of our ministry, to ensure that we are not guilty of such a grievous fault.

- Young people are attracted by lives of dedicated service, authentic holiness. In the western world with its cynicism about institutions we have a particular responsibility to minimise unnecessary bureaucracy and any inappropriate expressions of hierarchy which hinder the Church's vocation to reflect the service and humility of the Lord.

- While in some parts of the Communion resources are few, and communications difficult, there is more vibrancy and intimacy and more respect between young and old, but still bishops can seem remote and distant.

- We know the best evangelists of young people are likely to be other young people, yet there is an important place for the bishop in encouraging their Christian life and as a teacher of faith.

- The Holy Spirit is forever young. For those who live in the life of the Spirit, age need be no barrier to communication. The day of Pentecost transformed the possibilities for human relationships.

- Brothers and sisters, pray that God will grant you a youthfulness of spirit. Trust that generational and cultural difference is not a barrier in your own relationship with the young people in your diocese.

- We challenge you to meet with young people in your diocese. Although you may have priests or laity who work on your behalf with young people, we believe that it is likely that the structures seem to young people to separate you from them.

- Specifically we ask you to return to your diocese resolved to meet personally with a group of young people to listen to them to ask them about their hopes and vision and the way they understand the world, to pray with them, to open the scriptures with them, to break bread within six months of this conference, and that should become a regular part of your ministry.

- Such a resolution is a small beginning and yet if you respond it would mean that across the globe some tens of thousands of young people would be in direct touch with their bishops. It will involve a reorientating of your time and priorities. If you are too busy to meet with your young people, then brothers and sisters, you are indeed too busy.

- Your meetings should work towards a plan of action which allows young people to minister in appropriate ways, to participate in worship and contribute to the proclamation of Christ and to social action. It should also include the development of a voice of young people in the consultative process which leads to decision making in your diocese.

- We also suggest a network of people throughout the Communion committed to assisting bishops and others as they seek to understand and speak to the young people and their culture.

- The gift of episcopal ordination brings us many joys and weighty responsibilities. We believe that a renewed emphasis on our ministry with young people will enrich our lives, and theirs, and it is vital to the development of a world which better reflects the values of God's kingdom.

The Archbishop's address spoke of the dangers of loveless evangelism, when he quoted the Welsh poet R.S. Thomas. 'They listened to one preaching the unique Gospel of love, but our eyes never met.'

May the God-given eyes of the bishops meet with the God-given eyes of the young people! In such a meeting we shall surely be given a new vision for our life together, and in the strength of the ever youthful Spirit, be given the energy to proclaim the Gospel afresh in our generation.

The Bible, the World and the Church II
Dr David F. Ford, Regius Professor of Divinity, University of Cambridge, England

Introduction

How can we begin to do justice to the event that we have been taking part in during the past three weeks?

In the rest of this session there will be this address, two more videos, and a discussion between four bishops. This presentation has been drawn together by the group responsible for the earlier plenary presentation on The Bible, the World and the Church, and that group has been working closely with Angela Tilby and her video team. It is an interim attempt to tell something of what we have been experiencing here, and the guideline has been to try to understand the significance of the Conference in relation to the Bible, the world and the Church.

Realising Anglican Identity

Clearly it will take a long time after we leave here to discern what has been most significant in the events and experiences of the Conference. I think many of us feel overwhelmed in various ways. Yet at this stage we can perhaps agree with Brother Sam who said in the video that what he saw happening was a communion coming to life—and coming to life is not always easy. One bishop put it like this: 'These weeks at Lambeth have in many ways been a realisation, an embodiment, of Anglican identity'. So it is worth thinking a little about what has been happening here, in order to see better who we are.

Worship and the Bible

Asking people the question: Where has the Conference been most at home together? the same answer has been given time and again: we have been most at home in worship and in the small Bible study groups. The worship has never been without the Bible at its centre, and the Bible studies have been embraced by worship. And at the heart of both Bible and worship is what perhaps unites us most strongly: the desire for God, that hunger and thirst for God which is itself a gift of God.

Careful attentiveness to worship and scripture shapes our living. The reports of Bible study groups have been full of moving accounts of ordinary and extraordinary Christian living—and also Christian dying. The depth and intensity of life in and for Jesus Christ in our Communion, and the suffering which that can bring, has come home to us in first-hand accounts from all over the world. Through all this we have found others—and even ourselves—more transparent to God. As we have inhabited the Bible and our tradition of worship—which has now developed in so many ways around the whole world—we have recognized our family likenesses and realised the strength of our bonds—bonds which in Christ are stronger than death. 'It is my family that has been martyred', said a Canadian bishop.

Word and sacrament, our worship and our Bible studies: these have not on the whole made headlines, but they have been at the heart of the Conference, and they underlie the ability of the Conference to face sensitive issues in sections and in plenaries. How much easier it would have been if we had only come together to worship and discuss Second Corinthians!

Neither ruthless nor lawless: the ministry of unity

But this is a gathering of bishops with responsibilities in church and society in every continent. So besides word and sacrament, there is another feature of Anglican identity being embodied at Lambeth: our characteristic form of Church order. How has that been seen here?

The Anglican Church has always existed in a context of rival ways of ordering the Church. On the one hand, it has refused an authoritarian solution, where one central authority holds out the attractive possibility of getting rid of the messiness of debate, dissent and rival interpretations of scripture by pronouncements and commands which permit no argument. On the other hand, it has resisted the sort of diversity in which everyone is free to do according to their own interpretation and conscience, and no one is ultimately accountable to anyone else.

Anglicanism has characteristically tried to hold these tendencies in tension and develop good order. We in this Conference have welcomed the Virginia Report which explores the next stage in this complex order at the international level—and it is important that it is an order which takes account of united Churches and Churches in communion. It is an order which combines freedom of Christian conscience with mutual accountability, and in doing so we believe ourselves to be in continuity with the New Testament and the early Church.

And the practice of the Conference bears this out. We have been constantly trying to reconcile, on the one hand, diversity, independence and different contexts, with, on the other hand, mutual accountability, which calls bishops, who have a special ministry of unity, to be answerable to one another and for one another in the body of Christ. And as Bishop Rowan Williams reminded us, the body of Christ includes the communion of saints, past and future.

I think there is one place where this ministry of unity and reconciliation among bishops has been most evident. The subsection on human sexuality under Bishop Duncan Buchanan wrestled together on behalf of all of us. They have given us a sign of our agony but also of hope. Yet it is also clearly unfinished business. I suppose one question is: Can the Communion as a whole have something of that quality of engagement which has been possible here under special circumstances?

Mission in the world

We have glimpsed the potential of the episcopal ministry of unity and reconciliation in other ways too, especially in the Conference's concern to relate the Gospel to life in the world. Anglicanism is naturally deeply interwoven in the world, incarnational. That is why we struggle to interpret the Bible for our own situations, and why our Church is shaped in ways appropriate to life in different places. And we try, not only to discern what is right, but to find ways of making it effective in the life of the world. Our proclamation of the Gospel cannot be separated from what we do in ordinary life, including how we act for justice and human welfare. That was the remarkable achievement of those concerned with international debt and relations with Islam, and in the strong concern for full visible unity with other Christians.

Lively thought

Besides worship, the Bible, the shape of our common life, and our mission in the world, there has been a further characteristic mark of our Anglican identity here. There has been lively thought. Our tradition calls us to lively thought. Passionate seeking after wisdom is encouraged by the Bible. The love of God involves using all our minds.

It was clear that the Conference was never going to be able to read the solution to all our problems straight out of scripture. We have had to pay attention to a wide range of sources, we have listened to each other and to the past, and we have paid attention to what is going on in the world. And all of that is fully in conformity with what goes on in scripture. So there has been a great deal of hard thinking.

One member of the subsection on human sexuality said this about his experience: 'The processes of labour, clarification, taking responsibility for positions one was opposed to, paying attention to the demands of the truth of scripture and of pastoral concern: that had to be experienced to be believed.' There we see scripture, tradition, the world and reason together, internally related to each other within a worshipping community. And it has been a process of mutual accountability that has tried to avoid both authoritarianism and turning our backs on each other.

From many comments, I suspect that a major frustration has been the pressure of time and the short-cuts that have had to be taken. Lively thinking takes time and deep concentration if it is to arrive at wisdom. If we look at Church history and see how long it has often taken to come to a common mind, and then at how long it has taken for positions to be received or rejected by the Church, three weeks is the blink of an eye.

Beyond Lambeth 1998: The Next Ten Years

If those elements I have been discussing describe something of the reality of Anglican identity being lived out here, the obvious question on the final day of the Conference is: How are things to be taken further beyond Lambeth? Clearly the reports and resolutions offer substantial answers to that question. But I am sure all of us come away with some key thoughts, distillations of the significance of Lambeth 1998 for the future. I have been collecting and discussing some of these thoughts around the Conference, and I offer you just four of them now.

Worship and the circulation of news

The first is about our worship. Clearly our continuing prayer has to be: Come, Holy Spirit!—Come on ourselves and on our whole Communion. We are always together in worship before God. But how can our prayer for each other be specific? This marvellous document, the Anglican Cycle of Prayer, has been received by all of us. Now there are faces to many of the dioceses. Many of us have found here either that we were simply ignorant of each other's Churches and situations or that, especially in the case of those Churches more exposed to the media, we had a picture which had to be changed considerably when we heard some inside stories. CNN and the BBC have not given the same impression as that of a local bishop. Paul's letters and visits were inseparable from his prayer for his Churches and theirs for him. Perhaps we can find ways of sustaining something of the circulation of news and understanding which we have had here. As well as overcoming ignorance and stereotypes, that might inspire our intercession for each other. I suspect that this circulation of specific prayer might well be the most important single preparation for the next Lambeth Conference.

The Bible and the Communion of Saints

The second thought is about the interpretation of scripture. Many questions have been raised about this, and most of them still remain on the table. I had a moving letter from a Brazilian member of the conference asking a basic question: how can personal, prayerful reading of scripture be related to social and political interpretation and also to scholarly, academic interpretation?

After the next video we will hear four bishops discussing some basic points about scripture. In preparation for that I want to take what Bishop Rowan Williams said about us making moral decisions in the communion of saints, and extend it to make the point that we also read the Bible in the communion of saints, with whom we also worship. Their understandings of the Bible may have much to teach us before the next Lambeth Conference. One such understanding, the statement on scripture produced by the 1958 Lambeth Conference, will be the starting-point for the bishops' discussion in a few minutes.

The circulation of money

The third thought was suggested by studying parts of 2 Corinthians chapters 8 and 9 in a Bible study group. That is one of the great biblical statements about the generosity of God and how the circulation of wealth and the strengthening of communion go together. In the Archbishop of Canterbury's address to the spouses he told the story of his visit to southern Sudan in 1993. He saw the conditions there and wanted to do something. But there were no Anglican Communion resources he could call on, and he said that he realised then: 'We are not yet a Communion.' He announced the setting up of a fund, the Anglican Investment Agency, to help share money between Provinces and enable response to urgent need. In 2 Corinthians chapters 8 and 9 we have studied this, and several resolutions in the Conference make the same point. It may be that the sincerity of our demands that creditor nations should forgive unpayable debts will be judged—not least by God—by the scale of generosity our Communion practises. The last part of the Conference resolution on debt challenges dioceses to give 0.7 per cent of their total income for development programmes. What if that were to happen—in poorer as well as richer dioceses?

Networks and the circulation of theology

The fourth thought arises out of a bishop's remark that a remarkable number of resolutions mention networks. There are networks to do with dioceses, provinces, regions, communications of all sorts, migrants and refugees, ecology, mission and evangelism, cities, young people, ecumenism, inter-faith matters, and prayer. I am sure this is no accident. Networks serve circulation within the communion and beyond it, and they fit very well with a Church order which resists both authoritarianism and fragmentation. They are essential to a dynamic unity. They are perhaps the most significant transformation in the shaping of our

Communion life. Between Lambeth Conferences they might be seen as the extended embodiment of what we have experienced here in concentrated form.

And these networks place great demands on our capacity for lively and godly thought. As a theologian I am deeply concerned about how we develop centres and networks of those whose vocation is to love God with all their minds in the sphere of studying, teaching and researching. Whatever else we say about our young people, education is vital for them. It is vital for clergy too. And for laity. We will fail them all if they do not receive a Christian faith which invites them into a mind-stretching and lifelong pursuit of truth and wisdom.

Conclusion: Beauty and the Face of God

The Feast of the Transfiguration has long been my favourite feast. This week's celebration has undoubtedly been the most memorable ever. I see the statement of war responsibility by the Holy Catholic Church of Japan, distributed to us during the service, as perhaps the most important document to have come before the Conference.

Then Susan Cole-King told us in her sermon about her father, Bishop Leonard Wilson, and his experience of torture. She quoted him saying about one occasion in his cell: 'Something of God's indestructible beauty was conveyed to my tortured mind.' And she described the transformation of one of his torturers whom her father later confirmed: 'He looked gentle and peaceful'.

When Jean Vanier told us about the passion for unity that gripped him as he lived with those he called 'some of the weakest and least presentable members of the body of Christ', people with severe mental disabilities, he spoke of the revelation of their beauty. He said that the struggle for unity means loss, pain and effort, walking with the crucified Jesus, but that at the heart of unity is the mutual revelation of our beauty: frailty and suffering becoming transparent to God.

I hope that we too, in our struggles and suffering, have been able to glimpse in our Communion something of the love of God, something of the beauty of gentleness, of peace, of reconciliation—the indestructible beauty of God and the beauty of each other in God's image, so that we know there is nothing that 'is able to separate us from the love of God in Christ Jesus our Lord' (Romans 8:39).

And as we prepare for the closing service the question that was put at the end of the first plenary session after the drama of Jacob's wrestling at Jabbok Ford still stands. The question is: Can we now say to each other, as Jacob said to Esau in Genesis 33:10: 'To see your face is like seeing the face of God'?

RESOLUTIONS

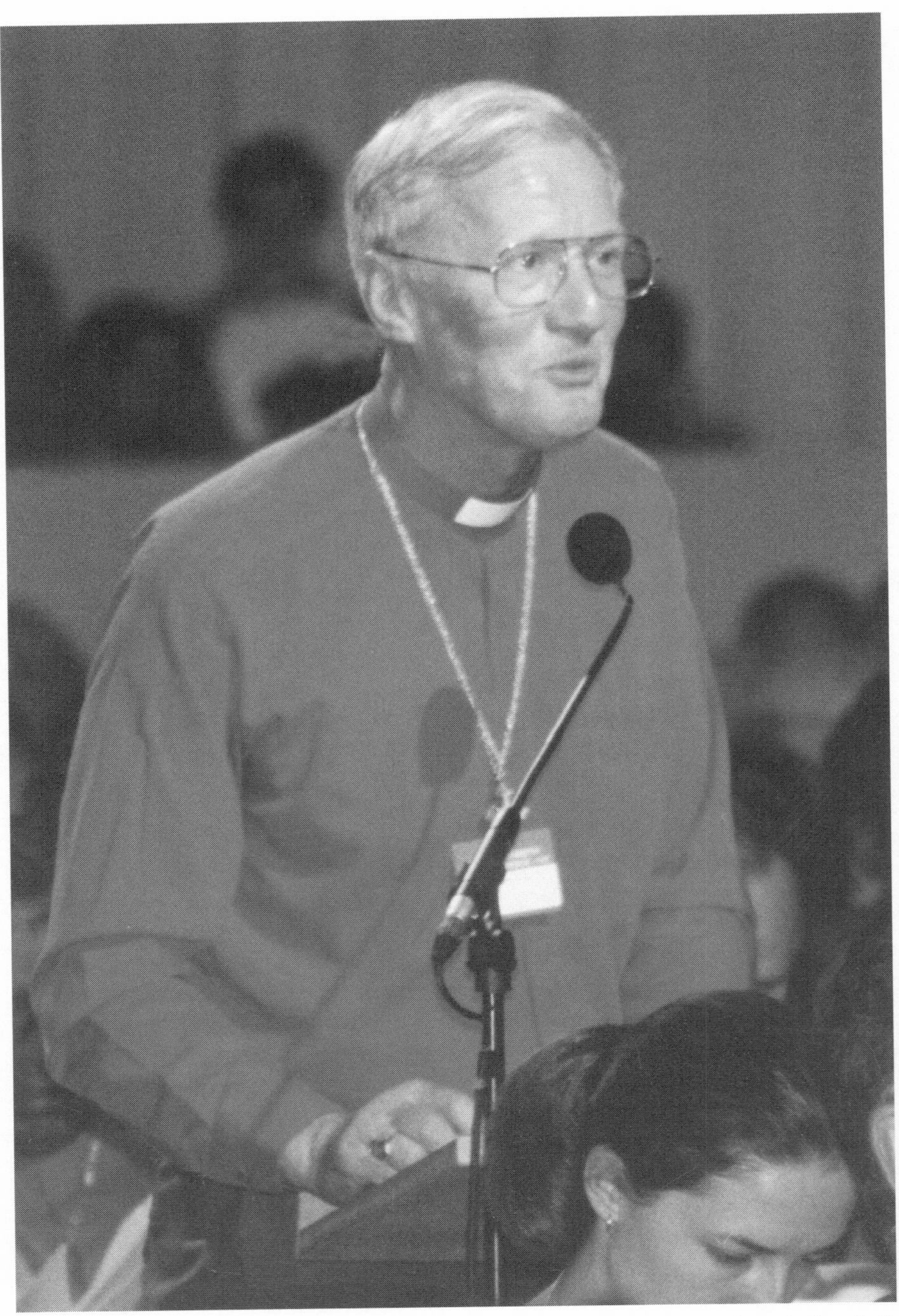

photo: *Anglican World*

Debating the issues.

Section I Resolutions

Resolution 1.1

Affirmation and Adoption of the United Nations Universal Declaration of Human Rights

On the fiftieth anniversary of its proclamation in December of 1948, this Conference:

(a) resolves that its members urge compliance with the United Nations Universal Declaration of Human Rights by the nations in which our various member Churches are located, and all others over whom we may exercise any influence; and

(b) urges extension of the provisions of the Declaration to refugees, uprooted and displaced persons who may be forced by the circumstances of their lives to live among them.

Resolution 1.2

Religious Freedom and Tolerance

This Conference, meeting at the dawn of the new millennium calls upon:

(c) all faith communities, especially the Christian Church, to acknowledge our responsibility to mobilise our spiritual, moral and material resources to promote and protect as absolute rights, each person's freedom of thought, conscience and religion;

(d) the leaders of all faith communities to encourage their congregations to reach out to people of all faiths among whom they live, move and have their being, in order to proclaim and demonstrate the imperatives of love and reconciliation as a pre-condition for a new world community; and

(e) governments of all the nations our Churches represent to strive for creation of just and free conditions for people of all religions to practice their beliefs "either alone or in community with others and in public or private, to manifest his (or her) religion or belief in teaching, practice, worship and observance." (UN Universal Declaration of Human Rights, Article 18)

Resolution 1.3

Justice for Women and Children

This Conference resolves that each member Church represented make an intentional effort to:

(a) discover the ways in which women and children are affected and victimised by the political, economic, educational, cultural or religious systems in which they live;

(b) discover the ways in which criminal elements of our societies victimise and exploit women and children;

(c) praise the level of public (local, national and international) awareness about such abuses; and

(d) work toward eliminating abuses through co-operation with existing groups such as ECPAT (End Child Prostitution in Asian Tourism) and the monitoring agencies of the United Nations and World Council of Churches.

Resolution 1.4

A Faithful Response to Aggression and War

This Conference:

(a) abhors the evil of war;

(b) repudiates and condemns the use of violence for settling religious, economic, cultural or political disputes;

(c) encourages the use of peacekeeping forces to prevent or forestall the escalation of conflicts, and to assist in their resolution;

(d) repudiates and condemns the use of terrorism;

(e) decries the production and proliferation of arms;

(f) commits its members to prayer, mediation, and any active, non-violent means we can employ to end current conflicts and wars and to prevent others; and

(g) urges the nations represented by our Churches and all those on whom we have any influence whatsoever to join us in this endeavour.

Resolution 1.5

Uprooted and Displaced Persons

This Conference commits its members to:

(a) promote within the Anglican Communion and beyond a greater awareness of the plight of uprooted and forcibly displaced persons, including indigenous peoples, and the causes of such disruption, including Third World Debt, religious conflict, economic deprivation, political oppression and environmental degradation;

(b) recognise the plight of our brothers and sisters who are victims of forcible displacement, and encourage prayer, worship, and study experiences which express the solidarity of the Anglican Communion with uprooted and forcibly displaced persons, commending the exceptional courage and leadership exercised on behalf of these victims by certain members of the Anglican Communion;

(c) encourage effective advocacy on behalf of uprooted and forcibly displaced persons within the Anglican Communion as well as within its individual provinces;

(d) promote greater co-operation within the Anglican Communion on behalf of uprooted and displaced persons by designating contact persons in every province whose responsibility would be to develop and guide this work, and by increasing the commitment of personal and material resources for this work*; and

(e) encourage the revitalisation of the Anglican Communion International Migrant and Refugee Network to assist the Anglican Communion in this work.

*All primates were requested to do this as expressed in Anglican Consultative Council 6, 1984. See Proceedings of ACC-6, Appendix 3, page 26, 1984.

Resolution 1.6

The Plight of the People of Northern and Western Uganda

This Conference, acknowledging the appalling suffering of the people of Northern and Western Uganda as a result of continued civil war waged by rebels, known as LRA and ADF (Lord's Resistance Army and Allied Democratic Forces), backed by forces from outside Uganda:

(a) urges the government of Uganda to continue to engage in a process which will lead to reconciliation, peace and justice. The process must include the Governments of Sudan and the Democratic Republic of Congo, representatives of the Rebels, representatives of main Religious bodies and Opinion Leaders of the areas affected; and

(b) calls upon the Anglican Consultative Council and appeals to the United Nations organisations to assist in bringing about a quick settlement of this armed conflict.

Resolution 1.7

The Plight of the People of the Sudan, Rwanda and Burundi

This Conference, expressing its horror at the human disaster in the Sudan, Rwanda and Burundi, urges that:

(a) the Episcopal Church of the Sudan be encouraged to establish a dynamic network of reciprocal communications with government bodies, sympathetic Muslims, and non-governmental organisations, including the All Africa Conference of Churches, the Anglican Consultative Council, the Primates of the Anglican Communion, the Anglican Observer at the UN, and specialised organs of the UN and the UN Security Council;

(b) the member Churches of the Anglican Communion find ways to help provide technology, equipment, vehicles and administrative support in order to make publicity about and response to the urgent situation in the Sudan, Rwanda and Burundi possible;

(c) the member Churches of the Anglican Communion contribute as generously as possible of expertise, labour, money, and material goods to aid in necessary rebuilding of these nations on all levels; and

(d) help be sought from existing organisations whose mission is the facilitation of peace processes, to aid in the implementation of this resolution.

Resolution 1.8

Creation

This Conference:

(a) reaffirms the Biblical vision of Creation according to which:
Creation is a web of inter-dependent relationships bound together in the

Covenant which God, the Holy Trinity has established with the whole earth and every living being.

(i) the divine Spirit is sacramentally present in Creation, which is therefore to be treated with reverence, respect, and gratitude;

(ii) human beings are both co-partners with the rest of Creation and living bridges between heaven and earth, with responsibility to make personal and corporate sacrifices for the common good of all Creation;

(iii) the redemptive purpose of God in Jesus Christ extends to the whole of Creation.

(b) recognises:

(i) that unless human beings take responsibility for caring for the earth, the consequences will be catastrophic because of:

- overpopulation
- unsustainable levels of consumption by the rich
- poor quality and shortage of water
- air pollution
- eroded and impoverished soil
- forest destruction
- plant and animal extinction;

(ii) that the loss of natural habitats is a direct cause of genocide amongst millions of indigenous peoples and is causing the extinction of thousands of plant and animal species. Unbridled capitalism, selfishness and greed cannot continue to be allowed to pollute, exploit and destroy what remains of the earth's indigenous habitats;

(iii) that the future of human beings and all life on earth hangs in balance as a consequence of the present unjust economic structures, the injustice existing between the rich and the poor, the continuing exploitation of the natural environment and the threat of nuclear self-destruction;

(iv) that the servant-hood to God's creation is becoming the most important responsibility facing humankind and that we should work together with people of all faiths in the implementation of our responsibilities;

(v) that we as Christians have a God given mandate to care for, look after and protect God's creation.

(c) prays in the Spirit of Jesus Christ:

(i) for widespread conversion and spiritual renewal in order that human beings will be restored to a relationship of harmony with the rest of Creation and that this relationship may be informed by the principles of justice and the integrity of every living being, so that self centred greed is overcome; and

(ii) for the recovery of the Sabbath principle, as part of the redemption of time and the restoration of the divinely intended rhythms of life.

Resolution 1.9

Ecology

This Conference:

(a) calls upon all ecumenical partners and other faith communities, governments and transnational companies:

(i) to work for sustainable society in a sustainable world;

(ii) to recognise the dignity and rights of all people and the sanctity of all life, especially the rights of future generations;

(iii) to ensure the responsible use and re-cycling of natural resources;

(iv) to bring about economic reforms which will establish a just and fair trading system both for people and for the environment.

(b) calls upon the United Nations to incorporate the right of future generations to a sustainable future in the Universal Declaration of Human Rights.

(c) asks the Joint Standing Committee of the ACC and the Primates to consider the appointment of a co-ordinator of an inter-national ecological network within the Anglican Communion, who would:

(i) work in co-operation with other ecumenical and interfaith agencies;

(ii) be funded through and responsible to the Anglican Consultative Council;

(iii) support those engaged in grass-roots environmental initiatives;

(iv) gather and disseminate data and information on environmental issues so that the Church can play an informed role in lobbying for ecological justice in both the public and private sectors; and

(v) contribute to the development of environmental educational programmes for use in the training of Christian leaders.

Resolution 1.10

Human Sexuality

This Conference:

(a) commends to the Church the subsection report on human sexuality;

(b) in view of the teaching of Scripture, upholds faithfulness in marriage between a man and a woman in lifelong union, and believes that abstinence is right for those who are not called to marriage;

(c) recognises that there are among us persons who experience themselves as having a homosexual orientation. Many of these are members of the Church and are seeking the pastoral care, moral direction of the Church, and God's transforming power for the living of their lives and the ordering of relationships. We commit ourselves to listen to the experience of homosexual persons and we wish to assure them that they are loved by God and that all baptised, believing and faithful persons, regardless of sexual orientation, are full members of the Body of Christ;

(d) while rejecting homosexual practice as incompatible with Scripture, calls on all our people to minister pastorally and sensitively to all irrespective of sexual orientation and to condemn irrational fear of homosexuals, violence within marriage and any trivialisation and commercialisation of sex;

(e) cannot advise the legitimising or blessing of same sex unions nor ordaining those involved in same gender unions;

(f) requests the Primates and the ACC to establish a means of monitoring the work done on the subject of human sexuality in the Communion and to share statements and resources among us;

(g) notes the significance of the Kuala Lumpur Statement on Human Sexuality and the concerns expressed in resolutions IV.26, V.1, V.10, V.23 and V.35 on the authority of Scripture in matters of marriage and sexuality and asks the Primates and the ACC to include them in their monitoring process.

Note: The resolutions referred to in subsection (g) of this resolution are set out in the appendix to this document.

Resolution 1.11

Nuclear Weapons

This Conference resolves to call upon our respective governments and through our governments, the United Nations and other instruments:

(a) to urge all nations to agree by treaty to stop the production, testing, stock-piling and usage of nuclear weapons; and

(b) to press for an international mandate for all member states to prohibit nuclear warfare.

Resolution 1.12

Calling for a Commission on Technology and Ethics

This Conference:

(a) calls for consideration to be given to the establishment of a commission through the Anglican Consultative Council to track technological developments, to reflect on them theologically and ethically, and to inform bishops and other church leaders as to what is taking place; and

(b) recommends that such a commission does its work and informs the church of it, as far as possible, through e-mail and Internet conferencing.

Resolution 1.13

Landmines

This Conference—attended both by bishops from nations suffering acutely from the presence of landmines in their own countries (Mrs. Winifred Ochola, wife of the Bishop of Kitgum in Uganda, was killed by a landmine), and by bishops from countries that have profited from the manufacture of landmines:

(a) calls upon all signatory Governments to ratify the Ottawa Convention (without exceptions) at the earliest possible date;

(b) calls upon all non-signatory Governments to sign and ratify the Ottawa Convention at the earliest possible date;

(c) calls upon all Governments to provide extra funding for mine clearance programmes, and to encourage the development of appropriate technology for mine clearance initiatives; and

(d) calls upon international organisations, all Governments, community level and local Government initiatives, NGOs, Churches and other people of good will, to engage in educational work on this issue, provide practical assistance to alleviate the consequences of the massive level of previous landmine deployment, and engage in practical schemes to reintegrate landmine survivors and their families into their communities.

Resolution 1.14

Euthanasia

In the light of current debate and proposals for the legalisation of euthanasia in several countries, this Conference:

(a) affirms that life is God-given and has intrinsic sanctity, significance and worth;

(b) defines euthanasia as the act by which one person intentionally causes or assists in causing the death of another who is terminally or seriously ill in order to end the other's pain and suffering;

(c) resolves that euthanasia, as precisely defined, is neither compatible with the Christian faith nor should be permitted in civil legislation;

(d) distinguishes between euthanasia and withholding, withdrawing, declining or terminating excessive medical treatment and intervention, all of which may be consonant with Christian faith in enabling a person to die with dignity. When a person is in a permanent vegetative state, to sustain him or her with artificial nutrition and hydration may be seen as constituting medical intervention; and

(e) commends the Section Report on euthanasia as a suitable introduction for study of such matters in all Provinces of the Communion.

Resolution 1.15

International Debt and Economic Justice

Recognising the importance and urgency of issues of international debt and economic justice, this Conference adopts the following statement:

(a) We see the issues of international debt and economic justice in the light of our belief in creation: God has created a world in which we are bound together in a common humanity in which each person has equal dignity and value. God has generously given to the nations immense resources which are to be held in trust and used for the wellbeing of all and also offered us in Christ Jesus liberation from all that which destroys healthy human life—a pattern of giving which God desires all to follow. The healthy pattern for relationships is of mutual giving and receiving of God's gifts. Borrowing has its place only in as much as it releases growth for human well being. When we ignore this pattern, money becomes a force that destroys human community and God's creation. The vast expansion in the power and quantity of money in recent decades, the huge increase in borrowing among rich and poor alike, the damaging material and spiritual consequences to many, bear testimony to this destructive force.

(b) Mindful of the work done by the political leaders, finance ministers, church leaders and people of creditor nations, we welcome the framework provided by the historic Heavily Indebted Poor Country Initiative (HIPC) of 1996. We particularly welcome the approach of bringing all creditors together to agree upon debt relief, and the emphasis on debtor participation. We welcome unilateral initiatives taken by governments to write off loans owed to Overseas Development Departments; and initiatives by governments and international financial institutions to strengthen the capacity of debtor nations to manage debt portfolios, and to co-operate together. We welcome the commitment by leaders of the eight most powerful economies (the G8—Canada, France, Germany, Italy, Japan, Russia, UK, US) in Birmingham May 1998; to consider withholding future taxpayer-subsidised loans intended for arms sales and other unproductive purposes.

(c) While recognising these achievements, we wish to assert that these measures do not as yet provide sufficient release for the hundreds of millions of people whose governments are diverting scarce resources away from health, education, sanitation and clean water.

(d) We have heard and understood the point of view that poverty reduction is more important than debt cancellation. Nevertheless we conclude that substantial debt relief, including cancellation of unpayable debts of the poorest nations under an independent, fair and transparent process, is a necessary, while not sufficient precondition for freeing these nations, and their people, from the hopeless downward spiral of poverty. Because indebted nations lose their autonomy to international creditors, debt cancellation is also a necessary step if these governments are to be given the dignity, autonomy and independence essential to the growth and development of democracy. We believe it vital that all of God's people should participate, on the basis of equal dignity, in the fruits of our interdependent world.

(e) The need for debt relief for the poorest nations is urgent. Children are dying, and societies are unravelling under the burden of debt. We call for negotiations to be speeded up so that the poorest nations may benefit from such cancellation by the birth of the new millennium. The imagination of many, rich and poor alike, has already been gripped by the stark simplicity of this call. This response can be harnessed for the cause of development.

(f) We call on the political, corporate and church leaders and people of creditor nations:

- to accept equal dignity for debtor nations in negotiations over loan agreements and debt relief;
- to ensure that the legislatures of lending nations are given the power to scrutinise taxpayer-subsidised loans; and to devise methods of regular legislative scrutiny that hold to account government-financed creditors, including the multilateral financial institutions, for lending decisions;
- to introduce into the design of international financial systems mechanisms that will impose discipline on lenders, introduce accountability for bad lending, and challenge corruption effectively, thus preventing future recurrence of debt crises;
- to introduce measures that will enable debtor nations to trade fairly with creditor nations. Fair trade will allow debtor nations to develop their domestic economies. This in turn will allow them to pay those debts which remain and to take their rightful place in the community of nations;
- to ensure that each of the OECD (Organisation for Economic Co-operation and Development) nations honour their commitment to set aside 0.7% of their GNP for international development.

(g) We call on political leaders, finance ministers, corporate executives traditional rulers, religious leaders and the people of debtor nation:

- to accept independent, fair and transparent procedures for agreeing debt relief;

- to adopt much greater transparency and accountability in the process of accepting and agreeing new loans, particularly as the burden of repayment of these loans will fall largely on the poorest; ensuring proper scrutiny by legislative bodies of each loan contract signed by government ministers;

- to adopt measures for disciplining elected and paid government officials who corruptly divert public funds and also to provide for sanctions against private sector persons and bodies who act corruptly; and

- to adopt measures for ensuring that additional resources generated from debt relief are allocated to projects that genuinely benefit the poorest sections of society.

(h) We call on political leaders and finance ministers in both creditor and debtor nations to develop, in a spirit of partnership, a new, independent, open and transparent forum for the negotiation and agreement of debt relief for highly indebted nations. In particular, we call on them to co-operate with the United Nations in the establishment of a Mediation Council whose purpose would be:

- to respond to appeals from debtor nations unable to service their debts, except at great human cost;

- to identify those debts that are odious, and therefore not to be considered as debts;

- to assess, independently and fairly, the assets and liabilities of indebted nations;

- to determine that debt repayments are set at levels which prioritise basic human development needs over the demands of creditors;

- to hold to account those in authority in borrowing countries for the way in which loans have been spent;

- to hold to account those in authority in lending nations for the nature of their lending decisions;

• to demand repayment of public funds corruptly diverted to private accounts;

• to consult widely over local development needs and the country's capacity to pay; and

• to ensure, through public monitoring and evaluation, that any additional resources made available from debt relief are allocated to projects that genuinely benefit the poor.

(i) We commit ourselves to supporting the objectives outlined above, in the countries in which we live, whether they are debtor nations or creditor nations. We will seek also to highlight the moral and theological implications. Mindful of the wisdom held within other faith traditions we shall work with them, as we are able, to examine the issues of credit and debit and the nature of the economy.

(j) Furthermore we call upon members of the Communion to co-operate with other people of faith in programmes of education and advocacy within our dioceses, so that we may help to raise public awareness of these vital economic issues that impact so deeply on the daily lives of the poor.

(k) Finally, we call on all Primates to challenge their dioceses to fund international development programmes, recognised by provinces, at a level of at least 0.7% of annual total diocesan income.

Section II Resolutions

Resolution II.1

The Theological Foundations of Mission

This Conference:

(a) believing that all our mission springs from the action and self-revelation of God in Jesus Christ and that without this foundation, we can give no form or content to our proclamation and can expect no transforming effect from it,

(b) resolves to:

(i) reaffirm our faith in the doctrines of the Nicene Creed as the basis of what is to be believed, lived and proclaimed by the churches of the Anglican Communion;

(ii) accept the imperative character of our call to mission and evangelism as grounded in the very nature of the God who is revealed to us.

Resolution II.2

Mission and The Structures of The Anglican Communion

This Conference:

(a) acknowledges gratefully the contribution of many individuals and agencies in serving, stimulating and assessing the work of the Decade of Evangelism, particularly the Church of Nigeria for its gift to the whole church through its role in initially resourcing the involvement of the ACC in this work by seconding Canon Dr Cyril Okorocha, the continuing contribution of MISSIO whose report we received, and whose work we wish to see continued, and the Anglican Communion Global Conference on Dynamic Evangelism beyond 2000 at Kanuga in 1995;

(b) believes that the instruments of unity (the Archbishop of Canterbury; the Lambeth Conference; the ACC and the Primates meeting) need to work much more closely together and to review their mutual accountability (e.g. the ACC and the Primates meetings should consider communicating the results of their deliberations to all Bishops in the Communion);

(c) considers that regional networks and relationships should be reinforced and encouraged and their work be fully publicised;

(d) requests that the Joint Standing Committee of the Primates' Meeting and the ACC consider, as a matter of urgency, how the budget and staffing of the Communion's official networks might come to reflect the priorities of mission and evangelism;

(e) similarly requests that the MISSIO be instructed to study further the most efficient and effective ways for the Communion to extend mission and evangelism (e.g. through a mission and evangelism secretary);

(f) suggests that the Lambeth Conference be recognised as a significant consultative body which gives a sense of unity and direction to the whole Communion, which should receive and review reports of significant activities carried out as part of the work of the Communion.

Resolution II.3

Companion Dioceses

This Conference:

(a) notes that many dioceses in the Anglican Communion have not as yet been able to establish companion relationships;

(b) believes that the time has come for significant new initiatives in encouraging all dioceses to develop companion relationships across provincial boundaries, as part of the process of developing the cross-cultural nature of the communion;

(c) believes that, in addition to the structures administered through Partners in World Mission and the Anglican Communion Office, dioceses should be encouraged to take initiatives in sharing information, contact and exchange;

(d) accordingly resolves that each diocese of the Communion should, by the time of the next Lambeth Conference, have made a serious effort to identify one or more dioceses as a companion, in formal and informal ways.

Resolution II.4

Christianity in Islamic Societies

This Conference:

(a) mindful of the great changes that have taken place in many nations with a substantial or majority Islamic population, and recognising the historic contributions of Islamic culture to ideals of justice and religious freedom;

(b) views with concern the tendency in some such nations to seek to enforce a legal code which encourages discrimination against, or harassment of, non-Muslim communities;

(c) resolves:

(i) respectfully to request the governments of nations where such discriminations and harassment are common occurrences to affirm their commitment to religious liberty; and

(ii) to pledge ourselves to support the civil and religious liberties of Muslims in situations where they are in a minority, and to combat prejudice and ignorance about Islam among Christians and others.

Resolution II.5

Iran

This resolution was not moved in view of a similar resolution from the South Asia/Middle East Region.

Resolution II.6

Future Priorities in Mission

As it moves towards the third millennium of Christian Witness, this conference;

(a) gives thanks to God for all the experience so far of the Decade of Evangelism, noting the Testimonies and challenges from many churches across the Communion;

(b) repents of our failures in mission and evangelism;

(c) expresses its determination that the impetus should not be lost. The primary task of every bishop, diocese and congregation in the Anglican Communion is to share in and show the love of God in Jesus Christ—by worship, by the proclamation to everyone of the gospel of salvation through Christ, through the announcing of good news to the poor and the continuing effort to witness to God's Kingdom and God's justice in act and word and to do so in partnership with Christians of all traditions;

(d) urges that priority should be given at every level in our Communion to reaching out to those who have never heard, or never responded to the gospel of Christ, and to reawakening those whose love has grown cold;

(e) commits ourselves to call our people to be a transforming church by practising Jubilee, and by sharing financial resources between different regions of our Communion, not only for responding to crises or disasters, but to enable local initiatives in outreach, service and evangelism;

(f) commits ourselves in the light of what is said in this Report to work to transform the dioceses we serve into communities that share fully at every level in the mission of God.

Resolution II.7

Urbanisation

This Conference:

(a) calls upon the Member Churches of the Anglican Communion to address the processes of urbanisation across the world, both in our cities and all other communities;

(b) asks our Member Churches to give urgent attention to "Living and Proclaiming the Good News" in our cities so that all that destroys our full humanity is being challenged, the socially excluded are being welcomed and the poor are hearing the Good News (Matthew 11:5); and in order to assist this priority in mission

(c) resolves:

(i) to ask the Anglican Consultative Council to give support to the formation of an Anglican Urban Network to share information and experience on urbanisation and urban mission;

(ii) to support the establishment of a "Faith in an Urban World" Commission, after due consultation with ecumenical bodies.

Resolution II.8

Young People

This Conference:

(a) recognises and celebrates the dynamic work of God among young people, and their infinite value in the human family. They are for us in the church, as they were for Jesus, signs of the Kingdom of God among us. Their presence and ministry in the church is essential for the whole family of God to be complete. As adults, we confess with deep humility and sorrow that the adult world has created children of war, children abused by neglect and sexual exploitation, and children who are victims of aggressive advertising. In joyful obedience to God we reaffirm our apostolic commitment to all young people everywhere.

(b) recognises the faithful and creative work by many Church members in ministry with children both within and beyond the church's borders.

(c) resolves, for the health and welfare of the whole Church:

(i) that the bishops of the Anglican communion will commit themselves, and will give leadership in their diocese, to ensure that the church is a safe, healthy, and spiritually enriching community for children and young people;

(ii) that the bishops will give more attention to the furtherance of ministry to children as a recognition of their importance to God and as a foundation for all future ministry;

(iii) that the bishops will commit themselves to give significant time over the next twelve months to meet with young people in their dioceses, listening to them, praying with them searching the Scriptures and breaking bread together with them, and providing ways for them to be trained in leadership skills and to exercise that leadership in the life and mission of the church;

(iv) that such meetings should open out into attempts to meet and hear young people who have not yet been touched by the Gospel;

(v) that teams of adults and young people in as many congregations as possible be trained for holistic ministry to young people outside the church, so as to speak of God's love in Christ in ways that can be heard, and that Christian young people be equipped, in the power of the Holy Spirit, for service in Church and Community;

(vi) that young people should be helped to find or maintain their spiritual home in the Anglican Church by giving particular attention to matters of liturgy including the use of music and silence; and

(vii) that urgent consideration be given to how best international Anglican networks of young people may be strengthened and serviced by the structures of the Communion.

Section III Resolutions

Resolution III.1

The Bible

This Conference, recognising the need in our Communion for fuller agreement on how to interpret and apply the message of the Bible in a world of rapid change and widespread cultural interaction:

(a) reaffirms the primary authority of the Scriptures, according to their testimony and supported by our own historic formularies;

(b) urges that the Biblical text should be handled respectfully, coherently, and consistently, building upon our best traditions and scholarship believing that the Scriptural revelation must continue to illuminate, challenge and transform cultures, structures, and ways of thinking, especially those that predominate today;

(c) invites our provinces, as we open ourselves afresh to a vision of a Church full of the Word and full of the Spirit, to promote at every level biblical study programmes which can inform and nourish the life of dioceses, congregations, seminaries, communities, and members of all ages.

Resolution III.2

The Unity of the Anglican Communion

This Conference, committed to maintaining the overall unity of the Anglican Communion, including the unity of each diocese under the jurisdiction of the diocesan bishop:

(a) believes such unity is essential to the overall effectiveness of the Church's mission to bring the Gospel of Christ to all people;

(b) for the purpose of maintaining this unity, calls upon the provinces of the Communion to uphold the principle of 'Open Reception' as it relates to the ordination of women to the priesthood as indicated by the Eames Commission; noting that "reception is a long and spiritual process" (Grindrod Report);

(c) in particular calls upon the provinces of the Communion to affirm that those who dissent from, as well as those who assent to, the ordination of women to the priesthood and eiscopate are both loyal Anglicans;

(d) therefore calls upon the Provinces of the Communion to make such provision, including appropriate episcopal ministry, as will enable them to live in the highest degree of Communion possible, recognising that there is and should be no compulsion on any bishop in matters concerning ordination or licensing;

(e) also affirms that "although some of the means by which communion is expressed may be strained or broken, there is a need for courtesy, tolerance, mutual respect, and prayer for one another, and we confirm that our desire to know or be with one another, remains binding on us as Christians" (Eames, p.119).

Resolution III.3

Subsidiarity

This Conference affirms the principle of "subsidiarity," articulated in Chapter 4, *The Virginia Report,* which provides that "a central authority should have a subsidiary function, performing only those tasks which cannot be performed at a more immediate or local level", provided that these tasks can be adequately performed at such levels.

Resolution III.4

Eames Commission

Noting that Resolution 1 of the 1988 Lambeth Conference (The ordination or consecration of women to the episcopate) recommended that the Archbishop of Canterbury, in consultation with the Primates, appoint a commission:

(a) to provide for an examination of the relationships between the provinces of the Anglican Communion and ensure that the process of reception includes continuing consultation with other Churches as well;

(b) to monitor and enumerate the process of consultation within the Communion and to offer further pastoral guidelines;

and noting that the Archbishop of Canterbury and the Primates having now received the completed work of the commission chaired by the Most Revd

Robin Eames, this Conference:

(a) accepts and endorses the report and thanks the members of the Commission;

(b) recognises the ongoing, open process of reception within the Communion;

(c) recommends the guidelines to every Province; and

(d) urges continuing monitoring within the Communion with regular reporting to the Primates' Meeting.

Note: This Resolution was conflated with Resolution IV.10.

Resolution III.5

The Authority of Holy Scriptures

This Conference:

(a) affirms that our creator God, transcendent as well as immanent, communicates with us authoritatively through the Holy Scriptures of the Old and New Testaments; and

(b) in agreement with the Lambeth Quadrilateral, and in solidarity with the Lambeth Conference of 1888, affirms that these Holy Scriptures contain 'all things necessary to salvation' and are for us the 'rule and ultimate standard' of faith and practice.

Resolution III.6

Instruments of the Anglican Communion

This Conference, noting the need to strengthen mutual accountability and interdependence among the Provinces of the Anglican Communion:

(a) reaffirms Resolution 18.2(a) of Lambeth 1988 which "urges that encouragement be given to a developing collegial role for the Primates' Meeting under the presidency of the Archbishop of Canterbury, so that the Primates' Meeting is able to exercise an enhanced responsibility in offering guidance on doctrinal, moral and pastoral matters";

(b) asks that the Primates' Meeting, under the presidency of the

Archbishop of Canterbury, include among its responsibilities positive encouragement to mission, intervention in cases of exceptional emergency which are incapable of internal resolution within provinces, and giving of guidelines on the limits of Anglican diversity in submission to the sovereign authority of Holy Scripture and in loyalty to our Anglican tradition and formularies;

(c) recommends that these responsibilities should be exercised in sensitive consultation with the relevant provinces and with the Anglican Consultative Council (ACC) or in cases of emergency the Executive of the ACC and that, while not interfering with the juridical authority of the provinces, the exercise of these responsibilities by the Primates' Meeting should carry moral authority calling for ready acceptance throughout the Communion, and to this end it is further recommended that the Primates should meet more frequently than the ACC;

(d) believing that there should be a clearer integration of the roles of the Anglican Consultative Council and the Primates' Meeting, recommends that the bishops representing each province in the Anglican Consultative Council should be the primates of the provinces and that—

> (i) equal representation in the ACC from each province, one presbyter or deacon and one lay person from each province should join the primates in the triennial ACC gathering;
>
> (ii) an executive committee of the ACC should be reflective of this broad membership, and;
>
> (iii) there should be a change in the name of the Anglican Consultative Council to the Anglican Communion Council, reflecting the evolving needs and structures to which the foregoing changes speak;

(e) reaffirms the role of the Archbishop of Canterbury as a personal sign of our unity and communion, and the role of the decennial Lambeth Conference and of extraordinary Anglican Congresses as called, together with inter-provincial gatherings and cross-provincial diocesan partnerships, as collegial and communal signs of the unity of our Communion.

Resolution III.7

The Lambeth Conference

Noting that:

(a) the members of the Anglican Consultative Council (ACC) were invited to Lambeth Conference 1988 and Lambeth Conference 1998;

(b) some assistant bishops were invited in 1978 and 1988 and that in 1998 all assistants were invited; and

(c) that in ten years' time numbers and costs will inevitably be much greater;

this Conference requests that those planning for the next Conference actively consider:

(a) the optimal size for the Conference;

(b) possible alternative locations; and

(c) optional Conference designs.

Resolution III.8

The Virginia Report

This Conference:

(a) welcomes the 1997 Report of the Inter-Anglican Theological and Doctrinal Commission (*The Virginia Report*) as a helpful statement of the characteristics of our Communion;

(b) recognises that the report, the fruit of ten years of careful work accomplished since the 12th Lambeth Conference, identifies and explores important questions about unity, interdependence and mutual accountability in the Anglican Communion;

(c) commends its discussion of our Trinitarian faith as the basis of our koinonia and interdependence, while recommending the need for further work to be done with respect to the report's discussion of reason in relation to the primacy of Holy Scripture;

(d) affirms that the Churches of our Anglican Communion are joined in the communion of God through Our Lord Jesus Christ by the gracious power of the Holy Spirit, celebrating the fact that our communion together is maintained in the life and truth of Christ by the gift to us of the Holy Scriptures, the Apostles and Nicene Creeds, the sacraments of Baptism and Eucharist, and the historic episcopate, and commending the fundamental importance of these to the consideration of our partners in ecumenical dialogue;

(e) values the instruments of Anglican unity as they are described in the *Virginia Report*, the Archbishop of Canterbury, the Lambeth Conference, the Anglican Consultative Council, and the meeting of Primates;

(f) values and discerns the Church to be held in *koinonia* by our liturgical tradition and common patterns of worship, by prayer and the communion of the saints, the witness of the heroes and heroines of our history, the sharing of the stories of our faith, and by our interdependence through exchanges of friendship between our dioceses and by service to others in the name of Christ;

(g) calls upon member Churches and the ACC in the next decade to facilitate the sharing of resources of theological education and training in ministry and to promote exchanges amongst the theological colleges and seminaries of our Communion so as to minister to a deepening unity of heart and mind;

(h) requests the Primates to initiate and monitor a decade of study in each province on the report, and in particular on *"whether effective communion, at all levels, does not require appropriate instruments, with due safeguards, not only for legislation, but also for oversight"* (para. 5.20) as well as on the issue of a universal ministry in the service of Christian unity (cf. Agros Report, para. 162, and the Encyclical Letter of Pope John Paul II, *Ut unum sint* 96);

> (i) requests that this study should include consideration of the ecumenical implications involved and that the Primates should make specific recommendations for the development of instruments of communion not later than the 14th Lambeth Conference.

Resolution III.9

Inter-regional groupings

This Conference requests that at a forthcoming meeting of the Anglican Consultative Council ways and means be explored for bishops to gather in inter-regional groupings at convenient intervals for communion, exchange, renewal and theological reflection whereby they might be enabled to take back home ideas for guidance distilled from the global experience of fellow bishops.

Resolution III.10

Marriage and Family Life

This Conference, recognising the need for the Church to respond to the destructive pressures on the integrity of marriage and family life on behalf of the families in our care and noting that the local congregation bears a serious responsibility for giving counsel about the Christian understanding of marriage and family life:

(a) endorses the summary report of the International Anglican Family Network (IAFN *Newsletter*–July 1998);

(b) affirms that the local Christian community should give such counsel; and

(c) believes that the institutions charged with training people for and in Christian ministry must include in their programmes thoughtful and practical courses to prepare clergy and laity to give counsel and encouragement in Christian marriage and family life in the congregations where they serve.

Resolution III.11

Religious Freedom

This Conference challenges Anglicans, as servants of Jesus Christ, our Lord and Saviour:

(a) to respect the rights and freedom of all faiths to worship and practice their ways of life;

(b) to work with all people of good will to extend these freedoms of worship, religious practice and conversion throughout the world;

(c) to stand by those who are being persecuted for their faith by our prayers, protests and practical support;

(d) to enter into dialogue with members of other faiths, to increase our mutual respect and explore the truths we hold in common and those on which we differ;

(e) to witness to our faith in the reconciling and saving activity of God in our Lord Jesus Christ working in us now through the power of the Holy Spirit; and

(f) to equip ourselves for our witness, dialogue and service by becoming better versed in the teaching and practice of our own faith, and of at least one other faith.

Resolution III.12

The Monitoring of Inter-Faith Relations

This Conference requests the Anglican Consultative Council to consider setting up a body in the Anglican Communion to monitor Christian/Muslim and other faith relations throughout the world for the purpose of, promoting, educating, and advising on inter-faith dialogue with Muslim and other faiths and to arrange for adequate support and relief for Christians who are persecuted.

Resolution III.13

Marriage and Family Life

This Resolution was not moved, having been conflated with Resolution III.10.

Resolution III.14

Inculturation of Worship

This Conference, rejoicing in its own experience of multi-cultural worship, reaffirms Resolutions 22 and 47 of the 1988 Lambeth Conference encouraging the inculturation of worship and urges each province to seek the best ways of inculturating its forms and practice of worship.

Resolution III.15

Co-ordinator for Liturgy

This Conference:

(a) thanks the Anglican Church of Canada for seconding the Revd Paul Gibson to the Anglican Consultative Council (ACC) in 1989 and for funding his work, and is grateful for his contribution to the Anglican Communion as its Co-ordinator for Liturgy in the years since then;

(b) urgently requests the Anglican Consultative Council to take steps to find, appoint and sustain a successor to him on his retirement; and

(c) calls upon all provinces to keep the Anglican Consultative Council fully informed about all official liturgical revision through the Co-ordinator for Liturgy or other members of the Council's staff as necessary.

Resolution III.16

International Anglican Liturgical Consultations

This Conference welcomes the emergence in the 1980s of the International Anglican Liturgical Consultations (IALCs); endorses the recognition given to the IALCs by, first the Standing Committee of the Anglican Consultative Council (ACC) and then in 1993, by the Joint Meeting of the Primates and the ACC; requests the IALCs to report regularly to the Primates' Meeting; commends to study of each diocese and province the publications of the IALCs; asks each province to send representatives to the Consultations held every four years in orde that these may represent the whole Communion; and commends to the provinces which can afford to send more representatives the principle of funding bursaries for those provinces which cannot.

Resolution III.17

Liturgical Revision

This Resolution was not moved, having been conflated with Resolution III.15.

Resolution III.18

The Mothers' Union

This Conference:

(a) expresses its gratitude to the Mothers' Union and related organizations, for all their work in supporting families and family life throughout the world;

(b) it is grateful for the many initiatives they have taken to address the needs of the disadvantaged in society; and

(c) encourages the Mothers' Union and the related organisations in the many ways that they are planning for further development of all this work in the next Millennium.

Resolution III.19

Urbanisation

This resolution was not moved in view of the similar Resolution II.7.

Resolution III.20

The Daily Offices

This Conference, affirming the importance of Bishops being faithful in the praying of the daily offices, urges the bishops present at this Conference to recommit themselves to this spiritual discipline and to endeavour to encourage their clergy and people in the discipline of daily prayer.

Resolution III.21

Young People

This resolution was not moved in view of the similar Resolution II.8.

Resolution III.22

Discipleship

This Conference:

(a) affirms our trust in the power of God's Spirit to ensure that all persons are made full disciples and equally members of the Body of Christ and the people or laos of God, by their baptism;

(b) while recognising the necessity of the ordained ministry and special responsibilities which are given to various members of the Body, also recognises that all the baptised share in the common priesthood of the Church;

(c) notes that the life, practice, polity and liturgy of churches everywhere should exemplify this understanding of our community and common life; and

(d) affirms that in baptism all are called to personal commitment to Jesus Christ and should be given education and opportunity for ministries which include worship, witness, service and acts of forgiveness and reconciliation in the setting of their daily life and work.

Section IV Resolutions

Resolution IV.1

Commitment to Full, Visible Unity

This Conference:

(a) reaffirms the Anglican commitment to the full, visible unity of the Church as the goal of the Ecumenical Movement;

(b) encourages the further explication of the characteristics which belong to the full, visible unity of the Church (described variously as the goal, the marks, or the portrait of visible unity); and

(c) recognises that the process of moving towards full, visible unity may entail temporary anomalies, and believes that some anomalies may be bearable when there is an agreed goal of visible unity, but that there should always be an impetus towards their resolution and, thus, towards the removal of the principal anomaly of disunity.

Resolution IV.2

The Chicago-Lambeth Quadrilateral

This Conference:

(a) reaffirms the Chicago-Lambeth Quadrilateral (1888) as a basis on which Anglicans seek the full, visible unity of the Church, and also recognises it as a statement of Anglican unity and identity;

(b) acknowledges that ecumenical dialogues and experience have led to a developing understanding of each of the elements of the Quadrilateral, including the significance of apostolicity, pastoral oversight (*episcope*), the office of bishop and the historic episcopate; and

(c) commends continuing reflection upon the Quadrilateral's contribution to the search for the full, visible unity of the Church, and in particular the role within visible unity of a common ministry of oversight exercised in personal, collegial and communal ways at every level.

Resolution IV.3

An Inter-Anglican Standing Commission on Ecumenical Relations

This Conference:

(a) while noting that expense will be involved, endorses the proposal of the Ecumenical Advisory Group, endorsed by the ACC–10 in Panama (Resolution 16), that the EAG be replaced by an Inter-Anglican Standing Commission on Ecumenical Relations; and

(b) proposes that the tasks of this Commission should be:

(i) to monitor and enable Anglican participation in multilateral and bilateral dialogues, both regional and international;

(ii) to monitor and encourage the process of response, decision and reception;

(iii) to ensure theological consistency in dialogues and conversations by reviewing regional and provincial proposals with ecumenical partners and, when an agreement affects the life of the Communion as a whole, after consultation with the ACC, to refer the matter to the Primates' Meeting, and only if that Meeting so determines, to the Lambeth Conference, before the Province enters the new relationship;

(iv) to give particular attention to anomalies which arise in the context of ecumenical proposals with a view to discerning those anomalies which may be bearable in the light of progress towards an agreed goal of visible unity, and to suggest ways for resolving them;

(v) to consider, when appropriate, if and how an agreement made in one region or Province can be adopted in other regions or Provinces;

(vi) to address issues of terminology;

(vii) to facilitate the circulation of documents and ecumenical resources throughout the Communion, as far as possible in the languages of the Communion.

Resolution IV.4

Local Ecumenism

This Conference:

(a) welcomes the initiatives taken in many provinces and dioceses to work together at the local level with Christians of other traditions; especially in the establishment of Co-operating Parishes, Ecumenical Shared Ministries and Local Ecumenical Partnerships;

(b) notes with interest the proposal for an Ecumenical Bishop in Wales and commends this proposal to the first meeting of the proposed Inter-Anglican Standing Commission on Ecumenical Relations for study;

(c) commends joint ministerial and theological formation, wherever appropriate and possible, including both pre-and post-ordination training;

(d) encourages Christians to join together to witness to justice and peace and to moral, social and environmental concerns entailed by life in Christ;

(e) notes with interest the *Covenant Agreement on Mutual Recognition of Ministers* of the Church Unity Commission in Southern Africa; and

(f) welcomes the continuing work of the Church Unity Commission on the ministry of *episcopé* and requests that the result of the study be reported to the proposed Inter-Anglican Standing Commission on Ecumenical Relations.

Resolution IV.5

Ecclesiology and Ethics

This Conference:

(a) recognising the centrality of ethical obedience and witness to life in Christ and hence to the visible unity of the Church, welcomes the ecumenical work done since the last Lambeth Conference on ecclesiology and ethics (*Life in Christ* [ARCIC], (1994), *Church and World* (1990), *Costly Unity* (1993), *Costly Obedience* (1996), and *Costly Commitment* (1995) [WCC]) and encourages the continuation of this work in the multilateral and bilateral dialogue;

(b) rejoices at the emerging consensus that racism, inequality between men and women, global economic injustice and the degradation of the earth's ecology are incompatible with the Christian faith; and

(c) calls for continuing work to identify, study and come to a common mind concerning ethical issues where contention threatens to divide the Anglican Communion and create new division amongst the churches.

Resolution IV.6

Churches in Communion

This Conference:

(a) recommends that the proposed Inter-Anglican Standing Commission on Ecumenical Relations reflect upon the implications of being in communion with the See of Canterbury with particular reference to the United Churches and Churches in Communion;

(b) welcomes the fact that the International Bishops' Conference of the Union of Utrecht and the ACC have agreed to the establishment of an Anglican-Old Catholic International Co-ordinating Council;

(c) recommends that consideration be given to ways of deepening our communion with the Old Catholic Churches beyond the Bonn Agreement, including means of taking counsel and making decisions together; the anomaly of overlapping jurisdictions; the implications of wider ecumenical relationships, particularly with the Roman Catholic, Orthodox and Lutheran Churches; and the importance of work together on issues of mission and common witness;

(d) welcomes the adoption by both churches of the Concordat between the Episcopal Church in the Philippines and the Philippine Independent Church (1997), which establishes a relationship of full communion;

(e) welcomes the relationship of communion established in Northern Europe between six Lutheran churches (Estonia, Finland, Iceland, Lithuania, Norway and Sweden) and four Anglican churches (England, Ireland, Scotland and Wales) by the signing of the Porvöo Declaration in 1996, and recognises the enrichment brought through the presence of Finnish, Norwegian and Swedish bishops at this Conference as bishops in communion; and

(f) welcomes the decision by the Porvöo Church Leaders Meeting in 1998 that the Lusitanian Catholic Apostolic Evangelical Church of Portugal and the Spanish Episcopal Reformed Church should be regarded as being covered by the Preamble to the Porvöo Declaration subject to their Synods' approval of the Declaration.

Resolution IV. 7

World Council of Churches

This Conference:

(a) greets the 8th Assembly of the World Council of Churches in Harare and congratulates the Council as it celebrates its Fiftieth Anniversary in 1998;

(b) expresses its gratitude to the WCC, which has enriched the Anglican Communion not least through the work of the Faith and Order Commission;

(c) commends the achievements and insights of the Ecumenical Decade of Churches in Solidarity with Women;

(d) affirms the importance of the study Towards a Common Understanding and Vision of the WCC as a first step in the renewal of the Council's life and work;

(e) recommends that the Assembly mandate the incoming Central Committee to undertake more focused work on:

(i) the vision of unity the Council should seek to nurture, building on the Canberra Statement adopted by the Seventh Assembly;

(ii) renewed structures of the Council which would most effectively promote that vision;

(iii) a radical reassessment of the basis and categories of membership in the WCC and what changes in the WCC would be required to make it possible for the Roman Catholic Church to be a full member; and

(iv) the nature of the fellowship shared by members of the Council;

(f) invites the Joint Working Group between the WCC and the Roman Catholic Church to consider what changes in the WCC would be required to make it possible for the Roman Catholic Church to be a full member; and

(g) requests that the Harare Assembly makes provision for a consideration of the concerns of the Orthodox Churches, expressed at the meeting at Thessaloniki (May 1998).

Resolution IV.8

A Common Date for Easter

This Conference:

(a) welcomes the work of the WCC on a common date for Easter, recognising that in the year 2001, according to calculations by both the Eastern and Western Churches, the date of the Easter/Pascha observance will coincide; and

(b) recommends:

(i) that the following procedures for achieving a commonly recognised date for the annual celebration of Easter, as the day of resurrection of our Lord Jesus Christ, should be agreed upon by all Christian Churches:

(1) maintain the Nicene norms (that Easter fall on the Sunday following the first vernal full moon);

(2) calculate the date of the vernal equinox from the data provided by the most accurate scientific and astronomical methods;

(3) use as the basis of reckoning the meridian of Jerusalem, the place of Christ's death and resurrection.

(ii) that each province of the Anglican Communion be invited to endorse the above resolutions and to report its endorsement to the Secretary of the Anglican Consultative Council by the Feast of the Nativity, AD 2000 and that these responses be reported to the WCC.

Resolution IV.9

The Virginia Report

This Resolution was not moved, having been conflated with Resolution III.8.

Resolution IV.10

Eames Commission

This Resolution was not moved, having been conflated with Resolution III.4.

Resolution IV.11

'Continuing' Churches

This Conference:

(a) believes that important questions are posed by the emergence of groups who call themselves 'continuing Anglican Churches' which have separated from the Anglican Communion in recent years; and

(b) asks the Archbishop of Canterbury and the Primates' Meeting to consider how best to initiate and maintain dialogue with such groups with a view to the reconciliation of all who own the Anglican tradition.

Resolution IV.12

Implications of Ecumenical Agreements

This Conference:

(a) encourages a fuller embodiment of the spirit and content of accepted agreed statements in the life and teaching of the Provinces; and

(b) urges that new Provincial liturgical texts and practices be consonant with accepted ecumenical agreements reached in multilateral and bilateral dialogues, for example BEM and ARCIC, and requests the Primates to consider appropriate ways for encouraging this in consultation with the International Anglican Liturgical Consultation.

Resolution IV.13

Unity within Provinces of the Anglican Communion

This Conference:

(a) notes with gratitude the ministry of support which the Archbishop of Canterbury has been able to give in Sudan and Rwanda, and recognises that he is called upon to render assistance from time to time in a variety of situations;

(b) in view of the very grave difficulties encountered in the internal affairs of some Provinces of the Communion, invites the Archbishop of Canterbury to appoint a Commission to make recommendations to the

Primates and the Anglican Consultative Council, as to the exceptional circumstances and conditions under which, and the means by which, it would be appropriate for him to exercise an extra-ordinary ministry of episcopé (pastoral oversight), support and reconciliation with regard to the internal affairs of a Province other than his own for the sake of maintaining communion within the said Province and between the said Province and the rest of the Anglican Communion.

Resolution IV.14

Assyrian Church of the East

This Conference:

encourages regional conversations between Anglicans and members of the Assyrian Church of the East in areas where their communities coincide.

Resolution IV.15

The Baptist Churches

This Conference:

recommends as a priority the implementation of resolution 10(3) of Lambeth 1988, by developing, in partnership with the Baptist World Alliance, co-ordinated regional and local discussions leading to the establishment of a continuing forum between Anglicans and Baptists at the world level.

Resolution IV.16

The Lutheran Churches

This Conference:

(a) welcomes the remarkable progress in Anglican-Lutheran relationships during the last decade in many parts of the world;

(b) commends for study the report of the Anglican-Lutheran International Commission, *The Diaconate as Ecumenical Opportunity (1996);*

(c) noting the approval by the Episcopal Church in the United States of America of the *Concordat of Agreement* with the Evangelical Lutheran

Church in America and the narrow vote against the *Concordat* by the ELCA, hopes that the draft revision of the *Concordat*, currently being undertaken by the ELCA in consultation with representatives from ECUSA, will provide a firm basis for the two churches to move to full communion;

(d) commends the progress toward full communion between the Anglican Church of Canada and the Evangelical Lutheran Church in Canada as set forth in the *Waterloo Declaration* (1997) for consideration by both churches in 2001;

(e) encourages the continuation of close relations with the Lutheran Churches of Denmark and Latvia, which participated fully in the Porvöo Conversations but have not so far become signatories;

(f) welcomes the development of dialogue in Australia, and of dialogue and collaboration in the search for justice and human rights and the joint pastoral care of scattered Christian communities in Africa;

(g) affirms the growing fellowship between churches of the Anglican and Lutheran Communions in other regions of the world, and encourages further steps toward agreement in faith, eucharistic sharing and common mission on the way to the goal of full, visible unity;

(h) rejoices not only in the *Porvöo Common Statement* between the Anglican Churches of Britain and Ireland and the Lutheran Churches of the Nordic and Baltic region, but also in the *Meissen Common Statement* with the Evangelical Church in Germany, which includes Lutheran, Reformed and United Churches, and looks forward to the proposed agreement between the Anglican churches of Britain and Ireland and the French Lutheran and Reformed churches; and

(i) recommends consultation with the Lutheran World Federation about the continuation of the work of the Anglican-Lutheran International Commission.

Resolution IV.17

The Methodist Churches

This Conference:

(a) greets with appreciation the report of the Anglican-Methodist International Commission, *Sharing in the Apostolic Communion*, and the unanimous adoption of paragraph 95 of this report by the World Methodist Council meeting in Rio de Janeiro in August 1996;

(b) invites member Churches of the Anglican Communion to study the report and, where appropriate, to develop agreements of acknowledgement that

(i) both churches belong to the one, holy, catholic and apostolic Church of Jesus Christ and participate in the apostolic mission of the whole people of God;

(ii) in the churches of our two communions the Word of God is authentically preached and the Sacraments duly administered;

(iii) our churches share in the common confession and heritage of the apostolic faith; and

(c) recommends the establishment as soon as possible of a Joint Working Group with the World Methodist Council to promote, encourage and monitor regional developments and when appropriate to

(i) consider ways of celebrating regional agreements of mutual acknowledgement;

(ii) prepare, in full accordance with the principles set out in the report of the Anglican-Methodist International Commission, guidelines for moving beyond acknowledgement to the reconciliation of churches and, within that, the reconciliation of ordained ministries and structures for common decision-making.

Resolution IV.18

The Moravian Church

This Conference:

(a) welcomes the Fetter Lane Agreement between the Church of England and the Moravian Church in Great Britain and Ireland;

(b) welcomes the adoption of the Agreement by the Church of Ireland; and

(c) commends the Common Statement for study in provinces of the Anglican Communion which overlap with Moravian provinces, and invites those provinces to consider whether the Common Statement offers a basis for similar agreements in their regions.

Resolution IV.19

The Oriental Orthodox Churches

This Conference:

(a) reaffirms resolution 5(9) of Lambeth 1988 that the Anglican-Oriental Orthodox International Forum should be upgraded to an International Theological Commission to seek an agreement on Christology in the light of the Christological agreements between the Orthodox Churches and the Oriental Orthodox Churches, between the Roman Catholic Church and the Oriental Orthodox Churches, and between the Oriental Orthodox Churches and the Reformed World Alliance and to consider other theological and ecclesial issues; and

(b) encourages bilateral discussions with individual member Churches of the Oriental Orthodox family on a regional basis.

Resolution IV.20

The Orthodox Churches

This Conference:

(a) invites the bishops of the Anglican Communion to study and respond to the Interim Agreed Statements of the International Commission of the Anglican-Orthodox Theological Dialogue, June 1998, and to forward these responses to the Anglican co-chair of the International Dialogue by 31 December 1999, namely *The Trinity and the Church; Christ, the Spirit and the Church; and Christ, Humanity and the Church;*

(b) notes that there is a continuing concern on the part of the Orthodox Churches in dialogue with the Anglican Communion about the issue of the ordination of women to the presbyterate and episcopate;

(c) requests that the *Dublin Agreed Statement 1984* be circulated to all provinces of the Anglican Communion for study as requested by resolution 6.3 of Lambeth 1988 and that responses be sent to the proposed Inter-Anglican Standing Commission for Ecumenical Affairs for collation and for forwarding to the Primates' Meeting and the ACC; and

(d) welcomes the emerging Christological agreement between the Orthodox and Oriental Orthodox Churches and requests that the provinces study this potentially major Christological agreement.

Resolution IV.21

Pentecostal Churches

This Conference:

in the light of Resolution 11 of Lambeth Conference 1988 and noting that the Roman Catholic Church, the Baptist World Alliance and the World Alliance of Reformed Churches respectively have been involved in bilateral conversations with some Pentecostal churches, invites the proposed Inter-Anglican Standing Commission on Ecumenical Relations to explore the possibility of such conversations between the Anglican Communion and the Pentecostal churches, at an appropriate level.

Resolution IV.22

The Reformed Churches

This Conference:

(a) encourages, in the light of resolution 7 of the Lambeth Conference 1988, regional initiatives and dialogues with the Reformed Churches on the basis of the convergence recorded in *God's Reign and Our Unity* (1984), the report of the Anglican-Reformed International Commission; and

(b) looks forward to the completion of the studies commissioned by the Joint Working Group of the Anglican Communion and the World Alliance of Reformed Churches, particularly a study of the exercise of personal episcopacy in the Reformed tradition and case studies of local Anglican-Reformed sharing in mission, justice issues and congregational life.

Resolution IV.23

The Roman Catholic Church

This Conference:

(a) continues to be grateful for the achievements of the Anglican Roman Catholic International Commission and, recognising that there are a number of outstanding issues which still need to be addressed, strongly encourages its continuation;

(b) welcomes the proposal for a high-level consultation to review Anglican-Roman Catholic relationships in the light of the agreements reached and the 'real though imperfect communion' already existing between the churches of the Anglican Communion and the Roman Catholic Church. The Conference requests that the consultation should include different local situations, including the movement of clergy from one Church to another; the experience of Christian solidarity under persecution [e.g., in the Sudan]; discussions of the implications of having agreed statements on *Eucharistic Doctrine* and *Ministry and Ordination*, and the status of *Apostolicae curae* in the new context brought about by the work of ARCIC;

(c) recognizes the special status of those Agreements which have been affirmed by the Lambeth Conference 1988 as 'consonant in substance with the faith of Anglicans' (*Eucharistic Doctrine, Ministry and Ordination*, and their *Elucidations*) and urges the provinces to receive them into their life;

(d) encourages the referral of *Salvation and the Church* (1987), *Church as Communion* (1991), *Life in Christ* (1994), and the anticipated completion of ARCIC's work on authority in the Church to the provinces for study and response back to the proposed Inter-Anglican Standing Commission on Ecumenical Relations and (through the Primates' Meeting and the Anglican Consultative Council) to the next Lambeth Conference; and

(e) welcomes warmly the invitation of Pope John Paul II in his Encyclical Letter *Ut unum sint* (1995) to consider the ministry of unity of the Bishop of Rome in the service of the unity of the Universal Church, strongly encourages the provinces to respond and asks the proposed Inter-Anglican Standing Commission on Ecumenical Relations to collate the provincial responses.

Resolution IV.24

WCC Faith and Order Commission

This Conference:

(a) welcomes the *Canberra Statement: The Unity of the Church as Koinonia: Gift and Calling* (WCC 1991) and commends it to the Provinces as an important statement on the unity of the Church;

(b) expresses gratitude for the insights of the 5th World Conference on Faith and Order in Santiago de Compostela (1993) on the theme *Towards Koinonia in Faith, Life and Witness;*

(c) looks forward to the publication of the convergence text on *The Nature and Purpose of the Church: A Step on the Way to a Common Statement* and the study *A Treasure in Earthen Vessels—An Instrument for an Ecumenical Reflection on Hermeneutics;* and

(d) supports the widespread use of the study guide *Towards a Sharing of the One Faith.*

Resolution IV.25

New Churches and Independent Church Groups

This Conference:

(a) encourages the development of relationships between members of Anglican Churches and members of New Churches and Independent Christian Groups bilaterally, multilaterally, locally and informally, where this is appropriate and possible; and

(b) asks the Primates to investigate ways and means of monitoring the development of New Churches and Independent Christian Groups, studying their characteristics, and offering advice to provinces and dioceses about initiating and developing relationships with them.

Resolution IV.26

Kuala Lumpur Statement

This Resolution was not voted upon, as the Conference agreed to move to next business.

Resolutions from the Regions

Resolution V.1

On the Authority of Scriptures in Matters of Marriage and Sexuality.

This resolution was moved as an amendment to Resolution I.10 and was lost.

Resolution V.2

On International Debt Cancellation and the Alleviation of Poverty

This Conference:

(a) noting that the beginning of a New Millennium affords the Church of Christ a timely opportunity to propose concrete, Christ-centred means by which to combat poverty, disease, unemployment and other forms of human suffering especially in the developing world, and that cancellation of the unpayable International Debt by poor countries is one such means;

(b) aware that many countries in the developing world suffer under the weight of unpayable external debt, unable to provide essential services;

(c) believing in the principles championed by the Jubilee 2000 Coalition;

(d) convinced that developed lender countries, institutions and individuals have the capacity and means to cancel this crippling, unpayable debt, given the necessary concern and goodwill;

(e) therefore calls upon all concerned to join hands with our Anglican Communion in exploring together the possible cancellation of debt, as well as other ways and means of enabling the poor at a grassroots level to escape the poverty cycle, for example by sponsoring projects which will equip and empower the poor to provide for their families; and

(f) noting that revolving micro-credit projects—such as those managed by Opportunity International, Grameen Bank, and ECLOF and others—equip the poor with the credit needed to start small businesses and create jobs with dignity, commends the efforts of these various development agencies. It further welcomes new initiatives such as the Five Talents

Project, a micro-credit development initiative designed to combat world poverty, and commends it for its implementation.

Resolution V.3

A Call for Solidarity in Working for Justice, Peace and Reconciliation in the World

Whereas the last millennium, especially the twentieth century, has been characterised by human division, conflict, war and violence, both religious and civil, as well as economic and social injustices;

Whereas the Kingdom Jesus proclaimed and established is to be marked by reconciliation between God and humanity, and between peoples and His creation;
Whereas the work of the power of evil is to create divisions between humans and ruin the harmony that God intended; and

Whereas we have particularly experienced the demonic effects of division and conflict most recently in African nations fuelled by selfishness and greed for power;

This Conference believes that the people's hopes and aspirations for the third millennium will only be achieved if they are founded on the message of peace, reconciliation and practical steps taken to achieve the same; and

Therefore calls upon all governments, religions and people of good will

(a) to work for Peace and Reconciliation in order to make this world a better place for all its inhabitants and for posterity; and

(b) to engage decisively in reconciliation within families, congregations, residential areas and nations, and among nations, so that we may participate in our calling to be peacemakers, as servants of the Prince of Peace.

Resolution V.4

On Transformation and Renewal

This Conference:

(a) noting that while Lambeth 1988 called for a Decade of Evangelism during which we have witnessed welcome changes in the world and enhanced efforts to share the Gospel of Christ many other injustices still disfigure our world and challenge our commitment to share the love of God;

(b) therefore calls our Church to build on what has been achieved in the Decade of Evangelism by working for a transformed humanity, transformed cultures, a transformed mission for the Church, and transformed relationships with other Christian communities. This will require a fair sharing of God's resources of personnel and funds.

(c) proclaiming the Gospel of the Kingdom of God, forgiveness through the cross of Christ and deliverance from the power of Satan, will seek:

(i) Spiritual renewal of God's people;

(ii) Transformation in the lives of children and youth, who form most of our growing churches;

(iii) Transformation in the relations between ethnic groups and the nations;

(iv) Transformation in Christian relations with Muslims, Hindus, Buddhists and other religions:

- True freedom of religion
- Study of the history of other major religions including Islam/Christian relations
- Assistance for converts from Islam and other religions
- Support of new Dioceses within the Anglican Communion

(v) Transformation in our churches, in our worship and in our proper use of Scriptures.

Resolution V.5

On Northern Ireland

This Conference:

(a) welcomes the recent peace process in Northern Ireland, culminating in the Good Friday Agreement, overwhelmingly endorsed by both North and South, and the election of the new Assembly;

(b) supports the Church of Ireland and the other Christian Churches in any efforts to build bridges between the communities, and to pursue their Christian duty as peacemakers;

(c) seeks to encourage the Churches in re-assessing any attitudes or alliances which may be perceived as sectarian, so that the body of Christ may be free from any divisiveness or bitterness as it seeks to live out the Good News of peace in Ireland.

Resolution V.6

Anglican Provincial Structure for Continental Europe

This Conference, noting with appreciation the progress made so far by the parallel Anglican jurisdictions in Continental Europe working both with each other and with churches in communion in the area, resolves to encourage:

(a) continued exploration towards appropriate provincial structures for Anglican Continental Europe in partnership with other Churches in the service of the common mission of the Church; and

(b) the Church of England and the Episcopal Church of the United States of America to consider the provision of appropriate funding for such a province.

Resolution V.7

Formation of an Iberian Forum

In order to facilitate a greater participation of the Iberian–Afro–Latin Region in the affairs of the Anglican Communion, this Conference resolves to request the Joint Standing Committee of the ACC and Primates to consider:

(a) the immediate formation of an Iberian–Afro–Latin American Consultative Forum that will meet periodically;

(b) the appointment by the Archbishop of Canterbury, with the advice of the Primates of the region, of a permanent advisor, as adjunct to the ACC Secretary-General, for the Iberian–Afro–Latin American world.

Resolution V.8

Reopening the Evangelism Secretariat

This resolution was not moved in view of Resolution II.2

Resolution V.9

Cuba

This Conference reaffirms the 1988 Lambeth Conference Resolution that called for the condemnation and cessation of the embargo of the USA against Cuba.

Resolution V.10

Traditional Sexual Ethics

This resolution became an amendment to Resolution I.10 and was withdrawn.

Resolution V.11

Millennium Logo

This Conference requests the Anglican Consultative Council to consider developing a logotype for the Anglican Communion that will focus on the birth of Jesus Christ in order to celebrate the Millennium.

Resolution V.12

Global Cease Fire

This Conference rejects the use of violence in the name of religion and supports the call for a 72-hour Global Cease Fire, December 31, 1999, to January 2, 2000, which will allow the world to end the old age in peace and to begin the new millennium in the spirit of reconciliation, healing and peace-making.

Resolution V.13

Episcopal Responsibilities and Diocesan Boundaries

This Conference:

(a) reaffirms Resolution 72 of the Lambeth Conference of 1988 "Episcopal Responsibilities and Diocesan Boundaries"; and

(b) requests the Primates to encourage the bishops of their Province to consider the implications of Resolution 72 of the Lambeth Conference 1988.

Resolution V.14

On Social Justice Issues in the Oceania Region

This Conference, noting that in the Churches of Oceania (Aotearoa, New Zealand and Polynesia, Australia, Melanesia and Papua New Guinea) there continues to be much concern about a variety of social justice issues affecting island nations, indigenous peoples and rural communities:

(a) reaffirms the recommendations of the 1988 Lambeth Conference Resolution 35 (Concerns of South Pacific Islands) on the right of indigenous peoples to self-determination, that they "be in control of their own affairs and especially of the use of the vital resources of their lands and seas", the development of a truly nuclear-free Pacific, the cessation of unjust exploitation of the region's natural resources and the need for international advocacy on these issues;

(b) affirms its support for the recognition of indigenous land title;

(c) expresses its concern that where existing indigenous land title is under threat whether through domestic legislation, globalisation, structural adjustment programmes and debt rescheduling, resulting in increased foreign ownership and control of indigenous land and resources;

(d) recognises the effect of unpayable international debt on island nations and calls for immediate relief as outlined by the Jubilee 2000 campaign;

(e) encourages the nations of Oceania to address corruption in government and business and to participate in the establishment of an international code of practice for financial management;

(f) supports the actions of churches, governments and other organisations to challenge those aspects of globalisation which are having a negative impact upon agriculture, forestry and fishing throughout Oceania;

(g) (i) stands in solidarity with Pacific island nations facing disaster because of global warming and rising sea levels;
(ii) encourages a broad range of research, education and action on global warming and its effects;
(iii) requests churches to urge their governments to fund this research, education and action;

(h) requests churches in Australia, Aotearoa/New Zealand, East Asia and other countries engaged in trade and economic activities in Oceania

(i) to become more aware of these activities by their governments and multi-national corporations in the region;

(ii) where these activities are unjust and exploitative, to become strong advocates of social justice to eliminate this exploitation.

Resolution V.15

An Appeal for Peace to the Governments of the Middle East and South Asia

This Conference, noting that peace is being threatened in the Middle East and South Asia region, appeals to all the governments of the region for disarmament, the up holding of human rights and harmony among people.

Resolution V.16

An Appeal to the Churches and Governments of South Asia

This Conference, noting the complex situation that exists in South Asia, which has been highlighted by recent events and is based upon ethnic and religious complexities, which have become great impediments to the harmony and development of its people, and also noting that such a milieu continues to be blatantly exploited by different political parties and fundamentalist religious groups for their own ends, and that such a scenario causes havoc amongst communities, especially the poor and the marginalised, calls upon the churches of this region to live and preach the Gospel, to promote the right of God's creation and to collaborate with other faith communities in acknowledging the sovereignty of God and in sharing their common values and resources for harmony and justice, and further calls upon the governments of this region to seek after serving its people, especially by providing universal education and proper health care in an atmosphere of security and stability and urges them to refrain from excessive militarisation and abuse of authority.

Resolution V.16A

Peace and Reconciliation

This Conference resolves that our Anglican Communion be called upon to take special initiatives to use its resources and efforts in facilitating peace and reconciliation between conflicting nations and communities of our human family.

Resolution V.17

Religions/World Faiths Desk

This Conference:

(a) noting that the major religions were born in Asia and recognising the complexities and challenges of religion, the role that religions have played in the lives of people and civilizations throughout human history and foreseeing, as we enter the third Christian millennium, that religious pluralism will bring many new challenges and dilemmas;

(b) recognizes that in this milieu faith should be the source of reconciliation and hope; and

(c) urges our Anglican Communion to give high priority to this challenge and invites the ACC to consider setting up a Religions/World Faiths desk at the earliest opportunity.

Resolution V.18

Economic Needs of Asia

This Conference:

(a) noting that the poverty and human deprivation in most parts of Asia (which is about $3/5$ of humanity) is acute and deplorable, that South Asia (c. 1.2 billion people) has recently been declared by the UN as the poorest region in the world, displacing sub-Saharan Africa, and that there are at least 400 million people in South Asia who live below the acute poverty line;

(b) urges the Western governments, Church bodies and aid agencies to give special attention to the economic needs of this region and to strive towards the eradication of this misery.

Resolution V.19

On Pakistan

This Conference notes with deep concern the following resolution of the Church of Pakistan, namely:

"The Church of Pakistan wishes to place before the Lambeth Conference their concern about the deterioration of Christian/Muslim relations ever since the introduction of the Blasphemy Law into the Pakistan Penal Code under Section 295 B and C."

While we affirm

1. our love for Pakistan as our homeland and our good wish for its safety and dignified position among the community of nations;

2. our continued participation in the building of the nation which has been the hallmark of individual Christians and our institutions;

3. our appreciation for Islamic moral values and the commonalities between the two faiths enabling us to live together;

we are deeply concerned with the increasing intolerance and call upon the Conference to condemn:

1. the rise of intolerance towards minorities, especially Christians;

2. the legal and judicial processes which marginalise minorities and isolate them from the national mainstream, such as the separate electorates.

and therefore at the Church's request—

(a) calls for

(i) the repeal of the Blasphemy Law (PPC 295 B and C) which is the source of victimization of the minorities in Pakistan;

(ii) the release of all prisoners unjustly accused under the Blasphemy Law, such as Ayub Misih; and

(iii) the restoration of the rights of minorities as given in the 1973 Constitution;

(b) requests the Anglican Consultative Council to use its good offices to promote and develop harmony between the two major communities in Pakistan.

Resolution V.20

On the Holy Land

This Conference:

(a) expresses its deep ongoing concern about the tragic situation in the Holy Land, especially as it affects the City of Jerusalem;

(b) affirms the following points:

(i) Jerusalem is holy to the three Abrahamic faiths, Judaism, Christianity, and Islam, and a home equally for Palestinians and Israelis;

(ii) The status of Jerusalem is fundamental to any just and lasting peace settlement and therefore it should serve as the capital of two sovereign states, Israel and Palestine, with free access to the adherents of all three faiths.

(iii) East Jerusalem is an integral part of the occupied territories, and should be included in all political arrangements relating to those territories, including self-determination, release of prisoners, right of return, and eventual sovereignty;

(iv) The continued serious decline of the Christian Community is a substantial threat to the threefold presence in the Holy City;

(v) The continued building and expansion of Jewish Settlements within East Jerusalem and the occupied territories remains a major obstacle to any just and lasting peace.

(c) urges the government of Israel to recognize the right of Palestinians, Christians and Muslims alike to build their own homes and establish their own institutions in Jerusalem;

(d) sends a message of love, hope and support to our fellow Christians in Israel and Palestine;

(e) encourages our own congregations in greater dialogue, understanding and fellowship with their brothers and sisters in that land;

(f) urges our political leaders to take every opportunity to encourage the Israeli Government and Palestinian Authority to work urgently for a just and lasting peace settlement, to include fair and proper provision for the right of return to the land of those Palestinians dispossessed by the conflicts of the past fifty years;

(g) urges the United Nations, and the governments of the United States and the European Community to use diplomatic and economic influence in support of the above and to demonstrate as firm a commitment to justice for Palestinians as they do for the security of the State of Israel;

(h) continues to uphold all those, in any nation, who have committed themselves to working for the cause of peace, praying that they may have wisdom and courage to bring this process to a just conclusion; and

(i) resolves to send copies of this resolution to the respective parties mentioned above as well as to the Prime Minister of Israel and the President of the Palestinian Authority.

Resolution V.21

Iran

This Conference:

(a) recording with gratitude the welcome received by the President Bishop of the Episcopal Church in Jerusalem and the Middle East on his recent visit to Iran and the courtesy accorded to him by the country's authorities,

(b) re-affirms the following resolution of Lambeth 1988, namely:

"This conference, recognizing the positive development of recent events in Iran, and in the light of a declared policy of religious tolerance in that land, respectfully requests the Islamic Republic of Iran to facilitate a positive response to the many requests, sent on behalf of the Diocese of Iran, the Primates of the Anglican Communion, and the President Bishop of the Episcopal Church in Jerusalem and the Middle East, concerning all the claims of the Church in Iran;"

(c) eagerly awaits the government of Iran's positive response to that resolution; and

(d) respectfully requests the Archbishop of Canterbury to pursue these concerns.

Resolution V.22

Iraq and Libya

This Conference:

(a) aware of the serious effects of economic sanctions on two of the major countries of the Province of Jerusalem and the Middle East (i.e. Iraq and Libya);

(b) concerned about the plight of the civilian populations of these countries, particularly those who are vulnerable because basic medicines and food are lacking;

calls upon the Security Council of the United Nations urgently to review the situation.

Resolution V.23

On the Kuala Lumpur Statement

This resolution was not voted upon, as the Conference agreed to move to next business.

Resolution V.24

Young People

This Conference, recognising the active participation and contribution of young people and young adults in the Churches of East Asia, calls on the Anglican Churches to continue to provide challenges and opportunities for young people to serve in the ministry of the Church.

Resolution V.25

Economic Difficulties in Asia

This Conference:

(a) supports the actions and initiatives of the churches in the East Asia region for the realization of economic justice through the restructuring of the economic system, including debt cancellation for the poorest countries; and

(b) expresses its concern to see that the economic difficulties in the countries in East Asia are resolved.

Resolution V.26

Korean Unification

This Conference, noting the desire of the Korean people for the reunification of Korea:

(a) supports the efforts of the National Council of Churches in Korea, including the Anglican Church of Korea, to achieve reunification;

(b) recognises that these efforts have promoted peace not only in Korea but also in Northeast Asia; and

(c) urges that the governments of the North and South improve their relationship by implementing peace, reunification and cooperation through the 'Agreement on Reconciliation, Non-aggression and Exchange and Cooperation between the South and the North' which was signed on the 13th December 1991 by the Prime Minister of the Republic of Korea and the Premier of the Administrative Council of the Democratic People's Republic of Korea.

Resolution V.27

Millennium

This Conference calls on:

(a) all Provinces of the Communion to take concrete steps to celebrate the dawn of a new millennium as a Christ-centered event, and to share these steps widely;

(b) all countries to celebrate the millennium by, *inter alia,* freeing all slaves, returning refugees to their homes, doing their utmost not to create any more refugees, and restoring land to those that have been deprived thereof.

Resolution V.28

Swords into Ploughshares

This Conference:

(a) endorses the call of the Bishops of the Church in Central and Southern Africa and of the Indian Ocean for Africa to be declared a weapons-free zone;

(b) encourages the rest of the Anglican Communion and the worldwide Christian Community to campaign against the international arms trade;

(c) calls upon all nations to invest their resources in the development of people, rather than in the manufacture of weapons of destruction.

Resolution V.29

Reconciliation

This resolution was not moved as it had been conflated with Resolution V.3

Resolution V.30

St. Helenians' Citizenship in the United Kingdom

This Conference:

(i) supports the members of the government of the United Kingdom who are urging that full British Citizenship be granted to the citizens of all the British Overseas Territories, and

(ii) respectfully draws their attention to the islanders of St Helena and the specially strong reasons for full British Citizenship to be restored to them.

Resolution V.31

Apartheid

This Conference:

(a) gives thanks to God for the end of apartheid rule and of centuries of colonial oppression in South Africa; and

(b) welcomes the first democratically elected government under President Mandela and sends greetings and good wishes to him and to all the people of South Africa.

Resolution V.32

Namibia

This Conference:

(i) gives thanks to God for the successful decolonisation process that led to the attainment of freedom and independence in Namibia; and

(ii) sends a message of good wishes to the President of Namibia, Dr Samuel Shafiishuna Nujoma and the people of Namibia, assuring them of our prayers for lasting peace, stability and prosperity.

Resolution V.33

Angola

This Conference:

(a) warmly welcomes the coming of Anglicans in Angola into the Church of the Province of Southern Africa, rejoicing in the prospect of the creation of a new diocese there; and

(b) calls on all involved in the political life of Angola to bring the peace process there to full fruition, using peaceful means.

Resolution V.34

Christian–Muslim Relations

This Conference:

(a) noting that—

(i) to the Muslim community, a secular state is a state of hostility to religion;

(ii) to the Christian community, a secular state is the separation of church and state and a guarantee of freedom of religion; and

(iii) the experience of Christian–Muslim relations calls attention to the issue of the appropriate relationship between politics and religion,

(b) supports the idea of a national state in which all religions are free to establish and propagate themselves without the state and religion becoming either interchangeable or mutually hostile.

Resolution V.35

On Homosexuality

This resolution was moved as an amendment to Resolution I.10 and was lost.

Resolution from the Inter-Faith Team

Resolution VI.1

On Relations with People of Other Faiths

This Conference:

(a) having heard about situations in different parts of the world where relations between people of different faiths vary from co-operation to conflict, believes that the approach of Christians to people of other faiths needs to be marked by:

(i) commitment to working towards genuinely open and loving human relationships, even in situations where co-existence seems impossible;

(ii) co-operation in addressing human concerns and working for justice, peace and reconciliation for the whole human community;

(iii) frank and honest exploration of both the common ground and the differences between the faiths;

(iv) prayerful and urgent action with all involved in tension and conflict, to understand their situation, so that everything possible may be done to tackle the causes of conflict;

(v) a desire both to listen to people of all faiths and to express our own deepest Christian beliefs, leaving the final outcome of our life and witness in the hands of God.

(vi) sharing and witnessing to all we know of the good news of Christ as our debt of love to all people whatever their religious affiliation.

(b) recognizes that by virtue of their engagement with people of other faiths in situations all over the world, Anglican Christians are in a special position to explore and develop genuinely Christian responses to these faiths;

(c) also recognizes that the Network for Inter-Faith Concerns (NIF-CON) has been established by the ACC at the request of the last Lambeth

Conference as a way for sharing news, information, ideas and resources relating to these concerns between provinces of the Anglican Communion;

(d) recommends:

(i) that NIFCON be charged to monitor Muslim–Christian relations and report regularly to the Primates Meeting and the ACC;

(ii) that the ACC consider how to resource NIFCON adequately both in personnel and finance;

(iii) that all the other official Anglican networks should be encouraged to recognise the inter-faith dimensions to their work.

Appendix

Resolutions of Sections and Regions referred to in Subsection (f) of Resolution I.10 (Human Sexuality)

Resolution IV.26 from Section IV

This Conference, noting that no province of the Anglican Communion has voted to change the traditional ethical teaching on homosexuality, in order to have and promote credibility with our brothers and sisters in New Churches and Independent Christian Groups, receives and recognises the *Kuala Lumpur Statement on Human Sexuality* as a contribution of the 'South—South Encounter' to the Anglican Communion.

Note: This Resolution was not voted upon, as the Conference agreed to pass to next business.

Resolution V.1 from Central and East Africa Region

This Conference:

(a) believes in the primary authority of the Scriptures, according to their own testimony; as supported by our own historic tradition. The Scriptural revelation of Jesus the Christ must continue to illuminate, challenge and transform cultures, structures, systems and ways of thinking, especially those secular views that predominate our society to day;

(b) consequently, reaffirms the traditional teaching upholding faithfulness between a husband and wife in marriage, and celibacy for those who are single;

(c) noting that the Holy Scriptures are clear in teaching that all sexual promiscuity is a sin, is convinced that this includes homosexual practices, between persons of the same sex, as well as heterosexual relationships outside marriage;

(d) believes that in this regard, as in others, all our ordained Ministers must set a wholesome and credible example. Those persons who practise homosexuality and live in promiscuity, as well as those Bishops who knowingly ordain them or encourage these practices, act contrary to the Scriptures and the teaching of the Church. We call upon them to repent;

(e) respects as persons and seeks to strengthen compassion, pastoral care, healing, correction and restoration for all who suffer or err through homosexual or other kind of sexual brokenness;

(f) affirms that it is therefore the responsibility of the Church to lead to repentance all those who deviate from the orthodox teaching of the Scriptures and to assure them of God's forgiveness, hope and dignity.

Note: This Resolution was put to the Conference in the form of an amendment to Resolution I.10 and was defeated.

Resolution V.10 from the Latin American Region

This Conference recognises the importance of strengthening Christian family values, and thereby reaffirms traditional Anglican sexual ethics.

Note: This Resolution was put to the Conference in the form of an amendment to Resolution I.10 and was withdrawn by the mover.

Resolution V. 23 from the South East Asia Region

This Conference receives the Kuala Lumpur Statement on Human Sexuality with gratitude as an authentic expression of Anglican moral norms.

Note: This Resolution was not voted upon, as the Conference agreed to pass to next business.

Resolution V.35 from the West Africa Region

This Conference:

(a) noting that—

(i) the Word of God has established the fact that God created man and woman and blessed their marriage;

(ii) many parts of the Bible condemn homosexuality as a sin;

(iii) homosexuality is one of the many sins that Scripture has condemned;

(iv) some African Christians in Uganda were martyred in the nineteenth century for refusing to have homosexual relations with the king because of their faith in the Lord Jesus and their commitment to stand by the Word of God as expressed in the Bible on the subject;

(b) stands on the Biblical authority and accepts that homosexuality is a sin which could only be adopted by the church if it wanted to commit evangelical suicide.

Note: This Resolution was put to the Conference in the form of an amendment to Resolution I.10 and was defeated.

GLOBAL POVERTY AND
UNPAYABLE DEBT

photos: *Anglican World*

British Prime Minister Tony Blair, Archbishop Carey, and Mrs Eileen Carey

Global Poverty and Unpayable Debt
The Right Honourable Tony Blair, MP
Prime Minister of the United Kingdom

Lambeth Palace 28 July 1998

I am particularly pleased and indeed honoured to address this Conference, with so many distinguished people from around the world, on a subject which could hardly be more important, the subject of global poverty and the unpayable burden of debt weighing down many of the world's poorest countries. I understand if I am right that the issue of debt was nominated by all Anglican Communion Provinces as the subject for today's discussion and I think that is enormously powerful and symbolic in itself.

And if I can say to the Archbishop of Canterbury and to all of you who are engaged in this work, sometimes the Church gets attacked and criticised a lot of the time as you will all know, and indeed, we are pretty familiar with that syndrome too in my business. But I do believe that the Church does tremendous work, certainly in this country and in towns, villages and cities around the world. Often unsung work, often work that goes totally unnoticed by the vast majority of people in a country, but work that is essential and has its own effect, in awakening the moral conscience, not just of a particular country, but indeed of the world. Not so very far from here, there is a centre for the homeless that is run by one of the Church charities, and to see the people there working with some of the most deprived, poorest, often psychologically disturbed members of the community, and to see people from the Church do that through sheer love of their common human beings, is a tremendous signal to the whole country. You may get attacked and criticised from time to time, but I think that the Churches in communities up and down this country, and throughout the world, contribute an enormous amount to the right spirit that should inform our society and indeed our political debates as well.

I also know that the Church, the Anglican Church, has played a great role, to pay tribute, to peace in Northern Ireland, which is something we have been working very, very closely for, and indeed have worked with the other churches there in order to bring about a greater spirit of reconciliation. Before I come to my topic and the detail of what I wanted to say to you today, I think one of the great things a gathering like this can do, is not just to send an international signal, but also to send a signal of openness from the Churches themselves towards people of other religions. I often reflect upon the fact that with all the differences in the world between Jews and Muslims and Christians, we are, after all, Abrahamic religions. We have actually got a lot in common in the values system that we share, and gatherings like this can send a very strong signal to that effect. These are the universal values of human progress, and it is important that we understand that and communicate that with people.

I remember a short time ago I went to visit a Hindu temple, and I saw some of the phrases that were written up on the wall there and some of the stories and parables that were there, and the stories that were told, and I thought how many echoes there were with our own religion. So, when a Conference like this meets, of course you will discuss the affairs particular to the Lambeth Conference, and of course you will discuss some specific issues as well like debt and world poverty, but it is also a powerful signal to the rest of the world.

I talk about globalisation as a politician very often, in terms of the trade liberalisation and the flows of capital, the opening of huge new markets, the revolution in technology and communications, and those are daunting challenges for the whole of the world. There are tremendous opportunities there, we should never forget that. I don't think we ever want to be people who simply sit there and say, globalisation should stop, technology is a threat and a danger. There are great opportunities for our people as a result of the new communications, the new technologies, the greater trade in the world. But, they also bring tremendous challenges, and I think the most important thing is that we don't let global change rule us, but that we drive it and subordinate it to the common good. The policies of our government are to open up the world in terms of technology and trade. We are doing it deliberately, and with a strategy that ensures that we don't just open up opportunities for more trade for one part of the world, when they are actually closing those opportunities off for another part. Now, there is no reason why that should happen if we get the right combination of policies to make it happen.

We live in a world today where as you know, 1.3 billion people, nearly a quarter of the world's population, two-thirds of the women, continue to live in extreme poverty with an income of less than US$1 a day. Eight hundred million people end each day hungry, 900 million people are illiterate, 30,000 children die each day from readily preventable diseases and malnutrition. The causes of this poverty can be very complex. In some countries people are poor, because they lack education and employment opportunities, because they lack access to land, to markets or technology. Elsewhere people are poor, because they live under unjust or corrupt governments who misuse their countries' resources and violate human rights. Then the poor often suffer most from bad health, or are victims of war or natural disasters, and frequently the poor are forced to over-exploit their own environment, destroying forests to get access to land, using trees for fuel and therefore causing solaration and problems for the environment.

The central point that we have tried to get across as a government, when talking about issues of aid and development, is that it is important to deal with these issues as a matter of moral duty and compassion, but we also believe that we have a common interest, mutually shared, in tackling these problems of poverty and injustice.

In our rapidly shrinking world, the fates of peoples across the world are more and more bound together. The new global challenges, whether it is climate change, or crime or terrorism, mass migration, these are problems that we solve together as one global community or not at all. But any of these issues can be solved if we work together. Take the global environment. Global environmental threats require co-ordinated global action. And that means marrying together the agendas of environment and the agendas of development. We know that developing countries fear that industrialised countries may seek to impose environmental controls which will prevent their development. It will be impossible, however, to reach effective global agreement on those major environmental challenges, unless we commit ourselves at the same time to securing real progress in development for the poorest countries. So the issues of environmental challenge and the issues of development, are intimately connected together. Again, you can see the same mutual interdependence in the area of security. Poverty is itself a major source of instability. Most of today's wars are fought within the poorest countries, and the poor are the principal victims of those wars. But the effects of that conflict are very rarely contained within the borders of one state. They have got the capacity to spill over boundaries, generate instability, refugees, further conflict, to demand for humanitarian assistance, and eventually for external intervention. So, there is a task there for peacekeeping and security, which has again to tie in with the agenda for poverty and development. One of the reasons why we in our country launched a major review of our defence forces, was so they could be better equipped for today's world. As well as obviously defending the country, they will be intervening in international situations of conflict where we require a different type of defence force and a different type of flexibility and mobility. The point that I am making, however, is that our action, whether it is on the environment or on poverty or on security is intimately linked together. Development, giving people a stake in their societies is, as Kofi Annan put it, "the prevention of conflict begins and ends with the promotion of human security and human development".

It is for all these reasons that we have tried to strengthen our commitment to international development. On taking office last year we created a department for International Development. Last November we published a White Paper on the Government's policy for development strategy, and that put a new and strong emphasis on the international poverty eradication strategy. A set of internationally agreed goals for poverty reduction, which derived from the great UN conferences of the past decade, commit us to halving the proportion of the world's population living in abject poverty by the year 2015, and providing education and health care for all by that date. Our aim then, as a government, is to mobilise international support for the achievement of these agreed targets and the policies necessary to do so. It means building partnerships with developing country governments, which are serious about reducing poverty, pursuing sensible economic policies, and upholding human rights. However, our policy on aid goes further than simply money. It is about investing in health and education, particularly the education of girls, it means promoting sustainable livelihoods, and it means creating a fairer international system of trade. Our development effort therefore, has gone far beyond merely the delivery of aid.

On trade we have tried to argue that the benefits of globalisation need to be spread more widely, so that developing countries feel that they, too, have a stake in the world's trading system. And during our presidency of the European Community recently we fought hard and successfully for a mandate for the renegotiation of the Lome Convention that should protect the trading interests of the seventy-one African, Caribbean and Pacific countries. That was a real achievement of our presidency.

Now, I know that today Gordon Brown and Clare Short have already set out the Government's policy on debt in some detail. I believe that we made some significant progress at the G8 conference in Birmingham. I know that many people feel that it wasn't enough, that is always the case, that is what you learn about being in Government, it is never enough, but we are trying to do more and we will try to do more, and this Government attaches the highest priority to doing that. We are working to ensure that by the year 2000 all highly indebted poor countries have embarked on a systematic process of debt reduction under the Mauritius Mandate. We are taking the initiative in accelerating IMF assistance to post-conflict countries; we set aside a special sum of money as a supplement for individual donors amounting to £60 million, and we must ensure that countries are getting the relief they need in order to secure a lasting exit to the debt problems that so dogged their development. So, on trade, again we have tried to push the boat out and move further. But on aid, we also need greater flows of official development assistance. That is why we have made a commitment to increasing spending on development, reversing a long period of years of decline, and we have begun to move towards the UN target of 0.7 percent of national income.

It will mean a cash increase in our aid and development budget of some £1.6 billion over the next three years. I think that is a clear measure of our commitment to development. This extra money will be spent on achieving measurable progress against the key international development goals. More access to primary education, lower maternal and child mortality, reversing the loss of environmental resources for a national strategy of sustainable development. As a concrete example of what I mean by this, we are today committing some £18 million to help eradicate polio in East Africa over the next three years. That is additional money. Working together with the World Health Organisation, we shall provide immunisation for all infants in Kenya, Tanzania and Uganda. Now, that is just one example of what we can do to give a whole generation of children the chance to lead healthier lives.

Sometimes, when we make the greater commitment, whether it is in aid or development, or in resources necessary to promote policies of sustainable development for the environment, people say to us, well, the country doesn't want to spend money on these things. People don't want to pay money out for these types of activity. I believe that that is wrong. I think that the British people do want Britain to provide a lead in the international efforts to eliminate poverty, and they want to feel pride and commitment in what we are doing, actually what they are doing through us to help others throughout the world.

I know that from time to time people will argue against this and say that it doesn't fulfil the purpose we have set out for it, but I do believe that to be fundamentally wrong. I also know that it will always be the desire of the Church to say, "You could do more; there are other and better and different things you could be doing" and that is always going to be the role of the Church—to warn and to criticise, to face power with truth.

But I think that we are embarked on a different era of international relations for the future. For a long period of time, people did regard issues of aid and debt simply as issues of compassion. And of course they are issues of compassion. We want to make sure that we are making a commitment to people who are in need, and we do that within our own society as well as outside it. But just as I would argue in Britain today that if we have a large group of young people who are permanently excluded from the work force, or you have got groups of people growing up in inner city estates without family stability, with crime and drugs and poor educational opportunity and high levels of unemployment; just as I would argue that in the end that problem affects all of Britain and all of our society, so, I would argue to you, that when we forget the needs of those countries that desperately have to develop and change over a period of time to become prosperous and do well, when we forget those needs we all lose as a result of that. It is not a situation in which we have to choose between the interests of our own country and the interests of others. That extra commitment that we are making to aid and development, is a commitment that I believe serves this country well, as well as the countries to whom we are making that commitment.

And that, after all, is the basic principle of community. It is the basic political philosophy that informs my life, the idea that we owe obligations to one another as well as to ourselves, but more than that, that in part we fulfil our own talent and potential through what we do with others. That essential guiding concept, a belief in the dignity and worth of each human being is not some platitude that we should dismiss. It is actually at the heart of ensuring that our nation and our world have some sense of purpose. We have the opportunity today for religion to be seen not as some exclusive sect, but as the possibility of opening up the world to other people and sharing certain common values that bring people together. The fact that we have that possibility as we approach the 21st Century, should be a cause for optimism. I am essentially optimistic about it. I know that sounds very strange when we look around the world today and we see all the poverty and the disease and the war, but I am optimistic because I think we can leave behind the prejudices that informed the worst part of the value system that used to dominate all our countries in the world, and we can leave in place and intact the best of the values of basic justice, of belief in community, the notion of society being important to advance the individual.

So, when I look ahead and I see all the challenges and I realise that my kids are going to grow up in a completely different world to the world that I inhabited; and if any of you have ever sat and watched your own children in front of a computer terminal, if you are fortunate enough to have one, and you see a child operating that computer, you feel a deep sense of humiliation and inadequacy. You know, they are going to grow up in a completely different world. But the values that they will need to make sense of that world are the values that people have used to make sense of the world since time immemorial. That never changes. And indeed, the more the world opens up, and the more the opportunities there are, the more those values are important. And if we ever forget that, then, of course, that is when we descend into the dark ages. The dark ages aren't a product of a lack simply of technology or advancement, they are a product of when people forget the basic values that make life worthwhile.

So, I am delighted and thrilled to come along here today to tell you some of the things that we have been doing in respect of aid and development, to say how immensely gratified we are that you are here, to make you feel very welcome and to say to you, as we look ahead, let's feel that sense of optimism. I think there is a lot to be hopeful for, and as you know better than me, there is a lot more work to do.

Thank you.

SERMONS AT SPECIAL OCCASIONS

photo: *Anglican World*

Jean Vanier of the L'Arche Community

Opening Service, Canterbury Cathedral

The Right Revd Simon E. Chiwanga, Bishop of Mpwapwa, Tanzania, Chairman of the Anglican Consultative Council

19 July 1998

Called to be Christlike
2 Cor. 4:7–11; Luke 6:27–36

In the name of the Father and of the Son and of the Holy Spirit. Amen.

I express my deepest appreciation to his Grace, the Archbishop of Canterbury, for giving me this rare and awesome honour of preaching at this Opening Service of Lambeth 1998. I accepted this honour on behalf of my Province and on behalf of the Anglican Consultative Council.

I thank the Dean and Chapter for their most warm welcome. I thank all of you for your prayers, for me and for all those who have been asked to undertake tasks more challenging than mine at this Lambeth Conference.

I count it a particular honour to worship today with His Royal Highness the Prince of Wales, with former Presidents of the Anglican Consultative Council, now retired Archbishops of Canterbury, and with all of you present at this great Eucharist where we ask for God's blessings upon the Lambeth Conference and the Spouses' Programme.

For Anglicans Canterbury Cathedral symbolizes both our common roots and our being part of that apostolic succession of costly witness through suffering and martyrdom. As we view its magnificence and grandeur during our time here let us be reminded of the majestic transcendence of God which rises far above our divisions both in the Church and society and draws us together in Christ as a pilgrim people.

During the great fourth-century period of spiritual renewal, when women and men were called by God to forsake their cultures and retreat to the desert, a great and powerful man of the royal court went to the desert to seek out a holy person.

Soon the pilgrim met an abbot walking with his young monks. He stopped the holy man and asked for a teaching upon which he could build his whole life. The abbot responded by picking up a tablet and on it he wrote one word "Awareness!"

Perplexed, the pilgrim asked if the abbot expected him to live his life seeking God on the basis of only one word. The abbot took back the tablet and wrote "Awareness, awareness, awareness!" "Whatever do you mean?" cried the pilgrim. The holy man bowed down humbly, picked up the tablet and wrote, "awareness, awareness, awareness, means awareness!"

For myself if there is one thing that I am in need of in my ministry, it is awareness, Christlike awareness.

I am aware that the world is desperately in need of a living demonstration of what it means to be a Christ-centred community of believable believers where every person is welcomed, accepted, loved, restored to wholeness and is encouraged to serve.

Like the pilgrim in the story, there are many people, particularly the youth, who are looking for Christ-like leaders in the Church—lay and ordained—who can demonstrate the awareness of the love of God and the way to a more meaningful life.

The scenario described in today's readings is a scenario that confronts many of the Bishops gathered in this Cathedral this morning. The Second Letter to the Corinthians, which forms the text of our daily Bible Studies at this Conference, speaks about episcopacy in time of crisis and leadership in the midst of struggle and suffering.

2 Cor. 4:7–11 reflects the difficult experiences that are faced by many within the Anglican Communion, who live and serve in places where there is both physical and spiritual deprivation. There are places where State disapproval is the normal context for some, as the recent tragic loss of the Roman Catholic bishop in Pakistan testifies. "We are afflicted in every way, but not crushed; perplexed, but not driven to despair, persecuted, but not forsaken; struck down, but not destroyed; always carrying in the body the death of Jesus, so that the life of Jesus may also be made visible in our bodies."

The stories of tribal conflicts in Africa, the violence in Northern Ireland, the terrorism that touches every person in the Western world; all this points to a world which is hungry for Christ's love and compassion; and this is the world that God so loved "that he gave his only Son, so that everyone who believes in him may not perish but may have eternal life." (John 3:16) God wants His Church and His servants to keep on growing more and more into a Christlike image in order to accomplish His purpose as St Paul says, "so that through the Church the wisdom of God in its rich variety might now be made known to the rulers and authorities in the heavenly places." (Eph. 3:10)

What this means for the Church is to turn itself inside out. The Decade of Evangelism was a call to turn the Church inside out, that is to move from being primarily a pastoral community, looking inward; to being primarily a missionary community looking outward. This call to Evangelism must remain our guiding principle as we develop the next step after the Decade.

The Church that is aware of, and is engaged in Christlike mission, will not spend its time bragging about being the only real missionary or the better evangelist. It will not occupy the seat of Moses judging others. The Christlike evangelist says with St John the Evangelist—"He must increase, but I must decrease." (John 3:30)

A Church that harbours bitterness, anger and disharmony is distorting its image of a living gospel and may be on the road to decay.

It is in mission in the world that we grow more into Christ's likeness. For Jesus, the constant moments of his encounter with the poor, the crippled, the lame, the blind, the sinner and the dead became moments of deeper awareness of his divine identity and mission. Likewise the identity and mission of the Church is discovered and deepened when we literally take up our cross and follow Jesus Christ into the midst of the poor, the crippled, the lame, the blind, and there reveal the love of Christ. The authority and power given to the Church and its leaders is discovered at the Holy Table in Holy Communion and in table fellowship with the poor, the outcast, the broken hearted and all who are in need of God and of freedom.

Our Communion's total commitment to the cause of cancelling International Debt that adds an unbearable burden on the poor is a powerful witness of our following Jesus into the midst of the disadvantaged.

Day by day our Anglican Communion continues to grow. We give thanks to God for the exciting developments, such as the formation of our new Province in Central America. The incredible work of the Karen Christians in Burma and Thailand is a tremendous inspiration to us all. The often hard-pressed situation of our Palestinian–Arab Christian friends, including our own Episcopalians in that country, is also most inspiring.

Christians who live in the midst of such conflict teach us to be aware of being Christlike in differences and in conflicts.

The passage from St Luke, read for the Gospel, speaks about the need for Christians to treat even those whom they find resentful, and who might have significant differences with them, in a way that is Christlike. Controversial issues and passionate debates do happen, and the Lambeth Conference cannot be an exception. What is essential for every participant to be aware of is that we have to look for the Christ in each other and to turn the other cheek, particularly when feel we have been offended.

In Barbados, a story is told of a woman in Church who always bowed profoundly whenever the name of Jesus was mentioned. But she was seen to bow equally profoundly whenever the name of Satan was mentioned. When she was questioned about this strange behaviour she explained "Well when I die I do not know whose hands I shall fall into, so I am making friends on both sides!"

Being Christlike in our differences does not mean having no convictions or clear position of your own. It is a call to interpretive charity in our Christian dialogues.

Interpretive charity can be defined as the ability to apply the most loving interpretation to actions and opinions of others. Interpretive charity means listening to one another in love. It demands that we restrain our impulse to start formulating our response before the other has finished what they are saying. It is difficult. It is a lot easier and more attractive to evaluate the first few words of the speaker and then plug that statement into a pre-constructed mental model.

Interpretive charity calls us to persevere with the discomfort of thoughtful silence and to use that time to prepare a loving response to what we have heard. Interpretive charity challenges us to avoid demeaning labels that we are so eager to apply to our opponents.

There are several examples we can give of Jesus' interpretive charity. When some men cut through the roof of a house where Jesus was staying so that they could lower their paralyzed friend into Jesus' healing presence, he did not call them vandals. He rewarded their faith. When an angry mob wanted to stone a woman caught in sin, Jesus challenged anyone who was without sin to cast the first stone. And even upon the cross, when he was being insulted, spat at and nailed, Jesus prayed "Father forgive them for they know not what they do."

Interpretive charity calls us to two further things: first not to disenfranchise or un-church anyone. Hold unswervingly to that which you believe to be of essential truth, but to God leave the final judgement in all matters. Change comes by enlightenment, not by force. Forcing your point of view by excluding from your circle those who disagree with you, or by compelling acceptance, is to usurp the place of God.

Remember what St Paul says in Romans: "Who are you to pass judgement on servants of another? It is before their own lord that they stand or fall." (Rom. 14:4)

In Philippians he says, "Let those of us then who are mature be of the same mind; and if you think differently about anything, this too God will reveal to you. Only let us hold fast to what we have attained." (Philippians 3:15, 16)

Second, do not give power to sin. Whenever you are the recipient of uncharity in any form, bear it, forgive it, rather than repeat it to others. The Apostle Peter says, "Above all, maintain constant love for one another, for love covers a multitude of sins." (1 Peter 4:8)

St Paul again says, "With all humility and gentleness, with patience, bearing with one another in love, making every effort to maintain the unity of the Spirit in the bond of peace. There is one body and one spirit,… one Lord, one Faith, one Baptism, one God and Father of all." (Eph. 4:2–6)

In our daily relationships with others and during this Conference, may we be aware that a critical remark, a gesture of rejection or an act of impatience can be remembered for life by those to whom it is directed. The Prophet Malachi cautions those in authority and leadership as follows: "For the lips of a priest should guard knowledge, and people should seek instruction from his mouth, for he is the messenger of the Lord of Hosts."(Malachi 2:7)

During the next few weeks, as we stand aware of God and the world, we have a tremendous opportunity before us. It is a holy moment, when we can once more demonstrate, through the power of the Holy Spirit, our ability to speak the truth in love—interpretive charity—and to show how truth can triumph over error in a way that is Christlike.

"But I say to you that listen, Love your enemies, do good to those who hate you, bless those who curse you, pray for those who abuse you." (Luke 6: 27, 28)

In the name of the Father, and the Son, and the Holy Spirit. Amen.

Homily at Ecumenical Vespers Edward Idris Cardinal Cassidy, President, Pontifical Council for Christian Unity

20 July 1998

Your Grace, dear brothers and sisters in Christ,

I am most grateful to the Archbishop of Canterbury for graciously inviting me to preach at this Ecumenical Vespers service as the Lambeth Conference gets underway. I am honoured to be asked to address you. As President of the Pontifical Council which assists Pope John Paul II and the whole Catholic Church with the task of promoting the unity of all the disciples of the one Lord and Saviour Jesus Christ, I take the invitation most seriously.

In what I make bold to say I cannot presume to speak for all the other ecumenical guests. However, I am sure that *I can say* on behalf of all how much we appreciate the opportunity to share this important moment in the life of the Anglican Communion as the second Christian millennium draw to a close. We will all be praying that the life in Christ of your churches, and their unity with one another, will be deepened through this Conference.

The last thirty years or so have seen our relationships renewed, our brotherhood and sisterhood rediscovered. Now a commitment to seek visible unity, enhanced contacts, dialogue and discussions are normal for most Christian Churches and communities. In particular, praying for unity, as we do here this evening, has become almost commonplace. This is all the fruit of God's grace for which we do not cease to give thanks. At the same time, as ecumenical commitment loses its novelty, there are new risks of which I will speak in a moment.

Our prayer for unity often returns to the priestly prayer of Jesus Christ in chapter 17 of St John's Gospel. Sometimes it may seem that its words are used almost like an ecumenical proof-text—when the going gets tough we turn to them to be reminded that here the New Testament speaks particularly clearly about unity. We need anchorholds in storms, but the significance of John chapter 17 is greater than that.

Among the many reasons for seeking Christian unity the primary one is the desire to do Christ's will. Slowly, our Churches have been relearning this lesson, especially by reflecting on the prayer of Christ in verses 20–21: "I pray not only for these, but for those also who through their words will believe in me. May they all be one Father, may they be one in us, as you are in me and I am in you".

When this prayer, which is our prayer too, is answered, there may indeed be greater efficiency, better husbandry of resources, or the elimination of competitiveness, perhaps solutions to other organisational concerns as well. But, crucially, we will have become more obedient to Christ's will for his Church.

It is clear that John's Gospel challenges us to seek unity of a particular and demanding kind. It is unity in the truth, a unity grounded in more faithful obedience to every aspect of the Gospel of Christ. Our oneness is to reflect the unity between Christ and his Father which was manifested in the Lord's obedience in all things, even unto death. He glorified his Father by finishing the work he was given to do (cf. Jn 17:3–4). "I know him and I faithfully keep his word", he says (Jn 8:55). "What I have spoken does not come from myself; no… What I had to speak was commanded by the Father who sent me" (Jn 12:49). To those who follow him he has made known everything he learned from his Father; they will be his "friends" if they do what he commands (cf. Jn 15: 14–15). "I have given them the teaching you gave to me" (Jn 17:8). Before praying for their unity, he asks the Father. "Consecrate them in the truth; your word is truth" (Jn 17:17). As the very first ARCIC statement on Authority put it, "The Church is a community which consciously seeks to submit to Jesus Christ".[1] The Lord give his Spirit to create and perfect this *koinonia.*[2]

If we are to reach a unity grounded in such deep faithfulness, there has to be continual conversion. The Second Vatican Council underlined this in its Decree on Ecumenism with those remarkable words: "There can be no ecumenism worthy of the name without a change of heart".[3] Pope John Paul II, in his Encyclical, similarly, prefaced his consideration of the practice of ecumenism by reflecting on renewal and conversion.[4] Indeed, having expressed the conviction that the Bishop of Rome's mission today is "particularly directed to recalling the need for full communion among Christ's disciples",[5] he asks everyone to join him *in praying for his conversion*—indispensable if, like Peter, he is to serve his brethren.[6] Truly to desire unity we have to pray for our conversion to Christ and his truth.

Why, then, mention risk, as I did earlier? For two reasons. The first comes if we lower our sights. Doubts are expressed about whether we shall ever reach the goal of full, visible unity. Should we not concentrate on shorter-term goals, greater understanding and co-operation, a peaceful coexistence (which, I believe, would itself prove illusory)? Three years ago Pope John Paul II said quite unambiguously that the Catholic Church continues to be irrevocably committed to the re-establishment of full, visible unity among all the baptised? If we believe the Church to be one, holy, catholic and apostolic then mutual understanding and doctrinal convergence, vital as they are, cannot be sufficient.

The second threat is more insidious. It comes when prayer for unity and ecumenical engagement are compartmentalised, hermetically sealed off from other areas of Church life and decision-making. If these are just part of a series of concerns, perhaps subtly marginalised. Different approaches, important decisions, in other areas of the Church's life can conflict with it and may even undermine it. The commitment to unity is relativised if diversity and differences that cannot be reconciled with the Gospel are at the same time being embraced and exalted. It is put in question when pluralism in the Church comes to be regarded as a kind of 'post-modern' beatitude. It will be lost sight of altogether if radical obedience, and the necessity of costly ethical choices for faithful discipleship, are swept aside by a naive overemphasis on our innate goodness, underestimating the reality of sin in our lives and our world and also the power of Christ's redemption and the grace-filled possibility of conversion. Are we not experiencing in fact new and deep divisions among Christians as a result of contrasting approaches to human sexuality for instance? When such attitudes are in the ascendant, disunity between Christians will remain unresolved. Moreover, disunity becomes an increasingly grave matter *within* the still-separated Churches as well. Authoritative proclamation of the Gospel of Christ is diminished.

I believe this Conference is to give considerable attention to *The Virginia Report*. It is concerned with how the Anglican Communion makes authoritative decisions which, in the final analysis, means how the Gospel is to be proclaimed authoritatively and faithfully. You have shared this report with your ecumenical partners. This is a sign of trust in us. It shows that we are joined in an imperfect but real degree of communion, as brothers and sisters in Christ, so that the lives of our Churches are increasingly bound up with each other. I hope it also represents an awareness of how important the renewal and strengthening[8] of Anglican instruments of communion is for progress towards full communion between the Anglican Communion and the Catholic Church.

From the beginning of Anglican-Catholic dialogue Authority in the Church has had a prominent place in our discussions. In fact, it lies at the heart of how and why we have diverged. Great progress was made by the first ARCIC, and the present Commission may soon to complete a further statement. More and more we are coming to realise in all our theological dialogue just how important the question of authority is for real progress towards unity. We are constantly faced with fundamental questions that demand an answer. What are the means with which the Church of Christ has been endowed to ensure the Good News is proclaimed with authority? How will it pass on its entirety what we ourselves have received (cf. 1 Cor 15:3), what was seen and heard (cf. 1 Jn 1:3)? How are Christians to respond to new questions and remain faithful to the Gospel of Christ? How is the authority of Christ appropriately exercised at different levels in the Church? And when we reach ecumenical agreement can our Churches recognise it authoritatively so as to be sure that the results will be taken into their life? Again and again, such questions bring us back to the Johannine vision of unity in loving, faithful obedience.

We are in dialogue because we know that brothers and sisters in Christ should be able to give united testimony to him. What happens in one Christian community affects others. The deepening of communion within any Christian Church is a gift to the others, its deepening of communion within any Christian Church is a gift to the others; its impairment diminishes us all. As you reflect on how Christian authority is exercised within the Anglican Communion, I pray that your deliberations may lead to a strengthening of those "restraints of truth and love", of which the 1920 Conference spoke. They are not a restraining of the Holy Spirit. Rather, they are his work, as he leads us to the complete truth by saying "only what he has learnt" (Jn 16:13). The Spirit, again to use some words of ARCIC, "safeguards [the People of God's] faithfulness to the revelation of Jesus Christ".[9]

I want to express in Christian love the concern of the Catholic Church when new and conflicting interpretations of the Gospel result in fresh disagreements, especially where these touch ministry and strain ecclesial communion, above all at the Eucharist. *The Virginia Report* is surely right to argue that "At all times the theological praxis of the local church must be consistent with the truth of the gospel which belongs to the universal Church"[10]; and that the universal Church sometimes has "to say with firmness that a particular local practice or theory is incompatible with Christian faith".[11] In ARCIC's words, "A local Church cannot be truly faithful to Christ if it does not desire to foster universal communion, the embodiment of that unity for which Christ prayed".[12] Is not some form of universal authority the necessary corollary of communion at a universal level, even while Christians are on the way towards full communion? Indeed the Spirit does bestow a diversity of gifts but their purpose is that "we all come to unity in our faith and in our knowledge of the Son of God" (Eph 4:13).

As we go into a third Christian millennium the Risen Lord still calls us to go and make disciples of all the nations (cf. Mt 28:19). Even where the Church has long been present there are many who have not heard the Gospel preached to them and in their search for meaning have turned to other beliefs and to superstitions. The ecumenical movement has taught us not to be complacent any longer about the effects on mission and evangelisation of our disunity and conflicting voices. Our divisions may have contributed to the growth in society of a do-it-yourself, *à la carte* attitude towards what should be and which decisions are important. In obedience to Christ we have to address the world sympathetically, but with clarity and conviction, about the Good News of everlasting life in Jesus Christ. May each of us hear the urgency in the Lord's prayer for unity—"May they be one in us, as you are in me and I am in you, *so that the world may believe it was you who sent me*" (Jn 17:2).

Edward Idris Cardinal Cassidy
President
Pontifical Council for Promotion Christian Unity

Notes

1. Anglican-Rome Catholic International Commission. [*Authority in the Church 1.4*].

2. Cf. *ibid* 1.4 and *passim.*

3. Second Vatican Council. Decree on Ecumenism *Unitatis Redintegration.* 4.

4. John Paul II. Encylical letter on Commitment to Ecumenism *Ut unum sint.* 15–17.

5. *Ut unum sint.* 4.

6. *Ibid.*

7. *Ibid.* 77.

8. Cf. Inter-Anglican Theological and Doctrinal Commission, *The Virginia Report.* 1.14. 3.54 and *passim.*

9. *Authority in the Church* 1.3.

10. *The Virginia Report.* 4.25.

11. *Ibid.*

12. *Authority in the Church* 1.13.

Vigil of Meditation, Prayer and Washing of Feet I
Jean Vanier, L'Arche Community

30 July 1998

I think you can imagine how moved I am to share with you, and how touched I was when I received the invitation from the Archbishop of Canterbury. I felt very moved because you are the good shepherds of the Anglican Communion, and the shepherds of an immense flock of disciples of Jesus.

I want to begin by saying how I rejoice in you; how I give thanks for you; how I give thanks for your beauty, for your fidelity. I give thanks for those of you who come from countries oppressed by poverty. I give thanks for you who live in oppression and fear of persecution. And I give thanks for you who are in our richest societies who have difficulty seeing our crucified Jesus and our risen Jesus.

So I am moved to be with you. I suppose that I accepted the invitation of the Archbishop of Canterbury, because I feel humbled to be the voice of people who have no voice. People with mental handicaps, disabilities are amongst the most oppressed people of our world, and I have visited institutions, asylums which are really places of death. Many of you maybe know of these institutions (they are in all our countries) where these very special people are crushed and hurt, broken, with no voice. And yet—and this is what I am going to try and share with you—they are precious people.

They are very precious people. St Paul had some sense of this when he said that God has chosen what is foolish in this world to confound the wise; that God has chosen the weak of this world to confound the strong; that God has chosen those that are despised. This is the incredible love of our God.

I'd like to begin by citing a text of Isaiah 53, where Isaiah says "Who can believe what we have heard? And to whom has the arm of God been revealed?" And then he goes on, and he talks of this man—no beauty, no comeliness in him—"we turned away our faces. He was a man of sorrows; despised." And then he goes on, "And we are healed by his stripes. And he has borne the sins or transgressions of many." This incredible vision of Isaiah: That man—dirty, ugly, beaten—who, in some mysterious way, brings us peace. Maybe this is a little bit of the mystery that we in L'Arche and Faith and Light, and maybe many of you, have had the privilege of living.

I want to begin by saying just a little word about a little boy of eleven. This little boy made his first communion, and there was a beautiful liturgy. After the liturgy, there was a family celebration. And the uncle of the little boy said to the mother (and the little boy was nearby) "Wasn't it a beautiful liturgy? The only thing that's sad is that he understood nothing." The little boy looked at his mother, with tears in his eyes, and said "Don't worry mummy, Jesus loves me as I am."

"Jesus loves me as I am." Are we able to say that? Sometimes maybe we'll add, "Jesus loves me IF..." Can we believe that we—with our handicaps, with our brokenness—that Jesus loves us as we are? Some of you may think that these words "Jesus loves me as I am", may be a bit sentimental or emotional. But those of you who have lived or been with people who are crushed; those of you who know something about the wounds and hatred of humanity; you who know something about what oppression is; You know that somebody who begins to say "Jesus loves me as I am", is on the road of transformation.

Maybe that's what we are all called to discover. Maybe it is those words of Isaiah 43, where Isaiah says "Do not be afraid for I have redeemed you, I have liberated you. I have called you by your name, and you are mine. If you pass through the waters I will be with you. If you pass through the rivers you will not be overwhelmed. If you pass through the fires you will not be burned. If you pass through the flame you shall not be consumed, for I am the Lord God your Saviour. You are precious to my eyes, and I love you. Do not be afraid because I am with you."

To understand the transformation that occurred in that little boy, because somewhere he had become conscious that he was precious to God, I would like to tell you a word about Moses, (not the big Moses, not the Moses of Exodus), just a little boy with a severe handicap, who was found in the streets of Harare Zimbabwe. We don't know about his mother, nor his father. My experience with people with disabilities is that sometimes a mother feels that she cannot cope. She has other children, she has emotional difficulties, so she puts her child somewhere in the streets—not because she does not love the child, but because she does loves the child. And she leaves the child in a place where the child will be found. And the little child was found by police and brought to the hospital. And there he spent something like three years, where the co-ordinator of our communities in Africa found him. And he was all closed up in himself. There was no beauty, no comeliness, in him. A little boy filled with anguish and fear—a little boy in pain. You see, a hospital can have beautiful and competent nurses, but they are not there to create family. And what that little boy needs is somebody who says, "you are my beloved son, in whom I have put all my pleasure." He needs his family—a place of belonging—and a hospital is not a place of belonging.

So what happens inside of the heart of this helpless little. When one is helpless one feels insecure, unsafe, in danger. When one is loved, then one feels safe. So there is a lot of fear in this little Moses. But also terrible anguish—anguish which comes from loneliness, anguish which comes from this feeling of hopelessness in an unsafe world, where there are so many forces of lack of love, of indifference, sometimes hate. And when a little boy feels unloved, when a little child feels not wanted, when a little child feels helpless and in anguish, very quickly he feels guilt. "I am not loved, I am not loveable. I am no good. If nobody wants me it is because I am dirty." So you find a lot of people in institutions, a lot of people with disabilities, roaming the streets. A lot of those they call mad. You find somewhere a desire to die, because why live? "If nobody loves me, if nobody wants me, there is nothing to live for. If I am dirty and despised, no comeliness, no beauty, and nobody looks at me with love or attention, then I want to die." This develops in us a broken self-image.

When I went to Zimbabwe last December for the official opening of the community of L'Arche, Moses had already spent four months in the community. And he was changing. Instead of being all closed up in himself, he was opening up. His face was being transformed, his eyes were becoming bright, and a smile was breaking out in his face. The incredible thing is that love transforms people. It really transforms people.

So I want to talk to you about this love that transforms us, that transformed Moses, that transformed that little boy of eleven who said "Don't worry mummy, Jesus loves me as I am." What is this love? This is the love which Jesus calls us to—his new commandment which is to love one another as he loves. John in his letter says, "Beloved, let us love one another." The person who loves is born of God and knows God, because God is love.

What is this love? This little word is so misused. But somewhere we don't quite know what it is. And my experience in L'Arche, as in Faith and Light—my experience with people like the little boy of eleven, or the little Moses—is that love has a special connotation, it means something very special. To love is not first of all to do things for other people, because we can do things for people and hurt them. We can do things for people and make them feel that they're no good, that they can't do it themselves. So what is this love?

First of all, to love is to reveal. And what do we reveal when we love someone? "You're special. You're unique. You're beautiful. Your life has a meaning." And how do we reveal that "you are beautiful, you are special"? This revelation which is primary—which is not first of all revealing what is no good, revealing the handicap or judging people. No, it is a way of looking at people, of touching people, of listening to people, of being attentive to people—and so revealing to them that they are special. Isn't that how a mother loves her little child. Does the mother give more to the child, or does the child give more to the mother?

But somewhere, to love is to reveal—through our eyes and hands and flesh. The Word became flesh, so our flesh becomes word. So that through our flesh, through our eyes and hands, and listening and attention, we reveal to people. But this is not some passing moment, because this revelation is a revelation of fidelity. It is a consciousness of belonging. Somewhere we belong to each other. There is a covenant between us. So to love is to reveal.

To love is also to understand. Living with people with disabilities, I have been very moved by their pain; their difficulties in expressing themselves; their difficulties in mobility. Their difficulty in never living up to the expectations of people—the pain they have because in some way they feel they are a disappointment to their family. And of course they are. Every mum and every dad, what do they desire? It is a healthy, beautiful child. And of course the heart of a mother, the heart of a dad, is wounded when they discover that this little child has had convulsions, brain damage; that their little child at the age of three has a meningitis; that the little child that is born, is born with a serious handicap. To understand the pain of people, to understand their suffering, to understand the suffering of parents is love. I have been very moved as I have listened to parents.

Maybe you wouldn't believe this, but how many feel somewhere in their guts that this is a punishment from God. This is something which is in the culture and in all cultures. It was in the culture of the Jewish people during the time of Jesus—that immediate reaction of the disciples of Jesus in the ninth chapter of Saint John. When they saw that man born blind crying out for money, their reaction, "was it because he has sinned, or his parents have sinned?" To have a child with a handicap is quickly seen as a punishment. The answer of Jesus is "No! They have not sinned. It is so that the work of God may be accomplished in them." What is that work of God? That they may be transmitters of love. That they may receive the love of Jesus and give the love of Jesus. This is the mission of all of us. It is the mission of every disciple and lover of Jesus. It is to receive the love, and to give the love. Each one of us, in some mysterious way, may manifest the presence of Jesus in our world—just by who we are and the way we are, and the way we are present to people, and particularly to people in pain.

To love is to reveal. To love is to understand. To love is to celebrate. It is to celebrate people. In my community a few years ago, we welcomed Fareed. And Fareed was quite a severely handicapped man. His great moment is when he goes to a restaurant and has a huge ice cream. You ought to see his eyes when he looks at the ice cream. I think if Jesus was talking to him, he would say "the kingdom of God is like a big ice cream". Fareed would then understand.

We are called to celebration, and to be celebrated. We are called to ecstasy. In our world and in our communities and in our faith, we are called to celebrate people.

To love is also to empower people. It is to bring them to freedom—to the freedom that they can have. It is not to control, it is to help each person make choices. I cannot make a choice for you; you cannot make a choice for me. When we live with people with disabilities it is to help them to own their lives, each one according to their possibilities. Each one of us as disciples of Jesus is called to own our lives. And to choose to follow Jesus, to be loved and to love; to be men and women of the resurrection; to struggle through the powers of selfishness which engulf us so quickly. To love is to empower.

To love is to forgive and to be forgiven. I feel this very deeply because sometimes I feel the need to be forgiven quite deeply by people with disabilities. To be forgiven by those who at times I didn't listen to correctly or well, or that I didn't empower them or reveal to them their beauty sometimes hidden under the ruins of their lives and their immense psychological difficulties.

So we are called to be people of love. And holiness, for me, is to receive this love and to give this love. Jesus comes to reveal to us, "You are precious, and I have called you to reveal the love of our Father to the world". And Jesus understands us. He understands our brokenness, our inner pain. He celebrates us. And Jesus empowers us. He calls us to make choices—to follow him on the path of love and reconciliation. Jesus is the gentle forgiver—the gentle lover.

I'd like to share with you now about a young man in my community who died a year and a half ago. His name was Antonio. Antonio spent twenty years in hospital. He could not move his legs or use his hands, he could not speak, he needed extra oxygen, and he had to be fed through the stomach because he could not swallow. So, he was a man weak and fragile, impoverished. But at the same time he was an incredible man with an incredible face. If you came up to him and called him by his name (you shouldn't call him Anthony nor Antoine but Antonio—his origins were Italian and there was no fooling around there). And if you called him Antonio, his face would light up with a huge smile. One of the moments I had with him just shortly before his death, he stuck his tongue out at me. And the person next to him said to me, "Do you know what he is saying to you?" I said, "No". He said, "He is saying to you that he hasn't received communion yet today." This is an incredible secret that is hidden in our people.

What touched us in our community was his total acceptance of himself. There was no anger, no depression (that didn't mean that now and again he wasn't "peeved" if the water of the bath was too hot or too cold, or if he didn't receive the attention that he needed), but there was incredible beauty in this man. He was a little lover. He couldn't love with the love of generosity. You know what generosity is. It is when someone has more power, more goods, more knowledge, and then bends down to somebody who has less power, less goods, less knowledge—hopefully to help the lowly person to rise up, and not for the glory of the giver. So Antonio couldn't love with generosity (which as you know is a one way street—I give). But he did love. He loved with a love that maybe sometimes we have lost—the love of trust.

Trust is something very beautiful. In trust I do not give things, I give my heart, I give myself. I give myself because I trust you. And in trust somewhere we become vulnerable because, as I give myself I can be hurt, if you don't receive the gift that I am. And that is how Jesus is hurt. It is the incredible vulnerability of our God. He gives Himself, but we don't always know how to receive Jesus. And of course this is the trust of Antonio to those that were around him (he lived in a small house where six of people like Antonio with six people who had the privilege to share their lives together with them). The trust of Antonio called forth the trust of the assistants, and brought them together to the place of communion—communion of hearts.

Communion of hearts is very different to generosity. In communion of hearts, I give and I receive. We give to each other. There is a mutual trust. We are safe in each other's hands. Fear has disappeared. I am not better than you, and you are not better than me. But somewhere, there is a belonging which has come together. I don't seek to possess you. No, I want to bring you to freedom. And you don't seek to possess me, but you also want to bring me to freedom. There is something very beautiful in communion. And I suppose in living with people with disabilities, I have discovered this mystery of the communion of hearts. That we are bonded together in a covenant, and we are there for each other. And in that bonding, God is present.

Maybe one of the greatest mysteries or words of the gospels is when Jesus takes a little child in his arms and says, "Whoever welcomes one of these little ones in my name, welcomes me. The person who welcomes me welcomes the one who sent me." What can those words mean? To welcome Antonio, or Moses is to welcome Jesus. How can the Word be unable to speak? This mystery is there when Jesus reveals himself in the poor and the broken, and those who cannot cope for themselves. But I would tend to say today, as I try to understand these incredible words from Jesus, that God is hidden in the broken child. God is hidden in the stranger, in the naked, in those in prison.

What does Antonio want? Does he want money, power, knowledge, and an important place in community? What is the fundamental question of Antonio? "Do you love me? Do you love me as I am? Do you rejoice in me?" What is the question of Jesus to each of us? Those words that he said to Peter after the resurrection, near the lake of Tiberias, when he took Peter aside and said, "Simon son of John, do you love me?" That is the question of Antonio to all of us. It is the question of Jesus to all of us. "Do you love me?"

If you had sat down beside an assistant in that little house and said to him or her, "How do you live with Antonio? Is it difficult for you?" You would be surprised. Many would say, "Antonio has transformed my life. He has changed me. I come from a world where I have to be aggressive, go up the ladder of promotion, to win. I have to succeed and I have to put all my energy into that success of knowledge, of power. Antonio is drawing me into another world—of mutuality, of tenderness, of mutual acceptation, a community where Jesus is present."

I'd like to say a word about how I feel many of us who live with the Antonios in our communities, how we have been transformed.

The Archbishop of Canterbury told you that I was a naval officer. In the navy they taught me to be efficient, to be quick, to use armaments, to kill people, not to get too sentimental, not to be too concerned by people. When I did studies I was taught to think. So I was somebody who was, during my adolescent and young adult period, somebody who was called to be efficient, rapid; to teach and to control. Where I have been led is somewhere where I didn't expect to be led—into a relationship through my body, to discover community of hearts, to enter into relationships of celebration, to discover tenderness. I suppose in some way my thirty-four years in L'Arche has brought my head into my heart, and my heart into my head. I think as a young man I had overdeveloped my intellectual and rational capacities or my powers to control and to organize, but I had underdeveloped my heart.

So I have been led little by little to understand this relationship of love, of communion. To love people intelligently, to bring them to freedom, not to hold on but to help each one just to be themselves, to empower them, to reveal to them that they are able to do beautiful things; that they are loved and that they are special.

So somewhere this living with people with disabilities has brought me into my own body. Maybe I understand a bit more the whole mystery of "the Word became flesh." To help me to discover what it is to be fully human. To be fully human is, somewhere, to become whole—for my heart and my head to be together. And then in this wholeness, to discover a presence of God.

But this relationship with people like Antonio and others has also had an element of great pain. I have discovered all my blockages, my fears, and my angers. I remember that when I left the responsibility of my community, I went to stay in one of our houses where I met a young man named Lucien. He was very severely handicapped—couldn't walk or talk. And Lucien had lived for thirty years with his mum—a beautiful relationship. He could not talk, but his mum understood every grunt and every movement, and responded to all his needs in a beautiful way. There was an incredible relationship between the two. But mum fell sick; mum had to go to hospital. Lucien had to be put into a hospital because obviously he couldn't live alone, and he lived a terrible anguish. Anguish is broken communion—loneliness, helplessness. And in the hospital there were good people, but he was lonely because nobody understood him. He eventually came to our community, and he used to scream a lot. And his scream was the scream of anguish, the scream of loneliness, because he was no longer with the one he loved. And this is understandable. But his scream entered into me, and awoke my scream. And I discovered, being with him, immense powers of anger inside of me. Living in community I was protected, but I could see how I could hurt a weak person. I don't dare say I could kill a weak person, but maybe that too is true. To discover powers within me, which in someway I'd never wanted to look at, but which came welling up inside of me. It is not always easy to live with people with disabilities, because they reveal all sorts of things within us. They reveal what is most precious, our capacity to love. They reveal also what is most broken.

Then I began to see that the truth only will set me free. It was important to know myself. It was important to know my shadow side. It was important to understand a little bit my character traits, my need for power or success, the fears that I might have in relationship with people who are broken.

At that time, I discovered a letter from Carl Jung, the Swiss psychoanalyst. And in this letter he wrote to a Christian woman and said this: "I admire you Christians, because when you see somebody hungry and thirsty you see Jesus. When you see somebody in prison or in hospital you see Jesus. When you see somebody who is strange, a stranger or naked you see Jesus. What I don't understand is that you don't see Jesus in your own brokenness. Why are the poor always outside of you? Can't you see they're inside of you; in your hunger and thirst? That you too are sick; that you too are imprisoned in your own fears or need for honour and power; that you too have strange things inside of you which you don't understand; that you too are naked?" That helped me. It helped me to discover that to be compassionate (and that is the heart of the message of Jesus—"Be compassionate as my Father is compassionate; do not judge and you shall not be judged; forgive and you shall be forgiven")—to be compassionate for Antonio, to be compassionate for Lucien, I have to be compassionate also towards myself. I have to understand myself. I have to understand what is happening inside of me, so that I can give all that to Jesus for the Kingdom.

One of the things that we discover when we live with the poor, is that they awaken our hearts as we tell each other's stories; they open us up to people; but they also reveal our own poverty. And it's then that we discover how each of us, to be a true a disciple of Jesus, we need the Paraclete—the defender, the advocate, the counsellor. The one who comes to us and reveals to us that we are loved, that we will receive a force.

Through living with people with disabilities, they've taught me about myself, they've taught me about Jesus. Jesus, meek and humble of heart—the Jesus that says, "come to me all you who labour and are overburdened and I will give you rest. Take upon you my yoke, for my yoke is easy and my burden is light." This is the Jesus who is hidden in the weak and the poor—the crucified Jesus, the risen Jesus. Who in some mysterious way calls us to be with him.

I suppose also the other thing that I have learned is a passion for unity, a unity in which people who are disabled might find their rightful place in the Church. Saint Paul says, as he describes the Church as the Body, that those parts of the

Body which are the weakest and the least presentable are necessary to the Body and should be honoured. They have their rightful place in the Church, for they are precious to Jesus. This passion for unity, because our world is too broken between the rich and the poor, the "have's" and the "have not's", the able and the disabled. But God wants us, and we become impassioned for unity.

L'Arche began on Roman Catholic soil. Then L'Arche developed in other countries, and there we discovered the wealth, the richness, and the beauty of living together with people from different Christian traditions. That has brought inside of me this passion for unity. I can tell you this morning, as I assisted at your incredibly beautiful Holy Eucharist, I began to weep because to be loyal to my tradition I did not go to communion. And the little tears I shed are the tears, I think, of Christ. How Jesus is calling us to oneness, to reconciliation, to mutual understanding, to revealing to each other that maybe there can be different theological visions. But we are disciples of Jesus, and he loves us and he calls us. And we are called to announce this good news, to receive love and to give love.

In our community in Calcutta we are Hindus, Moslems and Christians together. We are in an area of Calcutta where on one side there are Moslems and the other side Hindus. The Moslems sometimes kill cows, the Hindus bring up pigs, so occasionally (as you can imagine) it flares up and houses are burned. And somewhere in between, we are together, Hindus, Moslems and Christians. We are a sign of our common humanity—the sign that we are all children of God. A sign that we are all called together to struggle for peace and for unity.

But you know, as I know, to struggle for unity means loss. It means pain, it means effort. It means to listen to each other, to reveal to each other our mutual beauty, to enter not only into dialogue, but into this mystery of communion where God is present. And I am touched that it is the weakest, the most broken, those who have no voice, that have given me this thirst for unity and created in L'Arche and Faith and Light these communities where we are coming together as disciples of Jesus.

Sometimes we come in pain, but are we not able to accept pain? Are we not called to accept this pain in order to walk towards the resurrection? Don't we all have to walk with the crucified Jesus in order to rise up with the risen Jesus?

Vigil of Meditation, Prayer and Washing of Feet II
Jean Vanier, L'Arche Community

30 July 1998

"Before the festival of the Passover, Jesus knowing that his time had come to depart from this world and to return to the Father, having loved his own, he loved them fully, he loved them to the end." And then, in the middle of this rather solemn meal, he got up and started taking off his clothes—the outer garment. You can imagine the surprise of the disciples.

Jesus is always surprising us. He doesn't like it when we fall into little habits. He shakes us up. Imagine the disciples looking at Jesus and saying, "What's going on?"

Jesus took off his outer robe. We know in the nineteenth chapter of John that Jesus had an outer robe, and under the robe what we call the tunic. The robe must have been pretty dirty, the robe of a poor person. The soldiers cut it into four, and they would use it for cleaning up. But the tunic was particularly beautiful—it had been woven from head to foot. It was one beautiful piece, and so the soldiers drew lots to see who would have it. So when Jesus takes off the outer garment he is dressed in this flimsy tunic which could go down to the knees or the ankles, sometimes with sleeves and sometimes without. He fills a basin with water, puts a towel around his waist, and starts washing the feet of his disciples.

He comes to Peter to wash Peter's feet. Peter looks at him,

"You? Wash my feet?"

"You cannot understand now, you shall understand later."

"No! You shall never wash my feet!"

You see, Peter has a sense of hierarchy. There are people at the top and people at the bottom. He is quite prepared to wash the feet of Jesus. That is quite a normal and natural situation. And he would probably like people to wash his feet. That is to say, he has a sense of what all our societies are about—the vision of a pyramid. There are a few people at the top, and an immense number right at the bottom. Those at the bottom are the useless ones—people with disabilities, people maybe who are mentally sick, people out of work, immigrants. So Peter has this sense of hierarchy.

What would we do if Jesus appeared in our homes and started washing the dishes, washing the floor, and maybe washing the toilets? What would our attitude be? "No! Please go into the sitting room. I will bring you some food. Don't do that!" Peter has the same resistance, which maybe all of us have, to Jesus kneeling down at our feet. Maybe a very natural resistance even to have our feet washed. Peter had that resistance. "It is not in the order of things—it is not according to the culture. It shouldn't be like this!" So the attitude of Peter is a normal and natural reaction. This is the reaction of a loyal person, who in reality has a lot of difficulties with Jesus. (We see this throughout the Gospels.)

What is more surprising is the reaction of Jesus. "If I cannot wash your feet, you shall have no more part with me." These are very strong words and very powerful words. "If I cannot wash your feet, you cannot share in the Kingdom. The Kingdom will no longer be part of your heritage. You are no longer my disciple." In fact, it can be so strong as, "If I cannot wash your feet, there is the door!" These are very strong words. Sometimes it is difficult for us to take them seriously.

Peter panics. "Well then, not only my feet, my head and my hands!" You see, he is a loyal person. But he is panicking. He couldn't imagine that Jesus was going to put such a stake on the washing of the feet.

"If I cannot show that I want to be your servant, then you are no longer my friend. Because you must understand that message turns everything upside down." Those who are at the bottom come up to the top.

Jesus washes the feet, and then he puts the bowl of water aside, takes off the towel, and puts on again the outer garment. And he says, "Do you understand what I have done to you? You called me Lord and Master… so I am. So if I have washed your feet, you must wash each other's feet. I have done this as an example for you." This is the only time that Jesus says, 'I have done this as an example'. "So as I have done it to you, you must do it to each other. Verily, verily I say to you, the servant is not greater than the master, and the one who is sent is not greater than the one who sends. Knowing this, if you do it you shall be blessed."

You know that in the Gospel of Matthew there are the eight beatitudes or blessings. And in the Gospel of Luke there are the four blessings, or the four beatitudes. And here and there throughout the Gospels there are other beatitudes, other blessings. In L'Arche and Faith and Light there are two very special blessings. The first is in the fourteenth chapter of Luke when Jesus says "When you give a meal, don't invite the members of your family, don't invite your rich neighbours, don't invite your friends. But when you give a really good meal—a banquet—invite the poor, the lame, the disabled, and the blind. And you shall be blessed. You shall have the benediction of God. God will be with you." I say this is a special benediction for L'Arche and Faith and Light because, as you know to eat at the same table or to be invited to the same table, is not just to share roast beef, spaghetti and so on. It is to become a friend. That is what it is all about. If you become a friend of the poor, the lame, the disabled, and the blind—if you become vulnerable to them—you shall receive the blessing of God. And if you wash each other's feet, then you receive the blessing of God.

You know that in the Gospels of Luke and Matthew and Mark, at this last important meal, Jesus institutes the Eucharist. Here in the Gospel of John, it doesn't talk at all about the institution of the Eucharist. He talks only about the washing of each other's feet. It is a little sign that these two realities—the institution of the Eucharist and the washing of each other's feet—should not be separated. We are called to eat the Body of Christ so that we can wash each other's feet, and wash the feet of the poor and the lame, the broken and the blind.

I would like to go a little bit deeper and ask why does Jesus wash our feet? And why does he ask us to wash each other's feet? What is the signification behind it?

I think I discovered that a little bit living in L'Arche. And I said this afternoon that, after having been the leader in our community, I lived in one of our small homes where there were people with very severe disabilities. And I talked to you about the Lucien—the screams of Lucien, who brought up the screams in myself and brought up a lot of inner pain. We had also welcomed into that house Eric. Eric had lived for twelve years in the psychiatric hospital. He was blind, he was deaf, he couldn't walk, and he couldn't feed himself. He was a man with an immense amount of anguish—a man who wanted to die. In the psychiatric hospital the nurses rather avoided him because he wasn't gratifying, he could do nothing. He came to our community, and in him there was this terrible desire to die. He vomited everything that he ate. He was just in immense anguish and immense pain. His anguish and his desire to die were evident.

I said that, for us in L'Arche or in Faith and Light, our mission in welcoming Eric is to help him to move from the desire to die to a desire to live. We want him to move from a feeling of being no good to a sense of his value and his worth—from a feeling of guilt to a feeling of trust. I said this afternoon that the only way that this can come about is through the transforming power of love. Through that love which reveals that you are beautiful; love that understands your pain and your needs; love which celebrates; love which empowers and calls you to be and to be yourself; and a love that forgives. But for Eric, how will this be revealed to him? He is blind and he is deaf. So the only way of communication with Eric is through our hands. These are the incredible hands that we have been given by Jesus—hands that give security; hands that give peace; hands that manifest love. But hands that also can hurt; can take; can abuse.

I had the privilege of giving Eric his bath every morning, and to hold his little naked body in my arms. This was a fragile little man of sixteen. And through our hands (because it was not just me, but those of our community together) we revealed to him that he is beautiful. We are to touch people with a deep respect—to touch them with tenderness. Our hands, and not just our voices, may become vehicles of the love of Jesus. The Word became flesh, that our flesh may become word. Our flesh, through the power of the Holy Spirit, can reveal to people their value—that they are cherished and loved by God.

Our hands are, in some mysterious way, a source of revelation of communion. Jesus, as he knelt down in front of the feet of his disciples, knows that tomorrow he will be dead. But he wants to have with each disciple a moment. Not just to say goodbye. Up until now he has just talked with the group. When you talk with a whole group you don't have that individual contact with each person. Jesus wants that contact with each one of these people. He wants to touch them—to touch their feet; to touch their bodies; to touch them with tenderness and love. Maybe to each one he says a word; maybe looks each one in the eye. There is a moment of communion.

So there is communion through the Body of Christ, where Jesus says "do this in memory of me". But there is also this communion as he kneels at their feet. And later he will say "I have done this as an example for you. And what I have done to you, you must do one to another." So this is a gesture of communion, of tenderness.

Jesus touched their bodies—a realization that each one is the Temple of God. "Do you not know that your body is the temple of the Spirit. The Spirit of God is living in you." I believe that Jesus must have touched these bodies with an immense respect and love and tenderness. He was revealing to them, in a special way, his love for them. But he also revealed to them that each one of them is beautiful, is chosen, and is loved. To continue this mission, which is his mission, to announce the good news to the poor, freedom to captives, sight to the blind, liberty to the oppressed, and to announce a year of grace and forgiveness.

As you know water, in biblical language, refreshes but cleanses. And when Jesus is washing the feet of the disciples, he is cleansing their feet to show that he wants to cleanse their hearts. That is Jesus. He doesn't judge, he doesn't condemn; he cleanses. He just wants us to be people of the resurrection—people who stand up; people who believe in ourselves and in our gift; people who believe in the gift of Jesus—so that we can bring this gift to our broken world.

I believe also that as Jesus knelt at the feet of Judas, it must have been a particularly moving time. You see Judas already has the thirty pieces of silver in his pocket; he has already been to the priests of the Temple; he has already decided that he will show the guards where Jesus spends the night. (Because you know, they couldn't arrest Jesus in broad daylight or there would be a revolt.) They have to find out where he is going to spend the night, and here Judas tells them. So the feet of Judas, indeed his whole body, must be incredibly tense.

This man must have hardened his entire body in front of the incredible tenderness of Jesus kneeling at his feet. Somewhere I wonder whether Jesus looked at him and said, "whatever you do, I want you to know that I love you." And maybe the next day when Judas commits suicide, and as the noose tightens around his neck, maybe he remembers those eyes of Jesus. And maybe then his own eyes begin to be tearful. He remembers.

So Jesus washes the feet in a sense of cleansing. But also, Jesus is there on his knees as a servant, as a slave—to be there for us. There is something inconceivable that the Lord and master, in this flimsy tunic washing our feet, says to us "I want to serve you; I want to empower you. Because you will receive the Holy Spirit. And you must continue what I have done. You must be filled with the Spirit of God, so that you can go out to the ends of the earth, to bring that love to all people of all cultures."

So Jesus is the servant. "Jesus who didn't keep equality with God as something to be held on jealously. But he emptied himself." He became just a human being. And he humbled himself even more. This is the downward road of Jesus—going down and down and down. And he calls us to walk with him in that downward path.

I know, we all know, how difficult it is to exercise authority and power. Either we are too controlling, and want everything to be in order—preventing people, or not permitting them to be empowered. We try in every way just to hold on to things. Or else we run away—we do nothing. We want to be popular and want everyone to love us, so we don't make decisions. And we hurt people by making the decision not to make decisions.

Jesus knows that to exercise authority is not easy. I know myself. For many years I was responsible for my community. How quickly I could hurt people by not taking the time to listen to those who are weaker; to those who weren't of my idea; to those who maybe had a different vision; to those who could criticize things which were really citicizable in me or in things that I had done. I saw a lot of fear in me. It is not easy to exercise authority. It is not easy to be parents—to help children to gradually come to freedom, and not to be there just to control them. Instead to help each one to become themselves.

Everyone one of us here, we exercise power in some way—as parents, teachers, priests, bishops. And we know that it is not easy servant leadership—to really give ourselves to others; to help each one to rise up; to know when to make decisions. It is difficult. We need that power of the Holy Spirit, because without that power of the Spirit we will never be able to exercise authority as Jesus exercises it.

And Jesus, as he kneels at our feet, is saying, "I want you to exercise your authority in love. As a good shepherd who gives his life for his sheep. Exercise authority with tenderness and love. Exercise authority in truth and in forgiveness". So when Jesus is at our feet there is something unacceptable. But he is teaching us. He is teaching us how he wants us to exercise authority—not from the top of the pedestal, but close to people. Confirm them; call them forth; empower them; help them to grow to freedom in truth.

Then Jesus, washing the feet of the disciples is saying something else. You see, Jesus came to transform the pyramid into a body. The pyramid, we know what it is. Some few have power and privileges and wealth. And at the bottom is the immense number of the poor and the broken. And Jesus wanted to transform this into a Body. That is why Paul, in the first letter to the Corinthians, talks about the Church as Body. Where every person is different, and everyone is important. Where the eye is different to the foot and the eye is different to the ear and so on. And he goes on to say that those parts of the body which are the least presentable, the weakest, are necessary to the body and should be honoured. I believe Paul is saying something about people with disabilities—they are necessary to the body and should be honoured.

And Jesus is saying something more. He wants us to discover the Church as Body where each one is important—where leadership is important, because the body needs the element of the leadership. But we are all together as brothers and sisters in the same Body. That we are one together in the Body which is inspired, motivated and inhabited by the Spirit of God.

Jesus is saying also something important about the relationship between the master and the slave. He is reminding us that henceforth we must look downward. Because God is hidden in the weak, and the poor, and the disabled. God is in the Body. He is saying, "be attentive to the littlest, to the weakest, to the poorest, to those who are the most broken; for I am living there."

Jesus insists and says we are called to wash each other's feet. Obviously this is symbolic. Jesus is saying that all of us together must be servants of one and other—serving each other, empowering each other. We are not entering into that competitive game of 'I know more than you' or 'My culture is better than your culture.' But we are there to serve each other, to love each other.

So, the washing of the feet is symbolic. It is something about service; something about communion; something about mutual forgiveness, togetherness, and oneness. But at the same time Jesus insists so much about the washing of the feet, about touching the body, that I believe that this symbol is also sacrament. It is something very special. It is not just to talk with people, but to recognize that their body is the Temple of God. Recognize that the Spirit of God is living in them. Recognize that their body is precious. I believe that Jesus insists on the washing of feet because our bodies are precious, Temples of the Spirit.

We want to be in communion—one with another. We love each other. We may have divergences in vision, divergences in theological questions. This is normal. We come from cultures and backgrounds that are very different. Each one of us, we have our character traits. We have the wound in us. We have our fragility and our need to prove that 'I am better than you'. So Jesus is saying something about communion—how to be with each other with words that are not flowing from our woundedness, our darkness, and our need for power and superiority, but from a desire for oneness. And oneness is not exclusion of difference. Oneness is not fusion. Saint Paul says we are all different. It is the recognition of difference. But that doesn't mean to say that we crush difference.

So we are called to be in communion, to forgive each other, to serve each other, and to discover that together we are all called to walk the downward path.

We are all called to be small. "The camel cannot go through the eye of the needle." But we who carry authority and power, in some way we are called to be like little children. And we are called to serve each other in rectitude and in truth as Jesus. And as we become small, then maybe we can go through the eye of the needle.

And so this evening, that is what we are going to do. We do so in a witness of our desire to follow the humble Jesus, the broken Jesus, and the weeping Jesus—the Jesus who became little and humbled himself even more. In some way we want to follow Jesus on that downward path. This is the path which, as we go down, then with him we rise again to be a sign of resurrection in our world.

The Feast of the Transfiguration on Hiroshima Day
The Revd Canon Susan Cole King

6 August 1998

I am very grateful to Bishop Takeda for this invitation to speak at this service on this very significant day.

Last year I read the statement from the Anglican Church of Japan, the NSKK, on their war responsibility. I felt humbled and moved by its honesty and courage. Its acknowledgement of the suffering inflicted by Japan during the war, and their moving apology, had obviously come out of a process of painful self-examination and prayer. It is an example to us all.

The particular reason why this statement from the Japanese Church touched me so deeply was that my father was one of the many Japanese prisoners of war who suffered from the atrocities perpetuated by their captors, and I'd like to tell you something of his story. His name was Leonard Wilson and he was Bishop of Singapore.

On October 10, 1943 (the "double 10th" as it became known), the Japanese military police, the Gestapo or Kempei-tai, raided Changi and arrested fifty-seven of the prisoners. Among them was my father, the bishop. He was accused of being a spy and for many days he was subjected to torture.

Often he had to be carried back to his cell, that crowded, dark and filthy cell, almost unconscious from his wounds. On one occasion, seven men were taking it in turns to flog him, they asked him why he didn't curse them. He told them it was because he was a follower of Jesus who taught us to love one another.

He asked himself then how he could possibly love these men with their hard, cruel faces, obviously enjoying the torture they were inflicting. As he prayed he had a picture of them as they might have been as little children, and it's hard to hate little children.

But then, more powerfully, his prayer was answered by some words of a well-known Communion hymn which came into his mind: "Look Father, look on his anointed face, and only look on us as found in him."

In that moment he was given a vision of those men not as they were then, but as they were capable of becoming, transformed by the love of Christ. He said that he saw them completely change, their cruelty becoming kindness, their sadistic instincts changed to gentleness. Although he felt it was too blasphemous to use Christ's words "Father, forgive them," he experienced the grace of forgiveness at that moment.

After eight months he was released back to Changi—one of the few who survived the torture. For the rest of his life he emphasised the importance of forgiveness in his speaking and preaching.

How he would have rejoiced to be here today—I am sure he is. This year he would have been 100, and it is fitting to remember him now in this month which is the anniversary of his death.

Although he was able to forgive, and I and my family want to affirm that unconditional forgiveness, true reconciliation can only happen when there is an acknowledgement of wrongs done, when the truth is faced, and painful self-examination leads to confession and apology.

I and my brothers with me here today want to say to our Japanese brothers and sisters a heartfelt thank you for what you have done. The cycle of reconciliation is completed.

Today we celebrate the Transfiguration. Michael Ramsey, a former Archbishop of Canterbury, says: "Transfiguration is indeed a central theme of Christianity, the transforming of suffering and circumstances, of men and women with the vision of Christ before them and the Holy Spirit within them".

My father's experience was a transfiguration story, not just for himself but also for his captors. After the war he returned to Singapore and had the great joy of confirming one of his torturers.

This is how he described the moment: "One of these men who was allowed to march up from the prison to the cathedral, as a prisoner, to come for baptism, was one of those who had stood with a rope in his hand, threatening and sadistic. I have seldom seen so great a change in a man. He looked gentle and peaceful."

St Paul says in the second letter to the Corinthians: "All of us, with unveiled faces, seeing the glory of the Lord, are being transformed into the same image from one degree of glory to another; for this comes from the Lord the Spirit".

As we have been reminded, today we remember also something else. Hiroshima Day, the day when terrible suffering was inflicted on the Japanese people of

Hiroshima and then of Nagasaki three days later, when 8,000 Christians were killed instantly, and thousands later as a result of radiation.

How necessary were those bombs? Why was a second bomb dropped on Nagasaki even as the Supreme Council of War was meeting in Tokyo to decide whether to surrender? Those bombs ended the war, but at what terrible cost! I do not know the politics or the arguments, only that something horrendous was inflicted on the people of Japan by my country and its allies, which the world must never forget.

A few years ago I read a book, a little book called "The Bells of Nagasaki" by a Japanese doctor and physicist, who was also a Christian, Takashi Nagai. He witnessed the bombing of Nagasaki and describes in detail the terrible devastation and horror as it unfolded.

Everything was destroyed for him—his home, his wife and family, his hospital, his cathedral, the honour of his country, and thousands of fellow men and women. Heroically, in spite of his wounds and radiation sickness he worked to relieve the suffering of others.

How he survived to write the book and tell the story is a miracle. As Nagai tells the story of Nagasaki, he is also telling the story of his own transfiguration, his transformation through suffering and loss.

In his funeral address for the victims of the bomb he said that it was fitting that the Church in Nagasaki, which had kept the faith through 400 years of persecution, should bear the brunt of this bomb, and that through this sacrifice peace was given to the world.

He ends his book with a ringing message: "Men and women of the world, never again plan war! From this atomic waste the people of Nagasaki prostrate themselves before God and pray: Grant that Nagasaki may be the last atomic wilderness in the history of the world."

It is significant that we remember Hiroshima and Nagasaki on the Feast of the Transfiguration which links the glory of Christ with his suffering. Spiritual radiance and nuclear radiation, transfiguration and disfiguration. It is through Christ's disfiguration on the cross that God's glory is revealed.

Not only is suffering the means of reconciliation, but the transfiguring of suffering itself is attested to in Christian life and experience. My father experienced this transforming of suffering through the power of others' prayer.

When two of his companions in the cell, who had shared so much with him, died of their wounds and of hunger, he said a terrible loneliness descended. But, conscious of the prayers of others, he said, and I quote: "Here again I was helped by God, there was a tiny window at the back of the cell and through the bars I could hear the song of the golden aural, I could see the glorious red of the forest tree and something of God, of God's indestructible beauty was conveyed to my tortured mind.

"A great peace descended. Gradually, the burden of this world was lifted and I was carried into the presence of God, and received from him the strength and peace which were enough to live by day by day."

Many of you have experienced depths of suffering among your people or in your own lives beyond what most of us can imagine. You will know, too, the darkness and the cloud where God is mysteriously and awesomely present in the confusion and pain.

I would like to end with some words of Karl Barth: "Our tribulation without ceasing to be tribulation is transformed. We suffer as we suffered before, but our suffering is no longer a passive perplexity but is transformed into a pain which is creative, fruitful, full of power and promise. The road which is impassable has been made known to us in the crucified and the risen Lord."

Closing Service at the University of Kent at Canterbury, The Most Revd and Rt Hon George L. Carey, Archbishop of Canterbury

8 August 1998

Just a few days before the Conference began, two visitors from South Africa came to see me—a little girl aged four and her young mother. The girl's name is Dorah and, at the age of seven months, the shack she and her mother were living in, in a squatters' camp near Johannesburg, caught fire. She was trapped inside it and, as a result, her face was burnt away; she has no nose—simply a hole remains; she has no ears or eyelids and has just a little sight. She has no hands either because they were so badly damaged that they had to be amputated. But Dorah is a person even though she has no face and through the skill of surgeons and the love, the costly love, of her mother and her friends her new face is beginning to emerge. But in the most important sense of all Dorah, as with all of us, already has a face which she will never lose; the face known to God, unblemished and uniquely hers.

For the last three weeks we have been studying Paul's moving letter which we know as 2 Corinthians. In it, 'faces' are important. The 'glory' of Moses' face after he had met with God; our own 'unveiled' faces when we are open to the word of God; the glory of God 'mirrored' in each others' faces as we see Christ in each other; and then in Chapter 4 comes Paul's breathtaking picture: 'For God has shone in our hearts to give the light of the knowledge of the glory of God in the face of Jesus Christ'.

Faces. On the screen behind me we have seen so many faces; faces of speakers, faces of the musicians, faces of one another as the camera has roamed over us. Before we came here we knew about each other but we didn't know each other's faces. Now we have seen them. In doing so we have begun to see, and to know, each other. We have recognised too that mystery, that every face is unique. And we have also recognised that behind each face stands a Diocese which is unique, and a Province which is also unique.

That is one glory of a gathering of Christians like this. In beginning to see each other as unique, in all our diversity, we have also begun to glimpse something of the glory of God in the face of Jesus Christ in each other. And yet, in all that personal and cultural diversity, there is also that family likeness as Anglicans, as Christians, and as human beings whose ultimate source is to be found in the Trinity, in that mystery of the family likeness of the three Persons of the one God.

Our Anglican Communion has long declared its belief in the joy of that diversity. And while we have been here together that belief in the goodness of diversity has become a felt strength and a joyous reality to many, particularly in the marvellously varied worship we have experienced. We have come to know for our own selves that so to delight in each others' diversity is not—as some commentators sometimes seem to suggest,—in any way to "fudge" the hard questions. Quite the opposite. As the Virginia Report reminded us, God invites his people to enjoy diversity, to use it not to weaken but "for the building up of the body". So it is not an amiable compromise but a diversity through which we are strengthened to face the hard questions, based on our actual experience of the glory of God in the face of Jesus Christ, as we have seen it, seen it with our own eyes, in the faces of each other. A 'diversity-in-unity', I must remind you, founded in the personal God revealed to us in Jesus Christ and rooted in scripture and the creeds of the Church. That glory is given to us to celebrate and proclaim.

And we have seen that glory in so many ways! That wonderful Opening Service in Canterbury Cathedral; in the intimacy and opennness of our small Bible Study Groups; in the Vigil led so beautifully by our friend Jean Vanier; in the harrowing stories of pain and suffering through poverty, persecution and war, as well as in those of growth and success.

But perhaps it became less easy in some other situations, such as in the heat and length of some of the Section meetings and the Plenaries, particularly where a view was being put forward with which we did not agree. And so we know too what it is to move from a "diversity" which can be delighted in and celebrated, to something quite different: a "differing" from each other which gathers heat, and can turn into a very painful "dispute". That, too, has happened this week, hasn't it? It is so easy to "demonise" one another when that happens and to part company in the family. We must resist that and face the pain together, studying the scriptures together, praying together. Remember that wonderful play "Wrestling with Angels". It seemed impossible that Jacob could glimpse the glory of God in the face of Esau. Yet, you will recall the angel's reply when, in anguish, he pleads for God's blessing. "You have my blessing. Turn and receive it." And there, standing behind him, was Esau, offering his blessing of reconciliation.

That play offered us a vital Gospel insight. For the truth is that where, in the name and strength of the Christ, Christians work hard in honesty and pain to enter into each other's experience and understanding, the glory of the crucified Christ is found. At this Conference we have begun to see—and it has changed us. A bishop said the other day: " what this Conference has done for me is to blow my mind and heart right open to ways of living and thinking I hadn't begun to imagine. And out of that I begin to see just a little of how the face of Christ looks in cultures so unimaginably different from my own."

What an important discovery and how central to all that we have wrestled with together! For the kind of unity we have been seeking in this Conference, the kind of unity we want to achieve for the world's sake, is not the facile coming-together of the like-minded or the pretence of agreement where there is none. It is that profound unity which belongs to a family which has been tried and tested, not just by the diversity of its members and the variety of their life-styles, but by controversy and profound disagreements encircled by a still deeper love which holds a family together, the kind of unity that, for us, is bonded in blood and in love. Christ's blood was shed for us on the Cross because of the great love with which he loves us. As Bishop Glauco Soares de Lima commented at one of our Eucharists: 'Grace is free but it is never cheap'.

And so we shall remember faces long after words, statements and resolutions have been forgotten. For what God spoke to the world, what transformed it, was something greater even than the divine law written on tablets of stone. Tablets of stone have quite a lot in common with carefully honed Reports and Resolutions. They are necessary, to keep us on the right track. But ultimately God used a human face to bridge the profoundest division of all, between his own holiness and purity, and our intransigent, sinful humanity. It is then to the human face we must attend: each others', and the faces all round us of the world's needy, pressing in upon us because in them we see the face of Christ.

But whatever struggles towards that kind of unity we have won here are not an end in themselves, just as this Conference is not an end in itself. The only valid consequences of this coming-together will be, in the end, what we take back to our Dioceses and Provinces. Whatever Christ-like victories we have won in finding out how to live and work together under the Gospel, whatever victories of reconciliation in the Law and Grace of Christ, these are the offering we take back to our people, the food we bring them from the banquet we have shared, the dynamic we bring them from the power that has flowed through this gathering. T.S. Eliot, after whom Eliot College is named, had something very profound to say about the renewal of the Church in his play *The Rock*. It is that God's Church will only be renewed and rebuilt if all its members work together.

"Where the bricks are fallen
We will build with new stone
Where the beams are rotten
We will build with new timbers
Where the word is unspoken
We will build with new speech
There is work together
A Church for all
And a job for each"

(from Choruses from *The Rock*)

And therefore, my dear sisters and brothers, it is our responsibility to take back from here the materials to transform and renew our local churches, and the ministry of all our people, lay and ordained. For if we take back only rotten timbers eaten with the woodworm of criticism or suspicion; or if our bricks were the crumbling old bricks of unchanged vision; and if, above all, we had heard no new word from the Lord to take back a 'new speech' to our people, then we would, indeed, have failed.

But I do not believe for one moment that we have failed. I believe that we have learnt many things from our own experiences of 'Leadership under pressure' as we have listened to those moving accounts on video, linked with our Bible Studies and heard stories of victory and transformation under pressure. Above all, I believe we have been brought afresh to lay claim, not just for ourselves but for our churches, to the transforming, renewing power that is Christ's. As Paul wrote, 'If any one is in Christ, there is a new creation', and all else flows from that.

And that is the true purpose of Lambeth Conference. It represents a pause, a staging post, where we are refreshed in spirit, body and mind for the next stage of our journey. It marks a stage in the life of our Communion. And it marks a stage in our own personal journeys. So, what are the things that will you take out into the next stage of your own journey, your Diocese's journey and your Province's journey?

I hope you will take a keen awareness that you are not alone. You belong to a great family of God, and here you have come face to face with brothers and sisters from all over the world as we have spoken, prayed, eaten and worshipped together in the intimacy of that family.

I hope too you will take a renewed sense of the bonds of prayer binding you with your brothers and sisters right across the world, guarding you with that shield which only such fervent loving prayer can offer.

I hope you will leave here with an enriched theology which has led you deeper into your thinking about God. A sharper sense of the wonder of the Gospel and the Lord at its centre; and so into a closer and more profound love-relationship with him.

I hope you will also carry with you newly stimulated ideas about mission and the proclamation of the Gospel; new ideas gathered from across the world of new and different and challenging ways of telling the story of Jesus.

I hope, with all the passion I can muster, that together we will take out into the world from this 13th Lambeth Conference a strengthened Anglican Communion more deeply committed to the weak, the very poor, the suffering and the marginalised. May we be a great 'Protest' movement against anything that dehumanises our sisters and brothers anywhere, raising our voices about international debt and world poverty, speaking for young people and working for a strong and growing Anglicanism world wide.

But above all, of course, what you will be taking back to your diocese is yourself: the person you have become during these weeks. For you will remember that I said at the beginning that our first task as a Conference was to be transformed ourselves. So what will your Diocese see in your face, when you return? Will they see in you the sort of 'brightness' that Paul talks about, brightness like that of Moses when he had been with God; the brightness of 'unveiled faces' as they are open to the word of God; above all that light which shines from a renewed knowledge of the glory of God as you have glimpsed it in the face of Jesus Christ?

I want to end, as I began, with Dorah, that little girl with a face totally disfigured by fire who slowly, fraction by fraction, painfully, is being given a new face. It is not only fire that can almost obliterate the beauty of a human face. Long distress, hopes denied, vision blocked, trust withdrawn, calumny, humiliation, and apparent failure can all disfigure our countenance. And such has been and will be the experience of some of us, perhaps most of us, from time to time.

But just as Dorah's true face is known to God in heaven, so is yours. And inch by inch, slowly and painfully, that unique face that is already ours before God is being shaped and formed here in our earthly life. So, my dear sisters and brothers, as you prepare to return home and take up again the heavy burden that is yours, remember that your heavenly Father knows you not just by name but by face. And that one day, in his own good time, we shall see him, not just in part, as we do now, but we shall see him "face to face". It is in that hope and conviction, a hope and conviction not just for ourselves only, but for the whole world, that we have met here. It is in that hope and conviction that we shall go out from here to tell the world that there is a saving God, God incarnate, made known to us in the face of Jesus Christ.

And so, as we come to the point where I must say 'goodbye' I want to use T.S. Eliot's words from his poem *The Dry Salvages*: 'I do not say 'farewell' but 'fare forward, voyager!' Yes indeed, may we all 'fare forward'—into the next millennium, into God's future which is our hope and glory towards that goal of the high calling which we have in our Lord Jesus Christ.

But let Paul have the last word—that great Apostle whose profound letter has fed us these three weeks—and in his own final words to those fallible Corinthian Christians, so like us: "Finally, brothers and sisters… live in peace; and the God of love and peace will be with you'.

Amen. So be it.

REPORT OF THE SPOUSES' CONFERENCE

photo: *Anglican World*

Spouses' Programme Planning Group

Report of the Spouses' Conference
Mrs Eileen Carey

The 630 spouses participating in this programme wish to express their appreciation of the outstanding facilities provided for their separate activities. The 'village' has been of enormous benefit to our meeting, rehearsing, sharing, socialising and working together. Consultation with the spouses prior to Lambeth seems to have enabled good planning for the very varied provision requested for attention on an individual and collective basis.

The diversity and yet common experience and issues for ministry which have emerged are quite remarkably consistent, especially given the range of cultural, ecclesiastical and geographical backgrounds. The Plenary presentations, with the assistance of translation services, were under four major headings and in line with the bishops'. They were:

i. 'For Better, For Worse'—The Role of the Bishop's Spouse
ii. 'A Healthy World? Strategies for Hope'—Looking at Social Issues
iii. 'Together in God's Mission: The Vocation of the Anglican Communion in the 21st Century'
iv. 'Go into all the World', Mission and Evangelism Today and Tomorrow

The shared experience of personal and collective ministry was both impressive and deeply moving. The poignant stories of situations and poverty and its consequent cycle of deprivation, corruption and ill-health are an enormous challenge to our contribution in ministry and to the importance of empowering women within the structures of the Church, its organisations and setting an example within society.

The fellowship and worship of Bible Study groups (like the Bishops', based on 2 Corinthians), the commitment and participation of 100-plus workshops, the exploration and fun of outings, and the shared involvement in the presentation of 'Crowning Glory'—all created a sense of the common task in our changing world. Women in community, women in development, women in family, women and spirituality, women as victims of violence—all were recurrent themes. We heard from both individuals and groups particularly involved in support and the promotion of change such as the ACC Networks and the Mothers' Union. We were also privileged to have external contributions from Christian authors Susan Howatch, Michele Guiness and Jean O'Barr.

It was an important development to have some of our brother spouses for the first time. Increasing numbers of spouses are in formal employment as well as carrying their role within the lives of bishops in the Church. The pressures on family life and the place of children in bishops' households were raised.

It has been of major significance that we have worshipped together and been able to be part of the main plenary sessions of the Bishops' Conference. Yet the separate identity of the Spouses' Programme alongside this has been of immense value to us all.

PASTORAL LETTER
FROM THE ARCHBISHOP OF CANTERBURY

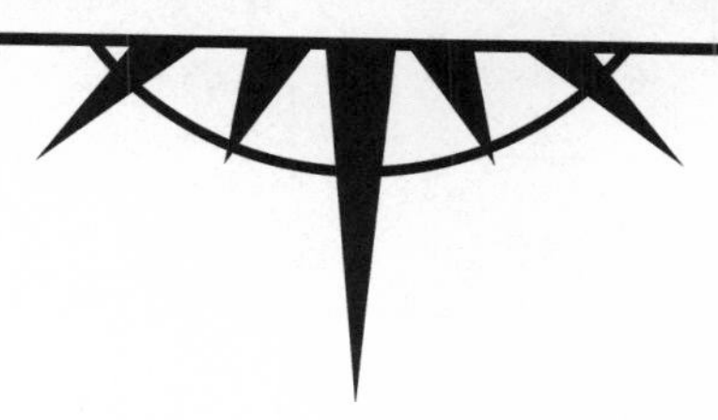

photo: *Anglican World*

Archbishop Carey

Pastoral Letter to the Communion

August 13, 1998

My dear Sisters and Brothers:

Just a few days ago the 13th Lambeth Conference, which brought together 750 Bishops and 650 spouses from the 37 Provinces of the Anglican Communion, ended. Thanks to the prayers of many, and the work of the Holy Spirit in our midst, the vast majority of those present agreed that it had been very worthwhile, with much blessing resulting from our common worship, study and dialogue—blessings which, I know, were experienced as much in the Spouses' Programme as in the Bishops' Conference.

At the heart of our Conference was our daily Bible study, in small groups, of Paul's Second Letter to the Corinthians, which we looked at under the title *Leadership under Pressure*—something which all of us could, I think, readily identify with. As we did so, I was struck by St Paul's emphasis on 'faces': The glory on Moses' face after he had met with God (3:12); the transforming glory on our faces when we turn to God (3:18) and then in 4:6, that wonderful passage where Paul speaks of the light which has shone in our hearts *'to give the light of the knowledge of the glory of God in the face of Jesus Christ'*.

And we have been transformed by being together over these three weeks. We have seen one another's faces. People who we might only have heard about in the past are now people we know as friends, whose faces are known to us. And many of us will never be the same again because we have been enriched by the stories those people have shared with us, of leadership under pressure, and of the goodness of God sometimes in the context of great hardship, poverty and persecution or, elsewhere, of secularity and indifference. How could any of us forget the Bishop of Kitgum's simple but moving account of the death of his beloved wife, Winifred, blown up by a landmine? And who was not challenged by his courage in maintaining a faithful witness in an area where terrorists regularly abduct children and take them away to train them as killers? Such an account is a vivid reminder of the context in which some of our brothers and sisters work as bishops and Christians.

In listening to each other and sharing common concerns we have also seen the face of the world in its agony and confusions. We have taken time together to study carefully some of the profound and perplexing problems which the

Provinces had requested for our agenda. Some of these problems press hard only on some parts of our Communion but they must be of concern to us all as members of one family. The burden of international debt; the changing pattern of inter-faith relations; the making of moral decisions in an increasingly relativistic climate; the need as a Church to bring peace and reconciliation in those parts of the world threatened by civil strife; the impact of technology on us all—all these were looked at in depth and our Report and Resolutions reflect that fact. What is more, we believe we made considerable progress in addressing these issues as we listened to each other in the context of scripture and the experience of the Communion; and the fruit of our discussions will, I hope, become evident in days to come. Of particular significance, I believe, is the issue of International Debt, and much more will flow from our commitment to press the moral argument for the relief of the burden of unpayable debt.

But there have been times when 'face to face' encounter has been difficult and potentially divisive. This was particularly so with regard to our discussions about human sexuality. Prior to the Conference no Province had asked for homosexuality to figure as a major item on the agenda, but, nonetheless, the issue was debated hotly and we found that our diversity of theology and culture, often a source of blessing, was becoming a 'differing' that could so easily have resulted in bitter confrontation.

But the result of those discussions was a Resolution, passed by a huge majority, that *'this Conference, in view of the teaching of Scripture upholds faithfulness in marriage between a man and a woman in lifelong union, and believes that abstinence is right for those who are not called to marriage'*. In the same Resolution we also affirmed that we would *'commit ourselves to listen to the experience of homosexual persons, and we wish to assure them that they are loved by God and that all baptised, believing and faithful persons, regardless of sexual orientation, are full members of the Body of Christ'*.

For the vast majority of us involved in that debate the friendships that had been established, coupled with a desire to listen to each other, enabled us to transcend our differences. Nevertheless, I recognise that for some parts of the Church, there was considerable pain to be endured both in the debate itself and its outcome and so the listening must go on, not only to Scripture but also to one another.

And the fact of division in the world and the Church is surely something that we should face up to with courage and faith. So much energy goes into maintaining divisions instead of working for unity. It is my strong belief that one of the greatest benefits of this Conference will be our experience as bishops of pursuing a oneness of aim in the midst of diversity. That, I believe, has strengthened rather than weakened our Communion.

But, if we have looked at the difficulties facing our Churches we have also perceived the effects in many Provinces of the Decade of Evangelism that was so wonderfully brought to our Communion by the last Lambeth Conference. We give thanks to God for all that has been achieved. We affirm under God that the Decade of Evangelism does not end in two years' time! Rather, the 201st decade begins then! The Millennium will, I believe, provide a unique opportunity of telling the story of Jesus Christ afresh to our world. Let every diocese aim to present our Lord as Saviour and Hope of the world and let us all seek to bring people to baptism and new life in Christ.

For through this marvellous Conference we have begun to see some of us for the first time, the growth and the vigour of the Communion. Anglicans are at work among the very poor as well as among the most privileged. We have thus gained true insights into our interdependence as Provinces. We know now that we ***must*** ensure that our structures are more accountable; we know that we must find new ways of supporting the poorest parts of the Communion (often rich in faith and joy); we know that we must become a more outward looking and serving Communion; we know that we must share together our resources in training and Biblical scholarship.

And strengthened by our fellowship together we return to our dioceses more ready to serve that Communion and all its members. Thank you, brothers and sisters, for making it possible for us to meet in Canterbury, because in meeting here we believe we have glimpsed something precious of the glory of God in the 'face of Jesus Christ' and the nature of a serving ministry which comes from following him.

And in the words of St Paul, from that letter which challenged us so very deeply, we salute you from the Lambeth Conference: *Finally, brothers and sisters... put things in order... agree with one another, live in peace and the God of love and peace will be with you.*

May God bless you in our faith and life together.

Your brother in Christ

+ George

PHOTOGRAPHS

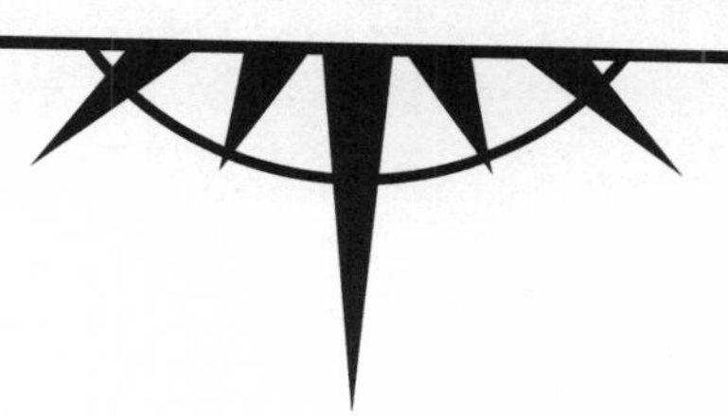

photo: Marcus Perkins

photo: Marcus Perkins

photo: Marcus Perkins

photo: Marcus Perkins

photo: Marcus Perkins

photo: Marcus Perkins

photo: Marcus Perkins

photo: Marcus Perkins

PARTICIPANTS

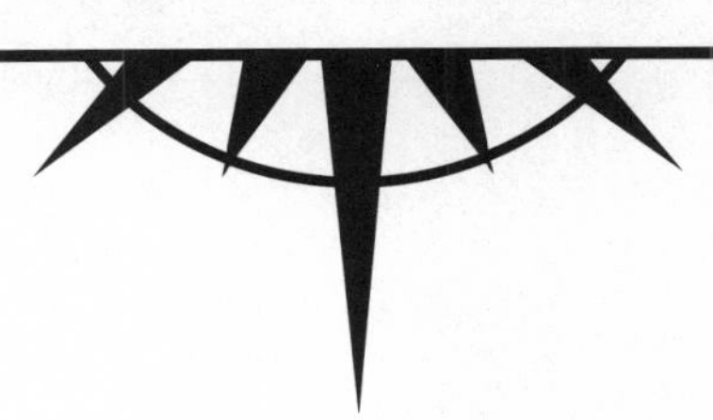

photo: *Anglican World*

Some of the participants at the Lambeth Conference 1998.

Participants

CONFERENCE STEERING GROUP

Chairman:
The Most and Rt Hon George L. Carey
Archbishop of Canterbury
Chair of the Design Group:
The Most Revd Keith Rayner
Secretary:
The Revd Canon John L. Peterson
Manager of the Conference:
Mr David Long
Chaplain to the Conference:
The Rt Revd Roger Herft
Episcopal Co-ordinator of Communication:
The Most Revd Robert Eames
Editor of Reports:
The Rt Revd J. Mark Dyer
Chair of Resolutions Committee:
The Rt Revd Michael Nuttall
Consultant to the Steering Group:
The Most Revd Frank T. Griswold
Spouses' Programme:
Mrs Eileen Carey
Chairs and Vice Chairs of Sections:
The Most Revd Njongonkulu Ndungane
The Rt Revd Kenneth Fernando
The Rt Revd Rowan Williams
The Rt Revd Yong Ping Chung
The Rt Revd Frederick Borsch
The Rt Revd Simon Chiwanga
The Rt Revd Jabez Bryce
The Rt Revd Stephen Sykes
Inter-Faith
The Rt Revd Michael Nazir-Ali

RESOLUTIONS COMMITTEE

Chair:
The Rt Revd Michael Nuttall
Vice Chair:
The Most Revd John Paterson

Canon Dr Christina Baxter
The Rt Revd French Chang-Him
The Rt Revd Barry Morgan
The Rt Revd Orlando Santos de Oliveira
The Rt Revd Peter J. Lee
The Rt Revd David Silk
Secretary:
Mr Philip Mawer
Legal Advisor:
Mr Brian Hanson
Consultant:
The Revd John Rees
Assistant:
Mr Robin Stevens

EDITORIAL TEAM

Chair:
The Rt Revd J. Mark Dyer

The Rt Revd Dr Emmanuel Gbonigi
The Rt Revd Mano Rumalshah
Dr Ruth Etchells
The Revd Canon Roger Symon

BIBLE STUDY TEAM

Convenor:
The Rt Revd Simon Barrington-Ward

The Rt Revd Sam Amirtham
Mrs Myrtle Baughan
The Rt Revd Sergio Carranza-Gomez
The Rt Revd Penelope Jamieson
The Revd Dr Israel Selvanayagam
The Rt Revd Dinis Sengulane

BISHOPS BY PROVINCE

Anglican Provinces and Dioceses

The number after the name of each participant indicates the Section to which the participant was assigned, viz:

1 Called to Full Humanity
2 Called to Live and Proclaim the Good News
3 Called to be a Faithful Church in a Plural World
4 Called to be One

The Anglican Church in Aotearoa, New Zealand & Polynesia

Diocese	*Bishop*		*Section*
Aotearoa	Hui Vercoe		1
	Ben Te Haara	(Northern Region)	4
	John Gray	(South Island)	4
	Muru Walters	(Wellington/ Taranaki)	4
Auckland	John Paterson	Primate	3
Christchurch	David Coles		4
Dunedin	Penelope Jamieson		3
Nelson	Derek Eaton		2
Polynesia	Jabez Bryce		4
	Viliami Hala'api'api	(Assistant)	2
Waiapu	Murray Mills		1
	George Connor	(Bay of Plenty)	3
Waikato	David Moxon		4
Wellington	Tom Brown		2
	Brian Carrell	(Palmerston North)	3

The Anglican Church of Australia

Internal Provinces:
New South Wales *NSW*
Queensland *Q*
South Australia *SA*
Victoria *V*
Western Australia *WA*
Extra Provincial *EP*

Diocese / Province	*Bishop*		*Section*
Adelaide SA	Ian George	Archbishop	1
	Phillip Aspinall	(Assistant)	2
Armidale *NSW*	Peter Chiswell		1
Ballarat *V*	David Silk		4
Bathurst *NSW*	Bruce Wilson		1
Bendigo *V*	David Bowden		2
Brisbane *Q*	Peter Hollingworth	Archbishop	1
	John Noble	(Assistant)	2
	Ronald Williams	(Southern Region)	4
	Raymond Smith	(Western Region)	4
Bunbury *WA*	Hamish Jamieson		2
Canberra & Goulburn *NSW*	George Browning		1
	Richard Randerson	(Assistant)	3
Gippsland *V*	Arthur Jones		2

Grafton *NSW*	Philip Huggins		3
Melbourne *V*	Keith Rayner	Archbishop & Primate	3
	Andrew Curnow	(Assistant)	3
	John Wilson	(Southern Region)	2
	John Stewart	(Eastern Region)	4
	Andrew St John	(Western Region–Geelong)	4
Newcastle *NSW*	Roger Herft		2
North Queensland *Q*	Clyde Wood		3
	Ian Stuart	(Assistant)	1
	Arthur Malcolm	(Assistant)	4
North West Australia *Q*	Anthony Nichols		1
Northern Territory *Q*	Richard Appleby		4
Perth *WA*	Peter Carnley	Archbishop	3
	David Murray	(Fremantle)	4
	Gerald Beaumont	(Goldfields Country Region)	4
	Brian Farran	(Northern Region)	2
Riverina *NSW*	Bruce Clark		3
Rockhampton *Q*	Ron Stone		2
Sydney *NSW*	Harry Goodhew	Archbishop	1
	Ray Smith	(Liverpool)	3
	Paul Barnett	(North)	1
	Peter Watson	(Southern Region)	3
	Reg Piper	(Wollongong)	3
Tasmania *EP*	Phillip Newell		2
The Murray *SA*	Graham H. Walden		4
Wangaratta *V*	David Farrer		2
Willochra *SA*	David McCall		3

Igreja Episcopal Anglicana do Brasil

Diocese	*Bishop*		*Section*
Brasilia	Almir dos Santos		3
Pelotas	Luiz Prado		1
Recife	Robinson de Barros	Cavalcanti	3
Sao Paulo	Glauco Soares de Lima	Primate	3
South Western Brazil	Jubal Pereira Neves		2
Southern Brazil	Orlando Santos de Oliveira		4

Eglise Episcopale du Burundi

Diocese	*Bishop*		*Section*
Bujumbura	Pie Ntukamazina		3
Buye	Samuel Ndayisenga		4
Gitega	Jean Nduwayo		2
Makamba	Martin Nyaboho		4
Matana	Samuel Sindamuka	Primate	2
	Bernard Ntahoturi	(Coadjutor)	1

The Anglican Church of Canada

Internal Provinces:
British Columbia *BC*
Canada *C*
Ontario *O*
Rupert's Land *RL*

Diocese / Province	*Bishop*		*Section*
	Michael Peers	Primate	1
Algoma *O*	Ronald Ferris		1
Athabasca *RL*	John Clarke		3
Brandon *RL*	Malcolm Harding		2
British Columbia *BC*	R. Barry Jenks		1
Caledonia *BC*	John Hannen		1
Calgary *RL*	Barry Curtis		3
	Gary Woolsey	(Assistant)	3
Cariboo *BC*	James Cruickshank		1
Central Newfoundland *C*	Edward Marsh		1
Eastern Newfoundland & Labrador *C*	Donald Harvey		2
Edmonton *RL*	Victoria Matthews		3
Fredericton *C*	George Lemmon		2
	William Hockin	(Coadjutor)	1
Huron *O*	Percy O'Driscoll	Archbishop	1
	C Robert Townshend	(Suffragan)	3
Kootenay *BC*	David Crawley	Archbishop	1
Montreal *C*	Andrew Hutchison		1
Moosonee *O*	Caleb Lawrence		3
New Westminster *BC*	Michael Ingham		2
Niagara *O*	Ralph Spence		4
Nova Scotia *C*	Arthur Peters	Archbishop	3
	Frederick J. Hiltz	(Suffragan)	4
Ontario *O*	Peter Mason	1	
Ottawa *O*	John Baycroft	4	
Qu'Appelle *RL*	Duncan Wallace	1	
Quebec *C*	Bruce Stavert	4	
Rupert's Land *RL*	Patrick Lee	4	
Saskatchewan *RL*	Anthony Burton	4	
	Charles Arthurson	(Suffragan)	2
Saskatoon *RL*	Thomas Morgan		3
The Arctic *RL*	Christopher Williams		4
	Paul Idlout	(Suffragan)	1
Toronto *O*	Terence Finlay		1
	Ann Tottenham	(Credit Valley)	3
	Douglas Blackwell	(Trent-Durham)	2
	Michael Bedford-Jones	(York-Scarborough)	2
	Taylor Pryce	(York-Simcoe)	2
Western Newfoundland *C*	Len Whitten		2
Yukon *BC*	Terrence Buckle		3

The Church of the Province of Central Africa

Diocese / Country	*Bishop*		*Section*
Botswana *Botswana*	Khotso Makhulu	Primate	1
Central Zambia *Zambia*	Clement Shaba		4
Eastern Zambia *Zambia*	John Osmers		2
Eastern Zimbabwe *Zimbabwe*	Elijah Masuko		4
Harare *Zimbabwe*	Jonathan Siyachitema		2
Lake Malawi *Malawi*	Peter Nyanja		4
Lusaka *Zambia*	Leonard Mwenda		4
Matabeleland *Zimbabwe*	Theophilus Naledi		4
Northern Malawi *Malawi*	Jackson Biggers		4
Northern Zambia *Zambia*	Bernard Malango		1
Southern Malawi *Malawi*	James Tengatenga		2

Iglesia Anglicana de la Region Central de America

Diocese	*Bishop*		*Section*
Costa Rica	Cornelius Wilson	Primate	3
El Salvador	Martin Barahona Pascacio		2
Guatemala	Armando Guerra Soria		1
Panama	Clarence Hayes		2

Province de L'Eglise Anglicane Du Congo

Diocese	*Bishop*		*Section*
Boga	Patrice Njojo	Primate	4
Bukavu	Fidèle Dirokpa		2
Katanga	Henri Kahwa		1
Kindu	Zacharie Masimango Katanda		2
Kisangani	Sylvestre Tibafa Mugera		2
	Antoine Mavatikwa Kany	(Assistant)	4
Nord Kivu	Musubaho Munzenda		4

The Church of England

Internal Provinces:
Canterbury *C*
York *Y*

Diocese / Province	*Bishop*		*Section*
Bath & Wells *C*	James Thompson		1
Birmingham *C*	Mark Santer		4
	John Austin	(Aston)	2
	David Evans	(Hon (Assistant))	2
Blackburn *Y*	Alan D Chesters		2
	Martyn Jarrett	(Burnley)	3
	Stephen Pedley	(Lancaster)	1
Bradford *Y*	David Smith		3
Bristol *C*	Barry Rogerson		3
	Michael Doe	(Swindon)	1

Canterbury *C*	George Carey	Archbishop & Primate	2
	Richard Llewellin	(Dover)	1
	John Richards	(Ebbsfleet)	4
	Frank Sargeant	(Lambeth)	1
	Gavin Reid	(Maidstone)	2
	Edwin Barnes	(Richborough)	4
Carlisle *Y*	Ian Harland		4
	Richard Garrard	Penrith	2
Chelmsford *C*	John Perry		1
	Roger Sainsbury	(Barking)	2
	Laurie Green	(Bradwell)	3
	Edward Holland	(Colchester)	3
Chester *Y*	Peter Forster		3
	Michael Langrish	(Birkenhead)	2
Chichester *C*	Eric Kemp		1
	Lindsay Urwin OGS	(Horsham)	4
	Wallace Benn	(Lewes)	1
Coventry *C*	Colin Bennetts		3
	Anthony Priddis	(Warwick)	1
Derby *C*	Jonathan Bailey		2
	Henry Richmond	(Repton)	4
Diocese in Europe *C*	John Hind		4
	Henry Scriven	(Suffragan)	2
Durham *Y*	Michael Turnbull		2
	Alan Smithson	(Jarrow)	3
Ely *C*	Stephen Sykes		4
	John Flack	(Huntingdon)	2
Exeter *C*	Hewlett Thompson		1
	Richard Hawkins	(Crediton)	2
	John Garton	(Plymouth)	3
Gloucester *C*	David Bentley		2
	John Went	(Tewkesbury)	4
Guildford *C*	John Gladwin		1
	Ian Brackley	(Dorking)	2
Hereford *C*	John Oliver		1
	John Saxbee	(Ludlow)	3
Leicester *C*	Thomas Butler		1
	Bill Down		4
Lichfield *C*	Keith Sutton		2
	David Hallatt	(Shrewsbury)	1
	Christopher Hill	(Stafford)	4
	Michael Bourke	(Wolverhampton)	3
Lincoln *C*	Robert Hardy		1
	Alastair Redfern	(Grantham)	3
	David Tustin	(Grimsby)	4
Liverpool *Y*	James Jones		1
	John Packer	(Warrington)	3

London *C*	Richard Chartres		1
	Brian Masters	(Edmonton)	3
	John Broadhurst	(Fulham)	4
	Michael Colclough	(Kensington)	2
	John Sentamu	(Stepney)	2
	Graham Dow	(Willesden)	1
Manchester *Y*	Christopher Mayfield		4
	David Bonser	(Bolton)	1
	Colin Scott	(Hulme)	3
	Stephen Venner	(Middleton)	2
Newcastle *Y*	Martin Wharton		3
	Kenneth Gill	(Assistant)	4
	Paul Richardson	(Assistant)	2
Norwich *C*	Peter Nott		2
	David Conner	(Lynn)	3
	Hugo de Waal	(Thetford)	1
Oxford *C*	Richard Harries		1
	Michael Hill	(Buckingham)	1
	Anthony Russell	(Dorchester)	1
	Dominic Walker OGS	(Reading)	2
Peterborough *C*	Ian Cundy		4
	Paul Barber	(Brixworth)	2
Portsmouth *C*	Kenneth Stevenson		2
Ripon *Y*	David Young		2
	Frank Weston	(Knaresborough)	2
Rochester *C*	Michael Nazir-Ali		1
	Brian Smith	(Tonbridge)	3
Salisbury *C*	David Stancliffe		2
	John Kirkham	(Sherborne)	4
Sheffield *Y*	Jack Nicholls		2
	Michael Gear	(Doncaster)	2
Sodor & Man *Y*	Noel Jones		1
Southwark *C*	Wilfred Wood	(Croydon)	3
	Peter Price	(Kingston-upon-Thames)	2
	Colin Buchanan	(Woolwich)	3
Southwell *Y*	Patrick Harris		1
	Alan Morgan	(Sherwood)	1
St Albans *C*	Christopher Herbert		1
	John Richardson	(Bedford)	2
	Robin Smith	(Hertford)	4
St Edmundsbury & Ipswich *C*	Richard Lewis		1
	Timothy Stevens	(Dunwich)	1
Truro *C*	Bill Ind		3
	Graham James	(St Germans)	1
Wakefield *Y*	Nigel McCulloch		2
	John T. Finney	(Pontefract)	2

Winchester *C*	Michael Scott-Joynt		1
	Geoffrey Rowell	(Basingstoke)	4
	Jonathan Gledhill	(Southampton)	4
Worcester *C*	Peter Selby		1
	Rupert Hoare	(Dudley)	4
York *Y*	David Hope	Archbishop	3
	John Gaisford	(Beverley)	2
	Humphrey Taylor	(Selby)	1
	Gordon Bates	(Whitby)	3

Hong Kong Sheng Kung Hui

(Became an autonomous Province on 25 October 1998)

Diocese	*Bishop*		*Section*
Hong Kong Island	Peter Kwong	Primate	3
	Louis Tsui	(Eastern Kowloon)	4
	Thomas Soo	(Western Kowloon)	3

The Church of the Province of the Indian Ocean

Diocese / Country	*Bishop*		*Section*
Antananarivo *Madagascar*	Remi Rabenirina	Primate	2
Mahajanga *Madagascar*	Jean-Claude		4
Mauritius *Mauritius*	Rex Donat		2
Seychelles *Seychelles*	French Chang-Him		4

The Church of Ireland

Internal Provinces:

Armagh *A*

Dublin *D*

Diocese / Province	*Bishop*		*Section*
Armagh *A*	Robert Eames	Archbishop & Primate	1
Cashel & Ossory *D*	John Neill		4
Clogher *A*	Brian Hannon		2
Connor *A*	James Moore		1
Cork, Cloyne & Ross *D*	Roy Warke		2
Derry & Raphoe *A*	James Mehaffey		2
Down & Dromore *A*	Harold Miller		4
Dublin & Glendalough *D*	Walton Empey	Archbishop	1
Kilmore, Elphin & Ardagh *A*	Michael Mayes		3
Limerick & Killaloe *D*	Edward Darling		4
Meath & Kildare *D*	Richard Clarke		1
Tuam, Killala & Achonry *A*	Richard Henderson		4

The Nippon Sei Ko Kai

(The Anglican Communion in Japan)

Diocese	*Bishop*		*Section*
Chubu	Francis Mori		4
Hokkaido	Nathaniel Uematsu		1

Kita Kanto	James Uno		1
Kobe	John Furumoto		2
Kyoto	Barnabas Muto		2
Kyushu	Joseph Iida		3
Okinawa	David Tani		2
Osaka	Koichi Takano		3
Tokyo	John Takeda	Primate	4

The Episcopal Church in Jerusalem & The Middle East

Diocese	*Bishop*		*Section*
Cyprus and the Gulf	Clive Handford		4
Egypt	Ghais Abdel Malik	Primate	2
Iran	Iraj Mottahedeh		2
Jerusalem	Riah Abu El-Assal	(Coadjutor)	3

The Anglican Church of Kenya

Diocese	*Bishop*		*Section*
Bungoma	Eliud Wabukala		3
Butere	Horace Etemesi		4
Eldoret	Thomas Kogo		3
Embu	Moses Njeru		1
Kajiado	Jeremiah Taama		2
Katakwa	Eliud Okiring Odera		1
Kirinyaga	Daniel Ngoru		1
Kitale	Kewasis Nyorsok		4
Kitui	Benjamin M. P. Nzimbi		3
Machakos	Joseph Kanuku		2
Maseno North	Simon Oketch		2
Maseno South	Francis Abiero		2
Maseno West	Joseph Wasonga		1
Mbeere	Gideon Ireri		4
Meru	Henry Paltridge		4
Mombasa	Julius Kalu Katoi		1
Mount Kenya Central	Julius Gachuche		2
Mount Kenya South	Peter Njenga		1
Mount Kenya West	Alf Chipman		1
Mumias	William Wesa		1
Nairobi	David Gitari	Primate	3
Nakuru	Stephen Njihia Mwangi		2
Nambale	Josiah Were		2
Nyahururu	Charles Gaikia Gaita		2
Southern Nyanza	Haggai Nyang'		2
Taita-Taveta	Samson Mwaluda		4

The Anglican Church of Korea

Diocese	*Bishop*	*Section*	
Seoul	Matthew Chung	Primate	4
Taejon	Paul Yoon		1

The Church of the Province of Melanesia

Diocese	*Bishop*		*Section*
Banks & Torres	Charles Ling		2
Central Melanesia	Ellison Pogo	Primate	4
Central Solomons	Charles Koete		4
Hanuato'o	James Mason		1
Malaita	Terry Brown		3
Temotu	Lazarus Munamua		2
Vanuatu	Michael Tavoa		4
Ysabel	Walter Siba		1

La Iglesia Anglicana de Mexico

Diocese	*Bishop*		*Section*
Cuernavaca	Martiniano Garcia-Montiel		3
Mexico	Sergio Carranza-Gomez		4
Northern Mexico	German Martìnez-Marquez		2
Southeastern Mexico	Claro Huerta Ramos		2
Western Mexico	Samuel Espinoza	Primate	1

The Church of the Province of Myanmar (Burma)

Diocese	*Bishop*		*Section*
Hpa-an	Daniel Hoi Kyin		4
Mandalay	Andrew Hla Aung		4
Mytikyina	John Shan Lum		2
Sittwe	Barnabas Theaung Hawi		1
	Aung Tha Tun	(Assistant)	2
Toungoo	John Wilme		1
Yangon	Andrew Mya Han	Primate	2
	Joseph Than Pe	(Assistant)	4

The Church of Nigeria (Anglican Communion)

Internal Provinces:
Province One *One*
Province Two *Two*
Province Three *Three*

Diocese / Province	*Bishop*		*Section*
Aba *Two*	Augustine Iwuagwu		2
Abakaliki *Two*	Benson Onyeibor		1
Abuja *Three*	Peter Akinola	Archbishop	1
Akoko *One*	Jacob Olowokure		1
Akure *One*	Emmanuel Gbonigi		2
Asaba *Two*	Chukwunweike Nwosu		4
Awka *Two*	Maxwell Anikwenwa		1
Bauchi *Three*	Laudamus Ereaku		3
Benin *One*	Peter Onekpe		3
Calabar *Two*	Wilfred Ekprikpo		4
Damaturu *Three*	Daniel Yisa		2
Dutse *Three*	Yesufu Lumu		2

Egba *One*	Matthew Owadayo		1
Egbu *Two*	Emmanuel Iheagwam		2
Ekiti *One*	Samuel Abe		2
Enugu *Two*	Emmanuel Chukwuma		3
Ibadan *One*	Gideon Olajide		1
Ife *One*	Gabriel B. Oloniyo		2
Ikale-Ilaje *One*	Joseph Omoyajowo		1
Ilesa *One*	Ephraim Ademowo		2
Jalingo *Three*	Tanimu Aduda		2
Jos *Three*	Benjamin Kwashi		2
Kabba *One*	Solomon Oyelade		2
Kaduna *Three*	Josiah Idowu-Fearon		3
Kafanchan *Three*	William Diya		2
Kano *Three*	Zakka L. Nyam		3
Katsina *Three*	James S. Kwasu		4
Kebbi *Three*	Edmund Akanya		2
Kwara *One*	Jeremiah Fabuluje		1
Lagos *One*	Joseph Adetiloye	Archbishop & Primate	1
Lokoja *One*	George Bako		3
Maiduguri *Three*	Emmanuel K Mani		1
Makurdi *Three*	Nathan Inyom		2
Mbaise *Two*	Cyril Anyanwu		1
Minna *Three*	Nathaniel Yisa		3
Niger Delta North *Two*	Samuel Onyuku Elenwo		3
Nnewi *Two*	Godwin Okpala		1
Nsukka *Two*	Jonah Iloñuba		2
Oke-Osun *One*	Abraham Awosan		2
Okigwe North *Two*	Alfred Nwaizuzu		4
Okigwe South *Two*	Bennett Okoro		2
On the Niger *Two*	Jonathan Onyemelukwe		2
Ondo *One*	Samuel Aderin		3
Orlu *Two*	Samuel Ebo		4
Osun *One*	Seth Fagbemi		4
Oturkpo *Three*	Ityobee Ugede		2
Owo *One*	Peter Adebiyi		1
Remo *One*	Elijah Ogundana		3
Sabongidda-Ora *One*	Albert Agbaje		4
Sokoto *Three*	Joseph Akinfenwa		1
The Niger Delta *Two*	Gabriel Pepple		2
Ughelli *One*	Vincent Muoghereh		3
Ukwa *Two*	Uju Obinya		4
Umuahia *Two*	Ugo Ezuoke		2
Uyo *Two*	Emmanuel E. Nglass		1
Warri *One*	Nathaniel Enuku		1
Wusasa *Three*	Ali Buba Lamido		2
Yewa *One*	Timothy Bolaji		2
Yola *Three*	Christian Efobi		3

The Anglican Church of Papua New Guinea

Diocese	*Bishop*		*Section*
Aipo Rongo	James Ayong	Primate	3
Dogura	Tevita Talanoa		4
Popondota	Reuben Tariambari		4
Port Moresby	Michael Hough		1

The Episcopal Church in the Philippines

Diocese	*Bishop*		*Section*
	Ignacio Soliba	Primate	4
Central Philippines	Ben Botengan		4
North Central Philippines	Joel A. Pachao		1
Northern Luzon	Renato Abibico		1
Northern Philippines	Edward Malecdan		4
	Miguel Yamoyam	(Suffragan)	1
Southern Philippines	James Manguramas		2

Province de L'Eglise Episcopal au Rwanda

Diocese	*Bishop*		*Section*
Butare	Venuste Mutiganda		4
Byumba	Onesphore Rwaje		2
Cyangugu	Kenneth Barham		2
Gahini	Alexis Bilindabagabo		2
Kibungo	Prudence Ngarambe		1
Kigali	Emmanuel Kolini	Primate	3
Kigeme	Norman Kayumba		4
Shyira	John Rucyahana Kabango		1
Shyogwe	Jered Kalimba		4

The Scottish Episcopal Church

Diocese	*Bishop*		*Section*
Aberdeen & Orkney	Bruce Cameron		2
Argyll & The Isles	Douglas Cameron		4
Brechin	Neville Chamberlain		1
Edinburgh	Richard Holloway	Primate	3
Moray, Ross & Caithness	Gregor Macgregor		1
St Andrew's Dunkeld & Dunblane		Michael Henley	4

The Church of the Province of Southern Africa

Diocese / Country	*Bishop*		*Section*
Bloemfontein *South Africa*	Patrick Glover		2
Cape Town *South Africa*	Njongonkulu Ndungane	Primate	1
	Edward MacKenzie	(Saldanah Bay)	2
	Christopher Gregorowski	(Table Bay)	1
	Merwyn Castle	(False Bay	1
Christ the King *South Africa*	Peter Lee		2

George *South Africa*	George Damant		3
Grahamstown *South Africa*	David Russell		3
	Nceba Nopece	(Assistant)	2
Highveld *South Africa*	David Beetge		4
Johannesburg *South Africa*	Duncan Buchanan		1
Kimberley & Kuruman *South Africa*	Itumeleng Moseki		1
Klerksdorp *South Africa*	David Nkwe		2
Lebombo *Mozambique*	Dinis Sengulane		2
Lesotho *Lesotho*	Andrew Duma		3
Namibia *Namibia*	Nehemiah Hamupembe		3
	Petrus Hilukiluah	(Suffragan)	4
Natal *South Africa*	Michael Nuttall		3
	Matthew Makhaye	(Natal North)	3
	Rubin Phillip	(Natal Coast)	1
Niassa *Mozambique*	Paulino T. Manhique		1
Order of Ethiopia *South Africa*	Sigqibo Dwane		4
Port Elizabeth *South Africa*	Eric Pike		2
Pretoria *South Africa*	Johannes Seoka		1
	Robin Briggs	(Suffragan)	3
St Helena	John Ruston OGS		4
St John's	Jacob Dlamini		2
St Mark the Evangelist *South Africa*	Philip Le Feuvre		2
Swaziland Swaziland	Lawrence Zulu		3
Umzimvubu South Africa	Geoff Davies		1
Zululand South Africa	Anthony Mdletshe		3

Iglesia Anglicana del Cono Sur de America

Diocese	*Bishop*		*Section*
Argentina	David Leake		4
Bolivia	Gregory Venables		3
Chile	Colin Bazley		1
	Hector Zavala	(Coadjutor)	1
	Abelino Apeleo	(Assistant)	2
Northern Argentina	Maurice Sinclair	Primate	3
	Humberto Axt	(Assistant)	4
Paraguay	John Ellison		2
Peru	William Godfrey		2
Uruguay	Miguel Tamayo		3

Church of the Province of South East Asia

Diocese / Country	*Bishop*		*Section*
Kuching *Malaysia*	Made Katib		3
Sabah *Malaysia*	Ping Chung Yong		2
	Chen Fah Yong	(Assistant)	1
Singapore *Singapore*	John Tan	(Assistant)	2
	Moses Tay	Primate	4
West Malaysia *Malaysia*	Cheng Lim		3
	Moses Ponniah	(Assistant)	2

The Episcopal Church of the Sudan

Diocese	*Bishop*		*Section*
Bor	Nathaniel Garang Angieth		1
Cueibet	Reuben Maciir Makoi		2
El-Obeid	Ismail Gibreil		1
Ezo	Benjamin Ruati		2
Ibba	Levi Hassan Nzakara		1
Kadugli & Nuba Mountains	Peter Elbersh Kowa		4
Kajo Keji	Manasseh Binyi		1
Khartoum	Bulus T. Idris Tia		2
Lainya	Eliaba L. Menasona		1
Malakal	Kedhekia Mabior		3
Maridi	Joseph Biringi Hassan		2
Mundri	Eluzai Munda		3
Port Sudan	Yousif Kuku		4
Rejaf	Michael Lugör		4
Renk	Daniel Deng Bul Yak		3
Rokon	Francis Loyo		1
Rumbek	Gabriel Roric Jur		2
Torit	Wilson Arop Ogwok Ocheng		2
Yambio	Daniel Zindo	Acting Primate	2
Yirol	Benjamin Mamur		3

The Anglican Church of Tanzania

Diocese	*Bishop*		*Section*
Central Tanganyika	Godfrey Mhogolo		2
	John Ball	(Assistant)	3
Dar-es-Salaam	Basil Sambano		1
Kagera	Edwin Nyamubi		4
Mara	Hilkiah Omindo		2
Masasi	Patrick Mwachiko		1
Morogoro	Dudley Mageni		2
Mount Kilimanjaro	Simon Makundi		1
Mpwapwa	Simon Chiwanga		3
Rift Valley	Alpha Mohamed		4
Ruaha	Donald Mtetemela	Primate	4
Ruvuma	Stanford Shauri		2
South West Tanganyika	John Mwela		2
Tabora	Francis Ntiruka		2
Victoria Nyanza	John Changae		3
Western Tanganyika	Gerard Mpango		4
Zanzibar and Tanga	John Ramadhani		4

The Church of the Province of Uganda

Diocese	*Bishop*	*Section*
Bukedi	Nicodemus Engwalas-Okille	1
Bunyoro-Kitara	Wilson Turumanya	4
Central Buganda	George Sinabulya	4

East Ankole	Elisha Kyamugambi		1
Kampala	Livingstone	Primate	2
	Eliphaz Maari	(Assistant)	3
Karamoja	Peter Lomongin		4
Kigezi	George Katwesigye		4
Kinkizi	John Ntegyereize		2
Kitgum	Macleord Ochola II Ameda		1
Lango	Melchizedek Otim		2
Luwero	Evans Kisekka		2
Madi & West Nile	Enock Drati		1
Mbale	Israel Wanambisi Koboyi		3
Mityana	Wilson Mutebi		4
Muhabura	Ernest Shalita		1
Mukono	Michael Senyimba		3
Namirembe	Samuel Balagadde Ssekkadde		1
Nebbi	Henry Orombi		2
North Kigezi	John Kahigwa		3
North Mbale	Nathan Muwombi		1
Northern Uganda	Nelson Onono-Onweng		1
Ruwenzori	Eustace Kamanyire		2
Soroti	Geresom Ilukor		1
South Rwenzori	Zebedee Masereka		1
West Ankole	William Magambo		4

The Episcopal Church in the USA

Internal Provinces *I–IX*

Diocese / Province	*Bishop*		*Section*
	Frank T. Griswold	Primate	4
	Charles Keyser	(Armed Forces and Micronesia)	3
	Clayton Matthews	(Bishop for the Office of Pastoral Development of the Episcopal House of Bishops USA)	1
Alabama *IV*	Robert Miller		2
	Henry Parsley Jr	(Coadjutor)	1
Alaska *VIII*	Mark MacDonald		2
Albany *II*	Daniel Herzog		4
Arizona *VIII*	Robert Shahan		4
Arkansas *VII*	Larry Maze		3
Atlanta *IV*	Frank Allan		1
	Onell Soto	(Assistant)	3
California *VIII*	William Swing		4
Central Florida *IV*	John Howe		3
	Hugo L. Pina-Lopez	(Assistant)	2
Central Gulf Coast *IV*	Charles Duvall		2
Central New York *II*	David Joslin		4

Central Pennsylvania *III*	Michael Creighton		2
Colombia *IX*	Bernardo Merino-Botero		1
Colorado *VI*	Jerry Winterrowd		2
Connecticut *I*	Clarence Coleridge		3
	Drew Smith	(Suffragan)	3
Dallas *VII*	James Stanton		1
Delaware *III*	Wayne Wright		3
Dominican Republic *IX*	Julio Holguin Khoury		2
East Carolina *IV*	Clifton Daniel		1
East Tennessee *IV*	Robert Tharp		3
Eastern Michigan *V*	Edwin Leidel Jr		1
Eastern Oregon *VIII*	Rustin Kimsey		4
Easton *III*	Martin Townsend		2
Eau Claire *V*	Bill Wantland		4
El Camino Real *VIII*	Richard L. Shimpfky		4
Europe, Convocation of American Churches in	Jeffery Rowthorn		3
Florida *IV*	Stephen Jecko		2
Fond du Lac *V*	Russell Jacobus		3
Fort Worth *VII*	Jack Iker		3
Georgia *IV*	Henry Louttit Jr		2
Haiti *II*	Zache Duracin		2
Hawaii *VIII*	Dick Chang		3
Honduras *IX*	Leo Frade		4
Idaho *VIII*	John Thornton		2
	Harry Bainbridge	(Coadjutor)	4
Indianapolis *V*	Catherine Waynick		1
Iowa *VI*	Chris Epting		4
Kansas *VII*	Bill Smalley		4
Kentucky *IV*	Edwin Gulick Jr		4
Lexington *IV*	Don Wimberly		1
Long Island *II*	Orris 'Ja' G. Walker Jr		1
	Rodney Michel	(Suffragan)	1
Los Angeles *VIII*	Frederick Borsch		3
	Chester Talton	(Suffragan)	3
Louisiana *IV*	Charles Jenkins		4
Maine *I*	Chilton Knudsen		1
Maryland *III*	Robert Ihloff		3
Massachusetts I	M. Thomas Shaw SSJE		1
	Barbara Harris	(Suffragan)	4
Michigan *V*	Stew Wood		1
Milwaukee *V*	Roger White		4
Minnesota *VI*	Jim Jelinek		3
Mississippi *IV*	Chip Marble Jr		1
Missouri *V*	Hays Rockwell		3
Montana *VI*	Ci Jones		1
Navajoland Area Mission *VIII*	Steven Plummer		1
Nebraska *VI*	James Krotz		1

Nevada *VIII*	Stewart Zabriskie		3
New Hampshire *I*	Douglas E. Theuner		3
New Jersey *II*	Joe Doss		3
New York *II*	Richard Grein		4
	Mark Sisk	(Coadjutor)	3
	Catherine S Roskam	(Suffragan)	3
	Don Taylor	Hon (Assistant)	2
Newark *II*	John Spong		1
	Jack McKelvey	(Suffragan)	2
North Carolina *IV*	Robert Johnson Jr		3
	Gary Gloster	(Suffragan)	1
North Dakota *VI*	Andrew Fairfield		3
Northern California *VIII*	Jerry Lamb		4
Northern Indiana *V*	Frank Gray		2
Northern Michigan *V*	Thomas Ray		3
Northwest Texas *VII*	C. Wallis Ohl Jr		2
Ohio *V*	Clark Grew II		3
	Arthur Williams Jr	(Suffragan)	1
Oklahoma *VII*	Robert Moody		3
Olympia *VIII*	Vincent W. Warner Jr		4
	Sandy Hampton	(Assistant)	3
Oregon *VIII*	Robert Ladehoff		2
Pennsylvania *III*	Charles E. Bennison Jr		1
	Franklin Turner	(Suffragan)	3
Pittsburgh *III*	Robert Duncan		3
Quincy *V*	Keith Ackerman		4
Rhode Island *I*	Gerry Wolf		1
Rio Grande *VII*	Terence Kelshaw		2
Rochester *II*	William Burrill		4
San Diego *VIII*	Gethin Hughes		2
San Joaquin *VIII*	John David Schofield		4
South Carolina *IV*	Edward Salmon Jr		3
	William J. Skilton	(Suffragan)	2
South Dakota *VI*	Creighton Robertson		3
Southeast Florida *IV*	Calvin Schofield Jr		1
	John L. Said	(Suffragan)	2
Southern Ohio *V*	Herbert Thompson		2
	Kenneth Price Jr	(Suffragan)	1
Southern Virginia *III*	David Bane Jr		2
	Donald Hart	(Assistant)	2
Southwest Florida *IV*	John Lipscomb		1
Southwestern Virginia *III*	Neff Powell		3
Springfield *V*	Peter Beckwith		2
Taiwan *VIII*	John Chien		3
Tennessee *IV*	Bertram Herlong		3
Texas *VII*	Claude Payne		2
	Leo Alard	(Suffragan)	4
	William Sterling	(Suffragan)	2

Upper South Carolina *IV*	Dorsey Henderson Jr		3
Utah *VIII*	Carolyn Irish		2
Vermont *I*	Mary Adelia McLeod		1
Virgin Islands *II*	Theodore Daniels		3
Virginia *II*	Peter James Lee		1
	David Jones	(Suffragan)	2
Washington *III*	Ronald Haines		1
	Jane Dixon	(Suffragan)	1
West Missouri *VII*	John Buchanan		3
	Barry Howe	(Coadjutor)	3
West Tennessee *IV*	Jim Coleman		4
West Texas *VII*	Jim Folts		2
	Bob Hibbs	(Suffragan)	3
Western Kansas *VII*	Vernon Strickland		2
Western Louisiana *VII*	Robert Hargrove Jr		4
Western Massachusetts *I*	Gordon Scruton		2
Western Michigan *V*	Edward Lee Jr		3
Western New York *II*	David Bowman		4
Western North Carolina *IV*	Bob Johnson		1
Wyoming *VI*	Bruce Caldwell		1

The Church in Wales

Diocese	*Bishop*		*Section*
Bangor	Barry Morgan		2
Llandaff	Roy T. Davies		3
Monmouth	Rowan Williams		2
St Asaph	Alwyn Jones	Primate	4
St David's	Huw Jones		4
Swansea & Brecon	Dewi Bridges		3
Assistant to all Welsh Bishops	David Thomas		4

The Church of the Province of West Africa

Diocese / Country	*Bishop*		*Section*
Accra *Ghana*	Justice Akrofi		3
Bo *Sierra Leone*	Samuel Gbonda		1
Cape Coast *Ghana*	Kobina Quashie		4
Freetown *Sierra Leone*	Julius Lynch		4
Gambia *Gambia*	S. Tilewa Johnson		3
Koforidua *Ghana*	Robert Okine	Primate	1
Kumasi *Ghana*	Edmund Yeboah		4
Liberia	Edward Neufville		1
Sunyani *Ghana*	Thomas Brient		3
Tamale *Ghana*	Emmanuel Arongo		3

The Church in the Province of the West Indies

Diocese	*Bishop*		*Section*
Barbados	Rufus Brome		1
Belize	Sylvestre Romero-Palma		3

Guyana	Randolph George		2
Jamaica	Neville de Souza		2
Jamaica–Kingston	Herman Spence	(Kingston)	4
Jamaica–Montego Bay	Alfred C. Reid	(Montego Bay)	1
Nassau & The Bahamas	Drexel Gomez		3
North Eastern Caribbean & Aruba	Orland Lindsay	Primate	1
	Leroy Brooks	(Coadjutor)	2
Trinidad & Tobago	Rawle Douglin		4
Windward Islands	Sehon Goodridge		1

The Church of Ceylon

Diocese	*Bishop*	*Section*
Colombo	Kenneth Fernando	1
Kurunagala	Andrew O. Kumarage	3

Iglesia Episcopal de Cuba

Diocese	*Bishop*	*Section*
Cuba	Jorge Perera Hurtado	1

Extra-Provincial to Canterbury

Diocese	*Bishop*	*Section*
Bermuda	Ewen Ratteray	2

Extra-Provincial to the Archbishop of Canterbury

Diocese	*Bishop*	*Section*
Lusitanian Church	Fernando Soares	3
Spanish Reformed Church	Carlos López-Lozano	4

Extra-Provincial to Province IX of the Episcopal Church USA

Diocese	*Bishop*	*Section*
Puerto Rico	David Alvarez-Velazquez	4
Venezuela	Orlando Guerrero	3

The Church of Bangladesh

Diocese	*Bishop*		*Section*
Dhaka	Dwijen Mondal	Moderator	3
Kushtia	Michael S. Baroi		3

The Church of North India

Diocese	*Bishop*	*Section*
Agra	Morris Andrews	1
Amritsar	Anand Chandu Lal	1
Barrackpore	Brojen Malakar	3
Bombay	Baiju Gavit	2
Chotanagpur	James Terom	4
Delhi	Karam Masih	3
Eastern Himalayas	Gerry Andrews	4
Gujarat	Vinodkumar Malaviya	1

Jabalpur	Sunil Cak		2
Lucknow	Anil R. Stephen		4
Nagpur	Vinod Peter	Deputy Moderator	1
North East India	Purely Lyngdoh		3
Patna	Philip Marandih		2
Rajasthan	Christopher Anthony		2
Sambalpur	Lingaraj Tandy		1

The Church of South India

Diocese	*Bishop*		*Section*
Coimbatore	William Moses	Moderator	4
Dornakal	Rajarathnam Allu		3
East Kerala	Joseph Kunnumpurathu		1
Jaffna	Subramaniam Jebanesan		1
Kanyakumari	Messiadhas Kesari		3
Karimnagar	Sanki Theodore		2
Karnataka Central	Vasanthakumar Suputhrappa		3
Karnataka North	Vasant Dandin		4
Karnataka South	Christopher Furtado		3
Krishna-Godavari	Prakasha Rao Thumaty		1
Madhya Kerala	Sam Mathew		3
Madras	Masilamani Azariah		1
Madurai–Ramnad	Thavaraj Eames		4
	David Pothirajulu	(Assistant)	3
Medak	Peter Sugandhar		3
Nandyal	Abraham Gondi		1
Rayalaseema	Chowtipalle Bellam Moses Frederick		4
South Kerala	John Gladstone		2
Tirunelveli	Jason S. Dharmaraj		2
Trichy–Tanjore	Daniel Srinivasan		1
Vellore	R. Trinity Baskeran		2

The Church of Pakistan

Diocese	*Bishop*		*Section*
Faisalabad	John Samuel		1
Hyderabad	S. K. Dass		2
Lahore	Alexander Malik		2
Multan	John Mall		1
Peshawar	Mano Rumalshah		4
Raiwind	Samuel Azariah	Moderator	4
Sialkot	Samuel Sant Masih		3
Assistant for the Arabian Gulf	Azad Marshall		3

BISHOPS FROM CHURCHES IN COMMUNION

CHURCHES SIGNATORY TO THE PORVÖO DECLARATION

The Church of Norway

The Rt Revd Andreas Aarflot | Bishop of Oslo

The Church of Sweden

The Rt Revd Dr Jonas Jonson | Bishop of Strängnäs

The Evangelical-Lutheran Church of Finland

The Rt Revd Dr Olavi Rimpiläinen | Bishop of Oulu

THE MAR THOMA SYRIAN CHURCH Of MALABAR

The Rt Revd Dr Zaharias Mar Theophilus | Bishop of North America and the United Kingdom

THE OLD CATHOLIC CHURCHES OF THE UNION OF UTRECHT

The Old Catholic Church of the Netherlands

The Most Revd Antonius Glazemaker | Archbishop of Utrecht

The Catholic Diocese of the Old Catholics in Germany

The Rt Revd Joachim Vobbe | Bishop

THE PHILIPPINE INDEPENDENT CHURCH

The Most Revd Alberto B. Ramento	Supreme Bishop
The Rt Revd Roman B. Tiples Jr	Chair, Supreme Council of Bishops
The Rt Revd Rhee M. Timbang	Bishop of Surigao
The Rt Revd Bartolome O. Espartero	Assistant Bishop of Antigue

PARTICIPANTS FROM THE ANGLICAN CONSULTATIVE COUNCIL

The Anglican Church in Aotearoa, New Zealand & Polynesia		
John Paterson	Vice Chairman (Episcopal)	3
The Anglican Church of Australia		
Phillip Newell	Episcopal	2
David Richardson	Clerical	2
Robert Tong	Lay	3
Igreja Episcopal Anglicana do Brasil		
Sumio Takatsu	Episcopal	4
The Church of the Province of Burundi		
Bernard Ntahoturi	Episcopal	1
The Anglican Church of Canada		
Stewart Payne	Episcopal	1
The Church of the Province of Central Africa		
Bernard Malango	Episcopal	1
Michael Kututwa	Lay	1

Province de L'Eglise Anglicane Du Congo		
Sylvestre Tibafa Mugera	Episcopal	2
Basimaki Byabasaija	Clerical	1
The Church of England		
Richard Harries	Episcopal	1
John Moses	Clerical	3
Christina Baxter	Lay	2
George Carey	President	2
Colin Craston	Former ACC Chairman	3
The Church of the Province of the Indian Ocean		
Roger Chung Po Chuen	Clerical	2
The Church of Ireland		
Michael Mayes	Episcopal	3
Brenda Sheil	Lay	4
The Nippon Sei Ko Kai (The Anglican Communion in Japan)		
Sam Koshiishi	Clerical	3
The Episcopal Church in Jerusalem & The Middle East		
Ghais Abdel Malik	Episcopal	2
The Anglican Church of Kenya		
Joseph Wasonga	Episcopal	1
Samuel Arap Ng'eny	Lay	1
The Anglican Church of Korea		
John Lee	Clerical	3
The Church of the Province of Melanesia		
James Mason	Episcopal	1
La Iglesia Anglicana de Mexico		
Ortega Reybal	Lay	1
The Church of the Province of Myanmar (Burma)		
Samuel San Si Htay	Episcopal	4
The Church of Nigeria (Anglican Communion)		
Maxwell Anikwenwa	Episcopal	1
Vincent Muogereh	Clerical*	3
G. O. K. Ajayi	Lay	3
The Anglican Church in Papua New Guinea		
Tevita Talanoa	Episcopal	4
The Episcopal Church in the Philippines		
Warren E. Luyaben	Lay	4
Province de L'Eglise Episcopal au Rwanda		
Prudence Ngarambe	Episcopal	1
Damien Nteziryayo	Clerical	3
Margaret Bihabanyi	Lay	4
The Scottish Episcopal Church		
John Rea	Lay	1
The Church of the Province of Southern Africa		
Petrus Hilukiluah	Episcopal	4
Maureen Sithole	Lay	1

* Was elected Clerical representative to the Council for ACC-8 in 1990; he was elected as Bishop in January 1998.

Iglesia Anglicana Del Cono Sur de America		
Hector Zavala	Episcopal	1
Church of the Province of South East Asia		
Bolly Lapok	Clerical	3
The Episcopal Church of the Sudan		
Michael Lugör	Episcopal	4
Nelson Nyumbe	Clerical	2
Is-hag Kannidi Kodi Kodi	Lay	4
The Anglican Church of Tanzania		
Simon Chiwanga	Episcopal, Chairman ACC	3
Mkunga Mtingele	Clerical	1
Joyce Ngoda	Lay	4
The Church of the Province of Uganda		
Livingstone Mpalanyi-Nkoyoyo	Episcopal	2
John Baganizi	Clerical	4
Edward Mungati	Lay	1
The Episcopal Church in the USA		
Mark Dyer	Episcopal	3
Judith Conley	Lay	3
The Church in Wales		
David Williams	Clerical	2
Sylvia Scarf	Lay	2
The Church of the Province of West Africa		
Adrian DeHeer-Amissah	Lay	1
The Church in the Province of the West Indies		
Leroy Brooks	Episcopal	2
Bernard Turner	Lay	1
Alvin Stone	Clerical	2
The Church of Bangladesh		
Samuel Sarkar	Lay	4
The Church of Pakistan (United)		
Alexander Malik	Episcopal	2
Theodore Phailbus	Lay	3
The Church of North India (United)		
Vidya Sagar Lall	Lay	1
The Church of South India (United)		
Peter Sugandhar	Episcopal	3
J. Prabhakara Rao Jeedipalli	Clerical	1
George Koshy	Lay	4
Co-opted		
Rachel Beleo	Lay	2
Lovey Kisembo	Clerical	2
Ghazi Musharbash	Lay	4
Lenore Parker	Lay	1
Candace Payne	Lay	4
Fernando Soares	Episcopal	3

Consultants

Denise Ackermann	South Africa	Section	1
Marcus Arruda	Brazil	Section	1
Patrick Augustine	USA	Inter-faith	
Alyson Barnett-Cowan	Canada	Section	4
Dean Borgman	USA	Section	2
Ashton Brooks	USA	Section	3
Colin Chapman	England	Inter-faith	
John Chew	Singapore	Section	4
Christopher Duraisingh	USA	Section	3
Bill Franklin	USA	Section	4
Raymond Fung	Hong Kong	Section	2
Kathy Galloway	Scotland	Section	2
Sebastiáo Gameleira Soares	Brazil	Section	2
Robin M Gill	England	Section	1
John Kater Jr	USA	Section	3
Peter Lenkoe	South Africa	Section	4
Jaci Maraschin	Brazil	Section	4
David Martin	England	Section	4
George Mathew	India	Section	1
Esther Mombo	England	Section	3
Ann Pettifor	England	Section	1
Michael Root	USA	Section	4
Courtney Sampson	South Africa	Section	1
Vinay Samuel	England	Section	2
Lamin Sanneh	USA	Section	2
John Sargant	England	Inter-faith	
Chris Sugden	England	Section	2

ECUMENICAL PARTICIPANTS

Archdiocese of Thyateira and Great Britain (Ecumenical Patriarchate)
Archbishop Gregorios of Thyateira and Great Britain

Armenian Apostolic Church, Catholicosate of Cilicia
The Very Revd Nareg Alemezian — Ecumenical Officer of the Armenian Catholicosate of Cicilia

Armenian Apostolic Church, Holy See of Etchmiadzin
Archbishop Vatche Hovsepian — Prelate of the Western Diocese of the Armenian Apostolic Church of America (Los Angeles, California)

Holy Apostolic Catholic Assyrian Church of the East
Bishop Mar Odisho Oraham — Bishop in Europe
The Revd Yonan Youil Yonan

Baptist World Alliance
The Revd David Coffey — General Secretary
The Revd Chris Ellis

China Christian Council	
The Revd Su De-Ci	General Secretary
The Revd Bao Jia-Yuan	Associate General Secretary
Christian World Communions	
Dr Milan Opocensky	
Dr Bert Beach	
Church of Cyprus	
Metropolitan Chrysostomos of Kition	
Coptic Orthodox Church	
Metropolitan Bishoi of Damiette, Barari, Kafr el Sheikh	
Council of Churches for Britain & Ireland	
The Revd John Reardon	
Ecumenical Patriarchate	
Metropolitan John of Pergamon	
Greek Orthodox Patriarchate of Alexandria and All Africa	
Archbishop Serafim Kykkotis	Archdiocese of Kenya and Tanzania
Lutheran World Federation	
The Revd Dr Ishmael Noko	General Secretary
The Revd Sven Oppegaard	
The Revd Richard Stetson	
Malabar Independent Syrian Church	
Metropolitan Joseph Mar Koorilose	
Malankara Orthodox Syrian Church, Catholicate of the East	
Metropolitan Geevarghese Mar Ivanios	Diocese of Kottayam
Russian Orthodox Church	
Metropolitan Vladimir of St Petersburg and Ladoga	
Archdeacon Andrei Chighov	
Greek Orthodox Patriarchate of Antioch and All the East	
The Revd Fr Samir Gholam	
Romanian Orthodox Church	
Bishop Nifon of Slobozia and Calarasi	
Roman Catholic Church	
His Eminence Cardinal Edward Cassidy	President, Pontifical Council for Promoting Christian Unity
The Rt Revd Pierre Duprey	Secretary, Pontifical Council for Promoting Christian Unity
The Revd Timothy Galligan	Pontifical Council for Promoting Christian Unity
The Most Revd Alex J. Brunett	Archbishop of Seattle
The Rt Revd Philip Pargeter	Auxiliary Bishop of Birmingham
Syrian Orthodox Patriarchate of Antioch and All the East	
Archbishop Mor Gregorios Yohanna Ibrahim of Aleppo	Metropolitan of Aleppo Archdiocese
World Alliance of Reformed Churches	
Dr Milan Opocensky *(Also representing CWC)*	
The Revd Dr Jana Opocenská	

World Council of Churches
The Revd Dr John Pobee
The Revd Dr Thomas FitzGerald
World Methodist Council
Bishop William B. Oden
Dr Geoffrey Wainwright

CONFERENCE STAFF

SECRETARY TO THE LAMBETH CONFERENCE
The Revd Canon John L. Peterson

MANAGER OF THE LAMBETH CONFERENCE
Mr David Long

ANGLICAN COMMUNION SECRETARIAT
Miss Paula Atkinson
Mrs Helen Bates
Mr Pete Bennett
Mr Dominic Brant
Mrs Joan Christey
Mrs Christine Codner
Mrs Nicola Currie
Mrs Veronica Elks
The Revd Dr Joan Ford
The Revd Paul Gibson
Miss Elizabeth Gordon Clark
The Revd Canon David Hamid
Mr Ian Harvey
Mrs Frances Hiller
Mrs Cate Irvine
Mrs Deirdre Martin
Miss Marjorie Murphy
Mr Mike Nunn
The Rt Revd James Ottley
Mrs Rosemary Palmer
Ms Ann Quirke
Canon James Rosenthal
The Revd Canon John Rye
Ms Caroline Shrieve
Mr Graeme Smith
Mrs Barbara Stanford-Tuck
Mr Jon Williams

ARCHBISHOP OF CANTERBURY'S STAFF
Ms Emily Boswell
The Revd Herman Browne
Ms Virginia De Boinod
The Revd Canon Andrew Deuchar
Ms Mary Eaton
Dr Ruth Etchells
The Revd Canon Colin Fletcher
Miss Catherine Harbord
Mrs Gill Harris Hogarth
The Revd Stewart Jones
The Revd Canon Richard Marsh
Miss Fiona Millican
Ms Lesley Perry
Ms Ruth Schroder
Mr Pete Ward

CHAPLAIN TO THE CONFERENCE

The Rt Revd Roger Herft, Bishop of Newcastle, NSW, Australia

CHAPLAINCY TEAM

The Revd Canon Ron Diss
Mr John Gereighty
Ms Maggie Hamilton
Mrs Cheryl Herft
Mrs Anne Shelburne Jones
The Rt Revd Ted Jones
The Revd Patrick Jones
The Revd Maurice Kidd
Ms Gerry Latty
Mr David Leeke
The Rt Revd Michael Marshall
Ms Jan Payne
Mrs Joan Priestman
Mrs Jenefer Randolph
Mrs Anne Rees
Ms Matilda Tullberg
Mr Geoff Weaver

COMMUNICATIONS TEAM

Director, Canon James Rosenthal
The Revd Dr Tom Ambrose
Mr Roland Ashby
The Revd Tim Barker
Ms Andrina Barnden
Mrs Bev Barnes
The Revd & Mrs Ron Barnes
Ms Carol Barnwell
Mr Cooper Barnwell
Ms Virginia Barrett-Barker
Ms Lisa Barrowclough
The Ven Beni Bataaga
Mrs Helen Bates
The Revd Dr Bill Beaver
Mr Dominic Brant
Mrs Barbara Braver
Mr Marc Burnette
The Revd Canon Brian Chave
The Revd Philip Chester
Miss Nan Cobbey
The Revd Robert Commin
Ms Courtney Cowart
The Revd Geoff Crago
Mr Christopher Cunningham
Mr Nicola Currie
The Revd Dorothy Curry
Mr Andy Day
Mrs Pat Donaldson
The Revd David Duprey
Mr Vincente Echerri
Mrs Veronica Elks
Mr Ian Endicott
Ms Susan Erdey
Mrs Rachel Farmer
The Revd Dr Joan Butler Ford
The Revd Timothy Fujii
Mrs Liz Gibson-Harries
Ms Jane Gitau
Mr Peter Gudaitis
Mr Martyn Halsall
Mrs Linda Hanick
The Revd Canon Greg Harvey
Mrs Sally Hastings
Mr Julian Hewitt
Mr Cliff Hicks
Mr Greg Holmes
Mr Steve Jenkins
The Revd Jonathan Jennings
The Revd David Johnston
Ms Arun Kataria
Ms Cindy Kent
Mr William Killough
Ms Liz Knowles
Mr Mark Larmour
Ms Shannon Ledbetter
The Revd Kris Lee

The Revd Randall Lee
The Revd Bob Libby
Mr Rob Lines
Miss Harriet Long
Mr Andy Male
The Revd Canon Ted Malone Jr
The Revd Rob Marshall
Ms Carole Miller
Mr Greg Mills
Mrs Alison Moore
The Revd Peter Moore
Ms Sarah Moore
Ms Marla Murphy
Mr Alexander Nicoll
The Revd Jan Nunley
The Revd Stanley Nyahwa
Mr Paul Olsson
Ms Sue Primmer
Mr Kenneth Quigley
The Revd Renato Raatz
The Rt Revd Andy Radford
Mr Allan Reeder
Mr Ian Robertson
Deaconess Margaret Rodgers
Ms Suzi Rohman
Mr John A. Rollins
Mrs Judy Ross
The Ven Lynn Ross
Ms Sarah Rowland Jones
Mr Yazeed Said
Ms Sally Sedgwick
The Revd Dr Jeff Sells
Mrs Hannah Sharp
Mr Stuart Sharp
Ms Katie Sherrod
The Revd Martin Short
Mr Federico Sierra
Mr Edward Simonton
Mr David Skidmore
The Revd Joanne Skidmore
Mr Brian Thomas
Mr James Thrall
Mr Doug Tindal
Mr Christopher Took
Mr Ricardo Tucas
Ms Ann Wetzel
Mr Bob Williams
Ms Sarah Williams
The Revd Don Witts

CONFERENCE SECRETARIAT

Director, Mrs Christine Codner
Ms Hazel Agar
Ms Mia Anderson
Mrs Tali Anderson
Mrs Gillian Bloor
The Revd Sunil Caleb
Mrs Elspeth Coke
The Revd Irv Cutter
Mrs Angela Doe
Mrs Julia Farrer
The Revd Stacey Fussell
Mrs Sheila Garner
Miss Judith Gracias
Mr Will Ingle-Gillis
Mr Brian Irvine
Ms Barbara Johnson
The Revd Gordon Light
The Revd Vanessa MacKenzie
Ms Pollyann Matson
The Revd Sean Mullen
Ms Jo Mutch
The Revd Joe Parrish
Mrs Helen Smallwood
Miss Sally Smith
Ms Brenda Stanley
Mr Eric Tanauan
The Revd Carolyn Tuttle
Mrs Wendy Ward
Mrs Maureen Webb
The Revd Paul Williams

ECUMENICAL TEAM

Director, The Revd Canon David Hamid
The Revd Dr Donald Anderson
The Revd Canon Richard Marsh
Dr Colin Podmore
Dr Mary Tanner

FINAL PLENARY TEAM

Mr Chris Calderhead
Mr Guy Collins
Professor David Ford
The Revd Professor Dan Hardy
Mr Mike Higton
Mr Tim Jenkins
Mr Ben Quash
Ms Joanna Spreadbury
The Revd Angela Tilby

INTERPRETERS

Director, Mrs Donata Colema
Miss Lucia Alvarez de Toledo
Mr Estanislao Arroyabe
Ms Laurence Bastit
The Revd Gilbert Beaume
Miss Joanna Benson
Mrs Renate Braun
The Revd Tony Coates
Miss Claire Debenham
Mr Robert Faerber
Mrs Tomoko Faerber-Evdokimov
Mrs Yoshimi Gregory
The Revd Dr Enrique Illarze Delgado
The Revd Canon Michael Ipgrave
Mr Nozomu Ishiyama
Ms Ruth Lambert
Mrs Dominique MacNeill
Mrs Estuko Maruyama
Mrs Christine Mèar
Mr Jerome Moriyama
The Revd Renta Nishihara
The Revd Rogelio Prieto
Miss Madeleine Richter
Mr Asato Saito
Mrs Ikuku Williams

LOCAL COMMITTEE

Mr Peter Carson
The Revd Derek Crabtree
The Revd Canon Reg Humphriss
Mrs Sue Humphriss
The Revd Stephen Laird
Mrs Su Rennison
Mrs Helen Thompson
The Revd Maurice Worgan

MARKET PLACE

Mrs Kathleen McCloskey
The Revd Bob McCloskey

PROVINCIAL STAFF

The Revd Canon Randolph Chase
The Revd Canon Anthony Jewiss
The Revd John Lewis
The Revd Patrick Mauney
The Revd Todd McGregor
The Revd Canon Dr George K Tibeesigwa

RELIGIOUS TEAM

The Revd Sr Rosina Ampah
Sister Carol CHN
Brother Alfred Leong SSF
Brother Anthony Michael SSF
Sister Catherine Oh
Sister Pamela Owens CAH
Brother Samuel SSF
Br Martin Smith SSJE

STEWARDS

Co-ordinator, The Revd Stephen Laird
Ms Sara Afshari
Mrs Julianah Ajayi
Mr Gibran Augustine
The Revd Bernard Bagaba
The Revd Joseph Bain-Doodu
Ms Melanie Baynton-Campbell
Mr Kevin Brown
Mr Mark Chalmers
The Revd Raymond Chamungu
Ms Elizabeth Chance
Miss Frances Chang-Him
Miss Michelle Chang-Him
Miss Lonah Cheptoo
Hai Joon Choung
Miss Helen Dalgleish
Ms Emma Davey
Naw Lah De Ne
Mr Ian Delinger
Mr Tommy Dillon II
Mr Markus Duenzkofer
The Revd Ben Enwuchola
The Revd George Fetiza
Mr Paul Flowers
Mr Joseph Galgalo
Ms Luciane Gomes dos Santos
Mr Scott Goodwin
Mr Simon Graham
Ms Miriam Hadcocks
Ms Jo Hancock
Ms Kim Hannah
Ms Libby Harper
Ms Kate Heywood
Mr Neil Hollis
Miss Anna Holt
Ms Sarah Horton
The Revd Stanley Jones
The Revd Canon Dennis Josiah
The Revd John Kaoma
The Revd Barnabas Sotoshi Kobayashi
Ms Claire Lambert
The Revd Moses Matonya
Mr Lester McKenzie
Miss Lynn McKenzie
Mr Paul McKenzie
Mr Jonathan Millard
Mr Rohintan Mody
Mr Lazarus Mokobake
The Revd Solomon Mugyenzi
Mr Paul Narayanasamy
Mr Ross Nazir-Ali
Mr Shammy Nazir-Ali
The Revd Joel Obetia
Mrs Jane Ongaye
The Revd Matthew Ongaye
The Revd Margaret Ouma
Miss Emily Peterson
Mr Geoff Phillips
Miss Mary Phiri
The Ven Sylvester Phiri
Ms Nicola Pritchard
Ms Jean Read
Mr Mario Ribias
Mr Nicholas Rose
Miss Erin Rutherford
The Revd Alfred Sebahene
The Revd Godfrey Sehaba
The Revd Samy Shehata
Mr Tim Smith
Miss Kayt Spall
Miss Megan Stoffregen
Ms Anupama Tandy

Mr Charles Varnum
Miss Louise Vincer
Mr Alphonse Watho-Kudi
Mr Dawan Wiggins-Owen
Naw Lu Yu Hpaw
Mr Andrew Zinhi